Crime and the Risk Society

The International Library of Criminology, Criminal Justice and Penology
Series Editors: Gerald Mars and David Nelken

Titles in the Series:

Integrative Criminology
Gregg Barak

The Origins and Growth of Criminology
Piers Beirne

Issues in Comparative Criminology
Piers Beirne and David Nelken

Criminal Detection and the Psychology of Crime
David V. Canter and Laurence J. Alison

Offender Rehabilitation
Francis T. Cullen and Brandon K. Applegate

International Criminal Law and Procedure
John Dugard and Christine van den Wyngaert

Crime and the Media
Richard V. Ericson

Psychological Explanations of Crime
David P. Farrington

Penal Abolition
Johannes Feest

State Crime, Vols I & II
David O. Friedrichs

Terrorism
Conor Gearty

Criminal Careers, Vols I & II
David F. Greenberg

Fear of Crime
Christopher Hale

Social Control: Aspects of Non-State Justice
Stuart Henry

Professional Criminals
Dick Hobbs

Crime, Deviance and the Computer
Richard C. Hollinger

Race, Crime and Justice
Barbara A. Hudson

Fraud: Organization, Motivation and Control, Vols I & II
Michael Levi

Violence
Michael Levi

Radical Criminology
Michael J. Lynch

Serial Murder
Elliott Leyton

Street Crime
Mike Maguire

Occupational Crime
Gerald Mars

Theoretical Traditions in Criminology
Ross Matsueda

Alternatives to Prison
Roger Matthews

The Sociology of Punishment
Dario Melossi

Gender, Crime and Feminism
Ngaire Naffine

White-Collar Crime
David Nelken

Comparative Criminal Justice
David Nelken and Richard K. Vogler

Crime and the Risk Society
Pat O'Malley

Organized Crime
Nikos Passas

Transnational Crime
Nikos Passas

Uses and Abuses of Criminal Statistics
Kenneth Pease

Criminal Justice and the Mentally Disordered
Jill Peay

Policing, Vols I & II
Robert Reiner

Victimology
Paul Rock

Criminal Policy Making
Andrew Rutherford

Prosecution in Common Law Jurisdictions
Andrew Sanders

Politics, Crime Control and Culture
Stuart A. Scheingold

Drugs, Crime and Criminal Justice, Vols I & II
Nigel South

Youth Crime, Deviance and Delinquency, Vols I & II
Nigel South

Crime and Political Economy
Ian Taylor

Rape and the Criminal Justice System
Jenny Temkin

The Sentencing Process
Martin Wasik

Social History of Crime, Policing and Punishment
Robert P. Weiss

Sex Crimes
Donald West

Crime and the Risk Society

Edited by

Pat O'Malley

La Trobe University

Ashgate

DARTMOUTH

Aldershot • Brookfield USA • Singapore • Sydney

Published by
Dartmouth Publishing Company Limited
Ashgate Publishing Limited
Gower House
Croft Road
Aldershot
Hants GU11 3HR
England

Ashgate Publishing Company
Old Post Road
Brookfield
Vermont 05036
USA

British Library Cataloguing in Publication Data
Crime and the risk society. – (The international library of
   criminology, criminal justice and penology)
   1. Crime – Sociological aspects
   I. O'Malley, Pat
   364.2'5

Library of Congress Cataloging-in-Publication Data
Crime and the risk society / edited by Pat O'Malley.
        p.   cm. – (The international library of criminology, criminal
   justice, and penology)
   Includes bibliographical references.
   ISBN 1–84014–027–5
   1. Crime   2. Crime prevention.   3. Criminal justice.
Administration of.   4. Risk–Sociological aspects.   5. Risk
assessment.   6. Risk management.   I. O'Malley, Pat.   II. Series:
International library of criminology, criminal justice & penology.
HV6025.C713   1998
364–dc21

98–12101
CIP

ISBN 1 84014 027 5

Printed and bound by Athenaeum Press, Ltd.,
Gateshead, Tyne & Wear.

A000006331870

Contents

PART III   ACTUARIAL JUSTICE

PART IV   THE POLITICS OF CRIME RISK MANAGEMENT

Acknowledgements

The editor and publishers wish to thank the following for permission to use copyright material.

American Society for Public Administration for the essay: Edwin W. Zedlewski (1985), 'When Have We Punished Enough?', *Criminal Justice Reform*, **45**, pp. 771–79.

American Society of Criminology for the essay: Malcolm M. Feeley and Jonathan Simon (1992), 'The New Penology: Notes on the Emerging Strategy of Corrections and its Implications', *Criminology*, **30**, pp. 449–74.

Blackwell Publishers for the essays: R.A. Litton (1982), 'Crime Prevention and Insurance', *Howard Journal of Penology and Crime Prevention*, **21**, pp. 6–22; J. Robert Lilly (1990), 'Tagging Reviewed', *The Howard Journal*, **29**, pp. 229–45.

Butterworths for the essay: John Pratt (1995), 'Dangerousness, Risk and Technologies of Power', *Australian and New Zealand Journal of Criminology*, **28**, pp. 3–31.

Canada Law Book Inc. for the essay: Clifford D. Shearing and Philip C. Stenning (1985), 'From the Panopticon to Disney World: The Development of Discipline', in Anthony N. Doob and Edward L. Greenspan, QC (eds), *Perspectives in Criminal Law*, Ontario: Canada Law Book Inc., pp. 335–49.

Carfax Publishing Limited for the essay: Stephen Mugford (1993), 'Social Change and the Control of Psychotropic Drugs – Risk Management, Harm Reduction and "Postmodernity"', *Drug and Alcohol Review*, **12**, pp. 369–75.

Duke University Press for the essay: Jonathan Simon (1987), 'The Emergence of a Risk Society: Insurance, Law, and the State', *Socialist Review*, **95**, pp. 61–89. Copyright © 1987, Center for Social Research and Education. Reprinted by permission of Duke University Press.

Fax Forlag for the essay: Trevor Bennett (1994), 'Police Strategies and Tactics for Controlling Crime and Disorder in England and Wales', *Studies on Crime and Crime Prevention*, **3**, pp. 146–67.

Global Options for the essay: Pat O'Malley and Stephen Mugford (1992), 'Moral Technology: The Political Agenda of Random Drug Testing', *Social Justice*, **18**, pp. 122–46.

Series Preface

The International Library of Criminology, Criminal Justice and Penology, represents an important publishing initiative designed to bring together the most significant journal essays in contemporary criminology, criminal justice and penology. The series makes available to researchers, teachers and students an extensive range of essays which are indispensable for obtaining an overview of the latest theories and findings in this fast changing subject.

This series consists of volumes dealing with criminological schools and theories as well as with approaches to particular areas of crime, criminal justice and penology. Each volume is edited by a recognised authority who has selected twenty or so of the best journal articles in the field of their special competence and provided an informative introduction giving a summary of the field and the relevance of the articles chosen. The original pagination is retained for ease of reference.

The difficulties of keeping on top of the steadily growing literature in criminology are complicated by the many disciplines from which its theories and findings are drawn (sociology, law, sociology of law, psychology, psychiatry, philosophy and economics are the most obvious). The development of new specialisms with their own journals (policing, victimology, mediation) as well as the debates between rival schools of thought (feminist criminology, left realism, critical criminology, abolitionism etc.) make necessary overviews that offer syntheses of the state of the art. These problems are addressed by the INTERNATIONAL LIBRARY in making available for research and teaching the key essays from specialist journals.

GERALD MARS
Professor in Applied Anthropology, University of Bradford
School of Management

DAVID NELKEN
Distinguished Research Professor, Cardiff Law School,
University of Wales, Cardiff

Introduction

What is 'the risk society'?

The thesis of 'the risk society' has recently moved to a central place in social theory and is increasingly becoming a major issue in criminology. Broadly speaking, a risk society is understood as a society which is organized in significant ways around the concept of risk and which increasingly governs its problems in terms of discourses and technologies of risk. While it is important to specify the meaning of risk (and its relationship to 'danger'), this cannot be done independently of an understanding of the concept of 'risk society' as developed in two principal, overlapping, but distinct schools of thought.

The first, and probably best known, approach in social theory is linked most closely with the work of Ulrich Beck (1992a, 1992b) and Mary Douglas (Douglas, 1992; Douglas and Wildavsky, 1986). This focuses primarily on the foundation of the risk society in historically unique risks and dangers – epitomized by nuclear radiation and environmental pollution – that are massive and global in their nature, affecting all, regardless of class, race or gender. These 'modernization risks' (Beck, 1992a) generate forms of consciousness and social organization that are distinct from those which characterized modern societies even 50 years ago. Thus for Beck, the 'risk society' is to be distinguished from 'class society', which was the dominant form from the early part of the nineteenth century until the middle of the twentieth. In class society the principal focus was on the problem of sustaining the legitimacy of the systematically required unequal distribution of wealth. In the risk society the key problem becomes that of the distribution and circumscribing of risks, and class consciousness is displaced by risk consciousness. This shift in mentality gradually circulates throughout the society and inhabits most fields of government, including that of crime control. In this society, knowledge becomes crucial. Science and expertises based on science are rendered responsible for the definition of risks, the establishment of standards of acceptable risk, and for making the population think in terms of risk: health and safety on the roads, at work and in our diet; crime risks; drug risks; pollution and waste risks; and so on. At the same time, and in the same moment, danger and security become central ways in terms of which problems of rule are conceptualized.

In the arguments of Beck and Douglas, therefore, risks are culturally or politically identified with the presence of (real) dangers – although we mainly rely on experts to identify these for us. Thus, while noting that the link between risk and probability calculations was formerly crucial, Douglas suggests that, under the impact of overwhelming dangers, the discourse has changed: 'the word *risk* means now means danger, *high* risk means a lot of danger' (Douglas, 1992, p. 24). This is not quite the case for the more Foucaultian line of thinking associated with a second approach to the risk society – one which has been far more influential in criminology. This is fairly agnostic about any connection between risk consciousness and 'real' dangers. Rather, it is concerned with what it sees as risk – in the probabilistic sense – becoming an ascendant framework for problematizing and dealing with matters for government. In this, the Foucaultian approach is at odds with that of Douglas, although it shares with Beck's line of thought the view that security has become a prime category in the *mentality* of those governing. This overlap in the approaches makes it possible for some writers in the field to bring the two together in a coherent argument (see, for example, Ericson in Chapter 5 of this volume). But the distinction between Douglas's thought and that of the more Foucaultian writers is crucial, for the focus on statistical and probabilistic problematization – rather than on the presence of posited real dangers – is at the heart of the crime and risk society literature. What is so crucial is the argument that in the field of crime control, as elsewhere in the risk society, problems are being governed in terms of statistical aggregates, populations and distributions rather than individuals. The governance of crime is becoming *actuarial* in its form.

Of course, we may readily recognize that statistical knowledge has long played a role in the governance of crime. But the crime and risk society thesis argues that actuarial criminology and criminal justice deploy such knowledge in a distinctive fashion. What Garland (1995) refers to as 'penal modernism' – the dominant approach over the past century – deployed actuarial knowledge to discover the causes of crime and to develop means whereby social engineering and therapeutic correctionalism could attack crime at its roots and reform individuals. In short, its aim was to normalize pathologies. Actuarialism was, in Foucaultian terms, subordinated to the purposes of a disciplinary regime and a disciplinary society. Actuarial crime control is, in a sense, the opposite. It regards crime as normal, rather than pathological, and subordinates disciplinarity to the purposes of actuarialism. This may need a little explanation here, although Jonathan Simon provides a brilliant extended analysis in Chapter 1.

Put simply, actuarial crime control is not directly concerned with the meaningful activities of individuals – involving intentions, motivations, understandings, guilt, fault and so on, that were the concern of disciplinarity and correctionalism. Instead, its focus is the distribution and effects of *behaviours* in the sense of 'external' physical dispositions rather than 'internal' states. It is concerned with the statistical distribution of behaviours primarily in order to assess and predict their consequences for security, rather than their moral affront; and it seeks to develop ways of manipulating risk-bearing behaviours in order to increase security. Thus if the figure of the panopticon was the symbol of penal modernism, perhaps that of the speed hump is its equivalent in actuarialism. As this suggests, actuarial justice is not concerned with the identity of the offender, and by implication it accepts that anyone can be an offender: crime in this sense is normal. It may certainly define some individuals as presenting a higher risk for security – although significantly it is as much concerned here with potential victims as with potential offenders – but their risk is merely the attribution to the person of the characteristics of a risk category to which they are assigned. As this implies, it is also markedly less theoretical and more pragmatic. Statistics are not merely the route to discovering causes or pathologies. Rather, statistics represent direct knowledge of *risk factors and risk distributions*: a correlation is not merely a possible register of abstract causation but a concrete map of probabilities. The response will not therefore be to address the causes of crime but to reduce or redistribute the risks. Governing through actuarial risk and its management thus becomes primary, while disciplinary practices (for example, training in personal security or building self-esteem) are put to work in order to achieve ends defined by actuarialism.

It is risk, in this distributional, probabilistic sense of dealing with the government of security, that is the nub of the issue for most concerned criminologists, and it is why 'Crime and the Risk Society', rather than say 'Crime and Risk' was selected as the title for this volume. The 'risk society' label distinguishes its content clearly from more familiar approaches to risk in criminology which have a long history and which are still active sites of development – notably, the literature on crime as risk-taking activity (for example, Katz, 1988; Collison, 1996; Lyng, 1990). Less clearly, it distinguishes it from the literature concerned with people's perceptions of crime risks – the 'fear of crime' literature (see, generally, Hale, 1994). The lack of clarity in this latter distinction is a reflection of the fact that, as the essays in this volume by Stanko and Walklate illustrate, the 'fear of crime' research exists in an ambiguous relationship with the concerns of the 'risk society' literature (see Chapters 19 and 20). Traditionally, fear of crime has been understood to be an indicator of the seriousness of the 'crime problem' and was often framed in terms of questions about whether or not the fear of crime was 'rational' – that is, whether it reflected a 'real' risk exposure. When deployed governmentally, (and prior to the 1980s it was a much more marginal field of criminology than is now the case), such research tended to be linked to law and order politics and calls for stronger policing powers. More recently, however, fear of crime work has occupied a more central place in criminology and has become linked to the government of crime through risk managerial techniques: in particular as a mobilizing force to create responsible victims who will reduce their exposure to risk (see Stanko, 1994 and Chapter 19 in this volume). In such contexts, community police may, in fact, make the reduction of 'irrational' fear of crime one of its goals, in order to encourage practical and effective risk avoidance behaviours on the part of potential victims (O'Malley, 1997). The fear of crime literature is thus unevenly relevant to the concerns of this book and is only marginally represented in it, for so much depends on how it is deployed.

But if the term 'the risk society' is a useful identifier, and one which would be immediately familiar to many criminologists, it has its dangers. Indeed, in general I would not otherwise favour using the term because it can be read to imply that whole societies are, or could be, oriented entirely around risk and risk management and in which people are effectively subordinated to such regimes – certainly an implication of Beck's thesis. The term is used, rather, to refer to what Mitchell Dean (1995) describes as a *telos* – as a pattern of activities and knowledges which are oriented toward a specific end but which do not necessarily achieve this. It is thus possible to speak of nineteenth-century Britain, for example, as a disciplinary society without implying that the population was disciplined or that all existing organizations were disciplinary. Part IV of this volume, which examines some of the opposing forces to actuarial justice and crime control, is provided as a corrective to more totalizing visions – and especially to those who would see the risk society as the inevitable endpoint of 'the way things are going'.

Crime in the Risk Society

Part I of this volume deals with broad attempts to theorize the rise of the risk society, with particular reference to crime control. Jonathan Simon's essay (Chapter 1) is a significant point at which to begin, because it sets out a general, broadly Foucaultian, thesis about the emergence of 'the risk society' out of the disciplinary society with which we are all familiar. Disciplinary society is a society in which the processes of instilling conformity and correcting (or punishing) deviance in individuals – 'training the soul' – are the primary governing techniques. For Simon, this world has been eroded over the past century by government which grasps security problems in terms of actuarial data and governs them with actuarial technologies. This essay, perhaps with greater detail and scope than any other of which I am aware, provides an introduction to the risk society thesis and clearly outlines its defining features. Much of Simon's analysis is not concerned with crime as such, for he is intent on outlining the extent to which this new technology of rule can be seen investing major areas of life and law – from the management of credit cards through the government of accidents. Indeed, this generalist scene setting is the principal reason why this essay has pride of place.

However, it also makes two further important contributions. The first is to speculate about the logic underlying the spread of actuarialism in the late twentieth century. This he controversially attributes to its economy, arguing that it is less visible than disciplinarity and thus provokes less resistance, and does not require the disciplinary sequestration of individuals or the difficult process of changing people's minds. It is also, in his view, a more tolerant technology in that it can allow much greater leeway in individual deviance than the normatively focused disciplinary techniques and is ostensibly more concerned with technical distribution of harms than with the enforcement of morality (see also Simon, 1988; Ewald, 1991; Defert, 1991). In this way, he suggests, it is well fitted to the late twentieth-century consumerist cultural milieux, whereas it would not have been adequate to deal with the dangerous classes which were confronted by – and rendered more tractable by – disciplinarity in previous centuries. It is perhaps disappointing that this stimulating, if somewhat technologically determinist, account has not been followed up in his later work. But as we will see, this may be because he devises more convincing arguments.

Simon's second subsidiary argument stresses that crime control is nevertheless an area in which sovereign technologies remain robust. Individual punishment, morality and coercion are still vital forces and remain in considerable tension with emerging actuarialism – what he refers to as 'the contest between "risk" and "sovereignty"'. This contest, he proposes (although arguably the two are allied as often as they are in conflict) must always remain in the forefront of thinking about crime and the risk society. This is a crucial point, for it is in the nature of explorations into new developments that the advances of the novel over the existing order are usually overstated.

The same theme of the fate of discipline in the face of emerging preventive and 'amoral' techniques also exercises Shearing and Stenning in their already classic essay 'From the Panopticon to Disney World' (Chapter 2). However, while Simon hypothesizes the displacement of discipline by actuarialism, Shearing and Stenning suggest that, in many important ways, this is mistaken. In particular, they stress that the emerging practices of rule are highly disciplinary – albeit in the form of a new 'instrumental' disciplinarity – in that they require or impose orderly restraint and self-government by knowledgeable subjects. But whether we describe it as actuarialism or as instrumental disciplinarity, like Simon, they see an order emerging that is 'embedded, preventative, subtle, co-operative and apparently non-coercive and consensual.... focuses on categories, [and] requires no knowledge of the individual' (p. 45). They, too, provide an explanation for the rise of this form of power, and begin their analysis by locating the dynamic force behind such changes in the private or market sector.

In this sector, profitability and cost-benefit analysis, rather than issues of morality and law, determine whether and/or how to proceed in relation to a crime problem. Securing against loss becomes more important than protecting legal morality, and likewise prediction and prevention are much more important to profitability than punishment or correction. The expansion of private sector crime control industries generalizes this orientation towards governing in terms of risks to profit and the security of capital. It occurs not only through the growth of private security but, more importantly, through the growth of 'mass private property' (of which Disney World is the selected example) which requires policing and order maintenance on an unprecedented scale. Shearing and Stenning thus see risk-based changes in crime control not as driven by the growth of actuarialism as a social technology, but rather as part of the spread of security-oriented 'instrumental discipline', driven by the expansion of private authorities and corporate power. However, they seem to concur with Simon on the judgement that the advancement of this technology of rule is founded in its efficiency and relative economy when compared to traditional disciplinary governance.

In Chapter 3 Nancy Reichman provides a third interpretation of the same set of trends in crime control. In her analysis of an emerging 'actuarial model of social control', the specifically insurantial identity of the techniques of risk management looms larger than in the other essays. Indeed, a valuable contribution, especially at this point in the collection, is her schematic outline of the insurantial nature of this range of techniques in terms of 'classification and selection of risk', 'loss prevention' (that is, controlling the hazards for those risks that you do assume), and 'transferring risk'. As with some of the other essays in this area, it is disappointing that analysis in such *insurantial* terms has not really been extended subsequently in the criminological literature, although there is a growing body theorizing insurance elsewhere (for example, Burchell *et al.*, 1991; O'Malley, 1996; Baker, 1994, 1996; Stone, 1994; Simon, 1988).

What is also valuable here are the brief but stimulating conclusions in which Reichman suggests that an explanation for the shift toward risk management is to be found in changes in the order of modern capitalism. Drawing on Claus Offe's (1985) analysis she suggests that the emergence of actuarial control may be a response to the contradictions between accumulation and legitimation – and in particular the problems of the fiscal and legitimation crises that confront the welfare states. By 'building control directly into the environment, insurance techniques socialize the costs of control without the need for a direct state intervention' (p. 167) – a process furthered by the trend in current insurance and crime prevention toward making potential crime victims more responsible for governing their own personal and property security. This, of course, appears to be in direct contradiction to the Beck model, as it locates actuarialism in the dynamics of 'class society' rather than in 'risk society'. More to the point, it takes as the key issue the relationship not between actuarialism and discipline, but the relationship between two different models of risk management – the socialized and the privatized. While it comes to the problem from a different theoretical position, this is the central issue for the following essay.

The first three essays hardly address each other (largely because they are pioneering pieces written almost simultaneously), and thus provide only an indirect and somewhat limited debate. However, O'Malley's later (1992) essay (Chapter 4) develops specifically as a critique of Simon's opening essay. It questions the elision of political and moral dimensions from analyses of actuarialism itself and thus questions the tension between actuarialism and sovereignty that is thereby posited. Its concern is to map out the extent to which many of the features of actuarial and insurance technologies – especially, but not only, in the field of crime control – have grown to prominence because they are linked closely with the ascend-ant politics of neo-liberalism (or perhaps more accurately 'advanced liberalism' (Rose, 1996a, 1996b)). Neo-liberalism rejects the forms of social insurance and socialized risk management that characterize welfarism and Keynesianism and seeks to govern through making individuals responsible and through the promotion of competition and the market model. The idea that we are witnessing the advance of actuarialism, O'Malley argues, is mislead-ing. Rather, we are witnessing a change in the *form* of actuarialism: from social forms (social insurances, the welfare state) to individual, private and market forms of 'prudentialism' (private insurances, individual purchase of security commodities and the like). This political shift, he argues, is also responsible for the currently rising tide of punitivism in penal discourses, which is seen as allied with, rather than hostile to, increased individual risk management. For example, both punitivism and prudentialism emphasize individual respon-sibility and promote a tight nexus between actions and consequences. In addition, many of the characteristics of risk-focused actuarial justice – such as the abandonment of correctionalism and the emphasis on incapacitation of high-risk offenders – are quite con-sistent with neo-liberal visions that punishment should not be alloyed with the provision of retraining in the prison – a benefit for which a free person would have to pay a market price. The spread of marketized, as opposed to socialized, actuarialism therefore appears as one aspect of a broader shift toward a resurgent neo-liberal individualism in contemporary politics, thus raising further questions about the divergence of actuarialism from disciplinarity.

Part I thus leaves us with an open and fascinating debate on several fronts. There is general agreement about the nature of the changes that are summarized in the term 'risk society' and about how these are manifested in crime control. But each theoretical account, while provocative, also appears wanting. Simon seems to flirt with technological determin-ism and assumes a contest between sovereignty, discipline and actuarialism that may not be there. Shearing and Stenning seem to have little place for a moral politics despite the fact that this is central to crime control (see, for example, Garland, 1991) and are perhaps open to accusations of an economism that does not pay sufficient attention to the innovative role of the public sector, especially under neo-liberals. Reichman has only the most shadowy of explanations for the appearance and spread of insurantialism, while O'Malley does not adequately account for the spread of actuarial techniques into areas that were never invested by the social and are not obviously the concern of resurgent neo-liberalism. The prominence of the risk society thesis in the field of criminology makes it unlikely that these differences and shortcomings will be left unaddressed for very long.

Policing the Risk Society

Part II moves away from generally broad-ranging attempts to delineate and account for the nexus between crime control and risk society and concentrates more specifically on the processes of policing. Despite this, Ericson's essay (Chapter 5) is significant in part because it is one of the few essays in this literature that has attempted to bring to bear the work of Ulrich Beck (see also Hebenton and Thomas, Chapter 9 in this volume). Ericson develops

Beck's thesis – particularly his stress on the strategic place occupied by knowledge and expertise relating to security – to account for what he perceives as the principal transformation of the police in the risk society. Rather than fighting crime, he argues, the police officer now 'produces and distributes knowledge for the risk management activities of security operatives in other institutions' (p. 99). Such institutions include local government, the private security industry, the insurance industry, community organizations and so on. In part, this knowledge-brokering function becomes identified with the police because police forces are security agencies with a historical licence to generate, receive and store such information but, equally, it is because they are, for much the same reason, situated at the intersection of a huge network of security-focused social relations and agencies. A corollary of this, Ericson suggests, is that, as risk consciousness generalizes throughout the society, responsibility for effecting security increasingly passes from the police to these other sites and agencies – to the potential victim, to the local community, to the insurance corporation and so on (cf. Stanko, Chapter 19). Thus for Ericson, the risk society thesis helps explain a number of other recognized changes in policing over the past few years that are not generally addressed in the risk society literature, or are not directly linked to its dynamics. These include the valorization of victim responsibility (which O'Malley attributes to linked political rationalities), and the devolution of policing and other crime control rules to a diversity of dispersed private agencies (which Mugford in Chapter 23 understands as an effect of postmodernization of the state). Certainly it would appear that there are promising avenues to be explored using Beck's model and, indeed, Ericson and his colleagues recently have made substantial contributions (Ericson and Haggerty, 1997). However, overall, the attraction of more Foucaultian themes focused on actuarialism seems to be blinkering analysts to its potential.

The essays by Litton and O'Malley (Chapters 6 and 7), dealing with insurance and crime prevention, are the first of several essays in the collection that do not orient themselves explicitly to the risk society thesis, but rather represent instances, or detailed maps, of processes highlighted by this model. Both are explorations of the police–insurance nexus that forms part of Ericson's reading of policing in the risk society, and thus also link back to Reichman's emphasis on insurance practices. Litton's essay provides an example of how the insurance industry's thinking and planning was already (in 1982) moving *self-consciously*, and with considerable sophistication, in the direction of reinventing crime control along the lines explored in Part I. Litton writes as an insurance practitioner seeking to move crime control's focus away from past-oriented causal theories and correctional models, and towards such preventive strategies as identifying and reshaping high risk crime situations – a process now referred to as 'target hardening' and 'situational crime prevention'. He identifies ways in which the insurance industry could play a part in this process, *inter alia*, by providing incentives to potential victims to implement such security knowledge. In terms later to be echoed almost identically by risk society theorists, Litton suggests that 'criminologists should not concern themselves with trying to change the individual – his dispositions, traits or personality – but instead should concentrate on modifying the environment with which the criminal is faced when carrying out his criminal acts' (p. 126).

O'Malley's analysis of how the insurance industry and police work together with respect to crime prevention links closely to the two previous essays, but focuses instead on a single empirical study of how this was practised at the 'grassroots' level in Australia. One aspect of this research explores the articulation between police and other non-state security organizations discussed by Ericson, here seen at work in cooperative projects to disseminate security-skilling material regarding domestic property, and to mobilize citizens in security-related practices. But we also see the concrete operation of new risk managerial practices in which responsibility for preventive security is privatized and located at the individual or family level through institutional arrangements built into the insurance contract – a theme developed theoretically in several of the previous essays. By chance, although its theoretical focus is not on the risk society, the chapter's overarching theoretical concern is that which also exercises Ericson (and later Mugford), – namely, the 'dispersion' of government in the current era.

In Chapter 8 Trevor Bennett provides us with an excellent outline of 'the large number of strategies and tactics targeted at particular "hot spot" locations, high-rate offences, high-rate offenders and high-risk victims' (p. 182) in Britain, and at the same time indicates just how many police forces are involved in such work. Taking issue with Ericson and others, he argues that police are highly active in prevention activities, rather than simply receiving and disseminating knowledge. It is quite possible that Ericson would defend his position by arguing that these activities are still small in scale when compared to information work. It could also be argued that these formal strategies are not always translated into practice by the police. Nevertheless, it is clear that Bennett is mapping out a major shift in police organizational thinking and planning around the central themes of the risk society thesis.

Ericson's reading of the Beck thesis is also at the centre of Hebenton and Thomas's recent work (see Chapter 9) on classifying and tracking sex offenders released into the community (see also Hebenton and Thomas, 1996). Here, much emphasis is placed on supporting Ericson's argument concerning the transmission of security-related information from the police and the criminal justice system to other community agents, including members of the public. Such 'agents' adopt a monitoring, or tracking role with respect to recorded sex offenders and, in this way, Hebenton and Thomas also register (with Lilly, Chapter 17) the impetus towards increased surveillance and regulation that risk managerialism provides. But perhaps one of their most important contributions to the literature is their insistence (following Beck) that the risk society does not produce security. In this view, schemes such as sexual offender registration paradoxically produce insecurity not only in the subjective sense, by heightening awareness of risks, but also by promoting devolution of responsibility to 'community' groups which, in practice, are not well equipped to deal with the matter and which are prone to media manipulation and moral panic. The effect, they note, is likely to be '"at odds" with the criminal justice system's "calculated knowledge" of risk assessment and management' (p. 199).

In the final chapter of Part II O'Malley and Mugford examine a development in policing almost quintessentially actuarial in its nature – random drug testing. Here, the key issue focuses on the way in which random drug testing has been introduced – especially in the workplace – ostensibly as a means of risk reduction. The essay argues that, despite the technology being presented as an amoral and technical exercise to increase safety, the evidence supporting this rationale is weak or non-existent. Much of the data indicating that drug use causes accidents in the workplace is questionable, while evidence that reductions in accidents can be attributed the effects of random drug testing are dubious. The authors suggest that, rather than workplace testing being part of a risk reduction exercise, it is rather more evidently part of a moral and disciplinary crusade to stamp out drug use. In a sense, risk-based actuarialism is deployed as a smokescreen for a very old-fashioned disciplinary project of moral exclusion.

Actuarial Justice

Part III begins with the essay by Feeley and Simon that brought the issues of actuarialist crime control and risk managerial criminology to the attention of most criminologists. Developing the model of actuarialism outlined in Simon's 'The Emergence of a Risk Society' (Chapter 1), this essay takes account of the rising punitivism of current penological discourses but, unlike O'Malley in his critique of Simon, sees this as just another swing of a political pendulum, quite distinct from the steady advance of actuarial language and technique. Focusing on penological trends, they suggest, makes it clear that the agenda has changed from individual reform to management or containment of dangerous categories. As normalization becomes irrelevant, so the criteria of institutional success move away from successful correctional outcomes to the efficiency of the system itself in which key issues are reduction of risk through incapacitation, successful security measures and cost-effectiveness. Feeley and Simon link this shift to the emergence of thinking about a new, politically defined 'underclass' mostly constituted by Black Americans who represent a significant categorical risk, and who are regarded as permanently excluded from the labour market by structural changes occurring during the last 30 years. For these people, reform is thus regarded as pointless for it is without economic, social or cultural anchors. They are now politically defined as no longer part of the normative universe of the larger community. This particular aspect of the argument is developed in more detail elsewhere (Simon, 1992) but, even so, it represents, in its present form, an important development of the position outlined in Simon's opening essay which posited that the retention of 'sovereign' punishments in relation to this sector of the populace represented 'one of the last traces to share a commitment to share a community with them' (p. 24). Five years later, the judgement appears to be that this commitment has been abandoned, and the 'contest between sovereignty and actuarialism' resolved in favour of the latter.

The issue of 'dangerousness' raised by Feeley and Simon, it needs to be stressed, is not a revival of the venerable debates over imprisoning dangerous offenders whose dangerousness was evaluated solely on the basis of their case histories and whose imprisonment was justified by reference to social utility and social defence. Rather, something new has come into consideration, and one highly visible turning point here was the 'Floud Report' (Floud and Young, 1981) which made a significant impact on British official penology in the 1980s. Jean Floud's (1982) overview of the report, reprinted as Chapter 12, makes clear the emerging logic which it expressed is one that explicitly rejects the social defence justification for inflicting imprisonment on people because they are judged to be dangerous. Rather it introduces a new logic, that 'we are thereby relieving someone else of a substantial risk of grave harm – that we are justly *redistributing a burden of risk that we cannot immediately reduce*' (p. 262, emphasis added). Indeed, she moves on to argue that dangerousness is not linked to the threat to a specific person, but rather that 'the strength of the case for a protective sentence must vary inversely with the size of the population at risk from the offender concerned' (p. 263). In this sense, Floud began to shift the penological emphasis away from the offender and on to the population at risk.

The Floud Report, although published in 1981, had been commissioned and under way since 1976. In the United States, an almost exactly contemporaneous process was taking place at the Rand Corporation, resulting in the publication, in 1982, of Peter Greenwood's report on *Selective Incapacitation*. This outlined a classification scheme based on statistical data rather than case records, which claimed to determine which offenders could be designated at 'high risk' of reoffending and should be incapacitated by long sentences, and which could be safely assigned to 'low-risk' status and low security programmes. Blackmore and Welsh in Chapter 13, outline the Greenwood Report and the response to it. In particular they provide a valuable summary of the risk-based vision of the research, and of how it was established that actuarial prediction seems to greatly reduce the problem of false positive predictions that afflict expert classification. It was this same problem that confronted the authors of the Floud Report, although their response was to create an actuarial discourse to justify expert-based sentencing under these conditions, rather than to recommend actuarial sentencing *per se*.

Blackmore and Welsh conclude their analysis by noting that, at the time of writing (1983), no state had adopted Greenwood's proposal. But, within a decade, a proliferation of 'dangerous offender' legislation had been introduced in a wide array of jurisdictions worldwide. This development led John Pratt to examine the broader genealogy of the concept of dangerousness. In Chapter 14, Pratt starts the examination with the 1970s disillusionment over the inability of experts to predict dangerousness in individual offenders (which had given rise to both the Floud and Greenwood reports). He maps out the extent to which jurisdictions, since the 1980s, have been implementing sentencing models of actuarial prediction based on the more reliable predictors produced from statistical profiles of dangerousness. As Castel (1991) has also argued, Pratt notes that, in such analyses, the concept or category of dangerousness has changed. No longer is it seen as a real attribute of individuals, but, instead, emerges as a probabilistic attribute of an aggregate: attributions of dangerousness now are made in terms of profiles built up from statistical data which are then matched to the individual. (In their essay Feeley and Simon note that an identical process works with the policing of drug couriers.) This, clearly enough, is one of the foundations of the recent 'three strikes and you're out' sentencing policies, in which all individual detail relating to the offender is abandoned in favour of a risk-based formula of the utmost crudity. Yet even this form of selective incapacitation is not the end of the line for risk-based sanctioning.

Among the many objections to 'three strikes' legislation has been the objection that prison is an expensive punishment, and it would not be feasible to expand capacity to accommodate all repeat offenders. As Jonathan Simon might suggest, this violates the 'system efficiency' element of actuarialist penology. However, economic rationalist analyses, such as that prepared by Edwin Zedlewski from the National Institute of Justice and reproduced here as Chapter 15, challenge such a view and provide a basis for expanding such strategies. Zedlewski argues that the full range of costs created by releasing offenders into the community has not been built into assessments that prison is an expensive sanction. If we include the costs of crime for victims (translating violence and injury into monetary equivalents), costs to the welfare system (many offenders are unemployed), costs generated by the increased crime prevention and policing created by released offenders being at large, costs to the court system for dealing with subsequent offending and so on, then the picture changes: '[I]ncapacitating borderline offenders now crowded out by today's space constraints would likely cost communities less in crime expenditure than they now pay in social damages and prevention' (p. 336). While such proposals have not been taken up, they provide a clear illustration of the extents to which the risk society logic may go in order to minimize harms through incarceration of its risky citizens.

The essay following, by Clear and Barry, is like Zedlewski's, in that it is written from within the advancing paradigm. It provides an important demonstration that we need to pay attention to diversity and dispute *within* what we define as actuarial penology – a matter almost entirely ignored by theoretical commentators. Indeed, Clear and Barry's argument indicates that the range of views about, and diversity of options available for, 'effective' actuarial sanctioning is potentially as great as that among correctionalists in penal modernism. In their complex, subtle and sometimes alarming essay, they express concern about the effectiveness of the present 'crude' incapacitative approach for achieving goals of risk reduction. Current approaches, they argue, are actuarially unsophisticated in many respects. They are also seen to be penologically inadequate because they treat incapacitation as a unity – whereas 'a *variety* of incapacitative measures [should] be considered as researchable, including relatively high failure-rate approaches' (p. 350). In other words, even where they are regarded as 'failing' according to orthodox evaluation, some approaches may nevertheless prove cost-effective with respect to certain categories of offender who represent an expensive risk if left at large. Such arguments are perhaps disturbing because they have the potential to expand imprisonment almost geometrically, but the authors' most striking claim is the complaint that 'legal agencies operate to limit the potential of incapacitation' (p. 351). For example, they note that the increased severity of a punishment ordinarily requires increased levels of proof, and this works against actuarially effective sanctioning. In other words, such aspects of legal tradition as due process, attrition of cases and discretion limit the effectiveness of actuarial sanctioning. Unless such issues are addressed, they suggest, we will prematurely judge incapacitation a failure.

The final two essays in the Part III, written a decade later and from a rather different perspective, begin an examination of 'progress' with respect to two of the matters raised by Clear and Barry: the development of alternative incapacitation and the actuarial transformation of justice.

Electronic monitoring or 'tagging' has been experimented with in most OECD jurisdictions, with uneven results. In Chapter 17 Lilly provides us with a succinct account of this development in the British and US contexts, noting, in the process, the ways in which many of the features of what Feeley and Simon define as 'the new penology' appear. As many observers have previously noted, electronic monitoring and related surveillance technologies form a kind of electronic panopticon in which 'it becomes ever more difficult to ascertain when and whether or not we are being watched and who is doing the watching' (p. 359). But Lilly's argument makes clear that this is not simply the extension of panoptical disciplinarity into the 'punitive society' (Cohen, 1979), for these technologies 'trigger a shift from targeting specific suspects to categorical suspicion' and facilitate 'anticipatory strategies [that] seek to reduce risk and uncertainty' (p. 359). In addition, as Stan Cohen (1985) has also observed, the new technologies enhance surveillance, but disconnect it from a concern about the individual and the disciplinary 'training of the soul'. *Behaviours* become the target of these new devices, which are overwhelmingly of use only in locating the whereabouts of individuals, facilitating home confinement, creating exclusion zones, recording activities and so on. Their attractiveness as an alternative sanction, he suggests, is partly a product of demands for system efficiency (costs are estimated to be 75 per cent lower than people watching people) and partly a result of the market pressure of the private sector security firms developing and marketing the technologies. In this there is much that accords with what earlier essays have defined as characteristic of the new penology. But despite all this, the success and adoption rate of the technology has been uneven, for reasons such as low profitability, lack of cost-effectiveness, political ambivalence and judicial resistance. There is, in short, nothing inevitable about the forms to be taken by actuarial sanctions, even when they appear so ideally to fit the criteria of theorists.

Part III closes with a further development of Feeley and Simon's argument, as they broaden the scope of their thesis from the idea of a 'new penology' to the emergence of 'actuarial justice'. While rehearsing and significantly elaborating a number of the arguments raised in their earlier essay, including a welcome extension of their location of the material origins of actuarial justice in the formation of a new underclass, they also begin new explorations into actuarial justice's intellectual origins. These they locate outside the sphere of punishment, in the emergence of risk management in tort law, the practical application of systems engineering and the rise of the law and economics movement. These claims are likely to give rise to further debate, if only because of their sometimes doubtful privileging of the legal arena and questionable sense of timing. For example, the transformation of tort law into an apparatus of risk management is linked clearly enough to the social actuarialism of the early part of the century and is not easily linked to recent developments in criminal justice. Thus while pointing to the displacement of torts by social insurance schemes as an exemplar of actuarialism – epitomized by the New Zealand case – Feeley and Simon fail to note that, under neo-liberal regimes, not only have these schemes failed to advance since their high watermark of the early 1980s, but they have been subsequently wound back (see, for example, Palmer, 1995). Furthermore, many of the non-actuarial and individualistic features of tort law – such as contributory negligence (individual fault) – have been experiencing a reassertion in the courts. The debate over relative contributions of the technical and the political–moral to the development of actuarialism evidently is yet to be resolved.

The Politics of Managing Crime Risks

In the final Part, the multiple oppositions and resistances to actuarial justice are addressed, partly as a way of emphasizing that the concept of the 'risk society' should not be read as implying an automatic or total investment of criminal justice by actuarial logics and techniques. Elizabeth Stanko has been one of the most prominent and trenchant critics of the British Home Office's risk managerial programmes for crime prevention, as they relate to women and personal safety. One aspect of her critique is that frameworks of risk management and security consciousness tend to reinforce the myth of 'stranger danger' – largely focusing on safety against intruders and on safety in public places and ignoring the fact that the main source of violence against women is men with whom they live or at least know. Another criticism is that, in keeping with current neo-liberal trends in such programmes, the victim is rendered responsible for managing her own security. But perhaps the most telling critique is that, by accepting the risk managerial framework, 'police advice to women about personal safety fails to ask the question why we are at risk' (p. 421). Addressing such a question – especially where its locus is in such deep causal foundations as men's violence to women – is not a problem congenial to risk management with its non-causal orientation and its focus on the more immediate and remediable 'criminogenic situations' (Garland, 1997).

Exactly this point is explored in greater depth by Sandra Walklate (Chapter 20) who suggests that risk management focuses on the 'symptoms' of crime, rather than its causes or cures, a point made, of course, in most theses of crime in the risk society. But Walklate moves the analysis forward by arguing that this reflects the fact that the concept of risk deployed is itself male-centred – that is, risk in the context of governing crime risks focuses on risk avoidance, which Walklate associates with male knowledges with their impetus to control the environment (and to seek 'zero risk' situations). Risk management, she stresses, need not be associated with risk *avoidance,* for the effect of this association is victim-blaming, and both men and women suffer the consequences of this outcome of gendered knowledge about risk. In the context of women's victimization, particularly in the field of sex, this is frequently and perniciously linked with the argument that a women who failed to avoid risks 'asked for it'. The current model of 'risk society', and the kinds of defensive risk avoidance and management agenda promoted by government crime prevention strategies in this context are, in other words, *gendered.*

Stanko and Walklate represent positions which reflect, or seek to generate, feminist resistance to prevailing models of crime control in the risk society. But it is by no means the case that opposition stems only from critics *outside* the system of crime control. In Chapter 21 Daniel Glaser provides us with an extremely lucid summary of the long history of actuarialism in US criminal justice. Tracing the history of actuarial analyses of criminal offending since the 1920s, Glaser shows that, since that time, actuarial tables have repeatedly been shown to predict offending, by classifying offenders into future risk categories, far more accurately than expert analysis based on case studies. He argues that the opposition to the predictively superior actuarial models has been based on several factors, including the persistence of the 'passion for punishment' that defines actuarial sentencing as amoral and insufficiently responsive to public demands; the resistance of the judiciary and affiliated experts to having their knowledges sidelined; and, (perhaps most importantly) the simple fact that sentencing officials on public and political support which is more attuned to traditional justice. This judicial and expert-based opposition was overcome, he argues, when historical compromises were struck, and sentencing was restructured to take account of both actuarial and expert/judicial considerations and interests. Even so, Glaser suggests, the result is unlikely to be any uniformity of sentencing because of the 'interference' of too many non-actuarial variables – most significantly, plea bargaining. (In this, of course, he precisely reflects Clear and Barry's observations.) To the extent that his analysis is correct, then we may have an explanation for one of the problems that haunts Simon's original thesis – namely, the long time lag between actuarial development in most fields of government and that in the field of criminal justice. Simon's 'contest between sovereignty and actuarialism' now takes on historical significance, for it has been the expression of this in public opinion and judicial politics that has set back the calendar of actuarialism – whose time, otherwise, would have come many years ago.

In the final two essays, Broadhead and Mugford each explore opposition to actuarialism in the field of crime and drug policy. Broadhead's analysis (Chapter 22) is particularly valuable because it brings the level of analysis down to the grassroots level, where it is possible to see the adherents of an actuarial (public health) model of drug regulation engaged in a war of manoeuvre with law and order crime controllers and their moralities. More precisely, we can also see that, while risk managerialism appears as amoral and technical, seeking to control HIV and other diseases though the management of risky behaviours, and while its opponents appear as driving a moral anti-drug agenda, there are rather two moralities in conflict: in short, a politics, one being a utilitarian morality of the least harm to the largest number; the other being the more familiar absolutist moralities of bourgeois rectitude. This same struggle is registered by Mugford (Chapter 23) on a somewhat broader organizational level. Noting that 'harm minimization' (an eminently risk managerial approach) has been state policy in Australia since the mid-1980s, Mugford demonstrates, in his analysis of a key drug policy agency, that, even so, the success of actuarialism is not secure. Struggles between supporters of actuarial harm minimization and the proponents of other models of drug control (including law and order and prohibitionism) continue within the very organizations which seem to be the fortresses of the new order. While at the level of formal policy it may appear that we are witnessing the triumph of actuarialism, the political contest is not over.

Whatever we may think of the 'risk society' and it approach to the governance of crime, the future, as actuarial practitioners themselves would aver, is no more than a set of possibilities.

References

Baker, T. (1994), 'Constructing the Insurance Relationship', *Texas Law Review*, **72**, 1395–433.

Baker, T. (1996), 'On the Genealogy of Moral Hazard', *Texas Law Review*, **75**, 237–92.

Beck, U. (1992a), 'Modern Society as A Risk Society', in N. Stehr and R. Ericson (eds), *The Culture and Power of Knowledge*, New York: de Gruyter.

Beck, U. (1992b), *Risk Society: Towards a New Modernity*, New York: Sage.

Burchell, G., Gordon, C. and Miller, P. (1991), *The Foucault Effect. Studies in Governmentality*, London: Harvester/Wheatsheaf.

Castel, Robert (1991), 'From Dangerousness to Risk', in G. Burchell, C. Gordon and P. Miller (eds), *The Foucault Effect: Studies in Governmentality*, Chicago: University of Chicago Press, pp. 281–98.

Cohen, S. (1979), 'The Punitive City. Notes on the Dispersal of Social Control', *Contemporary Crises*, **3**, 339–63.

Cohen, S. (1985), *Visions of Social Control*, London: Pluto Press.

Collison, M. (1996), 'In Search of the High Life. Drugs, Crime, Masculinities and Consumption', *British Journal of Criminology*, **36**, 428–44.

Dean, M. (1995), 'Governing the Unemployed Self in an Active Society', *Economy and Society*, **24**, 559–83.

Defert, D. (1991), 'Popular Life and Insurance Technology', in G. Burchell, C. Gordon and P. Miller (eds), *The Foucault Effect: Studies in Governmentality*, London: Harvester/Wheatsheaf.

Douglas, M. (1992), *Risk and Blame*, London: Routledge.

Douglas, M. and Wildavsky, A. (1986), *Risk and Culture*, Berkeley: University of California Press.

Ericson, R. and Haggerty, K. (1997), *Policing the Risk Society*, Toronto: University of Toronto Press.

Ewald, F. (1991), 'Insurance and Risk', in G. Burchell, C. Gordon and P. Miller (eds), *The Foucault Effect: Studies in Governmentality*, London: Harvester/Wheatsheaf.

Floud, J. and W. Young (1981), *Dangerousness and Criminal Justice*, London: Heinemann.

Garland, D. (1991), *Punishment and Modern Society*, Oxford: Oxford University Press.

Garland, D. (1995), 'Penal Modernism and Postmodernism', in Stanley Cohen and David Blomberg (eds), *Punishment and Social Control*, New York: Aldine.

Garland, D. (1997), '"Governmentality" and the Problem of Crime', *Theoretical Criminology*, **1**, 173–215.

Greenwood, P. (1982), *Selective Incapacitation*, Santa Monica: Rand Corporation.

Hale, C. (1994), *Fear of Crime: A Review of the Literature*, Canterbury: University of Kent, Canterbury Business School.

Hebenton, B. and Thomas, T. (1996), '"Tracking" Sex Offenders', *The Howard Journal*, **35**, 97–112.

Katz, S. (1988), *Seductions of Crime*, New York: Basic Books.

Lyng, S. (1990), 'Edgework: A Social Psychological Analysis of Voluntary Risk Taking', *American Journal of Sociology*, **95**, 887–921.

Offe, C. (1985), *Disorganized Capitalism*, Cambridge: MIT Press.

O'Malley, P. (1996), 'The Prudential Man Cometh. Industrial Insurance and the Government of Working Class Security', paper presented to the Law and Society Association Annual Meeting, Toronto.

O'Malley, P. (1997), 'Policing, Politics and Postmodernity', *Social and Legal Studies*, **6**, 363–81.

Palmer, G. (1995), 'New Zealand's Accident Compensation Scheme: Twenty Years On', *University of Toronto Law Journal*, **44**, 223–73.

Rose, N. (1996a), '"Governing Advanced Liberal Democracies", in A. Barry *et al.* (eds), *Foucault and Political Reason*, London: UCL Press.

Rose, N. (1996b), 'The Death of the Social? Refiguring the Territory of Government', *Economy and Society*, **25**, 326–54.

Simon, J. (1988), 'The Ideological Effects of Actuarial Practices', *Law and Society Review*, **22**, 772–800.

Simon, J. (1992), 'Doing Time. Punishment, Work Discipline and Industrial Time', paper presented to the Law and Society Association Annual Meeting.

Stone, D. (1994), 'Promises and Public Trust: Rethinking Insurance Law Through Stories', *Texas Law Review*, **72**, 1435–446.

Part I
Crime in the Risk Society

[1]

The Emergence of
a Risk Society:
Insurance, Law, and the State

Jonathan Simon

MODERN SOCIETY is colored by a concern for the risks that people face. One can debate whether or not modern life is more or less risky in an objective sense, but risk itself has been made problematic: individuals in their daily lives are immersed in practices concerned with risk; the methods through which we handle risk are overwhelmingly social. Whether or not this is positive is difficult to say, but the social practices we are creating to deal with risk, such as forms of insurance, are changing society.*

---

*My interest in the social effects of risk management techniques was inspired by the work of Michel Foucault. Foucault was interested in the way modern forms of power operated at the level of populations, in their attempts to represent and regulate the health and welfare of the social body. He used the term "Bio-power" to describe the focus of power on the biological existence of society. Nowhere is this more evident than in the apparatuses of social security and insurance that have spread in western societies since the end of the nineteenth century, what we call the "welfare state." See Foucault, *The History of Sexuality, Vol. I; An Introduction,* trans. Robert Hurley (New York: Random House, 1978), part five. Foucault's own research on this topic was cut short by his tragic death. One of his closest associates,

---

The author wishes to thank the following individuals for their comments and encouragement through various drafts of this paper: Marianne Constable, Keith Gandal, David Horn, Alan Hutchinson, Stephen Kotkin, Susan Lehman, Michael Merantze, Sheldon Messinger, Kerry Nelson, Paul Rabinow, Adam Simon, William Simon, and Jackie Urla. I would especially like to thank Jeff Escoffier for his tremendous help in editing this article. Whatever coherence it has achieved is substantially due to his help. As always, responsibility for all errors remains with the author. —J.S.

Insurance techniques alter the way we interact with each other, and, inevitably, the way we experience ourselves and our belonging together. Insurance represents individuals "actuarially" as instances of a population. This makes it more difficult to conceive of individuals as sovereign subjects, with moral and political dimensions. Actuarial methods aggregate individual experience to predict and plan for risk. They are becoming more prevalent in all parts of society. They represent collective life by "objective" characteristics, distinct from the kinds of bonds that individuals intentionally create with each other. This makes it more difficult to act together as groups, and to understand ourselves as members of a community.

The result of these changes is to make political and moral action appear increasingly irrational. I use these terms not in their generic sense, but as qualities of action and experience that have a history within our culture. When as individuals we speak publicly to condemn certain practices as wrong (not just "inefficient," "suboptimal," or "mistaken") and demand change, we are taking up cultural forms of moral and political character that depend upon a certain kind of community as an audience, and upon a certain kind of self-understanding I call *sovereign*.

These cultural forms are being eroded by the social practices we deploy to manage risk. A close look at the practices involved in the emerging rationality of risk and in the insurance model suggests two distinct cultural patterns: *aggregation,* and *security.**

François Ewald, has published an important study of the historical development of the state's capacity for, and interest in, risk management. See Ewald, *L'État Providence* (Paris: Bernard Grasset, 1986).

*By practice I mean a distinct way of doing things. This can pertain to any area of life, and not just economic life. The assembly line is a practice but so is the missionary position. To a certain degree what is discussed as a single practice may be capable of being interpreted as a number of smaller ones, or included in a set of others to make up a larger practice. What is crucial is a certain unity and mobility so that a practice may be shifted from one project to another without becoming unintelligible. Thus chess is a practice but moving queens isn't. The latter cannot be transferred out of its place in chess without becoming unintelligible.

It is useful to distinguish a phenomenon which is itself made up of specific practices, but is not unified in the way of a practice. I will call this, after Foucault, a *dispositif:* a cluster of practices that has a certain coherence, but one that is looser and more permeable. Foucault used the term to indicate a cluster of practices including both ways of exercising power, and systems of knowledge-gathering and deployment. The dispositif includes both practices and strategies for organizing and deploying its component practices. At the

Insurance and the Management of Aggregates

AT ITS SIMPLEST, insurance is a systematic way of organizing experience to provide for future contingencies. A number of features of this system are worth considering in detail.

1. The contingencies that may affect an individual's life are guarded against by aggregating a group of individuals together. Imagine insuring yourself with a savings account: the amount you would need to save would be calculated on the basis of what your earning capacity would be in the face of various possible events— if you lost your job, if you became ill for a prolonged period, if you became permanently disabled, etc. Obviously your present income, and whatever surplus over immediate need it provided, would place a constraint on the amount you could devote to savings. But, even assuming a high enough income and return on invested savings, the ability to provide for all contingencies is implausible for the average person. Imagine, however, the advantage of knowing in advance when the various contingencies would be realized, if at all. Knowing the amount of time you would have to save before the particular event arrived would make it far more possible to choose an investment strategy to meet that contingency. While such certainty is impossible for the individual, it can be approached if one is dealing with an aggregate of people.

2. The effectiveness of the insurance system depends upon the aggregation of the experience of a sample of the population at risk. The larger the sample provided, the more accurate the pattern indicated. The natural tendency of such a system then is to grow, to place the individual within a larger and larger group.

3. The knowledge gathered is more effective the more it magnifies the differences among individuals. By *dis*aggregating the individual's characteristics, the system can achieve even greater precision in assessing the pattern of negative occurrences within the population. The tendency of the system then is to know the individual in ever finer detail.

4. The knowledge collected concerning an individual does not aim at discovering the individual's "identity." Actuarial methods

---

cost of some confusion this essay will use the term "cultural pattern" to designate the same idea. Risk, for example, as used in this essay refers to a particular cultural pattern—a cluster of knowledge and power practices— which is gaining ascendancy in our society.

compile information about individuals to put together a picture of the population. Whatever response is specified for particular individuals comes from situating them within the population.

THE SET OF PRACTICES and techniques that make up the capacity to insure have a way of hanging together and also a certain dynamic. In order to secure the individual, these actuarial practices simultaneously aggregate and isolate individuals. While seeking to know individuals better and better, these practices disperse the individual in more and more precise fragments within this larger population. These techniques are familiar enough to many of us through interacting with the insurance system. But how do they function as practices that shape our lives? How do they work as rituals that help define how we live together?*

Many of us experience at some point the frustration of not being treated fairly as individuals when we come in contact with insurance. In purchasing auto insurance, for example, we are all subjected to producing information about ourselves that seems to have nothing to do with how safe a driver we are (the factor we invariably think is most important): where we live, how far we have to go to get to work, our level of education, or our grades. No matter how frustrating buying such coverage can be, it comes to an end and hopefully one walks out the door with the necessary insurance. All this aggregating and disaggregating only results in specifying how much we have to pay. The ultimate result is unassailably benevolent. We, and other people, are financially protected against some of the severe harms that can result from even minimally negligent driving. But actuarial techniques are not found exclusively in the provision of insurance. They show up in other forms of financial planning like pensions. They show up in direct marketing where the arrangement and sale of lists of people likely to purchase a certain product or service is carried out by a similar process. They can be found in hiring and admissions procedures. These techniques have become the hallmark of "rationality" in almost every instance where social costs and benefits are distributed.

---

*My use of the term "ritual" follows the long tradition in sociological and anthropological research that treats social practices as techniques for creating and reinforcing social identities. Cf. Erving Goffman, *Interaction Ritual* (Garden City, N.Y.: Anchor Books, 1967).

The Emergence of a Risk Society • *65*

O UR POLITICAL LIFE is increasingly organized in an analogous manner. Polls tell us which candidates are ahead. But the same process results in creating for the candidate a precise picture of the voting public as an aggregate that can be precisely mapped in terms of the distribution of interests and concerns. In just the same way that an insurer puts together a pool of variously assessed premiums to match an aggregate of more or less risky drivers, a politician can assemble a speech to appeal to the sentiments of a majority of voters. Now imagine Ronald Reagan.

Most of the criticism about polling and the political process has been directed at the effect of voters knowing more about the likely outcome of political contests.* But more disturbing is the power given to candidates and their organizations to get around traditional intermediate associations like unions and urban party machines. The union vote, for example, was once a group thought capable of being delivered in a presidential election by labor leaders, usually to Democratic candidates. If the last several elections have shown this pattern to be inoperable, it is not because union leadership has been challenged by a great grassroots union movement, but because politicians, using the actuarially defined social group as an aggregate, can effectively disaggregate workers. They can speak precisely to union members who own their own homes, go to church, or speak another language. This process has the potential to dissolve groups and thus change the environment in which politics is played out in western culture.

Aggregation is familiar enough to those of us who have always lived within social practices that constantly measure us, compare us to each other, and make everything from receiving a prison sentence to getting into law school more or less easy, depending on how we fit into a comparative picture of the population as a whole. It is difficult to go beyond this familiarity and begin to articulate how these practices color the experience we have of our shared world. But it is important to start with the understanding that these practices do not *merely* represent us. To represent us in a certain way is also to shape how we actually are, if our society makes vital choices based upon such representations.

---

*Criticism has been especially severe of television election-day voter-exit surveys, which allow networks to declare a winner before the polls have closed, and which sometimes trigger a concession as in Jimmy Carter's 1980 defeat.

Insurance, Security, and Welfare

S INCE THE END of the nineteenth century most western nations
have provided alternative systems that resemble insurance practices, pooling resources to cover the risks generated by collectivities of people. These alternatives are generally the politics of the
welfare state: pension provision for retirees, direct cash relief to
disabled or laid-off employees, direct payment of medical costs for
the poor and elderly, direct cash payments to insolvent families, as
well as such lesser operations as student and small-business loans.
Capitalist societies vary considerably in how extensive and gener-
ous these networks are, with the United States among the least
extensive and stingiest. Differences exist, as well, in terms of how
these systems are managed. Some are actuarially based investment programs like commercial insurance. Others are a direct tap
into the general revenue of the state. It is important to see both
privately purchased "security" and publicly provided "welfare" as
a single cluster of practices, providing security for all segments of
the population.*

Today some methods of risk management have become predominantly private relationships, while others, such as direct relief
to the poor, remain among the functions of the state. The private
forms serve those who belong to the official economy, while the
state provides emaciated versions of the same protection to those
who are not linked to that economy through regular employment
or family ties. The distinction between public and private in these
capacities may seem vital because of the enduring debate over
nationalization (of health insurance, for example) and privatization. But this debate is really about the generosity and accountability of social insurance measures.

The contemporary cultural concern with risk then is really com-

---

*This general emphasis on security is highly distorted by class stratification
in capitalist countries, particularly the United States. But this does not
undermine the basic point that security has become a fixture of contemporary rationality. Even conservative critics of the welfare state don't attack
the rationality of providing security. Indeed they argue that more unregulated choice by the private sector will provide this security more efficiently
than public provisions.

Securing a population has a double meaning. It involves guarding the
well-being of the population, and guarding the population against the dangers it poses to itself. Thus the word *police,* which we today understand in
the sense of guarding, in the eighteenth century also signified regulating and
fostering.

posed of the confluence of two different historical processes. On the one hand is the growth of a set of techniques for *aggregating* people, representing them as locations in a population distribution, and treating people on the basis of this distribution. On the other hand, a set of political and economic strategies have made *security* a pervasive task for the state and other large organizations.

The Legal History of Accidents

THIS COMBINATION, which I call *risk,* first proliferated within those social processes involved with handling the distribution of harms in society: law. Considerable scholarly attention has lately been given to the history of accident law. Dispute has arisen as to whether the early law of tort in the sixteenth and seventeenth centuries required the injured plaintiff to prove that the defendant behaved in an unreasonably faulty manner, or whether defendants were strictly liable for harms they caused regardless of how carefully they acted. In either case it is clear that the costs of accidents were distributed on an individual basis by either letting them lie where they fell, or through the legal joust between parties in court.

At the end of the nineteenth century in Europe, however, and a little later in the United States, legal forms began to facilitate the social management of harms. The first wave of development in the U.S. centered on workers' compensation. The system was authorized by acts of various state legislatures from 1911 until World War II.[1] It abolished the common-law action of injured employees against their employers, and required employers to maintain insurance to cover all injuries received by workers from their labor.

Controversy exists among legal historians today as to how valuable the common-law right really was. In a notorious 1842 ruling, Chief Justice Shaw of the Massachusetts Supreme Court laid down what became know as the "fellow servant rule."[2] Under this rule workers injured by unreasonably hazardous workplace incidents could only sue the person most directly at fault for the hazard. In industrial shops and railroads, this was most likely another employee. The owner of the enterprise (unless directly involved) was effectively immunized.* More recent scholarship has pointed out

---

*Friedman and Ladinsky argue that Shaw's opinion was really an exercise in risk management. Utilizing contract language Shaw attempts to show that workers choose a level of risk in employment by selecting dangerous jobs. Their return on this choice is higher pay, and thus they should not get the

that common-law recovery was becoming more attainable for workers by the end of the nineteenth century. The "fellow servant" rule, and other rules protecting business owners, were eaten away by lower courts and local juries with pro-worker sympathies.[3]

The effect on legal rights and their economic utility does not exhaust the social impact of workers' compensation. The new laws transformed the conception of an accident from one of anomaly, to one of normal and inevitable occurrence. The reform initially aimed at replacing litigation with administration. Although lawyers quickly reasserted their role in the management of the system, the new practices placed them within a different discourse, in a different forum, and thus gave them a different ritual effect.[4]

A SECOND WAVE of development took off after World War II and social insurance was expanded to cover new portions of the population harmed by either industrial production or consumer products. Unlike workers' compensation, this generation of accident-law reform was never viewed as replacing private common-law rights. On the contrary, the legal field of "products liability" was seen as an expansion of "private" rights to sue.

Traditionally accident law, or torts as it is known to lawyers, was subordinate to contract law. People injured by manufactured goods could only sue the party they bought them from. Since no contract existed between the initial producer and the ultimate consumer, no duty of care was implied. The right to sue the maker of the product was granted to consumers only gradually.

In the case of *MacPherson v. Buick Motor Co.* (1916), Justice Benjamin Cardozo (then on the high court of New York, and later on the U.S. Supreme Court) upheld lower courts in allowing a purchaser of an automobile, who had been injured when the wooden wheel collapsed, to sue its manufacturer.[5] The holding of the case ratified a movement toward consumer law suits that was already under way.

Cardozo's opinion reflects the problems of justifying social insurance in a discourse keyed to rights and obligations among individuals in the "private realm." He attempted to show that the right

---

additional windfall from the court of accident relief from the employer. Shaw's notion of risk however is a narrow economic one. A social conception of risk that highlights the wider spread of harm in the social body does not arise in the United States for a half a century or more.

The Emergence of a Risk Society • *69*

to sue the manufacturer was always embodied in a higher-level legal principle which, as he wrote, "has never in this state been [in] doubt." Using the close reasoning for which he is justifiably renowned, Cardozo took cases which had gone precisely the other way and argued that their different facts allowed that the judges writing might have been applying the same principle to different facts.

On his side Cardozo had a series of cases allowing consumers to sue manufacturers. This line was long-running but traditionally confined to a series of especially hazardous products, such as poisons which can be mislabeled, or explosives which can go off at the wrong time. Over the argument of the defendant in *MacPherson,* Cardozo weaves the two lines of cases together: dangerous things where the manufacturer can be sued, and ordinary things where the consumer is limited to suing the immediate seller.

Cardozo pulls this off by playing with the concept of dangerousness. That of poisons and explosives is an inherent matter: they are things made for the very purposes that make them dangerous. The lawyer for the defendants in *MacPherson* argued that an automobile is of a different order, not made to be dangerous but as a form of transportation which, under appropriate conditions, does not release harmful purposes. Cardozo rejected this argument and substituted a "functional" concept of dangerousness where previously an "ontological" concept had operated:

> The defendant argues that things imminently dangerous to life are poisons, explosives, deadly weapons—things whose normal function it is to injure or destroy. But whatever the rule...may once have been, it has no longer that restricted meaning. A scaffold...is not inherently a destructive instrument. It becomes destructive only if imperfectly constructed. A large coffee urn...may have within itself, if negligently made, the potency of danger, yet no one thinks of it as an implement whose normal function is destruction. What is true of the coffee urn is equally true of bottles of aerated water...[6]

The first wave of social insurance, workers' compensation, was pushed forward on the basis of factory and railroad injuries: a regulatory web of security and control was created but confined to industrial spaces with narrow corridors interconnecting them. Just as the automobile caused cities to fill in and sprawl outwards, it helped social insurance spread out in all directions. The legal infrastructure of risk moved from a few relationships tightly linked to employment or proximity, to the general population.

THE SHIFT IN DOCTRINE culminating in *MacPherson* opened up the legal possibility of suing manufacturers, but other restraints, both doctrinal and practical, prevented recoveries from being widely generated. Cardozo had announced a functional concept of dangerousness, but he left it circumscribed by the concept of *negligence,* a concept usually assigned given weeks of class time in law school. Here it will suffice to say that negligent conduct is conduct unreasonable in the light of prevailing practice. Judges have considerable power to define the standard of care against which defendants will be judged. By the end of World War II judges were often holding manufacturers to a strict enough standard to permit recovery. But the law moved through the language of negligence even as it pushed the standard of care higher and higher. This left negligence in place as an increasingly ambiguous concept.

Another famous state high court judge, Roger Traynor of California, suggested an alternative doctrinal formulation known as "strict liability" to make the law consistent with the operational web of social insurance that was being churned out under negligence. In *Escola v. Coca Cola Bottling of Fresno* (1944), a waitress was injured when a Coke bottle spontaneously shattered in her hands. The California Supreme Court upheld a jury verdict in her favor finding the bottler negligent. Traynor joined in voting to uphold the jury finding and award, but argued that the concept of negligence had become gratuitous:

> It is to the public interest to discourage the marketing of products having defects that are a menace to the public. If such products nevertheless find their way into the market it is to the public interest to place responsibility for whatever injury they may cause upon the manufacturer, who, even if he is not negligent in the manufacture of the product, is responsible for its reaching the market. However intermittently such injuries may occur and however haphazardly they may strike, the risk of their occurrence is a constant risk and a general one. Against such a risk there should be a general and constant protection, and the manufacturer is best situated to afford such protection.[7]

In this passage, Traynor makes several different moves to disentangle the manufacturer's liability from the question of whether or not the manufacturer acted unreasonably. Traynor uses responsibility not so much to imply blame as to mark the fact that Coke will be assigned the risk. When he says that the manufacturer is "responsible for [the dangerous product] reaching the market," he doesn't mean that it's the manufacturer's fault, but that in a functional sense the manufacturer actually does cause the good to get to the market.

Traynor also represents the risks of overcarbonation in a very different way. Bottles exploding are not treated as anomalies that break the rules of normal conduct, but as a regular by-product of the manufacturing process which is predictable in general, but not in its specific manifestations. The logic of his position is forward-looking. Manufacturers can provide the generalized form of security needed to counteract the social cost of this risk, regardless of whether they could prevent the risk in the first place.

> As handicrafts have been replaced by mass production with its great markets and transportation facilities, the close relationship between the producer and consumer of a product has been altered. Manufacturing processes . . . are ordinarily either inaccessible to or beyond the ken of the general public. The consumer no longer has means or skill enough to investigate for himself the soundness of a product, even when it is not contained in a sealed package, and his erstwhile vigilance has been lulled by the steady efforts of manufacturers to build up confidence by advertising and marketing devices such as trade marks. Consumers no longer approach products warily but accept them on faith, relying on the reputation of the manufacturer or trade mark. . . . The manufacturer's obligation to the consumer must keep pace with the changing relationship between them.[8]

Traynor's concurring opinion became the law in California almost twenty years later. Together with New Jersey and New York, California's lead has been widely followed by other states. The replacement of negligence by the doctrine of strict liability with respect to harms generated through the normal use of products has become predominant.* But in the form envisioned by Traynor,

---

*The development of a social insurance rationality in legal doctrine has been relatively slow. Certain legal scholars understood the importance of insurance for transforming law and the legal understanding of individual responsibility as early as the 1920s. Young B. Smith, writing on the subject of vicarious liability (the doctrine that allows an injured person to sue the employer of the person directly responsible for her injury) observed that "through the agency of insurance it would be possible to effectuate a spreading of practically all forms of losses, and it is the opinion of the writer that

strict liability leaves many problematic issues that can permit a successful defense by manufacturers.

One example is causation. Injuries caused by modern products are not always apparent at the time they occur. When they surface years later, as in the case of asbestos poisoning, or in the risk of cancer posed to daughters of women who took DES, it may be difficult to determine which of many possible manufacturers produced the specific item that causes the particular plaintiff's harm. In *Sindell v. Abbott Laboratories,* a DES case, the California Supreme Court moved doctrine further toward a rationality of risk.[9] The court held that the unlikelihood of determining which company actually produced the drug that the victim's mother took should not bar her from recovering if the jury found that the drug was dangerous. Noting that the action was only part of a whole wave of similar cases, the court apportioned damages according to each company's market share of DES sales.

Law and the Routinization of Risk

THE PRODUCTS LIABILITY SYSTEM continues to exist in a state of flux and controversy. Calls to extend it further emerge periodically from all sides of the political spectrum but face tremendous opposition from the organized legal profession. In the 1970s, for instance, proposals to spread the model of "strict liability" to areas like medical malpractice, or to eliminate the remaining "fault" issues from strict liability cases, were made by academics and legislatures.[10] In the 1980s, calls for replacing the liability system in cases of catastrophic losses, like the asbestos industry or Bhopal, have been made by the corporations, their insurers, and their politicians. Gary Hart, for example, who introduced legislation to socialize damage payments to asbestos victims, had close ties with John Mansville, which is the largest asbestos defendant.[11]

Below the level of those accidents for which liability is still hotly contested (predominantly very expensive ones), one finds more routinized procedures. The system as a whole can be pictured as a pyramid. At the base are first-party insurance policies that cover most of the harm suffered by most people no matter whose fault.

---

within the next hundred years the possibilities of insurance will lead to very marked changes in the prevailing attitude towards the whole subject of legal responsibility." Young B. Smith, "Frolic and Detour," 23 *Columbia Law Review* 444, 460 (1923).

At this lowest level the social rationality of risk operates almost without interference.

Higher up is a smaller pool of cases where the victim of the accident and the subject of the insurance policy are not the same (thus called third-party insurance), entailing a greater involvement of law. But here as well the principle of risk dominates. Law is reduced to a mechanism of deciding which of several large economic entities will pay for damages. It distributes losses among various risk communities rather than attributing blame and responsibility.

At the pinnacle are a smaller number of exceptionally huge losses due to accidents. Law continues to be a primary way of resolving the placement of these losses. Rather than being only an instrument of risk distribution in these cases, law operates as a ritual of sovereignty, allowing moral and political outrage to be mobilized.

The recent wave of public interest in reforming the tort system has focused on the catastrophic level of losses. But the role of accident resolution in changing our culture is more determinative at the base where many of us directly encounter the social practices of the accident system as rituals. The most important location for these encounters is the world of the automobile.

The Politics of Driving

THERE IS MUCH that differentiates managing a vehicle from managing a marriage, a career, or a life, but stressing some commonalities allows a glimpse at what is at stake in the further entrenchment of the rationality of risk. As in other areas of life, bad things happen while managing vehicles. Sometimes we are at fault, sometimes someone else, sometimes fault doesn't seem to apply at all, as when we run off the road in bad weather. Fault and damages are not always concurrent. Sometimes we hurt ourselves, sometimes we hurt another involved party, sometimes we hurt someone who was hitherto uninvolved. As individuals involved in motor vehicle accidents, we often hold it of considerable significance to determine just who was at fault and apportion the responsibility for damages accordingly. At the social level, this fault/ damage linkage has been nearly severed by insurance.

Today, in most jurisdictions, maintenance of a liability insurance policy is a requirement for all licensed drivers. Increasingly drivers also choose to carry insurance to protect themselves against collisions for which they are at fault, and for when the other driver is uninsured. This insurance is only loosely linked to notions like fault. Drivers with terrible accident records may indeed pay additional premiums, but these differences are paralleled and often surpassed by actuarially derived premium increases. For the most part premiums are based on the sub-population that the driver belongs to, rather than the driver's individual history. For instance drivers who live in poor neighborhoods and who are young, male, and not in school pay higher premiums than other motorists.

One effect of this insurance revolution is on the operation of the legal structure for handling accidents. The clearest example is in the states of New York and Massachusetts, which have largely eliminated recourse to tort litigation for vehicle injuries, replacing it with a so-called "no-fault" system that requires everyone to carry insurance and pays everyone for their injuries, regardless of fault. Even in those jurisdictions where the tort system has not been eliminated through legislative action, the reality has been largely modified by the fact that insurance companies are the real parties in most lawsuits arising from traffic accidents. So much has negotiated settlement come to dominate this field that some states allow an insured defendant to compel her insurance company to settle for an offer within the policy limit or face paying the damages decided by a jury regardless of whether they go beyond the policy limits.[12]

FAULT IS NOT ONLY being pushed aside by risk but in some sense is being annexed by it. A recent decision by the Ninth Circuit Court of Appeals points this out forcefully. The action arose in Hawaii, a state that requires drivers to carry liability insurance. One driver ran over a motorcycle deliberately. The bike's owner sued the driver for damages. The insurance company contested, arguing that its policy only covered "accidents," not intentional harms. The court disagreed and ordered the company to pay. The Court of Appeals upheld the decision, stating that "an event is accidental if it is neither expected nor intended from the viewpoint of the person who is injured."[13]

Today we don't feel that it is problematic for drivers to be relieved of the financial harm of their own faulty conduct. At the dawn of the insurance age during the 1920s, people were concerned that severing the link between fault and compensation would encourage less-careful driving. Managing a motor vehicle (within certain important limits) has become a field of conduct to which little moral judgment attaches. It has become *de-moralized.* This is rational to us because of the social context in which we frame our accidents.

The modern driver has disappeared as a moral subject because our practices for handling the negative consequences of driving don't rely on moral judgments about the parties involved. This is more than a sort of secularization, or a change in sentiment. What has changed are the practices for managing accidental losses, and the way these function as rituals, and the experience we have of ourselves and others in and through these practices. Even the economic subject celebrated by liberal theory is no longer sustained in our social practices of driving. The subject as a rational economic actor surfaces when the law seeks to prevent accidents through deterrence, altering future choices by sanctioning past actions. But modern social insurance techniques undermine deterrence by breaking the link between compensation and fault. Whatever room for deterrence really exists is generally accounted for by the driver's own fear of injury. The teenage hotrodder who isn't thinking about smashing up their body, their friends, and their car, isn't likely to be overly concerned about paying the damages on the other party's vehicle.

We are learning, if gradually, that external environmental controls, such as deliberately placed bumps in the road, traffic obstacles, and other similar devices, can be a more effective hedge against bad driving than those deterrent techniques that depend on the consciousness of the driver. Not only has the moral/political subject been displaced from behind the wheel, the rational/economic subject has been displaced as well. Left steering the car is a more or less great, more or less tolerable risk.

Not all drivers have been de-moralized. There is one kind of driver we can't help but feel deserves some punishment, and for whom we cling to a belief that punishment will deter—the drunk driver. Drinking seems to resuscitate the sovereign subject behind the wheel. In *The Culture of Public Problems,* Joseph Gusfield analyzes the social construction of the drunk-driving problem.[14] He doesn't seek to prove that intoxication is irrelevant to automobile accidents, but to show that the way accidents are treated and recorded highlights the role of alcohol against other factors. Gusfield's point is that the moral sanction that attaches to the drinking driver is rooted more in the cultural imagery of drinking than the rational parameters of policy analysis. Indeed while the problem of drunk driving is recently getting some much-needed public-policy attention, the solutions proposed are for the most part punitive. The devices for handling the problem come down to harsh and stigmatic sentences. One exception to this is efforts to raise the drinking age, a policy based clearly on a population-risk perception.

Class Channeling in an Access Society

WE HAVE LOOKED at the modern rationality of risk as a means of providing security. But the risk principle, and the techniques of aggregation and security that constitute it, are also a form of social control. These techniques operate to regulate the access each of us has to the commodities and opportunities that exist in society. The control works two ways. First, methods of risk assessment assure that the access people have is controlled. Second, people alter their behavior in order to receive access.

The world of credit cards is a clear example of this.[15] Credit cards are markers that determine access to goods and services. They are made available to people on the basis of actuarial risk-prediction techniques. Sometimes this is done by processing individual applications. In other cases, whole populations, assumed to be good credit risks, such as college students, people who live in certain neighborhoods, or who belong to certain organizations, are issued credit unsolicited. Even those who obtain cards are graded by risk assessment in terms of how much credit they receive. Thus the potential damage a consumer can do through fraud or simple irresponsibility is limited in advance by a risk system that allows limited access based on predictive assessment.

Another dimension of risk control in credit cards operates at the time of purchase. Store owners must determine when to check the card proffered against a computerized system that checks the validity of the account. If you observe carefully you will see that this is not done all the time. If the purchase is small enough they will simply take the card and get your telephone number, allowing for some kind of later contact if the credit turns out to be bad. Many cards have particularized codes on them that tell the store clerk what level of scrutiny the cardholder should be accorded. With an American Express Gold Card, for example, you can make a much larger purchase before the computer is checked than you can with the Green Card.

Credit cards then are a complete system of channeling. Rather than old-fashioned systems of security that allowed the simple binary choice of yes or no, the credit card system can offer an endless range of alternative levels of access. It is like a miniature solar system in which people are placed in various orbits around the shining sun of consumption depending upon their risk profile. The interesting thing about this vast system of social control (and credit cards are only a part) is that it operates most strongly on the most privileged elements of society. The daily lives of the middle and upper classes are crisscrossed with the social technologies of risk.

Security in some sense has always been the quest of the middle classes. But in an earlier era this was achieved by property owner-ship and private capital. Today security is achieved through insur-ance, and through access to social capital such as college loans. In the past one would ask a person if they had a savings account to determine if they were middle class; today we ask them if they are insured.

This is nicely captured by a passage from Don DeLillo's novel *White Noise,* where he describes the ritual assembly of middle-class families dropping off their progeny on the opening day of a college:

> The parents stand sun-dazed near their automobiles, seeing images of themselves in every direction. The conscientious suntans. The well made faces and wry looks. They feel a sense of renewal, *of communal recognition.* The women crisp and alert, in diet trim, knowing people's names. Their husbands content to measure the time, distant but ungrudging, accomplished in parenthood, *something about them suggesting massive insurance coverage.* This as-sembly of station wagons, as much as anything they might do in the course of the year, more than formal liturgies or laws, tells the parents they are a collection of the like minded and the spiritually akin, a people, a nation.[16] [Emphasis added.]

THE TECHNIQUES OF AGGREGATION and risk assessment have become constant rituals of privileged America. For example, the process of competitive admissions to colleges and professional schools, which has become the great rite of passage for both children and parents, is largely managed by actuarial techniques. High-school students shop for extracurricular activities not as forms of self-expression, but as objective markers that will land them in the right square of the admissions grid. To hear potential law students speaking in hushed tones of their LSAT/GPA scores is to be ushered into the central sacraments of our modern rituals of risk.

Outside the circle of affluence in America, the rationality of risk becomes attenuated. Harsher, more old-fashioned forms of security management, including police and prisons, become more central. Yet increasingly these harsher methods are directed by the same actuarial methods that operate the soft machinery of access channeling. Prison sentences, levels of parole supervision, and access to public benefits are more and more coming to be distributed through methods of risk assessment. Yet, at the level of ritual, the poor are exposed in their daily lives to a much more punitive and stigmatizing set of social practices than the rest of society. The poor, locked out of the access and security channels of insurance and credit, remain a constant reminder that capitalism cannot achieve the rationality of risk in its fullest sense. As an odd reward for their suffering, the poor remain the last sovereign subjects left to carry the economic and moral burden of their circumstances.

The Contest between "Risk" and "Sovereignty"

OUR CULTURE is undoubtedly a more complicated place than is captured by this talk of risk. My argument is that social technologies of aggregation, and strategies of securing the population, have increasingly colonized social practices of all sorts. But other traditions remain within the culture. I have briefly indicated that an alternative rationality, that of *sovereignty,* continues to play a role in our practices.

It is worth contrasting the two briefly. Social relations that are constituted by *risk* practices bring people together on the basis of "objective" social markers. Think about how we "belong" to our insurance companies, our credit-card companies, and increasingly our jobs as well. Relationships of *sovereignty* involve moral bonds that pass through the "subjective" self-understanding of individuals. Think how we belong to our families, some religious and political associations, and some sorts of jobs that still evoke our sense of communal attachment. Rather than being limited and easily modified, sovereign relationships are "sticky" and spill over into other areas of life.

Surviving in the midst of risk techniques, in a society increasingly wed to security, practices persist that call into being forms of political and moral life. You can tell them because the experience they give rise to has a different "texture" than the smooth cool surface of risk relationships. The drunk driver stands out from the "de-moralized" world of automobile accidents. No-fault divorces still carry a moral charge not found in no-fault compensation schemes. The people who are carted off by police from the gates of nuclear power plants take their stands on political and moral grounds that are foreign to the "cost-benefit" discourse of environmental impact studies. These practices are rituals that sustain a system of sovereign relations. In sovereign relationships people show up as subjects who are capable of praise and blame, rather than simply costs and benefits. We think of sovereignty and its attendant sense of "responsibility" as a quality of "moral" relationships, but in western culture political life also carries with it the sovereign dimension.

Practices of sovereignty have a loose cohesion, although one that is often sketchy and fragile. Prior to the rise of risk, they existed in a stronger and more coherent network which unified, via law, political and moral subjectivity. A sovereign community existed called the "body politic" and at the center of it was the state.[17] The state, from its inception, carried on regulatory and administrative functions which we recognize in a greatly expanded form in our own state: standardization of weights and measures, maintenance of property, and always, of course, taxation. But these regulatory functions existed amidst rituals that sustained the sovereignty of the network of social relations, such as public executions, coronations, royal funerals, the rituals of war.*

*It is true that these rituals operated to sustain the hegemony of society's rulers. See Antonio Gramsci, *The Prison Notebooks* (New York: International Publishers, 1971), and E. P. Thompson, Douglas Hay, et al., *Albion's Fatal Tree* (New York: Pantheon, 1975). Some may read my use of sovereignty as ignoring the ideological function it served. Instead I mean to highlight the way sovereignty exists as a quality of social relationships that survives beyond the structure of power that built it.

Sovereignty remains a potent form of power in the modern state. Despite the increasing hegemony of welfare and security as the functions of the state, sovereign imperatives operate in, and sometimes dominate, our social life. Despite efforts to consolidate the debate over public policy in risk terms, the moral and political discourses of sovereignty continue to flare up. More than others, certain areas of public life remain invested with moral and political significance. The problems of war, criminal punishment, and citizenship continue to haunt the twentieth century with the problem of sovereignty.

The power to make war. The persistence of the possibility of the state fighting a major war despite the evident threat of destroying our own population seems to contradict the conception of the state as an agent of security and welfare for its population. If the state exists to protect and facilitate the biological and economic growth of the social body, wars that risk massive damage to the domestic population seem irrational.

One way the modern state can justify fighting war is by presenting the social body as a national community. Wars can be fought in the name of securing resources and markets to enhance the welfare and security of the population. It was the genius of National Socialism to combine rituals of sovereignty with the welfare and security functions of the state and thus mobilize a social body for massive destruction.* War is, after all, one of the great rituals of sovereignty.

To the modern state war is a paradox. Its sovereignty requires war, but its welfare and security functions (i.e., risk rationality) are endangered by high-intensity conflict. On this basis three phenomena become a little clearer. First, short of fighting a nuclear war, the contemporary state maintains a constant dance on the edge of conflict, sometimes oscillating between arms negotiations and arms buildups, usually doing both simultaneously. Nuclear war, even if the state cannot carry it out, sustains the sovereign ritual of preparation. Second, the recent paradigm shift in strategic doctrine from "mutually assured destruction" (MAD) to "nuclear utilization theory" (NUTs) speaks directly to the need for the state to sustain this sovereign ritual. NUTs promises to revive

---

*The Reagan administration has come closer than any other modern American government in explicitly defining the use of military power in this way.

the possibility of fighting a nuclear war against our adversary, without destroying the whole population.[18] Third, little wars, such as those fought recently in the Malvinas/Falkland Islands by the British, and in Grenada by the Americans, also represent an opportunity to reinforce the sovereign features of the state. We know how much popular enthusiasm was generated by both these adventures. Indeed, the attempts of the press to question the rationality of these conflicts in terms of the state's welfare and security functions was greeted with scorn by the momentarily sovereignty-intoxicated publics of Britain and the United States.

Yet regional wars can also place sovereignty in danger when they go awry. When ritual adventurism turns to disaster, it reinforces the bankruptcy of the state's sovereign pretensions. The Vietnam memorial in Washington speaks eloquently to the absence of a national mission in that war. Its simple list of names against a black marble background highlights the meaning that the war now has for us: the stark biological fact that these people died.

In contrast to the symbolic representations of the glory of the body politic at war which we find in older monumental art (look at the Arc de Triomphe in Paris), the Vietnam memorial is a monument to a wounded social body.

The power to punish. For a very long time now, the problems of criminal justice have been posed in terms of the rationality of welfare and security (i.e., the rationality of risk). Foucault discussed at great length the deployment of disciplinary power within the institutions of punishment during the eighteenth and nineteenth centuries.[19] More recently control strategies consonant with the risk principle have begun to be widely considered and employed.

In the discourse of modern penal policy, the rationality of risk predominates.[20] Yet the passion to punish remains a powerful political phenomenon. Every state legislature is aware of the high demand for punishment. Some of this popular demand is, to be sure, a demand for security. Yet a demand that criminals suffer at the hands of the state remains. Those who feel some misgivings about the replacement of painful imprisonment with a risk-distribution scheme operated by electronic surveillance systems are not only concerned with the civil-liberties threat, but with something else as well. The state's effort to punish members of the underclass who commit crimes is one of the last traces of a commitment to share a community with them.

This is a painful hypocrisy to be sure. The abolition of this commitment may lead to the ominous acceptance of the permanent division of society. When we give up the myth of a political community, we will be left with a number of distinct and hostile social bodies.

Membership in the body politic. Recent economic and political displacements that have sent thousands of Haitian, Cuban, Mexican, and Central American people into the United States have no doubt helped to generate the tremendous policy concern that is now being given to the immigration issue. But nothing could be more central to the rituals and discourses of sovereignty than the question of who is a member of the body politic, who isn't, and what difference that should make. To see why, one need only go to south Texas. There the city of Brownsville stands across the international border from the Mexican city of Matamoros. Who can doubt that these two jurisdictions are one social body? Every morning hundreds of Mexican citizens cross that border to work in the United States. Americans cross to enjoy the cheaper and less regulated pleasures available on the other side. An epidemic in Matamoros would no more respect the border than a recession on the American side. But this thin juridical line is not inconsequential: it generates a whole series of oppressions, irrationalities, and systems of control.

The creation of a coherent national policy on immigration is stymied by the contradiction between legal form and social reality. While the legal concept of citizenship remains tied to a notion of sovereign participation, the "social body" is composed of many who are not part of the political community. This was highly visible in the recent battle over the new immigration law. The ostensible issue was one of sovereignty, but the debate again and again had to return to the basic social questions—employment, living conditions, crime.

A recent Supreme Court opinion nicely brings out this clash of rationalities. *Plyer v. Doe* (1982) arose out of a class-action suit on behalf of the children of undocumented aliens living in Texas against the attempt by the state of Texas to deny them access to free public education.[21] The state argued, in part, that its sovereignty included the discretion to choose whether or not to supply education to children who were not citizens—not, that is, members of the political community. In an opinion belonging to a discourse of welfare and security, Justice Brennan challenged the state's claims of sovereignty by exposing its irrationality in welfare and security terms:

> It is difficult to understand precisely what the State hopes to achieve by promoting the creation and perpetuation of a subclass of illiterates within our boundaries, surely adding to the problems and costs of unemployment, welfare, and crime. It is clear that whatever savings might be achieved by denying these children an education, they are wholly insubstantial in the light of the costs involved to these children, the State, and the Nation.[22]

But the majority of justices in the case, while voting with Brennan, included concurrences in which they found a way around Texas' sovereignty, rather than through it.

The court's decision in the *Plyer* case, to require the provision of free public education, may be salutary, but it offers little in the way of a coherent view of this problem. The conflict of the social body and the body politic remains even in the text of the opinion. In the meantime, the unsatisfactory status quo will continue indefinitely with its cruelties, wastefulness, and irrationalities. The creation of a coherent policy is stymied in part by the still vital struggle for the form of our own subjectivity.

The Society of Limited Liability

IN ORDER TO SEE BEYOND the struggle between risk and sovereignty, it may be useful to shed the burden of the present's complexities and imagine a world totally governed by the rationality of risk practices. This is not because such a world awaits inevitably beyond the next hill, but because such a vision provides an ideal type which concentrates the ritual aspects of risk and the ways it colors our actually existing social world.

Picture a society where individuals are relieved, at least financially, of every harm poor fortune or poor judgment can hurl at them. This is a society of limited liability. The term "limited liability" originally applied to corporations. The corporation was created to limit the liability faced by investors. The liability of its owners is strictly limited to their investment in the corporation. However great the losses they create, the owners are protected in their personal capital and thus their ability to remain solvent, capable of beginning anew.

In a risk society, individuals have the same kind of security. Individuals can engage in any experience their creditworthiness can get for them, while they remain as secure as the financial and medical resources of society allow.

What is wrong with this picture? In many respects nothing. It is the dream of social reformers for the last two centuries. At the heart of it is a certain paradox. The more individuals disappear as the subjects of juridical punishments, economic vulnerability, and moral judgment, the more free they become to act as individuals. Hooked into an integrated grid of risk assessment and security measures, the individual is free to act within their credit limits without the sanction of any of the communities that once might have laid claim to defining the self, such as the family, the neighborhood, or work organizations.

Sociologists and political scientists in the mid-twentieth century characterized our society as an organizational one, where the individual had largely been subordinated to the power of the organization.[23] The alternative and grimmer picture was that of totalitarianism, where the individual becomes subject to the all-powerful state.[24]

In a risk society, the individual disappears not into the organization but into this diffuse and comprehensive background of security measures. It is an access society, where the crucial parameter is not membership in any sovereign community but access to the security system itself. The tendency is for the system to become more encompassing so that we can switch organizations without becoming unhooked from this system. Think of the way banks have interconnected their automated teller systems so that you can put your card into any of their machines and get out cash. We may soon change organizations and families as easily as we do addresses or cars.

Something remains in our subjectivity that is repulsed by the smooth "digitally mastered" surface of a risk society.* Yet when

---

*Records are now made by a technique which allows the imperfections of the recording to be eliminated by electronically correcting for any interference. Music has been absorbed by the techniques of representation, which reproduce it without the inadequacies. Risk techniques carry out the same process in the human populations they represent and regulate.

The Emergence of a Risk Society • *85*

we consider any of the particular practices that are carrying us toward this kind of social life, it is hard to reject their utility. Social security, workers' compensation, health insurance, even consumer credit, are all things that have made social life less dangerous, and more merciful.

I F WE BEMOAN the passing of a certain kind of sovereign subject and community, we risk becoming like those conservatives who would restore the dignity of the individual by returning them to the harshness of Charles Dickens's London, where unemployed families starve, and twelve-year-olds are hanged for picking pockets. If we still feel that there is something disturbing in the domination of the lifeworld by risk principles, it can best be articulated by considering the system as a whole. Two different scenarios are worth envisioning.

The first is that the background security system could become intrusive and coercive. In the name of improving safety and lowering social costs, numerous social controls could be put in place to govern the way people work and live. These controls would differ markedly from traditional juridical social controls. One example is drug use. The 1960s stripped away much of the moral sanction against drug use. If drugs are out in the eighties, it is because they are perceived as driving accident risks up, and productivity down.

The control system is changing as well. In the near future the security system could effectively limit drug use by imposing urinalysis screening as a condition of employment. To use drugs would no longer be to challenge the moral sanction of the state and expose oneself to punishment, but instead to risk being denied access to the system. Rather than being defined as a deviant malefactor, the drug user becomes the self-selected occupant of a high-risk category that is channeled away from employment and the greater access it brings.*

The second scenario is that, as the security system becomes more comprehensive, and the effect of individual choices on society increasingly buffered by the proper channeling of risks, the society would come to make fewer and fewer claims on the con-

---

*As this essay is being written drug use has suddenly become the hot political issue of the moment. But it is a strangely unpolitical debate in which no one can articulate the moral dilemma. The policy thrust is toward systematic drug testing. And the rationale is pure risk. People who use drugs are harming themselves and hurting the economy.

duct or character of the individual. It is the opposite of the nightmare represented in the dystopias like *1984*. Rather than a world
where power must observe and respond to every act and thought,
we are envisioning a world where power doesn't care anymore. Is
this a vision of human freedom, or a world where the self, deprived of the oxygen of social attention (and, yes, coercion), dies?*

Conclusion

O NE WAY OF UNDERSTANDING the foregoing in political theory
terms is to speak of a crisis of liberalism. Liberal political
theory, in both its Lockean and Rousseauian moments, can be
seen as accommodating a conception of sovereignty to the emerging welfare and security functions of the state. As risk practices
become dominant in our culture, it has become far more difficult
to sustain the marriage. The central features on which it is based,
an autonomous individual vested with natural rights, and a legalistic state that administers those rights, are being rendered irrelevant by the techniques of risk and undermined by the experiences
these practices create.

One response to this crisis of liberal theory has come from a
loosely assembled group of thinkers called "communitarians."[25] In
Habits of the Heart, the authors posit both a psycho-social crisis of
liberal individualism, and the availability of a set of alternative
practices and conceptions. This alternative, which they identify as
"the civic republican tradition," situates individual sovereignty in a
context of community. Community provides both meanings and
limits, in the absence of which the self faces disintegration, and
society chaos. Bellah et al. claim that this tradition was once dominant in nineteenth-century American culture. Civic republicanism

---

*Fred Jameson's description of "postmodern" society accurately captures
many of the attributes discussed here as risk. Jameson, however, places his
description into a conventional marxist account of "monopoly capitalism."
Cf. Fredric Jameson, "Postmodernism or the Cultural Logic of Late Capitalism," *New Left Review,* no. 146 (July–August 1984), pp. 53–92. But this
framework doesn't get him very far in explaining what is at stake in postmodern culture. Postmodern architecture, for example, seems to dissolve
the individual who no longer has a location in a definable physical or social
geography. This description is powerful and accurate, but it explains next to
nothing to suggest that this architecture is produced by capitalists who are
part of a new global form of capitalism. How architecture works as a ritual
to organize the experience of the self inside it is something that, Jameson
himself argues, the capitalist builder didn't foresee, and something that isn't
very profitable.

was endangered by individualistic tendencies in the culture. But—and this is the crucial link in their argument—it remains alive in certain traditions which Americans are rediscovering, especially religion and political activism.

The account by Robert Bellah and his co-authors ignores the development of the risk practices discussed in this essay. They see in the instability of both individuals and organizations a fatal flaw that creates the conditions and needs for the return of community. But risk creates its own collective order. It is the subtle but totally coordinated order of an actuarial table. Without bringing people into a shared discourse or common rituals, it attaches precise linkages between them. Without punishing, moralizing, or redeeming, it provides for the security and harmony of the social body by coordinating risk and access, so that people are channeled through an environment designed to minimize their harm to each other.

We are together on the freeway during commuting periods. There we all are, individualized but coordinated. We are listening to our own music and thinking our own thoughts. Our being together has only one important quality for us on the freeway: that is the danger we create for each other. This order has no real connection to the purposes for which we are driving, where we are going, or where we are coming from.

The authors of *Habits of the Heart* see churches and political activism as the repository of communitarian renewal, groups that reflect the qualities of sovereignty. The practices they focus on may remain vital, but the real question is whether this old constellation can be revived as the dominant paradigm for collective ordering. The hegemony of risk is not merely an ideological fact. Its pervasive rationality is inextricably bound up with the way the social world develops. The practices we have called sovereignty, whether religious or political, have disintegrated and are too incoherent to replace risk. We may find it impossible to draw on this older sovereign tradition to make contemporary social choices.

The rituals of sovereignty—wars, crime and its punishment, citizenship—survive in our culture and help sustain a sense of integrity in individuals and their relations to each other. This is just as true of the forms of resistance they engender. The prospect of war in Central America today, for example, has helped generate communities of resistance which have been absent since the last war.

But these effects are incomplete. The sovereignty they sustain remains embedded in a pervasive set of risk practices for managing the business of daily life.

FOR THOSE OF US who remain responsive to both sets of practices, who still hear the call of the body politic as well as the social body, the situation is not comfortable. Perhaps the best we can do is struggle against those moments when the logic of one rationality becomes totally destructive of something basic in the other. We cannot sit back and allow the nuclear spasm of a sovereignty-hungry state apparatus to obliterate the population and perhaps the planet.

We should resist at those moments when the managers of the social body ask us to surrender, in the name of security, those precious remaining political spaces where new discourses and rituals might yet be born. We must necessarily face both ways, deciding in any moment which of the two orders threatens to utterly dominate the other, taking up the battle on the weaker side.

Future generations may experience far less of rituals and discourses that make being a part of a sovereign community possible. Those nurtured in local or familial traditions of sovereignty, who do continue to understand themselves as sovereign subject, will find it difficult to respond without a wider sovereign space in which to act. If isolated, they may show up as mad people. If they find one another, they may become terrorists, striking out against society, but without a program or an alternative.[26]

It is impossible, and presumptuous, to argue whether this is bad. If we were there, we might not even be able to recognize some altogether different system of social practices. We might not be able to differentiate it from what sounds to us like the discourse of risk, the sound of the social body, a hum of perfectly integrated circuits, the slumber of a certain kind of human soul.

REFERENCES

1 Wisconsin's was the first to stand up to a court challenge, in 1911. Mississippi was the last state to pass a workers' compensation law, doing so in 1948. Cf. Lawrence Friedman and Jack Ladinsky, "Social Change and the Law of Industrial Accidents," in Lawrence M. Friedman and Harry N. Scheiber, eds., *American Law and the Constitutional Order: Historical Perspectives* (Cambridge, Mass.: Harvard University Press, 1978).
2 *Farwell v. Boston & Worcester RR*, 45 Mass. 49 (1842).

The Emergence of a Risk Society • 89

3 For a useful discussion of the literature see Gary T. Schwartz, "Tort Law and the Economy in Nineteenth Century America : A Re-interpretation," 90 *Yale Law Journal* 1717 (1981).

4 Cf. Philippe Nonet, *Administrative Justice* (New York : Russell Sage Foundation, 1969).

5 *MacPherson v. Buick Motor Co.* (Court of Appeals of New York), 217 N.Y. 382 (1916).

6 Ibid., p. 387.

7 *Escola v. Coca Cola Bottling Co. of Fresno* (Supreme Court of California), 24 Cal. 2d 462 (1944).

8 Ibid., p. 467.

9 *Sindell v. Abbott Laboratories*, 26 Cal. 3rd 588 (1980).

10 Cf. Marc A. Franklin and Robert L. Rabin, *Tort Law and Alternatives* (Mineola, N.Y.: Foundation Press, 1983), pp. 684–766.

11 Paul Brodeur, *Outrageous Misconduct: The Asbestos Industry on Trial* (New York : Pantheon, 1985).

12 Cf. *Young v. American Casualty Co.*, 416 F.2d 906 (2d cir. 1969).

13 *State Farm Fire & Casualty Co. v. Tringali*, 686 F.2d 821 (9th cir. 1982).

14 Joseph Gusfield, *The Culture of Public Problems* (Chicago : University of Chicago Press, 1981).

15 Cf. James B. Rule, *Private Lives and Public Surveillance* (London : Allen Lane, 1973).

16 Don DeLillo, *White Noise* (London : Penguin Books, 1985), pp. 3–4.

17 See Ernest Kantorowicz, *The King's Two Bodies* (Princeton, N.J.: Princeton University Press, 1957), and F. Hinsley, *Sovereignty* (Cambridge, Eng.: Cambridge University Press, 2d edition 1986).

18 Cf. Robert Aldridge, *The Counterforce Syndrome* (Washington, D.C.: Institute for Policy Studies, 1978).

19 Michel Foucault, *Discipline and Punish* (New York : Pantheon, 1977).

20 See Jonathan Simon, "Back to the Future: Newman on Corporal Punishment," *American Bar Foundation Research Journal*, vol. 1985, p. 927.

21 *Plyer v. Doe*, 102 S.Ct. 2382 (1982).

22 Ibid.

23 William H. Whyte, Jr., *The Organization Man* (New York : Simon & Schuster, 1956); David Reisman, *The Lonely Crowd* (New Haven : Yale University Press, 1950).

24 Hannah Arendt, *On Totalitarianism* (New York : Harcourt Brace Jovanovich, 1973).

25 Robert N. Bellah, et al., *Habits of the Heart* (Berkeley : University of California Press, 1985); Michael Ignatieff, *The Needs of Strangers: An Essay on Privacy, Solidarity, and the Politics of Being Human* (London : Penguin, 1984); William Sullivan, *Reconstructing Public Philosophy* (Berkeley : University of California Press, 1982); Phillip Selznick, "Towards a Communitarian Morality," 75 *California Law Review* 445, 1987; Roberto Mangebiera Unger, *Knowledge and Politics* (New York : Free Press, 1975); Michael Sandel, *Liberalism and the Limits of Justice* (New York : Cambridge University Press, 1982); Alasdair MacIntyre, *After Virtue* (Notre Dame, Ind.: University of Notre Dame Press, 1981, 1982). Not all these thinkers would accept the label "communitarian."

26 Cf. Don DeLillo, *The Names* (New York : Vintage, 1982). DeLillo's protagonist is a professional political-risk analyst who becomes obsessed with a band of terrorists which commits a bizarre series of ritual killings.

[2]

FROM THE PANOPTICON TO DISNEY WORLD: THE DEVELOPMENT OF DISCIPLINE†

Clifford D. Shearing * *and Philip C. Stenning* **

In the literature on punishment an interesting and important debate has recently surfaced on the question of whether modern penal developments in the criminal justice system represent an extension of discipline (in the sense in which Foucault used the term) or a move away from it. In an influential article published in 1979, Cohen argued that modern penal practices provide evidence of a significant "dispersal of social control", in which the community is increasingly being involved in its administration. He also claimed, however, that this dispersal of social control is "merely a continuation of the overall pattern established in the nineteenth century" (p. 359), and described by Foucault, in which corporal punishment (based on the administration of pain and torture to the body) was replaced by carceral punishment (based on the exercise of sustained discipline over the soul).

In an incisive critique of Cohen's thesis, Bottoms has recently sought to show — successfully in our view — that while Cohen's conclusion that modern penal developments represent a significant dispersal of social control is correct, his conclusion that these developments are an extension of disciplinary punishment is not. Specifically, Bottoms argued that the most significant recent developments in penal practice — the greatly increased use of the fine, the growth of community service orders and the modern resort to compensation and related matters — are not essentially disciplinary in character. In making this argument, Bottoms makes the point that these new modes of punishment lack the element of "soul-training" which is the essential hallmark of disciplinary carceral punishment. He went on to speculate that this move away from disciplinary punishment within the criminal justice system may have been made possible, and encouraged, because

---

† We would like to thank Renée Shearing for her assistance in the development of this paper.
* Associate Professor, Centre of Criminology, University of Toronto.
** Senior Research Associate, Centre of Criminology, University of Toronto.

336   *Perspectives in Criminal Law*

more effective preventative social control measures are being implemented within the general society outside the criminal justice system.
This latter system, the argument goes, is increasingly being regarded
only as a "last resort" in social control, and as a result "juridical"
rather than disciplinary carceral punishments are being resorted to
within it (Bottoms, pp. 187-8, 191 and 195).

Thus far, Bottoms' argument is entirely consistent with similar
arguments we have made in our explanations of the implications for
social control of the modern growth of private security and private
control systems (Shearing and Stenning, 1983). These, we have
contended, are preventative rather than punitive in character, rely
heavily on strategies of disciplinary control, and make resort to the
more punitively oriented public criminal justice system only as a last
resort when their own strategies have failed to achieve their instrumentally conceived objectives.

Bottoms, however, went on to argue that we, too, are wrong to
characterize such private control systems as disciplinary in the
Foucaultian sense. This, he wrote, was because the systems we
described lack the essential ingredient of discipline, which he characterized as " 'the mechanics of training' upon the bodies and souls of
individuals" (Bottoms, p. 182). Work by Mathieson (1980 and 1983), in
which he characterized modern trends away from individualism as the
organizing focus of social control, and towards "surveillance of whole
categories of people" as "a change from open to hidden discipline", was
criticized by Bottoms for the same reasons (Bottoms, pp. 181-2). In
both cases, he argued that the mere extension of *surveillance*, without
the accompanying individualized soul-training, does not constitute
"discipline" as Foucault intended the term.

The explicit assumption which Bottoms makes in thus characterizing
modern non-penal systems of social control as not "disciplinary", is
that "discipline" necessarily involves individualized soul-training. In
this essay, we shall seek to argue that the concept of "discipline", as
used by Foucault, is much broader than this, and is appropriate to
describe many modern forms of social control which do not apparently
have individualized soul-training as their primary organizing focus.
More particularly, we shall argue that the identification of discipline
with individualized soul-training reflects a failure adequately to distinguish between Foucault's generic concept of discipline and his more
historically specific examination of it in the context of carceral punishment. Having made this argument, the essay will conclude with an
examination of a popular modern exemplar of non-carceral disciplinary

social control which, we believe, represents an important indication of what the "social control apparatus of society is actually getting up to" (Cohen, p. 339).

Discipline and Carceral Punishment

Central to Foucault's argument in *Discipline and Punish* is his contention that discipline as a generic form of power should be distinguished from the particular strategies through which it is expressed at any particular time.

> "Discipline" may be identified neither with an institution nor with an apparatus; it is a type of power, a modality for its exercise, comprising a whole set of instruments, techniques, procedures, levels of application, targets; it is a "physics" or anatomy of power, technology (p. 215).

This distinction between discipline, as a type of power, and its particular expression, is important for it allows for the possibility of the evolution of discipline through a series of different concrete expressions. Given this distinction it becomes apparent that carceral punishment, as exemplified in Bentham's Panopticon, should be seen as an instance of discipline that seeks compliance through individual soul-training. It is, however, only one possible expression, albeit the one that occupied Foucault's attention.

What, then, are the essential characteristics of "discipline" as a generic concept? There can be no doubt that training of one sort or another is an objective if not an explicit element of "discipline". Indeed, the very derivation of the word (from the Latin *disciplina* = instruction, tuition) confirms this. The nature of such training, however, and the manner in which it is accomplished, will vary according to the context in which discipline is applied. Of this we shall say more in a moment. For Foucault, there was another essential characteristic of discipline — namely, that it is a type of power that is embedded in, and dispersed through, the micro-relations that constitute society. Unlike monarchical power (which is expressed through terror and torture) it is not located outside and above the social relations to be controlled but is integrated into them. As it is part of the social fabric it is everywhere, and yet it is nowhere, because it does not have an identifiable locus.

> ... disciplines have to bring into play the power relations, not above but inside the very texture of the multiplicity, as discreetly as possible ... (Foucault, p. 220).

It is this embedded character that defines the Panopticon as an exemplar for discipline.

338   *Perspectives in Criminal Law*

> [The Panopticon] is an important mechanism, for it automizes and disindividualizes power. Power has its principle not so much in a person as in a certain concerted distribution of bodies, surfaces, lights, gazes; in an arrangement whose internal mechanisms produce the relation in which individuals are caught up. The ceremonies, the rituals, the marks by which the sovereign's surplus power was manifested are useless. There is a machinery that assures dissymmetry, disequilibrium, difference. Consequently, it does not matter who exercises power. Any individual taken almost at random, can operate the machine ... . (Foucault, p. 202).

The embedded nature of discipline makes it especially suitable as a preventative mode of control, as the surveillance (that is its basis) becomes part of the very relations to be controlled. Foucault illustrates this in discussing discipline in the context of the workshop:

> The discipline of the workshop, while remaining a way of enforcing respect for the regulations and authorities, of preventing thefts and losses, tends to increase aptitudes, speeds, output and therefore profits; it still exerts a moral influence over behavior, but more and more it treats actions in terms of their results, introduces bodies into a machinery, forces into an economy (Foucault, p. 210).

It is precisely because of this embedded character of discipline that its nature varies according to the context in which it is applied, and it is for this reason that, when applied in the context of carceral punishment, one of its distinctive elements is that of individualized soul-training. This is because the context of carceral punishment (unlike that, for instance, of the factory, the hospital or the workshop) is essentially a moral one rather than a primarily instrumental one. It is perhaps because Foucault was primarily concerned to explain "the birth of the prison" in *Discipline and Punish*, that the elements of carceral discipline have so easily come to be thought to be the fundamental elements of *all* discipline. As we shall try to illustrate, however, when applied in a context which is primarily instrumental rather than moral, the elements of discipline are significantly different.

Instrumental and Moral Discipline

The three models of control that Foucault identifies (monarchical, juridical and carceral), while fundamentally different in disciplinary terms, all share a moral foundation that defines them as "justice" systems. Foucault, in his analysis of these types of control, tended to take this feature for granted as it was common to all three models. As a result, if one works from within Foucault's framework in studying contemporary control, although one's attention will be directed towards discipline, the issue of whether the moral foundation of social control is changing will tend not to be considered. This is evident in the work of all the participants in the debate we have reviewed. Yet if contemporary control, especially as it appears in the private sector, is to be understood, it is precisely this issue (as the quotation above about disciplinary control in the work place suggests) that needs to be addressed. What makes private control different from traditional criminal justice is not its disciplinary character, which it shares with carceral control, but the challenge it offers to the moral foundation of the order-maintenance process (Shearing and Stenning, 1983).

Within criminal justice "order" is fundamentally a moral phenomenon and its maintenance a moral process. Accordingly, social order (and its enforcement) tends to be defined in absolute terms: one proper order expressing "natural justice". Within criminal justice the premise that shapes order maintenance is that order is the expression of a community of morally righteous people. Thus, the criminal process is concerned with the rightness and wrongness of acts and the goodness and badness of people. It defines the boundaries of moral order by stigmatizing certain acts and persons as morally tainted (Durkheim). Its methods are indignation, retribution and redemption. Each of the models of punishment Foucault identified represents a different set of strategies for doing this.

Every aspect of the criminal process is structured and shaped by its moral, absolutist foundation. Within it, discipline is a technology of power used to achieve this moral purpose. There is no better illustration of this than the carceral regime which targets the soul, the moral centre of the human being, so as to provide for its moral reformation. Not surprisingly, therefore, individualized soul-training is the essential hallmark of carceral discipline.

Private control, in sharp contrast, rejects a moral conception of order and the control process. Private security executives, for example, not only reject, as Wilson does, the present possibility of moral reform but reject the very idea of moral reform as a basis for control. Within private control, order is conceived primarily in instrumental rather than moral terms. Order is simply the set of conditions most conducive to achieving fundamental community objectives. Thus in a business corporation, for instance, order is usually whatever maximizes profit.[1]

In contrasting their definition of order with that of criminal justice, private control systems stress that for them "theft" is not a moral category and consequently does not deserve, or require, a moral response. Within private control the instrumental language of profit

340   *Perspectives in Criminal Law*

and loss replaces the moral language of criminal justice. This is not merely terminological (different terms for the same objects) but a reconstitution of the social world. "Loss" refers not simply to theft but includes, among other things, the cost of attempting to control theft. This redefinition has important implications for the way in which control is exercised and thus for order. For example, theft will not be subject to control if the cost of doing so is likely to be greater than the initial loss.

Where moral rhetoric appears in private control it does so not as principles that guide the order-maintenance process (as it does in judicial decision making) but simply as a control strategy. For example, employees may be given a lecture on morality not because control is conceived of in moral terms but because it creates attitudes that are good for profit. In such a context, training, as an element of discipline, need be neither individualized nor particularly directed at the soul. Indeed, from the point of view of the evolution of discipline, perhaps the most important consequence of the shift to an instrumental focus has been the move away from a concern with individual reformation to the control of the opportunities that permit breaches of order to occur. Accordingly, within private control it is prevention through the reduction of opportunities for disorder that is the primary focus of attention (Shearing and Stenning, 1982). This directs attention away from traditional offenders to a new class of delinquents: those who create opportunities for disorder. It is thus, to use banking as an illustration, not the employee who steals who is the primary focus of the control system's attention but the teller who creates the opportunity for the theft by neglecting to secure his/her cash drawer.

This transformation of the preventative thrust within discipline has important implications for other aspects of disciplinary control. The most visible is the change in the nature of surveillance as attention shifts from the morally culpable individual to the *categories* of people who create opportunities for disorder (Mathiesen, 1983; Rule *et al.*).

Although this focus on opportunities creates a need for mass surveillance it does not eliminate carefully pinpointed surveillance. Its purpose, however, changes; it is no longer soul-training, as such, but rather "tuning up the machine" (of which the human operator merely constitutes one part). While such scrutiny may, for this reason, focus on individuals, it is just as likely to target system deficiencies, for instance, in the paper systems that provide for ongoing surveillance, as well as retrospective surveillance, through the paper trails that they create.

In summary, the emergence of an explicitly instrumental focus in control has changed the nature of disciplinary power while reinforcing its embedded features. Thus surveillance, while changing both its focus and its purpose, has become increasingly embedded in other structures and functions. For example, the surveillance which Oscar Newman sought to achieve through "defensible space" is embedded both in the structure of the physical environment, as well as in the social relations it facilitates.

Finally, we may note that an instrumental focus implies a variety of orders, each reflecting the fact that different communities have different objectives. Thus, within private control systems, we find not one conception of order but many; not one societal order but many community-based orders.

Private Non-carceral Discipline

In seeking to identify the carceral model, and in explicating its relationship to disciplinary control, Foucault realized that, at any point in time, the actual control mechanisms in force would reflect the influences of both established and developing forms (p. 130). Thus in order to identify the nature and direction of these forms he turned to the ideas and projects of influential reformers. Hence his use of the Panopticon and recent prison developments, such as the Walnut Street prison, as exemplars of the disciplinary form as expressed through carceral strategies.

This approach suggests that in seeking to understand contemporary control we should direct our attention to strategies in arenas relatively immune from the influence of the carceral model. As public sector control has been dominated over the past century by the soul-training of the carceral model we are likely to find that the control strategies within this arena will reflect a mix of both established and newer forms, so that although it will be possible to identify disciplinary initiatives, we are not likely to find exemplary instances of contemporary embedded control here. The reverse, however, is likely to be true with respect to private control systems which, because they were in decline for most of the nineteenth and the first half of the twentieth centuries, are remarkably free of carceral overtones (Spitzer and Scull; Shearing and Stenning, 1981, 1983). Their contemporary manifestations, however, display precisely the embedded features that characterize disciplinary control (Shearing and Stenning, 1982, p. 101). Thus, in seeking an exemplar of contemporary discipline, we turn to the private arena.

342 *Perspectives in Criminal Law*

Our focus on private control, as a way of examining the features of contemporary discipline, is especially appropriate in a volume honouring John Edwards. Much of the existing Canadian research on private control systems was initiated by him during his term as Director of the Centre of Criminology. His enthusiastic encouragement of such research at a time when few others recognized its significance, either as a source of theoretical insight or as a burgeoning empirical phenomenon, is a mark of his considerable insight and foresight. It gives us the greatest pleasure to be able to recognize this in this essay.

Disney World: An Exemplar of Instrumental Discipline

As the discussion to this point has indicated, research on private security has already confirmed the development of a contemporary form of discipline outside of the moral restraints of criminal justice and begun to identify some of its distinguishing features. To elucidate the notion of instrumental discipline we contrast it with moral discipline by identifying the analytic equivalents of the carceral project and the Panopticon so as to highlight the nature of the changes that have been occurring in the development of discipline. As the identification of order with profit provides the most explicit example of an instrumental order, corporate control is an appropriate equivalent to the carceral model. As the features of corporate control are highly developed in the recreational facilities operated by Disney Productions and as these facilities are so widely known (directly through visits or indirectly through media coverage and Disney advertising), Disney World, in Orlando, Florida, provides a suitable exemplar to set against the Panopticon. In order to avoid lengthy descriptions of security strategies we will draw our illustrations from consumer controls which every visitor to Disney World encounters.

The essential features of Disney's control system become apparent the moment the visitor enters Disney World. As one arrives by car one is greeted by a series of smiling young people who, with the aid of clearly visible road markings, direct one to one's parking spot, remind one to lock one's car and to remember its location and then direct one to await the rubber-wheeled train that will convey visitors away from the parking lot. At the boarding location one is directed to stand safely behind guard rails and to board the train in an orderly fashion. While climbing on board one is reminded to remember the name of the parking area and the row number in which one is parked (for instance,

"Donald Duck, 1"). Once on the train one is encouraged to protect oneself from injury by keeping one's body within the bounds of the carriage and to do the same for children in one's care. Before disembarking one is told how to get from the train back to the monorail platform and where to wait for the train to the parking lot on one's return. At each transition from one stage of one's journey to the next one is wished a happy day and a "good time" at Disney World (this begins as one drives in and is directed by road signs to tune one's car radio to the Disney radio network).

As one moves towards the monorail platform the directions one has just received are reinforced by physical barriers (that make it difficult to take a wrong turn), pavement markings, signs and more cheerful Disney employees who, like their counterparts in other locations, convey the message that Disney World is a "fun place" designed for one's comfort and pleasure. On approaching the monorail platform one is met by enthusiastic attendants who quickly and efficiently organize the mass of people moving onto it into corrals designed to accommodate enough people to fill one compartment on the monorail. In assigning people to these corrals the attendants ensure that groups visiting Disney World together remain together. Access to the edge of the platform is prevented by a gate which is opened once the monorail has arrived and disembarked the arriving passengers on the other side of the platform. If there is a delay of more than a minute or two in waiting for the next monorail one is kept informed of the reason for the delay and the progress the expected train is making towards the station.

Once aboard and the automatic doors of the monorail have closed, one is welcomed aboard, told to remain seated and "for one's own safety" to stay away from open windows. The monorail takes a circuitous route to one of the two Disney locations (the Epcot Center or the Magic Kingdom) during which time a friendly disembodied voice introduces one briefly to the pleasures of the world one is about to enter and the methods of transport available between its various locations. As the monorail slows towards its destination one is told how to disembark once the automatic doors open and how to move from the station to the entrance gates, and reminded to take one's possessions with one and to take care of oneself, and children in one's care, on disembarking. Once again these instructions are reinforced, in a variety of ways, as one moves towards the gates.

It will be apparent from the above that Disney Productions is able to handle large crowds of visitors in a most orderly fashion. Potential

344   *Perspectives in Criminal Law*

trouble is anticipated and prevented. Opportunities for disorder are minimized by constant instruction, by physical barriers which severely limit the choice of action available and by the surveillance of omnipresent employees who detect and rectify the slightest deviation.

The vehicles that carry people between locations are an important component of the system of physical barriers. Throughout Disney World vehicles are used as barriers. This is particularly apparent in the Epcot Center, the newest Disney facility, where many exhibits are accessible only via special vehicles which automatically secure one once they begin moving.

Control strategies are embedded in both environmental features and structural relations. In both cases control structures and activities have other functions which are highlighted so that the control function is overshadowed. Nonetheless, control is pervasive. For example, virtually every pool, fountain and flower garden serves both as an aesthetic object and to direct visitors away from, or towards, particular locations. Similarly, every Disney Productions employee, while visibly and primarily engaged in other functions, is also engaged in the maintenance of order. This integration of functions is real and not simply an appearance: beauty *is* created, safety *is* protected, employees *are* helpful. The effect is, however, to embed the control function into the "woodwork" where its presence is unnoticed but its effects are ever present.

A critical consequence of this process of embedding control in other structures is that control becomes consensual. It is effected with the willing co-operation of those being controlled so that the controlled become, as Foucault (p. 170) has observed, the source of their own control. Thus, for example, the batching that keeps families together provides for family unity while at the same time ensuring that parents will be available to control their children. By seeking a definition of order within Disney World that can convincingly be presented as being in the interest of visitors, order maintenance is established as a voluntary activity which allows coercion to be reduced to a minimum. Thus, adult visitors willingly submit to a variety of devices that increase the flow of consumers through Disney World, such as being corralled on the monorail platform, so as to ensure the safety of their children. Furthermore, while doing so they gratefully acknowledge the concern Disney Productions has for their family, thereby legitimating its authority, not only in the particular situation in question, but in others as well. Thus, while profit ultimately underlies the order Disney Productions seeks to maintain, it is pursued in conjunction with other objectives that will encourage the willing compliance of visitors in maintaining Disney profits. This approach to profit making, which seeks a coincidence of corporate and individual interests (employee and consumer alike), extends beyond the control function and reflects a business philosophy to be applied to all corporate operations (Peters and Waterman).

The coercive edge of Disney's control system is seldom far from the surface, however, and becomes visible the moment the Disney-visitor consensus breaks down, that is, when a visitor attempts to exercise a choice that is incompatible with the Disney order. It is apparent in the physical barriers that forcefully prevent certain activities as well as in the action of employees who detect breaches of order. This can be illustrated by an incident that occurred during a visit to Disney World by Shearing and his daughter, during the course of which she developed a blister on her heel. To avoid further irritation she removed her shoes and proceeded to walk barefooted. They had not progressed ten yards before they were approached by a very personable security guard dressed as a Bahamian police officer, with white pith helmet and white gloves that perfectly suited the theme of the area they were moving through (so that he, at first, appeared more like a scenic prop than a security person), who informed them that walking barefoot was, "for the safety of visitors", not permitted. When informed that, given the blister, the safety of this visitor was likely to be better secured by remaining barefooted, at least on the walkways, they were informed that their safety and how best to protect it was a matter for Disney Productions to determine while they were on Disney property and that unless they complied he would be compelled to escort them out of Disney World. Shearing's daughter, on learning that failure to comply with the security guard's instruction would deprive her of the pleasures of Disney World, quickly decided that she would prefer to further injure her heel and remain on Disney property. As this example illustrates, the source of Disney Productions' power rests both in the physical coercion it can bring to bear and in its capacity to induce co-operation by depriving visitors of a resource that they value.

The effectiveness of the power that control of a "fun place" has is vividly illustrated by the incredible queues of visitors who patiently wait, sometimes for hours, for admission to exhibits. These queues not only call into question the common knowledge that queueing is a quintessentially English pastime (if Disney World is any indication Americans are at least as good, if not better, at it), but provides evidence of the considerable inconvenience that people can be

346   *Perspectives in Criminal Law*

persuaded to tolerate so long as they believe that their best interests require it. While the source of this perception is the image of Disney World that the visitor brings to it, it is, interestingly, reinforced through the queueing process itself. In many exhibits queues are structured so that one is brought close to the entrance at several points, thus periodically giving one a glimpse of the fun to come while at the same time encouraging one that the wait will soon be over.

Visitor participation in the production of order within Disney World goes beyond the more obvious control examples we have noted so far. An important aspect of the order Disney Productions attempts to maintain is a particular image of Disney World and the American industrialists who sponsor its exhibits (General Electric, Kodak, Kraft Foods, etc.). Considerable care is taken to ensure that every feature of Disney World reflects a positive view of the American Way, especially its use of, and reliance on, technology. Visitors are, for example, exposed to an almost constant stream of directions by employees, robots in human form and disembodied recorded voices (the use of recorded messages and robots permits precise control over the content and tone of the directions given) that convey the desired message. Disney World acts as a giant magnet attracting millions of Americans and visitors from other lands who pay to learn of the wonders of American capitalism.

Visitors are encouraged to participate in the production of the Disney image while they are in Disney World and to take it home with them so that they can reproduce it for their families and friends. One way this is done is through the "Picture Spots", marked with signposts, to be found throughout Disney World, that provide direction with respect to the images to capture on film (with cameras that one can borrow free of charge) for the slide shows and photo albums to be prepared "back home". Each spot provides views which exclude anything unsightly (such as garbage containers) so as to ensure that the visual images visitors take away of Disney World will properly capture Disney's order. A related technique is the Disney characters who wander through the complex to provide "photo opportunities" for young children. These characters apparently never talk to visitors, and the reason for this is presumably so that their media-based images will not be spoiled.

As we have hinted throughout this discussion, training is a pervasive feature of the control system of Disney Productions. It is not, however, the redemptive soul-training of the carceral project but an ever-present flow of directions for, and definitions of, order directed at every visitor. Unlike carceral training, these messages do not require detailed knowledge of the individual. They are, on the contrary, for anyone and everyone. Messages are, nonetheless, often conveyed to single individuals or small groups of friends and relatives. For example, in some of the newer exhibits, the vehicles that take one through swivel and turn so that one's gaze can be precisely directed. Similarly, each seat is fitted with individual sets of speakers that talk directly to one, thus permitting a seductive sense of intimacy while simultaneously imparting a uniform message.

In summary, within Disney World control is embedded, preventative, subtle, co-operative and apparently non-coercive and consensual. It focuses on categories, requires no knowledge of the individual and employs pervasive surveillance. Thus, although disciplinary, it is distinctively non-carceral. Its order is instrumental and determined by the interests of Disney Productions rather than moral and absolute. As anyone who has visited Disney World knows, it is extraordinarily effective.

Conclusions

While this new instrumental discipline is rapidly becoming a dominant force in social control in this year, 1984, it is as different from the Orwellian totalitarian nightmare as it is from the carceral regime. Surveillance is pervasive but it is the antithesis of the blatant control of the Orwellian State: its source is not government and its vehicle is not Big Brother. The order of instrumental discipline is not the unitary order of a central State but diffuse and separate orders defined by private authorities responsible for the feudal-like domains of Disney World, condominium estates, commercial complexes and the like. Within contemporary discipline, control is as fine-grained as Orwell imagined but its features are very different.

In this auspicious year it is thus, paradoxically, not to Orwell's socialist-inspired Utopia that we must look for a picture of contemporary control but to the capitalist-inspired disciplinary model conceived of by Huxley who, in his *Brave New World*, painted a picture of consensually based control that bears a striking resemblance to the disciplinary control of Disney World and other corporate control systems. Within Huxley's imaginary world people are seduced into conformity by the pleasures offered by the drug "soma" rather than coerced into compliance by threat of Big Brother, just as people are today seduced to conform by the pleasures of consuming the goods that corporate power has to offer.

348 *Perspectives in Criminal Law*

The contrasts between morally based justice and instrumental control, carceral punishment and corporate control, the Panopticon and Disney World and Orwell's and Huxley's visions is succinctly captured by the novelist Beryl Bainbridge's observations about a recent journey she made retracing J. B. Priestley's celebrated trip around Britain. She notes how during his travels in 1933 the centre of the cities and towns he visited were defined by either a church or a centre of government (depicting the coalition between Church and State in the production of order that characterizes morally based regimes).

During her more recent trip one of the changes that struck her most forcibly was the transformation that had taken place in the centre of cities and towns. These were now identified not by churches or town halls, but by shopping centres; often vaulted glass-roofed structures that she found reminiscent of the cathedrals they had replaced both in their awe-inspiring architecture and in the hush that she found they sometimes created. What was worshipped in these contemporary cathedrals, she noted, was not an absolute moral order but something much more mundane: people were "worshipping shopping" and through it, we would add, the private authorities, the order and the corporate power their worship makes possible.

REFERENCES

[1]   While it may be argued that social order, as traditionally conceived, has always had an implicitly instrumental function (that is, criminal justice supports an order that is conducive to capitalism). It is the explicitly instrumental character of private control system which distinguishes them from traditional criminal systems.

BIBLIOGRAPHY

Bottoms, Anthony E., "Neglected Features of Contemporary Penal Systems", in *The Power to Punish: Contemporary Penality and Social Analysis*, David Garland and Peter Young, eds. (Atlantic Highlands, N.J., Humanities, 1983), p. 166.

Bainbridge, Beryl, Television interview with Robert Fulford on "Realities", Global Television, Toronto, October, 1984.

Cohen, Stanley, "The Punitive City: Notes on the Dispersal of Social Control", 3(4) Contemporary Crisis 339 (1979).

Durkheim, Emile, *The Division of Labor in Society* (New York, Free Press, 1964).

Foucault, Michel, *Discipline and Punish: The Birth of the Prison* (New York, Vintage Books, 1977).

Mathiesen, Thomas
    "The Future of Social Control Systems — the Case of Norway", 8 International Journal of the Sociology of Law 149 (1980).
    "The Future of Social Control Systems — the Case of Norway", in *The Power to*

Punish: Contemporary Penality and Social Analysis, David Garland and Peter Young, eds. (Atlantic Highlands, N.J., Humanities, 1983), p. 130.

Newman, Oscar, *Defensible Space: Crime Prevention Through Urban Design* (New York, Macmillan, 1972).

Peters, Thomas J. and Waterman, Robert H. Jr., *In Search of Excellence: Lessons from America's Best-run Companies* (New York, Warner Books, 1982).

Priestley, J.B., *English Journey: Being a Rambling but Truthful Account of What One Man Saw and Heard and Felt and Thought During a Journey Through England the Autumn of the Year 1933* (London, Heinemann & Gollancz, 1934).

Rule, James B., McAdam, Douglas, Stearns, Linda and Uglow, David, "Documentary Identification and Mass Surveillance in the United States", 31(2) Social Problems 222 (1983).

Shearing, Clifford D., and Stenning, Philip C.

"Private Security: Its Growth and Implications", in *Crime and Justice — An Annual Review of Research*, vol. 3, Michal Tonry and Norval Morris, eds. (Chicago, University of Chicago Press, 1981), p. 193.

"Snowflakes or Good Pinches? Private Security's Contribution to Modern Policing", in *The Maintenance of Order in Society*, Rita Donelan, ed. (Ottawa, Canadian Police College, 1982).

"Private Security: Implications for Social Control", 30(5) Social Problems 493 (1983).

Spitzer, Steven, and Scull, Andrew, "Privatization and Capitalist Development: The Case of the Private Police", 25(1) Social Problems 18 (1977).

Wilson, James Q., *Thinking about Crime* (New York, Basic Books, 1975).

[3]

MANAGING CRIME RISKS:
TOWARD AN INSURANCE BASED MODEL
OF SOCIAL CONTROL

Nancy Reichman

> IBM recently announced plans to test job applicants for drugs. According to company officials the tests will help to avoid productivity, safety and security problems.
>
> U.S. concern over the illegal export of high technology products has prompted the Commerce Department to distribute a profile of illicit transfer. Persons working in high technology industries who observe the 12 "red flag" signals are encouraged to report the suspected violation.
>
> Computerized Arson Warning and Prevention Systems (AWAPS) search through city records, tax collections, and building inspections to locate properties matching profiles of arson.

These three examples illustrate part of an important trend in crime control: the use of insurance concepts and techniques to manage the uncertainties of losses due to crimes that have or might occur. Insurance is more than simply a product bought and sold in the marketplace. It is a particular form of social arrangement organized around a set of procedures for allocating risk across a community of risk takers. Under an insurance model, crime, like other "accidents," is conceptualized as a contingency

Research in Law, Deviance and Social Control, Vol. 8, Pages 151–172.
Copyright © 1986 by JAI Press Inc.
All rights of reproduction in any form reserved.
ISBN: 0-89232-536-4

for which the technology of insurance (independent of the insurance product) provides an effective management ethos.

The future of control systems is currently receiving much scholarly attention (see, for example, Spitzer, 1983a, the articles collected in Garland and Young, 1983 and in Cohen and Scull, 1983; as well as Cohen, 1985). The dialectic of control defies easy classification. As soon as one trend is identified an alternative often conflicting trend can be found. Debates rage as to whether control is becoming more or less intrusive, more centralized or decentralized, more extensive or intensive.

This paper adds to that general debate by conceptualizing the growing reliance on probability, opportunity reduction, and loss prevention as part of a trend toward an insurance or actuarial model of social control. These techniques offer an alternative to, not necessarily a replacement for, existing control strategies.[1] An insurance or risk management perspective toward social control tends to treat crimes not as moral wrongs but as fortuitous events, the effects of which can be spread across communities of risk takers. Control represents an administrative solution to a technical problem. The communities across which risks are spread do not appear to express a collective conscience or a particular form of moral solidarity. They simply form instrumental networks or relays through which control can be exercised over dispersed populations (Donzelot, 1979; Smart, 1983).

In the speculative analysis presented below, I consider how insurance and risk management are increasingly integrated into the processes and practices of crime control. I suggest that classifying, predicting, and redistributing crime risk may be increasing relative to apprehending and punishing offenders as law enforcement goals for certain types of offense. Redistributing crime risks provides a means for regulating the more abstract postindustrial violations that are not easily monitored through conventional forms of control. Just as theorists have critically examined policies for redistributing the "risks" of poverty or lost income (Rimlinger, 1971; Piven and Cloward, 1982),[2] those involved in the study of crime control must look beneath the surface of similar attempts to redistribute the risks of crime. How and when these techniques might be used, for what purposes, and with what implications and/or contradictions are the subjects of this paper.

THE INSURANCE CONCEPT OF CRIME CONTROL

Insurance is a technique for sharing and consequently reducing and managing individual risks. Risk refers to the uncertainty of loss or the probability that losses will occur. The concept of risk should not be confused with that of peril. Perils are the causes of risk. Typically, we think of perils as due to "natural" disasters—fires, earthquakes, floods, etc. But socially defined behaviors such as crime may also be so regarded.[3] Insurance permits individuals facing similar risks of victimization to combine and redistribute their resources to face them collectively. Should these perils (offenses) occur, individuals can claim relief or compensation from the community across which the "cost" of that risk has been spread.

Theoretically, the insurance mechanism disregards the notion of individual responsibility for losses. Neoclassical models of utility and welfare which form the foundation for insurance practice are grounded in assumptions about the independence of events. Those assuming risk[4] trust that the risks they assume are objective ones—unrelated contingencies beyond individual control.[5] Only under such assumptions can risk be efficiently and profitably redistributed according to mathematical formulae based largely on past experience.

In practice, however, the certainty of losses may be influenced by social and environmental factors. Hazards are those conditions which contribute to the probability of loss. They may include things as diverse as oily rags stored in a basement, liability laws, or broken door locks. Some hazards are more or less fixed; for example, the natural conditions of property, and their effects can be predicted with relative ease. Other hazards are reactive, i.e., due to the actions of those participating in loss sharing arrangements (Heimer, 1985). Because they are harder to predict, social factors, or reactive hazards, complicate the risk calculus. When the peril is itself a behavior, for example crime, risk evaluations become even more problematic.

An integral part of the insurance function, therefore, has been to develop strategies for minimizing or neutralizing those hazards which complicate the risk calculus (i.e., those conditions affecting the likelihood of loss). Among the strategies imposed to manage reactive and/or behavioral risks are excluding those who present "excessive" loss exposure, loss prevention activities, as well as contractual arrangements creating "communities of fate" between risk takers and risk assumers (Heimer, 1985).[6]

Many of the techniques currently being introduced, and in some cases reintroduced, as forms of social control can be conceptualized according to insurance or risk management metaphors. Techniques such as "defensible space," "forensic identification" "profiling," "opportunity structures" "target hardening" and "security accountability" are analogous to the hazard reduction strategies found in more conventional insurance contexts. The computerized arson profiling systems mentioned earlier illustrate the potential for predicting and reducing loss probabilities. By identifying which buildings are at risk of being burned, these systems open up the possibilities for neutralizing or minimizing losses through preventive action. Crime losses may also be reduced by eliminating the opportunities for hazards to develop in the first place, or if they do, to exist over time. Through conscious planning of physical space, Crime Prevention Through Design (CPED) programs build social control directly into the environment.

The application of insurance techniques to crime control is part of a more general trend toward behaviorism in social control (Cohen, 1985). Behaviorism is based on the assumption that what one is doing or has done in the past, relative to what is expected, is more important than why one acts the way that one does. A behaviorist approach to crime control focuses on the effects of crimes, not their causes, and is oriented toward changing behaviors, not people.[7] Social engineering, the planned manipulation of whole groups and categories of behavior, is characteristic of the behaviorist approach (Mathieson, 1983). Control activities produce what Shearing and Stenning (1984) refer to as "instrumental discipline," a concern not for individual reformation but for controlling the opportunities that permit violations to occur.

The objectives of insurance based systems of control, i.e., to anticipate and minimize crime loss probabilities, exemplify the behaviorist approach. Insurance-like techniques are pre-emptive, but only to a degree. The losses due to criminal victimization are contained, not eliminated. Hazards are reduced until they can be easily predicted. Once their probability of occurrence can be estimated, it is assumed that these events can be efficiently allocated among the community of risk sharers.

Insurance-based techniques of risk management are more likely to be applied to offenses which tend on average to involve relatively high degrees of uncertainty as to their effects. Uncertainties may exist because the extent of losses may be hard to predict, or because there is some doubt that once exposed, conventional law enforcement efforts will be effective at containing future losses. Organizational crimes where victimization is diffused, hidden, or hard to define are examples of such low certainty crimes. Other examples include computer crimes where the consequences of criminal action are unknown because the crimes occur over time or across institutional space. Crimes like employee theft or antitrust violations where the justice system response is often unpredictable might be usefully categorized as crimes having low certainty as well.

Although effects may be uncertain, the behavior must be relatively easy to predict or anticipate if risk management is to be successfully applied. Crimes involving behaviors which take advantage of patterned organizational transactions and activities are more susceptible to a risk management approach than more opportunistic offending. Repetition is often imperative for implementing a risk management approach. When the same offender commits the same crime in different contexts (see the discussion of selective incapacitation and major offender programs below), or when different actors always use the same organizational process to commit their crimes, prediction is possible. The requirement of high predictability also demands that there be some limit on the number of theoretically relevant variables that are essential to the explanatory model.

The combination of low certainty impacts and high predictability in incidence means that insurance based systems of control tend to be applied to crimes which are often perceived as private matters. Offenses which occur in bounded (private) environments are more likely to lend themselves to the development of modeling techniques whereas offenses in the public arena present a more fluid and difficult situation for risk analysis. When risk management is applied in the public arena, it is usually applied to habitual offenders and offenses where the patterns of behavior are relatively easy to discern.

Information is central to effective crime risk management. To better predict offenses and to interdict them before they can occur, social control must be "front loaded." Greater and greater amounts of personal data need to be collected and analyzed on the behavior of all individuals, not just those under suspicion. A recent example of front loading social control is the Internal Revenue Service's acquisition of commercially compiled direct marketing lists to identify tax non-compliance. The IRS is using these lists to correlate income estimates (based on car driven, neighborhood, etc.) with tax returns in an effort to determine whether anyone on that list is under-reporting their tax liability (see also Reichman and Marx, 1985).

The demand for more extensive and intensive information has given rise to new agents of surveillance. The topography of current social control reflects an interesting dialectic between, on the one hand, the trend toward specializing social control functions and functionaries, and on the other hand, embedding social control within other forms of social interaction and organization. We are beginning to witness the blending of private and public authorities and the creation of new public-private enterprises with access to private sector data that once eluded public authorities (Reichman, 1983). Specialized security personnel have emerged to patrol and protect new forms of "mass private property" such as shopping centers, manufacturing complexes, public arenas and the like (Shearing and Stenning, 1983). At the same time, surveillance has been added to the routine activities of many organizational actors. Insurance adjusters, bank tellers, welfare workers, department store clerks as well as others have added surveillance to the list of their official duties.

New technological paraphernalia are being employed to assist these actors in the processes of screening, classifying, and sorting behavior.

Electronic beepers, video scanners, computer matches, light amplifying devices, parabolic microphones, breathalyzers, brain wave scanners, voice stress analyzers, and toxic drug screens have profoundly changed the nature and amount of personal data that can be abstracted, standardized, measured, and compared. By transforming the meaningless (e.g., sound waves) into the meaningful (words), by joining that was heretofore unjoinable (matching previously disparate data), and by making what was hidden (body chemicals) apparent, these new techniques have increased the intensity and scope of what can be exposed and analyzed (Marx and Reichman, 1984).

Information disclosure does not depend solely on these techniques of extraction and abstraction, however. Much information is "voluntarily" revealed in the course of daily transactions. Control often requires the knowing, if not willing, participation of those being watched. It has the appearance of consensus as potential victims and offenders police themselves. Consider, for example, the metal detectors at airports designed to prevent those with weapons from boarding an aircraft. Or how much information about one's financial health and personal life style is revealed when applying for or even using a credit card. By "voluntarily" participating in everyday transactions, victims unwittingly bear much of the responsibility for the success and failure of social control.

That private actors, sometimes even the victims and offenders themselves, are becoming responsible for carrying out control functions once reserved for the state is consistent with the general trend toward privatization of social control (Spitzer and Scull, 1977). But unlike the "big stick" techniques used by a coercive state or by much more traditional forms of private police, insurance based systems of control offer a more subtle and "rational" approach (see Shearing and Stenning, 1984).

As has been noted elsewhere, the processes of "rationalizing" the social control apparatus is not without problems, contradictions and limits (Spitzer, 1983a). Redistributing crime risks, for example, may do little to prevent future crimes and may, in fact, support them. Some of the contradictions surrounding the redefinition of "crime as risk" may be illustrated by exploring specific techniques of insurance and risk management. Following this exploration, it will be possible to consider some of the forces which explain both the current use and the more far reaching implications of a risk-based approach to social control.

TECHNIQUES OF RISK MANAGEMENT

The insurance mechanism manages the problem of risk by efficiently allocating the probable effects of losses due to criminal victimization across a community of risk takers. Through the spreading or transferring of risk, the uncertainties associated with individual losses can be reduced or redistributed according to mathematical formulae. Efficiencies in risk allocation depend on reasonable risk calculations. These are achieved by assuming only the best risks and then minimizing the hazards for those risks which are assumed.

Classification and exclusion, opportunity reduction, and redistribution are the major objectives of risk management programs. The application of these insurance related techniques to crime control will be discussed below.

Classification and Selection

One way to manage the problem of crime is to prevent those who present high risks of offending from entering into certain types of social relationships. In general, this strategy is as old as crime control itself. The objective is to change, divert, exclude, or eliminate threatening behaviors by identifying and isolating suspicious acts before an offense actually is committed. What may be a novel variation on this old theme is that new techniques of information gathering and prediction are permitting social controllers to make exclusionary decisions without any direct indicators that offending behavior has or might occur. Statistical probabilities are driving exclusionary decisions.

In the insurance context, classification and exclusion have been used to prevent individuals from joining risk pools. What insurers refer to as "selective discrimination" is the backbone of the industry. By choosing only to insure risks that conform to the standards they impose, companies can improve their abilities to allocate risk efficiently and effectively. "Selective discrimination" also serves to protect insurance companies from applicants who present "excessive" loss exposure and from dishonest applicants who they believe do not deserve the coverage at all. An insurance maxim, "Select or be selected against" illustrates this piece of insurance philosophy (Launie, et al. 1976; Webb, et al. 1980). Because applicants for insurance tend to represent a biased sample (i.e., those facing the greatest risk or those wishing to profit from insurance), insurance companies must select carefully in order to obtain a reasonable distribution of profitable risk.[8]

These selection principles are consistent with what is becoming a dominant trend toward screening prospective employees. According to U.S. Representative Steward McKinney, sponsor of a bill to prohibit the use of lie detectors by private firms, more than half of the nation's retail companies use polygraph tests in an attempt to find dishonest employees or to turn down undesirable applicants (Denver Post, October 24, 1985). Strategies for weeding out those with the potential to harm corporate order are being developed to identify workers who may be using drugs on the job. The management of Kaiser steel plants, for example, requires employees who "behave oddly" to provide urine samples for drug testing (Newsweek, August 22, 1983). Urinalysis tests were performed on over four million persons in 1983 according to one estimate (Marx, 1986;147). The development of drug courier and hijacking profiles as well as those to predict dangerousness are consistent with the principles of classification and exclusion as well.

The Federal Insurance Administration uses profiles developed by the Arson Early Warning Systems to cancel insurance on inner city properties with high risk of arson. The logic here is that by canceling insurance (i.e., excluding participation in the risk pool) you may negate at least one of the profit motives for the crime. Cancellation criteria are based on variables identified as being significant indicators of arson. They include, among other things, unpaid taxes, code violations, vacancy rates and previous fires at a site (Insurance Committee for Arson Control, Fact Sheet /13, March, 1981).

Selective incapacitation, preventive detention, and major offender prosecution programs might be seen as examples of the exclusion principle operating in the public sector. These policies are aimed at getting offenders who commit the most crimes off the streets. They target career criminals identified according to profiles based largely on the number of prior convictions. Given fixed prison space, policies that target the most serious offenders are perceived as economical, even though legally and ethically questionable (Blumstein, 1983).

Controlling the Hazards For Those Risks You Do Assume
(Loss Prevention)

A second strategy for managing crime risks shifts the focus of control from the offenders to categories of potential victims. Concepts like target hardening and opportunity reduction attempt to minimize losses by changing the behavior of those who might be affected by losses. These strategies differ from exclusionary policies in so far as they are not focused directly on anticipating offending behaviors. Instead, they attempt to structure the environment so that those offenses which do occur can be managed and/or contained.

The insurance industry recognizes three kinds of hazards which increase the probability of losses due to crime. Physical hazards include such things as poor security systems (doors with no locks), or dark parking lots. Legal hazards are statutes, or judicial decisions which increase the probability of losses due to criminal behavior. Some of the more conservative scholars consider the exclusionary rule to be an example of a legal hazard since the rule may allow the release of individuals who go on to commit further crimes.[9] Moral hazards, the third type identified by the industry, include those attitudes and characteristics of insured persons which increase the probability of crime. Carelessness about where one walks at night, absentmindedness about locking car doors, or fraudulent intent would be examples of moral hazard. Insurance-based techniques of risk management are designed to minimize the influence of these hazards. This can be accomplished by taking control over activities that were once regarded merely as as externalities or by tightening up internal systems of control.

The concept of defensible space or control through design fits in with the general idea of hazard reduction. Rather than focusing directly on a problem population, control is built into physical and organizational structures. Social control is no longer a specialized duty focused on a particular clientele [see Shearing and Stenning's (1984) description of the social control system built into the design of DisneyWorld]. Instead there is an attempt to build control and containment into organizational life. Computer systems, for example, are being designed in ways to limit their vulnerability to potentially disruptive human agents. Remote access aids reduce the need for the physical presence of system programmers. Central processing units are physically separated from peripherals while maintenance functions are organized so that they can be carried out from a distance. Techniques of camouflage, such as computer encyrption, may also be built into computer systems to shield them from potential threats.

Many of the new surveillance techniques such as closed circuit televisions monitoring banking transactions, x-ray machines at airports, or electronic markers on consumer goods may be conceptualized as attempts to control the hazards associated with crime. These new technologies temporally and spatially extend an individual's or organization's field of vision, making them ever more aware of what's going on around them. Little is left to chance. Prevention is often possible when publicity about the use of these techniques serves to deter potential offenders.[10]

Some undercover operations, particularly those that facilitate crimes in order to prevent them, are consistent with the concept of hazard reduction. Contract homicides where police play the role of fake hit men may actually limit the extent of harm from crimes that are at least partially carried out (Marx, forthcoming).

Attempts to improve victims' awareness of frauds being committed against them is another example of hazard reduction. Auto theft and bodily injury fraud profiles designed by insurance companies to sensitize insurance adjusters to the possibilities of fraud illustrate some of the new techniques in victim education. These profiles are actually a set of "red flags" which outline factors associated with several fraud scenarios. They were designed to make companies less vulnerable to frauds committed against them. Certain types of auto theft claims, e.g., those involving stolen cars recovered totally burned, are immediately suspect.

Moral hazards may be reduced by making the victims more financially and legally accountable for losses they incur. This is the logic behind insurance company deductibles for crime losses. It also is the logic behind the extension of employee accountability to include responsibility for workplace security (O'Block, 1981). Parker (1983) for example, suggests that employees of computer-related firms be evaluated on whether they use safeguards and/or adhere to security regulations. Signs in restaurants and parking garages warning that those establishments are not responsible for items left in their care implicitly shift the legal burden of protection on to the potential victim. Holding boards of directors liable for failing to safeguard assets may be seen as another example of attempts to reduce moral hazard.[11]

Transferring Risk

When crime risks cannot be avoided or controlled, they may be transferred. A market exists for the trading of many types of crime risk (e.g., thefts, embezzlement, forgery, arson). The insurance commodity, a contract or policy, establishes these risk sharing arrangements. One party (the insurer) in consideration of a premium undertakes indemnification of another party (the insured) against a particular kind of loss. Those paying premiums give up current capital in exchange for the security that should it be necessary in the future, financial compensation would be forthcoming. Those assuming risks gamble that careful financial management of premium dollars would more than offset any losses that would have to be paid.[12] A financial community emerges out of such risk trading.

Crime risks also may be redistributed by passing along the costs of crimes which have occurred. This is seen most clearly in the case of shoplifting where the costs of that crime are passed along in the prices of consumer goods. As much as 15% of the cost of supermarket goods, for example, may be attributed to allowances for shoplifting (Bonn, 1984:278).

The obvious irony in the resort to risk spreading and transfer is that it sets up the very conditions or hazards that often lead to the loss opportunities in the first place. Because the effects of risk are spread across the community of risk takers, the incentives to protect against future losses are very much reduced. Thus, the marketing of risk ultimately recreates the very uncertainties that the techniques of risk management were designed to reduce.

EXPLAINING THE TREND

The application of insurance techniques to crime control appears to have developed hand in hand with the generation of the new technological paraphernalia. But we must guard against a technological determinism when explaining this trend. New methods for screening, sorting, classifying, and excluding behaviors have occurred in, and been spurred by a receptive social context. Some factors that appear to be important to the explanation or perhaps justification of the emergence of "crime as risk" may be found in the sources of uncertainty with crime itself. These include: the changing nature of social organization and offense patterns which make it difficult to disentangle criminal from other behaviors; a certain degree of moral uncertainty about offending behavior; as well as system constraints and contradictions which appear to be rocking the foundations of traditional forms of control for certain types of offense.

In contemporary society, the growth of bureaucracies has meant a significant increase in the proportion of violations that may be embedded in and shielded by organizations (Coleman, 1982 and Vaughan, 1984). Crimes which occur in organizational settings are often hard to locate and contain. Some offenses may be hidden intentionally or deceptively masked as legitimate organizational transactions (Katz, 1978; Altheide and Johnson, 1980; Vaughan, 1984). Because organizational infractions tend to occur along with many similar, legitimate transactions, their effects are not readily apparent.

Insurance based techniques of risk management are attractive strategies for minimizing or neutralizing the hazards that organizational structures create. They take advantage of the routinized and depersonalized character of organizational life which created the dilemmas for conventional social control in the first place. Aggregate models of rule violation which need no knowledge of personalized attributes can be applied categorically to entire populations of potential offenders (see the discussion in Marx and Reichman, 1984; Reichman and Marx, 1985). They permit risk managers to take the offensive and shape the environment before the "risky" can enter into positions to offend.

Insurance based techniques which focus on managing the effects or consequences of crime also divert attention away from an examination of their causes. An instrumental approach of this sort would seem to have practical and ideological advantages, when deeper analysis of the causes of crime would lead us to conclude that the processes of capital accumulation ought to be modified or dismantled. In a world where the opportunities for and varieties of corporate crime have expanded as rapidly as corporations themselves, the boundaries between legitimate and illegitimate behavior have become increasingly murky. The latest scandals involving E.F. Hutton, General Dynamics and United Baldwin remind us that many offenders look and act just like legitimate players (Loomis, 1985). The juxtaposition of legitimate and illegitimate behaviors may create conditions of moral uncertainty which then undermine the confidence or trust in these institutions. This, in turn, is likely to influence the perception of being at risk (Short, 1984). Risk management provides a means for restructuring confidence without looking into what has caused confidence to wane in the first place. By focusing on effects rather than causes, crises of legitimacy often can be averted.

The resort to insurance based systems which do not require the state to so actively intervene also may be viewed as an administrative response to the constraints welfare states face. The fiscal crisis facing many welfare states means that they can no longer raise taxes sufficient to cover the increased demand for social control services. Claims for more regulatory resources stem not only from real or perceived increases in the incidence of violations, but also from the state's expansion of social rights, entitlements, and obligations which have created "legalistic inflation:" an increase in the number of rules that must be enforced (Ericson and Shearing, 1985). That some of these rules are themselves contradictory[13] creates new sources of tension. System overload combines with claims that "nothing works" (Martinson, 1974) or that we simply don't know what works or why it might or might not (Greenberg, 1976 and Klein, 1979) to create a crisis of legitimacy for state sponsored forms of control.

Finally, although even harder to demonstrate empirically, it would appear that changes in social control mirror changes in the economy in general. In advanced capitalist states, the reproduction of capital often occurs apart from the industrial or directly productive process. The problems confronting postindustrial societies are increasingly grounded in issues of financing, distributing, and servicing, or in questions about how productive capital will be used. New financial instruments are being invented to trade the more abstract commodities of the burgeoning capital markets. For example, in addition to the more traditional investments in particular securities, traders now are able to buy and sell the index or proxy for a universe of stocks (e.g., the Standard & Poors 500 Index or the New York Stock Exchange Index). Trades have become even further removed from tangible products as arbitragers deal in the spread between the index and the underlying securities. Because such so-called finance capital is more abstract, it introduces greater uncertainties in the quest for accumulation. It is not surprising, therefore, that the cover story of a recent *Business Week* was introduced as the "Casino Society" (September 16, 1985).

The introduction of new financial commodities has created new opportunities for theft and new challenges for regulators. Many postindustrial violations involve thefts of "symbolic commodities"—insurance policies, pensions, stock options, or patents—that represent some future transaction or outcome. Offenders take advantage of the physical and temporal cushions "futures" commodities offer to separate themselves from their offenses and/or to cover up their misdeeds (Shapiro, 1984). Violations that involve commodities such as insurance or stock options which are grounded in uncertain or contingent outcomes provide few clues or red flags alerting regulators to their occurrence or effects. Lacking certainty about what shape legitimate outcomes should take, illegitimate outcomes are hard for regulators to recognize. The expansion of secondary financial markets[14] and increased reliance on fiduciaries have also changed the locus and scope of regulatory control. Since many offenses occur over time and across institutional space, a more extensive apparatus is necessary to control them.

The "administrative revolution," and the techniques of risk management to which it has given birth, have developed, in part, as responses to new forms of uncertainty and risk in the economy. Faced with the dilemma of maintaining creative flexibility while at the same time ensuring the orderly accumulation of capital, regulators have pursued strategies that enable them to shape rather than react to their environments. Insurance based techniques, for example, allow crime risk managers to incorporate what previously were perceived as externalities. Through extensive planning and monitoring, the parameters of activity can be defined so that problem behaviors can be treated as instances of *manageable* risk (see also, Short, 1984).

IMPLICATIONS

Using insurance or risk management metaphors to understand current control practices alerts us to ways in which the contours of social control might be changing. Rather than directly apprehending and punishing offenders, a risk management approach focuses on minimizing potential threats. Unlike conventional policing which relies on state sponsored agents of coercion, insurance techniques are embedded in other organizational functions and are carried out by non-specialized agents. As the theater of policing becomes ever more the theater of everyday life, social control practices become part of the routine. Classification, opportunity reduction, and risk spreading are built into the marketplace. The traditional resort to coercion is being supplemented with forms of engineering. But the subtlety should not blind us to the power nor to the changes in control that insurance based techniques are likely to bring.

164   NANCY REICHMAN

Some of the implications of applying risk management to crime control
will be discussed below. These include: (1) the decline of the moral and the
inevitability of crime; (2) changing criteria justifying the imposition of
sanctions; (3) abstraction of punishment; (4) the generation of new elites;
and (5) the limits of routinization.

The Decline of the Moral and the Inevitability of Crime

The insurance model of crime control does not explicitly impose a
moral weight on criminal behavior. Blame is less important than reducing
future threats. Crime is assumed to be an "accident," or "contingency"
which can be managed according to criteria that are assumed to be neutral
and fair. In this sense crime becomes an "act of God" rather than an act
against him. The rationality of science, manifest in laws of probability and
administration, appears to replace control based on conflicts of interest.
Crime is perceived as a technical rather than a moral problem. Consequently, technical solutions take their place along side of law as important
sources of legitimacy and mystification (Ericson and Shearing, 1985).
Science and expertise are granted an allegiance previously reserved for
religion or the state. By appearing to bleed the morality out of crime
control, risk management techniques tend to depoliticize the process of
social regulation.[15] However, the claims to moral neutrality should be
empirically examined. Implicit moral choices and unintended consequences often occur hand in hand with social interventions despite
appearances to the contrary.

Assuming that crime is the result of "accidents" also assumes and
legitimates its inevitability. A risk management approach to crime does not
offer any promises to eliminate crime by seeking out and correcting its
underlying causes or by rehabilitating offenders. Paradoxically, the assumption that crime is inevitable or natural may actually serve to legit-
imize the creation of problem populations by those with the means to
exert forms of control. It also may support coercive measures against
certain real or imagined offenders under the guise of rationality. Mathieson
(1983) for example predicts that expanding control systems "out there in
society" will provide the prisons with new legitimacy.

> in the shadow of the new control system, with its increased emphasis on the efficient
> control of whole categories of people, the prisons will regain a sense of rationality as a
> kind of last resort, used unwillingly against the utterly uncontrollable." (p. 140)

Changes in the Criteria Justifying the Imposition of Sanctions

One of the most significant effects of utilizing risk management systems
for controlling crime is a shift in the locus of criminal responsibility from

identifiable (guilty) offenders to categories of behavior. Conditions, characters, and modes of life supplement traditional moral choice as sufficient justification for the imposition of criminal penalties. When regulation shifts from individual offenders to the probability that some offense might occur, traditional presumptions of innocence are transformed into assumptions of guilt. When guilt is inferred from how closely your behavior matches some profile of likely offenses—a form of "statistical justice"—constitutional premises based on reasonable doubt may be undermined.

The Abstraction of Punishment

Redistributing or transferring the risks of crime from the individual to an instrumentally defined community means more than simply sharing the cost of crimes. Allocating crime risks has implications for traditional notions of punishment.

The concept of punishment may become more abstract and unconscious than it was previously. We can use Durkheim's sociology of punishment to make this notion of abstraction clearer.[16] In communities bound by mechanical solidarity, punishments are concretely expressed and their consequences are recognized by all. Indignations, revenge, and redemption are public expressions that tend to have an impact on the community at large. Communities bound by organic solidarity also tend to express punishment concretely, but the consequences of punishment are no longer collectively felt. Restitution and rehabilitation are experienced individually, on a case by case basis. However, when communities are defined according to instrumental, insurance based criteria, punishment can be neither concretely expressed nor felt. Since the spreading of risk theoretically disregards the notion of individual culpability, there are no particular offenders who can be logically punished. This does not mean that there are no longer penalties imposed. Instead, punishment becomes part of a collective unconscious. It is absorbed by us all, for example in the increased costs of goods and services, but rarely recognized as such.[17]

The abstraction of punishment and the absorption of the responsibility for crime losses across a community of risk takers also helps to form a veil over the sources of power in these social control arrangements. The paths of accountability for defining particular behaviors as offensive or risky are not clear. The reference to science only serves to further conceal or mask the sources of power that inhere in insurance relationships. Actuarial models tend to assume equality, but the redistribution of risk has rarely been fair—falling disproportionately on the powerless or poor (O'Riordan, 1983).[18]

Generation of New Elites

Accompanying the development of risk management as a form of crime control is a new group of technical elites with expertise in classifying, sorting, and excluding. Because their control functions tend to be blended into other activities, their status as elites and their relationship to the state apparatus may be hard to discern. That elites may become pockets of future resistance has been discussed elsewhere (Spitzer, 1983a as well as others).

The Limits of Routinization

Insurance based techniques of control are largely mass produced and data dependent, and, thus, they require a level of routinization that has not been typical of social control in the past. Information that is used to screen, sort, classify, and exclude needs to be standard, and clearly defined so that it can be quickly evaluated. The standardization and routinization characteristic of these forms of control are also sources of their limitations. Before they can be implemented, control models must be clearly specified. Overt specification of the social control system may also provide deviants with the blue prints for rule breaking. Once aware of what prompts detection and control, potential offenders, to the extent that they can, may take all necessary steps to avoid them. For example, knowing that insuring property under the same name will trigger the arson profiling system described above, potential offenders may use different family member names, corporate names or even aliases each time they insure a property with the intent to burn it down. It is an interesting irony that the publicity about social control which is necessary to deter future offenders is also the source of information from which sophisticated offenders learn how to beat the system.

The efficiency that categorical social control appears to offer may be illusionary. The standardization and routinization such techniques require may produce a sort of "tunnel vision." Focusing attention on specific indicators, i.e., those that can be quickly evaluated, may systematically divert attention away from other, perhaps more important ones. Categorical models are also limited to the extent that they can be applied only to those types of rule breaking that can be standardized easily. Since aggregate models cannot accommodate extenuating or atypical circumstances, many innocent people may be caught in the enforcement net. This may also mean that more sophisticated and innovative offenders will operate with impunity. Should these inefficiencies become publicly known, the legitimacy of these techniques may be undermined.

Finally, an insurance based or risk management approach to crime control tends to assume success absent behavior. The efficacy of the control system is a given. But when prevention is the enforcement goal, there is always the risk that resources will be wasted on preventing things that would not have occurred in any case.

CONCLUSIONS

This paper has attempted to sensitize the reader to the concepts of insurance based systems of control. Although the task of locating these techniques in their proper historical and socioeconomic context is beyond the scope of this work, a few speculative comments are appropriate. The contradiction of contemporary welfare states as expressed in the fiscal and legitimacy crises that face them means that: capital can no longer depend on the direct coercive action of the state and must search for additional forms of legitimation and regulation (Offe, 1984). Insurance based techniques of control built into the rhythms of social life may offer one such alternative. By building control directly into the environment, insurance techniques socialize the costs of control without the need for direct state intervention, and without undermining the legitimacy of private authority. Risk spreading concepts support integration, but they do so in a way that does not directly challenge private interest (see also Donzelot, 1979).

Insurance based techniques may be similar to the strategy of ad-hoc consensus formation that Claus Offe (1985), identifies as a new kind of rationality in capitalist states—a rationality that seeks to manage the contradiction between accumulation and legitimacy. Under these conditions, individual citizens may be called in to assist in the operation of state functions. Since outcomes represent "the result of a 'co-production' of the administration and its clients," the state no longer needs to rely solely on the authoritative implementation of rules (Offe, 1985;310). Insurance based techniques which implicitly ask potential victims (and that includes just about everyone) to police themselves may be a social control version of the consensus that Offe describes. They help to separate controls which support the processes of capitalist accumulation (investment) from controls which absorb the social discontent that accumulation processes generate (expense). Although structural segregation may ease the pressure on the state, it is far from clear that it will resolve the fundamental contradictions welfare states face.[19] Further work needs to be done to clarify the relationship between insurance based control and the socioeconomic structure of societies.

Using insurance concepts to understand current trends in crime control raises many questions. These include, among others, questions about the relationships between this and other forms of control and between the different types of crime risk that may be managed through insurance based tactics. I have suggested that patterned offenses which occur in bounded private environments are more susceptible to an insurance based approach than the more opportunistic offending that occurs in the public sphere. As corporate capital extends its reach into more and more spheres of our existence, will more and more of our activities be subject to such forms of control? What are the sources or resistance and limitation? When control is built into the environment, are there ways to hide or fight back? The appearance of consensus should not numb us to the power of insurance based systems of control.

NOTES

1. Stanley Cohen (1985) reminds us that even with all the new styles of social control, traditional forms remain, sometimes stronger than ever. Community corrections have not replaced prisons. In fact prison populations continue to rise. The interesting question is why we continue to impose new and deeper layers of social control and how these are likely to affect traditional forms.

2. Many social insurance programs can be conceptualized not simply as direct transfers or gifts, but rather as attempts to redistribute the risk of such social contingencies as poverty, old age, and disability (see, for example, Stevens, 1984).

3. This is so despite the fact that crimes differ from other perils because they are socially defined. Since there is no behavior that is essentially criminal, the risk itself must be socially defined.

4. Today, this generally means insurance companies as fiduciaries for policyholders and/or company stockholders.

5. The parties to an insurance contract agree that when the actions of nature become known, those most favorably affected will transfer resources to those who turn out to be less fortunate. If the contract is to provide protection in this way, it is essential that there be (at least substantial) independence in the actions nature takes with respect to different insured individuals (Kihlstrom and Pauly, 1971).

6. The concept of contributory negligence is important here. Many insurance policies will not cover losses when it is determined that the policyholder (victim) substantially contributed to the loss.

7. Implanting electrodes in prisoners' skulls, electric shock or psycho surgery would be consistent with this approach in so far as these techniques are less concerned with the general motivation to crime than the immediate desire to carry it out.

8. Political decisions to make some types of insurance mandatory (i.e., auto liability) have removed some biases and created others.

9. See Schlesinger's (1983:195) discussion of the exclusionary rule and reference to the National Institute of Justice finding that the "arrest [that] ended in release because of the exclusionary rule was only a single incident in a larger criminal career." Others (for example, Walker, 1985) question whether the exclusionary rule has had any effect on future crimes.

10. As Marx (1985:30) suggests, should offenders not be deterred, the surroundings have been so structured that there is a great likelihood that offenders will either be caught in the act or leave enough evidence of their identity and guilt.

11. Interestingly, the legal uncertainties associated with the liabilities of corporate officers and directors has prompted insurance companies to refuse to trade in those types of

risks. This has created problems for new companies trying to assemble prestigious boards of directors. Without insurance protection, qualified people are refusing to sit on the boards (Newsweek, November 4, 1984).

12.　Net premiums written for property-casualty insurance increased nearly threefold between 1970 and 1980 (Best Company, 1981). Even controlling for inflation this represents substantial growth. How much of that growth is associated with threat of crime loss cannot be determined. Many consumers purchase policy packages which cover a number of different perils.

13.　Some of the contradiction inherent in capitalist legal systems were recognized by Lukacs (1971). For a discussion see Spitzer 1983b.

14.　Secondary financial markets would include the reinsurance market where the insurance business is insured, or mortgage companies that sell the mortgages they write to other financial institutions. Given the temporal, spatial and administrative dispersion of transactions, monitoring and regulation can no longer hope to effectively tie these transactions to particular persons or organizations.

15.　Habermas (1970) suggests that ideologies constructed on purposeful-rational action often serve to neutralize the social choice aspects of action.

16.　Note that I am begging the question of whether Durkheim's *theory* of punishment makes empirical or logical sense (see Garland, 1983; Lukes and Scull, 1983; and Spitzer, 1975). I am simply borrowing Durkheim's vocabulary to provide "sensitizing concepts" in order to make the image of abstraction clearer.

17.　Mathieson (1983) discusses the shift from open to hidden discipline.

18.　For example, higher auto insurance premiums place disproportionate burdens on lower income policyholders. Insurance is a form of regressive tax.

19.　For a discussion see Offe (1984) and Alford and Friedland (1985).

REFERENCES

Alford, Robert and Roger Friedland
　1985　　Power of Theory: Capitalism, the State, and Democracy. New York: Cambridge University Press
Altheide, David and John Johnson
　1980　　Bureaucratic propaganda. Boston: Allyn and Bacon, Inc.
Best Company
　1981　　Aggregates and Averages
Blumstein, Alfred
　1983　　"Prisons: population, capacity and alternatives." Pp. 229–250 in James Q. Wilson (ed.), Crime and Public Policy. San Francisco: Institute for Contemporary Studies.
Bonn, Robert L.
　1984　　Criminology. New York: McGraw Hill.
Brodeur, James F.
　1984　　Risk Analysis and the Security Survey. Boston: Butterworth.
Business Week
　1985　　"Playing with Fire." Sept. 16:78–90.
Cohen, Stanley
　1985　　Visions of Social Control. New York: Basil Blackwell.
Cohen, Stanley and Andrew Scull
　1983　　Social Control and the State: Comparative and Historical Essays. Oxford: Robert Martinson.

170   NANCY REICHMAN

Coleman, James
  1982   The Assymetric Society. New York: Basic Books.
Denver Post
  1985   October 24.
Donzelot, Jacques
  1979   "The poverty of political culture." ideology and consciousness 5:73–87.
Ericson, Richard and Clifford Shearing
  1985   "The scientification of police work." In G. Bohme and N. Stehr (eds.), The
            Impact of Scientific Knowledge on Social Structures. Sociology of the Sciences
            Yearbook, 10. Dordrecht: Reidel.
Foucault, Michel
  1977   Discipline and Punish: The Birth of the Prison. New York: Pantheon.
Garland, David
  1983   "Durkheim's theory of punishment: a critique." Pp. 37–61 in Garland and Young
            (eds.), The Power to Punish. Atlantic Highlands, NJ: Humanities Press.
  1985   Punishment and Welfare. Brookfield, VT: Gower Publishing.
Garland, David and Peter Young
  1983   The Power to Punish. Atlantic Highlands, NJ: Transactions Books.
Greenberg, David
  1976   "The correctional effects of corrections: a survey of evaluations." Pp. xx in
            David Greenberg (ed.), Corrections and Punishment. Beverly Hills, CA: Sage
            Publications.
Habermas, Jurge
  1970   Toward A Rational Society. Boston: Beacon.
Heimer, Carol
  1985   Reactive Risk and Rational Action. Berkeley: University of California Press.
Insurance Committee for Arson Control
  1981   Arson Fact Sheets. Fact Sheet #13 (March).
Katz, Jack
  1978   "Concerted Ignorance: The Social Construction of Cover-Up." Urban Life
            8:295–316.
Kihlstrom, Richard and Mark Pauly
  1971   "The role of insurance and the allocation of risk." Proceedings of the American
            Economic Review 61 (May):371–379.
Klein, Malcolm
  1979   "Deinstitutionalization and diversion of juvenile offenders: a litany of impedi-
            ments." Pp. 145–200 in N. Morris and N. Tonry (eds.), Crime and Justice: An
            Annual Review of Research. Chicago: Chicago: Chicago University Press.
Launie, et al.
  1976   Principles of Property and Liability Underwriting. Malvern, PA: American Insti-
            tute of Property and Liability Underwriters.
Loomis, Carol
  1985   "The unlimited war on white collar crime." Fortune (July 22):90–100.
Lukacs, G.
  1971   History and Class Consciousness. Cambridge, MA: MIT Press.
Lukes, Steven and Andrew Scull
  1983   Durkheim and the Law. New York: St. Martins Press.
Martinson, Robert
  1974   "What Works? Questions and Answers About Prison Reform." The Public
            Interest (Spring):25.
Marx, Gary T.

1984   "I'll be watching you: the new surveillance." Dissent Winter:26–34.

1986   "The iron fist in the velvet glove: totalitarian potentials within democratic structures." Pp135–162 in J. Short Jr (ed) The Social Fabric. Beverly Hills: Sage Publications.

forthcoming A Necessary Evil: The New Police Undercover Work.

Marx, Gary T. and Nancy Reichman

1984   "Routinizing the discovery of secrets: computers as informants." American Behavioral Scientist 27(4):423–452.

Mathieson, Thomas

1983   "The future of control systems—the case of Norway." Pp. 130–145 in David Garland and Peter Young (eds.), The Power to Punish. Atlantic Highlands, NJ: Humanities Press.

Newsweek

1983   "Taking Drugs on the Job." August 22:52–60.

O'Block, Robert

1981   Security and Crime Prevention. St. Louis: Mosby Company.

1984   "Insurance: Now it's a Risky Business." Nov. 4:48–50.

O'Conner, James

1973   The Fiscal Crisis of the State. New York: St. Martins Press.

Offe, Claus

1984   Contradictions of the Welfare State. Cambridge, MA: MIT Press.

1985   Disorganized Capitalism. Cambridge, MA: MIT Press.

O'Riordan, Timothy

1983   "The cognitive and political dimensions of risk analysis." Journal of Environmental Psychology 3:345–354.

Parker, Donn C.

1983   Fighting Computer Crime. New York: Scribners.

Piven, Francis Fox and Richard Cloward

1982   The New Class War. NY: Pantheon Books

Reich, Charles

1964   "The New Property." Yale Law Journal 73:733–787.

Reichman, Nancy

1983   Ferreting Out Fraud: The Manufacture and Control of Fraudulent Insurance Claims. Unpublished PhD Thesis: Cambridge, MA: MIT.

1984   "Screening, sorting, classifying and excluding: social control in the welfare state." Paper presented at the annual meeting of the American Society of Criminology, Cincinnati, Ohio.

Reichman, Nancy and Gary T. Marx

1985   "Generating organizational disputes: the impact of computerization." Paper presented at the annual meeting of the Law and Society Association, San Diego, CA.

Rimlinger, Gaston

1971   Welfare Policy and Industrialization in Europe, America and Russia. New York: John Wiley & Sons.

Schlesinger, Steven R.

1983   "Criminal procedures in the courtroom." Pp. 183–206 in J. Q. Wisons (ed.), Crime and Public Policy. San Francisco, CA: Institute for Contemporary Studies.

Shapiro, Susan

1984   Wayward Capitalists. New Haven, CT: Yale University Press.

1985   "The Social Control of Trust." (unpublished manuscript).

Shearing, Clifford D. and Philip C. Stenning
  1981   "Private security: its growth and implications." Pp. 193–245 in Michael Tonry
          and Norval Morris (eds.), Crime and Justice—An Annual Review of Research, 3.
          Chicago: University of Chicago Press.
  1983   "Private Security Implications for Social Control." Social Problems 30(5):493–
          506.
  1984   "From the panoptican to Disney World: the development of discipline." Pp.
          335–349 in Essays in Honour of John L. J. Edwards. Toronto: Canada Law Book.
Short, James F., Jr.
  1984   "The social fabric at risk: toward the social transformation of risk analysis."
          American Sociological Review 49:711–725.
Smart, Barry
  1983   "On discipline and social regulation: a review of Foucault's genealogical analy-
          sis." Pp. 62–83 in Garland and Young (eds.), The Power to Punish. Atlantic
          Highlands, NJ: Humanities Press.
Spitzer, Steven
  1975   "Punishment and social organization: a study of Durkheim's theory of penal
          evolution." Law and Society Review 9:613–637.
  1982   "The dialectics of formal and informal control." In Richard Abel (ed.), The
          Politics of Informal Justice, 1. New York: Academic Press.
  1983a   "The rationalization of crime control in capitalist society." Pp. 312–333 in Cohen
          and Scull (eds.), Social Control and the State: Comparative and Historical
          Essays. Oxford: Robert Martinson.
  1983b   "Marxist perspectives in the sociology of law." Pp 103–124 in R. H. Turner and
          J. F. Short (eds.), Annual Review of Sociology 9.
Spitzer, Steven and Andrew Scull
  1977   "Privatization and capitalist development: the case of the private police." Social
          Problems 25(1):18–29.
Stern, Richard and Mark Clifford
  1985   "Trouble At Home." Forbes (August 12):31–33.
Stevens, Beth
  1984   In the shadow of the welfare state: corporate and labor development of em-
          ployee benefits. Unpublished PhD. Dissertation, Cambridge, MA: Harvard Uni-
          versity.
Vaughan, Diane
  1984   Controlling Unlawful Organizational Behavior. Chicago: University of Chicago
          Press.
Walker, Sam
  1985   Sense and Nonsense About Crime. Monterey: Brooks/Cole Publishing.
Webb, Bernard, J. T. Launie, W. P. Rokes, and N. Baglini
  1981   Insurance Company Operations, 2. Malvern, PA: American Institute for Prop-
          erty and Liability Underwriters.
Wilson, James Q.
  1983   Crime and Public Policy. San Francisco: Institute for Contemporary Studies.
Yang, Catherine
  1985   "Watching Pinocchio's nose" Forbes (November 4):73.

[4]
Risk, power and crime prevention

Pat O'Malley

Abstract

This paper addresses the development of post-disciplinary 'actuarial' or risk-based technologies of power. Arguing against models which focus on increased efficiency as an evolutionary criterion for emerging technologies of power, it suggests that such technologies' place and form are largely determined by the nature and fortunes of political programs with which they are aligned. Thus the rise of neo-conservatism and related programs have extensively modified and curtailed programs based on risk models, and expanded those based on punishment and discipline. The paper examines the nature of situational crime prevention in the light of these ideas, and moves on to consider certain broader theoretical implications.

Risk-based society

Almost the defining property of Foucault's conception of disciplinary power is that it works through and upon the individual, and constitutes the individual as an object of knowledge. In the disciplines, the central technique is that of normalization in the specific sense of creating or specifying a general rule (norm) in terms of which individual uniqueness can be recognized, characterized and then standardized. Normalization in the disciplinary sense thus implies 'correction' of the individual, and the development of a causal knowledge of deviance and normalization.[1] Thus, in the prison, Foucault (1977) saw discipline as acting directly and coercively upon the individual, producing thereby 'a biographical knowledge and a technique for correcting individual lives' which should follow the delinquent's life course 'back not only to the circumstances but also to the causes of his crime' (Foucault 1977: 251–2).

Rejection of the focus upon individuals and on causation therefore would reflect not merely a redirection of particular policies but rather a shift away from the disciplinary technology of power itself.[2] In the field of crime and crime management, a number of commentators have noted the development of programs and policies based on the regulation of behaviours and their

Economy and Society Volume 21 Number 3 August 1992
© Routledge 1992 0308-5147/92/2103-0252 $3.00/1

consequences – in which 'actuarial' (Cohen 1985) or 'insurance' based (Reichman 1986; Hogg 1989) assumptions and techniques are brought into play. Perhaps the most striking statement of the changes implied has been provided by Cohen (1985) who observes that the conception of a mind-control society envisaged in Orwell's *1984* is mistaken, for although such key Foucauldian elements as surveillance continue to develop, there is little or no concern with individuals as such. Thus in situational crime prevention, one of the fastest growing techniques of crime control, concern is with the spatial and temporal aspects of crime, thought out in terms of the opportunities for crime rather than its causal or biographical origins:

> What is being monitored is behaviour (or the physiological correlates of emotion and behaviour). No one is interested in inner thoughts . . . 'the game is up' for all policies directed to the criminal as an individual, either in terms of detection (blaming and punishing) or causation (finding motivational or causal chains). . . . The talk now is about 'spatial' and 'temporal' aspects of crime, about systems, behaviour sequences, ecology, defensible space . . . target hardening . . .
>
> (Cohen 1985: 146–8)

While such writers are concerned primarily with understanding the management of crime, there is a considerable literature which identifies this as merely one instance of the supercession of disciplinary techniques across a very broad spectrum of social sites (e.g. Donzelot 1979, 1991; Ewald 1986, 1990, 1991; Simon 1987, 1988; Castel 1991; Defert 1991; Miller and Rose 1990). Analysis of this shift is largely based on the observations of Foucault, who differentiated between two basic forms of power emergent in the seventeenth century – the disciplines, 'an anatomo-politics of the human body', and 'regulatory controls: a bio-politics of the population'. The latter were concerned not with the individual's deviation from the norm, but with managing populations at an aggregate level, notably through regulation in terms of statistical distributions about a mean (Foucault 1984: 139). Familiar examples include the development of social security arrangements such as unemployment relief and public health insurance as techniques of governing general physical and economic characteristics of the population. Thus state unemployment insurance manages the risks and effects of unemployment and spreads them across time and space to reduce their impact on public security. A disciplinary strategy, by contrast, would identify 'problem' individuals and intervene directly in their lives in an attempt to 'normalize' their status. One of the earliest examples of a disciplinary agency in this area, of course, was the workhouse.

Despite identifying the emergence of regulatory controls as occurring early in modern history, Foucault perceived that they have become ascendant over other technologies of power only during the last century, although in his discussion of this in *The History of Sexuality* it is not made altogether clear why this should have been so. One of the clearest and most developed elaborations

254   *Pat O'Malley*

accounting for such a change is given by Jonathan Simon (1987, 1988), Jacques Donzelot (1979) and Francois Ewald (1986) who generally regard these risk-based, insurance, or actuarial techniques as becoming dominant because they function to intensify further the effectiveness of power:

> While the disciplinary regime attempts to alter individual behaviour and motivation, the actuarial regime alters the physical and social structures within which individuals behave. The movement from normalization (closing the gap between distribution and norm) to accommodation (responding to variations in distributions) *increases the efficiency of power* because changing people is difficult and expensive.
>
> (Simon 1988: 773, emphasis added)[3]

It is argued that such risk-based techniques are more effective means of control than discipline, primarily because they do not need to resort to the inefficient methods of direct coercion of individuals.[4] In consequence, they are more subtle in their operation, and less likely to generate resistance (see also Donzelot 1979; Ewald 1990).

Whereas disciplines evolved in the early part of the modern era, as defensive strategies for managing the 'dangerous classes' by coercion, exclusion and correction, the risk-based tactics and categories are more incorporative and meliorating. Although developed earlier (insurance strategies go back to the emergence of modern capitalism) they have been employed predominantly in the twentieth century, in which the population has been extensively pacified by the operation of the disciplines and by the improvement in living and working conditions associated with the development of industrial capitalism. According to this view, because of the generally pacified nature of the populace, modern societies are able to tolerate greater degrees of individual deviance than was possible in the age of disciplinary control. Under such conditions, risk-based technology – which is more tolerant of individual deviance and thus less overt and coercive in its interventions – may operate effectively.

Thus such quintessential examples of this technology of power as social insurance, workers' compensation, and income tax 'created forms of management that did not need to rely on the cumbersome techniques of individual discipline' (Simon 1988). Further, through its utilization of risk-based techniques to detect and manage social problems, this emergent form of power divides the population into statistical and behavioural categories organized around risk, that tend not to correspond to people's lived experiences. Thus they do not lend themselves readily to the purposes of social recognition and mobilization, around which group resistance could form.[5]

In such accounts, these shifts are encapsulated in the idea that there is involved a movement from discourses of control to discourses of security (e.g. Donzelot 1991). Insurance apparatuses provide security by spreading the costs of breakdown (in health, employment, legality etc.), and in so doing:

> Insurance practice results in the dedramatization of social conflicts by eliding the question of assigning *responsibility* for the origin of 'social evils'

and shifting the issue to the differing technical options . . . required to optimise employment, wages, allowances etc. Also on the other hand, it creates a passive social solidarity, eliminating the forms of collective self defence.

(Donzelot 1979: 81. See also Ewald 1991; Gordon 1991)

These interpretations of actuarialism resonate strongly with a number of other accounts of the management of multiplicities, notably that of 'dispersed social control' (e.g. Cohen 1979; Abel 1982). While key differences exist between these accounts (for example over the integration of the whole into a control 'system'), all put stress on regulatory management, on reduced visibility and coercive intervention, and on a consequently reduced resistance to this emergent form of power. In particular, in each there is a clear case being made that a more efficient form of power has been developed – efficient that is in terms of a political and economic cost/benefit calculus. Correspondingly, in such accounts, there is also a very strong tendency toward a totalizing vision of regulation. Largely because of its greater efficiency, actuarial power is seen to permeate virtually all social fields replacing 'the punitive city' (Cohen 1979) with the 'risk society' (Simon 1987; Gordon 1991) or 'post-disciplinary order' (Castel 1991).

Such a position implies that technologies of power can be ranked hierarchically in terms of efficiency, and even that there is a kind of natural selection among technologies such that the most efficient survive. Certainly such interpretations may gather support from Foucault's discussions in *Discipline and Punish* which assert that technologies of power advance according to three criteria:

firstly, to obtain the exercise of power at the lowest possible cost (economically by the low expenditure it involves, politically, by its discretion, its low exteriorization, its relative invisibility, the little resistance it arouses); second to bring the effects of this power to their maximum intensity, to extend them as far as possible, without either failure or interval; thirdly to link this 'economic' growth of power with the output of the apparatuses . . . within which it is exercised; in short to increase both the docility and the utility of all the elements of the system.

(1977: 218)[6]

While a reading of Foucault in terms of a unilinear model of efficiency and power is possible, clearly it runs against an insistence on the fragmentary nature of social relations across time and space. Moreover, it collides with Foucault's (1984) recognition of discipline and regulation as 'two poles of development linked together by a whole intermediary cluster of relations', characterized by 'overlappings, interactions and echoes' (Foucault 1984: 149). Thus, rather than there being an implied redundancy, there comes into being a dynamic interaction:

We must consequently see things not in terms of substitution for a society of sovereignty of a disciplinary society and the subsequent replacement of a

256   *Pat O'Malley*

disciplinary society by a governmental one; in reality we have a triangle: sovereignty-discipline-government, which has as its primary target the population and as its essential mechanism apparatuses of security.

(Foucault 1979: 19)[7]

Such instances do not imply any hierarchy of efficiency, nor competition between forms of power, although such forms may be expected to collide as well as to collude.

Of course, Foucault cannot speak *ex cathedra*, but the clear implication is not to map out the unfolding of an evolution, but to understand the dynamics of such triangular relations and the conditions which affect the roles taken by the various elements in specific combinations. With respect to the nature and impact of actuarial techniques therefore we need to think out their relationships with sovereign and disciplinary forms, in terms of articulations and alliances, colonizations and translations, resistances and complicities between them rather than in terms of the 'pure logic' of their unilateral or unilineal development (cf. Fitzpatrick 1988).[8] Among the theorists of social risk, only Simon appears to have grappled with this issue.

Market relations, risk and residual sovereignty

Simon's focus on an evolutionary model of power and its efficiency means that while the force of sovereignty is recognized it appears as a technologically irrational anomaly, primarily explained by the resistance of moral reactions to more efficient instrumental methods of control.[9] In the case of punishment 'the state's effort to punish members of the underclass who commit crimes is one of the last traces of a commitment to share a community with them' (Simon 1987: 82).

To retain the force of his overall argument nevertheless, he claims that actuarial techniques are spreading into this deprived arena. This occurs partly because 'access to public benefits is more and more coming to be distributed through methods of risk-assessment' and partly because of the displacement of penal sanctions by the 'behavioural regulation' measures discussed by Cohen in *Visions of Social Control* (Simon 1987: 78). Both claims are dubious.

Viewing the enormous contraction of public benefit welfare and related strategies which has occurred under 'economically rationalist' regimes in many western states, the first claim seems a rather determined attempt to rescue the thesis of extending socialized security. It is evident that risk-based 'targeting' of benefits is increasingly a feature of welfarism. For example, the short-term unemployed may be targeted for 'retraining' or 'redeployment' while the long-term unemployed may be excluded from benefit or put on a lower rate of benefit (cf. Hatt *et al.* 1990). The distinct possibility here is that actuarial discourses are being used as means not simply of redistributing benefits, but rather as a way of downscaling welfare, at least on a per capita basis. This surely is something rather different to theorizing actuarial technologies in terms of the necessary centrality of 'apparatuses of security' (Foucault 1979), the 'hegemony of welfare' (Simon 1987) or the 'society of security' involving 'a distinctive circuit of interdependence between *political security* and *social security*' (Gordon 1991). Indeed, the focus of such approaches on the (presumed) politically pacifying effect of social security seems to blind these theorists to other possible relations between political and social security.[10] Thus, in such models there is no recognition of the increasing severity and scope of the 'sovereign' dispositions accompanying resurgent philosophies of 'just deserts', 'truth in sentencing' and 'protecting the public'. As levels of imprisonment begin to surpass those extant for generations, and as the rationales for imprisonment *increasingly* tend toward the punitive and away from the correctional, it becomes unsatisfactory to see certain forms of power as efficiently managing the population, and other forms as 'surviving' or 'persisting' because of the failure of the system to incorporate some of the population (Greenberg 1990; Brown 1989).[11]

Such difficulties can in part be traced to a subtle transition, already alluded to, in the nature of risk-based practices. The examples upon which Simon, Gordon, Donzelot and others draw to illustrate actuarial power refer largely to techniques developed in relation to state-centred means for managing the risks primarily confronted by those temporarily forced out of the labour market, or who exist on its margins. Such analysis seems to assume that the existence of a discourse of social security reflects the continued growth of the corresponding agencies (summed up by an implausible reference by Simon (1987: 80) to a currently 'increasing hegemony of welfare'). However, the past decade or more, I would argue, has not witnessed the continuation of this process. Rather it has witnessed the partial transformation of socialized actuarialism into privatized actuarialism (or *prudentialism*) as an effect of political interventions promoting the increased play of market forces. More specifically this has involved three integrally related changes: the retraction of socialized risk-based techniques (public benefit) from managing the risks confronting the poor; their progressive replacement by disciplinary or sovereign remedies; and the privatization of public benefits as an aspect of the extension of privatized risk-based technique.

Overall, this suggests a major revision of the conceptualization of actuarialism and the 'logic of power' that drives it. It implies movement from a model of technologies of power and their efficiencies, toward a model of substantive political programs which deploy such technologies in ways which cannot be reduced to any simple or direct formula.

From power to political programs

In order to avoid the difficulties associated with creating Power as a new subject, motor or logic of history, Donzelot (1979) has suggested that it be reconceptualized in terms of technologies, political programs and strategies.

In this conceptualization, technologies, of which the panopticon and insurance are examples, emerge as 'always local multiple, intertwining, coherent or contradictory forms of activating and managing a population' (Donzelot 1979).[12] Technologies, although they have their own dynamics, nevertheless develop primarily in terms of their role in relation to specific political programs.

Political programs focus upon doing something about a 'practical object', for example the reduction of levels of unemployment, rates of crime or youth homelessness. They are recipes 'for corrective intervention ... (and) redirection'. In turn, such programs are formed in terms of more abstract strategies – 'formulae of government, theories which explain reality only to the extent that they enable the implementation of a program' (Donzelot 1979: 77). Keynesianism and laissez-faire political economy provide examples of the latter.

Moving on from Donzelot's sketchy position, it can be argued that technologies do not simply come into being as a result of a logic of power, but are developed with specific purposes in mind (Miller and Rose 1990).[13] Subsequently they may be generalized to other purposes and fields. Institutional risk-management planning, for example, developed initially in relation to insurance, then was adapted unevenly to distinct purposes in relation to the formation of programs such as welfarism (Hacking 1991). However, the continued spread of technologies is by no means assured once commenced. The appeal of technologies may be based on a variety of criteria other than perceptions of effectiveness; and even the latter are subject to fluctuations not easily accounted for in any deterministic narrative – as the continuing oscillation between institutionalizing and de-institutionalizing tendencies in the field of mental policy suggests (Scull 1975; La Fond and Durham 1991).

What influences the spread of technologies is most likely to be their appropriateness to particular ends, and this in large measure will be related to political struggles which establish programs on the social agenda. The history of the prison or of actuarial techniques in crime prevention, this suggests, is not to be understood as the gradual encroachment of a more efficient technology of power, but the uneven and negotiated (and thus partial) implementation of a political program and the consequent (equally partial) installation of the appropriate techniques. The development of public benefit welfarism may thus be understood as the outcome of struggles between political programs (informed by broader 'strategies' such as Keynesianism), in each national instance taking different forms shaped by local conditions and the outcomes of struggles and negotiations.[14]

This (familiar) manner of thinking about technologies of power leads to a more overtly political understanding of the developments reviewed so far. Further, it has major consequences for an understanding of risk-based techniques. These may initially be examined with respect to two issues central to this case – the amorality and the efficiency of actuarial technology.

Morality, risk and the free market

In the analyses of Donzelot, Simon, Ewald *et al.*, it is clear that what they see as the spread of risk-based techniques is a power focused interpretation of the rise of the welfare and interventionist state (e.g. Gordon 1991: 38–41). Welfarism is thus represented as a technique for the management of populations, a construction also common in Marxist theory (Gough 1984). Because in their day-to-day operations these techniques work bureaucratically and on categories, it is argued that they are thought by the populace to work amorally. As seen, this very characteristic is interpreted as a source of efficiency, as it reduces opposition. However, in many western industrial states in the present day it can scarcely be thought that 'actuarial' welfarism is publicly understood as made up of amoral and apolitical programs. An alternative construction of such programs is to see them as the outcomes of moral and political struggle, which continue to be the objects of major conflict. The achievement of workers' compensation, of graduated income taxes and of various schemes of social insurance (unemployment relief, public health schemes, legal aid, etc.) has normally been set against considerable resistance in the political arena. Even their formation *in the discourse of actuarialism* has been fought out in moral and political terms (Pal 1986; Cuneo 1986).[15] As must be self-evident in the current era, their preservation is still a matter of bitter moral conflict, notably in the face of neo-conservative economic rationalism.

Certainly within the strategic vision of other political programs, such as those of a large sector of the New Right, such opposition takes on the form of a *moral* crusade against the coils of the welfare state which is sapping the energy and enterprise of individuals (Gamble 1988).[16] Moreover, the moral banner under which they carry forward this fight is that of the free market – the free market that reinstates the morally responsible individual and sets it against the collectivization inherent in public risk-management techniques.

This is not to deny that in many instances socialized risk-management techniques work invisibly and amorally. Rather, it is to deny that they can usefully be reduced to merely instrumental techniques for managing masses, the success of which is attributable in large measure to intrinsic characteristics or effects, the existence and operation of which can be taken for granted.[17] Rather I would argue that such matters are always problematic. As frequent objects of political struggle, not only are actuarial techniques both long-term political and overtly moral issues, but currently they are on the retreat as a result of distinctly moral inventions.

Efficiency: governance and market relations

Can power be more or less efficient, as is assumed in the above readings of Foucauldian accounts? In a recent paper, Miller and Rose (1990) point out

260   *Pat O'Malley*

that one of the peculiarities of discourses of governmentality is that they are eternally optimistic, assuming

> that a domain or a society could be administered better or more effectively ... (and as a result) the 'failure' of one policy or set of policies is always linked to attempts to devise or propose programs that would work better.
>
> (1990: 4)

Such 'optimism' may thus appear as an important characteristic of governmentality, but as such it should be distinguished sharply from the idea that governmentality (or any other manifestation of 'power') can *actually* perfect itself. Rather, programs incorporate discourses of success and failure as part of their political character.

> The imperative to evaluate needs to be viewed as itself a key component of the forms of political thought under discussion: how authorities and administrators make judgements, the conclusions that they draw from them, the rectifications they propose and the impetus that 'failure' provides for the propagation of new programs of government.
>
> (Miller and Rose 1990: 4)

From such a viewpoint, efficiency is not so much an abstract universal property, but as argued earlier, a political claim couched in terms of the achievement of fairly specific political goals. Thus the arguments of many of those proposing the establishment of such risk managerial techniques as social insurance was that they would increase the efficiency of nations by improving the productivity of labour, and by reducing conflict generated by unemployment and other vicissitudes created by market relations (Gough 1984). Such arguments parallel those of Simon, Donzelot and others. However, this is not in any simple sense a factual representation of what welfarism is or was. It is, rather, a restatement of a political argument put forward initially in favour of welfarism and more recently (at least conditionally) against it (e.g. Gough 1984). It is an account in which efficiency is constructed in relation to particular criteria and goals of class domination.

Again, such assumptions of efficiency are challenged by conservative opponents in the political arena. For the New Right, socialized actuarial developments have sapped the efficiency of the population. Proper efficiency will be achieved only by restoration of free market relations and by the reassertion of individual intitiative and entrepreneurialism.[18] Social insurances of all sorts and all other devices that have removed the spur provided by the need to fend for oneself in open competition, must be stripped back and replaced by privatized arrangements (Gamble 1988).

In the New Right vision, this is not to deny that individuals should be prudent. On the contrary, they should cover themselves against the vicissitudes of sickness, unemployment, old age and so on by making such private provisions as they see fit – including taking out the private insurances they can afford. In this fashion, risk-management techiques certainly play a vital role, but this is not the socialized actuarialims of Donzelot, Simon, Ewan and others. Better understood as prudentialism, it is a construct of governance which removes the key conception of regulating individuals by collectivist risk management, and throws back upon the individual the responsibility for managing risk. This may be advocated by its supporters as 'efficient', for individuals will be driven to greater exertion and enterprise by the need to insure against adverse circumstances – and the more enterprising they are, the better the safety net they can construct.[19]

This specific program for creating an efficient economy, as is clearly understood by the New Right and its allies, will create a need for a Strong State to deal with the major conflicts that can be expected to emerge (Gamble 1988). First among these involves struggles with the class of public employees and officials which has grown up around the apparatuses of public risk management, and whose political power will need to be countered. Second, and more vital, are those conflicts generated by people whose lives will be dislocated by the return to market relations. These include struggles against organized labour which can be expected to resist the dismantling of arrangements it has long fought for. They will also include conflicts with those already unemployed who will need to learn to redeploy themselves rather than depend upon the state (but who can be expected to resist the stripping away of welfare support). It also includes the newly unemployed who will be created by the inevitable dislocations created by the reformation of the economy – as bloated, counterproductive state agencies are closed or cut back, as inefficient companies go to the wall, and as 'flabby' organizations shed workers and become 'lean' and 'hungry' (Gamble 1988, 1989). This scenario of large numbers of people dislocated and dispossessed by the impact of advancing market relations is very similar indeed to that under which the disciplines first emerged (Foucault 1977). Accordingly, the kinds of measures developed and expanded in relation to new 'dangerous classes' are precisely what have come to be understood theoretically as the 'inefficient' coercive and divisive means of sovereignty.[20]

Putting these points together, therefore, in place of a model of increasingly efficient forms of power, what Simon and others interpret as actuarialism must be understood in its place as a technology geared to specific kinds of political programs. In turn, this is not characterized by an inevitable expansion of the social field under its sway. Rather, in the present era, the success of programs inspired by economic rationalists and neo-conservatism has been stripping away socialized risk management, and replacing it with a programmatic combination of privatized prudentialism and punitive sovereignty. While Simon's model constructs a 'struggle between risk and sovereignty', the policies of the New Right reveal no such conflict. Rather, the two technologies are systematically related to each other in a mutually augmenting, symbiotic fashion – albeit that contradictions inherent in the amalgam must be managed carefully.

In order to give these rather general comments more precise form, the

262 *Pat O'Malley*

second part of this paper will take up these themes in the analysis of situational crime prevention with which the analysis began.

Situational crime prevention as risk management

As indicated earlier in Stan Cohen's striking passage, situational crime prevention may be understood as quintessentially 'actuarial'. It deals hardly at all with individual offenders, is uninterested in the causes of crime, and generally is hostile or at best agnostic toward correctionalism. Its concern is with crime control as risk management (Reichman 1986). In a fairly aggressive self-description, the National Crime Prevention Institute outlines the following basic assumptions of what it grandly calls 'the contemporary perspective' in criminology:

> *Prevention (and not rehabilitation) should be the major concern of criminologists;
> *No one is sure how to rehabilitate offenders;
> *Punishment and/or imprisonment may be relevant in controlling certain offenders;
> *Criminal behaviour can be controlled primarily through the direct alteration of the environment of potential victims;
> *Crime control programs must focus on crime before it occurs rather than afterward; and
> *As criminal opportunity is reduced, so too will be the number of criminals.
> (National Crime Prevention Institute 1986: 18)

As Cohen also indicates (but see too Bottoms 1990; O'Malley 1991; King 1989; Iadicola 1986; Hogg 1989) situational crime prevention is enjoying a period of extraordinary success in Britain, the United States, Australia and elsewhere – at least in the political sense of its influence as a program of crime control. Certainly it is tempting to follow earlier arguments and regard this as due to the increased efficiency of actuarial techniques. But the rapidity of its rise to prominence can scarcely be attributed to evidence of its superiority over correctionalism and causal/social criminologies. Rather what emerges, as might be expected from Cohen's (1985) original account of the 'politics of failure', is a political struggle over the definition and the criteria of failure and success. This may be seen in several ways.

First, advocates of situational crime prevention take inexorably rising crime rates as its evidence of the failure of criminology (e.g. Geason and Wilson 1988, 1989).[21] Yet while this may be a politically persuasive argument, it is scarcely an indisputable fact, since between the 1960s and 1980s social criminologies progressively undermined the validity of crime rates in this respect. The meaning and validity of crime rates in other words is part of the politics of failure rather than a neutral gauge for the measurement of efficiency.[22]

Second, the assault on social and causal criminologies' ineffectiveness, even where accepted, is readily turned aside by the argument that at no point have the insights of these theories been translated properly into policy. This point is one seized upon by Miller and Rose (1990) who point out that all policies 'fail' for this reason – because no policy is ever unadulterated in practice. Perhaps more to the point, is the fact that no matter how 'pure' is the theoretical lineage of a policy, among adherents there will always be disputes over the 'correct' means of implementing the programs on which it is based. 'Failure' is always attributable to the mode of implementation rather than to the policy itself.

Third, situational crime prevention's own claims to success are undermined by counterclaims that it achieves merely the displacement of crime to softer targets (e.g. Wilson 1987; Cornish and Clarke 1986). More vitally, it is countered that it reacts only to symptoms, and thus fails to address the enduring social problems that crime merely manifests (King 1989; Bottoms 1990; MacNamara forthcoming). At this point, of course, the two approaches rather cease to converge – for the goals of each are regarded as misguided to the other, and the already disputed criteria of success and failure therefore lose the semblance of shared standards.

Such debates are endless. They reveal only that the politics of success and failure normally are struggles over the status of criteria, and can rarely be reduced to any universally accepted scale of efficiency. If this is the case, then the question of why situational crime prevention has proven so influential a technique will need to be answered in terms of its relationship to political programs and strategies, and especially to those currently in ascendance. I believe that the broader political and ideological effects of situational crime prevention reveal that its attractions to economic rationalist, neo-conservative and New Right programs provide such an answer (although not unrelated attractions to police forces are also significant). The primary attractions, I will argue, link directly with core ideological assumptions of the New Right, and through these with the two directions of population management – increasing punitiveness with respect to offenders, and with respect to victims, the displacement of socialized risk management with privatized prudentialism. While it is by no means the case that this is the only possible construction of situational crime prevention (others will be discussed briefly toward the end of this paper), for a variety of reasons it is a particularly durable and readily mobilized version under current conditions.

Neo-conservative readings of crime prevention

Situational crime prevention and the offender

Situational crime prevention destroys the disciplines' biographical individual as a category of criminological knowledge, but the criminal does not disappear. Opportunities only exist in relation to potential criminals who convert open windows into windows of opportunity for crime. To install such an agent, situational crime prevention replaces the biographical criminal with a polar opposition – the abstract and universal 'abiographical' individual – the 'rational choice' actor (see also Geason and Wilson 1989; Heal and Laycock 1986; National Crime Prevention Institute 1986).

However, while abstract and abiographic, this rational choice individual nevertheless is clearly structured. It thinks in cost-benefit terms – weighing up the risks, potential gains and potential costs, and then committing an offence only when the benefits are perceived to outweigh the losses. This construction may be thought of as having a source very close to the foundations of actuarialism. It is of course the amoral rational choice individual beloved of classical economics, the *homo economicus* which inhabits the world of insurance – the home base of risk management discourses, and an industry closely connected with the promotion of situational crime prevention (O'Malley 1991).

This same being, but invested with additional moral and political characteristics is the denizen of neo-conservative and New Right discourses. It single-mindedly pursues the entrepreneurial ideal, as an atomistic being it is 'naturally free', self-reliant, and responsible (Gamble 1988). It is the underlying form of the human being that the Right would liberate from the debilitating 'public benefit' shackles of the welfare state which have progressively been imposed upon it especially since the end of the Second World War (Levitas 1986). Indeed, the demolition of socialized risk management and the restoration of social conditions approximating 'freedom' of the responsible individual is central to neo-conservative thinking about crime.

> When the traditional family is undermined, as it has been, self reliance tends to be lost and responsibility tends to disappear, both to be replaced by a dependence often long term, on the government and manipulation by social engineers. It also provides the setting which leads young people to the treadmill of drug abuse and crime.
>
> (Liberal Party of Australia 1988: 15)

Already it is possible to see how it might be that the neo-conservatives who are concerned to dismantle so much that Simon understands as actuarialism, might nevertheless embrace and foster the actuarialism of situational crime prevention. But there are other reasons as well.

Situational crime prevention's rejection of concern with biographical-causal approaches to understanding crime, and the focus on the targets of crime rather than on offenders, combine to deflect attention from the social foundations of offending. This effect is achieved in the case of the rational choice model by its rejection of or agnosticism toward conditions which may have given rise to the offenders' action, but also and especially by constructing the offender as abstract, universal and rational. Like the abstract legal subject explored by Pashukanis (1977) and Weber (1954), the abstract individual appears logically to be 'free' and thus a voluntary agent. Such abstract and universal, equal and voluntary individuals are free to act in a perfectly 'rational' self-interested fashion, maximizing gains and minimizing costs. They are free to commit crime or not to commit crime.

This latter point suggests that not only is the knowledge of the criminal disarticulated from a critique of society, but in turn, both of these may be disarticulated from the reaction to the offender. As Foucault made clear, what he saw as the 'criminological labyrinth' was constructed around the assumption that crime is caused, and that cause reduces responsibility (1977: 252). Elimination of cause from the discourse of crime obviously restores responsibility and this has its effects on punishment. Thus the logical corollary of situational crime prevention from the point of view of a New Right discourse, is a policy of punitive or just desserts sentencing, rather than a program of sentencing for reform. Compatibility of crime prevention thinking with these models is furthered by the argument that salutary punishment in the form of imprisonment incapacitates offenders and thus acts directly as a means of behavioural crime prevention.

Thus the criminal becomes individually responsible and our concern with offenders as such ceases with that knowledge. In consequence, any class, race, gender or similar foundations of crime, especially as identified by causal criminology, are automatically excluded from consideration except in their role as risk-enhancing factors. If bothered with at all they are taken to be predictive of behaviours, not explanatory of meaningful actions.

This shift in understanding eschews also the moral dimensions of the sociological criminologies, condemned to the status of 'failures' by situational crime prevention theorists (e.g. National Crime Prevention Institute 1986; Geason and Wilson 1989). Out with them go their respective agendas linking crime and social justice – for example that of strain theory and its concerns with relative deprivation and inequality of opportunity, and the appreciative recognition of cultural variability and of the impact of material degradation of the inner city poor that was the hallmark of ecological analysis. Academically as well as politically and administratively, it now becomes respectable to regard criminals as unconstrained agents, and to regard a crime control policy as divorced from questions of social justice.

Finally, the 'politics of failure' provide a technical gloss to justify punitiveness. If correction and deterrence do not work, then sanctions based on these ideas must be swept away. What is left for the offender but punishment, retribution and incapacitation?[23]

Situational crime prevention and the victim

If situational crime prevention short-circuits the link between criminality and social justice, then it might be expected that the victim of crime moves more into the centre of concern. In some sense this is undoubtedly the case, as the rhetoric of 'protecting the public' rings loud throughout this program (e.g. Home Office 1990). However, just as the offenders are disconnected from the political dimensions of their existence, so too are the victims, for victims like offenders are to be understood as rational choice actors, responsible and free individuals.

Prevention now becomes the responsibility of the victim. This view is by no means the construct of academic reflection but permeates crime prevention thinking at all levels. At one level, this position emerges no doubt because it reduces pressure on police forces, which have not noticeably reduced crime victimization and which are therefore vulnerable to political pressure for this reason. Thus a senior official of the Australian insurance Council has noted: 'Severely restricted police resources and the sheer frequency of crime, means that any improvement in the situation will rely heavily on property owners accepting responsibility for their own property and valuables' (Hall 1986: 243).

At broader political levels similar arguments are being presented for much the same reasons. Responding to news that crime rates in Britain have reached record levels, 'the Prime Minister, Mrs Thatcher, blamed a large portion of the crimes on the victims' carelessness. "We have to be careful that we ourselves don't make it easy for the criminal" she said' (*Age* 28 September 1990).

Not only does responsibility and thus critique shift, but so too do costs. Privatization of security practice and costs – to be seen in the trend toward private security agencies, security devices, domestic security practices, neighbourhood watch schemes (with attendant insurance underwriting) – generate the rudiments of a user pays system of policing security.[24] Closer to the heart of neo-conservatism, the rational choice public will come to see the justice in this:

> The general public's apathy about self-protection arises mainly from ignorance of the means of protection, and a perception that somebody else – 'the Government' or insurance companies – bears most of the cost of theft and vandalism. The community is beginning to realise however that crime rates are rising despite increased penalties, that the judicial system cannot cope, and that it is the individual who eventually foots the bill for crime through increased taxes for expanded police forces and more jails, and through higher insurance premiums.
>
> (Geason and Wilson 1989: 9)[25]

In this process, security becomes the responsibility of the private individuals who through the pursuit of self interest, and liberated from enervating reliance on 'the state' to provide for them will participate in the creation of the new order.

Putting these points together, it can be seen that in this construction of situational crime prevention there is no conflict between risk management *per se* and punitiveness. Quite to the contrary, in the privatization of the actuarial techniques are the same notions of individual responsibility and rational choice that are present in the justification for expanding punitiveness. Reliance on the state, even for protection against crime, is not to be encouraged.[26] Quite literally therefore it represents the expression in one field of the New Right ideal of the Strong State and the Free Market, combining to provide crime control in a period when the threat of crime generated by the Right's own market oriented practices can be expected to increase.

Crime prevention and social justice

The discussion of situational crime prevention thus far has been one-sided, for it has deliberately focused on developments illustrative of the ways in which risk-based and punitive techniques may be rendered compatible and mutually reinforcing under neo-conservatism. It will not have escaped recognition that situational crime prevention is by no means *necessarily* associated with neo-conservatism. The French Bonnemaison program for example incorporates much that is focused on social justice (King 1988). Likewise, in the Australian state of Victoria situational crime prevention is integrated quite explicitly with a government focus on social justice and is shaped accordingly (Sandon 1991a, 1991b; Victoria Police 1991). Thus with respect to the status of women, an issue on which situational crime prevention has been soundly criticized,[27] such policies have extended well beyond narrowly defensive and privatized risk bearing, and have embedded preventative techniques in socializing reforms, being 'concentrated on reducing violence against women by targeting the involvement of the community to change male behaviour and attitudes, empower women in unsafe situations and change community perceptions and understandings about violence toward women' (Thurgood 1991).

Clearly this social justice contextualization of situational crime prevention conflicts considerably with the behavioural regulation model reviewed above and criticized by Cohen. Not only is this because of the focus on changing people's attitudes and 'inner states', but also because it reflects a series of value assertions and policy directions which are remote from rational choice individualism. Such articulation between situational crime prevention and collective responses to crime as an issue of *social justice* of course reflects precisely that social risk-based model actively discarded by conservatives, and which was highlighted by the analyses of Simon *et al*. Articulation of situational crime prevention with social justice is intelligible in terms of the construction of risk as shared among large sectors of the populace – a precondition of socialized actuarialism. Thus with the welfare model, 'The concept of social risk makes it possible for insurance technologies to be applied to social problems in a way which can be presented as creative simultaneously of social justice and social solidarity' (Gordon 1991: 40).

268   *Pat O'Malley*

It is therefore intelligible that risk-based techniques may be allied to socializing political programs through their discursive construction in terms of shared risk. Conversely it is equally clear that it may be articulated with a conservative political program through discursive construction in terms of rational choice individuals. As witnessed, this construction fosters the combination of a variety of disciplinary, punitive, and risk-based techniques in order to achieve effects consistent with neo-conservative programs.

Conclusions

Perhaps the central point in the argument of this paper is that history and the future are more contingent than is implied in the arguments of those theorizing the implications of risk-based social technologies. I have tried to argue that while such technologies undoubtedly have their own internal dynamics of development, these are neither prefectly autonomous nor do they have intrinsic effects which follow automatically from their nature. Rather, the direction of development, the form in which they are put into effect in specific policies, their scope *vis-à-vis* that of other technologies, and the nature of their social impact are all quite plastic. Hopefully this will not be taken to imply that history is entirely contingent, for it should be clear that in the analysis above there are constants produced by the central place taken by risk in modern societies (cf. Giddens 1990). Thus I would not object to the assertion common to theorists of actuarialism that (in Gordon's words noted earlier) 'The concept of social risk makes it possible for insurance technologies to be applied to social problems in a way that can be presented as creative simultaneously of social justice and social solidarity'.

My point is simply to confirm that 'social risk' and 'insurance technologies' make this move *possible* rather than necessary. They make possible also a variety of other innovations with quite different implications, notably forms of privatized social risk management which have as their likely effects neither social justice nor solidarity. In addition these developments make possible many other hybrid developments with complex and varied possible effects – the nature of which has not yet been determined with any certainty by social research or theory. For example, state sponsored advertising campaigns concerning private property insurance against burglary may be linked to the development of neighbourhood-watch programs. Under some circumstances these may lead to vigilantism, victim-oriented pressure groups seeking harsher sentencing of offenders, and a fortress mentality. Under other circumstances they may lead to increased police responsiveness to community demands and a rise in levels of community solidarity and interaction. The point here is simply to reaffirm the openness of social forms based on risk management, and to question the extent to which any linear pattern can be discerned. If it is still the case after so many years that critical examination cannot lead to any definitive answers on the nature and direction of quite specific developments such as neighbourhood watch, why should it be anticipated that this task is less problematic when directed at developments at a broader level which are themselves conceptually distilled from a myriad of such specific programs?

Furthermore, one of the emergent outcomes of new social technologies is opposition, formed in important ways by the form and anticipated impact of the technology itself. Such opposition may never turn back the clock. The emergence of social technologies of risk mean that laissez-faire, for example, could never be resurrected in its original form, and the policies of neo-conservatism obviously reflect this. Nevertheless, the resurgence of neo-conservatism and economic rationalism has clearly created developments unanticipated by a previous generation of welfare state theorists. The difficulty, evidently, is working out the forms of oppositional resurrection and innovation which will be generated by new social technologies. Of even greater difficulty is working out what their degree of success will be, and how the struggle will change the nature of the emergent technology, and its place in the ensemble of technologies arrayed to deal with social problems.

National Centre for Sociolegal Studies
La Trobe University
Melbourne, Australia

Notes

1   Ewald (1990) points out that normalization need not imply the disciplinary process of standardizing individuals, but merely implies the establishment of a norm in the sense of a point within a distribution. Strategies of normalization imply only the manipulation of distributions around the norm, and thus extend to what are referred to in this paper as actuarial or insurential technologies (in which, categories or indeed the entire population may be manipulated).

2   The use of the term 'technology' in this paper will be outlined later in more detail, but broadly speaking refers to any set of social practices which is aimed at manipulating the social or physical world according to identifiable routines. The three principle forms identified by Foucault are sovereign, disciplinary and insurential. 'Techniques' here refer either to distinct forms of application, or to distinct components, of technologies . For example, the prison and the school, examination and the case record may all be thought of as techniques of the disciplinary technology.

3   It will be evident that there is confusion over the terminology used to describe this technology. Simon (1987, 1988) refers to it as 'actuarial', for one foundation is in the management of multiplicities based on knowledge of the laws of large numbers. Stan Cohen (1985) also refers to the actuarial nature of these techniques, although in his analysis they are more usually referred to as 'behavioral regulation'. However, the latter term is too restrictive, omitting many closely related actuarially based processes such as property insurance or unemployment insurance (thus reflecting the field which he reviewed in *Visions of Social Control*). On the other hand the preference of commentators such as Donzelot (1979) for 'insurance' or 'insurential techniques' is likewise too restrictive, for it does not cover the practices outlined by Cohen. I suggest that what all analyses share in common is a focus on *risk* as the core concept underlying

270   *Pat O'Malley*

such diverse practices as the modification of the physical environment (e.g. installation of speed humps, improved security on property), interventions based on identification of high-risk categories of person, and various insurance based programs. Thus while there will be no hard and fast usage in the paper, the overall preference is for 'risk' and 'risk based' technologies.

4   Compare also Stan Cohen's (1985) paraphrase of contemporary crime control philosophy: 'solving problems by changing people is simply unproductive. People are not amenable to persuasion, resocialisation, counselling, treatment, re-education. We have to accept them as they are, modify their circumstances or deal with the consequences of their intractability'.

5   For example, in dealing with 'at risk' categories of young people, crime prevention strategies may quite deliberately intervene with respect to whole schools or even all schools in an area, rather than particular groups of individuals. Here, one of the intentions is to reduce the likelihood of identification (and thus the 'labeling') of potential offenders (Potas *et al.* 1990). As this example also makes clear, the effects to which Simon and others seek to draw attention are by no means deliberately or malevolently brought about.

6   This is consistent also with Foucault's account of the emergence of the disciplines, which were derived from the need to deal with the large 'floating populations' generated in the eighteenth and nineteenth centuries. In this account, Foucault (1977: 217–19) makes clear that is was the need to develop means of handling 'social multiplicities' with limited resources which stimulated the disciplinary strategies, a process strengthened by the fact that emerging capitalism required social technologies to manage its production in a cost-effective fashion.

7   For Foucault, it was specific *combinations* of disciplinary and regulatory techniques which gave rise to 'the four great lines of attack' in the modern politics of sex (1984: 146). Thus with birth control and the psychiatrization of perversions, 'the intervention was regulatory in nature, but it had to rely on the demand for individual disciplines and constraints'. On the other hand, the sexualization of children and the hysterization of women rested on the requirements of regulation (e.g. collective welfare) in order to obtain results at the level of discipline.

8   This will be a primary aim of the second part of the present paper where situational crime prevention will be assessed in such terms.

9   'The problems of war, criminal punishment and citizenship continue to haunt the twentieth century with the problem of sovereignty' (Simon 1987: 81–2).

10   Gordon and Ewart even go so far as to resurrect the old chestnut that the welfare state is an insurance against revolution (Gordon 1991: 41).

11   It would also be unconvincing to argue as would Garland (1990) that this is the result of an upsurge in moral outrage against crime, since the connection between popular feelings and public policy is variable and very indirect.

12   Between his 1987 and 1988 papers, Simon moved from an essentialist position in which Power existed more or less as the subject of history, to a position in which actuarialism is regarded as a technique or technology. However, in contrast to the position adopted in this paper, it then appears as a technique-at-large, not geared to or shaped by any particular programme. It retains its status as a more efficient form of power. And significantly in terms of my earlier point, the later usage refers almost solely to privatized forms of actuarial practice.

13   This is not to suggest that they are simply ingeniously constructed *de nova*. Many may come into existence more or less accidentally and are then refined, others are generated by drawing together disparate elements from other technologies, and so on. The process envisaged is one in which elements are drawn together pragmatically, and the ones that 'catch on' do so because they work for present purposes at hand. The 'logic' of growth is not therefore one of absolute efficiency, but of pragmatic appropriateness.

14   Thus in the Australian case the formation of a welfare state as a 'safety net' was developed in relation to such conditions as chronic shortages of labour, vulnerability of the economy to fluctuations on the international commodity market, early formation of unions and so on (O'Malley 1989). The result is quite distinct from that existing in the colonial core in Great Britain, even though the latter dominated the political, economic and cultural formation of Australia until well into the present century.

15   Reference should here be made to Pal's (1986) and Cuneo's (1986) analyses of the role of actuarial ideology in the construction of Canadian Unemployment Insurance (UI). In the debate between these scholars it emerges very clearly that the concept of the rational choice individual was an intrinsic component of an overtly socialized actuarial state policy. In other words, even where a policy is constructed around socialized forms then at least in a capitalist economy ideologies of the rational choice individual still are active. In this case, a struggle developed between those pressing for a universal benefit, and those who used rational choice models to argue for a strictly contributory scheme – because (rational choice) workers otherwise will 'naturally' cease to work for an income. This struggle played a major part in shaping the nature of the policy concerned, with the result that UI reflected simultaneously, if unevenly, the stamp of rational choice and social justice discourses.

16   I am fully aware of the dangers in ascribing any narrow band of views to the New Right, or indeed to any political movement or collectivity. However, my purpose in this paper is not to provide a complex analysis of the welfare and penal philosophies of the various groupings that can be collectively referred to as New Right. My purpose is to indicate in very broad terms the importance of examining the relationships between social technologies and political programs or strategies.

17   This point parallels the argument made by Garland (1990) that the reduction of punishment to an instrument of power is the central weakness of Foucauldian approaches to explaining legal sanctions, precisely because it is thereby unable to address the importance of the moral dimension.

18   Gamble (1986: 40–1) comments on Friedmanesque economic visions in much the same tone that this paper adopts toward assertions of absolute efficiency in crime management. Noting their claims that market solutions invariably are more efficient than governmental solutions, Gamble points out that the belief that economic propositions can be proven to be true is part of the political strategy used to discredit Keynesianism – rather than being a real foundation of such discrediting.

19   For a fascinating account of how yet another discourse on (national) efficiency generated still different reactions, see Miller and O'Leary (1987). While their account bears many similarities to that of actuarial approaches, the end point of the process examined is to *deepen* the understanding of the individual and to build such understanding into the nature of the organizational context.

20   Even debates over the 'failure' of imprisonment are by no means dead and buried. For example, as Garland has argued

> the prison might be evaluated in terms of its ability to deprive offenders of their liberty in accordance with a court order, to exclude them from society for a period of time, or to inflict mental suffering in ways that satisfy a punitive public – in which case the only failures would be occasional escapes and unwonted leniences.
>
> (1991: 165)

It is significant to note that even the hitherto taken for granted point that prisons are not cost effective when compared with community corrections is under challenge. Recent economic rationalist positions have been developed in favour of imprisonment as cost-effective in combating crime (e.g. Zedlewski 1985, 1987).

21   Such a view for example recently has been promoted by the Australian Institute of Criminology.

272   *Pat O'Malley*

The traditional approach to crime prevention has been to try to identify the social and psychological causes of crime and to attempt to remedy these deficiencies by treating the individual offender and/or designing special educational, recreational and employment services for groups regarded as being at risk. The escalating crime rate suggests that this approach is not working.

An alternative is 'situational crime prevention'. It rests on two assumptions: that the criminal is a rational decisionmaker who only goes ahead with a crime where the benefits outweigh the costs or risks; and the opportunity for crime must be there.

(Geason and Wilson 1988: 1)

22   Such debates are extremely complex, and show no signs of resolving themselves. The position on the Left has been confused by the infusion of a qualified respect for crime rates as understood by Left realists (MacLean 1991), while more orthodox criminologists cannot agree even as to whether crime rates are rising or falling (Steffensmeier and Harer 1987) and many other Left commentators retain their very critical stance toward the entire exercise (Greenberg 1990).

23   The dimensions of this criminological stance no doubt are familiar, although of course all aspects and subtleties cannot be rehearsed here. Related matters concern the justification of punishment as respecting the dignity of the individual offender, and broader issues of 'truth in sentencing' and its relationship to the calculus of pleasure and pain thought to be intrinsic to the rational choice offender (see for example Van den Haag 1975).

24   A further element in emergent crime prevention practices consistent with the New Right credo is the focus 'cost effectiveness' and 'cost-benefit' analysis. Thus for example *Young People and Crime* (Potas *et al.* 1990) produced by the Australian Institute of Criminology as part of its recently established series of publications dealing with crime prevention, ultimately asserts that no program of crime prevention should be established without prior and rigorous cost-effectiveness assessment (for which it duly provides a model). Indeed, for the more aggressively entrepreneurial versions of crime prevention

this does not mean merely that it is important to keep the costs of security as low as possible (consistent with good security), it also means that he [i.e. the crime prevention analyst] should apply his knowledge of risk-management in as creative a way as possible, looking for opportunities for profit or other benefit as well as other ways to minimise loss.

(National Crime Prevention Institute 1986: 51)

25   Of course, what this kind of argument tends to forget is that user pays models generally disadvantage the poor. In keeping with the tendency to abandon social justice, crime preventionism – through the progressive underdevelopment of public sector services – tends to leave the weak to fend for themselves (see O'Malley 1989).

26   Yet of course there is nothing in situational crime prevention that implies the diminution of police forces' powers and establishment. One of its major attractions for police is that it is an 'add-on' technique, augmenting traditional policing rather than replacing it. Moreover in many of its forms, for example neighbourhood watch, the police have been extremely active both in promoting it, in controlling the form of its development, and in maintaining control over its routine activities (e.g. O'Malley 1991).

27   Consider for example Lake (1990)

In one sense women have gained a measure of freedom. A real measure of freedom. Yet . . . everywhere we are confined and I mean physically, mentally, psychologically confined. We know because we are told often enough that we must not walk the streets at night. We must not now, it seems, travel on trains. Or public transport. Nor must we walk to dimly lit car parks. We must also every night securely lock ourselves up at home. And even then, of course, our security is illusory, for men force their way through windows into one's house or, they may already live in one's house . . . most domestic violence is committed on women known to the men who assault them, that is, it is committed on their wives, friends, daughters, sisters.

References

Abel, Richard (ed.) (1982) *The Politics of Informal Justice*, New York: Academic Press.

Bottoms, Anthony (1990) 'Crime prevention facing the 1990s', *Police and Society* 1: 3–22.

Castel, Robert (1991) 'From dangerousness to risk', in G. Burchell, C. Gordon and P. Miller (eds), *The Foucault Effect. Studies in Governmentality*, London: Harvester/Wheatsheaf.

Cohen, Stanley (1979) 'The punitive city. Notes on the dispersal of social control', *Contemporary Crises* 3: 339–63.

—— (1985) *Visions of Social Control: Crime, Punishment and Classification*, London: Polity Press.

Cornish, Derek and **Clarke, Robert** (1986) 'Situational prevention: Displacement of crime and rational choice theory', in Kevin Heal and Gloria Laycock (eds), *Situational Crime Prevention: From Theory into Practice*, London: Home Office.

Cuneo, Carl (1986) 'Comment: Restoring class to state unemployment insurance', *Canadian Journal of Political Science* 19: 93–8.

Defert, Daniel (1991) 'Popular life and insurance technology', in G. Burchell, C. Gordon and P. Miller (eds) *The Foucault Effect: Studies in Governmentality*, London: Harvester/Wheatsheaf.

Donzelot, Jacques (1979) 'The poverty of political culture', *Ideology and Consciousness* 5: 71–86.

—— (1991) 'Pleasure in work', in G. Burchell, C. Gordon and P. Miller (eds), *The Foucault Effect: Studies in Governmentality*, London: Harvester/Wheatsheaf.

Ewald, Francois (1986) *L'Etat Providence*, Paris: Grasset.

—— (1990) 'Norms, discipline and the law', *Representations* 30: 138–61.

—— (1991) 'Insurance and risks', in G. Burchell, C. Gordon and P. Miller (eds),

The Foucault Effect: Studies in Governmentality, London: Harvester/Wheatsheaf.

Fitzpatrick, Peter (1988) 'The rise and rise of informalism', in R. Matthews (ed.), *Informal Justice?* London: Sage.

Foucault, Michel (1977) *Discipline and Punish*, London: Peregrine Books.

—— (1979) 'Governmentality', *Ideology and Consciousness* 5–21.

—— (1984) *The History of Sexuality* Vol. 1, London: Peregrine Books.

Gamble, Andrew (1986) 'The political economy of the New Right', in Ruth Levitas (ed.), *The Ideology of the New Right*, Oxford: Basil Blackwell.

—— (1988) *The Free Economy and the Strong State*, London: Macmillan.

Garland, David (1990) 'Frameworks of inquiry in the sociology of punishment', *British Journal of Sociology* 41: 1–15.

—— (1991) *Punishment and Modern Society*, Oxford: Clarendon Press.

Geason, Susan and **Wilson, Paul** (1988) *Designing Out Crime*, Canberra: Australian Institute of Criminology.

—— (1989) *Crime Prevention: Theory and Practice*, Canberra: Australian Institute of Criminology.

Giddens, Anthony (1990) *The Consequences of Modernity*, Stanford: Standford University Press.

Gordon, Colin (1991) 'Governmental rationality: An introduction', in G. Burchell, C. Gordon and P. Miller (eds), *The Foucault Effect. Studies in Governmentality*, London: Harvester/Wheatsheaf.

Gough, Ian (1984) *The Political Economy of the Welfare State*, London: Macmillan.

Greenberg, David (1990) 'The cost benefit analysis of imprisonment', *Social Justice* 17: 49–75.

Hacking, Ian (1991) 'How should we do the history of statistics?', in G. Burchell, C. Gordon and P. Miller (eds), *The Foucault Effect. Studies in Governmentality*, London: Harvester/Wheatsheaf.

274 *Pat O'Malley*

Hall, John (1986) 'Burglary: The insurance industry viewpoint', in S. Mukherjee (ed.), *Burglary. A Social Reality*, Canberra: AIC.

Hatt, Ken, Caputo Tullio and Perry, Barbara (1990) 'Managing consent: Canada's experience with neo-conservatism', *Social Justice* 17: 30–48.

Hogg, Russell (1989) 'Criminal justice and social control: Contemporary development in Australia', *Journal of Studies in Justice* 2: 89–122.

Home Office (1990) *Crime, Justice and Protecting The Public*, London: HMSO.

Iadicola, Peter (1986) 'Community crime control strategies', *Crime and Social Justice* 25: 140–57.

King, Michael (1988) *How to Make Social Crime Prevention Work: The French Experience*, London: NACRO Occasional Paper.

—— (1989) 'Social crime prevention à la Thatcher', *Howard Journal of Penology* (October).

La Fond, J. Q. and Durham, M. (1991) *Back to the Asylum. The Future of Mental Health Policy in the United States*, New York: Oxford University Press.

Lake, Marilyn (1990) *Transcipts of Public Human Rights Debates*, Melbourne: National Centre for Socio-Legal Studies.

Levitas, Ruth (1986) 'Introduction. Ideology and the New Right', in Ruth Levitas (ed.), *The Ideology of the New Right*, Oxford: Basil Blackwell.

Maclean, Brian (1991) 'In partial defence of socialist realism. Some theoretical and methodological concerns of the local crime survey', *Crime, Law and Social Change* 15: 213–54.

Macnamara, Luke (Forthcoming) 'Retrieving the law and order issue from the Right', *Law in Context*.

Miller, Peter and O'Leary, Ted (1987) 'Accounting and the construction of the governable person', *Accounting, Organizations and Society* 12: 235–65.

Miller, Peter and Rose, Nikolas, (1990) 'Governing economic life', *Economy and Society* 19: 1–31.

National Crime Prevention Institute (1986) *Crime Prevention*, Louisville: National Crime Prevention Institute.

O'Malley, Pat (1988) 'The purpose of knowledge', *Contemporary Crises* 12: 65–80.

—— (1989) 'Redefining security. Neighborhood watch in context', *Arena* 86: 18–23.

—— (1991) 'Legal networks and domestic security', *Studies in Law, Politics and Society* 11: 181–91.

Pal, Leo (1986) 'Relative autonomy revisted: The origins of Canadian unemployment insurance', *Canadian Journal of Political Science* 19: 71–92.

Pashukanis, Evgeny (1977) *Law and Marxism*, London: Ink Links.

Potas, Ivan, Vining, Aidan and Wilson, Paul (1990) *Young People and Crime*, Canberra: Australian Institute of Criminology.

Reichman, Nancy (1986) 'Managing crime risks: Toward an insurance based model of social control', *Research in Law and Social Control* 8: 151–72.

Sandon, Mal (1991a) *Safety and Security*, Melbourne: Ministry of Police and Emergency Services (Victoria).

—— (1991b) *Ministerial Statement: Safety, Security and Women*, Melbourne: Parliament of Victoria.

Scull, Andrew (1975) *Decarceration. Community Treatment and the Deviant. A Radical View*, New York: Spectrum Books.

Simon, Jonathan (1987) 'The emergence of a risk society: Insurance, law, and the state', *Socialist Review* 95: 61–89.

—— (1988) 'The ideological effects of actuarial practices', *Law and Society Review* 22: 772–800.

Steffensmeier, Darrel and Harer, Miles (1987) 'Is the crime rate really falling?', *Journal of Research in Crime and Delinquency* 24: 23–48.

Thurgood, Pat (1991) 'Safety, security and women', Paper Presented at the Crime Prevention seminar, Ministry of Police and Emergency Services, Melbourne, 30 August.

Van den Haag, Ernest (1975) *Punishing Criminals*, New York: Basic Books.

Weber, Max (1954) *Max Weber on Law in Economy and Society* (ed. Max

Rheinstein), Harvard: Harvard University Press.
Zedlewski, Edwin (1985) 'When have we punished enough?', *Public Administration Review* 45: 771–9.

—— (1987) *Making Confinement Decisions*, Washington DC: Department of Justice.

Part II
Policing the Risk Society

[5]

Richard Ericson

The division of expert knowledge in policing and security[*]

ABSTRACT

The tenets of research on policing and security are criticized and an alternative model is developed. Myriad security institutions demand knowledge from the police that is relevant to their own forms of risk management and security provision. Reactive policing is therefore not only a matter of individual demand through requests for service, but also institutional demand through requirements of knowledge. The police have become knowledge brokers, expert advisors and security managers to other institutions. The claims to expertise and attendant knowledge requirements of institutions concerned with a given field of security determine the nature and degree of police jurisdiction in that field. An understanding of how policing and security have become constituted by institutional communications in the late modern 'risk society' is advanced. Implications for police discretion, community policing, and the perpetuation of insecurity are addressed.

POLICING AND SECURITY

Research on policing and security focuses almost exclusively on how the police secure a territory. The emphasis is on how military-type bureaucracy, discipline, deployment and coercion fight criminal sources of insecurity. For example, research on patrol policing examines how police deployment influences crime rates and public perceptions of security (Kelling *et al.* 1974; Ericson 1982; Sherman *et al.* 1989; Sherman 1992). Research on private security displays the same concern with securing a territory, the only difference being a focus on 'mass private property' sites (Shearing and Stenning 1981, 1983). Research that examines how environmental designs affect crime and public perceptions of security is concerned with how spatial arrangements, surveillance technologies and security hardware secure a territory (Newman 1972; Shearing and Stenning 1984; Wilson

150   *Richard Ericson*

and Kelling 1982; Skogan 1990a). This is General Schwartzkopf Criminology.

Securing territories is only one aspect of how contemporary societies provide for the security of their populations. There are three additional fields of security provision that offer populations a sense of predictability, assurance and guarantees.

There is security of an environment conceived in terms of matters that transcend particular physical spaces. For example environmental pollution and the health and safety features of consumer products move freely across territorial boundaries. These problems are often of greater public concern than crime (Gunter 1987; Ericson *et al.*1991). While there has been some attention to the policing of these matters in the research literature on regulation and compliance (Hawkins 1984; Friedland 1990), the implications of this research have not been incorporated into the prevailing models of research on policing.

There is security of life course of individuals (insuring the viability of one's earning and lifestyle capacity as a 'human resource'), and of organizations (insuring the viability of 'organizational resources'). For example, in the case of individuals there are a wide range of insurance products available both through private companies and state social security provision that protect against loss as a result of health problems, unemployment or underemployment, retirement, and other welfare risks. There is some attention to the policing of these matters in the literature on social welfare and administration (Donzelot 1979; Burchell *et al.* 1991; Chunn 1992), and on the insurance industry (Reichman 1986; Simon 1987, 1988; O'Malley 1991; Ewald 1991), but the implications of this field of security have not been addressed adequately within the literature on public policing and security.

There is security of cultural and personal identities, defined for example racially, ethnically, regionally, and in terms of gender. While questions of racial, ethnic, regional and gender discrimination in policing have been addressed, it is largely with regard to how these characteristics are variables in police decision-making, rather than in terms of the politics of cultural identities and the construction of subjectivities as contributors to security.

In terms of how they spend their time, the public police are as much oriented to these additional fields of security provision as to securing territories and dealing with crime. For most police officers crime arises infrequently, and when crime is dealt with it is usually in the context of other business, or as a completed event that requires paper to meet insurance and other security needs of the complainant. In Canada a police officer on average records one indictable crime occurrence a week, makes one indictable crime arrest every three weeks and secures one indictable crime conviction every nine months (McMahon 1992). Even in New York City, which has an extraordinarily high serious crime rate, officers spend an extraordinarily low amount of time dealing with crime and capturing criminals. Walsh (1986) found that among 156 patrol officers assigned to a high crime area in New York, 40 per cent did not make a single felony arrest in a year, and 69 per cent made no more than three felony arrests in a year.

POLICE AS KNOWLEDGE WORKERS

If police officers spend relatively little time on directly protecting persons and property against criminal threats, what else are they up to? An answer is available in viewing police as knowledge brokers, expert advisors and security managers to other institutions. It is knowledge for security that constitutes their trade. The police officer produces and distributes knowledge for the risk management activities of security operatives in other institutions. Consider Case I, which reproduces a story written by a police officer. The officer describes how he is called to the scene of an automobile accident, determines that there is personal injury and serious damage to the vehicle, and decides to charge one driver with impaired driving. He relates that he was required to fill out 16 different forms in relation to this incident, and that he spent three times as long doing this paper work as he spent at the scene in direct investigation.

CASE I:
An officer attended the scene of a serious motor vehicle accident involving personal injuries. Upon arrival he discovered that one of the drivers involved in the accident appeared to be impaired by the consumption of alcohol, and the necessary steps were taken to gather the evidence required for a conviction in criminal court. The result of the hour-long investigation was that one individual was criminally charged with impaired operation of a motor vehicle causing bodily harm, operating a motor vehicle with excess alcohol, and had his driver's licence suspended for 12 hours under the authority of the Criminal Code. After completing the investigation, the investigating officer then completed and submitted a total of 16 separate reports and forms regarding the incident. This total included: a motor vehicle accident report; a general occurrence report; an arrest report; a 12-hour suspension of drivers licence report; 2 itemized reports of property (including vehicles) seized for safekeeping; a certificate of analysis of a qualified breathalyser technician (prepared by the technician but processed by the investigating officer); a notice of intention to produce the certificate of analysis at the accused's trial; a form to be sent to the local driving records registry to generate a certified copy of the accused's driving record; a notice of intention to produce the certificate of analysis at the accused's trial; a 'crown brief' court package to be forwarded to

the office of the Crown attorney; a 'Promise to Appear' form which the accused was required to sign to facilitate release from custody and compel appearance in court; a 'CPIC' form to facilitate the entry of the accused, the charges, and the court date information into the national police computer; 2 'statistical tickets' to be forwarded to the headquarters of the force to give the officer 'credit' for laying the charges: and any information regarding the charges to be sworn before a justice of the peace and then lodged in the local criminal courthouse for processing. With the exception of the general occurrence report and the arrest report which were keyed into the police computer data base, the rest of the reports were completely by hand. Patrol officers perceived this to be another form of 'donkey-work' that required very little policing skill, particularly when it is considered that each of these reports contained basically the same information: the date, time and location of the incident, the particulars about the accused, and the charges laid. There was very little officers could do to reduce the amount of repetitive paperwork because each form was categorically different from the other and designed for different purposes. There was no possible way for the officer to accommodate a reduction in the workload to any lesser degree without neglecting force policy and due process . . . Processing the incident, including dealing with any associated property, evidence and persons, included first and foremost the routine processing of paper. In the one case above this took three times as long as it took the officer to initially investigate the incident. One hour to investigate, and three hours to write about it: to account for it, and to bureaucratically process it. Reporting incidents was integral to investigations; in fact, the reporting of events, that is, accounting for them, amounted to the rationale and primary purpose behind many investigations, particularly those that could not be 'solved'. (Shadgett 1990)

Who is demanding the knowledge reported in the various forms and for what purposes? The story suggests that public police work is entwined with a number of institutions involved in the provision of security. The police serve not only the criminal court judge but also the regulatory agency judge, the insurance adjuster judge, the doctor judge, and so on. The state motor vehicle registry requires knowledge about the place of the accident, vehicles involved, and persons involved for risk profiling that can be used in accident prevention, traffic management, resource allocation, and automobile industry compliance. The automobile industry requires knowledge about the safety of its vehicles to improve their safety and to address the compliance law enforcement concerns of regulatory agencies and consumer groups. Insurance companies require knowledge that allows allocation of blame and responsibility in the particular case, as well as statistical profiling for the general determination of risks, premium levels and compensation levels. The public hospital system requires knowledge about how the specific injuries occurred, and knowledge for statistical profiling as it relates to its provision of emergency services in the future. The criminal courts require knowledge that will provide adequate evidence for prosecution, and demonstrate proper procedure in generating the evidence. The police administration requires knowledge to account for property seized and persons processed, knowledge for the national computerized records system and its own records system, and knowledge for scientific 'human resources' management of police officer activity.

An institution consists of the relations, processes and patterns associated with particular interests. It includes material components (e.g. buildings, mechanical technologies), cultural aspects (e.g. traditions, rituals, scientific and legal technologies), political processes (e.g. it must be legitimated) and social dimensions (e.g. all of the above are reproduced through social knowledge and action). Institutions do 'a lot of regular thinking on behalf of individuals' (Douglas 1986: 47) through the perpetual elaboration of classifications which are designed to provide for entropy reduction, problem solving and routine decisions. Thus Manning (1988) views the public police institution as a coding system for indexing disorder in an orderly manner. A central activity of institutions is the social production and distribution of knowledge for risk management. 'The centrality of risk assessment and risk management to complex organizations testifies to the institutionalization of risk in modern society' (Reiss 1989: 392).

The fact that the police are one among many security institutions does not mean that their work is duplicated by other institutions, or that all institutions are reducible to their common functions as risk managers and security providers. On the contrary they each thrive as large scale and important institutions precisely because they offer distinctive knowledge about risks and distinctive security services; and, because each distinctive contribution is important to the overall provision of a security quilt for the population. It is their unique contribution to the security quilt that gives each institution its legitimacy as an aspect of government (cf. Hume 1978: 553).

Existing research focuses almost exclusively on how the police try to access other institutions for knowledge, argues that access is severely restricted because of the rights of private property owners and requirements on the state to protect privacy, and concludes that this is the major reason why the police have a limited capacity to deal with crime as the major aspect of their security provision (e.g. Stinchcombe 1963; Reiss 1971; Shearing and Stenning 1981, 1983). Reiss (1983: 78) correctly observes that 'All policing in an important sense is the policing of organizational life . . . Intelligence gathering, processing information, and directly controlling behaviour are impossible except in the context of organized life.' Yet Reiss, in keeping with other researchers (e.g. Marx 1988), only pursues the implications of this view in terms of how police penetrate other organizations for detection of violations, rather than in terms of the ways in which these other organizations involve the police in their expert systems of security. Research has not examined how other institutions manage to access the police for knowledge, and how this constitutes reactive policing at the level of institutions rather than individuals.

Regardless of the type of incident they deal with, the police are to provide knowledge about it not only for their own internal purposes but also to help fulfil the security mandates of other institutions. The expert systems – technologies, bureaucratic forms and formats, and professional operatives (Perrow 1984) – of these other institutions fundamentally shape and guide the knowledge the police provide. As new needs are defined and technologies refined, new ways of institutional categorizing, classifying, thinking and acting develop that demand police participation. Hacking (1991: 192) recalls, for example, how the French lawyer and statistician A. M. Guerry

> devised a series of classifications of suicides that now seem to us almost crazy, yet a good many of them became part of what the police were required to put into formal reports. When the avalanche of numbers began, classifications multiplied because this was the form of this new kind of discourse . . . the very fact of classifications and accounting was internal to a new practice.

The police are moving to a compliance model of law enforcement because they are driven by the knowledge requirements of other institutions that police in terms of compliance model themselves. This consideration is also absent from the research literature on public policing. Reiss (1984a: 85–6) argues that the compliance function of the public police is exhibited when informal discretionary decisions are taken not to arrest. He ignores how the public police service the compliance functions of other institutions through the ways in which they do FORMAL reports on incidents in forms that are formatted for the security requirements of these institutions. He thus fails to consider the crucial but neglected question of how the rationalities of risk and security from other institutions become part of the work of the police institution and vice versa.

Case I suggests that the police are first and foremost knowledge workers. The officer relates that the 16 reports of the incident were 'integral' to the work and provided the 'rationale and primary purpose' of the work. Elsewhere he reports, contrary to other researchers (e.g. Chatterton 1989: 108), that this knowledge work was 'real police work . . . a central aspect of the craft of policing', not least because doing it well was seen as the key to promotion and a successful career (Shadgett 1990: 30, 72).

Many researchers have found that the police spend a great deal of time doing knowledge work (Policy Studies Institute 1983; Kinsey 1985; Chatterton 1989; Skogan 1990b: 9), although the type and intensity of police knowledge work varies by function. For example, Ericson (1981) reports that detectives spend approximately one-half of their time in the office doing reports, and much more time reporting on their investigations than investigating directly through contact with persons and things involved in cases (see also Miyazawa 1992). In calls for service and dispatch units, there is nothing but knowledge work (Manning 1988). In addition to such line officer activity, police departments have substantial administrative staffs with employees working full-time in servicing the knowledge requirements of insurance companies, social service agencies, compliance law enforcers, freedom of information act requests, etc. Shadgett (1990) reports that in an Ontario Provincial Police detachment he studied, only 20/46 officers were assigned to routine patrol policing, with 15 officers in various administrative posts and 11 officers in knowledge-intensive special units.

While existing research has conceptualized and studied the police as knowledge workers, it has done so in very particular and narrow terms. The emphasis has been on knowledge production rather than knowledge distribution, and in particular on how the lowest ranks use their discretion and function as gatekeepers to the police organization and criminal justice system. Where knowledge distribution is considered, it is only in terms of the internal knowledge needs of the police bureaucracy. Following Goldstein (1960), researchers have examined how lower ranking officers maintain 'low visibility' of their knowledge to sustain some autonomy from their superiors, and, how all personnel control knowledge available to various publics, for example regarding what is released to the news media (Ericson 1989). These emphases have led to the view that when police produce knowledge in traceable form, it is largely for the purpose of internal management, control and accountability. Thus in a recent paper Chatterton (1991: 8) makes the extraordinary claim that the police

> have not been information-driven. On the contrary they have made information police property. They have interpreted it in accordance with their own interests and within their own cultural assumptions and typifications.

It is impossible to say just how, and how much, the police are 'information driven' because existing research fails to address the ways in which the police serve the knowledge for security needs of other institutions. However, it seems peculiar indeed to argue that the police unilaterally and uniformly convert all knowledge into their exclusive property for internal purposes. The police also produce knowledge for the security needs of other institutions. The police officer does not do this work only in terms of his own assumptions and those of the police culture, but also in terms of the assumptions built into the expert systems of other security institutions.

POLICE EXPERTISE

Research on police organization is a chronicle of how the expert systems of law and science fail to control line police officers. Police officer common sense knowledge, as it is collectively realized in the occupational culture of fellow officers, is imputed as paramount. The occupational culture is said to operate according to its own code that selectively ignores or translates official rule systems and other bureaucratic and technical systems and their rationalities (Manning 1992). Alternatively the police are said to reason and take action in terms of figurative language rather than in relation to rules and technical rationalities (Shearing and Ericson 1991). Thus laws of criminal procedure and administrative rules are seen to be deflected or absorbed by an obdurate police culture (Skolnick 1966; Manning 1977; Ericson 1981, 1982). Expert systems for knowledge management are said to have minimal impact. Chatterton (1991: 17) echoes Manning and Hawkins (1989: 150) in asserting that 'unless the traditional culture and structure of policing are addressed, they will condition the information technology much more than the information technology will condition police work'. Manning and Hawkins (1989: 150) see the expert system as simply being absorbed into the existing culture: 'The technology is used to produce and reproduce traditional ways of doing things or practices, and is slowly modifying them' (see also Manning 1992). The conventional academic wisdom is that scientific management of police work does not work (Bayley and Bittner 1984). This is expressed bluntly by Van Maanen (1983: 277)

> Because police tasks at the lower levels are ill-defined, episodic, nonroutine, accomplished in regions of low visibility, and are dispatched in ways that most often bypass the formal chain of command in the organization, control over the work itself remains largely in the hands of those who perform the work . . . In this sense police agencies resemble symbolic or mock bureaucracies where only the appearance of control, not the reality, is maintained.

The emphasis on common sense knowledge has led to an underestimation of the significance of expert knowledge and expert systems in policing. Expert systems deal with the disjuncture between expert knowledge – more abstract, formal, methodical and inaccessible knowledge – and common sense knowledge. Contrast the statement of Van Maanen quoted above with the officer in the story (Case I) who said he was performing 'donkey-work'. The officer had no discretion to avoid work in this situation, short of putting his career in jeopardy. He could not have ignored the accident without risking a charge of neglect of duty. Furthermore it is arguable that apart from omissions, lies or errors, he had little discretion in completing the reports more or less within the criteria formatted in the official forms.

Research emphasizes that police department manuals are full of instructions on what police officers should not do, but say little on what they should do as a basis for taking action (Bittner 1970; Manning 1977; Shearing and Ericson 1991). Research has largely ignored the ways in which instructions on how to behave are embedded in the bureaucratic forms of police departments. For example, in the Metropolitan Toronto Police Department there are 350 operational forms, while in the Royal Canadian Mounted Police they number over 2000! Manuals provide the 'do not', bureaucratic forms the 'do', the capacity to act. The bureaucratic forms and formats provide the police officer with the framework for knowing that he knows enough to act. Matters that do not fit the format are not actionable as real police work. This is the central aspect of the work the novice officer learns from a training officer when first on the job. Moreover, as considered earlier, to the extent that these classifications, categories and formats are influenced by other security institutions, police officers are thinking and acting in their terms.

Police common sense knowledge is reflexively constituted by expert systems. While expert systems deal with the disjuncture between expert and common sense knowledge, the disjuncture is itself the creation of the expert systems. The reliance upon expert systems

is a matter of the calculation of benefit and risk in circumstances where expert knowledge does not just provide that calculus but actually CREATES (or reproduces) the universe of events, as a result of the continual reflexive implementation of that very knowledge. (Giddens 1990: 84)

That is, the expert system is not only a means of discovering a condition but actually brings about a condition through embedding forms of thinking and persuasion in institutional classification schemes. For example the police, acting in terms of the classification requirements of law and insurance systems, must assign individual responsibility for accidents. Therefore, scientific use of police statistics on accidents confirms the view that accidents are more the fault of drivers – and in that sense are not accidents at all – than of, for example, road conditions or vehicle conditions, and that in turn the legal and insurance systems are the obvious mechanisms for traffic risk management. An expert system does not first establish some set of facts and only later mobilize them. The terms in which the facts are conceived, classified and understood as true facts are part of a hybrid construction process integrating heterogeneous elements in the expert system. As such the facts or reality have no single authorship, but develop from multiple elements within the system. Expertise, and expert authority, is based much more in the system than in the individual.

Expertise is transferred into organizational forms, the standardized 'paper' of bureaucracies. These forms deskill labour or, as the officer in the story expressed it, turn the labour into 'donkey-work'. While police officers avoid and alter expert systems through their practical decisions (Ericson and Shearing 1986), there is an obdurate character to these systems that is beyond the officers' control or field of experience. Altheide (1985:245) has shown how the reporting requirements of police officers as structured into bureaucratic forms frame 'perception, expectation and legitimation'. Bureaucratic reporting formats generally are tight and closed, offering simplified and even binary reductions to foster explicit meanings (Poster 1990). They freeze the communication process to make the familiar explicit and to give it a transituational meaning (Manning 1988).

Discretion lies at the level of those involved in devising and refining expert systems. One can no more understand the expert system of policing by limiting inquiry to what police officers do 'on the street' than one can understand retailing by reducing it to what the store clerk does while serving customers. The thought of a McDonald's Restaurant employee dispensing hamburgers is enough to indicate that those in 'McJobs' on the ground are constructed by expert systems. These considerations are not limited to the more obvious deskilled service jobs such as working in fast food restaurants or as a private security guard. Even in medicine the doctor on the ground becomes a subordinate of expert systems and those who manage them. She becomes one of many contributors to the expert system of risk management that makes up the patient's dossier, and therefore loses control over particular outcomes as well as the career of cases. Moreover, the dossier not only constitutes the particular medical biography, it also provides data for operating various hospital, insurance, educational and strategic planning systems. 'The operative on the ground now becomes a simple auxiliary to a manager whom he or she supplies with information derived from the activity of diagnosis expertise. These items of information are then stockpiled, processed and distributed along channels completely disconnected from those of professional practice' (Castel 1991:281). In turn the hospital, insurance, educational and planning schemes form how doctors think, act and organize.

Discretion also lies in the expert knowledge of police officers as professionals on security at all levels of the police hierarchy. The police have an ability to define and defend a wide range of problems and tasks, and to seize new problems, in terms of abstractions of 'security'. For example, middle management officers are involved in ongoing transactions with other security institutions regarding their knowledge requirements, formats and classifications for providing knowledge, and who pays for the knowledge. They also seek and give advice on security products. Senior police administrators have become experts in many areas of public policy, for example in urban planning and law reform (Reiner 1991).

> [T]he senior police officers have become the core of an autonomous police professionalism, with considerable discretion in the formulation of police policy within the state. Bureaucratization has enabled the police to become subordinate officials of the state AND autonomous experts. (Dandeker 1990: 125)

POLICE AND SURVEILLANCE

The focus on how police work takes place in conditions of 'low visibility' and 'secrecy' means that researchers have not adequately examined the ways in which the police distribute knowledge and thereby raise visibility. The contemporary police officer spends most of her time in the production and distribution of technologically-mediated and bureaucratically-formatted communications for other security institutions, and coterminously, taps into the already-processed knowledge of these other institutions to help fulfil the security mandates of her own organization. A lot of this production is 'second-level'(Böhme 1984: 39), appropriating knowledge already constructed in other bureaucratic settings, and presupposes 'a society that is bureaucratically conditioned and prepared for data processing' (*ibid.*).

A related research focus is on street-level, face-to-face, police-citizen transactions. However, as seen in the story (Case I), there is often a blend of face-to-face and extrasituational communication arising in a particular case. Moreover, the police are also increasingly involved in myriad activities and communications that do not involve any face-to-face communications with persons subject to their activity. The police officer serves as a 'faceless bureaucrat' or 'iconocrat'. For example a substantial proportion of calls for service do not result in the dispatch of a police officer to meet the complainant, and there is an increasing proportion of occurrences recorded over the telephone. Informants are recruited using the mass media, with a guarantee of anonymity through avoidance of face-to-face contact (Carriere and Ericson 1989). Investigations are conducted through computer matching that involves various institutions but no direct dealings with suspects (Marx 1988). This is policing by human absence, where the 'sights' prescribed by communication technologies are more significant than the 'sites' of face-to-face communication.

Here policing is not only a matter of the initial precipitating event or incident and how knowledge is produced about it, but also how that knowledge is distributed and used as it moves across various institutional boundaries into new settings. Modern institutions are not things. They do not occupy a particular place nor are they frozen in time. They consist of expert systems that are connected in time and space by communication media. Institutional activity transpires in space, that is in relations between absent others in different places. Moreover, any given place is penetrated by knowledge from elsewhere, so that 'what structures the locale is not simply that which is present on the scene; the "invisible form" of the locale conceals the distanciated [at a distance] relations which determine its nature' (Giddens 1990: 18–19). In a great deal of institutional activity a local interaction is also part of a transaction across distance involving expert systems and media.

What makes institutions 'social' is precisely the ways in which communications circuitry can be plugged into at any point in time and place. Police social interaction increasingly transpires within the communications circuitry of other institutions (Manning 1988, 1992). Communications media are part of the system of interaction, establishing patterns of knowledge flow and therefore patterns of interaction itself (Meyrowitz 1985; Ericson *et al.* 1989; Poster 1990). Moreover, communications media have a 'social' significance as a shared arena beyond their specific knowledge capacities or content. Their formats are held in common by all those who engage them, and it is media formats along with knowledge and trust that provide security.

The police phenomenal world is no longer only unified through a correspondence of territorial settings. It is also unified through an ability to move through myriad places as members of expert systems of security.

> [T]he individual enters the social realm as a connection, a terminal or code, that is, by means of a key, which gives him access to the social networks. Although this does not mean that someone who does not have the necessary connections . . . does not exist at all, it does mean that he does not exist socially. (Böhme 1992)

In the very act of plugging into an expert system to take action, the police officer creates knowledge that allows others to take action in relation to him. It is in this respect that expert systems create visibility. For example Manning (1988) observes that the police calls for service operators he studied were controlled through seven distinct monitoring means (see also Ericson and Shearing 1986).

> In order for society to be controllable through knowledge, it must itself be organized in terms of knowledge. Social processes must be differentiated according to function and arranged according to models, and social actors must be disciplined in a way which makes

their behaviour amenable to data collection or makes their social role and activities relevant only insofar as they produce data. (Böhme 1992)

The myriad electronic technologies and bureaucratic forms that are part of police organization provide surveillance and raise visibility with respect to both citizens and police officers. Surveillance is the production of knowledge about (monitoring), and supervision of (compliance), subject populations. Knowledge production and supervision are mutually reinforcing, and together they create surveillance as a system of rule (Dandeker 1990). Bureaucracy is itself a kind of surveillance system. Surveillance is THE vehicle of risk management. Modern bureaucracies are distinguished by 'the concentrated reflexive monitoring they both permit and entail. Who says modernity says not just organizations, but organization – the regularized control of social relations across indefinite time-space distances' (Giddens 1991: 16).

This view of surveillance differs from 'undercover' and 'spy' connotations of the term. Surveillance entails raising visibility for the practical task of routine action and administration. Surveillance mechanisms are established to have subject populations produce knowledge about themselves, and to do so routinely and obligingly. Undercover surveillance itself is simply part of a wider environment of surveillance in which various technologies and strategies are spawned and reinforce undercover uses (Marx 1988).

While 'the population has been disciplined to surveillance and to participating in the process' (Poster 1990: 93), one should not make the inferential leap, as Poster (1990) and Marx (1988) do, that we are therefore becoming a more totalitarian or 'maximum security society' (*ibid.*). Although modern institutional forms and surveillance mechanisms have totalitarian potential, this potential is tempered by the reflexivity that surveillance provides. The very surveillance technologies that allow one group to produce and distribute knowledge about another also facilitate counter-knowledge (Ericson and Shearing 1986; Marx 1988). For example a California-based company, TRW-MONITOR, uses credit-rating data produced for corporate institutions to provide a client with regular reports on her credit rating with these same institutions. The expert system is used to monitor risks entailed in the expert system's construction of the person as a risk. It is a general feature of electronic technologies that they not only allow the monitoring of the many by the few, but also the few by the many (Meyrowitz 1985; Mathiesen 1987).

The growth in surveillance is linked to key features of modernity (Giddens 1985, 1990, 1991; Dandeker 1990). Surveillance has grown in the context of state security provision, including the security of territories (e.g. police and military bureaucracies), environment (e.g.

corporate regulation), life course (e.g. welfare administration), and identities (e.g. rights claims). Surveillance also proliferates because of advances in communication technologies. 'The age of bureaucracy is also the era of the information society' (Dandeker 1990: 2), in which 'the circuits of communication are the supports of an accumulation and a centralization of knowledge' (Foucault 1977: 217). The communications technologies themselves become 'informers' (Marx 1988: 208ff), allowing surveillance to transcend physical barriers and time and therefore to be more intensive and extensive; to operate invisibly while providing visibility; and, to foster subjects' participation in their own monitoring (self-policing), sometimes involuntarily. These components of modernity foster distrust. The more a society is based on relations that are not primary and face-to-face, the greater the importance of trust. At the same time there is greater opportunity for deception and fostering of distrust. Distrust is then another source of growth in surveillance. Surveillance technologies proliferate in the workplace (Marx 1988), entertainment place (Shearing and Stenning 1984), marketplace (Reiss 1984b) and even at home (Wilson 1988), and distrust becomes an endemic feature of a society built on risk management (Short 1990).

COMMUNITY POLICING AS COMMUNICATIONS POLICING

Police research is reductionist and essentialist. The police have been conceived in terms of militarism (order maintainers), or legalism (law officers), or professionalism (public servants), or communitarianism (community agents). The latest popular model is communitarianism, which includes the view that the police should not longer be militaristic, legalistic, or professional in the old bureaucratic style. Rather, the police should be agents of community tradition, cooperation and consensus by working through local organizations in special face-to-face relationships to help members take direct action for their own security provision.

Literature that is critical of the community policing model is itself reductionist and essentialist. For example Klockars (1989) criticizes recent efforts to essentialize the police under the rubric of community policing. In his opinion community policing is part of a lineage of attempts to essentialize the police, a successor to the military, legal and professional models. However, Klockars' response to this problem is to follow the tendency, noted at the beginning of this paper, to essentialize the police in terms of their efforts to secure a territory (see also Waddington 1984). Klockars, following Bittner (1970), sees the essence of policing in state monopoly on the legitimate use of force within a political territory. Klockars explains the rise and fall of the various models in terms of their capacity to make more palatable the fact that the police are essentially there to be violent when necessary. The models are merely efforts to cover the 'when necessary' legitimation of police violence. Klockars does not see that the monopolization of force is inter-dependent with the various models and the mechanisms they urge. The monopolization of force is an achievement of bureaucracy and its mechanisms of militarism, professionalism and accountability to the community (Dandeker 1990: 66; Giddens 1990: 59). In other words Klockars fails to appreciate that the police are coercive, militaristic, legalistic, professional, community-oriented, and more.

Models not only inform but form police practices. The community policing model is a way of capturing changes in police discourse and practice. Like all discourse, the discourse of community policing should be taken seriously as constitutive of practice and as being constituted by practice, rather than simply dismissed as ideological camouflage.

Community policing is part of late modern surveillance as outlined in the previous section. Community policing is best understood as the policing of communications about risk and security in late modern society (Ericson *et al.* 1993). In early modern and modern societies, community was characterized by communications that included sharing, tradition, quality face-to-face relationships, and local organization with a sense of immediacy and direct results. Late modern society is characterized by institutions organized in relation to fear, risk assessment and the provision of security. These institutions – for example, insurance companies, social security agencies and regulatory agencies – refigure the community into communications about risk in every conceivable aspect of life. Indeed, late modern society has become a 'risk society' (Giddens 1990, 1991; Beck 1992a, b). Communications about risk have the opposite qualities to those enumerated above. For example, they involve relationships that are not face-to-face, but are between absent others who are connected by electronic media that transmit and record their transactions impersonally. These transactions offer no sense of immediacy or direct action, nor are they tied to a given place. Community becomes institutional methodologies for communicating risk management and security provision.

Community policing shifts responsibility for crime to other institutions. The police admit the 'impossible mandate' (Manning 1977) of efficient crime control and central responsibility for social order. Other state bureaucracies, private corporations, businesses, home owners and individuals are all to become more responsible for security provision.

[C]rime and disorder problems are the JOINT PROPERTY of the community as 'client' as well as the police as the local agency delivering public security services. Underlying this ownership principle is the core assumption that the level of crime, disorder and fearfulness in a community is closely related to the level of public participation in policing. (Leighton 1991: 487)

Crime is to be diverted into other institutional mechanisms of control and resolution or, better still, handled in the first instance within other institutions so that the police are 'no more than a catalyst, involving people in efforts to police themselves' (Trojanowicz and Bucqueroux 1990: 16). The process is documented in O'Malley's (1991) analysis of how the Australian police are involved with the insurance industry through neighbourhood watch schemes. Mainly funded by the insurance industry, neighbourhood watch schemes are distribution centres for security lessons and technologies, and for the selling of insurance. They allow the simultaneous promotion of insurance and of police as partners in security.

Community policing is at the same time designed to expand the police by involving them in a wider range of security activities with other institutions. In 'problem-solving policing' (Goldstein 1990) there is no limit to police participation in the construction and management of social problems. While the police give up some of their direct responsibilities for crime and the security of territories, they take on new responsibilities for security of the environment, life course and identities.

> [C]rime prevention through social development is recognized as the long-term solution in which prevention strategies focus on the reduction of the motivation of potential offenders or recidivists to engage in criminality by removing the root causes of these motivations. Under this framework, prevention tactics address poverty, unemployment, poor education and work skills, inadequate housing, poor health, and other underlying causes of crime. (Leighton 1991: 494–5)

In short, community policing accords with the role of the police as knowledge brokers, expert advisers and security managers analysed above.

As de-skilled knowledge brokers, the police plug into the circuits of various institutional networks to draw upon the currents and generate knowledge. Analyses of community policing emphasize that knowledge work is central (e.g. Trojanowicz and Bucqueroux 1990; Skolnick and Bayley 1986; Farrell 1988). The success of community policing

> depends on how well its personnel operate as *information managers* who engage in '*interactive policing*' by routinely exchanging information on a reciprocal basis with the community members through

formal contacts and informal networks. (Normandeau and Leighton 1990: 45)

Community policing also constitutes the police as professional advisors on security, able to offer expertise in diagnosis, treatment and inference (cf. Abbott 1988: chap 2). Police security expertise is exemplified in 'problem-solving policing' (Goldstein 1990), in which the police focus on underlying causes of problems in their diagnosis and treatment, and cooperate with other professions and institutions as sources of expertise and as collaborators in finding solutions. Part of the treatment mandate is to serve as clinician-like *counsellors* about security. Following the 'broken windows' thesis (Wilson and Kelling 1982), the focus is on creating a sensibility of security by reducing fear of threats or dangers regardless of the epidemiology of threatening incidents (Moore, Trojanowicz and Kelling 1988; Skogan 1990a, b). The community police officer is also an advisor on security products. 'The recommendations range from home target hardening (locks, strengthening doors etc.) to street and business design' (Moore, Trojanowicz and Kelling 1988: 10). Within this range there is also, for example, regular advice communicated via the mass media, at schools, and at community meetings on the best time and place for activities and on what to wear and how to appear (Voumvakis and Ericson 1984). In giving such advice the community police professional becomes an endorser and promoter of security products in a society absorbed by the commodification of security (Spitzer 1987; O'Malley 1991).

Community policing discourse also articulates with police practices in the management of security arrangements of others. As discussed previously, the police move in the direction of compliance law enforcement because of the knowledge-for-security demands of other institutions and their compliance mechanisms. Expertise and advice are not just given on a demand basis or in response to a particular instance of victimization, they are engrained in ongoing relationships similar to those that exist between regulatory agencies and organizations from whom they seek compliance. Community police professionals are complaint managers or ombudsmen (Goldstein 1990) who respond to grievances about the operations of other security institutions. They form a compliance inspectorate that drops security check notices at households and scrutinizes security at schools, halfway houses, hospitals, and on public transit (Skolnick and Bayley 1986). They also serve as advocates for others who need better legal or technological resources to meet their security needs (Goldstein 1990) while these others in turn become advocates for police (Fleissner *et al.* 1991: 61–2).

'Community' solutions are not peculiar to police or criminal justice. The 'community solution . . . is . . . a specialized regime of environmental intervention designed to contain high levels of concentration of risk' (Gordon 1991: 46). The direct task of discipline, control and security provision are left to members of the 'community' institutions concerned, while the governmental agencies avoid confrontations by posing as 'advisors, resource persons and friends' (Lasch 1980: 182). There is a decentralization of state security operations, resulting in

> a pluralization of the centre, enabling the problems of the state to rebound back on to society, so that society is implicated in the task of resolving them, where previously the state was expected to hand down an answer for society's needs. (Donzelot 1991: 178)

State legal and scientific expertise is mobilized to decide how to delegate matters in dispute and to distribute risks in a just manner.

COMMUNICATIONS POLICING IN THE RISK SOCIETY

The very idea of modern government was conceived in terms of policing and surveillance for security. In early modern Europe there was faith that scientific knowledge of security would yield wealth and welfare (Reiner 1988; Andrew 1989; Burchell *et al.* 1991). A science of police developed for the administration of populations and of individuals, in the hope of yielding both individual and collective prosperity through security. The science of police – led by figures such as Cesare Beccaria, who held the chair of Political Economy and Science of Police at the University of Milan from 1769 – both rationalized order and provided feelings of security about the order it was creating. Over the seventeenth and eighteenth centuries there were approximately 3,200 titles pertaining to the science of police in the German language alone (Pasquino 1991: 109). Among them was Johann Peter Frank's six-volume *System For A Complete Medical Policing* that included detailed regulations designed to 'prevent evils through wise ordinances', and covered every then imaginable aspect of health care including, for example, the regulation time for resting after a dance in order to avoid catching a cold on the way home (Bok 1979: 215–16).

The ideas of early modern scientists of police, and the eventual embodiment of their ideas in social institutions, set in motion the contemporary risk society. The goal of police was to develop precise knowledge of every conceivable risk, and to convert their assessments into the management of 'everything ... unregulated, everything which can be said ... to lack order or form' (Pasquino 1991: 111). In the words of Duchesne's 1757 *Code of Police*, 'The objects which it embraces are in some sense indefinite' (*ibid.*: 109), a statement echoed 200 years later by a senior administrator in France interviewed by Brodeur (1983), who declared that his task is nothing less than an omniscient 'police journalism on behalf of the state'.

Risk society is constituted by three logics that influence police (cf. Beck 1992a, b). First, there is a negative logic. Threats and dangers, and fears about them, are dealt with by the construction of 'suitable enemies' (Christie 1986) and attendant negative labelling, denial, avoidance and exclusion. Solidarity is based in a communality of fear. In some cases, such as the 'war on drugs', insecurities are cultivated and focused on unfortunate people to gain political purchase and to offset the endemic insecurity experienced more generally in everyday life (Christie 1986; McGaw 1991).

Second, there is a logic of controlling the irrational by rational means. Fear becomes a basis for rational action. People turn to expertise to rationalize fears and to make probability choices. Science displaces traditional controls of fear and insecurity, such as those provided by religion. There is a secularization of risk and danger and an attendant awareness that risks cannot be counteracted through knowledge that is not scientific. There is no escape from scientific production of risks. 'No amount of collective coughing, scratching or sighing helps. Only science does' (Beck 1992a). Science becomes a rhetorical force in the politics of risk, yet the more rigorous the scientific standard of risk, the greater the perceived risk and fear, and the greater the likelihood that other risks will be overlooked.

Third, there is a logic of insurance. The concept of risk is a neologism of insurance. In modernity the institution of insurance is central to the rationalization of risk (Ewald 1991; Reiss 1989; Lau 1992). Insurance makes risks objectified, as an accident; calculable, as a matter of probability; collective, as a distribution among groups; capital, as a means of capital accumulation and as a guarantee against loss of capital; and legal, as subject to contract and adjudication. Insurance has become a 'generalizable technology for rationalizing societies' (Defert 1991: 215) and selves in everyday life. It produces social configurations based on particular interests and membership in risk categories, which in turn affects inclusion and exclusion, hierarchy, solidarity, and justice.

The three logics of the risk society refigure institutional logic. Social integration is enhanced through a communality of fear which joins the communality of need as a socially binding force and basis for solidarity (Beck 1992a). There is a drift in the public agenda away from economic inequality to the distribution and control of risks. The values of the unsafe society begin to displace those of the unequal society (*ibid.*; Lau 1992). This sensibility is enhanced by the logic of insurance in particular, which offers solidarity and justice through common interests in the distribution of risk. Risks cut across traditional categories and boundaries based on class, labour and property, blurring and even disintegrating the bases of hierarchy and boundary maintenance.

In risk society the focus on deviance-control-order is beginning to be displaced by a focus on knowledge-risk-security. The concern is less with the labelling of deviants as outsiders, and more on developing a knowledge of everyone to ascertain and manage their place in society. The concern is not so much control of deviants in a repressive sense, but the constitution of populations in their respective risk categories. The concern is not only order in the form of a predictable spatial environment, but a plethora of security mechanisms that guarantee healthy, productive 'human resources' and 'organizational resources'. The risk society is also a 'transmission society' (Castell (1991) refers to a two-speed society) because it regulates the pace of contributions to society in terms of educational credentials, handicaps, productivity, and so on. Some are destined for the autobahn, others relegated to the highways with speed limits, and still others to local roads with speed bumps. The police spend a great deal of time and energy helping various security institutions regulate traffic in the transmission society. As we have seen, they undertake their work in terms of official paper formatted for the needs of other institutions; refer clients directly to these institutions; serve as experts on 'social development' and the inter-institutional provision of social security; provide educational instruction services to these institutions; and, rely on these institutions for knowledge useful in their own investigations.

POLICING, RISK AND INSECURITY

Risk society cannot escape the problem of insecurity. Consider Case II, which reproduces a description of a new police station in a suburb near Toronto. At the time the police station was built in the early 1980s, this suburb had a comparatively low crime rate. For example, with a population of about 400,000 the jurisdiction averaged fewer than five murders a year, and most of its murders occurred in domestic settings. Moreover, this police station was built at a time when models of community policing were being fostered (Task Force 1974).

CASE II:

The basic idea is to control the movement of everyone who approaches and enters the building. The movement of policemen will be controlled by computer access cards. There are eighteen security doors, and only some cards will be programmed for all of them. All entries will be recorded – with card number, date and time – and entries that are unauthorized will trigger an alarm.

If an intruder still gains entry despite cameras outside that can pan, zoom and tilt by remote control, he will find himself in a square corridor looking into full-length security mirrors and more steel-encased tamper-proof cameras.

Controlling and monitoring all these cameras and other items,

The division of expert knowledge in policing and security   169

such as electronic door hinges that signal when a door has failed to shut automatically, will be specially trained civilians working 24 hours a day. They will sit in front of a large console with a graphic of an entire building, lights signalling exists and entries, and TV monitors for the 18 security cameras. Certain top-security areas also have sonic intrusion alarms, and the entire outside of the building is lit by high-intensity sodium lights.

The windows are all strip, ribbon windows, their double glass tilted at a 45-degree angle to deflect bullets and stones and placed seven feet above ground so they need not be draped. Besides, they are reflective, to make viewing impossible even if apartment buildings are erected around the structure. (Kashmeri 1981)

This police station stands as an icon of insecurity. It is designed not only with an eye on an untrustworthy public that must be kept at a distance, but also with a view that police officers themselves are only trustworthy at some times and in some places. While it signifies acceptance of certain forms of security expertise as the best way to feel progressive, it also stands for future acceptance, indeed institutionalization, of hostility, distrust and insecurity.

This police station is a prime example of what Foucault (1988) termed 'the scandal of rationality' in security provision. Typical of modern rational systems of security, it is also irrational and signifies insecurity. All efforts to socially isolate and reduce risks via human and technological reproductive forces, and legal and social welfare protections and regulations, depend on the release of new or different risks and attendant insecurity. In the risk society 'knowledge is always embedded in ignorance, safety is surrounded by unsafety and rational planning inevitably frays out to uncalculable evolution' (van den Daele 1992).

The tendency for operatives in each particular institution and organizational unit to measure their success in the narrow terms of their specialization, while ignoring the systemic consequences of their rationality (Perrow 1984), ensures that knowledge for security produces insecurity.

Voluntary blindness to systemic consequences is the unavoidable CONDITION of expert success . . . Expertise thrives thanks to the skills of atomization, of splitting natural systems into an ever growing multitude of ever smaller and hence more manageable tasks . . . the very progress of expert knowledge and practice adds to the unpredictability and uncontrollability of the system. (Bauman 1992)

Security experts necessarily play on insecurities. Security expertise perpetually creates and enhances the need for itself in the very process of doing its work. All expertise fosters insecurity as part of showing the indispensability of its knowledge. For example in the case of insurance technology 'each new measure of protection makes visible a new form of insurable insecurity' resulting in 'an inexhaustible market' (Defert 1991).

Security depends upon a balance of trust and acceptable risk. However a sense of balance, or of how much one is out of line, is only available through forms of expertise. Everyone is regulated by the various professions of surveillance and adjustment who continuously track and counsel people to 'most effectively realize their potential' and 'least disrupt the flow of organizational life' (Abbott 1988: 148–9). Security experts make every person and organization highly reflexive about

> adequate provision for the preservation, reproduction and reconstruction of one's own human capital . . . [including a] stress on the individual's own civic obligation to moderate the burden of risk which he or she imposes on society. (Gordon 1991: 44)

While the 'burden of risk' lies with particular individuals and organizations, the burden of rationality about risks is externalized to experts and everyone becomes dependent upon expert knowledge for security.

Dependency is strengthened by a pervasive cultural assumption that solutions to security problems are available from experts and their products. This assumption makes living with unresolved problems unbearable, and therefore the demand for expertise is insatiable. However, 'each successive step in the endless problem-solving, experienced as another extension of freedom, further strengthens the network of dependency' (Bauman 1992).

As Bauman suggests, the proliferation of security expertise also occurs in the context of a pervasive cultural assumption that security experts are the key to greater liberty. This assumption is central to liberal theory. For example Bentham conceived liberty as a branch of security and both as a principle object of law. It is therefore ironic that security expertise, as the basis upon which liberal law and government develops liberty, can also provide a kind of counter-law that undermines liberty.

In spite of models such as 'community policing' which express consensus, the political system for promoting security is marked by conflicts over risks which create insecurity. The divisions and conflicts of the security society are based on the definition of risks, the distribution of scarce resources for the management of risks, the just distribution of risks, and risks created by the security institutions themselves. Political opposition mobilized in terms of insecurity is very effective because it is impossible to deny claims for safety expressed in terms of health and life itself; and, because it allows for critiques of some fundamental structural features of society that would be difficult to address in public culture otherwise. The result is intensified law and regulation even where scientific knowledge is lacking. At the same time there is no clear structure to political conflict as was the case in the past, for example with conflicts between labour and capital. Political alliances, and their bases in knowledge and fiscal resources, are dispersed and complex. Moreover, it is relatively easy for the conflicts to be displaced or redrawn because the dangers addressed remain largely unknown and invisible, and because experts must be deferred to for credible claims about risk management (Beck 1992a, b).

Security is marketed within a system seen as having limitless potential, and this system therefore augments insecurity. As with all forms of commodification, the more one experiences security products the more they become objects of desire and insatiable appetite. 'The more we enter into relationships to obtain the security commodity, the more insecure we feel; the more we depend upon the commodity rather than each other to keep us safe and confident, the less safe and confident we feel; the more we divide the world into those who are able to enhance our security and those who threaten it, the less we are able to provide it for ourselves' (Spitzer 1987: 50).

Security is always within us as a yearning rather than without us as a fact. The problem is that security experts have no basis within their own knowledges for establishing limits. Limitations can only come from sources outside their knowledges. As nation states in Europe and North America are now realizing painfully, there are finite resources that impose limits on security provision. As nation states in Eastern Europe are also experiencing painfully, limits are crystallized and changes made when security institutions themselves become too threatening, when the fear of loss of liberty at the hands of security institutions surpasses fear of loss of liberty at the hands of some other source.

(Date accepted: September 1992)

Richard V. Ericson,
Green College,
University of British Columbia.

NOTE

* Earlier versions of this paper were presented as public lectures at the Urban Security Research Institute, Tokyo, University of Sydney, University of Western Ontario, and University of Toronto. I am grateful to Kevin Carriere, Anthony Giddens, Kevin Haggerty and Peter Manning for their detailed comments on the penultimate draft of this paper. Preparation of this paper was funded by a research grant from the Social Sciences and Humanities Research Council of Canada, and by the Contributions Program of the Solicitor General of Canada to the Centre of Criminology, University of Toronto.

BIBLIOGRAPHY

Abbott, A. 1988 *The System of Professions: An Essay on the Division of Expert Labor,* Chicago: University of Chicago Press.

Altheide, D. 1985 *Media Power*, Beverly Hills: Sage.

Andrew, D. 1989 *Philanthropy and Police: London Charity in the Eighteenth Century*, Princeton: Princeton University Press.

Bauman, Z. 1992 'Life-world and Expertise: Social Production of Dependency', in N. Stehr and R. Ericson (eds) *The Culture and Power of Knowledge*, Berlin and New York: de Gruyter.

Bayley, D. and Bittner, E. 1984 'Learning the Skills of Policing,' *Law and Contemporary Problems* 47: 35–59.

Beck, U. 1992a 'Modern Society as a Risk Society', in N. Stehr and R. Ericson (eds) *The Culture and Power of Knowledge*, Berlin and New York: de Gruyter.

Beck, U. 1992b *The Risk Society*, London: Sage.

Bittner, E. 1970 *The Functions of Police in Modern Society*, Rockville, Md.: NIMH.

Böhme, G. 1984 'The Knowledge-Structure of Society', in E. Bergendal (ed.) *Knowledge Policies and the Traditions of Higher Education*, Stockholm: Almqvist and Wiksell Int.

Böhme, G. 1992 'The Technostructures of Society', in N. Stehr and R. Ericson (eds) *The Culture and Power of Knowledge*, Berlin and New York: de Gruyter.

Bok, S. 1979 *Lying*, New York: Vintage.

Brodeur, J. P. 1983 'High Policing and Low Policing: Remarks about the Policing of Political Activities'. *Social Problems* 30: 507–20.

Burchell, G., Gordon, C. and Miller, P. (eds) 1991 *The Foucault Effect: Studies in Governmentality*, Chicago: University of Chicago Press.

Carriere, K. and Ericson, R. 1989 *Crime Stoppers: A Study in the Organization of Community Policing*, Toronto: Centre of Criminology, University of Toronto.

Castell, R. 1991 'From Dangerousness to Risk', in G. Burchell, C. Gordon and P. Miller (eds) *The Foucault Effect: Studies in Governmentality*, Chicago: University of Chicago Press.

Chatterton, M. 1989 'Managing Paperwork', in M. Weatheritt (ed.) *Police Research: Some Future Prospects*, Aldershot: Gower.

Chatterton, M. 1991 'Organizational Constraints on the Uses of Information and Information Technology in Problem-

Focused Area Policing', British Criminology Conference, York, July 1991.

Christie, N. 1986 'Suitable Enemies', in H. Bianchi and R. Van Swaaningen (eds) *Abolitionism – Towards a Non-Repressive Approach to Crime*, Amsterdam: Free University Press.

Chunn, D. 1992 *From Punishment to Doing Good*, Toronto: University of Toronto Press.

van den Daele, W. 1992 'Scientific Evidence and the Regulation of Technical Risks: Twenty Years of Demythologizing the Experts', in N. Stehr and R. Ericson (eds) *The Culture and Power of Knowledge*, Berlin and New York: de Gruyter.

Dandeker, C. 1990 *Surveillance, Power and Modernity: Bureaucracy and Discipline from 1700 to the Present Day*, New York: St. Martin's Press.

Defert, D. 1991 '"Popular Life" and Insurance Technology', in G. Burchell, C. Gordon and P. Miller (eds) *The Foucault Effect: Studies in Governmentality*, Chicago: University of Chicago Press.

Donzelot, J. 1979 *The Policing of Families*, New York: Pantheon.

Donzelot, J. 1991 'The Mobilization of Society', in G. Burchell, C. Gordon and P. Miller (eds) *The Foucault Effect: Studies in Governmentality*, Chicago: University of Chicago Press.

Douglas, M. 1986 *How Institutions Think*, Syracuse: Syracuse University Press.

Ericson, R. 1981 *Making Crime: A Study of Detective Work*, Toronto: Butterworths.

Ericson, R. 1982 *Reproducing Order: A Study of Police Patrol Work*, Toronto: University of Toronto Press.

Ericson, R. 1989 'Patrolling the Facts: Secrecy and Publicity in Police Work', *British Journal of Sociology* 40: 205–26.

Ericson, R., Baranek, P. and Chan, J. 1989 *Negotiating Control: A Study of News Sources*, Milton Keynes: Open University Press.

Ericson, R., Baranek, P. and Chan, J. 1991 *Representing Order: Crime, Law and Justice in the News Media*, Milton Keynes: Open University Press.

Ericson, R., Haggerty, K. and Carriere, K. 1993 'Community Policing as Communications Policing', in D. Dölling and T. Feltes (eds) *Community Policing*, Holzkirchen: Felix-Verlag.

Ericson, R. and Shearing, C. 1986 'The Scientification of Police Work', in G. Böhme and N. Stehr (eds) *The Knowledge Society: The Growing Impact of Scientific Knowledge on Social Relations*, Dordrecht: Reidel.

Ewald, F. 1991 'Insurance and Risk', in G. Burchell, C. Gordon and P. Miller (eds) *The Foucault Effect: Studies in Governmentality*, Chicago: University of Chicago Press.

Farrell, M. 1988 'The Development of the Community Patrol Officer Program: Community – Oriented Policing in the New York City Police Department', in J. Greene and S. Mastrofski (eds) *Community Policing: Rhetoric or Reality*, New York: Praeger.

Fleissner, D. *et al.* 1991 *Community Policing in Seattle: A Descriptive Study of the South Seattle Crime Reduction Project*, Seattle Police Department.

Foucault, M. 1977 *Discipline and Punish*, New York: Pantheon.

Foucault, M. 1988 'Social Security' in L. Kritzman (ed.) *Michel Foucault: Politics, Philosophy, Culture*, London: Routledge.

Friedland, M. (ed.) 1990 *Securing Compliance*, Toronto: University of Toronto Press.

Giddens, A. 1985 *The Nation-State and Violence*, Berkeley: University of California Press.

Giddens, A. 1990 *The Consequences of Modernity*, Cambridge: Polity.

Giddens, A. 1991 *Modernity and Self-Identity: Self and Society in the Late Modern Age*, Stanford: Stanford University Press.

Goldstein, H. 1990 *Problem-Oriented Policing*, Philadelphia: Temple University Press.

Goldstein, J. 1960 'Police Discretion Not to Invoke the Criminal Process: Low Visibility Decisions in the Administration of Justice', *Yale Law Journal* 69: 543–94.

Gordon, C. 1991 'Governmental Rationality: An Introduction', in G. Burchell, C. Gordon and P. Miller (eds) *The Foucault Effect: Studies in Governmentality*, Chicago: University of Chicago Press.

Gunter, B. 1987 *Television and the Fear of Crime*, London: John Libbey.

Hacking, I. 1991 'How Should We Do the History of Statistics?' in G. Burchell, C. Gordon and P. Miller (eds) *The Foucault Effect: Studies in Governmentality*, Chicago: University of Chicago Press.

Hawkins, K. 1984 *Environment and Enforcement: Regulation and the Social Definition of Pollution*, Oxford: Clarendon Press.

Hume, D. 1978 *A Treatise on Human Nature*, Oxford: Oxford University Press.

Kashmeri, Z. 1981 *The Globe and Mail*, Toronto.

Kelling, G., Pate, A., Dieckman, D. and Brown, C. 1974 *The Kansas City Preventive Patrol Experiment*, Washington, D.C.: The Police Foundation.

Kinsey, R. 1985 *Survey of Merseyside Police Officers*, Liverpool: Merseyside County Council.

Klockars, C. 1989 'The Rhetoric of Community Policing', in C. Klockars and S. Mastrofski (eds) *Thinking About Police*, 2nd edition, New York: McGraw-Hill.

Lasch, C. 1980 *The Culture of Narcissism: American Life in the Age of Diminishing Expectations*, New York: Norton.

Lau, C. 1992 'Social Conflicts about the Definition of Risks: The Role of Science', in N. Stehr and R. Ericson (eds) *The Culture and Power of Knowledge*, Berlin and New York: de Gruyter.

Leighton, B. 1991 'Visions of Community Policing: Rhetoric and Reality in Canada', *Canadian Journal of Criminology* 33: 485–522.

McGaw, D. 1991 'Governing Metaphors: The War on Drugs', *The American Journal of Semiotics* 8: 53–74.

McMahon, M. 1992 *The Persistent Prison?*, Toronto: University of Toronto Press.

Van Maanen, J. 1983 'The Boss: First-Line Supervision in an American Police Agency', in M. Punch (ed.) *Control in the Police Organization*, Cambridge, Mass: MIT Press.

Manning, P. 1977 *Police Work*, Cambridge, Mass.: MIT Press.

Manning, P. 1988 *Symbolic Communication*, Cambridge, Mass.: MIT Press.

Manning, P. 1992 'Information Technologies and the Police', in M. Tonry and N. Morris (eds) *Modern Policing*, Chicago: University of Chicago Press.

Manning, P. and Hawkins, K. 1989 'Police Decision-Making', in M. Weatheritt (ed.) *Police Research: Some Future Prospects*, Aldershot: Gower.

Marx, G. 1988 *Undercover: Police Surveillance in America*, Berkeley: University of California Press.

Mathiesen, T. 1987 'The Eagle and the Sun: On Panoptical Systems and Mass Media in Modern Society', in J. Lowman, R. Menzies and T. Palys (eds) *Transcarceration: Essays in the Sociology of Social Control*, Aldershot: Gower.

Meyrowitz, J. 1985 *No Sense of Place: The Impact of Electronic Media on Social Behaviour*, Oxford: Oxford University Press.

Miyazawa, S. 1992 *Policing in Japan: A Study on Making Crime*, Albany, N.Y.: State University of New York Press.

Moore, M., Trojanowicz, R. and Kelling, G. 1988 'Crime and Policing' Perspectives on Policing, Paper No. 2. National Institute of Justice.

Newman, O. 1972 *Defensible Space: Crime Prevention through Environmental Design*, New York: Macmillan.

Normandeau, A. and Leighton, B. 1990 *A Vision of the Future of Policing in Canada: Police Challenge 2000*, Ottawa: Solicitor General.

O'Malley, P. 1991 'Legal Networks and Domestic Security', *Law, Politics and Society* 11: 171–90. Greenwich, Conn.: JAI Press.

Pasquino, P. 1991 'Theatrum Politicum: The Genealogy of Capital – Police and the State of Prosperity', in G. Burchell, C. Gordon and P. Miller (eds) *The Foucault Effect: Studies in Governmentality*, Chicago: University of Chicago Press.

Perrow, C. 1984 *Normal Accidents: Living with High-Risk Technologies*, New York: Basic Books.

Policy Studies Institute 1983 *Police and People in London*, London: Gower.

Poster, M. 1990 *The Mode of Information: Poststructuralism and Social Context*, Cambridge: Polity.

Reichman, N. 1986 'Managing Crime Risks: Toward an Insurance Based Model of Social Control', *Research in Law and Social Control* 8: 151–72.

Reiner, R. 1988 'British Criminology and the State', in P. Rock (ed.) *A History of British Criminology*, Oxford: Oxford University Press.

Reiner, R. 1991 *Chief Constables: Bobbies, Bosses or Bureaucrats?*, Oxford: Oxford University Press.

Reiss, A. 1971 *The Police and the Public*, New Haven: Yale University Press.

Reiss, A. 1983 'The Policing of Organizational Life', in M. Punch (ed.) *Control in the Police Organization*, Cambridge, Mass.: MIT Press.

Reiss, A. 1984a 'Consequences of Compliance and Deterrence Models of Law Enforcement for the Exercise of Police Discretion', *Law and Contemporary Problems* 47: 83–122.

Reiss, A. 1984b 'Selecting Strategies of Social Control over Organizational Life', in K. Hawkins and J. Thomas (eds) *Enforcing Regulation*, Boston: Kluwer-Nijhoff.

Reiss, A. 1989 'The Institutionalization of Risk', *Law and Policy* 11: 392–402.

Shadgett, P. 1990 *An Observational Study of Police Patrol Work*, M.A. dissertation, Centre of Criminology, University of Toronto.

Shearing, C. and Ericson, R. 1991 'Culture as Figurative Action', *British Journal of Sociology* 42: 481–506.

Shearing, C. and Stenning, P. 1981 'Private Security: Its Growth and Implications', in M. Tonry and N. Morris (eds) *Crime and Justice: An Annual Review of Research*, Chicago: University of Chicago Press.

Shearing, C. and Stenning, P. 1983 'Private Security: Implications for Social Control', *Social Problems* 30: 493–506.

Shearing, C. and Stenning, P. 1984 'From the Panopticon to Disney World: The Development of Discipline', in A. Doob and E. Greenspan (eds) *Perspectives in Criminal Law*, Toronto: Canada Law Book.

Sherman, L. 1992 'Attacking Crime: Policing and Crime Control', in M. Tonry and N. Morris (eds) *Modern Policing*, Chicago: University of Chicago Press.

Sherman, L., Gartin, P. and Buerger, M. 1989 'Hot Spots of Predatory Crime: Routine Activities and the Criminology of Place', *Criminology* 27: 27–55.

Short, J. 1990 'Hazards, Risks and Enterprise: Approaches to Science, Law and Social Policy', *Law and Society Review* 24: 179–98.

Simon, J. 1987 'The Emergence of a Risk Society: Insurance Law and the State', *Socialist Review* 95: 61–89.

Simon, J. 1988 'The Ideological Effects of Actuarial Practice', *Law and Society Review* 22: 772–800.

Skogan, W. 1990a *Disorder and Decline*, New York: Free Press.

Skogan, W. 1990b *The Police and the Public in England and Wales*, London: H.M.S.O.

Skolnick, J. 1966 *Justice Without Trial*, New York: Wiley.

Skolnick, J. and Bayley, D. 1986 *The New Blue Line: Police Innovations in Six American Cities*, New York: The Free Press.

Spitzer, S. 1987 'Security and Control in Capitalist Societies: The Fetishism of Security and the Secret Thereof', in J. Lowman, R. Menzies and T. Palys (eds) *Transcarceration: Essays in the Sociology of Social Control*, Aldershot: Gower.

Stinchcombe, A. 1963 'Institutions of Privacy in the Determination of Police Administrative Practice', *American Journal of Sociology* 69: 150–60.

Task Force on Policing Ontario 1974 *The Police are the Public and the Public are the Police*, Toronto: Solicitor General of Ontario.

Trojanowicz, R. and Bucqueroux, B. 1990 *Community Policing: A Contemporary Perspective*, Cincinnati: Anderson.

Trojanowicz, R., et al. 1982 *An Evaluation of the Neighbourhood Foot Patrol Program in Flint, Michigan*, East Lansing: Michigan State University.

Voumvakis, S. and Ericson, R. 1984 *News Accounts of Attacks on Women: A Comparison of Three Toronto Newspapers*, Toronto: Centre of Criminology, University of Toronto.

Waddington, P. 1984 '"Community Policing": A Sceptical Appraisal', in P. Norton (ed.) *Law and Order and British Politics*, Aldershot: Gower.

Walsh, W. 1986 'Patrol Officer Arrest Rates: A Study of the Social Organization of Police Work', *Justice Quarterly* 2: 271–90.

Wilson, J. and Kelling, G. 1982 'Broken Windows', *The Atlantic Monthly*, March, pp. 29–38.

Wilson, K. 1988 *Technologies of Control: The New Interactive Media for the Home*, Madison: The University of Wisconsin Press.

[6]

The Howard Journal Volume XXI 1982, pp. 6-22

Crime Prevention and Insurance[1]

By R. A. LITTON

Assistant Director, Bowring Scholfields Limited,
Insurance Brokers, Manchester.

Abstract

Crime prevention is hampered by a lack of incentives. A "situational" approach to crime is consistent with the view that environmental measures can help in its prevention. The fitting of crime prevention devices should help to reduce the incidence of certain types of crime and insurers are uniquely positioned to provide incentives for such devices to be installed. This paper explores the interaction between insurance and property crime and suggests some ways in which insurers can influence the behaviour of potential victims in such a way as to prevent the crimes from which they may otherwise have suffered.

The role of insurance as a potential force in the field of crime prevention has been sadly neglected in the criminological literature although a few writers (e.g. Pease 1979a, b) have attempted some preliminary explorations of its possible influence and some recent work (Association de Geneve 1980) is indicative of a further trend in this direction. This paper will attempt to show why crime prevention is important to insurers and to suggest some ways in which they can help to reduce crime.

Crime and criminal activities are important to insurers. In some cases the activities of criminals merely affect insurers' profit and loss accounts; at the other extreme, whole classes of insurance exist only because crime exists. However, not only can crime affect insurance, insurance can affect crime. This latter effect can manifest itself almost accidentally or the effect can be a deliberate one — planned to benefit insurers. The provision of insurance can constitute a powerful means by which financial incentives or disincentives can be offered for the adoption of crime prevention measures. In many ways, and for many reasons, the insurance industry has been slow to recognise and use this potential and it is hoped that this paper will demonstrate some of the ways in which insurance can be used to contribute to the prevention of crime and thus how the insurance industry, which is often castigated for being uncaring, can help to contribute both to its own welfare and to that of its policyholders (and perhaps even to a wider society) without being asked to do anything which would necessarily interfere with its primary objective of writing profitable insurance business.

The "Situational" Approach to Crime Prevention

Explanations of the causes of criminal behaviour range from genetic explanations (Eysenck 1977) through social and socio-political factors (e.g. Hall and Scraton 1981) to explanations of the environment in which crime is particularly likely to occur (Clarke 1977, 1980). The latter, "situational", approach is grounded in the work of behaviourist and social learning theorists (e.g. Mischel 1968; Bandura 1977). Many determinants of behaviour will be difficult, if not impossible, to change, especially in the short term, but some environmental contingencies can be altered and can lead to changes in behaviour. Thus theorists such as Mischel and Bandura would contend that it is preferable to concentrate on those factors — the environmental ones — which can be changed or manipulated rather than expend effort and energies endeavouring to influence the causes of behaviour which are not, in fact, susceptible to change.

Mischel (1968) argues that changing the environment can, and does, change behaviour. If Mischel is correct in his emphasis then perhaps criminologists should not concern themselves with trying to change the individual — his dispositions, traits or personality — but instead should concentrate on modifying the environment with which the criminal is faced when carrying out his criminal acts — to make the commission of specific crimes less likely by making those acts more difficult or more certain of detection. Such an approach does not amount to behavioural manipulation, in the sense which some people regard as ethically insupportable, by directly manipulating a specified person but rather seeks to change behaviour in general by manipulating the circumstances in which the behaviour is manifested. It is in this environmental context that insurers can potentially play a part by providing the financial motivation for their clients to modify the environment by the adoption of crime prevention measures and by stimulating the improvement of crime prevention technology.

This approach, termed "situational", is well defined by Clarke and Hough (1980):

> It consists of a detailed analysis of the way in which particular crimes in particular places occur; from this an assessment is made of the ways in which situational inducements and environmental opportunities to commit crime can be reduced, and of the extent to which specific organisations and individuals can be held responsible for those reductions. (p. 11)

Thus the approach is concerned with situational factors surrounding the commission of crime and with the way those factors might be manipulated to reduce opportunities for crime. As Hough *et al.* (1980) make clear, situational measures are not necessarily complex or expensive to implement and are not necessarily new in concept. That situational measures, of widely differing kinds, can in fact work has been attested by many studies; and, in fact, some measures have proved to have useful crime-preventive attributes as an adjunct to their main purpose. Thus Clarke (1980) reports a study in Birmingham which demonstrated a marked drop in the suicide rate between 1963 and 1969 attributed largely to the very substantial reduction in the toxicity of domestic coal-gas during the period which made it more

7

difficult for people to kill themselves by turning on the gas taps. Mayhew (1979) cites the activities of the Post Office who were able virtually to eliminate thefts from telephone kiosks by replacing the vulnerable aluminium coin-boxes with much stronger steel ones.

Legislation required that from 1 June 1973, all riders of motor cycles had to wear crash helmets. Whilst the law was intended to save lives it also had the, probably unanticipated, effect of reducing thefts of motor cycles (Mayhew *et al.* 1976) probably because intending thieves were deterred by their increased conspicuousness if not wearing a crash helmet. In West Germany in 1963 steering column locks, or similar security devices, were made compulsory on all cars; this action apparently achieved a permanent reduction of more than 60% in the rate of car thefts (Mayhew *et al.* 1976).

In a different field, large-scale thefts of copper from one of Britain's major ports were greatly reduced by the simple expedient of the port authority's refusing to accept consignments until immediately before the date of sailing (Clarke and Mayhew 1980). Each of these examples illustrates that, by a simple manipulation of the situational contingencies, it proved possible to change the criminal activities of a large number of people without attempting to change their dispositions or influence their motivation.

Insurance and Crime

Crime impinges upon insurance in many ways. Insurance may be provided against the results of criminal acts against the person — for example insurance is available against injury caused to an employee in the course of a robbery of his employer's money; in extreme cases, life assurance policies might be called upon to pay for a death caused by criminal activity. However, insurers are more often concerned with crime in the fields of theft from premises, theft of property in transit, criminal damage to property, theft of or from motor vehicles and fraud and theft by employees of their employers' property.

The impact of crime upon the major traditional classes of property insurance can be considered individually.

(i) *Fire Insurance*

This class of insurance provides cover for goods against fire and explosion and may be extended to cover additional perils ranging from storm to damage caused by "riot and civil commotion or by malicious persons". The interface between this class of insurance and crime will thus usually consist of its cover for the malicious damage and cover for any of its basic perils — usually fire — caused deliberately. Arson is a serious and growing problem for fire insurers; since the early 1950s when recorded "malicious ignition" fires were counted in hundreds, the number has soared to over 15,000 a year (Woodward 1979).

Whilst fire insurers can, and do, regularly offer advice to industry and commerce about the methods of reducing the fires in general, the role of insurers in relation to the prevention of arson fires is probably more limited — fire insurers are, by training and experience, more used to directing their preventive measures against the very extensive

8

range of naturally-induced fire hazards rather than against the human agency involved in arson. The influence of fire insurers is therefore at the present time probably limited to their considerable contribution to the prevention and minimisation of fire losses generally, by such measures as the allowing of premium discounts to encourage policy-holders to install fire detection devices and alarms, sprinkler systems and fire-fighting devices.

Fire insurers do not generally take the initiative in offering advice — or, more positively, stipulating requirements — aimed specifically at preventing, or minimising the effects of, arson. Similarly there is no evidence that they take measures against criminal damage in general, except the extreme sanction of refusing insurance for that peril.

(ii) *Theft Insurance*

Theft insurance policies now generally cover "theft involving entry to or exit from the premises by forcible and violent means" or some similar wording. By thus restricting their cover in relation to the wider meaning of the word "theft" in the 1968 Theft Act, insurers are deliberately excluding the more common forms of theft — theft by employees and shoplifting. These two forms of theft are often regarded together, or are indistinguishable, and are frequently euphemistically dismissed as "shrinkage". Carter (1974) estimates the total value of property stolen in known thefts in 1971 within the United Kingdom as £73.8m; he estimates that the total loss in the same year due to pilferage by employees and shoppers was nearer £400m. An employer may well take the view that acceptance of a certain level of pilferage is acceptable as an alternative to the high costs of preventing such losses plus, possibly, worsening labour relations. (The complexities of the relationship between employer and employee in crimes against both firms and customers are well illustrated by Ditton (1978)). Insurers for their part are unwilling to offer insurance cover for what they see as an inevitable loss (although see Perry (1976)); apart from the difficulty of calculating losses due to either staff thefts or customer thefts, or both, in isolation from the many other causes of unexplained stock shortages, insurers are not inclined to insure this type of theft because they see their role as offering protection against an event which may or may not happen, not as insuring an inevitable loss about which the only uncertainty is its size.

In the areas where they do offer cover, theft insurers attempt to influence crime by encouraging crime prevention measures (although not equally in all cases). They employ specialist surveyors (or, in some cases, non-specialist members of staff) who survey risks to establish the standard of theft protection.

Recommendations — or, in some cases, requirements — will be made if necessary for the improvement of protections. Some risks (but by no means all) will be surveyed when a proposal is presented to the insurer for insurance; some risks will be surveyed after a claim. In each case the purpose of the survey is to establish the adequacy of the current levels of protection and, if thought necessary in the light of the type of goods being proposed for insurance and the loss history of the

9

B

risk, to suggest improvements to bring the protections to a standard regarded as acceptable to the insurer. (Such surveys are similar to the crime prevention surveys offered by the police; insurers will seldom, if ever, undertake this exercise in conjunction with police C.P.O.'s and will not usually, when they think a survey necessary, accept a police survey in lieu of a report from their own surveyor).

If the protections are thought, by the insurers, to be below an acceptable standard and the client either cannot or will not improve them, then the insurer's sanction is to refuse insurance cover. This sanction must potentially constitute one of the most potent pressures currently available for the adoption of crime prevention measures.

(iii) *Household Insurance*

This class of insurance used to be profitable for insurers but several insurers' household accounts are now showing an underwriting loss. Whilst several factors have contributed to this result, the increase in theft losses is probably a major cause. Not only are theft losses in general increasing but thieves have apparently been diverting their attention away from commercial premises and towards private dwellings.

As Companyman (1977) notes:

> Throughout the 60s however the insurance market turned its attention to the improvement of protections on commercial risks and for at least five or six years the market showed such a combined (albeit unofficial) strong front that there was a great deal of success in substantially improving protections on commercial risks. . . . This indeed started to make things rather difficult for the professional thief and there was a noticeable turn by the criminal fraternity to the private house risk. (p. 2094)

Other writers (e.g. Pugh 1976) make the same point about the success of the concerted action by insurers to obtain a better general standard of protection for commercial premises and suggest a possible displacement of at least some criminal activity from commercial to private risks.

This trend is manifesting itself in a tendency for insurers to require householders to take better theft precautions (Carter 1974). Similar displacement effects have also been noted in the U.S.A. (Maltz 1972; Reppetto 1974) where the increase in the number of intruder alarms installed in commercial premises has coincided with a reduction in the rate of increase of commercial burglaries concurrently with (and possibly at the expense of) a greater increase in residential burglaries.

Most insurers do not survey the large majority of risks proposed for household insurance as they regard it as uneconomic to do so. Premiums for this class of insurance are small in relation to those charged for commercial insurances and the theft premium forms a relatively small proportion of the total premium charged for a household insurance. Thus, only the premises with higher values at risk and the premises situated in the more hazardous areas of the country (where, in any event, the theft element of the premium is set at a higher level) are surveyed. Given that most householders do not respond to publicity campaigns exhorting them to take more care

10

(Burrows and Heal 1980; Riley 1980a, b) it is apparent that, unless they expend more money on conducting more surveys of private dwellings, the potential for insurers to influence theft losses in this area is limited given their current range of conventional options. Whether the offer of a discount for the fitting of specified theft protection devices would be effective is a matter for debate. If the object of such an exercise was to cut survey costs, then the granting of such a discount would have to rely on the honesty of the householder in actually fitting the device for which the discount was claimed (the absence of the device would probably become apparent in the event of a claim but some insurers would be reluctant to incur the adverse publicity of turning down a claim on those grounds). As household premiums are relatively low, and the theft premium is only a proportion of the total household premium, the amount of premium available to offer as a discount is limited and might not be sufficient to induce householders to incur the expense of fitting the devices.

(iv) *Money Insurance*

Policies are issued to cover loss of money by any cause, subject to certain exclusions. The "money" covered will usually include not only cash but also, for example, cheques, postal orders and postage stamps. The main perils encountered in money insurance are those of theft and robbery (accidental loss of money, which is covered by the policy, is, surprisingly, relatively rarely encountered). Money is at risk when in transit (for example to or from a bank or to a construction site for the payment of wages), on the insured's premises (perhaps in the form of shop takings or money for wages) and on the insured's premises overnight (the policy will usually cover small sums of money whilst not in a safe when the premises are closed for business but, for larger sums, a safe is usually an insurer's requirement); other locations at which money is covered will also be specified.

The policy provides cover for losses caused by the dishonesty of an employee but only for such losses discovered within a specified number of days.

The area of concern to most money insurers is large shipments of cash. The most vulnerable point in the operation is often seen as that part of the journey between the bank and the insured's premises, particularly at the point where cash is being carried into or away from the carrying vehicle (if indeed a vehicle is used). It is now standard practice for most insurers to require cash in transit to be accompanied by a specified number of able-bodied employees, ranging from perhaps one person for cash up to £1,500 to four persons for cash between £6,000 and £10,000. For transits in excess of this latter figure the insurer would probably stipulate that an approved security company must be used to transport the cash. Until a few years ago, it was the usual practice for the stipulation to read "able-bodied adult male employees"; since the Sex Discrimination Act 1975 the tendency has been for insurers to drop the reference to "male". It could be argued that for an employer to expose a female employee to the potential dangers of an attempted robbery of cash in transit would be a breach of the Health and Safety at Work etc. Act 1974; to send only male employees to accompany cash could constitute a breach of the Sex Discrimination Act (it is to avoid being accused of promoting a breach of this latter Act that insurers have tended to drop the word "male"). The employer is thus, perhaps, faced with a dilemma. If both male and female employees are available for such duties, most employers will probably prefer to send a male.

If, as might be assumed, a male employee is able to give better protection to cash than is a female employee then it appears that one possible means by which insurers could influence crime losses in this field (by stipulating that only males shall accompany cash transits) has been denied to them, perhaps as an unintended consequence of legislation enacted with different aims in view. However, insurers are still able to influence crime losses by other means: they stipulate safes of a specified quality to safeguard cash; they sometimes require the installation of intruder alarms; and they specify how cash in transit shall be accompanied. All such actions should reduce the chances of a crime-related loss from that particular insured risk.

(v) *Goods in Transit Insurance*

Policies are usually issued to provide cover against all risks of loss or damage to goods whilst in transit. Whilst the cover afforded by the policy is very wide, and therefore embraces many different perils, for example fire and accidental damage, in recent years increasing theft losses have focused the attention of insurers upon that aspect of the cover (French 1970).

It is generally recognised that the most hazardous goods, from the point of view of transit losses, are wines and spirits and tobacco (such items as bullion and jewellery are usually insured only by specialist insurers and thus tend not to receive detailed attention from the insurance industry in general); some goods in transit insurers regard these goods as being so hazardous that they refuse to provide insurance for them.

The wines and spirits industry and the tobacco industry have each formed liaison organisations charged with recommending and investigating methods of reducing losses from crime. Since the formation of these organisations, losses in the respective industries have fallen dramatically. Tobacco losses in transit fell by nearly 83% in real terms over the period 1969 to 1978 (Tobacco Advisory Council 1979) and losses of wines and spirits have fallen by more than 91% over the period 1971 to 1978 (Wine and Spirit Security Liaison Limited 1979).

The Tobacco Advisory Council emphasises two main types of theft of tobacco products — theft from transit premises and from delivery vehicles in the street — and suggests that in most cases the offences were either committed by employees of the firm concerned or were made possible by employees' negligence. Both causes of loss would be covered by the standard goods in transit insurance policy and both appear to be areas where, if they wished, insurers could have an influence. Insurers could insist, by a policy condition, on adequate vetting of new staff (including the retention by employers of photographs of employees such as drivers); such checks might help to reduce the number of losses due to employee dishonesty but staff carelessness would be more difficult to eradicate. Thefts of loads from vehicles parked in the street could be reduced by an increased use of vehicle security parks; there is, as yet, little sign that insurers are demanding use of such parks although for many years individual writers (e.g. Hart 1962) have been deploring their lack of use.

The success of both the wine and spirit and the tobacco industries in reducing theft losses suggests that a determined effort to reduce transit crime can succeed, although the cost of the measures needed is not reported. Such success suggests that there is scope for crime prevention measures in other industries and insurers could perhaps take some of the initiative.

(vi) *Fidelity Guarantee Insurance*

The policy covers an employer against loss sustained by him through the fraud or dishonesty of his employees. The policy covers any of the employer's property and this will embrace theft of stock as well as of money but does not cover mere unexplained shortages or "shrinkage" from unknown (or unprovable) causes. The loss has to be proved by the employer and the proof includes identifying a specific loss or losses and the identifying of a specific employee or employees. Like the theft insurance policy, crime is the only reason for the existence of this class of insurance; unlike, for example, the money policy accidental losses are not covered and are not intended to be covered.

Insurers are naturally concerned to prevent losses and thus to prevent the crime which gives rise to the losses and can endeavour to do this in two main ways; by vetting the employer's system of check and supervision and by ensuring that employers obtain satisfactory references at least for specified categories of employee.

The proposal form will ask searching questions about the system of check in force for money payments and receipts and for stock. If the insurers are dissatisfied with the answer to any of the questions they will either impose restrictions on the policy relating to the areas with which they are not satisfied or they will refuse to grant cover unless changes are made in accordance with their requirements. Many clients, or potential clients, view this vetting of their systems of check and supervision as being one of the more valuable services provided by a fidelity guarantee cover; it is the contention of the few insurers who specialise in this field that they have extensive knowledge of the methods adopted by employees to defraud their employers and that they are, therefore, in a good position to advise clients how to avoid, or at least minimise, the possibility of incurring such losses. The proposal form will also ask whether the insured, as a standard practice, obtains references, at least for those employees having responsibility for money or stock. If the reply is in the negative the insurer will either decline to accept the insurance unless the references are obtained for all new staff or, in the case of certain insurers, will offer to obtain (for a fee) references for employees on behalf of the employer. Such reference enquiries are conducted by the insurer in the strictest confidence and the individual employee concerned will, after enquiry, either be accepted or declined for cover.

The main scope for crime preventive action by insurers in this field is twofold. First, the insurers can disseminate to prospective insureds the experience of types of losses accumulated over many years of providing insurance; such advice might enable an insured to avoid thefts perpetrated in a manner which would not otherwise have occurred to him. Second, insurers can, by their vetting process, insist on the remedying of what they regard as unsatisfactory check systems in the hope that thefts will thereby be rendered more difficult.

(vii) *Motor Insurance*

Whilst motor insurers frequently encounter crime, in the sense that the vehicles they insure can be involved in criminal offences (e.g. infringement of speed limits or parking regulations) or even involve payment for the result of a criminal act (e.g. bodily injury resulting from dangerous driving) the main effects of crime involve the theft (or unauthorised taking) of, and theft of property from, motor vehicles and, to a lesser extent, damage claims for criminal damage to vehicles ("vandalism").

Only a small proportion of motor insurance claims paid by insurers relate to theft of a vehicle or to theft from a vehicle; the bulk of payments relate to damage to the vehicles themselves or third party claims for injury or damage. Thus, only a relatively small proportion of the total motor insurance premium relates to the theft risk and insurers would find it uneconomic to try to reflect any increases or decreases in the theft risk in a particular case by significantly varying the level of this small portion of the premium; in any event, with only a small portion of the premium relating to the theft risk, any incentive or disincentive effect of such a move would, in itself, be miminal.

The Actions of Insurers

It is apparent that insurance and crime interact although the degree to which this is true varies between classes of insurance. Of the classes of insurance discussed, where property crime is a relevant feature, it appears that the reactions of insurers to crime range from relative disinterest to an active involvement in an endeavour to prevent crime. It is suggested, either implicitly (Reppetto 1974; Rupprecht 1978) or explicitly (Carter 1972; Companyman 1974) that insurance may even be criminogenic.

Whilst fire insurers deplore vandalism and arson there are no apparent signs that they are taking any positive steps towards their reduction except for advice and exhortation (Bailey 1979; Woodward 1979). Insurers could, by the offer of premium discounts, ensure that their clients insist that architects consult with insurers at the time when advice can have most effect and when crime prevention devices can be incorporated most cheaply — at the design and planning stage. However, fire insurers appear to choose not to exert this influence to prevent property crime, even when the crime impinges directly on their

14

area of concern. Nor is this state of affairs restricted to the U.K. (Robertson 1979).

In other classes of insurance, insurers appear to regard crime as being peripheral to their activities. Motor insurance is such a class. The main impact of crime upon motor insurance is in the area of theft or unauthorised taking of motor vehicles. However, whilst the amounts of money involved are not insignificant, as a proportion of motor insurance claims as a whole they are relatively small.

The few steps which insurers take in this regard appear to be aimed rather at obtaining a more equitable contribution to the premium pool than at attempting to encourage crime preventive behaviour; for example, it is usual for a proposal form question to enquire whether the vehicle is customarily kept in a securely-locked garage overnight — a negative reply will usually attract only a small premium loading. Insurers appear to make no attempt, for example, to encourage the use of anti-theft devices either by premium concessions or policy requirements (a policy requirement would, in any event, probably be impractical because of the difficulty insurers would encounter in establishing, once the vehicle had been stolen, that the devices had not been used). One writer, although perhaps not an unbiased one, holds different views:

> The managing director of one of the country's biggest vehicle security specialists [Simba Security Systems] has called on motor insurers to introduce discounts for policyholders who maintain strict security over their vehicles . . . [and] complains that insurance companies look upon discounts as a "dirty word". [He] argues that the more secure a motorist . . . makes his vehicles, the less should be the premium he pays.
> . . . The problem is that insurance companies fight shy of giving any sort of incentive despite the fact that everyone would benefit — that is, except the thief. Some years ago on an insurance proposal form it asked if the car was garaged overnight. If the answer was "no" then it meant an automatic 25 per cent [premium] loading. This was waived if, as an alternative, the car had an approved security alarm fitted. But . . . these loadings disappeared as victims of the cut price war. They have now been re-introduced, but without the benefit of the authorised alarm fitting as an alternative. This has been to the detriment of the careful motorist and crime statistics throughout the country. (*Policy Holder Insurance Journal*, 25 May 1979, p. 15)

An interesting recent development, although only on the part of one insurer, is the offer of premium discounts on vehicles protected by a system which involves the engraving of the vehicle's registration number on each of the vehicle's windows. This system is said to be a considerable deterrent to professional car thieves as all the glass in a stolen vehicle would have to be replaced before its identity could be hidden (*Policy Holder Insurance Journal*, 2 April 1981, p. 892).

Thus whilst insurers will occasionally endeavour to reflect an increased theft risk in the premium (e.g. by a premium loading where a car is not kept in a securely-locked garage overnight) their positive attempts to influence the reduction of this type of crime appear to be either non-existent or insignificant. As an example, most motor insurers appear to be completely unaware that steering column locks were introduced for all new motor cars, in 1971. Insurers know that cars are now fitted with such locks but do not know that 1971 was the operative year; thus they do not, for example, discriminate between otherwise-identical 1970 and 1972 cars.

For other classes of insurance, for example goods in transit insurance, crime is an important factor but the need for insurance would still exist even if criminal activities were eliminated. Thus whilst, as French (1970) argues, the theft risk is the most costly single risk for goods in transit insurers, the successes of the Tobacco Advisory Council and of Wine and Spirit Security Liaison Ltd. demonstrate that, given the incentive, the problem can be tackled.

Conversely, however, crime is the *raison d'être* of some classes of insurance such as theft insurance and fidelity guarantee insurance. In these classes of insurance, insurers have a direct financial incentive to reduce such crime; if less crime occurs (and if the average amount lost in the remaining crimes does not increase) then, in the short term, insurers' profits will increase. Therefore, active steps are taken to reduce crime by, in theft insurance, stipulating security protections (and insisting that they are used); in fidelity guarantee insurance, insurers vet systems of check and insist that references are obtained for certain categories of employees.

The economist's distinction between private costs and benefits on the one hand and social costs and benefits on the other (Carter 1974) is relevant to an understanding of the decisions of insurers and their clients as to the extent of crime prevention measures to be taken. Private costs include all those costs directly borne by the individual whereas social costs include the costs of public services either in trying to prevent crime or in processing the results of crime (including a part or the whole of expenditure on the police, courts and prison service). Insurers, and their clients, will take account only of private costs — social costs will be ignored.

In general individuals (including, in this context, insurers as well as their policyholders) acting rationally will take crime prevention measures up to the point at which the additional, marginal expenditure on security equals the anticipated marginal benefits in the form of extra crime prevention. Whilst this holds true for the individual, it would pay society as a whole to incur additional expenditure on reducing crime by the various means available, to the point where the additional marginal cost is equal to the additional marginal social benefit it produces. Thus if the social costs of crime were taken into account, marginal benfits would be manifested at a higher level and more crime prevention measures would, from an economic view-point, be justified.

If some means could be devised whereby insurers could be induced to take account of social costs, as well as the private costs which they already consider, then, to the extent that insurers' actions are effective in reducing crime, society would benefit. Whether such an end could be achieved by government subsidies to policyholders to cover the extra costs of protecting to the level required to recognise social costs (or, more logically, such subsidies to all persons with property to protect, whether

16

insured or not — see Pease 1979b) or whether a formal liaison between insurers and, say, the Home Office would be effective are questions for debate.

Future Options

Suggestions (e.g. Pease 1979a) that insurers are indifferent to the levels of losses, as long as they can obtain a premium commensurate with the risk, are, at best, only partly true and are, at worst, a travesty of the true position. It is in the interest of any individual insurer to prevent, or at least minimise, losses. If an insurer can, by whatever means, ensure that the insurance business he writes will have a below-average, (or, better still, a nil) chance of sustaining a loss or that any loss which occurs will be smaller rather than larger, then his profit will be enhanced. It is thus in the interests of both insurers and policy-holders that losses be controlled. Similarly, from a wider viewpoint, it would also appear to be generally accepted that crime prevention is desirable from the point of view of society as a whole.

Carter (1974) summarises the point very well in relation to crime losses (and must be one of the earlier writers to advocate the situational approach to crime prevention):

> So-called "short cuts" to crime control like loss prevention may be regarded as a very unambitious approach to the problem. They only attempt to reduce the opportunities and temptations to crime instead of tackling its fundamental causes . . . [but] in the present state of knowledge, measures which alter opportunities and temptations possibly offer the simplest, surest, and least expensive methods of control. (p. 13)

Whilst it is undoubtedly in the interests of insurers to prevent crime, they cannot do so directly. They can, however, provide the motivation for others to take crime prevention measures.

It is suggested (Carter 1974) that insurers could provide this incentive by involving policyholders in the financial consequences of losses (as a deliberate measure and separate from the results of unintended under-insurance or non-insurance). Three methods are proposed:

> Policyholders . . . may be required to bear the first £x of any loss (an "excess" or "deductible") ; or an agreed percentage of a loss (co-insurance) or the balance of a loss over an agreed amount (first loss insurance). (p. 55)

The universal application of compulsory excesses to, for example, theft insurance would probably not be practical except by agreement among insurers; there are no signs at present that such an agreement could be reached, or is desired, and the competitive advantages to be gained by the insurer breaking the agreement would render its future uncertain. In addition, insurers would find it difficult to assess the correct level of excess to provide just the right degree of incentive; too small an excess would be virtually irrelevant whereas too large an excess could be financially crippling. The optimum level would vary from policyholder to policyholder and, even for the same policyholder, might change over time. However, the more general introduction of voluntary excesses, accompanied by appropriate premium discounts is

17

c

perhaps a more promising area. The premium saved could be spent (or so the insurers would hope) on better protections which the insured would more readily install because of his greater financial involvement in any loss.

The loss of premium to the insurers would, hopefully, be offset by a reduction in claims (certainly because the amount of the excess would be saved on each claim and, it would be hoped, because the better protections would prevent or minimise some losses) and insurers — and insureds — might benefit from reduced handling costs if small losses, below the amount of the excess, were no longer reported to insurers (this latter argument begs several questions not least of which are the effects of such a change on the police and the fact that insurers would still wish to know of any thefts or attempted thefts as part of their on-going assessment of the risk). Of the other two measures, voluntary co-insurance is virtually unknown and compulsory co-insurance is used more as a coercive measure by insurers. The "first loss" basis is not primarily intended as a means of involving the insured in a loss but is rather intended to recognise the unlikelihood of an entire stock being stolen.

The deficiencies of the intruder alarm industry have been well documented, especially in relation to the unacceptably large number, and proportion, of false alarms (e.g. Carter 1974; Cross 1976; Randall 1976). Although it is contended (Callaghan 1974, 1976) that the existence of the British Standard for intruder alarms and, latterly, of the National Supervisory Council for Intruder Alarms, have improved the standard of alarm installations and reduced the number of false alarms — at least from systems complying with the Standard and from systems installed by N.S.C.I.A. members — it is still generally agreed that the situation is deplorable. (For example, in 1978 the Metropolitan Police received 169,307 calls from intruder alarms of which 166,153 were false calls — a false alarm rate of 98%). Despite the fact that insurers are well represented on the N.S.C.I.A. and were, and are, involved in the drawing up and review of the British Standard, insurers appear to be indifferent to the poor quality and performance of alarm systems. This is perhaps partly explained by the fact that they go out of their way to be seen to be impartial as between one alarm company and another and are thus denied one weapon — that of specifically recommending a particular alarm company — which might have a better record for avoiding false alarms. Also, to a certain extent, false alarms are seen as being a problem between the insured and his alarm company and not as an area which directly affects insurers.

Insurers should, despite their historical attitudes, move more directly into the debate. With the co-operation (and, undoubtedly, the willing co-operation) of the police, insurers could keep records of false alarms and other alarm failures and grade alarm companies accordingly. They should recommend only alarm companies with above-average records and make their data available to their policyholders as justification for their recommendation. Such a move would exert the best of all pressures — commercial pressure — on alarm companies to hasten their research and development programmes to eliminate, or at least reduce, alarm failures as it would be apparent that for the first alarm company to succeed, the rewards would be enormous. Such a move would cost insurers very little but could yield potentially large benefits.

Insurers should also take more positive steps to improve standards both within the British Standards and outside them. The security industry in general is not in favour of imposed Standards (Randall 1976) as, it is contended, manufacture, in those circumstances, tends to be down to the Standard at the cheapest price rather than upwards to the best quality attainable. In contrast, however, there is clear evidence that Standards appear to work well with locks and they are reputed to be working with alarms so the argument in favour of insurers' supporting Standards would appear to outweigh those against.

Insurers do not usually offer discounts from theft insurance premiums to recognise the presence of an intruder alarm; their view tends to be that they will only insure a risk if the protections are adequate and their rates already reflect that assumption. However, insurers could perhaps consider the offer of a discount for an alarm which does not act solely as an intruder alarm. The insurance industry tends to compartmentalise its thinking so that fire insurance departments make recommendations for fire detectors, theft departments stipulate requirements for intruder alarms and the engineering department might stipulate that freezer units be monitored by an alarm. Similarly (and, perhaps, in part consequently) the security industry has also tended to compartmentalise its thinking; if the customer (or his insurers) asks for an intruder alarm, the alarm company will install an intruder alarm but will go no further. One alarm company, for example, provides intruder alarm services to South Wales from Bristol but fire alarm services to the same area from Plymouth! There are, however, signs that on occasions integrated systems are offered to customers on the lines suggested by Randall (1976):

> Basically . . . [the customer] wants to guard his assets when he is not there; he is, therefore, looking for automated protection. As an aside we might remind ourselves that his assets are not just exposed to the risk of theft, there is also the risk of fire and flood. There might also be, within the protected premises, processes which need to be monitored outside the course of working hours. (p. 138)

If such needs can be satisfied by an integrated alarm system monitoring all vital aspects of the business then the whole question of discounts for security measures could perhaps be considered in a different light. If the insured was buying, in one system, a fire alarm, an intruder alarm, a device to monitor the temperature (thus helping, perhaps, to prevent burst water pipes), a device to monitor his cold rooms and freezers and a device to monitor the activity of his automatic production processes, then the discounts available from the various insurance premiums could cumulatively make such an installation an economically attractive proposition. Again, the initiative would probably have to come from insurers as client demand would otherwise be difficult to co-ordinate; for their part security companies appear to react to requests rather than to innovate, despite, or perhaps because of, the competitive state of the alarm industry. Such an initiative would probably also hasten the development of a British Standard, the absence of which is possibly at present inhibiting the more widespread use of such integrated alarm systems.

There is considerable overlap between the duties of a burglary insurance surveyor and some of the services offered by the police crime prevention officers. As already mentioned, insurers will not usually accept a survey report from a crime prevention officer in lieu of a report from their own surveyor — probably on the argument that as well as recommending risk improvements, a surveyor's function is to present all the facts of the risk to the underwriter and those facts might well go beyond a mere description of the physical protections. However, there has recently been a welcome sign of a small, but perhaps significant, change. Outside the major cities, some branches of major insurers have been known to ask a prospective insured to obtain a report from the police C.P.O. (in lieu of a survey by the insurer's surveyor) and to implement any recommendations as a condition of theft insurance. This practice should be extended in the form of formal liaison between insurers and the police. Costs could be reduced and requirements standardised with a little more co-operation which should extend beyond insurers' representation on joint Home Office committees and working parties and presence on local crime prevention panels. The question whether this increased co-operation should be with the police or with the Home Office is of less importance than that it should, in fact, take place.

The influence of an insurance company is potentially critical as it is probably the only agency in a position to offer a property owner financial incentives for crime prevention measures. There is substantial evidence that, when they do choose to act, insurers can function to prevent crime or to change the type of crime which occurs (as witness the apparent displacement of burglaries from commercial to private properties in the 1960s). In fact, insurers are probably uniquely positioned to intervene effectively to influence crime prevention — given that the ability can be recognised and that the incentive can be appreciated and mobilised.

NOTE

[1] The views expressed in this paper are those of the author and should not be taken to represent the views of his employer.

REFERENCES

Association de Geneve (1980) *Crime and Insurance* (Etudes et Dossiers Nr. 44). Geneva, Internationale pour l'Etude de l'Economic de l'Assurance.

Bailey, F. E. (1979) "Getting to grips with vandalism", *Policy Holder Insurance Journal*, (Part 1) 2 November, 25-8; (Part 2) 9 November, 34-9.

Bandura, A. (1977) *Social Learning Theory*, New Jersey, Prentice-Hall.

Burrows, J. and Heal, K. (1980) "Police car security campaigns", in: R. V. G. Clarke and P. Mayhew (Eds.), *Designing Out Crime*, London, H.M.S.O.

Callaghan, D. N. (1974) "The NSCIA — a broad survey", *Policy Holder Insurance Journal*, 12 July, 1576-80.

Callaghan, D. N. (1976) "Activities, policies and trends in the security industry", in: P. Young (Ed.), *Major Property Crime in the United Kingdom*, Edinburgh, University of Edinburgh, School of Criminology and Forensic Studies.

Carter, R. L. (1972) *Economics and Insurance*, Stockport, P. H. Press.

Carter, R. L. (1974) *Theft in the Market*, London, The Institute of Economic Affairs.

Clarke, R. V. G. (1977) "Psychology and crime", *Bulletin of the British Psychological Society*, 30, 280-3.

Clarke, R. V. G. (1980) "'Situational' crime prevention: theory and practice", *British Journal of Criminology*, 20, 136-47.

Clarke, R. V. G. and Hough, J. M. (Eds.) (1980) *The Effectiveness of Policing*, Farnborough, Gower.

Clarke, R. V. G. and Mayhew, P. (Eds.) (1980) *Designing out Crime*, London, H.M.S.O.

Companyman (1974) "An economist in the thieves' market", *Policy Holder Insurance Journal*, 22 November, 2616-25.

Companyman (1977) "Spare a copper, Guvnor?", *Policy Holder Insurance Journal*, 18 November, 2094-6.

Cross, B. (1976) "Alarms and response", in: P. Young (Ed.), *Major Property Crime in the United Kingdom*, Edinburgh, University of Edinburgh, School of Criminology and Forensic Studies.

Ditton, J. (1978) *Part-Time Crime*, London, Martin Robertson.
Eysenck, H. J. (1977) *Crime and Personality*, London, Routledge and Kegan Paul.

French, A. H. (1970) "The underwriting of carriers' liabilities", *Journal of the Chartered Insurance Institute*, 67, 35-46.

Hall, S. and Scraton, P. (1981) *Class and Control*, Milton Keynes, Open University Press.

Hart, C. V. (1962) "Can the insurer reduce crime?", Lecture before the Insurance Institute of London, 13 February, (mimeo).

Hough, J. M., Clarke, R. V. G. and Mayhew, P. (1980) "Chapter 1: Introduction", in: R. V. G. Clarke and P. Mayhew (Eds.), *Designing Out Crime*, London, H.M.S.O.

Maltz, M. D. (1972) *Evaluation of Crime Control Programs*, Washington, D.C., U.S. Government Printing Office.

Mayhew, P. (1979) "Road accident prevention; the lessons for crime control", in: *Home Office Research Bulletin No. 7*, London, Home Office Research Unit.

Mayhew, P., Clarke, R. V. G., Sturman, A. and Hough, J. M. (1976) *Crime as Opportunity* (Home Office Research Study No. 34), London, H.M.S.O.

Mischel, W. (1968) *Personality and Assessment*, New York, Wiley.

Pease, K. G. (1979a) "Reflections on the development of crime prevention strategies and techniques in Western Europe, excluding Roman Law countries", Report to the United Nations Centre for Social Development and Humanitarian Affairs, 31 October, Department of Social Administration, University of Manchester, (mimeo).

21

Pease, K. G. (1979b) "Some futures in crime prevention", in: *Home Office Research Bulletin No. 7*, London, Home Office Research Unit.

Perry, S. (1976) "Insurance and crime prevention", in: P. Young (Ed.), *Major Property Crime in the United Kingdom*, Edinburgh, University of Edinburgh, School of Criminology and Forensic Studies.

Pugh, J. (1976) "Insurance and crime prevention", in: P. Young (Ed.), *Major Property Crime in the United Kingdom*, Edinburgh, University of Edinburgh, School of Criminology and Forensic Studies.

Randall, W. E. (1976) "Activities, policies and trends in the security industry", in : P. Young (Ed.), *Major Property Crime in the United Kingdom*, Edinburgh, University of Edinburgh, School of Criminology and Forensic Studies.

Reppetto, T. A. (1974) *Residential Crime*, Cambridge, Mass., Ballinger.

Riley, D. (1980a) "An evaluation of a campaign to reduce car thefts", in: R. V. G. Clarke and P. Mayhew (Eds.), *Designing out Crime*, London, H.M.S.O.

Riley, D. (1980b) "An evaluation of a campaign to reduce vandalism", in: R. V. G. Clarke and P. Mayhew (Eds.), *Designing out Crime*, London, H.M.S.O.

Robertson, A. (1979) "General insurance under the microscope", *Policy Holder Insurance Journal*, 16 November, 40-2.

Rupprecht, R. (1978) "The problems of prevention — ten assertions: ten demands", in: *The Proceedings of the 1978 Cranfield Conference on the Prevention of Crime in Europe*, London, Peel Press.

Tobacco Advisory Council (1979) *Report on Security of Goods in Transit for the Year 1978*, London, (mimeo).

Wine and Spirit Security Liaison Ltd. (1979) *Director's Annual Report for 1978*, London, (mimeo).

Woodward, C. D. (1979) "Getting to grips with arson", *Policy Holder Insurance Journal*, 5 October, 33-5.

[7]

LEGAL NETWORKS AND DOMESTIC SECURITY

Pat O'Malley

Much sociological debate has focused on the proposition that state power is being dispersed from coercive, formal state agencies to an expanding 'soft' periphery of less formal, ostensibly less coercive nonstate control agencies. It is argued that these penetrate civil society in the forms familiar to that field and thus more effectively and covertly carry out regulatory functions (Abel 1982; Cohen 1985; Selva and Bohm 1987). Such accounts have been extensively criticised for their view of law and regulation as state centred and/or as systematically integrated. An increasingly influential body of theory and research has fostered the opposite view of laws as emerging in a large number of relatively autonomous social relations or fields, of which the state is only one important instance, and not necessarily the central one (Henry 1983; Merry 1988; Fitzpatrick 1988; Griffiths 1986). Furthermore, state law itself is subjected to pluralizing analysis, so that:

> The 'legal system' is neither totalised nor enclosed. There is no unity to the complex of written codes, judgements, institutions and agents and techniques of judgement which make up 'the law' . . . Legal regulation of different relations and processes has emerged at different

Studies in Law, Politics, and Society, Volume 11, pages 171-190.
Copyright © 1991 by JAI Press Inc.
All rights of reproduction in any form reserved.
ISBN: 1-55938-375-5

times and in relation to different concerns. They have defined their terms differently and utilise diverse forms of judgement and mechanisms of enforcement. They do not operate in terms of a single division of public and private—spaces, activities and relations which are within the scope of regulation for one purpose are outside it for another (Rose 1987, p.66).

By extension, such analyses suggest that any social setting is likely to be traversed by a variety of state and nonstate legal agencies, and that the integration or coordination of these agencies and their effects is always problematic. Hence what constitutes "the law" in any specific site therefore will depend on which legal agencies intersect in that context, how these orders are mobilized, and how they interact. Law becomes a congeries of:

activities which may support, complement, ignore or frustrate one another, so that the 'law' which is actually effective on the 'ground floor' of society is the result of enormously complex and usually in practice unpredictable patterns of competition, interaction, negotiation, isolation and the like (Griffiths 1986, p. 39).

Such an interpretation of legal pluralism coincides with postmodern tendencies, such as those of Rose, to react against a naive monolithic model of law by positing a radically disarticulated array of laws and agencies. Yet Griffiths' recognition of the importance of competition, interaction and negotiation clearly indicates that in place of such *a priori* polarizations, the need rather is to to develop understandings of how diverse legal agencies interact, and to what extent, in what ways, and under what conditions they may cohere in systematic legal networks.

Beyond merely analyzing the nature and extent of networks *between* diverse legal agencies, attempts have been made to explore the dialectical relations that may emerge therefrom, as the parties involved are themselves mutually constituted and reconstituted by the process. For example, Stuart Henry's (1983) research on private justice in the workplace reveals complex relations between two relatively autonomous spheres of law, in which:

state law relies on private justice to excercise some of its control functions, but private justice itself relies on state law to excercise its discipline. The one form is not separate from the other but each are [sic] necessary parts of the other. At the same time, however, each part has its own limited autonomy (Henry 1983, pp. vii-viii).

Moreover, the work of writers such as Donzelot (1979) and Fitzpatrick (1988) indicates that such interactions may create new social phenomena in their own right, such as the "tutelary complex" of Donzelot and the "synoptic power" of Fitzpatrick. These are characterized by the emergence of a common and integrating discourse and set of practices worked out between interacting agencies. Such negotiation involves suppression of incompatible elements of the different participating agencies' knowledges and practices, translation of other elements into more compatible forms, and the integration of all into a workable whole, albeit often inconsistent, labile and conflicting. In this process emergent, synthetic or synoptic social practices and knowledges may appear. A clear example is provided by Donzelot's (1979) analysis of social work as a synopsis that emerged around the turn of the century from interaction between a variety of regulatory professions, and that in its turn changed important aspects of those professions.

Part of the attractiveness of this concept of a tutelary complex is that it allows recognition of the emergence of delimited networks that may transcend the form and content of their constituent agencies, without catapulting analysis directly into an assumption of a single grand control system or a single functionalist logic of legal order. Such an approach by no means leads to the rejection of the insights of Abel, Cohen and their colleagues. Quite to the contrary, it suggests that they be taken very seriously as requiring more detailed investigation. This would aim to trace specific networks of legal coercion and control rather than to assume systematic overall unity: to provide networking "maps" from which to build up a theoretical and empirically based knowledge of the systematization of legal powers—of the formation, operation, transcendance and dissolution of networks of legal and social control. It would also involve raising questions often overlooked or sidelined by theories of state centred and unified social control systems.

First, the "state expansionary" processes identified by state centrist theories may be reconceptualized as effects of network formation—but without this implying any necessary centre (in the state or elsewhere) from which expansion grows. These processes in some instances may involve state-centred expansion, but equally may involve networks that form and operate entirely within civil society, or even instances of expansion "into" the state sphere by autonomous private legal orders and their knowledges What may pass as the expansion of social control or of state regulation may be re-examined in terms of power and knowledge relations within and between networks. Such relations, it goes without saying may be conflictual and contradictory as well as cooperative and synthetic. They may break down as well as extend, and they may transform the nature of all participating agencies rather than merely transmit the powers and effects of one. Moreover, as suggested, they could well include tutelary complexes or synoptic powers and strategies extending *across* the boundaries of the state.

In such analysis, current terminology referring to the "blurring" or "merging" of the public/private distinction emerges as too simplistic, concealing more than it reveals. Under these blanket terms may be hidden a great variety of processes that not merely negate that distinction, but that in ways yet to be theorized adequately generate new discourses, practices and agencies out of the synthesis of state and nonstate forms (cf. Freiberg and O'Malley 1984).

Such considerations lead back via a more methodical route to the important questions posed by grander theorizations: of whether in these processes the nature of and meaning of "control" is changed in significant ways. They may allow us to carry out such analysis in a less all-embracing fashion: to allow recognition that instead of a single overall pattern there is a multiplicity of logics, processes and sites of control.

In this paper, some of these questions will be developed through inspection of operations of the network of Australian insurance companies policing domestic property. This network is in the process of forming a tutelary complex with the state police organized around specific concepts of "risk" and "security" which, in their turn, are associated with important shifts in the conception, means, targets, and strategies of social control.

INSURANCE, RISK AND COMMODIFICATION OF SECURITY

To a very large extent, the meaning of security is symbolically constructed in tandem with that of a specific threat or danger (cf Spitzer 1987, p.47). Thus to provide security as a commodity involves specification of the danger in such a way that the potential consumer is made aware of it as an immediate problem whose resolution or abatement requires the purchase of the security commodity. A case in point concerns the definitions of (commodified) security provided by insurance companies. In recent years, Australians have been subjected to a pervasive information and advertising campaign on the subject of "domestic security," largely the outcome of combined efforts by the insurance industry and the state police forces. Whereas much of this activity focuses on neighborhood watch schemes jointly funded and promoted by these agencies (of which, more later), also prominent has been a program to educate the public about "secure living." A typical example of such material is the brochure entitled "Security and You" (Commercial Union 1988). Published by Commercial Union Insurance, sponsor of the neighborhood watch program in all Australian states, this booklet is distributed on its behalf by the Victoria Police (at such significant popular occasions as the Royal Melbourne Show). It opens with the following passage:

> While everyone fears violence, the odds of becoming a victim of murder or attack are slight. There is, however, one very serious crime to which we are all vulnerable—Burglary (Commercial Union 1988, p.1).

Certain fairly obvious points may be made quickly at this point. First, security is defined explicitly in terms of violence to property rather than as violence to the person. Second, burglary is defined as "a very serious crime," therefore catapulting it through the ranks of criminal offences, to be mentioned alongside murder. Third, danger is defined as coming from sources outside the domestic household—even though the effective denial of domestic violence as a major and ubiquitous threat to security must appear as extraordinary. This construction of threats to domestic security is possibly a product of patriarchal miopia among insurance executives. However, it is also directly reflective of the form of security—the security commodity—that is being offered. For obvious reasons, a corporation selling household contents insurance will present the principal danger to domestic security in terms of external threats to the security of domestic property rather than of domestically based threats of violence to the person.

It follows that the set of practices that operationally define domestic security in this publication—as in the broader campaign of which it is part—define security as a matter of creating a safe, private refuge rather than a matter concerning a secure social milieu. These practices may be summed up under four headings:

1. rendering the outer surface of the home impervious to strangers by means of mechanical interventions (bolts, doors, locks, and so forth) and other techniques (locking away tools that could be used to force entry, removing screening bushes and so on);
2. controlling the production of signs (for example, creating the illusion of occupancy by leaving on lights, radios, having mail collected while on holidays);
3. rendering moveable objects less available to theft (for example, marking items within the house for purposes of identification, concealing valuables and so on); and
4. insuring the contents of the homes.

As this outline intimates insurance enters the informative literature as part of the rational scheme of security. In "Security and You" there is a twenty-four page section on points (1) through (3), the final section of the brochure deals with "Home security and your insurance" and stresses that "Adequate insurance plays an important role in any security plan." (Commercial Union 1988, p. 26). This is predictable, for the sale of household insurance is the rationale behind the production of this document and the rationale informing its definition of danger and security. The point scarcely needs to be made that what is happening is that the commodity to be sold is shaping the entire definition of what security is and how it is to be achieved.

In this process of definition, the attempt is made to identify the interests of the insurer with those of the householder, by the very process of defining security itself. This is attempted in several ways. First, the bulk of the booklet is technical advice on securing houses, the insurance company appears as a technocratically neutral expert on security, and that insurance is a technical aspect of the security field (so defined). This "security," a security of fortified private spaces, is presented not as a value-laden set of social practices, embedded in discourses of private property and social atomism, but as a set of scientifically rational, objective techniques that are the solution to a technical problem (Spitzer 1987; Wilson 1986a, 1986b). The insurance company is now symbolically set into a place that permits its visible public identification with the state police, as a neutral anti-crime agency.

In this process of defining security, the prominence given to techniques of security do not simply sell insurance, but also maintain it as a profitable activity. Identification of the homeowner as the agent and beneficiary of security practices conceals the fact that domestic security practices (if effective) would secure not only the property of the householder but in so doing would reduce the risk borne by the insurer of this property. Whereas this consideration is obviously a basic rationale for the insurers' participation in the domestic security program, it is never mentioned in public relations material. However, it is quite explicit in the systematic actuarial discourse underlying insurance as a capitalist industry, where it emerges in conjunction with the pivotal concept of "moral hazard."

CONTRACT LAW AND THE INSURANCE RELATION

Within the discourse of insurance, moral hazard refers to "a subjective characteristic of the insured that increases the probability of loss" to the insurer (Mohr and Cammack 1961, p. 53), and may be broadly classified into two forms.[1] The first, is the possibility that a policyholder will seek financial gain by fraudulently calling on the policy—for example by destroying insured property or dishonestly claiming its loss by theft. This form, not being tied directly to the conceptions and practices of domestic security, will not be the subject of this paper. The second, legally legitimate form, results from a calculation by the insured that once the premium has been paid and the risk transferred to the insurer, it is economically irrational to take steps to secure the insured property. Clearly, such a model assumes a homo economicus valuing possessions only in money terms. Yet ironically, this discursive monster is a creation of the insurance relation, for insurance can only replace goods with a money equivalent. Things valued only for their subjective meaning cannot be replaced by a monetary value and could not be insured as such.[2] Yet to the extent that domestic property owners do think in commodity terms and are converted into amoral economic rationalists, then they create the loss-bearing moral hazards noted earlier.

These new hazards—the anticipated actions of the insured rather than those of the potential thief—become the primary object of insurance policing. To protect its profits, especially against forms of moral hazard that are not prohibited under criminal law (and thus potentially subject to state policing), the insurance company must establish its own legal order within the framework of the insurance contract. The insurance contract (and more remotely, the law of insurance contracts) establishes the coercive conditions for the operation of an enforcement network aimed at disciplining householders, in order to minimize the economic impact of assumed moral hazard.[3]

Policing domestic security: The insurance inspectorate

Typically, an insurance contract grants the insurer access to two sources of economically coercive power. The first is cancellation of the policy, which—subject to the broad parameters of the Insurance Contracts Act—can be effected at any time by giving written notice. Although this option is also open to the insured, the coercive effect on the insurer is minimal—given the large number of insured parties and minimal corporate reliance on any single household policyholder. Cancellation of the policy has a far more coercive effect on the insured, however, because it leaves that party to bear the entire risk of property loss. The second and more immediately tangible sanction is the right of the insurer to refuse a claim on the policy and thus inflict what may be a massive financial loss on the policyholder. The following extract from a typical home insurance policy makes clear what is at stake here:

> We may refuse a claim, or cancel this Policy or do both if:-
> (a) you are not accurate and frank in any statement you make in the claim form or in connection with a claim.
> (b) your home building, residential building or site or part of it is used for the purposes of a business, trade or profession unless you tell us beforehand and we agree to cover you in writing.
> (c) you do not comply with any security requirements imposed by us.
> (d) you keep flammable liquids or explosives in your residential building or the site illegally.
> (e) you do not immediately report to the police if you suspect or should reasonably have suspected that:-
> *something has been stolen from your residential building or site.
> *someone has acted maliciously and deliberately or intentionally to your residential building or site or something in it.
> *an attempt has been made to do any of these things.[4]

For the moment, attention should be directed to item (c) concerning security requirements, which inserts into the contractual relationship the crucial space and the coercive resources for the insurance company's enforcement of domestic security. The concrete manifestation of this process begins with the activation of the insurer's own policing agents subsequent to a claim being made by an insured party.[5]

Typically, the policing process commences with an interview with the insurance loss assessor. Virtually the entire period of every inspection emerges as an investigation into moral hazards created by the insured, the three phases being

1. assessment of the possibility of fraudulent claims or unintentional exaggeration in the amount of the claim;
2. assessment of the possibility of deliberate under-insurance (in which case the right to compensation is reduced on a pro-rata basis); and
3. assessment of the adequacy of security arrangements.

For the purposes of this paper, only the latter element of this process (that takes about half of the time of most interviews) is of concern, as it is the component concerned with domestic security.

The first step in a typical interview involves the assessor enquiring about the means of entry used by the intruders.[6] In part, this is to assess how far the claim of loss is plausible, but it is also intended to indicate the kinds of advice or instruction that the agent will give to the claimant. If entry were forced, then advice would focus on such matters as fitting better locks; if doors or windows were left open, additional stress was placed on the need to lock up when leaving the house. Whereas the particular details varied according to the case, the overall aim and content of the interview was a generalized course of instruction on the discipline of domestic security.

In a normal interview, assessors tour the entire home with the burglary victim, giving detailed advice on matters of security at each point of possible entry. This advice constitutes part of a discipline, the strategies for which are outlined earlier in this paper, and that appear both in insurance literature (such as "Security and You"), and in the advice given in assessment interviews. This account of the discipline of security makes it appear purely voluntary. In practice, it is actively and coercively enforced by the insurance companies. Within a week of the interview, claimants receive a letter from the insurance company that outlines the amount of compensation granted. However, accompanying this letter is another that requires the insured to implement certain specified changes in the security arrangements in their home. A typical example is as follows:

> Dear . . .
> As a result of the recent burglary in your home, it was recommended that the security at the property be improved as follows . . . [changes are then listed] . . . it is extremely important that these recommendations be implemented as soon as possible and you advise this office that this has been done or similar measures undertaken to improve the security. It is essential that you confirm this by returning the attached slip duly completed to enable our records to be noted accordingly.

These changes reflect fairly closely the verbal advice given at the interview. Frequently, changes will involve the policyholder in an expense of a considerable sum, especially if tradespeople are to be employed to install items required in this review. After the policyholder notifies the insurer in writing that these changes have been effected payment of the claim follows automatically. The implication is clear enough: either the insured carries out the changes, or the present or a subsequent claim, together with the continuation of the policy is placed in jeopardy.

Policyholders do have a degree of leeway open to them. They can simply refuse to make the changes, and accept the risk to their claim and possible cancellation of the policy. Naturally enough, this appears to be a relatively unusual course of action. Alternatively, a policyholder may dishonestly notify the insurer that the changes have been effected. However, given the possibility of future claims and inspections, this is a high-risk strategy. One apparent way around the problem would be to dishonestly inform the company that changes had been made, to collect the claim, and then to cancel the policy—then take out a new policy with another insurer. Against this possibility major insurance companies require applicants to specify in the proposal for insurance whether another insurer has made continuation of insurance conditional on security measures to prevent further loss. Informed accordingly, the new insurer will usually require the applicant to bring the property up to the specified level of security before issuing the policy.[7] Thus the insurance industry as a whole appears as a network of agencies cooperatively and coercively policing domestic security, and empowered for this role by the potential for economic coercion established in the conditions of the insurance contract.[8] However, it is by no means the case that these coercive powers establish an isolated, private legal order, for they are also used to enforce internetworking with other legal agencies.[9]

CONTRACTUAL OBLIGATIONS AND MOBILIZATION OF LAWS

As argued earlier, the conception of risk embodied in property insurance is balanced on a model of perfectly rational homo economicus. Following a calculation of risk, the individual would then assess the most cost-effective means for economic loss prevention. This might include capital outlay on property security and/or on insurance. However, such calculation will not necessarily, nor even probably maximize the efficacy of a control *system*. This much is clear in the discourse of insurance economics:

> Ideally when deciding how much to spend on loss prevention the individual should allow
> for social costs and benefits but, as in other private economic decisions, he will normally

be concerned only with items which affect his own pocket. At present after a theft the individual incurs only a little part of the cost of apprehending, convicting and punishing the thief [for example the cost of appearing in court]; . . . Consequently private decisions are taken without regard to their effect on the total opportunities and costs for thieves, or on the demands for public law-enforcement services (Carter 1974, p. 31).

It may be argued that the economics of private risk calculation do include a systematic factor, as insurance premiums frequently reflect the prevalence of risk in specific areas. However, such arguments are weakened by the fact that the expenditure required for any individual to secure their own property is likely to greatly exceed the economic savings resulting from reduced premiums resulting from a generalized lowering of risk. Indeed, insurance companies face considerable risk in such perfect economic calculation. It is quite plausible that in high risk areas, individuals may calculate it to be more rational to pay increased insurance premiums rather than to outlay considerable sums on security measures.

As will be recognized, we have returned to the field of "moral hazard," of costs to the insurer generated by the actions of an economically rational policyholder. As with other examples of moral hazard, the insurance company exercises the economic coercion conferred by the insurance contract to exert a disciplining force to foster security and thus protect its profits. However, whereas previously enforcement was concerned with securing the domestic space, now attention is directed to securing the connection between policing of the domestic space and policing in the broader social setting. To this end, the insurance contract may be used to coerce networking practices. These practices fall into several categories:

Private Actions

Many household insurance contracts contain provisions compelling the policyholder to act as an agent of the insurance company in relation to legal actions against third parties. The form of compulsion and the form of action are usually spelt out quite unambiguously as in the following example, so that the policyholder can be left in no doubt as to the consequences of non-cooperation:

Any benefits which this policy gives to you or you family depend upon you and your family giving us any information and help as we require, including attendance in court to give evidence. You or your family must assist us even where we have paid a claim for we may attempt to recover the amount of our payment from the party who caused the loss or damage . . . [10]

Evidently, what is primarily at issue here is the effort by the insurer to defend profitability, but the networking implications are clear. Such contractual provisions form the basis of part of an intermeshing network of control directed at controlling offenders: monetary damages in a civil action acting in the same deterrant capacity as the fine (O'Malley 1982). This is all the more so because in the Australian context, as elsewhere, it has for some time been advocated that civil actions be articulated with criminal prosecution as a means of providing double deterrance against offending (see Freiberg and O'Malley 1984).

Police Mobilization

Without exception, insurance contracts require the policyholder to contact police as a condition of the company commencing to process a claim. Moreover, in the policy section quoted at length earlier, it was stated that

> We may refuse a claim, or cancel this Policy or do both if . . . [e] you do not immediately report to the police if you suspect or should reasonably have suspected that . . . something has been stolen from your residential building or site.

Networking is thus coerced on the policyholder, and mobilization of the police is required—formally, at least—even in comparatively trivial instances of burglary where a claim on the policy is not made.

In both instances of **compulsory** networking, therefore, policyholders become the direct subjects of legal interventions, disciplining them into activating or enlisting in the broader framework of public (rather than purely domestic) security. Yet in terms of the current political developments, this compulsory process of networking is secondary to a more subtle, noncoercive process—that is, of enlistment in neighborhood watch programs

Neighborhood Watch and the Socialization of Risk

In raising the questions of moral hazard and the compellability of policyholders to participate in networking enforcement, we confront a dilemma of domestic policing: that whereas it focuses attention inward, to the security of the domestic space, it cannot afford to leave unsurveyed the public spaces from which the dangers emanate. It is in this respect that the neighborhood watch program becomes important from the point of view of the insurers. Insurance companies have invested very heavily in the neighborhood watch programs throughout Australia, both funding the schemes virtually in their entirety, and providing direct and indirect publicity through multi-media advertising (Settle 1987). In certain obvious respects, this participation takes a form that reflects general insurance concerns for the discipline of security. In the first place, neighborhood watch schemes are distribution centers for security material. Television cassettes under the subtle and evocative title of "Secure living," are made available to such groups, and newsletters are funded that give information of local crime profiles, information about domestic security practices and how to identify "suspicious behaviour." Neighborhood watch groups also provide engraving tools for marking valuable household items, in order to make them less easy to dispose of. Coupled with all of this, periodic meetings are attended by the police, in which local members of the scheme are given information pertaining to crime and security, largely focused on burglary and closely related matters. On this basis alone, it is easy to see that neighborhood watch is organizationally and functionally integrated with the broader insurance-based program for policing a discipline of domestic security.

Whatever the disputed effectiveness of these schemes in countering burglary, enhancing domestic security, and thus protecting the profitability of insurance, what cannot be in doubt is that the programs are used to sell insurance. Not only does neighborhood watch proselytize the conception of security in which insurance is embedded, but the promotional material, literature, warning signs and advertising of the program are everywhere and always carried out under the sponsoring insurance company's logo. Thus, because the insurers and the state police are incorporated as co-promoters, the program offers priceless attractions for insurers, for police distribution of neighborhood watch brochures and related material involves them in distributing advertising material at the same time as presenting an authoritative identification of the burglary problem as immediate and massive. Furthermore, by such association with the state police forces, the status of the insurer as a neutral expert is enhanced, and insurance appears as an integral component of a national strategy of crime control.[11]

PUBLIC POLICE AND THE PRIVATIZATION OF SECURITY

It should already be clear that the strategy of the insurance industry in promoting a public discipline of security relies extensively on active support from the state police. In practice this cooperation is truly symbiotic, for the extensive direct and indirect services provided by police to the insurance corporations are balanced by equally significant and strategic reciprocal benefits provided to the police. In order to understand the details of this process, it is necessary to look at the situation confronting police in Australia in the 1980s.

Over the past decade the police have demonstrably been unsuccessful in curbing the rate of burglaries, and have been solving a declining proportion of these.[12] Burglary thus presents something of a political liability for police, appearing as a failure to protect the public. In the words of one senior Victoria Police representative,

> Burglary . . . remains an offence which has a strong influence on public perception of police professionalism and competence. The solution rate for burglary is low and it has continued to decline . . . Many experienced police officers and criminologists have expressed virtual powerlessness to do anything about this, taking into account traditional police methods and available resources (Braybrook 1986, p. 91).

Although the problem may provide a basis to calls for increased establishment or powers, there seems to be little reason for confidence that such expansionary changes would have a significant effect on rates of offending.[13] In Australia, as in Britain and elsewhere, this recognition has been associated with a shift in thinking about crime prevention, away from an imagery of effective proactive police deterrence, and toward a policy of "target hardening" or "situational prevention" (Clarke and Hope 1984, pp. 5-12; South 1987). In other countries, as in Australia, this shift has been associated with neighborhood watch programs, and police or state sponsored and managed media campaigns—such as the British "Protect your home" series—to create "community awareness" of the necessity for domestic vigilance.[14] Police in virtually all western nations have been involved in some way with variations on the theme of "Operation identification" in which valuables are marked by an engraving machine. Specialist crime prevention officers give free advice on domestic security, very much along the lines of the "service" offered by insurance companies in Australia (Bennett and Wright 1984, pp. 22-23).

The increasingly high public profile of insurance companies in generating, disseminating, and policing a discipline of domestic security cannot, therefore, be understood in isolation from a parallel, but independently generated, strategy of state police. From the point of view of the police, strategies of target hardening represent a complex effort to resolve a series of contemporary problems, which tend to merge with problems confronting insurers. Each of these problems may be looked at independently, although in practice they merge together in the broader complex of police politics and strategies.

Containing Burglary and Improving Clearance Rates

Unable to contain the threat in the public domain, attention is being given to the creation of secure "defensible" domestic spaces (South 1987). In Australia, we cannot yet tell how successful this strategy will prove to be. Where resort has been made to police advice as a source of security information, penetration of the discipline of security has been poor. In the United Kingdom, for example, only 0.5 percent of households per year receive a police security survey; only 7-10 percent of households have ever been reached by these police services, and there is no information available on how far (and for how long) such free advice is followed (Mayhew 1984, p. 32). At this point the articulation of state and insurance policing in Australia becomes significant because, as seen, insured claimants are subject to economically coercive and long-term policing of their domestic security by the insurance agencies. Such procedures, in all probability will be more effective than the state police counterpart. Whereas we may not talk of a system of control being created, the convergence of the interests of the police and the insurance industry in a strategy of target hardening, combine to produce a policing arrangement which extends the discipline sought by state police into the domestic arena, where their own powers apparently do not effectively penetrate.

Privatizing Responsibility for Domestic Security

For the state police, one of the organizational benefits of the strategy of target hardening is that in a subtle fashion, it shifts primary responsibility for policing onto the owners of property. As a senior official of the Australian Insurance Council has noted,

> Severely restricted police resources and the sheer frequency of crime, means that any improvement in the situation will rely heavily on property owners accepting responsibility for their own property and valuables . . . (Hall 1986, p. 243).

Whereas police retain responsibility for the policing of public spaces, their role in securing private spaces is made more indirect and reactive (cf Shearing and Stenning 1983).[15] Such effects are consequences both of the domestic security push and of neighborhood watch—with its stress on "neighbours helping neighbours," and communities surveying their own streets.

Whereas this process reflects organizational and political interests of the state police, it is clear that these articulate very closely with the distinct but symbiotic concerns of the insurance industry. To the extent that the police urge target hardening, and develop their own policies accordingly, then the commodified, or privatized definition of security (and its component, the insurance commodity) that has been articulated by the insurance industry is supported and extended.

Public Relations

Neighborhood watch programs have been a major advance in the police penetration of popular consciousness. By identifying crime with a direct threat to the mass of householders, by bringing this threat down to the local level through presentation of local statistics, news and illustrations of crime, and by creating at least the illusion of popular participation at the local level, neighborhood watch has re-established a police presence in the communal void left by the withdrawl of the beat patrol officer. Police control over the organization and orchestration of the watch meetings provides them with a political platform in which their presence and perspectives gain a foothold at the local level. The intersection of insurance and police organizations in these programs likewise reflects their symbiotic relation. To the extent that the program succeeds in raising the public fear of burglary, then both insurer and police are pushed into the forefront of consciousness. Their cooperation in this excercise, in the manifold ways already mapped out, secures for both parties independent but interacting benefits.

FAMILY AUTONOMY AND DOMESTIC SECURITY

It is by no means the case that homeowner insurance necessarily (or even overwhelmingly) relates to the family. Despite this, the family, contractually defined as "any member of your family ordinarily residing with you" is universally accorded a special status in insurance contracts. The insured is contractually defined to include not only the individual named in the policy (the contractual "you") but "you and your family," benefits accrue to the insured or "your family," and these benefits "depend upon you or your family" giving information and cooperating. The contents insured refer to property "owned by you or a member of your family" and so on. One way of looking at this is simply to recognise that the family is united in law with respect to property ownership in ways that do not apply to non-relatives. The insurance contract simply recognizes this legal fact. However, the implications of the unification of the family have major consequences for understanding the policing of domestic spaces. In the case of insurance dealing with co-resident family members, the terms of the contract clearly imply or assume relations of familial responsibility and/or subordination. Other family members are contractually bound by the policy issued in the name of the insured. Thus the processes of economically coercive policing that are enforced in the ensurance relation, implicitly enlist the relations of authority within the family in the process of domestic security. In the most obvious case, the implication is that an insurance policy taken out in the name of a father or mother will involve the excercise of parental authority in order to enforce the disciple of security on the children. As Donzelot (1979) would argue, the autonomy and internal structure of the family are not destroyed by the intrusion of these new forces, but are being enlisted in the support of a new regime. The process is one in which the family is becoming "the nexus of nerve endings of a machinery that was exterior to it . . . a transition from a government of families to a government through families" (Donzelot 1979, pp. 91-92).

CONCLUSIONS

By focusing primarily on the semi-autonomous relations of policing domestic security developed by private insurance companies, it has emerged quite clearly that major processes of law enforcement are located in the nonstate field, and that these are formed in very significant ways independently of state initiatives for control. Moreover, it would appear that important changes in policing over the past decade owe much to social regulatory conceptions, initiatives, and interests located in the private sector. Yet the character and implications of this program of enforcing domestic security cannot be understood without taking into account the symbiotic relation that has formed between private sector agencies and state police, each following a similar course in relation to relatively distinct organizational purposes. From this mutually beneficial arrangement has emerged a common project based on a formal and informal networking of legal powers and enforcement practices. Yet what has emerged is something more than a simple alliance between agencies, for it has generated an unprecedented public focus on commodified and privatized conceptions of domestic security. Part of this development has involved the formation of specific "synoptic organisations"—the neighborhood watch committees being the most salient example—that involve the participation both of police and insurance interests (or more accurately, some elements of each) and that also involve community activists and participants. This emergent synopsis, in its turn, has acted back on the component organizations. The police forces' alliance with the insurance industry in this project, especially (but not only) in promoting neighborhood watch, has greatly strengthened tendencies toward "community" policing practices. The insurance companies, in their turn, have moved themselves into a prominent place in law and order politics and practices, and into an overt alliance with the police.

Such considerations must also lead to the re-examination of the question of whether we are witnessing an "expansion" of the state, or indeed of control and surveillance generally. Rather than expansion, what would appear to be occurring is a redistribution of responsibility for control and a change in its form. "Control," if that vague and slippery term is of any use at all, is not simply becoming more extensive. Rather, the process, the targets, methods and meanings of control are being transformed. To all appearances, what is occurring in the policing of domestic security is not the penetration of state control into civil society in ingenious disguises, but a rearrangement of forces involving some strategic displacement of state agencies and their traditional enforcement practices by privatized forms. This is not to suggest that state police are somehow being removed (albeit willingly) from the scene. Rather, private agencies are being inserted into a more complex set of policing relations, enabling police to redeploy resources and achieve other political and legitimatory ends.

The increasingly disciplinary role of insurance companies in this field brings to bear powers nominally outside of the criminal law and criminal justice networks. Property, insurance and contractual laws are engaged to enlist and enforce the active participation of householders. Thus the strategic rearrangement of forces enmeshes both burglars and householders as objects of control in a broader network of legal relations. It may well be that there is a "widening" of the control net or a fining of its mesh (Cohen 1985), but much of this is in order to discipline the potential *victims* of crime into a regime of crime prevention. The approach, as Nancy Reichman (1986) makes clear, is based on a risk-based model of social regulation, indigenous to the insurance industry but increasingly characteristic of other areas of social control. Its concern is not with categories of offender, motivation, and guilt, but with hazards and their minimization. In the process, breaches of morality are reconstructed: from moral reprehensibility to moral hazard. The "moral" thus conceived becomes merely the behavioral, a point expanded on by Cohen (1985) in other contexts. The distinction between the criminal and the victim is reduced to the distinction between two hazardous elements in a formula of risk management.

At first glance, this facilitates the merging or blurring of the public and private, as police and insurance companies cooperate in a common project that downgrades the moral meanings characteristic of state interventions in criminal law. Closer inspection reveals otherwise, for it is precisely the "private" corporate identity and powers of the insurers that facilitate their entry into the domestic space. At the same time and for the same purpose insurers nevertheless have enlisted ideologies of "public" order (for example, via neighborhood watch) to assist with this entry. Conversely, police adoption of the risk based models of social regulation, stimulation of neighborhood watch schemes and action on behalf of insurers, represents some privatization of the character of state practice. The public and the private thus are not collapsed together and "blurred" or "merged" by what we have witnessed, but neither do they retain a character defined relative to state or nonstate spheres of action. Rather they may be seen as strategic conceptions—ideological notions that faclitate the use of particular strategies of intervention that need not be confined to agencies in the corresponding state or private "sector." Thus, they may be coordinated, transferred and orchestrated by specific networks of legal power that traverse the boundaries of the state. Further attention to such processes and to their ideological effects may provide us not only with a more complete understanding of systematization among agencies of law and social control, but also help to clarify our currently weak conceptual grasp of the dimensions in which they operate.

ACKNOWLEDGMENTS

This research was made possible by a research grant from the La Trobe University School of Social Sciences. I would like to thank Peter Fitzpatrick, Stuart Henry and Martin Chanock for their useful and constructive commentaries on earlier drafts of this paper.

NOTES

1.   For an extended analysis of the definition of moral hazard, see Heimer (1985, pp. 8-9, 29-36).

2.   It is not being suggested that insurance agents need deny subjective meaning. It is simply that a monetary or commodity perspective is the only one which forms the direct nexus with insurance discourse on economic risk, calculation and so on.

3.   Similar illustrations may be drawn from the work of insurance loss adjustors in the automobile insurance business. See for example Reichman (1987), Guarino Ghezzi (1983) and Ross (1970).

4.   Extracts from Home Insurance Policies, unless otherwise stated, are taken from the 1988 policy wording of the RACV General Insurance Pty Ltd. The selection of this particular policy is merely based on convenience and has no significance, as the conditions for such policies vary little between most major companies. The conditions laid out in this section of the contract must be material to loss suffered by the policyholder, but as will be seen, this leaves open a broad range of intervention by the insurer.

5.   It is not clear in what proportion of claims such investigations are initiated. In 1986 a senior official of the Insurance Council of Australia indicated that the proportion was limited by the costs of inspection rather than by the wishes of the insureres, but that in any case the frequency of inspections would rise appreciably in the following years. (Hall 1986, pp. 246-248).

6.   Data concerning interviews with insurance assessors were drawn from a non-random snowball study of 43 Melbourne residents who had been interviewed by insurance assessors following a burglary.

7.   In Australia, as in Britain and elsewhere, the contract of insurance is subject to the doctrine of **uberrimae fides** or "utmost good faith." Thus the Insurance Contracts Act 1984 specifies (s13) that "A contract of insurance is a contract of utmost good faith." Failure to act in accordance with this principle—for example, to answer dishonestly to the questions outlined in the text— may therefore be grounds for cancellation of the contract, or for the reduction or refusal of any claims made under the terms of the contract.

8.   Hall (1986, pp. 247-248) notes that in Australia in 1982 a "filing cabinet" of such claims information was set up by the Insurance Council of Australia for access by all major insurers. This is also used in the policing of fraudulent claims.

9.   It is worth remarking at this point that the development and expansion of these insurance policing practices cannot easily be attributed to some structural demiurge, pressing for increased control. Hall (1986) indicates that the interest of insurers in these developments primarily arose out of the fact that during the late 1970s the Australian Trade Practices Commission disallowed tariff setting practices. To that date, such practices had rendered of lesser consequence. With the abolition of tariffs, profitability fell and losses due to moral hazard were of lesser consequence. With the abolition of tariffs, profitability fell and losses due to moral hazard emerged as a critical issue.

10.   As this suggests, the insurer may have grounds for procedding against the insured for breach of contract where, after the payment of a claim, the latter refuse to cooperate in a civil action.

11. Settle (1987, p. 1) provides an illustration from Melbourne radio advertising, part of which runs as follows:

Son: "Who are the good guys?"
Father: "Well the police . . . and people like us . . . and Commercial Union."
Son: "Who's Commercial Union?"
Father: "The insurance company that sponsors Neighbourhood Watch."

12. After theft, burglary is the most frequently reported crime in most Australian states. The average official rate of increase in burglary has long been about 10 percent per annum, increasing by about 214 percent in the last decade. Clearance rates average about 9 percent (Mukherjee 1986; Braybrook 1986).

13. Clarke and Hope (1984, pp. 5-6) report that in Britain clearance rates for burglary have fallen to about 6 percent. The hopelessness of reliance on police patrols as a deterrent is illustrated by their calculation that (at 1984 levels) a patrolling officer might expect only once in every eight years to be within 100 meters of a burglar entering or leaving a residence.

14. See, for example "Practical ways to crack crime" produced by the Central Office of Information (1988) in Britain and published by Her Majesty's Stationery Office.

15. Compare Sir Robert Mark's (1978) statement that "police and courts are of little relevance from the point of view of the victim and insurer . . . the belief that the state can, or even wishes to protect people effectively from burglary and theft should be abandoned . . . ".

REFERENCES

Abel, R. 1982. "The Contradictions of Informal Justice." Pp.186-235 in *The Politics of Informal Justice*, Vol. 1, edited by R. Abel. New York: Academic Pess.

Bennett, T. and R. Wright. 1984. *Burglars on Burglary: Prevention and the Offender*. London: Gower.

Braybrook, R. 1986. "Burglary in Victoria." Pp. 81-96 in *Burglary. A Social Reality*, edited by S. Mukherjee. Canberra: AIC.

Carter, R.L. 1974. *Theft in the Market*. London: Institute of Economic Affairs.

Clarke, R. and T. Hope. 1984. *Coping with Burglary. Research Perspectives on Policy*. Boston: Kluwer Nijhoff.

Cohen, S. 1985. *Visions of social control: Crime punishment and classification*. London: Polity press.

Commercial Union Insurance. 1988. *Security and You*. Melbourne: Commercial Union Insurance.

Donzelot, J. 1979. *The Policing of Families: Welfare Versus the State*. London: Hutchinson.

Fitzpatrick, P. 1988. "The Rise and Rise of Informalism." Pp. 178-98 in *Informal Justice?*, edited by R. Matthews. London: Sage.

Freiberg, A. and P. O'Malley. 1984. "State Intervention and the Civil Offense." *Law and Society Review*. 18:373-94.

Griffiths, J. 1986. "What is Legal Pluralism?" *Journal of Legal Pluralism and Unofficial Law* 24:1-55.

Guarino Ghezzi, S. 1983. "A Private Network of Social Control: Insurance Investigation Units." *Social Problems* 30:521-531.

Hall, J. 1986. "Burglary 1985: The Insurance Industry Viewpoint." Pp. 241-54 in *Burglary. A Social Reality*, edited by S. Mukherjee. Canberra: AIC.

Heimer, C. 1985. *Reactive Risk and Rational Action: Managing Moral Hazard in Insurance Contracts*. Berkeley, CA: University of California Press.

Henry, S. 1983. *Private Justice*. London: Routledge & Kegan Paul.

Mayhew, P. 1984. "Target-Hardening. How Much of an Answer?" Pp. 29-44 in *Coping with Burglary. Research Perspectives on Policy*, edited by R.Clarke and T. Hope. Boston: Kluwer Nijhoff.

Merry, S. E. 1988 "Legal pluralism." *Law and Society Review* 22:865-96.

Mohr, R.I. and E. Cammack. 1961. *Principles of Insurance*. New York: Irwin.

Mukherjee, S. 1986. "The Nature and Extent of Burglary in Australia." Pp. 5-26 in *Burglary. A Social Reality*, edited by S. Mukherjee. Canberra: AIC.

O'Malley, P. 1982. "The Invisible Censor. Civil Law and the State Delegation of Press Control." *Media, Culture and Society* 4:323-338.

Reichman, N. 1987. "The Widening Webs of Surveillance." Pp. 247-267 in *Private Policing*, edited by C. Shearing and P. Stenning. Beverly Hills: Sage.

————. 1986 "Managing Crime Risks: Toward an Insurance Based Model of Social Control." *Research in Law and Social Control* 8:151-172.

Rose, N. 1987. "Beyond the Public/Private Division: Law, Power and the Family." *Journal of Law and Society* 14:61-76.

Ross, H. 1970. *Settled Out of Court. The Social Process of Insurance Claims Adjustments*. Chicago:Aldine.

Selva, L. and R. Bohm. 1987. "A Critical Evaluation of the Informalism Experiment in the Administration of Justice." *Crime and Social Justice* 29: 43-58.

Settle, R. 1987. "Some Ideological Functions of the Neighborhood Watch Programme in Victoria." Unpublished paper, La Trobe University, Melbourne.

Shearing, C. and P. Stenning. 1983. "Private Security: Implications for Social Control." *Social Problems* 30:493-506.

South, N. 1987. "The Security and Surveillance of the Environment" Pp. 139-152 in *Transacarceration. Essays in the Sociology of Social Control*, edited by J.Menzies and J.Lowman. London: Gower.

Spitzer, S. 1987. "Security and Control in Capitalist Societies: The Fetishism of Security and the Secret Thereof." Pp.43-58 in *Transacarceration. Essays in the Sociology of Social Control*, edited by J.Menzies and J.Lowman. London: Gower.

Wilson, L. 1986a. "Neighborhood Watch." *Legal Service Bulletin* (April), pp. 86-90.

————. 1986b. "A Response." *Legal Service Bulletin* (July), pp. 175-176.

[8]

Police Strategies and Tactics for Controlling Crime and Disorder in England and Wales

By Trevor Bennett

Abstract

The main aim of the paper is to explore, describe, conceptualise, and categorise some of the strategies and tactics currently implemented by the police to reduce crime and disorder. The results of an analysis of data from a national survey of police forces in England and Wales show that the police use a large number of strategies and tactics targeted at particular "hot spots" locations, high-rate offences, high-rate offenders, and high-risk victims. The paper concludes that the view that the police no longer engage in crime prevention and (if they do) do no more than offer advice to others is incorrect. Instead, it is argued that the police engage in a broad and complex range of crime prevention activities which in effect comprise the "hidden" face of crime prevention. The paper recommends that further research is done in order to identify and to evaluate the broad range of policing strategies and tactics for controlling crime and disorder. *(Studies on Crime and Crime Prevention Vol. 3 1994. National Council for Crime Prevention).*

Keywords: police, policing, strategies, tactics, crime prevention, targeted patrols.

*R*ecent research on the police and crime prevention has offered a challenge to two widely held beliefs about the ability of the police to control crime. The first belief is that the police spend little or no time in attempting to prevent crime. Instead, it is thought that they spend most of their time responding reactively either to calls for service or to offence investigations. The second belief is that (when the police do attempt to prevent crime) their efforts are ineffective. It is now a widely held view that the outcome of ten years of experimentation with innovative policing programmes is that "nothing works".

There is substantial evidence available which can be drawn upon to find support for these propositions. The view that the police spend little time on crime prevention work is given support by recent surveys of police work which show that the police (even community constables) spend relatively little time on community-oriented or crime prevention activities (Bennett & Lupton, 1992; Brown & Ilse, 1985). The belief that the police spend little time on crime prevention is also reflected in recent studies of the crime prevention work of the police which in Britain tends to focus almost exclusively on the specialist work of police crime prevention officers (Harvey et al., 1989; Johnston et al. 1993). A similar view has been expressed in a more theoretical study recently published which concluded that community policing is no more than "communications policing" because the major function of the police is now receiving and disseminating information about crime prevention rather than doing it (Ericson, 1992).

The view that the police are ineffective in the prevention of crime is also supported by a large amount of research. The classic studies of foot patrols in Newark, New Jersey (Pate et al., 1986) and of vehicle patrols in Kansas City (Kelling et al. 1974) each found that changing the levels of policing had no effect on reducing crime. A similar study by Fisk (1970) found no evidence that increases in the number of patrol cars led to crime reduction and a more recent study by Bennett (1991) showed no evidence that increases in time spent patrolling reduced reported victimisations or police-recorded crime.

The kinds of research evidence cited above certainly appear to support the belief that the police have a limited role in crime prevention. Nevertheless, there are other research studies which have arrived at more positive conclusions.

The most encouraging research findings have derived from studies of targeted policing strategies. Targeted strategies have been referred to by a number of different names. The term police "crackdown" has been used to describe a sudden increase in some kind of law enforcement activity which is targeted on a particular type of person, offence, or place (Sherman, 1990). These strategies have also been referred to as proactive "crime attack" strategies (Sherman, 1986). A broader range of strategies is encompassed under the headings of "focused" or directed" patrols (Chatterton, 1989; Burrows, 1988) or "specific" patrols (Sherman, 1992). The main elements

which these strategies have in common is that they are all proactive and all have the effect of concentrating crime prevention efforts onto particular targets of crime, criminals, places or victims.

Evidence from published evaluations and other sources have produced some encouraging findings. A recent review of the literature on police "crackdowns" concluded that fifteen of the eighteen programmes investigated showed signs of initial deterrent effects and two of them showed signs of long-term deterrent effects (Sherman, 1990). Another review by the same author of specific policing strategies directed at offenders, places, times and victims as targets also showed examples of programme effectiveness (Sherman, 1992). Studies which have examined the effects of saturation patrols have also provided some favourable findings (Schwartz & Clarren, 1977). Similar successes have been identified in a study of policing an alcohol-free zone in the city centre of Coventry in England which showed a reduction in the number of incivilities reported in the area (Ramey, 1990). Another study of policing an alcohol-free zone in Sweden also showed a reduction in drunkenness and disorderly behaviour following the implementation of the programme (Bjor et al., 1992).

The idea that concentrating and focusing crime prevention efforts onto specific high-risk targets might be more effective than dispersing these efforts across a wide range or targets has an intuitive appeal. It also has some empirical support from recent fundamental research which has shown substantial clustering in terms of offences, offenders and victims. This research has shown that offences tend to be clustered into a relatively small number of locational "hot spots" (Sherman, 1992); offending tends to be clustered among a relatively small number of offenders (West & Farrington, 1977); and victimisation tends to be clustered among a relatively small number of victims (Farrell, 1992).

However, there is still little known about the use of these strategies or their effectiveness. In order to explore the potential value of these programmes more work needs to be done in identifying and conceptualising these kinds of strategies and tactics and in evaluating their effectiveness.

The current paper aims to explore the first of these two issues by discussing the findings of a recent national survey of police strategies and tactics operating in England and Wales.

THE NATIONAL SURVEY OF POLICE STRATEGIES AND TACTICS

The national survey of policing strategies and tactics was part of a larger survey of community-oriented policing in England and Wales conducted in 1990 (Bennett & Lupton, 1990).

Methods

The principal aim of the methods was to collect information on policing "strategies" and "tactics" which in some way benefitted the local community (e.g. reduced crime, detected offenders or provided reassurance). The meaning of the terms "strategies" and "tactics" was not differentiated as it was hoped that the officers completing the questionnaire would include everything which they thought fell within the definition of either term. Nevertheless, it is necessary to comment briefly on the way in which the terms are used in this paper.

The concepts of "strategies" and "tactics" have been defined in various ways in the literature. In a broad sense "strategies" are regarded as generally formulated plans of actions while "tactics" are regarded as more specific plans of action. Felson refers to "strategies" and "tactics" as military terms with the term "strategy"

referring to an overall plan and the term "tactic" referring to the specific method for carrying out the "strategy" (Felson, 1992).

The definition which has informed the current paper is taken from the Oxford English Dictionary which refers to the terms in their original military sense but makes a distinction between "strategies" which involve the deployment of troops and setting the conditions of contact with the enemy and "tactics" which refer to actions taken after contact with the enemy has been made.

This definition of the terms "strategies" and "tactics" can be applied to policing programmes. For example, a policing "strategy" to prevent crime might be to allocate a team of officers to a residential area (i.e. a deployment plan before contact with the community has been made) while a policing "tactic" to prevent crime might be for the team of officers to arrest known offenders operating in the area (i.e. an action plan after contact with the community has been made).

However, in practice the distinction between deployment plans and action plans is often difficult to make and does not always help conceptually (especially when other typologies of categorisation are used simultaneously). Hence, while acknowledging that there are differences between "strategies" and "tactics" the following discussion for simplicity refers to all policing programmes as "strategies".

Details on policing strategies and tactics (henceforth strategies) were collected by distributing a self-administered questionnaire to representatives of every police division (or sub-division when no divison existed) in the country. In total 40 out of the 43 police forces in England and Wales were included in the survey and a completed questionnaire was returned from 297 of the 304 eligible divisions or subdivisions (98%).

The divisional or sub-divisional (henceforth divisional) respondents were asked to write details of every proactive policing initiative currently operating in their division. The questionnaire included a preamble to the section which outlined which kind of programmes should be included in the replies. An extract from part of this section of the questionnaire is shown below:

> The aim of this section is to find out about any special measures currently operating within the division which might affect the quality of the police service to the community within its area.
>
> The measures included in this section:
>
> (1) should be in some way "different" from routine methods of using patrol officers;
>
> (2) should in some way affect or aim to affect the deployment, organisation or operation of patrol officers; and
>
> (3) should in some way benefit the community being policed (rather than designed specifically to make policing easier or cheaper).
>
> Please write below in the space provided details of all policing "strategies" and "tactics" currently operating in this division which you think fall into the categories described above.

The questionnaire included space for a programme name and about ten ruled lines for the programme details. The respondents could include any number of programmes which they thought fitted our criteria of inclusion.

The survey resulted in details on over 1,000 policing programmes currently operational in police force areas during the period of the research.

Validity and reliability

The remainder of the paper is based on what was reported in the completed ques-

tionnaires. Hence, it is relevant to comment on the nature of the replies received.

The first point concerns the nature of the information provided about each programme. The respondents typically provided a name for each programme and about six lines of text explaining the programme. There were no rules given on what the text should cover as it was largely unknown what kinds of programmes would be revealed by the survey. Hence, the information provided in the programme summaries varied. However, most summaries included information on the key programme elements (programme type, target and objectives) and the following analysis has been confined to these specific pieces of information.

A second and related point concerns the nature of the programmes discussed in the paper. The programmes and programme elements described in the following analysis derived from textual descriptions. Strictly speaking, it would be necessary to qualify most statements about programmes and programme elements with the phrase, "it was reported that" a programme or programme element existed. In order to avoid this repetition the qualification is sometimes omitted (e.g. the statement "the majority of programmes were targeted on crime and disorder" might be used in preference to the statement "in the majority of programmes summaries it was reported that the programmes were targeted on crime and disorder").

The third point concerns counting programmes. In the following analysis the programmes have been categorised and counted. It is not intended that the count of programmes should represent a reliable estimate of the actual number of different kinds of programmes in existence. It is possible that some programmes existed which were not included in the completed questionnaire. It is also possible that one of a type of programme was included in the questionnaire which in a sense "stood in for" a number of programmes of a similar type.

There are a number of reasons for counting the number of programmes even though the counts might not be reliable. First, the number of programmes counted provide a minimum (or an "at least") score of the number of programmes in existence. This argument would also hold true on the occasions when one or a small number of programmes were used to "stand in for" a larger number of programmes. Second, the number of programmes referred to can provide an estimate of the proportion of each type of programme in existence. A difference in proportions would not be considered important when only small variations existed between programme types. However, when the difference in proportions was very large, attention might be drawn to this fact.

The fourth point concerns the objectives of the research and the analysis. The primary purpose of the analysis is to attempt to conceptualise, categorise, and describe the main programme types used by the police to tackle crime and disorder as revealed by the survey. Hence, the research concerns primarily exploration and hypothesis generation rather than hypothesis testing. The current research cannot test the validity of conceptualisations and descriptions discussed in the paper nor the reliability of the frequency estimates. In order to do this it would be necessary to carry out another and different kind of research project.

POLICING STRATEGIES AND TACTICS

The primary aim of the paper is to draw on the information generated by the National Survey of Police Strategies and Tactics to conceptualise and describe the range of policing strategies and tactics used by the police to control crime and disorder.

The presentation part of the paper is divided into two main parts. The first part concerns what the police alone do to prevent crime and disorder. The second part concerns what the police do in combination with others to prevent crime and disorder.

POLICE STRATEGIES AND TACTICS INVOLVING THE POLICE WORKING ALONE

The programmes which have been identified as strategies and tactics which the police alone do include many of the programmes described above under the headings of "crackdowns" and targeted patrols. While these programmes could be categorised in a number of different ways an obvious choice is to categorise them (as they have already been categorised in the literature) in terms of the target or the focus of the programme. In the following analysis these programmes have been grouped primarily in terms of the four main targets to which they were directed: places, offences offenders and victims.

The total number of strategies within each target type is shown in Table 1.

TABLE 1. *Type of patrol strategies*

Category	n	%
Location-oriented	232	46.9
Offence-oriented	198	40.0
Offender-oriented	28	5.7
Victim-oriented	37	7.5
	495	100.1

BENNETT/POLICE STRATEGIES AND TACTICS FOR CONTROLLING CRIME AND DISORDER

The table shows that a total of 495 strategies could be classified as representing proactive attempts to control crime or disorder and involving the police operating (for the most part) alone. The table also shows that the most frequently reported strategies were targeted at specific locations (47 %) or specific offences (40 %).

Tables 2 and 3 show the number of each type of strategy for all forces grouped into four categories based on the total number of officers allocated to the force. Table 2 shows, as might be expected, that the larger forces reported a larger number of each type of policing strategy than the smaller forces. Table 3 shows the number of strategies calculated as a rate per 1,000 officers and per 1,000 population of the police force area. The table shows that after controlling for force and population size the number of strategies reported is fairly even across police force areas.

TABLE 2. *Type of strategy by police force strength total number of officers allocated to the force*

Strength	Location oriented	Offence oriented	Offender oriented	Victim oriented
High	132	89	19	24
Medium-High	43	57	9	8
Medium-Low	20	35	0	2
Low	37	17	0	3
Total	232	198	28	37

TABLE 3. *Number of strategies per thousand officers and per thousand population of police force areas by strength (total number of officers allocated to the force)*

Strength or Population of police force area	Number of strategies per 1,000 officers	Number of strategies per 1,000 population
High	40.8	0.12
Medium-High	48.7	0.10
Medium-Low	39.9	0.08
Low	52.8	0.11

The remainder of this section examines in detail each of the four primary types of target on which the strategies focus: (1) location-oriented strategies, (2) offence-oriented strategies, (3) offender-oriented strategies, and (4) victim-oriented strategies.

LOCATION-ORIENTED STRATEGIES

The term location-oriented strategy is applied to those programmes which focus on crime and disorder clusters at particular locations.

Table 4 shows five main categories of location to which these programmes were targeted and the number of strategies allocated to each of these categories. The most frequently reported locational "hot spots" were town centre areas and residential areas (accounting for over 70% of all locational strategies). The remainder comprised strategies aimed at public places, out-of-town areas, and other high-crime areas.

BENNETT/POLICE STRATEGIES AND TACTICS FOR CONTROLLING CRIME AND DISORDER

TABLE 4. *Type of location-oriented patrol strategies*

Type of strategy	Forces n	Strategies n	%
Town centre areas	32	72	31.0
Residential areas	26	93	40.1
Public places	13	21	9.1
Out-of-town areas	15	26	11.2
High-crime areas	12	20	8.6
All combined*	39	232	100.0

* Multiple responses possible (e.g. 32 forces reported at least one town centre area strategy while 26 forces reported at least one residential area strategy).
Source: National Survey of Policing Strategies and Tactics.

Table 4 also shows the number and percentage of forces reporting at least one of each of the five types of "hot spot" patrol strategies. The table shows that at least 80 % of all police forces were currently using town centre strategies and that at least 65 % of all forces operated some kind of proactive residential area strategy. About one-third of all forces reported each of the remaining locational policing strategies. All bar one (39 of 40) of the police force areas reported operating at least one type of locational strategy at the time of the survey.

TABLE 5. *Breakdown of type of location-oriented patrol strategies*

Town centre areas	Residential areas	Public places	Out-of-town areas	High-crime areas
town centres	housing estates	universities	villages	streets
		hospitals	tourist areas	beats
shopping areas	specific communities	military buildings		problem areas
			holiday areas	
licensed premises	high rise areas	warehouses		
leisure areas	red light districts	car parks		
		football stadia		
food bars		schools		
		public parks		

BENNETT/POLICE STRATEGIES AND TACTICS FOR CONTROLLING CRIME AND DISORDER

A breakdown of the various types of locational strategy is shown in Table 5. The table includes all the main types of programmes reported in the survey summaries. The main town centre strategies comprised strategies which were described as being focused on town centre areas (without further elaboration) or to shopping areas. Strategies targeted on residential areas were typically allocated to specific housing estates or other special housing areas (such as areas comprising ethnic minorities or areas owned by local authorities). The survey revealed a number of strategies targeted on highly specific public places such as local universities, hospitals and military buildings. Strategies aimed at out-of-town areas were generally focused on the centres of villages which had become the location for local youths to hang about. Other out-of-town areas included holiday areas and tourist attractions. Strategies located at specific high-crime areas most frequently were deployed at specific roads or streets or intersections.

A brief description of some of these programmes is given below.

Town centres

Town centre programmes comprised three main types of policing strategy: police shops, high-profile patrols, and saturation patrols.

The main function of town centre police shops (as defined here and as described in the police returns) was to advertise crime prevention literature and to provide crime prevention advice to members of the public using the town centre area. Town centre police shops were often located in mobile and temporary offices such as caravans or trailers.

Town centre high-profile patrols typically comprised a small number of uniformed officers (e.g. two to four) who patrolled the town centre area (covering a broader area than just shopping areas)

with the primary function of maintaining order or providing reassurance to the public, as well as providing a full police service when necessary. These patrols were often time specific and limited to the weekends or just Saturdays.

Town centre saturation patrols were more frequently described as having a deterrent and order maintenance function. Typically, they comprised a carrier van of two or three cars which patrolled the town centre area during "hot times" such as weekends and at the time when people begin returning home during the evening after drinking or visiting other leisure and entertainment centres. Their main aim was to deal with any "trouble" that occurred during these busy times.

Shopping areas

The descriptions of shopping area strategies suggested that at least three main types of strategy were used to police shopping areas: police shops, police teams, and high-profile patrols.

Police shops in town centre shopping areas were often located in actual shops or in offices made available to the police by a consortium of shop-owners or by the local council. The main objectives with the shops were to provide a contact point for the general public and to provide a base for policing the area. Police shops were typically time specific, operating only during shop opening hours.

Police teams operating in shopping areas usually comprised plainclothed squads which had the task of preventing and detecting crimes associated with shopping complexes, such as shop lifting. Covert teams were sometimes permanently deployed in a shopping area and sometimes deployed during periods of special need such as during the Christmas period or at weekends. Their duties sometimes included training shop staff and providing crime prevention advice to shop managers.

High-profile patrols in shopping areas generally provided a reassurance function for people while they were using the shopping area and provided a preventive and deterrent function in relation to potential offenders. They also provided a general police service during the periods when the officers patrolled the area.

Residential areas

Strategies for policing targeted residential areas comprised a full range of programmes. The most frequently mentioned were: police shops, police surgeries, police teams, high-profile patrols, and general-purpose patrols (saturation patrols were less frequently mentioned as operating on a routine basis in housing estates).

Housing estate police shops tended to differ from town centre police shops (which were mainly used for displaying crime prevention advice) and shopping area police shops (which were predominantly used as local contact points). Police shops in residential areas most frequently consisted of office or dwelling accommodation which the police used primarily as a base or as a contact point for the public. The main objectives with police shops reported in the programme summaries were to provide a full police service to the local community. The use of police shops on housing estates was typically associated with the permanent or semi-permanent deployment of officers to the area.

Police surgeries differed from police shops in that they were open to the public for a relatively short period of time. Police shops were normally open to the public during office hours or up to two shifts per day. Police surgeries were normally open to the public for just one or two hours one day of the week. The main objectives of police surgeries noted in the police returns were to provide an opportunity for the public to meet the police

and to discuss local problems.

The concept of police teams is used here to refer to the permanent or semi-permanent deployment of two or more officers to a residential area. Police teams were typically directed to tackle a full range of policing functions in a particular residential area although they were also deployed to tackle particular crime problems. The police team differed from officers working from a local police shop in that they were deployed from the sub-divisional or divisional police station rather than from a local base.

High-profile patrols usually were made up of two or more foot patrol officers who patrolled residential areas in order to provide public reassurance or to prevent crime. The work of the officers was typically described as providing a visible presence and speaking to members of the community. They differed from the police teams and police shops in that they generally confined their activities to patrolling the streets rather than engaging in problem-oriented or other proactive police work.

The category of general-purpose patrols has been included here as many residential areas used (instead of, or in addition to, the above strategies) community beat officers who provided a more general policing function. Beat officers were typically permanently or semi-permanently attached to a beat to provide high-profile patrols and a range of other police services.

Public places

The category of strategies directed at public places covered specific public places rather than general public places such as town centre areas and shopping areas. The term is used here to describe strategies directed at single buildings or single locations. The types of strategy tended to be limited mainly to high-profile patrols and (less frequently) police shops.

High-profile patrols were typically deployed to specific permanent or temporary locational "hot spots" such as particular car parks and public parks as a means of deterring and preventing crime. These patrols were also used as a means of providing a visible presence and public reassurance at vulnerable locations such as hospital complexes, military establishments and university campuses.

The police sometimes established a police shop or police office at these sites as a permanent base. Police bases of this kind were established in particular hospitals and particular schools which were thought of as troublesome in some way.

OFFENCE-ORIENTED STRATEGIES

The term offence-oriented strategies is applied to strategies in which the offence (rather than the location) is described as the primary target.

TABLE 6. *Type of offence-oriented patrol strategies*

Type of strategy	Forces n	Strategies n	%
Crime-oriented	29	77	38.9
Disorder-oriented	26	69	34.8
Problem-oriented	29	52	26.3
All combined*	37	198	100.0

* Notes as Table 4.

Table 6 shows the total number of strategies defined as offence-oriented programmes and the distribution between the three main categories. The table shows that the distribution of crime, disorder and problem-oriented strategies is fairly even. It also shows the distribution among police forces in England and Wales. Over 90 % of forces reported at least one offence-oriented programme in operation at the time of the survey.

TABLE 7. *Breakdown of type of offence-oriented patrol strategies*

Crimes	Disorder	Problems
robbery	nuisance	unspecified
burglary	vice	
vehicle crime	drink-related	
traffic offences	drugs-related	

Table 7 provides a breakdown of the various sub-categories of offence-oriented strategies. The table shows that the most frequently reported crime-oriented strategies were targeted at the offences of robbery, burglary, and vehicle crime. Disorder-oriented programmes were most frequently focused on drink and drug-related behaviour and on general nuisance. The category of problem-oriented strategies covers all references to strategies directed at particular problems which were not specified in the police returns. These were typically described as programmes targeted at "specific problems as they arose" and almost certainly included the same kinds of crime and disorder problems as noted above.

The detailed information provided on each programme can be used to identify some of the key programme types. A brief description of some of these programmes is shown below.

Burglary

One of the most frequently mentioned strategies for tackling burglary was to use a police team. The names given to these teams varied and included: burglary units, squads and teams. They were typically composed of a small group of officers who worked full-time for either short or long periods dealing with burglary wherever it occured. The work of these teams included plain-clothes operations and general information gathering and dissemination. Their primary stated function was detection and prevention.

Burglary-oriented strategies also included high-profile patrols deployed in order to provide a visible presence in areas which were experiencing problems with burglary. High-profile patrols also operated in collaboration with the CID and other units in providing and sharing information.

Vehicle crime

The most frequently mentioned offence on which offence-oriented strategies were targeted was vehicle crime. These also could be divided into police teams and high-profile patrols.

Vehicle crime teams were also referred to by a variety of names including: auto crime squads, anti-car theft units and vehicle crime teams. Typically, they were charged with investigating vehicle crime, obtaining information about crimes against vehicles and disseminating it to other uniformed and CID officers. Vehicle crime teams were frequently cited as being involved in observation and surveillance activities which often involved plain-clothes operations and stake-outs. The primary objectives of these programmes were detection and prevention.

The use of high-profile patrols to tackle vehicle crime was mentioned much less frequently than the use of police teams. High-profile patrols were directed to whatever areas were currently experiencing particular crime problems with the primary objective of deterring potential offenders.

Nuisance

The strategies used to combat various kinds of disorder were similar to those used to combat various kinds of crimes. The category of disorder strategies targeted against "nuisances" covered a range of behaviours including noise from youths riding motor cycles to late-night disturbances by people returning home from evening entertainments.

Strategies aimed at general nuisance typically made use of police teams or general–purpose (response) strategies. Police teams tackled disorder offences by collecting information and making inquiries including speaking to the people involved. The most frequent strategy mentioned was to deploy additional generalpurpose patrols with a small number of officers to deal with (react to) disorder situations as they arose.

OFFENDER-ORIENTED STRATEGIES

The term offender-oriented strategy is used to describe strategies which were targeted of specific known offenders or offender groups.

BENNETT/POLICE STRATEGIES AND TACTICS FOR CONTROLLING CRIME AND DISORDER

TABLE 8. *Type of offender-oriented patrol strategies*

Type of strategy	Forces n	Strategies n	%
Targeted criminals	8	11	39.3
Offence-specific criminals	4	5	17.9
Potential criminals	7	12	42.9
All combined*	16	28	100.1

* Notes as Table 4.

The number of offender-oriented strategies identified in the survey is shown in Table 8. The term "targeted criminals" has been used to refer to programmes in which specific individual or specific groups of offenders were referred to in the programme details (e.g. a programme directed towards "suspects" or "known criminals" or "mobile criminals" who travelled large distances to commit their crimes). The term "offence-specific criminals" has been used to describe programmes aimed at catching offenders associated with the commission of a particular kind of offence (e.g. a programme directed at shoplifters). The category of "potential criminals" is used to refer to groups who were in danger of becoming criminals (e.g. truants). 40 % of police forces reported at least one offender-oriented policing strategy in operation at the time of the survey.

A breakdown of some of the key type of offender-oriented strategy is shown in Table 9. A brief summary of some of these programmes is given below.

TABLE 9. *Breakdown of type of offender-oriented patrol strategies*

Targeted criminals	Offence-specific criminals	Potential criminals
suspects	drug dealers	truants
known criminals	shoplifters	beggars
mobile criminals	car thieves	youths
	disqualified drivers	strangers

Suspects

All of the programmes described as targeted against suspected or known offenders made use of some kind of police team. These were typically a small number of uniformed officers working in collaboration with a small number of CID officers. The unit or team was charged with gathering information on individual suspected offenders. This was used to detect offences and arrest offenders. The teams might also be involved in surveillance operations and targeting or tracking individual offenders.

BENNETT/POLICE STRATEGIES AND TACTICS FOR CONTROLLING CRIME AND DISORDER

Shoplifters

There were very few programmes mentioned in the police returns which comprised offender-oriented strategies aimed at specific offence types. The most frequent use of this kind of strategy was in relation to shoplifters. The offence category "shoplifting" defined the group of offenders "shoplifters" as the target of the strategy. The only programmes mentioned as a means of tackling "shoplifters" were police teams or squads which worked in plain-clothes with the specific aim of arresting offenders in the targeted offence group.

Truants

One of the most frequently mentioned offender-oriented strategies directed at potential offenders concerned truants. Either police teams or general-purpose patrols were used. Police teams comprised a small number of officers who searched an area during school hours looking for potential truants. Children who were stopped and identified as truants were returned to their school or to their parents. General-purpose patrols were also used to perform a similar function during the course of their normal patrol duties. Their task was essentially the same and involved looking out for children of school age who were not in school during school hours.

VICTIM-ORIENTED STRATEGIES

The term victim-oriented strategies is used to refer to programmes which aimed to prevent crime by targeting known victims of crime. Table 10 shows that the small number of victim-oriented strategies identified were fairly evenly distributed across the four programme subtypes. Just over one-third of police forces reported at least one victim-oriented strategy during the period of the survey.

TABLE 10. *Type of victim-oriented patrol strategies*

Type of strategy	Forces n	Strategies n	%
Domestic violence	3	8	21.6
Elderly people	8	10	27.0
Racial groups	2	6	16.2
Victims (unspec.)	9	13	35.1
All combined*	14	37	99.9

* Notes as Table 4.

Only three distinct sub-categories could be identified from the police returns: programmes aimed at victims of domestic violence, programmes aimed at elderly victims and programmes aimed at victims of racial violence.

Domestic violence

Some forces tackled domestic violence by forming specialist domestic violence units which apart from assisting the victim also provided a base for gathering information and for taking action to prevent repeat attacks. Domestic violence units sometimes included female officers who gave advice to victims. They also gave advice and made presentations at local meetings as part of a general educational function.

Domestic violence was also tackled using general-purpose patrols. Individual officers were sometimes charged with responding to incidents of domestic violence. Some forces also trained all patrol officers to take positive action in cases of domestic violence.

Elderly victims

Elderly victims were targeted by some forces by using police teams or units who collected information on crimes against elderly people including burglary and deception. This information was used to detect and prevent crimes against the elderly. Elderly victims were also targeted using general-purpose patrols which were given the task of patrolling near to the homes of elderly people at risk of victimisation in order to prevent crime and to reassure the residents. Other tactics included general-purpose patrols who made contact with elderly people and offered them advice on security and other matters.

Racial groups

Racial groups were targeted by some forces using either police teams or general-purpose patrols. Police teams were used primarily to collect and disseminate information on racial attacks and to conduct follow-up visits on victims. General-purpose patrols (mainly permanent beat officers) were also used to follow up cases of racial attack and to provide back-up to current investigations. General-purpose patrols were also used to supply information packages to victims of racial attack in order to reassure them and to prevent repeat attacks.

POLICE STRATEGIES AND TACTICS INVOLVING THEIR WORKING WITH OTHERS

The programmes identified as strategies and tactics for controlling crime and disorder which involved the police working with others included many programmes which might be thought of as traditional crime prevention strategies. The returns from the national survey revealed over 500 programmes which fell under this heading. In the following analysis the programmes have been categorised into strategies which involved collaboration with the general public, with specific individual groups and with multiple groups (multi-agency cooperation).

BENNETT/POLICE STRATEGIES AND TACTICS FOR CONTROLLING CRIME AND DISORDER

TABLE 11. *Police strategies and tactics involving the police working with others*

Category		n	%
General public			
Crime prevention panels		23	4.4
Neighbourhood watch		90	17.3
Crime prevention campaigns/advice		27	5.2
Home security surveys/advice		13	2.5
Property marking		16	3.1
	Subtotal	169	32.5
Specific individual groups			
Licensed premises projects		84	16.2
Business projects/advice		55	10.6
Youth projects		51	9.8
Schools projects		87	16.8
	Subtotal	277	53.4
Specific multi-agency groups		73	14.1
Total		519	100.0

A summary of the programmes identified and their frequency counts is shown in Table 11. The main programmes involving the general public included few surprises and covered the principle community crime prevention measures including crime prevention panels, neighbourhood watch, crime prevention campaigns involving the general community, home security surveys and property marking.

The main projects involving specific targets included those concerning licensed premises, businesses, youth programmes and schools. Programmes involving multi-agencies were wide ranging and included many of those reported in other sections as well as some additional programmes which required collaboration between a number of agencies.

TABLE 12. *Number of strategies per thousand officers and per thousand population of police force areas by strength (total number of officers allocated to the force)*

Strength or population of police force area	Number of strategies	Number of strategies per 1,000 officers	Number of strategies per 1,000 population
	n=519		
High	210	32.3	.09
Medium-High	149	61.5	.13
Medium-Low	78	54.6	.11
Low	82	75.1	.15

Table 12 shows the numbers of strategies reported among forces in terms of the total number of officers and the total population within the different police force areas. A straight count of the programmes reveals, as might be expected,

that the forces with larger numbers of established officers reported a greater number of programmes than forces with lower number of officers. After controlling for force size in terms of number of officers and number of the population it

BENNETT/POLICE STRATEGIES AND TACTICS FOR CONTROLLING CRIME AND DISORDER

can be seen that the number of strategies reported tended to be inversely correlated with police force size. The larger police forces recorded fewer programmes (expressed as a rate per 1,000 officers or per 1,000 population) than the smaller forces. While the frequency counts might not provide reliable estimates of the actual number of programmes within each

police force area, this distinct trend is worth noting. One possible explanation for the relationship is that larger forces have a larger reactive workload which results in proportionately fewer resources being used for proactive tasks (although neither the phenomena nor the cause of the phenomena can be verified from the current data).

TABLE 13. *The number and percentage of forces reporting police strategies and tactics involving the police working with others*

Category	n	%
General public		
Crime prevention panels	17	42.5
Neighbourhood watch	33	82.5
Crime prevention campaigns/advice	17	42.5
Home security surveys/advice	10	25.0
Property marking	11	27.5
Specific individual groups		
Licensed premises projects	30	75.0
Business projects/advice	20	50.0
Youth projects	21	52.5
Schools projects	31	77.5
Specific multi-agency groups	27	67.5

The total number of forces recording examples of the various types of collaboration in crime prevention is shown in Table 13. The table shows that over three-quarters of all forces reported at least one neighbourhood watch programme, licensed premises project and schools project. Over half reported activities (in addition to the above) consisting of business projects, youth projects and multi-agency programmes. Overall, the table shows that a large number of forces were engaged in a large number of community crime prevention strategies and tactics during the period of the survey.

Crime prevention panels

Crime prevention panels consisted of small groups of people who worked as a committee in analysing local crime patterns and in recommending appropriate

crime prevention actions. The police returns indicated a fairly even division between "senior" crime prevention panels involving adults and "junior" crime prevention panels involving schools and young people. The senior panels typically comprised various combinations of people drawn from the police, local residents, school, social workers, probation officers, local council officials and representatives of business. The junior panels were typically organised within schools using local children who made recommendations about youth crime, and other problems concerning particular schools.

Neighbourhood watch

Neighbourhood watch is one of the most prolific community crime prevention programmes in Britain in terms of its level of community support. While only

90 discrete references to neighbourhood watch programmes were found in the returns most of these referred to more than one programmes and the figure of over 80 % of all forces operating neighbourhood watch schemes is a more realistic estimate (although probably still an underestimate) of the total involvement in the programme. The schemes reported in the returns covered the typical model of neighbourhood watch which consisted of police collaboration with local communities in looking out for suspicious behaviour and reporting this to the police. The schemes also included less typical community-based programmes such as university watch and hospital watch.

Crime prevention campaigns/advice

Crime prevention campaigns and advice (excluding home security surveys and advice discussed in the next section) included a range of activities involving collaboration between the police and the community. This category differed from crime prevention advice given in town centre police shops in that the programmes were focused on the community rather than on particular locations.

One common method of informing and educating the public made use of various kinds of crime prevention displays. These were sometimes mobile displays using a police bus or police caravan which travelled to various locations and provided a range of information about security and crime prevention in general. Displays were also based in fixed locations such as shops or offices or in vacant houses in residential areas. The display method not only provided information for the public but also provided an opportunity for the police to speak to members of the public who showed an interest in the display. Other crime prevention campaigns included various vehicle crime campaigns such as writing to owners of cars left in an insecure state to inform

them of the dangers of vehicle crime together with various burglary campaigns such as delivering audio tapes to householders informing them of the risks of burglary and the precautions that the might take.

Home security campaigns

Home security campaigns are dealt with here as a separate category because of the unique nature of the programme. Typically, campaigns involved community beat officers or other specialist officers (e.g. crime prevention officers) visiting the homes of residents and assessing their current level of security and offering advice on security hardware and security behaviour. Home security surveys usually were conducted only when a member of the public contacted the local police and requested one. However, some forces "flooded" particular high-crime areas with officers who travelled door-to-door offering home security advice.

Property marking

Property marking campaigns were often an integral part of neighbourhood watch schemes and were not always reported separately by the police in their returns. Nevertheless, a wide range of other kinds of property marking schemes were reported. One of the most frequent was bicycle marking schemes in which the police stamped the frame of the bicycle with a postcode or some other identifying mark. Other property marking campaigns included horse riding equipment stamping to reduce theft, motor vehicle coding by etching the vehicle number on the windscreen, boat and boat equipment marking schemes to prevent theft from harbours and residential property marking schemes which usually involved supplying householders with marker pens.

Licensed premises projects

One of the most frequently mentioned programmes directed at licensed premises was the "pub watch" scheme. This comprised an association between the licensees and the police which had various functions including an "early warning system" for crime and disorder. Licensees who observed drink-related disorder, drugs misuse or other kinds of criminal activity within or outside their public houses, were instructed to telephone or contact by radio-pager both other licensees in the area and the police. The pub watch schemes were usually set up and administered by the police with the objective of preventing and detecting alcohol-related offences.

Another frequent programme involving the police and licensed premises was supervision and site visits. The broad aim of police supervision of licensed premises is to ensure that the licensee conforms to the legislation on the sale of alcohol. However, supervision visits also had a broader function of generating a relationship between the police and the licensee, exchanging information and providing an opportunity to offer crime prevention advice.

Another scheme organised by the police in collaboration with managers of licensed premises was the use of identity cards. Identity card schemes were usually organised and supervised by the police with cards made available to young people so that they could authenticate their identity and age. This worked to the benefit of young people who were just at the legal age to purchase alcohol as they then had proof of identity and age and could enter licensed premises with impunity.

Business projects

The police also collaborated with shops and other businesses in developing "early warning schemes" similar to the pub watch schemes mentioned above. Schemes involving shopkeepers and business in the town centre and shopping areas were referred to as "shop watch", "store watch", or "business watch" schemes and involved staff working in business areas in informing the police and other shopkeepers and businesses of any signs of disorder or other criminal activity.

Various other "watch" schemes were used in relation to non-residential premises such as "industrial watch" (collaboration between the police and factory owners on industrial estates), "farm watch" (involving collaboration with and between farmers), "hotel watch" (relating to hoteliers) and many others including "marine watch", bank watch", "poacher watch" and "taxi watch".

Youth projects

The most frequently mentioned youth projects comprised some kind of collaboration between the police and young people in providing sporting or other activities. Popular schemes at the time of the survey were the "SPLASH" or "SPACE" projects which involved the police in organising activities and events for children during the summer holidays.

The police also provided a range of other sporting and outdoor activities including setting up youth clubs, involvement in the Duke of Edingburgh Award Schema, scout and military cadet services, camping and sailing schemes, swimming and hiking clubs, and football and boxing clubs.

Other police programmes for young people included police discos which aimed to provide alcohol-free and drug-free leisure facilities for young people. These were usually organised for juveniles under the age of 16 with various stated objectives including those of keeping children off the streets and away from crime and broader social functions.

In addition to activity-based programmes the police organised a number of educational programmes designed to educate children and young people away from criminal activities and into non-criminal activities. These educational programmes include drugs-prevention programmes, publicity material about drug use and community activities projecting moral messages by means of plays and pantomimes for young people.

Schools projects

Schools projects are dealt with here as a separate category because they were different from the youth programmes in that they were based at particular schools and involved different tactics. The main form of schools programmes involved representatives of the police (usually home beat officers) visiting local schools regularly and establishing a personal relationship with the teachers and pupils.

One element of this programme involved the police in giving presentations at schools on a number of issues concerning crime and crime prevention and general morality. The aim of the programmes was stated in the programme summaries as making young people aware of criminal activities and to prevent them from becoming involved. Broader objectives referred to in the returns included generating a general social awareness among young people and a sense of social responsibility.

Police visits to schools also had broader objectives including attempts by the police to break down barriers between the police and young people and attempts to show that the relationship between the police and young people could be non-confrontational.

Another general objective of the schools programmes was to set up a liaison with teaching staff as a means of gathering and disseminating information which might be used in a variety of ways.

The police and the schools also worked together to identify and to solve particular crime or disorder problems in specific schools.

Multi-agency cooperation

The programmes reported above comprised schemes which involved the police collaborating with one other agency to tackle specific problems. Many other programmes were described in the programme summaries which were referred to as multi-agency approaches which involved the police collaborating with a number of agencies. The programmes described below comprise schemes reported by the police either as multi-agency projects (and the number of agencies was unknown) or as schemes which were reported as involving more than one other agency.

The number of agencies (and other bodies) reported in the programme summaries as currently involved in multi-agency programmes with the police was wide ranging and included local authorities, probation, social services, education, pressure groups, voluntary associations, residents groups, the media, youth clubs, businesses, private security companies, taxi drivers, transport companies, hoteliers, political pressure groups and public service industries.

The number of problems tackled by multi-agency approaches was also wide ranging and covered many of the initiatives described earlier in this section. The problems identified were mainly concerned with crime, disorder, quality of life, offenders and victims. Programmes targeted on offences included general prevention of crime and disorder (non-specific), burglary prevention and traffic law enforcement. Those targeted on disorder included drug and alcohol abuse. Programmes targeted on the quality of life included fear of crime, general statements about the quality of life, litter, general cleanliness and graffiti. Those targeted on (potential) offenders included youth projects, youth clubs and truants. Finally, programmes targeted on victims included domestic violence and racially-motivated crime.

CONCLUSION

The main aim of this paper has been to explore, describe, conceptualise and categorise some of the programmes currently implemented by the police to reduce crime and disorder. The result of an analysis of data from a national survey of police forces in England and Wales has shown that the police use a large number of strategies and tactics. These include programmes which are implemented mainly by the police alone and programmes which are implemented mainly by the police in collaboration with others.

The programmes involving the police working alone comprise a large number of targeted patrols and "crackdowns" which are focused on particular "hot spot" locations, high-rate offences, high-rate offenders and high-risk victims. The research has shown that within each category there exists a number of quite distinct sub-categories of strategy involving a range of different structures and functions. In a general sense targeted patrol activities have received relatively little attention in the academic literature with most attention being paid to programmes where the police work with others.

The programmes where the police work with others include the more widely known crime prevention activities of the police, such as a large number of situational measures, e.g. security advice, property marking and neighbourhood watch. The programmes also embrace a large number of social measures including a complex array of youth projects designed to reduce offending or reduce offender development. While there is

some literature on some examples of these programmes, the research has shown that there are many versions of these programmes which have not been fully documented or evaluated.

There are a number of general findings and general conclusions which derive from the research.

The first point is that the view that the police no longer engage in crime prevention and (if they do) do no more than offer advice to others is incorrect. It would appear that in fact the police engage in a broad and complex range of crime prevention activities which might be thought of as the "hidden" face of crime prevention.

The second point is that there are a large number of policing strategies and tactics which have not been evaluated and, to a large extent, have not even been documented. It would seem that there is much to be gained from broadening the range of research evaluations to include the crime prevention work of the police to a greater extent than has been done in the past.

The third point concerns the potential effectiveness of policing strategies. The research evidence to date indicates that crime is clustered in terms of location, time, offender and victim. Targeted policing strategies are designed to make explicit use of these known characteristic of crime and in so doing offer a good chance of success. Focusing crime prevention efforts on high-rate places or on high-risk offenders and victims not only directs crime prevention efforts to where they are most needed but also it has the effect on concentrating crime prevention at a level which would not be feasible if applied more widely.

The fourth point concerns the issue of displacement. While the chance of preventing crime seems to be higher using targeted rather than general strategies, the likelihood of displacement also seems higher. For example, it is easy to imagine a group of young people being deterred from committing acts of vandalism in a public place or a group of drug dealers being deterred from open street dealing in a particular section of the town centre. It is also easy to imagine that these people would then simply move elsewhere and continue their deviant or criminal acts. The phenomenon of displacement need not, however, undermine the value of the policing strategy or the value of evaluative research into the policing strategy. It is possible that displacement (especially repeated displacement) might change the characteristics of the offending behaviour in some way which might make it less of a social problem. For example, repeated displacement might result in some kind of "weakening" of the original deviant activity as it is displaced from ideal to less than ideal conditions. The possible benevolent effects of displacement have been discussed in more detail by Barr and Pease (1990).

Additionally, the phenomenon of rapid repeated prevention and subsequent displacement could offer an excellent research opportunity to investigate both phenomena in ways which could not be done with programmes which might take years to become effective. The benefits of expanding knowledge about these two processes would not only advance understanding but also would inform preventive efforts.

The fifth point concerns the nature of research that could be done on police strategies and tactics to reduce crime and disorder. The current paper has attempted to document and explore these programmes from data collected from a larger research project. There is a great deal more research that could be done which might be able to tackle specific issues more systematically than could be done within the framework of the present research. Such specific research might, for example, focus on time of day for the programme, whether officers were permanent or temporary, life-time length of the programme, objectives of the programme, details of the programme target, number of officers involved and the effectiveness of the programme. Information of this kind could help to generate an effective typology of policing strategies and might help a fuller range of policing programmes to enter into current debates about crime prevention.

REFERENCES

Barr, R. & Pease, K. (1990). Crime placement, displacement and deflection. In: Tonry, M. & Morris, N., eds. *Crime and justice: A review of research.* Vol. 12. Chicago: University of Chicago Press.

Bennett, T. H. (1991). The effectiveness of a police-initiated fear reducing strategy. *British Journal of Criminology.* 31: 1–14.

Bennett, T. H. & Lupton, R. (1990). *National review of community-oriented patrols: Report.* Report to the Home Office Research and Planning Unit. Cambridge: Institute of Criminology.

Bennett, T. H. & Lupton, R. (1992). A national activity survey of police work, *The Howard Journal of Criminal Justice,* 31: 200–223.

Bennett, T. H. & Lupton, R. (1992). A national survey of the organisation and use of community constables. *British Journal of Criminology* 32: 167–182.

Bjor, J., Knutsson, J. & Kühlhorn, E. (1992). The celebration of Midsummer Eve in Sweden: A study in the art of preventing collective disorder. *Security Journal* 3: 169–173.

Brown, D. & Iles, S. (1985). *Community constables: A study of a policing initiative.* Home Office Research and Planning Unit Paper No. 30. Home Office. London: HMSO.

Burrows, J. & Lewis, H. (1988). *Directing patrol work: A study of uniformed policing.* Home Office Research Study No. 99. London: HMSO.

Chatterton, M. & Rogers, M. (1989). Focused patrol. In: Morgan, R. & Smith, D. J. eds. *Coming to terms with policing: Perspectives on policy.* London: Routledge.

Ericson, R. (1992). *Community policing as communications policing.* Paper presented at a conference at the University of Heidelberg.

Farrell, G. (1992). Multiple victimisation: Its extent and significance. *International Review of Victimology* 2: 85–102.

Felson, M. (1992). Routine activities and crime prevention: Armchair concepts and practical action. *Studies on Crime and Crime Prevention* 1: 30–34.

Fisk, D. (1970). *The Indianapolis Police Fleet Plan.* Washington D.C.: Urban Institute.

Harvey, L., Grimshaw, P. & Pease, K. (1989). Crime prevention delivery: The work of crime prevention officers. In: Morgan, R. & Smith, D., eds. *Coming to terms with policing.* London: Routledge.

Johnston, V., Shapland, J. & Wiles, P. (1993). *Developing police crime prevention: Management and organisational change.* Police Research Group. Crime Prevention Unit Series. Paper 41. London: Home Office.

Kelling, G. L., Pate, T., Dieckman, D. & Brown, C. E. (1974). *The Kansas City Preventive Patrol Experiment.* Washington D. C.: Police Foundation.

Pate, A., Wycoff, M. A., Skogan, W. & Sherman, L. W. (1986). *Reducing fear of crime in Houston and Newark: A summary report.* Washington D. C.: Police Foundation.

Ramsey, M. (1990). *Lagerland Lost: An experiment in keeping drinkers off the streets in Coventry.* Home Office Crime Prevention Unit Paper No. 22. London: Home Office.

Schwartz, A. L. & Clarren, S. N. (1977). *The Cincinnati Team Policing Experiment: A summary report.* Police Foundation, Washington D. C.

Sherman, L. (1986). Police communities: what works?. In: Reiss, A. & Tonry, M., eds. *Communities and crime. Crime and justice: A review of research, Vol. 8.* Chicago: University of Chicago Press.

Sherman, L. (1990). Police crackdowns: Initial and residual deterrence. In: Tonry, M. & Morris, N., eds. *Crime and justice: a review of research, Vol. 12.* Chicago: University of Chicago Press.

Sherman, L. (1992). Policing and crime control. In: *Modern policing: Crime and justice, Volume 15.* Chicago: University of Chicago Press.

West, D. J. & Farrington, D. P. (1977). *Who becomes delinquent.* London: Heinemann.

Received July 1993

Trevor Bennett
University of Cambridge
Institute of Criminology
7 West Road
Cambridge CB3 9DT
United Kingdom

[9]

International Journal of the Sociology of Law 1996, **24**, 427–443

Sexual Offenders in the Community: Reflections on Problems of Law, Community and Risk Management in the U.S.A., England and Wales

BILL HEBENTON* and TERRY THOMAS†

University of Manchester and †Leeds Metropolitan University, U.K.

As new needs are defined and technologies refined, new ways of institutional categorizing, classifying, thinking and acting develop that demand police participation. (Ericson 1994: 154)

Introduction

In designing criminal justice and penal policy, we are not simply deciding how to deal with a group of people on the margins of society — whether to deter, reform or incapacitate them, and if so how. Nor are we merely deploying power or financial resources for penological ends. We are also, as David Garland has so eloquently argued, "at the same time defining ourselves and our society in ways which may be quite central to our cultural and political identity" (Garland 1990: 276). The representations projected by criminal justice and penal practice are not just threats aimed at offenders; they are also positive symbols which help produce subjectivities, forms of authority and social relations. It is in this context that the authors want to consider the nature of the 'response' in England, Wales and the U.S.A. to one group of offenders at the margins, namely convicted sexual offenders, and, in particular, the matter of their release back into the community.

Correspondence should be addressed to: Bill Hebenton, Lecturer in Criminology, School of Social Policy, Faculty of Economic and Social Studies, University of Manchester, Oxford Road, Manchester M13 9PL, U.K.

0194–6595/96/040427 + 17 $25.00/0

428   *W. Hebenton and T. Thomas*

In considering this issue, the authors suggest that current legal and policy responses to sexual offenders in the community both reflect and constitute some deeper and emerging transformations in contemporary society, in particular the social production and distribution of knowledge for 'risk' management in modern societies. In part, some recently completed field research, undertaken by the present authors last autumn in the U.S.A., is drawn upon.

The Nature of the Beast

Public concerns about mobile yet anonymous ex-offenders are not new. Radzinowicz and Hood in their magisterial survey of developing English penal policy in the Victorian era argue that the 19th century perception of a mass of offenders, mobile yet anonymous, fostered an escalating fear of a dangerous criminal class — vast, self-contained, self-perpetuating and largely irreclaimable (Radzinowicz & Hood 1990). They contextualize these concerns in relation to the abandonment of transportation to the colonies and its replacement with penal servitude, rapid urban growth and mobility and the expansion of the 'new' police. In respect of penal servitude, established in 1853, it was the intention that even though the period in separate confinement and the period of public works might be performed in this country, the period on 'licence to be at large' was to be spent in the colony. In the event, it became increasingly necessary for the period on licence to be spent at home in England.

Public confidence in this 'ticket-of-leave' system, as it was known, was extremely low, and those on licence were often harassed (Tobias 1972). As a policy option, it rapidly proved increasingly ineffectual, with the problem of incapacitating the habitual criminal through the granting and revoking of licences proving almost impossible in practice because of a lack of a central and national record system (see Radzinowicz & Hood 1990: 250). By 1868, a new strategy to effect the necessary 'supervision' of those on licence was presented as proposals to Parliament, with a proposed tightening up of leave conditions and registering of all those convicted of a crime on a national 'Habitual Criminals Register' (see Hebenton & Thomas 1993: Chapter 2 for an analysis of the limitations of these early 'tracking' arrangements). The flavour and tenor of the parliamentary debate on the 1869 Habitual Criminals Bill has, as evidenced shortly, a contemporary resonance. For example, the Earl of Kimberley introducing the Bill described the aim to "establish a complete system of communication throughout the country, so as to form a complete network of supervision of criminals in every part of the country" [*Hansard* [Lords] Vol CXCIV (194) February 26 col 341]. Speaking in the debate, Earl Shaftesbury agreed that "...the principle is a perfectly legitimate one, that those who have been guilty of repeated offences should, after the expiration of their sentences, for the better security of society be placed under constant supervision" (ibid. March 5 col 697). In the Commons, Sir Charles Adderley opined in critical response that the proposals would enact "...a wholesale system of police surveillance, so that another considerable portion of people would be in a state of out-door imprisonment, tied, as it were, by the leg to the police" (*Hansard* [Commons] Vol CXCVIII (198) August 4 col 1261).

In modern society, the spectre of the mobile and anonymous sexual offender holds a special place in its demonology, and such offending occupies a particular space *both* in official (criminological) discourse and in the popular imagination. We are living in an age when sex crime dominates the headlines (see, for example, Caputi 1987; Soothill & Walby 1991; Soothill & Grover 1995; Aldridge 1995; and in the U.S.A. Benedict 1992). As one British commentator recently remarked:

> A crude stereotype of a violent, calculating and perpetually dangerous offender has been built up in the popular press, and to a worrying level, in the 'respectable' writing about sexual crime (Sampson 1994: 124).

Studies of media coverage (see citations above) of imprisoned sexual offenders suggests that sexual offending is a narrow band of activity committed by a narrow band of offenders who have been convicted in the past for sex crimes and would be a danger in the future if released from prison too soon (or ever).

The underlying theme of the stories is that *if only* adequate records could be maintained, women and children could be protected. New sexual offences committed by convicted offenders are blamed on failures in record-keeping, while the discovery of offenders working with 'vulnerable' people is regarded as an unacceptable risk, which could have been avoided through more effective and efficient 'tracking'. In their analysis of the year 1985, Soothill & Walby (1991) note numerous headline calls for a national index of sexual offenders, particularly those who offended against children.

The present authors would argue that this 'cultural repertoire' around sexual offending connects, in a reflexive way, with official (criminological) discourse on sexual offenders. Criminology is not simply an instrumental/problem-oriented science, but can also be usefully seen as a cultural discourse (Garland 1990). It is one of the modern ways in which social problems are represented and understood. It is one of several discourses which compete to define the way we think about and act towards dangerous individuals and about the threats they pose to our security. Although 'specialized', the discipline is open-ended, trailing off into everyday understandings of lay people. As a consequence, the discourse of criminology also relies upon a repertoire of narrative modes, explanatory devices, as well as images, metaphors — which draw upon the symbolic resources of the wider culture. The '*special*' nature of sexual offending and more importantly the problems of *reoffending (recidivism)* and '*treatment*' act as crucial reference points in understanding public perception.

Although criminological research on sexual offending now has a substantial pedigree, it is clear that there is little in the way of settled ground — particularly as regards recidivism and prediction (see recent reviews by Monahan & Steadman 1994; Menzies *et al.* 1994; Quinsey *et al.* 1995) and the efficacy of treatment programmes. In respect of reoffending, Barker & Morgan (1993) in addressing recidivism discuss the problem of methodological differences between studies and also in the heterogeneity of this population (see also Marshall 1994). Indeed, because of the high level of under-reporting of sexual offences, they point out that known offenders are probably a highly select population anyway. Nevertheless, as Mair (1993) points out, while studies have been made looking at factors such as age of victim, sex of victim, relationship to victim and a wide range of personal and demographic variables, none of these seem to discriminate as effectively as previous offending history. While Broadhurst & Maller (1992) in their Australian study found little support for the notion of sexual offenders as 'specialists', they still conclude that "there is sufficient evidence of repetition to warrant that *special attention be given to offender tracking...by police and corrections agencies*" (ibid: 73, emphasis added). The limited evaluation studies of treatment which have been conducted also point to uncertainty and inconclusiveness. Beckett *et al.* (1994) in their research for the British Home Office point to differing 'success' rates depending on the assessed risk of a particular offender and variation by type of sexual offender.

Forming the Response: Risk and Security

Post-prison release arrangements for sexual offenders into society can be usefully considered in terms of two inter-related concepts: 'risk' and security. The importance of these two notions for understanding contemporary life is now well rehearsed (see Giddens 1990; Wagner 1994). The processes of rapid social and economic change which characterize modern societies have generated unprecedented wealth and mobility, have generated increased opportunities for crime, and have eroded particular forms of social cohesion which can be said to have characterized many previous social formations. Significant advances in transport and communications, and in administrative systems and information technology, have tended to 'lift out' social relations from localized contexts, and to attenuate traditional family and community ties. Erosion of these tends not only to increase the crime rate (as 'indigenous' social control is diminished), but also to create a greater potential for feelings of personal anxiety among the population, since ties of this kind have been strongly related to the maintenance of individual psychological (personal) security. Social order is increasingly thought of as something which cannot merely be protected and maintained but which must, rather, be actively constructed and managed if the social and personal costs of insecurity are to be minimized. In debates about social ordering practices, the concept of risk increasingly furnishes a discursive framework within which 'responses-to-problems' are being conceived, designed, implemented and legitimated (Beck 1992, 1994).

This 'institutionalization of risk' in modern society is evidenced by the centrality of risk assessment and risk management to almost all complex organizations. A governing activity for these organizations becomes the social production and distribution of *knowledge* for risk management (Reiss 1989). Late modern society is characterized by institutions such as police, probation, insurance and other regulatory bodies organized in relation to fear, risk assessment and the provision of security. Such institutions can be said to reconfigure society into communications about risk.

Ericson (1994) has recently considered how much forms of risk management and security provision are negotiated between police and other institutions. He points out that the technologies, bureaucratic forms and formats, and professional operatives of these other institutions fundamentally shape and guide the knowledge the police provide. New needs are defined and ways of classifying that demand police participation. More broadly, the rationalities of risk and security from other institutions become part of the police institution and vice versa. In terms of police expertise itself, here they have an ability both to define and defend a wide range of problems and tasks, and to 'grasp' new problems, in terms of abstractions of 'security'.

Production and distribution of knowledge become bureaucratically formatted communications for other security institutions, which also tap into the already-processed knowledge of these same agencies. In this context, one can see "surveillance as the production of knowledge about (monitoring), and supervision of (compliance), subject populations" (Ericson 1994: 161). Knowledge production and supervision are mutually reinforcing, and together they create surveillance as a system of rule. Surveillance is *the* vehicle of risk management — with subject populations producing knowledge about themselves, routinely. Moreover, growth in this surveillance has to be seen in the context of security provision itself and expansion of technologies. Finally, the knowledge-for-security

432   *W. Hebenton and T. Thomas*

demands of other institutions and their compliance mechanisms move the police in the direction of compliance law enforcement.

In the remainder of this paper, the legal and policy response to the release of convicted sexual offenders in England, Wales and the U.S.A. will be considered within this interpretive framework.

England and Wales

The current arrangements that exist for monitoring released offenders can be set out briefly. The Probation Service has a statutory responsibility for parole conditions and supervision for all offenders, with reporting conditions set out by the Home Office (Home Office 1995). Under the early release provisions of the Criminal Justice Act 1991, offenders sentenced to periods of time between 12 months and under 4 years are subject to Automatic Conditional Release (ACR) on licence at the half-way point, with supervision until the three-quarter point. If a Discretionary Conditional Release (DCR) on licence decision on those serving more than 4 years is not made by the Parole Board by the time of the two-thirds point in the sentence, release becomes automatic for that prisoner (Home Office 1995), with supervision to the three-quarter point. For both ACR and DCR, the judge at sentence has the discretion to direct that some sex offenders be supervised until the end of their full sentence — in effect the last quarter. The licence allowing the prisoner to serve the remainder of a custodial sentence in the community under Probation supervision is signed by either the Parole Board (DCR) or the Prison Governor (ACR). Both act on behalf of the Home Secretary and both can attach conditions to a licence.

In relation to offenders *against children*, arrangements have long been in place in England and Wales to allow local authorities to have notice of discharge from prison. A 1964 Home Office circular advised that "it has been the practice of the Home Office for many years" to inform a local authority when a prisoner convicted of incest is due for release (Home Office 1964: para. 6). The same circular outlined wider arrangements to be implemented from 1 February 1964, and to include those convicted of any sexual offence against a child listed in Schedule One of the 1993 Children and Young Persons Act or any offence against a child involving cruelty or ill treatment.

In bringing the new release arrangements into line with Part 2 of the Criminal Justice Act 1991, the recent H.M. Prison Service guidance to governors on so-called 'Schedule-One' offenders effectively makes only minor adjustments to earlier guidance (for example, D.H.S.S. (1978) *The disclosure of criminal records on release on prisoners who have committed offences against children in the home, Circular LAC (78) 2*). Governers are asked to notify and consult with local authorities and the Probation Service at the start of a period of custody, during custody if there is likely to be home leave or temporary release, and towards the end of the period of custody. The final notification continues the practice of allowing local authorities to check out the possibility of any unresolved child protection implications, if a prisoner should go to a given address (H.M. Prison Service 1994: para. 41). This could include a requirement not to reside in the same household as a child below a given age, or not to approach or communicate with specified family or extended family members without the prior approval of a supervising officer and the relevant social services department. Breaches of conditions would result in either a court hearing (ACR) or recall (DCR) (H.M. Prison Service 1994: para. 41). Even after supervision under licence ends, surveillance may still continue on the known 'Schedule One' offender by social services staff, if the offender comes into contact with children in a household. The surveillance may be triggered off by accident or chance but it has been held that social services do have a duty to maintain this surveillance in the interests of child protection. In the case of *R. v. Devon County Council ex parte L* (1991 2 FLR 541 Divisional Court), 'L' tried to prevent social services continually 'catching up with him' as a suspected child abuser to notify the women he had moved in with that their children might be considered 'at risk'. In this case 'L' actually had no convictions but the court still held that social workers were under a duty to inform women 'L' came into contact with as part of their duty to protect children (see Hayes 1992 for a critique of the ruling).

'Risky' sexual offenders and protecting the public

The effect of the 1991 Criminal Justice Act early release provisions has been to increase the number of sexual offenders released from custody, and the Home Office projections are of some 1700 offenders released annually of which some 700 will have been sentenced to 4 or more years (for a discussion of this and general sentencing trends, see Hebenton & Thomas 1996*a,b*). Indeed, Sampson (1994) suggested a quadrupling of the number of sexual offenders on licence in the community as a result of the overall package of changes brought in by the 1991 Act. However, the legislation enacted by the Criminal Justice Act 1991 was seen by government and others as enhancing the role of the Probation service in protecting the public. Protection (security) from 'risky' sexual offenders is indeed foregrounded in the introduction to the 1992 version of the government's *National Standards for the Supervision of Offenders in the Community.*

> Some offenders...present a significant potential risk to the public.
> While guarantees cannot be given about offenders' future behaviour,
> the standards give consistent support to positive management of risk:
> (by)...careful assessment of individual offenders to devise suitable
> programmes of supervision... (Home Office 1995: para. 1·4).

Recognizing that "more potentially dangerous offenders who might not
have been granted parole under the old system will now become a statutory
responsibility of (Probation)" (ACOP 1994: 2), the Association of Chief
Officers' of Probation (ACOP) issued a 'Position Statement' on
management of risk and public protection which called for a 'culture shift'
in the work of Probation towards a more active recognition of responsibility for assessing risk to the public and its subsequent management (ACOP
1994: 1). ACOP's review of practice for 1993 pointed to a situation where
very few Probation areas had adequate internal guidance on risk
assessment or management and a lack of 'common procedures' which
could potentially hinder 'safe' supervision of cases transferred between
geographical areas (ibid.: 3). ACOP's guidance saw the following as
essential:

— Risk assessment in all cases with regular review;
— Inter-agency working, which may require the establishment of formal
   protocols covering information exchange; and
— Need for common computerized and integrated recording systems for
   cases.

The instantiation of the centrality of risk in such guidance is clear,
together with the paramountcy of 'information sharing' and formatted
knowledge with other agencies. However, the inherent reflexive 'insecurity' of risk is also evident with ACOP's paper also noting the importance
of not creating 'unrealistic expectations' about their ability to provide
'public protection' from 'risky' sexual offenders (ibid.: 1).

The discursive framework provided by notions of risk and protection
(security) within which policy and practice are conceived, designed,
implemented and legitimated is well evidenced in another recent report.
The thematic inspection by H.M. Inspectorate of Probation, highlighted as
a source of particular concern by Probation officers, the growing number
of sexual offenders under statutory supervision (H.M. Inspectorate of
Probation 1995: 39). In the introduction to their report, they
contextualized their work in terms of growing public concern and media
attention to particular cases (see, for example, 'Sex attacker struck while
on parole' *The Times* 23 August 1994; 'Freed paedophile still a threat to
children' *The Times* 3 December 1994). Definitionally the Inspectorate's
report takes *risk assessment* as "an assessment carried out to establish

whether the subject is likely to cause serious physical or psychological harm to others (ibid.: 12), *risk management* as "action taken to monitor a person's behaviour and attitudes, and to intervene in his/her life, in order to try to prevent them harming others" (ibid.: 13) and *public protection* as "the desired outcome of risk assessment and risk management" (ibid.: 13). The report itself criticizes inadequacies of current policy and practice in some Probation areas, and recommends adoption of 'good policy and practice' systems for future risk management and public protection.

Among the public protection key principles informing the Inspectorate's approach are the need to work at all times to reduce the risk to the public, and the priority of information sharing over notions of confidentiality (ibid.: 17). The report recommends: the need for risk assessment for all and clear case marking involving, if necessary, a "no-risk" classification; case information in 'high-risk' cases to be kept for a minimum of 10 years; central registration at Probation area level for 'high-risk' offenders; agreement of joint policies, procedures and strategies with police and other agencies; the need to consider development of a national risk assessment system. The Inspectorate also highlights the important requirement of what it calls centralized notification for serious sexual offences and Schedule One offenders:

> incidents where public protection has been compromised by a person subject to statutory supervision by the service should be investigated by a chief officer. A written report should be prepared for the probation committee. Home Office Circular 41/95 'Incident Reporting' sets out the requirements for the Home Office to be notified. (Ibid.: 24).

The framework set out by the Inspectorate fully reflects the recently revised *National Standards for the Supervision of Offenders in the Community* (Home Office 1995), and, in particular, the standard on 'Supervision Before and After Release from Custody'.

While the centrality of 'risk' and security are now fully instantiated in post-release supervision of sexual offenders, the adequacy of current arrangements for monitoring and managing 'the risk' are increasingly questioned. Keeping *active track* of released offenders beyond the length of supervised licence, particularly Schedule One paedophiles, is now advocated by the police, academics and professionals in child sexual abuse work as crucial for effective risk management (Parker *et al.* in press; Hughes *et al.* 1996). Hughes *et al.* point to local area systems that cannot deal with aspects of the known behavioural strategy of many such offenders — namely, that these offenders are extremely mobile, often searching out families and likely targets in distant police and probation areas. They describe current arrangements as "haphazard and it is very easy for offenders to become invisible" (Hughes *et al.* 1996: 34). Existing police

436   *W. Hebenton and T. Thomas*

systems are described as "inaccessible and not amenable to the manipulation of data" (ibid.: 31). In a similar vein, it is argued by Parker *et al.*, "that
the development of (police) intelligence systems, tracking the movements
and activities of known and suspected perpetrators is needed" (Parker *et
al.*, in press). Only by 'knowing' perpetrators can we "ensure more effective
risk assessment and allow protective strategies to be more accurately
tailored" (ibid.).

Hughes *et al.* (1996) in their recent report to the Home Office Police
Research Group recommend both the setting up of a co-ordinated
intelligence system for paedophiles (convicted and suspected) for
proactive work, and the establishment of a national, accessible and
effective database of convicted sexual offenders for 'tracking' purposes.
The intelligence system "would properly store and manipulate information
which is in fact already available within the police officers' 'heads' and with
their colleagues in Probation and Social Services" (ibid.: vii). The proposed
system would allow:

—A local and nationally linked network;
—Interaction between the intelligence system and other computer
   systems;
—Access to all police officers and other agencies;
—Inputs by all agencies via the police; and
—Suspects/offenders would be 'starred' on other databases so that
   whenever their name is retrieved on any matter, they are identified as a
   paedophile suspect.

The report's recommendation of a national database echoes calls from
police organizations and others (see comments by President of The Police
Superintendents' Association of England and Wales in *Independent*
4 October 1995; and the Labour Party's letter to the Home Secretary on
the matter *Independent* 4 August 1995). The Home Secretary, at the ACOP
annual conference on 22 March 1996, announced for the first time that a
national register for sexual offenders is being considered and that a
consultation paper is to be published shortly setting out detailed proposals
(*The Guardian* 23 March 1996). In terms of risk and security, such a register
can be seen as reifying the 'permanence' and 'prevalence' of risk attached
to sexual offenders.

The U.S.A.

Statutes and registers

In the U.S.A., the sexual offender registration phenomenon is almost now completely pervasive and yet very recent. At the state level, the 'legislative surge' in popularity of this method of responding to the risk of released offenders into the community has been exponential. By the end of 1995, some 40 states now have registration statutes, 16 were enacted in 1994 alone, with over two-thirds enacted since 1989 (for a full review of state laws, see Bedarf 1995; Thomas & Lieb 1995). With the passage of the Violent Crime Control and Law Enforcement Act 1994, federal government now requires all states to have registries in place by the end of 1997 (Pub L. No. 103-322, 108 Stat.2038 (codified at 42 U.S.C. 14071).

In general, the current laws follow a similar pattern, with variations in specific provisions such as the specific sexual offences that trigger registration requirements, the penalties for failure to register, and the type of information held by the register. Statutes conform in many respects:

— The registry is usually maintained by a state agency;
— Local law enforcement (the chief of police in cities, the local county sheriff elsewhere) is responsible for collecting information and forwarding it to the administering agency;
— Typical information includes an offender's name, address, fingerprints, photograph, data of birth, social security number, criminal history, place of employment, vehicle registration details, and DNA profile;
— The period for initial registration varies from 'prior to release' or 'immediately' to 12 months; the modal period is within 30 days;
— Duration of registration is in excess of 10 years, but an increasing majority require lifetime registration; and
— Most registration is 'passive' in nature, and updates are provided only when the offender notifies law enforcement (although this is set to change to active address verification procedures under federal Attorney General's guidance).

Rationales, risk and 'community protection'

The legislative rationales identified in statute reveal a regulatory intent to manage 'risk' which has allowed registration, so far, to survive constitutional challenge (at the time of writing no appeal has gone as far as the U.S. Supreme Court). To take two typical examples:

> The legislature finds that sex offenders often pose a high risk of re-offense, and that law enforcement's efforts to protect their communities, conduct investigations, and quickly apprehend offenders who commit sex offenses, are impaired by the lack of information available to law enforcement agencies about convicted sex offenders who live within the law enforcement agency's jurisdiction. Therefore, this state's policy is to assist local law enforcement agencies' efforts to

protect their communities by regulating sex offenders by requiring sex
offenders to register with local law enforcement agencies as provided
in [RCW 9A·44·130–140]. (Revised statutes of Washington State)

And in New Jersey:

The Legislature finds and declares:

a. The danger of recidivism posed by sex offenders...requires a system
of registration that will permit law enforcement officials to identify (sex
offenders)...and provide law enforcement with additional information
critical to preventing and promptly resolving incidents involving sexual
abuse and missing persons (New Jersey Stat.Ann.2C:7–1)

In this context of justification through risk, sexual offender registration has
withstood challenges on *ex post facto* arguments and cruel and unjust
punishment grounds (for example, see opinion in *State* v. *Noble*, 829 P.2d
1217, 1218 (Ariz.1992); *State* v. *Ward*, 869 P.2d 1062, 1965 (Wash.1994); *Doe*
v. *Poritz*, Nos. A-170/171–94 (N.J. decided 25 July 1995)).

In spite of the popularity of registration, its effectiveness is largely
empirically untested, and in those states which have attempted evaluation,
the results reveal the inadequacies of 'passive' and poorly financed systems,
with low compliance rates and inaccurate registers (see Bedarf 1995:
900–903). To enhance 'risk' management still further in pursuit of security,
some states have now enacted *community* notification statutes, and the list of
states considering such provisions grows steadily.

Indeed, under the requirements of the federal Violent Crime Control
and Law Enforcement Act 1994, eventually all states are likely to enact
some version of a community notification law. Bedarf (1995) points to four
basic types or models of community notification: mandatory self-
identification, discretionary or mandatory police identification, public
access to police book, and public access by telephone.

The self-identification model requires the person both to identify
himself to the community as a sexual offender and to register with the
police (operational in Louisiana since 1992). In the second model, police
either use discretion over whether to release information (in Washington
State since 1990), or are mandated to do so statutorily (in New Jersey since
1995). The federal 1994 Act adopts the discretionary approach. In the
third model, individuals decide when they want to know about sexual
offenders in their community (in California since 1995). It permits
individuals to go to their local sheriff's office and examine the register data
and photographs of offenders in particular areas. Finally, the telephone
request model allows people to find out whether a particular individual is
an offender by calling a '900' telephone number. Callers must provide very

specific information, such as the exact street address, birth date, or detailed physical description of the person in question, in order to verify registration status (in New York state since 1995).

Community notification statutes have also, so far, successfully withstood constitutional challenge (for example *State* v. *Ward; Doe v. Poritz,* see above). The legislative rationale of Washington State is illustrative of the risk-based justificatory context:

> overly restrictive confidentiality and liability laws governing the release of information about sexual predators have reduced willingness to release information that could be appropriately released under the public disclosure laws, and have increased risks to public safety. Persons found to have committed a sex offense have a reduced expectation of privacy because of the public's interest in public safety and in the effective operation of government. Release of information...to public agencies and under limited circumstances, the general public, will further the governmental interests of public safety... so long as the information released is rationally related to the furtherance of those goals. Therefore, this state's policy is to...authorize the release of necessary and relevant information about sexual predators to members of the general public. (Wash. Laws of 1990: ch.3, 116).

Analysis of the statutory legislation and derived implementing guidance in Washington State, New Jersey and State of New York reveals the central importance of calibration of degree of notification to the degree of risk (see, for example, New Jersey Attorney-General's 'Guidelines for Law Enforcement for Notification to Local Officials and/or to the Community of the Entry of a Sex Offender into the Community', dated 9/14/95). In addition, it is evident that 'objective' risk assessment processes increasingly define this calibration process. New York, for instance, will utilize the services of a Board of Examiners for Sex Offenders (State of New York Bill 1059-C, 1995-6), while New Jersey's Prosecutor must use a Sex Offender Risk Assessment Scale (SORAS) and can consult a task force of 'experts' on sexual assault. In some counties of Washington State, where the first modern notification law was enacted in 1990, 'Classification and Release Committees' are now established (see, for example, 'Protocol for the Public Notification of Sex Offenders Released into Clark County, Washington', Clark County Prosecutor's Office September 1995).

Discussion

It has been argued that security through knowledge and the instantiation of 'risk management' processes can be said to characterize our legal and policy response to the problem of the release of sexual offenders back into

440   *W. Hebenton and T. Thomas*

the community. The efficient formatting and availability of detailed knowledge about offenders becomes the major concern. With the development of community notification, a wider public can be said to become knowledge empowered as 'consumers' and 'producers'. However, risk management in this context is itself paradoxical in that the process is rooted in, and itself constitutes, 'insecurity'.

Our risk society cannot escape the problem of insecurity. As Ewald (1986) argues, risk problems are characterized by having no unambiguous solutions; rather they are distinguished by a fundamental ambivalence. Typical of modern risk management systems of security, sexual offender registration is also irrational and stands as an icon to insecurity — indeed institutionalizing distrust and insecurity. All efforts to isolate socially and reduce risks via legal protection and regulation depend on the release of new or different risks and attendant insecurity. In the risk society, "knowledge is always embedded in ignorance, safety is surrounded by unsafety and rational planning inevitably frays out to uncalculable evolution" (van den Daele 1992). In modern conditions, trust both of 'expertise' and of institutional systems, such as criminal justice, becomes problematic — in particular, trust between experts (or the criminal justice professionals) and lay public, based as it is on technical competence, is inherently 'revisable' (Giddens 1992). In addition, the prevalence of institutional reflexivity means that there is a continuous filter-back of expert (professional) theories, concepts and findings to the lay public. That is, "the routine incorporation of new knowledge or information into environments of action that are thereby reconstituted or reorganised" (Giddens 1991: 243). Such a reconstitution is continual and has no necessary stopping point.

Risk also carries with it its own political economy. In the context of modern societies, the divisions and conflicts of 'security' are based on the definition of risks, the distribution of scarce resources for risk management, the just distribution of risk, and even risk created by the 'security' institutions themselves. Here, political arguments can be viewed as illustrative of tensions in the political economy of risk. Thus, for example, mobilization by victim groups in terms of insecurity ('better protection') is very effective because it is impossible to deny claims for protection expressed in terms of life itself; and because it allows for criticism of some fundamental structural features of society that would be difficult to address in public culture otherwise. The result is intensified law and regulation even where scientific (expert) knowledge is lacking. At the same time, there is no clear structure to political conflict around legislation such as community notification or the proposed national sexual offender registration scheme in England and Wales. Political alliances and their bases in knowledge are dispersed and complex. Moreover, it is relatively easy for the conflicts to be redrawn or displaced because the 'threat' addressed always contains residual uncertainty, and because experts must be deferred to for credible claims about management of this 'risk' (Beck 1992).

However, risk society is by tendency also a self-critical society. Redistribution of risk between offender-victim–community-criminal justice professional is always in tension. To take the community notification example, American citizens of many states are not convinced that mere registration provides adequate security from repeat sexual offenders who, in their opinion, may be incapable of rehabilitation. This sentiment often results from the highly publicized occurrence of heinous sexual crimes committed by repeat offenders who were known to the police but not to the general community. Washington State, for example, enacted its community notification law after a 7-year-old boy was taken by a repeat offender, orally and anally raped by him and then the boy's penis was cut off. New Jersey's law followed after 7-year-old Megan Kanka was raped and murdered by a twice-convicted sexual offender who, unbeknownst to Megan's parents, had moved in across the street — "Why, they asked, had they not been told?" (*New York Times* B1 August 4 1994). In this context, public discussion (discursivity) of the sexual offender threat is related to everyday life, drenched with experience and plays with cultural symbols. It is also highly media-dependent and manipulable. It is 'at odds' with the criminal justice system's 'calculated knowledge' of risk assessment and management. Notification 'speaks of' a system that will address the threat by allowing parents to advise children to avoid certain individuals, by facilitating community monitoring of released sexual offenders, and by deterring future crimes by such offenders by increasing the likelihood of apprehension; it 'speaks of' an awareness that may motivate parents to educate their children about sexual crimes and will vest communities with a sense of control over their homes and neighbourhoods. From supervision, to registration, to community notification, the anonymity afforded to repeat offenders in the impersonal environment of large, increasingly transient modern communities is increasingly being regulated. However, the salient point here is that the expansion and heightening of the intention of control ultimately ends up producing the opposite.

Acknowledgements

A version of this paper was delivered to the Socio-Legal Studies Association Annual Conference, University of Southampton, 1–3 April 1996. The authors gratefully acknowledge the financial support of the British Academy to the project 'Sexual offenders and community protection' under Grant No. APN 3022.

442   *W. Hebenton and T. Thomas*

References

Aldridge, M. (1995) UK national press treatment of Frank Beck affair. *Sociological Review* **43**, 658–674.

Association of Chief Officers' of Probation (ACOP) (1994) *Position Statement: Guidance on Management of Risk and Public Protection.* ACOP: Wakefield.

Barker, M. & Morgan, R. (1993) *Sex Offenders: A Framework for the Evaluation of Community Bas Treatment.* Home Office: London.

Bedarf, A. (1995) Examining sex offender community notification laws. *California Law Review* **83**, 885–939.

Beck, U. (1992) *Risk Society: Towards a New Modernity.* Sage: London.

Beck, U. (1994) The reinvention of politics: towards a theory of reflexive modernization. In *Reflexive Modernization* (Beck, U., Giddens, A. & Lash, S., Eds). Stanford University Press: Stanford.

Beckett, R., Beech, T., Fisher, D. & Fordham, A. (1994) *Community-Based Treatment for Sex Offenders: An Evaluation of Seven Treatment Programmes.* Home Office: London.

Benedict, H. (1992) *Virgin or Vamp: How the Press Covers Sex Crimes.* Oxford University Press: New York.

Broadhurst, R. & Maller, R. (1992) The recidivism of sex offenders in the Western Australian prison population. *British Journal of Criminology* **32**, 54–80.

Caputi, J. (1987) *The Age of Sex Crime.* Women's Press: London.

van den Daele, W. (1992) Scientific evidence and the regulation of technical risks: twenty years of demythologising the experts. In *The Culture and Power of Knowledge* (Stehr, N. & Ericson, R., Eds). de Gruyter: New York.

Ericson, R.V. (1994) The division of expert knowledge in policing and security. *British Journal of Sociology* **45**, 149–175.

Ewald, F. (1986). *L'Etat Providence.* Grasset: Paris.

Garland, D. (1990) *Punishment and Modern Society.* Clarendon Press: Oxford.

Giddens, A. (1990) *The Consequences of Modernity.* Polity Press: Cambridge.

Giddens, A. (1991) *Modernity and Self-Identity.* Stanford University Press: Stanford.

Giddens, A. (1992) *The Transformation of Intimacy.* Polity Press: Cambridge.

Hayes, M. (1992) R v. Devon County Council ex parte L. Bad practice, bad law and a breach of human rights? *Family Law* June, 245–257.

Hebenton, B. & Thomas, T. (1993) *Criminal Records: State, Citizen and the Politics of Protection.* Avebury: Aldershot.

Hebenton, B. & Thomas, T. (1996*a*) Beyond good and evil. *Community Care* 5 January.

Hebenton, B. & Thomas, T. (1996*b*) Tracking sex offenders. *Howard Journal of Criminal Justice* **35**(2), 97–112.

Her Majesty's Inspectorate of Probation (1995) *Dealing with Dangerous People: The Probation Service and Public Protection. Report of a Thematic Inspection.* Home Office: London.

Her Majesty's Prison Service (1994) *Release of Prisoners Convict of Offences Against Children or Young Persons Under the Age of 18, Guidance Notes to: Instruction to Governors 54/1994.* H.M. Prison Service: London.

Home Office (1964) *Children and Young Persons Act 1933: parts I and II.* Circular 22/1964.

Home Office (Department of Health and Welsh Office) (1995) *National Standards for the Supervision of Offenders in the Community.* Home Office (Department of Health and Welsh Office): London.

Hughes, B., Parker, H. & Gallagher, B. (1996) *Policing Child Sexual Abuse: The View from Police Practitioners.* Home Office Police Research Group Report: London.

Mair, K. (1993) The nature of the act: a neglect dimension in the classification of sex offenders. *British Journal of Criminology* 33, 267–275.

Marshall, P. (1994) Reconviction of imprisoned sexual offenders. In *Home Office Research Bulletin No. 36.* Home Office Research and Statistics Department: London.

Menzies, R., Webster, C., McMain, S., Staley, S. & Scaglione, R. (1994) The dimensions of dangerousness revisited: assessing forensic predictions about violence. *Law and Human Behavior* 18, 1–28.

Monahan, J. & Steadman, H. (1994) *Violence and Mental Disorder: Developments in Risk Assessment.* University of Chicago: Chicago.

Parker, H., Gallagher, B. & Hughes, B. (in press) The policing of child sexual abuse in England and Wales. *Policing and Society.*

Quinsey, V.L., Lalumiere, M., Rice, M. & Harris, G. (1995) Predicting sexual offenses. In *Assessing Dangerousness.* (Campbell, J.C., Ed.). Sage: London.

Radzinowicz, L. & Hood, R. (1990) *The Emergence of Penal Policy in Victorian and Edwardian England.* Clarendon Press: Oxford.

Reiss, A. (1989) The institutionalization of risk. *Law and Policy* 11, 392–402.

Sampson, A. (1994) *Acts of Abuse: Sex Offenders and the Criminal Justice System.* Routledge: London.

Soothill, K. & Grover, C. (1995) Changes in the newspaper reporting of rape trials since the Second World War. *Research Bulletin, No 37. Home Office Research and Statistics Department.* Home Office: London.

Soothill, K. & Walby, S. (1991) *Sex Crime in the News.* Routledge: London.

Thomas, S. & Lieb, R. (1995) *Sex Offender Registration: A Review of State Laws.* Washington State Institute for Public Policy: Olympia.

Tobias, J.J. (1972) *Crime and Industrial Society in the Nineteenth Century.* Penguin: Harmondsworth.

Wagner, P. (1994) *A Sociology of Modernity: Liberty and Discipline.* Routledge: London.

[10]

Moral Technology: The Political Agenda of Random Drug Testing

Pat O'Malley and Stephen Mugford

Introduction

T HIS ARTICLE HAS A DUAL AIM. THE FIRST IS TO CONTRIBUTE TO THE POLICY debate on drug testing. The second is to link that specific debate to an analysis of social control in contemporary society.

Random drug testing in the workplace (RDT) has become widespread in American industry. Protagonists offer various claims to justify this spread. The more common claim is that RDT reduces accidents and improves productivity — in short, that it is efficient, actuarial risk management. Less commonly, it is argued that by reducing illegal drug consumption, demand for those drugs will be severely reduced, thus furthering the War on Drugs — in short, that RDT is part of a moral crusade. We argue that the evidence reveals that the first, and ideologically less challenging, of these claims is largely unsupported; that the second is nearer the truth, but glosses over complex questions; and, finally, that if RDT is introduced on a very widespread basis, a probable major effect will be a hardening of divisions within the labor market, with associated divisions along class and racial lines. In particular, the result will be a deterioration of the employment prospects of the underclasses and a continuation of the tendency to consign those people to unemployability or, at best, to employment in marginal occupations.

Second, in establishing this argument, we seek to contribute to theoretical debates about social control in contemporary capitalist societies. One school of thought — epitomized by Donzelot (1979, 1991), Reichman (1986), Simon (1987, 1988), Castel (1991), and Ewald (1986, 1991) — argues that modern forms of control are "demoralized" and that actuarialist modes of reasoning and action supplant older forms of regulation that hinge on the discipline and

PAT O'MALLEY is the director of the National Center for Socio-Legal Studies, La Trobe University, Bundorra Victoria, Australia 3083.

STEPHEN MUGFORD is a Senior Lecturer in the Department of Sociology, Faculty of Arts, Australian National University, GPO Box 4, Canberra ACT 2601, Australia. He acknowledges the support of the Institute for Scientific Analysis and of the School of Public Health, University of California, both in Berkeley, California, during the period when this article was completed. He is also grateful to Jerry Beck, Jim Jacobs, and John Morgan for help with sources on random drug testing.

punishment of the individual deviant. Whereas the latter forms concern themselves with detection, correction, or retribution with respect to individuals who have offended, actuarial techniques are concerned with the distribution of behaviors and the regulation of their effects. In place of guilt, offending, fault, and a variety of other negatively sanctioned personal failings and pathologies there are instead impersonal risks and their prevention or management. Two brief examples will suffice to illustrate the distinction, one from criminal and one from noncriminal regulation.

One of the pioneering developments in actuarial power was that of unemployment insurance. Under the disciplinary mode, the unemployed were subjected to the disciplinary procedures of the workhouse. Segregated, working in silence on repetitive tasks, the individual would be shaped into a docile body compliant to the demands of the labor routine. Actuarialism, on the other hand, does not operate upon the individual to ensure conformity. Rather, it takes the distribution of employment/unemployment and works on it at a population level to spread the risk and thus mitigate and manage the impact of unemployment for the social collectivity. Either by direct contributions into a fund, or through indirect payment via taxation, the fiscal damage wrought by unemployment is spread across the population and across time.[1]

With respect to the regulation of crime — say, housebreaking — the same broad model is seen in a different form. In the disciplinary mode, after the offense is committed and the offender is captured, moral and causal responsibility is assigned to offenders, who are duly punished or disciplined. In the actuarial, or insurance mode, on the other hand, the identity of the offender — as opposed to the offense — is not even vital. Rather, the aim is to identify the risk created by offenses and to minimize it by rendering the house (as nearly as possible) burglary-proof, while spreading the risk among a population of those who share a similar risk (insurance) and/or to identify categories of risk creators (for example, householders who are not security conscious, or young people "at risk" of becoming criminal). Corrective action may then be taken against risk creators, although this differs from disciplinary intervention, for it is preventive rather than reactive, focuses on victims as much as on offenders, is not concerned with moral responsibility, and seeks to change behaviors rather than attitudes (see O'Malley, 1991a). Similarly, while actuarial interventions may bear directly on individuals, rather than hinging on "proof beyond reasonable doubt," the application is probabilistic — those "at risk" are assumed to be probable offenders until tests show otherwise.[2] This, of course, creates a limited reversal of the criminal law assumption of "innocent until proven guilty." As Stan Cohen argues of this emergent mode of regulation:

> What is being monitored is behaviour (or the physiological correlates
> of emotion and behaviour). No one is interested in inner

thoughts..."the game is up" for all policies directed to the criminal as an individual, either in terms of detection (blaming and punishing) or causation (finding motivational or causal chains).... The talk now is about "spatial" and "temporal" aspects of crime, about systems, behaviour sequences, ecology, defensible space...target hardening... (1985: 146–148).

In actuarial approaches, the individual is replaced by the category and the context. Suburbs are designed to minimize opportunities for crime, streets are given roundabouts and speedhumps to prevent speeding, robbery is reduced by increasing the range of the credit economy, and so on. Thus, "while the disciplinary regime attempts to alter individual behaviour and motivation, the actuarial regime alters the physical and social structures within which individuals behave" (Simon, 1988: 71).

The actuarial mode is concerned with risks, that is, with the calculable effects of future events. As noted earlier, one major account of RDT describes it as a risk-management technique, designed to improve safety and productivity. If so, such a development fits the actuarialist account of social control. Indeed, Simon's brief account of RDT within such a framework seems to complete this logical circle:

One example of [this process] is drug use. The 1960s stripped away much of the moral sanction against drug use. If drugs are out in the eighties, it is because they are perceived as driving accident rates up, and productivity down.

The control system is changing as well. In the near future the security system could effectively limit drug use by imposing urinalysis screening as a condition of employment. To use drugs would no longer be to challenge the moral sanction of the state and expose oneself to punishment, but instead risk being denied access to the system. Rather than being defined as a deviant malefactor, the drug user becomes the self-selected occupant of a high risk category that is channelled away from employment and the greater access it brings (1987: 85).

This passage contains two (linked) assertions. The first concerns the way that drugs are perceived — the claim being that drugs have been moved out of the moral domain and are dealt with via actuarialist risk management. The second is a description, offered in the second paragraph, of what is happening in drug control and what the likely effects will be. To prefigure our difference with Simon, we disagree with the analysis offered in the first paragraph, arguing instead that RDT hinges on a "remoralization" of illicit drug use.[3]

Moreover, as we shall show below, actuarial power bears a more complex relation to risk management than Simon perceives, for even when taking on the
rhetorical gloss of moral neutrality, actuarialism may be linked directly to
strongly moral claims. On the other hand, we endorse Simon's description as a
sensible account of RDT and of its likely consequences such as depoliticiza-
tion. In the body of the article, we will explore the contours of the actuarialism
debate in more detail, examine some evidence on the practice of RDT, and
then weave the two together to make better sense of both.

From the Punitive City to Risk Society

Initially, Cohen (1979) foresaw that the spread of surveillance would lead
its gaze to penetrate every nook and cranny of society. This extension of
surveillance he understood as part of the formation of "the punitive city," an
integral element of the efflorescence of disciplinary technologies of power.
More recently, however, Cohen, Simon, and many others have conceived of
surveillance as increasingly disarticulated from the other, "normalizing" elements of the disciplinary technique and as forming part of an actuarial mode
that retains an emphasis on surveillance and monitoring, but articulates this
with quite distinct, statistical, and actuarial patterns of knowledge and power
construction. Consequently, in place of the "disciplinary society" (*Ibid.*), such
theorists now speak of the "post-disciplinary society" (Castel, 1991) or "risk
society" (Simon, 1987). The clear implication is that a new technology of
knowledge/power will ultimately result in colonization of all social institutions
and agencies. The underlying assumption of such reasoning is technological
evolutionism, which presumes that social transformation is being driven in
vital ways by the internal "logic" of social technologies in a continuous refinement of population-management techniques. To critically assess the implications of this model, it is thus necessary to look first at the adequacy of its
theoretical foundations.

In the work of Simon (1987, 1988), Donzelot (1979), and others (Ewald,
1986, 1991; Castel, 1991), actuarial techniques are seen as becoming dominant because they function to further intensify the effectiveness of power:

> While the disciplinary regime attempts to alter individual behaviour
> and motivation, the actuarial regime alters the physical and social
> structures within which individuals behave. The movement from
> normalization (closing the gap between distribution and norm) to ac-
> commodation (responding to variations in distributions) increases the
> efficiency of power because changing people is difficult and expen-
> sive (Simon, 1988: 773).

Such developments allegedly are more efficient means of managing social order than is discipline, primarily because they avoid the inefficient methods of direct coercion — inefficient because the redeployment of political and economic resources is required to overcome resistance to overt, coercive manipulation. Efficiency is increased by reducing resistance. As Cohen (1985) has commented, in the view of these writers:

> solving problems by changing people is simply unproductive. People are not amenable to persuasion, resocialization, counselling, treatment, reeducation. We have to accept them as they are, modify their circumstances, or deal with the consequences of their intractability.

Compared with "the cumbersome techniques of individual discipline" (Simon, 1987), actuarial techniques are argued to be more subtle and less likely to generate resistance. First, since it is largely unconcerned with the attribution of guilt or the coercive correction of offenders, actuarialism is less intrusive and (can be) more tolerant of individual deviance than are disciplinary regimes. In addition, actuarial techniques masquerade as "technical" solutions to problems, thus seeming to be morally and politically neutral (Donzelot, 1979; Castel, 1991; Ewald, 1991). Furthermore, actuarial power divides the population into statistical and behavioral categories organized around "risk." Because risk categories tend not to correspond closely to traditional forms of ordering social experiences, it is argued, they do not generate social recognition or social mobilization. Thus, by minimizing resistance through an amoral form, employing categorical rather than individual intervention, and exercising low coerciveness, actuarialism appears to be more efficient than the disciplines.

This reasoning presupposes that techniques of power can be ranked hierarchically and that through selection the most efficient survive. The gradual transformation of social orders to accord with the form of the ascendant technology is an obvious corollary. We believe, however, that power cannot be divorced so positivistically from the social context and programs in which it is embedded, and "efficiency" is not a technical issue, but rather a politically evaluated and contested one. Consequently, we argue that there is no unilinear evolution toward actuarialism or "risk society." The evidence suggests instead an accumulation of regulatory technologies — punitive, disciplinary, and actuarial — with their arrangement and combination in specific patterns under specific regimes so as to achieve specific political-moral effects.

The point may be made illustrated by reference to the fate of African Americans in the United States. This sector of the American population currently is experiencing virtually unprecedented rates and volumes of imprisonment (Duster, 1987). Further, such imprisonment long ago abandoned any pretense of being disciplinary regimes of correction. At best understood as warehousing, the regime increasingly is justified by a neoconservative discourse of just deserts and retribution, linked to strongly moral conceptions of criminal responsibility. This is a return to what Foucault calls sovereign power — the negative form of coercive sanctification of "core" moral values. Remoralization and punitiveness would surely appear to be more prominent than demoralization and actuarialism, and for the past 25 years, this appears to be a high tide on the flow rather than a low tide on the ebb.

Almost alone among theorists of actuarialism, Simon (1987) has attempted to face this issue. He argues essentially that the resort to sovereign power represents the failure of capitalism to manage certain sectors of the population through rationalization. Actuarial power, he argues, works through the market, accessing only market participants: "the poor, locked out of the access and security channels of insurance and credit, remain a constant reminder that capitalism cannot achieve the rationality of risk in its fullest sense" (*Ibid.*: 78). Sovereign power, an obsolete form, continues to "haunt" modern societies because no other solution can be found for managing the underclasses (*Ibid.*: 80–82).

Although this is a plausible effort to rescue technological determinism, it cannot explain why "actuarial" technologies, such as state unemployment insurance, are being stripped back while the punitive prison regime concurrently expands. Indeed, the pinnacle of social actuarialism probably occurred several decades ago and as often happens in social theory, identification of a "new trend" occurs not when it appears, but rather as it confronts a crisis that threatens its viability. We suggest that actuarialist technologies currently are being commandeered in a selective and morally explicit fashion by a broad neoconservative political program.[4] In this program, actuarial processes that provided socialized insurances against individual risk — such as health, unemployment, disability, and related "insurances" — commonly are being dismantled or reduced. Paradoxically, such "downsizing" often is justified by actuarialist rhetoric such as "targeting" benefits to those "most at risk." Yet such actuarial claims are made on moral grounds, contrasting those "genuinely at risk" with the "undeserving," or those in jeopardy of disempowerment by welfarism. Preaching individual liberty, dignity, responsibility, and efficiency, neoconservatives have disemboweled actuarialist, socialized insurance and replaced it with individualistic competition "unfettered" by the welfarism and regulation (Levitas, 1986; Gamble, 1986, 1988). Simultaneously, they have expanded and reshaped punitive institutions, displacing correctionalism with "sovereign" forms of retribution, claiming both to expose free and responsible individuals to their just deserts and to accord them the "dignity" of punishment free from the tampering of social engineers (van den Haag, 1975).

Returning to the arguments of Simon and his colleagues, then, we stress that while actuarialism may be advancing in some sectors (for example, situational crime prevention), it is being dismantled and condensed in others. Moreover, far from the direct "demoralization" of social regulation, actuarialism has a complex relationship with moral discourses. Indeed, it may be linked with covert moral programs in a variety of ways. For example, it may be offered as a technically neutral justification for their activities. Alternatively, it may be condemned as generating "welfarist" waste and inefficiency. It might even be tied to overtly moral programs. Consider, for example, the question of "efficiency."

In the debates over welfarism, actuarialism generally is regarded by neo-conservatism not as more "efficient" than discipline and punishment, but rather as counterproductive, stifling the freedom necessary to a dynamic society (Gamble, 1988). Rather than a purely technical exercise in achieving maximum regulatory effect for minimum resource expenditure, the estimate of efficiency is thus inextricably linked to moral agendas (concerning individual responsibility). To be clear, we are not arguing that actuarialism is unimportant as a regulatory technology. Quite to the contrary. In particular, Jonathan Simon's work — including his comments on random drug testing and its place within actuarialism — are of great value. Our point, rather, is that it is a mistake to see actuarialism as impelled by a technological logic of power's efficiency into the dominant form of regulation or to see this "efficiency" as linked in any simple fashion to its capacity to appear amoral.

Rather, we wish to press the following points: that actuarialism has been added to the pantheon of regulatory technologies instead of displacing all others; that its "efficiencies" are matters determined as much by moral agendas as by instrumental effects; and that its operation must be examined in context to understand its effects. These points are relevant to this article's main concern — random drug testing. We shall argue that RDT, despite displaying features accurately depicted by Simon, is not an example of actuarialism. First, drug testing is not geared to technical concerns with productivity levels so much as to moral discourses. Second, the exclusion associated with RDT appears to have a definite set of consequences that are geared directly to the morality lodged within the drug-testing program itself.

Workplace Drug Testing — The U.S. Experience

Reviewing the U.S. literature on RDT and its implementation in the workplace, it appears that two clusters of alleged aims and objectives can be outlined — the first concerns safety, productivity, and security within the workplace, the second concerns furthering the "War on Drugs." We might usefully label these the "internal" and the "external" clusters, viewed from the workplace.

The "Internal" Cluster of Reasons

With respect to safety, productivity, and security — and, in passing, some other things as well — Schottenfeld puts the case well:

> Workplace testing programs to detect substance abuse have been advocated primarily as a way of preventing or curtailing drug- or alcohol-related impairment in the workplace and consequently of enhancing safety and productivity in the workplace. Besides this primary objective, workplace testing programs have also been advocated as a way of achieving some closely related, secondary objectives. These secondary objectives include expediting identification and referral for treatment of impaired workers, fostering public trust in the business or industry using such programs, decreasing the likelihood that employees will engage in illegal activities (such as stealing from the employer or betraying company secrets) so as to support expensive drug habits or to avoid blackmail, and complying with federal regulations or orders requiring such testing (1989: 415).

Schottenfeld here offers a rationalistic history for RDT (that is, that given certain demonstrated potentials, the technique is adopted for practical reasons) and in doing so mimics the technological evolutionism implicit in many actuarialist accounts that presume a selection toward the most efficient technique. Does this history withstand investigation? In the section preceding the quotation, the author explains that the technology for RDT had been developed in the previous 20 years for "medical" purposes. In rehabilitation programs such testing is "invaluable in confronting denial." Or, in plain English, some people tell lies about their drug use and testing can show up those lies. That is, testing technologies were developed as part of coercive drug-treatment strategies that are more social-control activities than they are medical. The translation to the workplace context remains unexplained, implying that the availability of the technology was sufficient to account for its use. This is problematic, for the availability of a technology is rarely sufficient to account for its use.[5] Thus, the history of RDT is not convincingly illuminated by Schottenfeld's own account. Jacobs and Zimmer (1991) offer quite a different and much more compelling account. They argue that RDT was rendered more politically palatable by being linked to treatment and to Employee Assistance Programs (EAPs), thus masking the social-control implications. They also show that the impetus toward testing is strongly linked to the profits to be made from testing when linked to EAP treatment — a double irony when we recall that the treatment sector is itself based on techniques that have not been scientifically established and are of dubious efficacy.

Determining whether a connection between RDT and workplace gains *could* be demonstrated for RDT would require an established corpus of research. Improvements in safety and productivity should be shown to occur in both "before-after" designs within given workplaces and in comparisons between employers, with some but not others employing RDT. Moreover, such studies would need to be cognizant of the "Hawthorne effect" (that is, *any* treatment results in change, simply because the work force is under scrutiny). Sensitivity to this dimension seems singularly lacking in most attempted studies. So, too, is any sensitivity to confounding effects, such as the possibility that some correlations (for example, between drug use and accidents) do not reflect a causal tie (accidents result from incapacity) so much as a common cause (propensity to take risks).[6] Were such evidence forthcoming, employers and others might then make rational calculations to apply new forms of control, and, in turn, we could concede that Schottenfeld correctly describes the evolution of RDT.

In practice, however, it is difficult to sustain this account of RDT. Indeed, we find no established corpus of research evidence that clearly shows the benefits that employers might enjoy as a result of RDT. On the contrary, recent material collected by Morris (1991) argues a reverse relationship to that frequently posited. He cites studies showing, among other things, that per capita Utah Power and Light spent $215 per annum *less* on health benefits for drug users than for a control group, while Georgia Power (examining data from a "for cause" testing procedure) found that employees testing positive for illegal drugs had a *better* promotion record than those who did not.[7] Moreover, a *Scientific American* investigation, also cited by Morris, indicates that only *one* of the many studies allegedly demonstrating the dangers of drugs in the workplace had been subjected to normal scientific peer-review procedures. This represents a serious departure from the normal standards of scientific enquiry and looks suspiciously like a moral crusade. Not surprisingly, then, it seems likely that dispassionate calculation of risk might prevent RDT from being adopted.[8]

The literature does show, however, that the serious impact of drugs on safety and productivity arises not from illicit but from licit drugs. Indeed, Schottenfeld himself draws attention to the problem of alcohol, which "is by far and away the most abused substance in the work force and a major cause of impaired safety and performance...." In terms of lost productivity, tobacco is also a major problem, far exceeding the impact of marijuana, cocaine, or heroin:

> In 1985, the direct health care cost of smoking-related illnesses exceeded $16 billion annually: the indirect smoking-related cost, if lost productivity and earnings from excess morbidity, disability, and pre-

mature death are considered, totaled more than $37 billion.... *The approximate cost to a typical employer in 1988 was at least $1,000 extra per year per smoking employee compared to an otherwise similar non-smoking employee....* The costs to an employer for employees who smoke include the expense of increased accidents, fire risk, disability, retirement, absenteeism, life insurance, health insurance, property and/or business insurance premiums, cleaning, worker's compensation, effects of passive smoke, occupational health risks (especially involving synergies with smoking), damage to property and furnishings, productivity losses, and time wasted in actual smoking-related activities (Sees, 1990: 479, emphasis added).

Sees relies upon material published in 1983, 1985, and 1989, the authors of which in turn were drawing upon earlier material. These data were therefore available for calculating safety and productivity loss in the 1980s, as were data about alcohol and pharmaceutical drugs such as benzodiazepines and ephedrine. Any dispassionate calculation of drug-related risks, therefore, would have concentrated on the licit drugs. Furthermore, if safety and productivity were principal employer concerns, it is uncertain that any drug use — licit *or* illicit — would top the list of relevant problems. In transportation, for example, poor maintenance and declining investment have been the main source of problems for the railway system (*San Francisco Chronicle*, 1991), while in quite another direction, the extensive discussion of sexual harassment following the controversial hearings into the nomination of Clarence Thomas to the U.S. Supreme Court revealed that productivity is higher in companies with strong anti-harassment policies (Strom, 1991). To these disparate examples may be added others, including (where safety is concerned) bonus systems designed to encourage risk taking or (where productivity is concerned) the contested terrain of labor relations. A rational employer might well concentrate scarce dollars on improving the production plant, improving inter-employee relations and improving labor relations, long before monitoring the level of employee drug use. Above all, given the objective evidence, a rational-actuarial employer would not have been drawn either to illicit drug use, nor to RDT as a method of controlling that activity. Here was a new and largely untried technique, with considerable costs attached to it, involving complex labor relations and legal questions that might (or might not!) have an impact upon a small sector of the problem of safety and lost productivity, while leaving the major sources of drug problems untouched. Why would that employer have chosen to employ RDT?

One answer is a moral crusade by politicians, "experts," and moral entrepreneurs using rhetorical persuasion rather than rational argument. Central to such a strategy have been cautionary tales, not dissimilar to Aesop's fables. Miller et al. provide one plausible example:

> Movement in this direction accelerated when the United States Navy instituted routine laboratory testing for drugs after a Navy jet crashed on the aircraft carrier, USS *Nimitz*, in 1981. The crash left 14 sailors dead and 42 injured. The finding that changed the Navy's operating procedure was that drug use was determined to be directly responsible for the crash. A prior survey in 1980 revealed that one-third to one-half of the Navy's junior enlisted officers smoked marijuana regularly. The Navy reduced the size of this problem by instituting drug testing for all military personnel. By August 1986, the number of sailors testing positive for drugs was less than 10% (1990: 239).

We are invited to make the following connections: (1) there was a 1980 survey that showed high levels of marijuana use in the Navy, but nothing much flowed from that; (2) in 1981, there was a terrible accident, and it turned out that drugs (marijuana?) "caused" the accident; (3) therefore, drug testing was introduced; and (4) the consequence of testing was that use dropped from a high range of 30% to 50% of sailors to only 10%.

We are also invited *not* to ask awkward questions, such as the following: Wasn't *anyone* concerned and lobbying as a result of the 1980 survey, which showed high levels of illicit drug use in the armed forces of the country that leads the world in anti-drug public sentiment? What else was happening between 1980 and 1986 that could account for the change in drug use patterns? Are survey data and RDT data comparable (i.e., was the change a real change)? Is it really this easy for a deterrence program to shift behavior so radically? If safety is such a concern, what was being done about licit drug consumption, which in most contexts is a far more common cause of serious accidents?

Miller et al. are silent about the improvement (or lack of it!) in the U.S. Navy's safety record since implementation of RDT. Instead, we are offered data about the reduced incidence of drug use, variously described as decreasing from one-third to one-half down to 10% and from 43% down to less than 2%. The example of the crash, as they present it, implies a connection between illicit drugs and a poor safety record, on the *Nimitz* and in general. Thus, evidence of spectacular reductions in drug use among sailors — allegedly a result of RDT — suggests that the U.S. Navy can sail again with safety. Yet this "conclusion" is unwarranted in both the specific and the general sense. Specifically, one "difficulty" frequently overlooked by supporters of RDT — who are unwilling to allow mere facts to spoil a good tale — is that the Miller tale is not true:

> A postmortem toxicological screen found that the pilot had probably ingested a decongestant. The crash, however, occurred at night in poor weather and a new guidance system may not have functioned adequately. Some of the deck crew killed in the crash had cannabinoid residue in bodily fluids on postmortem exam. *None of these killed was responsible for guidance or contributed to the accident.*
>
> The finding that the men at sea probably had access to cannabis surely contributed to the zeal for testing. *However, the accident on the* Nimitz *was not caused by drug use* (Morgan and Puder, 1989: 385, emphasis added).

As Morgan and Puder make quite clear, this is an attempt to persuade by rhetorical force rather than by marshalling evidence.

At the general level, anecdotal evidence at least as compelling as the *Nimitz* case suggests that no improvement in safety followed from the Navy's RDT program. The spectacular explosion aboard the USS *New Jersey* post-dates RDT, as do a number of less memorable accidents, which at one point led the Navy to take the drastic step of suspending all sea-going operations while safety procedures were reviewed.[9] An alternate interpretation of the Navy's actions is that illicit drug use in the U.S. Navy was extremely politically embarrassing and the *Nimitz* provided an alibi for introducing RDT. While RDT may have reduced drug use — in politically rewarding ways — it had little impact on the alleged goal of improved safety. Since safety, however, was an excuse rather than a real impetus to change, the lack of payoff in the safety area was not devastating for the RDT program and its protagonists.

We suggest that this account of the data — polemically phrased though it is — is at least as warrantable as that offered by Miller et al. The Navy's testing program was not an "actuarial" response in which an objective threat was met with a calculated response designed to manage the effects of that threat. Furthermore, the Navy persisted with the program despite high costs, few tangible benefits, and serious quality-control problems (Morgan and Puder, 1989) — again suggesting that symbolic politics, not rational risk calculation, lay at the heart of the exercise.

Moreover, even if the U.S. Navy had demonstrated a "success" for RDT in the terms initially canvassed (that is, safety improvement, absenteeism reduction, and removal of security threats), it is unclear what lesson, if any, this might be thought to offer to civilian employers. Even in the U.S., where labor unions do not exert the industrial and political muscle that they do in many other countries, the existence of unions, of labor-relations legislation, of industrial arbitration schemes means that employers cannot introduce RDT by fiat. Indeed, the introduction of RDT has been a bonanza for lawyers, with cases contested up to the U.S. Supreme Court, which, despite several decisions that favor RDT in certain instances, has refused to give the practice *carte blanche*. As McCunney (1989: 597) notes, "legal challenges to random testing have been upheld in nearly every occupational setting, aside from the military." U.S. Congress and Senate votes in October 1991 extended testing in the transportation industry, where safety issues seem more prominent and where public acceptance of testing is highest (Latessa et al., 1988; see also poll data cited by Jacobs and Zimmer, 1991: 349). The fact remains, however, that for most U.S. employers, the introduction of an RDT program is not simple, requiring both complex procedures to ensure reliable testing and also a commitment, in the first instance, to referring workers to EAPs for rehabilitation.

In addition, any wise employer knows that the formal apparatus of labor relations is matched by an informal web of understandings and practices that the employer is prudent not to disturb without a good cause and strong evidence that the disturbance will be worthwhile (Gouldner, 1955). For example, employers often tolerate pilferage in the workplace if they believe that losses through disruption would exceed losses due to theft (Henry, 1978). In the case of drug use, there are at least two kinds of use that employers might rationally choose to ignore. These are drug use in employees nonwork hours, if work performance is not markedly affected, and drug use in and around the workplace, where risks of accidents or of litigation are low. RDT, of course, cannot discriminate between these uses and instances of use where direct peril is created. Indeed, most RDT technologies, especially urine testing, have a lag time of days or even weeks, so if an employee is incapacitated, this is not revealed until long afterwards. Thus, any impact on safety (or on productivity) has to be indirect, through deterrence of use and/or retrospective dismissal of "problem" workers. Here is yet another irony of RDT — that it discovers drug use of limited relevance to employers while partially neglecting use of the most perilous kind! The enthusiasm for RDT despite this weakness is, we suggest, another symptom of the fact that RDT is more about moral crusade than risk control.

The absence of confirmatory evidence to support RDT is highly significant, for there is no doubt that if these data existed, they would be widely trumpeted. Schottenfeld's first explanation, then, which is the commonest single ground for explaining and justifying RDT, turns out to be highly questionable. Yet we should note also that Schottenfeld mentions other "secondary" reasons and aims. The form he specifically mentions are "expediting identification and referral for treatment of impaired workers, fostering public trust in the business or industry using such programs, decreasing the likelihood that employees will engage in illegal activities..., and complying with federal regulations or orders requiring such testing." Let us look at each of these in turn.

1. *Identification and referral for treatment of impaired workers.* In itself, this aim is not inherently problematic. Yet the implication is that the users identified are drug addicted, which is why they need "treatment" and why they have "expensive habits." Nowhere has Schottenfeld suggested, however, that RDT will identify addicts as opposed to casual users. Since the drug most likely to be detected is marijuana — not a drug of addiction — and given the high ratio of casual users to addicts and the broad time frame (several days) over which use of the drug is detected by a urine test, it is clear that most users detected by testing are not addicts. Indeed, the data cited by Miller et al. (1990: 240) that use in the U.S. Navy apparently fell from 43% to less than 2% following the introduction of RDT — a fall of some 95% — is hardly congruent with addicted use. What will happen to non-addicted users? Will they be "referred to treatment"? What "treatment" is appropriate for such people? What if, as the data from the Georgia and Utah power studies cited earlier might imply, some non-addicted users are "better" employees than non-users?

2. *Fostering public trust in the business or industry using such programs.* Here the underlying logic risks circularity. That is, it presumes that RDT is publicly accepted and seen to be desirable, thus begging two questions. First, how is it publicly acceptable to allow licit drug use to pass with little comment and yet be excited about illicit use, which causes less harm in aggregate terms? More importantly, how did RDT become accepted to begin with? The latter is crucial, for we are otherwise offered a circular account that confuses *explanans* and *explanandum*. In practice, it seems likely that it was the government that "accepted" RDT before employers, so that reasons four and two are heavily interconnected.

3. *Decreasing the likelihood that employees will engage in illegal activities.* This reason raises the old specter that users will indulge in security breaches and theft, either to support expensive habits or to conceal use when blackmailed. There is no doubt that such things can happen. The question that needs to be posed is whether RDT is a useful way to handle such threats. Since most users of drugs do not represent this kind of risk, and since risks can arise from many other sources (for example, greed for gain, bad gambling debts, blackmail because of sexual preference or extramarital affairs), the overlapping set of those who both test positive and are a risk is very small. In terms of traditional criteria for diagnostic tests, as a way of identifying employees whose drug use makes them a risk in other illegal ways, RDT is low on both specificity and sensitivity. Both type one and type two errors are rife in the system.

4. *Complying with federal regulations or orders requiring such testing.* Here, perhaps, is the nub of the issue. The U.S. federal government has been actively introducing RDT for federal employees and, through secondary action such as the Drug-Free Workplace Act, 1988 (Harrison and Simpler, 1989), it

has caused others to implement it too. Placing this as a *secondary* reason for introducing RDT is a confusion, however. An employer who introduces a new technique because she or he is pressured to do so is not acting to achieve the ends that RDT purportedly produces, but rather because of that pressure. Such behavior cannot, therefore, be usefully added to the list of explanations of why RDT was introduced, because it merely raises the further question of why the government chose to introduce RDT.

In short, the "internal" cluster of reasons that are cited as explaining the trend toward RDT do not stand scrutiny. Of the explanations cited by Schottenfeld, the only one that can be supported is that companies are moving toward RDT because of external pressure from the U.S. federal government.[10] Of necessity, then, the inadequacy of the internal reasons leads us to explore external reasons.

The "External" Cluster of Reasons

When we turn to this topic, an entirely different set of reasons for adopting RDT emerges, embedded in a different discourse — a discourse, as we shall see, of moral crusade. One of the main protagonists here is Robert Dupont and it may be simplest to let his own words outline the position:

> The company policy about off-duty drug use needs to be clear. The clearest policy is one that states that no on-duty *or* off-duty illicit drug use will be accepted (Dupont, 1989: 149).

> In general, punishment...is not appropriate for employees who refer themselves voluntarily for help, including treatment for drug use.... In contrast, employees who do not refer themselves for help and who are identified as drug users by company drug use prevention programs should, in my view, be punished by suspension without pay or even firing.... Testing all employees is essential to the company's overall program. This program is in the interest of non-users because it reduces the "chemical dependence tax" which all workers pay. It also helps drug users and their families. Unless the non-drug user is tested, then the people with drug use-associated problems will not be tested. This is similar to having the Internal Revenue Service check one's tax return, or having the police stop one at a road-block looking for drunk drivers, or going through a metal detector entering a security area, such as an airport. *All these intrusions on privacy are necessary to protect everyone. They are part of the price paid for living in interdependent communities (Ibid.*: 151–152, emphasis added).

> There is a brighter side to the problem of chemical dependence at work. Even as the United States has begun to recognize the limits of

cutting off the supply of drugs, because of the billions of dollars involved in drug sales...it is beginning to recognize that a key to ending the imputed "drug use epidemic" is to take the profit out of the drug trade. That can only happen when the user decides not to use, and therefore not to buy, drugs. *Workplace drug use prevention programs are a central element in an anti-drug, pro-people national strategy* (*Ibid.*: 158, emphasis added).

Drug testing in the workplace holds great promise for the nation and for individual employers and employees. For that potential to be realized, drug testing policies need to distinguish clearly between nonmedical drug use (that should be prohibited on and off the job) and the use of legitimate medicines (that should be encouraged).... *Drug testing which prohibits nonmedical drug use and promotes legitimate medical treatment is rooted in easily understood values that are the foundation of American drug-control laws. Such a policy reflects commitment to the needs of the organization, of employees in the organization and their families and the nation as a whole* (Dupont, 1990: 458, emphasis added).

Dupont in these pieces proposes quite a different account of RDT. In a nutshell, the explicit and implicit case may be summarized as follows: the use of some drugs is un-American ("testing holds great promise for the nation"), rejecting "easily understood values" and undermining families. It is hard to contain this activity and supply-side efforts have limited utility, so we must attack demand. In a liberal democracy with strong constitutional defenses to intrusion on privacy, this can be hard to achieve through direct law enforcement. A large majority of Americans, however, are either waged or salaried employees or are dependent upon such employees. If one can link drug surveillance to employment, through binding contracts, one can shift enforcement from the criminal domain (where standards of proof are exacting and defendants have the right not to testify against themselves) to a civil arena, where standards of proof are lower and penalties are likely to be higher (compare the likely fine for possession of a small quantity of marijuana with the costs of losing employment for testing positive to marijuana use). By pursuing civil enforcement through contract law, we can replace ineffective criminal law enforcement. *To this end, RDT, which demonstrates merely that one has at some time used an illegal drug, is an ideal strategy.* The fact that such testing does not speak to current incapacity to perform safely and effectively is thus irrelevant.[11]

In this case for RDT, we are faced with some familiar positions. Implicitly, Dupont relies upon an old-fashioned, structural-functionalist view of the world. In this view, a society has an underlying core of values that are almost universally shared and that it is in the interest of all to have reiterated and maintained. The minority who do not share those values, or whose behavior departs from the norms based upon them, are deviants who threaten to undermine the system, perhaps as much through weakness and poor socialization as through willful evil. It is in their best interests, as well as the best interests of their families, co-workers, and friends, if their deviance is corrected. Once equilibrium is restored, we will all be happier and better off.

Such a view cannot comprehend the fact that social systems in fact contain a wide variety of norms and values, or that even within one "set" of values, there are contradictions and conflicts. In viewing drug use an un-American, for example, Dupont wishes to sidestep such unpleasant realities as the fact that Americans consume and export large quantities of drugs. At many professional football stadia, for example, despite NFL campaigns supported by the DEA and Department of Justice in which football stars exhort young people to "do your thing without drugs," the main scoreboards are flanked by enormous advertising slogans for tobacco (Marlboro), alcohol (Budweiser), and caffeine (Coca Cola). Alcohol, tobacco, and caffeine, of course, are the "Holy Trinity" of American drugs and involve multibillion dollar industries that are indissolubly intertwined with daily life. Moreover, as the scoreboard advertising symbolizes, such drug use is part of a hedonist ethic that, far from being un-American, might be argued to epitomize at least one central strand of contemporary American culture (Mugford and O'Malley, 1991). As opposed to deviating from American culture, drug use might be more usefully be understood as conforming to it, at least in the sense of conforming to the hedonistic imperative to seek commodity-based pleasure, albeit by illegal and socially contested means.[12]

In the face of these realities, the position adopted by Dupont does not constitute an attempt to describe and analyze a problem. Rather, it constitutes a moral crusade — a polemical attempt to impose both a politico-moral discourse that will justify a variety of exercises in social control and the set of exercises themselves. In particular, drug use becomes a terrain in which the representatives of "Middle America" can wrestle with those forces to which they are opposed, attempting all the while to claim the right to speak "for America" — but an America conceived in their own image.[13] At the core of this struggle we see a search for morally pure urine specimens, a search not unlike that for the Holy Grail, both centering on a search for powerfully valued signs of the ultimate good. In such a context, evidence of the efficacy of RDT in the employment context is almost irrelevant. The argument that RDT would improve safety and productivity was always at best a gloss upon the truth, so evidence that it has little or no impact upon them is of limited significance (see *fn.* 8). Further, in pursuit of such objectives, the employers themselves become subject to scrutiny. As Dupont makes clear, we must insist upon random, as oppose to purposive ("for cause"), testing programs, for when for-cause programs are the basis for testing, there are too few tests carried out. Rather:

> random testing...is fair and impartial. It also can do the major thing that cause-testing does not do: it can deter drug use and prevent drug-use-caused-associated problems by making it clear to every single employee that they may be tested every day at work. That is the source of the preventive power of random testing. It also solves the problem of supervisor reluctance to ask for tests and the bias of top management to deny and overlook chemical dependence problems (Dupont, 1989: 158).

Here Dupont mixes two issues — deterrence and labor relations. On the first, he is no doubt empirically correct. Frequent testing that creates a climate of certainty of apprehension is likely to have maximum deterrent impact. Yet from an employer's perspective, pursuing deterrence makes sense only if there is an objective payoff in terms of accidents avoided or productivity gained, especially if testing disrupts good labor relations. In the absence of documented gains, the ruthless pursuit of testing is not a good employer strategy, it is actually economically foolish. In such a climate, this is not to "deny" drug use — deny being a code word for moral disapproval of anyone who does not share your cause — but to act sensibly in terms of the shareholders economic interests. The extent to which Dupont is prepared to overlook the economic question in the search for employer (and hence employee) conformity is a measure of his commitment to RDT not as an internal workplace device, but rather as a Trojan Horse for wider social control.

The objects of that social control, the people who will suffer most if RDT becomes a widespread activity in large companies, will be those who already are more marginal in American society. In various testing programs, there is a tendency for African Americans and other minority groups to show up as having higher rates of positive urine tests than others (e.g., Normand et al., 1990: 633). Systematic application of such testing programs, therefore, will be more likely to affect such minority groups, squeezing them even more from employment in secure jobs with large employers, perhaps from employment altogether. This activity will take place under the guise of an objective "actuarialist" logic. It is not that employers discriminate against African Americans, we will be told, it is simply that they wish to eliminate high-risk employees and that any disproportionate effect upon any one category "merely" reflects its risk status.

Conclusion

We set out with two projects in mind — to understand RDT as a practice and through it to illuminate current debates on social control. These two projects may now be completed.

With respect to RDT, our analysis shows it to be a deeply moral activity, designed to impose, via civil law and the employment contract, a particular view of what it is to be an American — sober, reliable, conforming to Middle American views of drugs, supporting a traditionalist pro-family, pro-nation view of the world. This activity, however, is wrapped to a great degree inside packaging that purports to offer a scientific and rational account of RDT and its effectiveness — that claims, in part, to offer a nonmoralizing account while in fact remoralizing the issue.[14] In reality, the discourse is scientistic, not scientific, relying upon a series of rhetorical devices and tales to persuade the listener, with tales substituting for the research data that a rational account would require, but that, despite many efforts, do not exist. Moreover, those tales often do not stand up to scrutiny even within themselves.

This recalls the point made earlier about Simon's vision of RDT as an actuarialist mechanism. It can be argued that he too readily accepts the claim that these new controls are based on efficiency and risk management. In reality, the "why" of RDT is more problematic than he imagines. Yet at the same time his description of "how" seems well founded. RDT, conceived as a surveillance technique designed to deter use of certain drugs, is technically well conceived. Within the ranks of those with the educational, social, and economic resources that permit participation in the market economy, and who are also psychologically committed to such participation, there are good *a priori* reasons to suppose that RDT will act to deter drug use. Moreover, such evidence as is available tends to confirm deterrent effects. Whatever our doubts regarding the precision of the statistics marshalled by Miller et al. (1990) with respect to the U.S. Navy, it would be difficult to suggest that all the evidence of reduced use is an illusion. Although systematic research exploring the effects of RDT within corporate ranks is not available, anecdotal evidence from some drug researchers suggests that young, corporate executives are now offering accounts of their behavior in which potential recreational drug use has been dissuaded by testing.[15] At the same time, the willingness of other, lower-status groups to desist from illicit drugs is less clear. For example, a report in the *San Francisco Chronicle* (1988) describes a major problem in recruiting new police officers because a high proportion fail drug testing, despite foreknowledge of testing. It quotes a rejection rate of between 45% and 80% of the candidates who pass the written examinations because of drug test results. Thus, Simon's prediction of fragmentation of the marketplace for employment, as well as his characterization of this process as occurring in a nonpoliticized context, is well made.

Thus, debates on social-control theory are illuminated further by this concrete example. In some areas of social life there may be a genuine growth in actuarialism — some developments in traffic control and strategies for crime prevention fit such a model. At the same time, there is a growth, perhaps a larger growth, in social control justifications that deploy *rhetorics* of actuarialism as a mask for activities that are deeply moralized and in which the real contours of the activity are much closer to "punishment" or to "discipline" in the sense intended by Foucault[16] — that is, RDT seems more part of the punitive city than the risk society. We do not foresee the creation of categories of people who are controlled because of the objective risk they create, for those objective risks either do not exist, or, at the very least, have not been demonstrated to exist. Objective examination of risk, indeed, would lead to quite different attempts at actuarialist control. Rather, ostensible risks are assigned by sleight of hand and populations are dealt with in terms of these alleged risks. As such, control is exercised over people not in terms of reducing employment problems, but rather in terms of contrasting acceptable Americans to unacceptable Americans, a task quite different from that which proponents of RDT claim and probably quite different from what many of them understand themselves to be doing.[17] Moreover, while this results, as predicted, in a less politicized form of control, it is not clear whether that is an intended effect or a "fortunate" spin-off. As noted earlier, Simon argues that different techniques are available for controlling those in and those not in the market. In the case of RDT, if Dupont's approach is to be taken seriously, one of the reasons for relying on testing is that one can then improve demand control by linking it, via civil law, to employment, thus sidestepping other, less-effective forms of control. That sounds like classic actuarialism, but in a context not of amoral risk reduction so much as of a deeply moral crusade against drug use per se.

In short, actuarialism is easily as much of a rhetorical resource as it is a social-control process. The confusion is reduced if we examine the evidence for the rhetorical claims rather than accepting them at face value. When Simon says, in the passage cited earlier, that if "drugs are out in the eighties, it is because they are perceived as driving accident rates up, productivity down," he accepts too easily the claims of the drug warriors. As we have argued in this article, these claims cannot be seriously sustained. Moreover, if the rational-actuarialist impulse to improve safety and productivity were the main motive, we should expect to see very different types of control activity from employers. RDT, in short, is not a technique to improve efficiency, but rather a technique designed to pursue deeply moral goals. Despite its façade, it owes more to disciplinary tactics such as exclusion and moral condemnation than to actuarial control. In short, RDT is more a moral crusade than is actuarialism, but like many crusades, its real effects should not be confused with the stated goals of the self-appointed crusaders.

NOTES

1.   As this example suggests, the general view is that actuarial power — although developed long ago — has only comparatively recently become a feasible technology for managing populations. It is argued that it is only in the 20th century that actuarialism emerges from the margins of governance to its present central position. This is because it is viable only where the populace basically consents to the economic and political arrangements. In particular, it is argued that such conditions have been created in part precisely by the success of such disciplinary institutions as the school and the factory — these being the coercive institutions developed to manage the "dangerous classes" thrown up by capitalist industrialization (Foucault, 1979, 1984; Simon, 1987, 1988). Thus, ironically they create the conditions of their own obsolescence.

2.   In one sense, this revives the medieval notion of partial proof justifying partial punishment (cf. Langbein, 1977).

3.   Indeed, not merely of illicit use. For many years, one polemical tactic available to drug-law critics was to point to the contradiction involved in permitting the use of alcohol and tobacco — which together account for over 90% of drug-related deaths in Western countries — while maintaining bans on drugs like marijuana. This strategy presumed that the response that "we should, therefore, ban alcohol and tobacco too" was not culturally available. In recent years, however, a progressive rise in "prohibitionist" sentiments seems to have spread even to legal drugs. See, for example, Rose (1991) for a recent popular account of the phenomenon and Wagner (1987) for an historical comparison.

4.   For a more detailed explication of this argument, see O'Malley (1991b).

5.   Moreover, in many cases, the development of technology follows, rather than precedes the social changes that are associated with it. For example, Banks' (1954) classic study of the connection between (rubber) technology and the development of contraceptive practice indicates that while the technical skill to produce condoms existed for some time, it was not until economic depression squeezed middle-class families, creating a desire for fewer children, that the rubber condom was developed.

6.   There is always a danger with this argument, for in the 20th century "personality" can be, as Samuel Johnson said of patriotism, the last refuge of a scoundrel. Also, it is not beyond the bounds of possibility that personal qualities — psychological or genetic — could be the basis of politically motivated "risk-hunting," a topic dealt with in different ways by Wagner (1987), Duster (1990), and Nelkin and Tancredi (1989). Nonetheless, we have to challenge the basis for some alleged "evidence" because, like the story about the crash on the USS *Nimitz* detailed below, RDT zealots do not allow niceties like evidence and logic to obstruct their cause. Thus, if drug use is associated with poor safety — and evidence even for that is sketchy — we need to know whether the association is causal or coincidental.

7.   These data are excerpted from Crouch et al. (1989) and Sheridan and Winkler (1989) respectively. In both cases, the authors are supportive of RDT and present a wide range of data that purport to support its efficacy. While this is not the forum for a detailed analysis of these articles, two things might be noted. First, they are both funded by NIDA and published in a (nonrefereed) NIDA outlet, which does raise some concerns about objectivity. Second, in at least some of the calculations, questionable practices are visible — such as arbitrarily doubling some estimates to allow for "double jeopardy," or calculating losses where "users" have higher costs than "controls,"

The Political Agenda of Random Drug Testing

but neglecting to calculate gains that occur when controls have higher costs than users. In short, these articles are less convincing than their authors might have us believe.

8.   Although our data so far are anecdotal, preliminary investigations in some areas of the Australian mining industry indicate that some large companies, initially attracted by the promise of increased safety and productivity are now, on expert advice, shying away from RDT *because it cannot deliver the goods*. If this proves widespread it will be an interesting twist, for the scientistic rhetoric used to justify RDT will have led to precisely the kind of investigation that undermines the practice.

9.   The USS *New Jersey* case is also interesting with respect to rhetorics and tales. The Navy claimed at the time of the explosion — in which over 40 crew lost their lives — that a crew man, driven by depression over a failed (implicitly homosexual) relationship had committed murder/suicide by sabotage. Over two years later, in October 1991, this posthumous calumny was finally withdrawn and the sailor's family received an apology. The apology received less press coverage than the allegation, and it is probable that the original accusation is still widely believed. Here again, we see a process whereby blame is attached to less-conventional behavior, entirely by innuendo.

10.   We might add, in a speculative vein, that large companies are no more immune from questions of intellectual "fashion" than anyone else. That is, we should not neglect the possibility that once a particular trend emerges, many of those who swell its ranks do so because it is the "in" thing to do. Such an explanation is silent on the origins of the trend, but helps us understand its subsequent development. Of course, this line of reasoning is not stressed by those who believe — or profess to believe — that RDT arises as a rational response to objective conditions, since an explanation that implies faddism and fashion is incompatible with an explanation that centers on rational and objective logics.

11.   On this last point, it should be noted that Dupont does exert considerable effort to deal with the question of incapacity, developing intriguing arguments about the differences between drugs like alcohol — where the form of intoxication tends to be gross and socially identified through such signs as slurred speech, staggering, smell of drink on the user's breath — and drugs where intoxication is more subtle, may not be obvious to co-workers, but might cause impairment of higher-order discriminatory functions. Yet it is clear that his argument is heavily glossed at this point, continually sliding from statements of what might be possible toward the implication that such intoxication is common and a well-established cause of danger and loss, without any substantiation of the latter. As we have already demonstrated, however, it is very difficult on the evidence available to support the claim that these other forms of intoxication are actually responsible for accidents or lost productivity. That is, Dupont frequently resorts to an actuarialist rhetoric to complete the chain of his argument, but does so without demonstrating any real link to risk.

12.   We say "socially contested" because it is clear that very substantial proportions of the population do not consider some forms of illegal drug taking to be morally wrong, even while those same people would acknowledge that the activity remains outside the current law. Trying to gloss away such acceptance as constituting a small minority view, rather than accepting contestation, epitomizes the drug-war stance of writers like Dupont.

13.   The argument about Middle America is developed in detail in Mugford (1992, forthcoming).

14.   Indeed, to some extent this represents an attempt to have one's cake and eat it too. When the audience is more "scientifically" oriented and less obviously concerned with drugs as a moral issue, one can draw upon rhetorics of risk, but when the audience is explicitly concerned with drugs as a moral issue (voters, parents, etc.), the more explicitly moral discourse surfaces.

15.   Marsha Rosenbaum, personal communication.

16.   For example, Simon (1987) argues that the expansion of actuarialism is exemplified by the increasingly targeted planning of welfare distribution. Since he also argues that welfarism is a primary instance of actuarialism, that targeting is being used to scale down welfarism, and that

144   O'MALLEY AND MUGFORD

Simon himself recognizes that the consequence of this process is to subject many ex-recipients to penal control, then we may see that he is confusing form and substance. The fact that actuarial rhetoric is being used to implement disciplinary and sovereign social technologies does not constitute evidence of the expansion of actuarialism.

17.   That is, it would be equally naïve to suppose either that all proponents are involved in a conscious conspiracy, on the one hand, or that they are all misguided, on the other hand. More likely, many middle-level practitioners believe, unreflectively, that they are participating in an activity that is based on sound and established research.

REFERENCES

Banks, Joseph
    1954   Prosperity and Parenthood: A Study of Family Planning among the Victorian Middle Classes. London: Routledge and Kegan Paul.
    1991   "From Dangerousness to Risk." G. Burchell and C. Gordon (eds.), The Foucault Effect. Studies in Governmentality. London: Harvester/Wheatsheaf.
Cohen, Stanley
    1985   Visions of Social Control: Crime, Punishment, and Classification. London: Polity Press.
    1979   "The Punitive City. Notes on the Dispersal of Social Control." Contemporary Crises 3: 339–363.
Crouch, Dennis J., Douglas O. Webb, Lynn V. Peterson, Paul F. Buller, and Douglas E. Rollins
    1989   "A Critical Evaluation of the Utah Power and Light Company's Substance Abuse Management Program: Absenteeism, Accidents, and Cost." Steven W. Gust and J. Michael Walsh (eds.), Drugs in the Workplace: Research and Evaluation Data. NIDA Research Monograph No. 91. Rockville, MD: National Institute on Drug Abuse: 169–193.
Donzelot, Jacques
    1991   "Pleasure in Work." G. Burchell and C. Gordon (eds.), The Foucault Effect. Studies in Governmentality. London: Harvester/Wheatsheaf.
    1979   "The Poverty of Political Culture." Ideology and Consciousness 5: 71–86.
Dupont, Robert L.
    1990   "Medicines and Drug Testing in the Workplace." Journal of Psychoactive Drugs 22,4: 451–459.
    1989   "Drugs in the American Workplace: Conflict and Opportunity. Part II: Controversies in Workplace Drug Prevention." Social Pharmacology 3,1–2: 147–164.
Duster, Troy S.
    1990   Backdoor to Eugenics. New York: Routledge.
    1987   "Crime, Youth Unemployment, and the Black Underclass." Crime and Delinquency 33,2: 300–315.
Ewald, François
    1991   "Insurance and Risk." G. Burchell and C. Gordon (eds.), The Foucault Effect. Studies in Governmentality. London: Harvester/Wheatsheaf.
    1986   L'Etat Providence. Paris: Grasset.
Foucault, Michel
    1984   The History of Sexuality. Volume 1. London: Peregrine Books.
    1979   "Governmentality." Ideology and Consciousness 5: 21.
Gamble, Andrew
    1988   The Free Economy and the Strong State. London: Macmillan.
    1986   "The Political Economy of the New Right." Ruth Levitas (ed.), The Ideology of the New Right. Oxford: Basil Blackwell.

Gouldner, Alvin
    1955   Wildcat Strike: A Study of an Unofficial Strike. London: Routledge and
                    Kegan Paul.
Harrison, Bruce S. and Gary L. Simpler
    1989   "Antidrug Rules and Regulations." EAP Digest (September/October): 19–24.
Henry, Stuart
    1978   The Hidden Economy: The Context and Control of Borderline Crime. Oxford:
                    Martin Robertson.
Jacobs, James B. and Lynn Zimmer
    1991   "Drug Treatment and Workplace Drug Testing: Politics, Symbolism, and Or-
                    ganizational Dilemmas." Behavioral Sciences and the Law 9: 345–360.
Latessa, Edward J., Lawrence F. Travis III, and Francis T. Cullen
    1988   "Public Support for Mandatory Drug-Alcohol Testing in the Workplace."
                    Crime and Delinquency 34,4: 379–392.
Langbein, R.
    1977   Torture and the Law of Proof. Chicago: University of Chicago Press.
Levitas, Ruth
    1986   "Introduction. Ideology and the New Right." Ruth Levitas (ed.), The Ideology
                    of the New Right. Oxford: Basil Blackwell.
McCunney, Robert J.
    1989   "Drug Testing: Technical Complications of a Complex Social Issue." Ameri-
                    can Journal of Industrial Medicine 15: 589–600.
Miller, Norman S., A. James Giannini, Mark S. Gold, and James A. Philomena
    1990   "Drug Testing: Medical, Legal, and Ethical Issues." Journal of Substance
                    Abuse Treatment 7: 239–244.
Morgan, John P. and Pamela S. Puder
    1989   "Urinary Testing for Drugs of Abuse in the Military." Behavioral Sciences
                    and the Law 7,3: 379–386.
Morris, David
    1991   "Evidence Mounts That Drug War Cure Worse Than U.S. Ailment." St. Paul
                    Pioneer Press (May 6): 7A.
Mugford, Stephen K.
    1992   "Cocaine in Australia: A Comparative Perspective." Harry Levine and Craig
                    Reinarman (eds.), Crack in Context. New York: Basic Books.
Mugford, Stephen K. and Pat O'Malley
    1991   "The Demand for Intoxicating Commodities: Implications for the 'War on
                    Drugs.'" Social Justice: A Journal of Crime, Conflict and World Order 18,4
                    (Winter).
Nelkin, Dorothy and Laurence Tancredi
    1989   Dangerous Diagnostics: The Social Power of Biological Information. New
                    York: Basic Books.
Normand, Jacques, Stephen D. Salyards, and John J. Mahoney
    1990   "An Evaluation of Pre-Employment Drug Testing." Journal of Applied Psy-
                    chology 75,6: 629–639.
O'Malley, Pat
    1991a   "Legal Networks and Domestic Security." Studies in Law, Politics, and Soci-
                    ety 11.
    1991b   "After Discipline? The Strong State, a Free Market, and Crime Prevention."
                    Paper presented at the Annual Meeting of the Law and Society Association
                    and International Sociological Association, Amsterdam.
    1989   "Redefining Security. Neighbourhood Watch in Context." Arena 86: 18–23.
Reichman, Nancy
    1986   "Managing Crime Risks: Toward an Insurance Based Model of Social Con-
                    trol." Research in Law and Social Control 8: 151–172.
Rose, Frank
    1991   "If It Feels Good, It Must Be Bad." Fortune 124,9: 91–108.

146   O'MALLEY AND MUGFORD

San Francisco Chronicle
    1988   "Cop Recruiters Have Hard Time Finding Drug-Free Jobseekers." (August
                    30).
San Francisco Chronicle
    1991   "Rail Safety Is of Major Concern." [Editorial] (October 19): A20.
Schottenfeld, Richard S.
    1989   "Drug and Alcohol Testing in the Workplace — Objectives, Pitfalls, and
                    Guidelines." American Journal of Drug and Alcohol Abuse 15,4: 413–427.
Sees, Karen Lea
    1990   "The Smoke-Free Workplace." Journal of Psychoactive Drugs 22,4: 479–483.
Sheridan, John and Howard Winkler
    1989   "An Evaluation of Drug Testing in the Workplace." Steven W. Gust and J.
                    Michael Walsh (eds.), Drugs in the Workplace: Research and Evaluation Data.
                    NIDA Research Monograph No. 91. Rockville, MD: National Institute on
                    Drug Abuse: 195–216.
Simon, Jonathan
    1988   "The Ideological Effects of Actuarial Practices." Law and Society Review 22:
                    772–800.
    1987   "The Emergence of a Risk Society: Insurance, Law, and the State." Socialist
                    Review 95: 61–89.
Strom, Stephanie
    1991   "Many Companies Assailed on Sexual Harassment Rules." New York Times
                    (October 20): 1, 15.
van den Haag, Ernest
    1975   Punishing Criminals. Concerning an Old and Painful Question. Chicago:
                    Harper Torchbooks.
Wagner, David
    1987   The New Temperance Movement and Social Control at the Workplace. Con-
                    temporary Drug Problems 14: 539–556.

Part III
Actuarial Justice

[11]

THE NEW PENOLOGY: NOTES ON THE EMERGING STRATEGY OF CORRECTIONS AND ITS IMPLICATIONS*

MALCOLM M. FEELEY
University of California at Berkeley

JONATHAN SIMON
University of Michigan

The new penology *argues that an important new language of penology is emerging. This new language, which has its counterparts in other areas of the law as well, shifts focus away from the traditional concerns of the criminal law and criminology, which have focused on the individual, and redirects it to actuarial consideration of aggregates. This shift has a number of important implications: It facilitates development of a vision or model of a new type of criminal process that embraces increased reliance on imprisonment and that merges concerns for surveillance and custody, that shifts away from a concern with punishing individuals to managing aggregates of dangerous groups, and that affects the training and practice of criminologists.*

It is often observed that penal ideology and practice became more conservative during the 1970s and 1980s (trends that may well continue in the 1990s). As important as this shift in the political valence of penal policy has been, it is only one part of a deeper change in conception—discourse, objectives, and techniques—in the penal process. These shifts have multiple and independent origins and are not reducible to any one reigning idea (e.g., getting tough on criminals). Despite their different origins, the elements of this emerging new conception have coalesced to form what may be thought of as a new strategic formation in the penal field, which we call (for lack of a more descriptive term) the *new penology*.[1]

---

* An earlier version of this paper was originally presented at the California Conference on Growth and Its Impact on Correctional Policy, University of California at Berkeley, June 1992.

Support for this study was provided in part by the Daniel and Florence Guggenheim Criminal Justice Program at Berkeley and a grant from Berkeley's Committee on Research. We deeply appreciate this support. We also wish to thank Albert Alschuler, Piers Beirne, Alfred Blumstein, John Berecochea, Rosann Greenspan, Sheldon Messinger, and Franklin Zimring for helpful comments on an earlier draft of this paper. We also wish to thank Kiara Jordan for her extraordinary editorial assistance.

1. By *strategy* we do not mean a conscious and coherent agenda employed by a determinate set of penal agents or others. Just as structural elements in a building conjoin to create a pattern of force relations quite different from their individual properties, the loose

450   FEELEY AND SIMON

The transformations we call the new penology involve shifts in three distinct areas:

1. The emergence of new discourses: In particular, the language of probability and risk increasingly replaces earlier discourses of clinical diagnosis and retributive judgment.[2]

2. The formation of new objectives for the system: The objectives we have in mind are not simply new to the system (some of them have old antecedents) but are in some sense newly "systemic." We are especially interested in the increasing primacy given to the efficient control of internal system processes in place of the traditional objectives of rehabilitation and crime control. Goals like reducing "recidivism" have always been internally shaped in important ways (Maltz, 1984), but in the contemporary setting the sense that any external social referent is intended at all is becoming attenuated.

3. The deployment of new techniques: These techniques target offenders as an aggregate in place of traditional techniques for individualizing or creating equity.

It is fun to trace patterns in the runic distribution of institutional changes (for the same reasons academics are such inveterate crossword puzzle fans). However, we also think that the new penology has served a significant function in locking together some of the external factors impinging on the criminal justice system and in determining the prevailing responses of the system.

No other fact seems as defining for the current moment as the massive increase in the level of incarceration undertaken over the past decade and a half, during which rates of reported crime have risen only modestly and victimization rates have declined.[3] The conventional understanding of this rise links it to demographic changes, social changes (like increased drug use),

---

set of interconnected developments that we call the new penology increasingly shapes the way the power to punish is exercised. Foucault's (1978:94) notion that power is both "intentional and nonsubjective" (which often seems like an academic "koan") provides a useful methodological tool here. The point is not to deny that people have deliberate strategies but that the overall configuration created by multiple strategies is itself "strategic" without being deliberate in the same way (Foucault, 1982:225).

2. Some have argued that contemporary penality evidences a concern for behavior rather than intentions or mental states (Cohen, 1985; Wilkins, 1973). We extend this argument. Below, we show how increasingly the individual, even as locus of behavior, is less and less salient as the penal enterprise shifts away from a concern with reforming the individual to managing segments of the "population."

3. The incarceration rate (per 100,000 resident population of each sex) has gone from 102 in 1974 to 244 in 1988 (Bureau of Justice Statistics, 1989:582).

improvement in the efficiency of law enforcement, and increases in the punitiveness of sentencing systems.[4] More can be accomplished with models that allow for the contingent interaction of all these factors (Zimring and Hawkins, 1991:157). A shortfall of this approach, however, is that it in effect holds constant the nature of the penal enterprise while varying external pressures and internal policy shifts. Our analysis of the new penology emphasizes more holistic features of the current penal formation.

The new penology is found among criminal justice practitioners and the research community.[5] However, it certainly has not (yet) emerged as a hegemonic strategy for crime and crime policy. For instance, it contrasts in many respects with the "tough on crime" rhetoric in the political arena. Political themes do get translated into the administrative practice of agencies like corrections and police. The problem (for the administrator at least) is whether they translate into anything that can provide a viable handle on the agency's tasks. Even the seemingly coherent command of legislatures and governors to "lock 'em up" leaves much unsaid about how to do it with existing resource allocations. The new penology has helped fill that gap even as it competes with crime control and other options as a master narrative for the system.

THE OLD PENOLOGY

The outlines of the "old" penology become most visible when one considers what has been shared across the perceived lines of opposition in modern corrections and criminal law. Modern American law, whose concepts still form the core of law school education, concentrates on individuals; the individual is the unit of analysis. This concern is especially emphasized in the criminal process. Criminal law focuses on intention in order to assign guilt. Criminal procedure has erected barriers to conviction to test evidence and protect the accused individual in the face of the powerful state. Criminal sanctioning has been aimed at individual-based theories of punishment.

---

4. A critical analysis of claims based on all these factors can be found in Zimring and Hawkins (1991).

5. In this paper we do not deal at length with the methodological underpinnings of our approach. We should note, however, that it is informed by discussions that treat law as a communicative process, a system of discourse that, as it were, has a "life of its own." Thus, our objective is not to point to identifiable individuals who have articulated the positions or made the types of decisions we describe in this paper. Rather, we seek to identify the elements of the strategic formation that are becoming more salient—both consciously and unconsciously—to the operation of the penal process. This strategic field, as we shall argue, provides a new way of perceiving reality and as such becomes reality itself (Foucault, 1978; Garland, 1985; Habermas, 1974, 1985; Hay, 1975; Krygier, 1989; Nelkin, 1982; Teubner, 1989).

In contrast, the new penology is markedly less concerned with responsibility, fault, moral sensibility, diagnosis, or intervention and treatment of the individual offender. Rather, it is concerned with techniques to identify, classify, and manage groupings sorted by dangerousness. The task is managerial, not transformative (Cohen, 1985; Garland and Young, 1983; Messinger, 1969; Messinger and Berecochea, 1990; Reichman, 1986; Wilkins, 1973). It seeks to *regulate* levels of deviance, not intervene or respond to individual deviants or social malformations.

Although the new penology is much more than "discourse," its language helps reveals this shift most strikingly. It does not speak of impaired individuals in need of treatment or of morally irresponsible persons who need to be held accountable for their actions. Rather, it considers the criminal justice *system*, and it pursues systemic rationality and efficiency. It seeks to sort and classify, to separate the less from the more dangerous, and to deploy control strategies rationally. The tools for this enterprise are "indicators," prediction tables, population projections, and the like. In these methods, individualized diagnosis and response is displaced by aggregate classification systems for purposes of surveillance, confinement, and control (Gordon, 1991).

DISTINGUISHING FEATURES OF THE NEW PENOLOGY

What we call the new penology is not a theory of crime or criminology. Its uniqueness lies less in conceptual integration than in a common focus on certain problems and a shared way of framing issues. This strategic formation of knowledge and power offers managers of the system a more or less coherent picture of the challenges they face and the kinds of solutions that are most likely to work. While we cannot reduce it to a set of principles, we can point to some of its most salient features.

THE NEW DISCOURSE

A central feature of the new discourse is the replacement of a moral or clinical description of the individual with an actuarial language of probabilistic calculations and statistical distributions applied to populations. Although social utility analysis or actuarial thinking is commonplace enough in modern life—it frames policy considerations of all sorts—in recent years this mode of thinking has gained ascendancy in legal discourse, a system of reasoning that traditionally has employed the language of morality and been focused on individuals (Simon, 1988).[6] For instance, this new mode of reasoning is found

---

6. A number of influential scholars have commented on this process, often calling attention to what they regard as the shortcomings of traditional individual-based legal language when applied to the problems of the modern organization-based society. See, e.g., dan–Cohen (1986), Stone (1975).

THE NEW PENOLOGY 453

increasingly in tort law, where traditional fault and negligence standards—which require a focus on the individual and are based upon notions of individual responsibility—have given way to strict liability and no-fault. These new doctrines rest upon actuarial ways of thinking about how to "manage" accidents and public safety. They employ the language of social utility and management, not individual responsibility (Simon, 1987; Steiner, 1987).[7] It is also found in some branches of antidiscrimination law, wherein the courts are less interested in intent (i.e., discrimination based on identifying individuals whose intentions can be examined) than in effects (i.e., aggregate consequences or patterns that can be assessed against a standard of social utility [Freeman, 1990] and corporate misconduct [dan-Cohen, 1986; Stone, 1975]).[8]

Although crime policy, criminal procedure, and criminal sanctioning have been influenced by such social utility analysis, there is no body of commentary on the criminal law that is equivalent to the body of social utility analysis for tort law doctrine.[9] Nor has strict liability in the criminal law achieved anything like the acceptance of related no-fault principles in tort law. Perhaps because the criminal law is so firmly rooted in a focus on the individual, these developments have come late to criminal law and penology.

Scholars of both European and North American penal strategies have noted the recent and rising trend of the penal system to target categories and subpopulations rather than individuals (Bottoms, 1983; Cohen, 1985; Mathieson, 1983; Reichman, 1986). This reflects, at least in part, the fact that actuarial forms of representation promote quantification as a way of visualizing populations.

Crime statistics have been a part of the discourse of the state for over 200 years, but the advance of statistical methods permits the formulation of concepts and strategies that allow direct relations between penal strategy and the population. Earlier generations used statistics to map the responses of normatively defined groups to punishment; today one talks of "high-rate offenders," "career criminals," and other categories defined by the distribution

---

7. In contrasting the "old" and the "new" tort law, Steiner (1987:8) observes: "They [judges with the new tort law] visualize the parties before them less as individual persons or discrete organizations and more as representatives of groups with identifiable common characteristics. They understand accidents and the social losses that accidents entail less as unique events and more as statistically predictable events. Modern social vision tends then toward the systemic-group-statistical in contrast with the vision more characteristic of the fault system, the dyadic-individual-unique."

8. There has been considerable resistance to the actuarial logic in this area as well. See *McCleskey v. Kemp*, 107 S. Ct. 1756 (1987).

9. But even here there are signs that this is changing. Although they do not frame their discussion in our terms, a number of scholars have observed that many of the provisions in the Racketeer Influenced and Corrupt Organizations (RICO) statute run counter to the traditional individual-based orientation of the criminal law and in fact are designed to facilitate regulation of organizational behavior, not individual conduct.

454   FEELEY AND SIMON

itself. Rather than simply extending the capacity of the system to rehabilitate
or control crime, actuarial classification has come increasingly to define the
correctional enterprise itself.

The importance of actuarial language in the system will come as no surprise to anyone who has spent time observing it. Its significance, however, is
often lost in the more spectacular shift in emphasis from rehabilitation to
crime control. No doubt, a new and more punitive attitude toward the
proper role of punishment has emerged in recent years, and it is manifest in a
shift in the language of statutes, internal procedures, and academic scholarship. Yet looking across the past several decades, it appears that the pendulum-like swings of penal attitude moved independently of the actuarial
language that has steadily crept into the discourse.[10]

The discourse of the new penology is not simply one of greater quantification; it is also characterized by an emphasis on the systemic and on formal
rationality. While the history of systems theory and operations research has
yet to be written, their progression from business administration to the military and, in the 1960s, to domestic public policy must be counted as among
the most significant of current intellectual trends. In criminal justice the
great reports of the late 1960s, like *The Challenge of Crime in a Free Society*
(see note 10), helped make the phrase "criminal justice system" a part of
everyday reality for the operatives and students of criminal law and policy.[11]

Some of the most astute observers identified this change near the outset and
understood that it was distinct from the concurrent rightward shift in penal
thinking. Jacobs (1977) noted the rise at Stateville Penitentiary of what he
called a "managerial" perspective during the mid-1970s. The regime of War-
den Brierton was characterized, according to Jacobs, by a focus on tighter
administrative control through the gathering and distribution of statistical
information about the functioning of the prison. Throughout the 1980s this
perspective grew considerably within the correctional system. Jacobs
presciently noted that the managerial perspective might succeed where traditional and reform administrations had failed because it was capable of handling the greatly increased demands for rationality and accountability coming
from the courts and the political system.

---

10. A good example of this is the President's Commission on Law Enforcement and
Administration of Justice, created in 1966. Its report, *The Challenge of Crime in a Free
Society* (1967), combined a commitment to the rehabilitative ideal with a new enthusiasm
for actuarial representation. Indeed, that document represents an important point of coa-
lescence for many of the elements that make up the new penology.

11. Not everyone believes that this has been a positive change. For a critical perspective see Kelling (1991).

THE NEW PENOLOGY 455

THE NEW OBJECTIVES

The new penology is neither about punishing nor about rehabilitating individuals. It is about identifying and managing unruly groups. It is concerned with the rationality not of individual behavior or even community organization, but of managerial processes. Its goal is not to eliminate crime but to make it tolerable through systemic coordination.

One measure of the shift away from trying to normalize offenders and toward trying to manage them is seen in the declining significance of recidivism. Under the old penology, recidivism was a nearly universal criterion for assessing successor failure of penal programs. Under the new penology, recidivism rates continue to be important, but their significance has changed. The word itself seems to be used less often precisely because it carries a normative connotation that reintegrating offenders into the community is the major objective. High rates of parolees being returned to prison once indicated program failure; now they are offered as evidence of efficiency and effectiveness of parole as a control apparatus.[12]

It is possible that recidivism is dropping out of the vocabulary as an adjustment to harsh realities and is a way of avoiding charges of institutional failure. Nearly half of all prisoners released in eleven of the largest states during 1983 were reconvicted within three years (Flanagan and Maguire, 1990). In 21 of the 48 states with adults on parole supervision in 1988, more than 30% of those leaving parole were in jail or prison on new criminal or parole-revocation charges (Bureau of Justice Statistics, 1989:100); in 8 of them more than half of those leaving parole were returned to confinement (including a spectacular 78% in California and 70% in Washington).[13] However, in shifting to emphasize the virtues of return as an indication of *effective* control, the new penology reshapes one's understanding of the functions of the penal sanction. By emphasizing correctional programs in terms of aggregate control and system management rather than individual success and failure, the new penology lowers one's expectations about the criminal sanction. These redefined objectives are reinforced by the new discourses discussed above,

---

12. This is especially true for a number of new, intensive parole and probation supervision programs that have been established in recent years. Initially conceived as a way to reintegrate offenders into the community through a close interpersonal relationship between agent and offender, intensive supervision is now considered as an enhanced monitoring technique whose ability to detect high rates of technical violations indicates its success, not failure.

13. Probation, which involves huge numbers, many first offenders, and caseloads too huge even to apply techniques like drug testing to, does not send as high a proportion to incarceration. Still, nationwide, almost a fifth of all adults leaving state probation in 1988 either absconded or were incarcerated (Bureau of Justice Statistics, 1989:27). In California, 44% of adults leaving probation were incarcerated on the original charge for which they received probation (ibid.).

456   **FEELEY AND SIMON**

which take deviance as a given, mute aspirations for individual reformation, and seek to classify, sort, and manage dangerous groups efficiently.

The waning of concern over recidivism reveals fundamental changes in the very penal processes that recidivism once was used to evaluate. For example, although parole and probation have long been justified as means of reintegrating offenders into the community (President's Commission, 1967:165), increasingly they are being perceived as cost-effective ways of imposing long-term management on the dangerous. Instead of treating revocation of parole and probation as a mechanism to short-circuit the supervision process when the risks to public safety become unacceptable, the system now treats revocation as a cost-effective way to police and sanction a chronically troublesome population. In such an operation, recidivism is either irrelevant[14] or, as suggested above, is stood on its head and transformed into an indicator of success in a new form of law enforcement.

The importance that recidivism once had in evaluating the performance of corrections is now being taken up by measures of system functioning. Heydebrand and Seron (1990) have noted a tendency in courts and other social agencies toward decoupling performance evaluation from external social objectives. Instead of social norms like the elimination of crime, reintegration into the community, or public safety, institutions begin to measure their own outputs as indicators of performance. Thus, courts may look at docket flow. Similarly, parole agencies may shift evaluations of performance to, say, the time elapsed between arrests and due process hearings. In much the same way, many schools have come to focus on standardized test performance rather than on reading or mathematics, and some have begun to see teaching itself as the process of teaching students how to take such tests (Heydebrand and Seron, 1990:190–194; Lipsky, 1980:4–53).

Such technocratic rationalization tends to insulate institutions from the messy, hard-to-control demands of the social world. By limiting their exposure to indicators that they can control, managers ensure that their problems will have solutions. No doubt this tendency in the new penology is, in part, a response to the acceleration of demands for rationality and accountability in punishment coming from the courts and legislatures during the 1970s (Jacobs, 1977). It also reflects the lowered expectations for the penal system that result from failures to accomplish more ambitious promises of the past. Yet in the end, the inclination of the system to measure its success against its own production processes helps lock the system into a mode of operation that

---

14. This does not mean that recidivism ceases to be a meaningful concept, but only that in its new mode of operation the penal system no longer accords it the centrality it once had. Recidivism remains a potent tool of criticism of the system, especially given its former significance. See, e.g., the California Legislative Analyst's *Report to the 1989/1990 Budget* (Sacramento), which contains a strong attack on the parole process for emphasizing the high rate of recidivism.

has only an attenuated connection with the *social* purposes of punishment. In the long term it becomes more difficult to evaluate an institution critically if there are no references to substantive social ends.

The new objectives also inevitably permeate through the courts into thinking about rights. The new penology replaces consideration of fault with predictions of dangerousness and safety management and, in so doing, modifies traditional individual-oriented doctrines of criminal procedure. This shift is illustrated in *U.S. v. Salerno*,[15] which upheld the preventive detention provision in the Bail Reform Act of 1984. Writing the opinion for the Court, then Associate Supreme Court Justice William Rehnquist reasoned that preventive detention does not trigger the same level of protection as other penal detentions because it is intended to manage risks rather than punish. While the distinction may have seemed disingenuous to some, it acknowledges the shift in objectives we have emphasized and redefines rights accordingly.[16]

NEW TECHNIQUES

These altered, lowered expectations manifest themselves in the development of more cost-effective forms of custody and control and in new technologies to identify and classify risk. Among them are low frills, no-service custodial centers; various forms of electronic monitoring systems that impose a form of custody without walls; and new statistical techniques for assessing risk and predicting dangerousness. These new forms of control are not anchored in aspirations to rehabilitate, reintegrate, retrain, provide employment, or the like. They are justified in more blunt terms: variable detention depending upon risk assessment.[17]

---

15. 107 S. Ct. 2045, 2101-2 (1987).

16. There is a rapidly growing literature on the Supreme Court's shift away from individual rights in the area of criminal procedure. See, e.g., the Supreme Court's recent decision finding that forced medication for a mentally ill prisoner is subject to diminished procedural review because it is essentially a risk-management decision on the part of custodial managers rather than a punitive deprivation, *Washington v. Harper*, 110 S. Ct. 1028, 1039-40 (1990). For a discussion of shifts in criminal procedure more generally, see Greenspan (1988).

17. In recent years one of the authors has spent time with corrections officials in Japan and Sweden as well as the United States and found that significantly different language is used to characterize penal policies. In Sweden he heard the language of therapy and rehabilitation (the offender is not properly socialized and requires rehabilitative therapy). In Japan he heard the language of moral repsonsibility (the offender is morally deficient and needs instruction in responsibility to the community). In the United States, he heard the language of management (in a high-crime society, we need expanded capacity to classify offenders in order to incapacitate the most dangerous and employ less stringent controls on the less dangerous). Juxtaposed against each other, the differences are dramatic.

There is a similarity in approach between the new penology and the views expressed by Soviet legal theorist Eugenii Pashukanis (1978). He predicted that under socialism, law

458   FEELEY AND SIMON

Perhaps the clearest example of the new penology's method is the theory of incapacitation, which has become the predominant utilitarian model of punishment (Greenwood, 1982; Moore et al., 1984). Incapacitation promises to reduce the effects of crime in society not by altering either offender or social context, but by rearranging the distribution of offenders in society. If the prison can do nothing else, incapacitation theory holds, it can detain offenders for a time and thus delay their resumption of criminal activity. According to the theory, if such delays are sustained for enough time and for enough offenders, significant aggregate effects in crime can take place although individual destinies are only marginally altered.[18]

These aggregate effects can be further intensified, in some accounts, by a strategy of selective incapacitation. This approach proposes a sentencing scheme in which lengths of sentence depend not upon the nature of the criminal offense or upon an assessment of the character of the offender, but upon risk profiles. Its objectives are to identify high-risk offenders and to maintain long-term control over them while investing in shorter terms and less intrusive control over lower risk offenders.

Selective incapacitation was first formally articulated as a coherent scheme for punishing in a report by a research and development organization (Greenwood, 1982), but it was quickly embraced and self-consciously promoted as a justification for punishment by a team of scholars from Harvard University, who were keenly aware that it constituted a paradigm shift in the underlying rationale for imposing the criminal sanction (Moore et al., 1984).[19]

THE NEW PENOLOGY IN PERSPECTIVE

The correctional practices emerging from the shifts we identified above

---

would "wither away" and be replaced with management based upon considerations of social utility rather than traditional individualized considerations. See, e.g., Sharlet (1978).

18.   Incapacitation then is to penology what arbitrage is to investments, a method of capitalizing on minute displacements in time; and like arbitrage it has a diminished relationship to the normative goal of enhancing the value of its objects.

19.   Throughout the book the authors acknowledge the significance of their approach. They warn, "When one holds these tests [use of correlates to serious criminal activity as a basis for formulating sentences] to a more exacting standard emphasizing individual justice, however, the proposed tests have greater difficulty; inaccuracy, resulting in false positives, and the inclusion of variables that are not entirely under the control of individuals and are not in themselves dangerous criminal conduct" (p. 76).

Throughout the book, they repeatedly express similar warnings, e.g., "A . . . question is whether narrowing the focus of the system weakens the power and stature of the criminal law." (p. 90); "At the foundation of selective incapacitation is the distinctly illiberal view that people differ in their capacity for evil and that these differences are not the result of broad social processes but of something inherent in the individual" (p. 91). Ultimately, they conclude, "In our view the threshold objections to selective incapacitation do mark out important areas of vulnerability and uncertainty, but none stands as an absolute barrier to further consideration on the issue" (p. 92).

present a kind of "custodial continuum." But unlike the "correctional continuum" discussed in the 1960s, this new custodial continuum does not design penal measures for the particular needs of the individual or the community. Rather, it sorts individuals into groups according to the degree of control warranted by their risk profiles.

At one extreme the prison provides maximum security at a high cost for those who pose the greatest risks, and at the other probation provides low-cost surveillance for low-risk offenders. In between stretches a growing range of intermediate supervisory and surveillance techniques. The management concerns of the new penology—in contrast to the transformative concerns of the old—are displayed especially clearly in justifications for various new intermediate sanctions.

What we call the new penology is only beginning to take conherent shape. Although most of what we have stressed as its central elements—statistical prediction, concern with groups, strategies of management—have a long history in penology, in recent years they have come to the fore, and their functions have coalesced and expanded to form a new strategic approach. Discussing the new penology in terms of discourse, objective, and technique, risks a certain repetitiveness. Indeed, all three are closely linked, and while none can be assigned priority as the cause of the others, each entails and facilitates the others.

Thus, one can speak of normalizing individuals, but when the emphasis is on separating people into distinct and independent categories the idea of the "normal" itself becomes obscured if not irrelevant.[20] If the "norm" can no longer function as a relevant criterion of success for the organizations of criminal justice, it is not surprising that evaluation turns to indicators of internal system performance. The focus of the system on the efficiency of its own outputs, in turn, places a premium on those methods (e.g., risk screening, sorting, and monitoring) that fit wholly within the bureaucratic capacities of the apparatus.

But the same story can be told in a different order. The steady bureaucratization of the correctional apparatus during the 1950s and 1960s shifted the target from individuals, who did not fit easily into centralized administration, to categories or classes, which do. But once the focus is on categories of offenders rather than individuals, methods naturally shift toward mechanisms of appraising and arranging groups rather than intervening in the lives of individuals. In the end the search for causal order is at least premature.

In the section below we explore the contours of some of the new patterns represented by these developments, and in so doing suggest that the enterprise is by now relatively well established.

---

20. The mean of a multinomial variable is incoherent.

NEW FUNCTIONS AND TRADITIONAL FORMS

Someday perhaps, the new penology will have its own Jeremy Bentham or Zebulon Brockway (Foucault, 1977:200; Rothman, 1980:33), some gigantic figure who can stamp his or her own sense of order on the messy results of incremental change. For now it is better not to think of it so much as a theory or program conceived in full by any particular actors in the system, but as an interpretive net that can help reveal in the present some of the directions the future may take. The test of such a net, to which we now turn, is not its elegance as a model but whether it enables one to grasp a wide set of developments in an enlightening way (in short, does it catch fish?). Below we reexamine three of the major features of the contemporary penal landscape in light of our argument—the expansion of the penal sanction, the rise of drug testing, and innovation within the criminal process—and relate them to our thesis.

THE EXPANSION OF PENAL SANCTIONS

During the past decade the number of people covered by penal sanctions has expanded significantly.[21] Because of its high costs, the growth of prison populations has drawn the greatest attention, but probation and parole have increased at a proportionate or faster rate. The importance of these other sanctions goes beyond their ability to stretch penal resources; they expand and redistribute the use of imprisonment. Probation and parole violations now constitute a major source of prison inmates, and negotiations over probation revocation are replacing plea bargaining as modes of disposition (Greenspan, 1988; Messinger and Berecochea, 1990).[22]

Many probation and parole revocations are triggered by events, like failing a drug test, that are driven by parole procedures themselves (Simon, 1990; Zimring and Hawkins, 1991). The increased flow of probationers and parolees into prisons is expanding the prison population and changing the nature of the prison. Increasingly, prisons are short-term holding pens for violators deemed too dangerous to remain on the streets. To the extent the prison is organized to receive such people, its correctional mission is replaced by a management function, a warehouse for the highest risk classes of offenders.

From the perspective of the new penology, the growth of community corrections in the shadow of imprisonment is not surprising.[23] The new penology does not regard prison as a special institution capable of making a

---

21. In 1988, 3.7 million adults were under some form of correctional sanction in the United States, a 38.8% increase since 1984 (Bureau of Justice Statistics, 1989:5).

22. In 1988 there were 14 states in which more than a quarter of all prison admissions came from parole revocation (Bureau of Justice Statistics, 1989:69). In California, in 1988, 59% of admissions were from parole revocations (ibid.).

23. The importance of supervisory sanctions is all the more interesting given the effort

THE NEW PENOLOGY 461

difference in the individuals who pass through it. Rather, it functions as but one of several custodial options. The actuarial logic of the new penology dictates an expansion of the continuum of control for more efficient risk management. For example, the various California prisons are today differentiated largely by the level of security they maintain and, thus, what level risk inmate they can receive. Twenty years ago, in contrast, they were differentiated by specialized functions: California Rehabilitation Center, for drug users; California Medical Prison at Vacaville, for the mentally ill; Deuel Vocational Institute, for young adults.

Thus, community-based sanctions can be understood in terms of risk management rather than rehabilitative or correctional aspirations. Rather than instruments of reintegrating offenders into the community, they function as mechanisms to maintain control, often through frequent drug testing, over low-risk offenders for whom the more secure forms of custody are judged too expensive or unnecessary.[24]

The new penology's technique of aggregation has been incorporated in a number of sentencing reforms. Minnesota and, more recently, the U.S. Sentencing Commission have made population an explicit concern. The U.S. Sentencing Guidelines, which provide for "fixed" sentences as determined by a 238-cell grid, specifies that the presumptive sentence is a function of prior record and seriousness of offense, but as Alschuler (1991) has shown, although these guidelines have been defended as a step toward providing equal justice, in fact they are based upon "rough aggregations and statistical averages," which mask significant differences among offenders and offenses. The guidelines movement, he observes, marks "a changed attitude toward sentencing—one that looks to collections of cases and to social harm rather than to individual offenders and punishments they deserve . . . [and rather than] the circumstances of their cases" (p. 951).

DRUGS AND PUNISHMENT

Drug use and its detection and control have become central concerns of the penal system. No one observing the system today can fail to be struck by the increasingly tough laws directed against users and traffickers, well-publicized data that suggest that a majority of arrestees are drug users, and the increasing proportion of drug offenders sent to prison.[25]

---

of recent sentencing reform to remove discretion from corrections offices and establish juridical control through legislatures, judges, and prosecutors (Zimring and Hawkins, 1991).

24. The public remains interested in punishment for its own sake, and the expansion of parole and probation is tied in some degree to the ability of penal managers to convince the public that these supervisory sanctions can be punitive as well as managerial.

25. Incarceration for drug offenses grew at twice the rate of other offenses between 1976 and 1984 (Zimring and Hawkins, 1991:164).

462   FEELEY AND SIMON

In one sense, of course, the emphasis on drugs marks a continuity with the past 30 years of correctional history. Drug treatment and drug testing were hallmarks of the rehabilitative model in the 1950s and 1960s. The recent upsurge of concern with drugs may be attributed to the hardening of social attitudes toward drug use (especially in marked contrast to the tolerant 1970s),[26] the introduction of virulent new drug products, like crack cocaine, and the disintegrating social conditions of the urban poor.

Without dismissing the relevance of these continuities and explanations for change, it is important to note that there are distinctive changes in the role of drugs in the current system that reflect the logic of the new penology. In place of the traditional emphasis on treatment and eradication, today's practices track drug use as a kind of risk indicator. The widespread evidence of drug use in the offending population leads not to new theories of crime causation but to more efficient ways of identifying those at highest risk of offending. With drug use so prevalent that it is found in a majority of arrestees in some large cities (Flanagan and Maguire, 1990:459), it can hardly mark a special type of individual deviance. From the perspective of the new penology, drug use is not so much a measure of individual acts of deviance as it is a mechanism for classifying the offender within a risk group.

Thus, one finds in the correctional system today a much greater emphasis on drug testing than on drug treatment. This may reflect the normal kinds of gaps in policy as well as difficulty in treating relatively new forms of drug abuse. Yet, testing serves functions in the new penology even in the absence of a treatment option. By marking the distribution of risk within the offender population under surveillance, testing makes possible greater coordination of scarce penal resources.

Testing also fills the gap left by the decline of traditional intervention strategies. One of the authors spent a year observing parole supervision in California, where drug testing was the predominant activity for agents (Simon, 1990). If nothing else, testing provided parole (and probably probation) agents a means to document compliance with their own internal performance requirements. Agents are supposed to meet with their parolees twice a month on average, but with few parolees working, they can often be hard to find. When they are located, there is often little to do or talk about since the agent cannot offer them a job or coerce them to take one.[27] Testing provides both an occasion for requiring the parolee to show up in the parole office and a purpose for meeting. The results of tests have become a network of fact and

---

26. Support for the legalization of marijuana, e.g., peaked among first year college students in 1977 at 52.9% and has since declined, reaching 16.7% in 1989 (Flanagan and Maguire, 1990:195).

27. The law no longer requires that parolees be employed, and jobs are not available in the communities where many parolees reside.

THE NEW PENOLOGY 463

explanation for use in a decision-making process that requires accountability but provides little substantive basis for distinguishing among offenders.

INNOVATION

Our description may seem to imply the onset of a reactive age in which penal managers strive to manage populations of marginal citizens with no concomitant effort toward integration into mainstream society. This may seem hard to square with the myriad new and innovative technologies introduced over the past decade. Indeed the media, which for years have portrayed the correctional system as a failure, have recently enthusiastically reported on these innovations: boot camps, electronic surveillance, high security "campuses" for drug users, house arrest, intensive parole and probation, and drug treatment programs.

Although some of the new proposals are presented in terms of the "old penology" and emphasize individuals, normalization, and rehabilitation, it is risky to come to any firm conviction about how these innovations will turn out. If historians of punishment have provided any clear lessons, it is that reforms evolve in ways quite different from the aims of their proponents (Foucault, 1977; Rothman, 1971). Thus, we wonder if these most recent innovations won't be recast in the terms outlined in this paper. Many of these innovations are compatible with the imperatives of the new penology, that is, managing a permanently dangerous population while maintaining the system at a minimum cost.

One of the current innovations most in vogue with the press and politicians are correctional "boot camps." These are minmum security custodial facilities, usually for youthful first offenders, designed on the model of a training center for military personnel, complete with barracks, physical exercise, and tough drill sergeants. Boot camps are portrayed as providing discipline and pride to young offenders brought up in the unrestrained culture of poverty (as though physical fitness could fill the gap left by the weakening of families, schools, neighborhoods, and other social organizations in the inner city).

The camps borrow explicit from a military model of discipline, which has influenced penality from at least the eighteenth century.[28] No doubt the image of inmates smartly dressed in uniforms performing drills and calisthenics appeals to long-standing ideals of order in post-Enlightenment culture. But in its proposed application to corrections, the military model is even less appropriate now than when it was rejected in the nineteenth century; indeed, today's boot camps are more a simulation of discipline than the real thing.

In the nineteenth century the military model was superseded by another

---

28. The prison borrowed from the earlier innovations in the organization of spaces and bodies undertaken by the most advanced European military forces. See, e.g., Rothman (1971:105–108).

464   FEELEY AND SIMON

model of discipline, the factory. Inmates were controlled by making them work at hard industrial labor (Ignatieff, 1978; Rothman, 1971). It was assumed that forced labor would inculcate in offenders the discipline required of factory laborers, so that they might earn their keep while in custody and join the ranks of the usefully employed when released. One can argue that this model did not work very well, but at least it was coherent. The model of discipline through labor suited our capitalist democracy in a way the model of a militarized citizenry did not.[29]

The recent decline of employment opportunities among the populations of urban poor most at risk for conventional crime involvement has left the applicability of industrial discipline in doubt. But the substitution of the boot camp for vocational training is even less plausible. Even if the typical 90-day regime of training envisioned by proponents of boot camps is effective in reorienting its subjects, at best it can only produce soldiers without a company to join. Indeed, the grim vision of the effect of boot camp is that it will be effective for those who will subsequently put their lessons of discipline and organization to use in street gangs and drug distribution networks. However, despite the earnestness with which the boot camp metaphor is touted, we suspect that the camps will be little more than holding pens for managing a short-term, mid-range risk population.

Drug testing and electronic monitors being tried in experimental "intensive supervision" and "house arrest" programs are justified in rehabilitative terms, but both sorts of programs lack a foundation in today's social and economic realities. The drug treatment programs in the 1960s encompassed a regime of coercive treatment: "inpatient" custody in secured settings followed by community supervision and reintegration (President's Commission, 1967). The record suggests that these programs had enduring effects for at least some of those who participated in them (Anglin et al., 1990). Today's proposals are similar, but it remains to be seen whether they can be effective in the absence of long-term treatment facilities, community-based follow-up, and prospects for viable conventional life-styles and employment opportunities.[30] In the

---

29. The model of industrial discipline was rarely fully achieved in prisons, but at least it had a clear referent in the real world, one that provided a certain coherence and plausibility to the penal project. The boot camp, like so much else in our increasingly anachronistic culture, is a signifier without a signified.

30. In his important 1966 essay "Work and Identity in the Lower Class," Rainwater suggested that members of the lower class often choose "expressive" life-styles of deviance in the absence of opportunities for the most prestigious and desirable roles in the occupational structure. But he argued they also predictably burn out and accept the identification offered by even low-level employment of the good worker and provider. Rainwater urged that keeping entry-level employment available and tolerable was essential to fostering that transition. Today, when entry-level employment has shrunk to levels not imagined in the mid-1960s, the transition of those who are dissuaded or simply burn out on crime cannot be assumed (Duster, 1987).

meantime it is obvious that they can also serve the imperative of reducing the costs of correctional jurisdiction while maintaining some check on the offender population.

Our point is not to belittle the stated aspirations of current proposals or to argue that drug treatment programs cannot work. Indeed, we anticipate that drug treatment and rehabilitation will become increasingly attractive as the cost of long-term custody increases. However, given the emergence of the management concerns of the new penology, we question whether these innovations will embrace the long-term perspective of earlier successful treatment programs, and we suspect that they will emerge as control processes for managing and recycling selected risk populations. If so, these new programs will extend still further the capacity of the new penology. The undeniable attractiveness of boot camps, house arrest, secure drug "centers," and the like, is that they promise to provide secure custody in a more flexible format and at less cost than traditional correctional facilities. Indeed, some of them are envisioned as private contract facilities that can be expanded or reduced with relative ease. Further, they hold out the promise of expanding the range of low- and mid-level custodial alternatives, thereby facilitating the transfer of offenders now held in more expensive, higher security facilities that have been so favored in recent years. Tougher eligibility requirements, including job offers, stable residency, and promises of sponsorship in the community can be used to screen out "higher risk" categories for noncustodial release programs (Petersilia, 1987). Thus, despite the lingering language of rehabilitation and reintegration, the programs generated under the new penology can best be understood in terms of managing costs and controlling dangerous populations rather than social or personal transformation.

SOCIAL BASES OF THE NEW PENOLOGY

The point of these reinterpretations is not to show that shifts in the way the penal enterprise is understood and discussed inexorably determine how the system will take shape. What actually emerges in corrections over the near and distant future will depend on how this understanding itself is shaped by the pressures of demographic, economic, and political factors. Still, such factors rarely operate as pure forces. They are filtered through and expressed in terms in which the problems are understood. Thus, the strategic field we call the new penology itself will help shape the future.

THE NEW DISCOURSE OF CRIME

Like the old penology, traditional "sociological" criminology has focused on the relationship between individuals and communities. Its central concerns have been the causes and correlates of delinquent and criminal behavior, and it has sought to develop intervention strategies designed to correct

466   FEELEY AND SIMON

delinquents and decrease the likelihood of deviant behavior. Thus, it has
focused on the family and the workplace as important influences of socialization
and control.

The new penology has an affinity with a new "actuarial" criminology,
which eschews these traditional concerns of criminology. Instead of training
in sociology or social work, increasingly the new criminologists are trained in
operations research and systems analysis. This new approach is not a criminology at all, but an applied branch of systems theory. This shift in training
and orientation has been accompanied by a shift in interest. A concern with
successful intervention strategies, the province of the former, is replaced by
models designed to optimize public safety through the management of aggregates, which is the province of the latter.

In one important sense this new criminology is simply a consequence of
steady improvements in the quantitative rigor with which crime is studied.
No doubt the amassing of a statistical picture of crime and the criminal justice system has improved researchers' ability to speak realistically about the
distribution of crimes and the fairness of procedures. But, we submit, it has
also contributed to a shift, a reconceptualization, in the way crime is understood as a social problem.[31] The new techniques and the new language have
facilitated reconceptualization of the way issues are framed and policies pursued. Sociological criminology tended to emphasize crime as a relationship
between the individual and the normative expectations of his or her community (Bennett, 1981).[32] Policies premised on this perspective addressed
problems of reintegration, including the mismatch among individual motivation, normative orientation, and social opportunity structures. In contrast,
actuarial criminology highlights the interaction of criminal justice institutions
and specific segments of the population. Policy discussions framed in its
terms emphasize the management of high-risk groups and make less salient
the qualities of individual delinquents and their communities.

Indeed, even the use of predictive statistics by pioneers like Ernest Burgess
(1936) reflected sociological criminology's emphasis on normalization. Burgess's statistics (and those of most other quantitative criminologists before the
1960s) measured the activity of subjects defined by a specifiable set of individual or social factors (e.g., alcoholism, unemployment, etc.). In the actuarial
criminology of today, by contrast, the numbers generate the subject itself
(e.g., the high-rate offender of incapacitation research). In short, criminals
are no longer the organizing referent (or logos) of criminology. Instead,

---

31. Again, we would point to the 1967 President's Commission report as a critical
point of emergence for the actuarial criminology that dominates today, especially the Task
Force report on "Science and Technology" (Ch. 11).

32. The research relied on ethnography and life histories. See, e.g., the work of Blumstein et al. (1986), Burgess (1974), Shaw (1931), Sutherland (1934).

THE NEW PENOLOGY 467

criminology has become a subfield of a generalized public policy analysis discourse. This new criminal knowledge aims at rationalizing the operation of the systems that manage criminals, not dealing with criminality. The same techniques that can be used to improve the circulation of baggage in airports or delivery of food to troops can be used to improve the penal system's efficiency.

THE DISCOURSE OF POVERTY AND THE "UNDERCLASS"

The new penology may also be seen as responsive to the emergence of a new understanding of poverty in America.[33] The term *underclass* is used today to characterize a segment of society that is viewed as permanently excluded from social mobility and economic integration. The term is used to refer to a largely black and Hispanic population living in concentrated zones of poverty in central cities, separated physically and institutionally from the suburban locus of mainstream social and economic life in America.

In contrast to groups whose members are deemed employable, even if they may be temporarily out of work, the underclass is understood as a permanently marginal population, without literacy, without skills, and without hope; a self-perpetuating and pathological segment of society that is not integratable into the larger whole, even as a reserve labor pool (Wilson, 1987). Conceived of this way, the underclass is also a dangerous class, not only for what any particular member may or may not do, but more generally for collective potential misbehavior.[34] It is treated as a high-risk group that must be managed for the protection of the rest of society. Indeed, it is this managerial task that provides one of the most powerful sources for the imperative of

---

33. Although in this paper we emphasize recent significant shifts, a management approach is not wholly unprecedented. For instance, during the formative years of the development of the modern criminal justice system, the late eighteenth and the early nineteenth century, the term "dangerous classes" was used widely in discussions of English criminal justice policies. Influenced in part by Malthusian thinking and burgeoning urban populations, policy analysts of the time often treated criminal justice policy in aggregate management terms, treating crime as an indicator of the dangerousness of a larger group, rather than of individuals. For instance, transportation of convicted felons was often regarded as but one of several interrelated policies to export the dangerous classes. Other policies accomplishing similar ends were voluntary emigration and indentured servitude, both of which were actively promoted by the government. The invention of the large-scale prison helped to individualize crime policy.

34. A recent study estimated that on any one day in 1988 roughly one in every four young (between ages 20 and 29) black males was under some form of correctional custody (Mauer, 1990). More recently, a similar study calculated that on a given day in 1990 some 42% of all young black males in Washington, D.C., were in custody. The growing visibility of the link between penality and race is likely to reinforce the sense that crime is the product of a pathological subpopulation that cannot be integrated into the society at large, as well as the perception that the penal system can do no better than maintain custody over a large segment of this population.

preventive management in the new penology. The concept of "underclass" makes clear why correctional officials increasingly regard as a bad joke the claim that their goal is to reintegrate offenders back into their communities.

Reintegration and rehabilitation inevitably imply a norm against which deviant subjects are evaluated. As Allen (1981) perceived more than a decade ago, rehabilitation as a project can only survive if public confidence in the viability and appropriateness of such norms endures. Allen viewed the decline of the rehabilitative ideal as a result of the cultural revolts of the 1960s, which undermined the capacity of the American middle classes to justify their norms and the imposition of those norms on others. It is this decline in social will, rather than empirical evidence of the failure of penal programs to rehabilitate, that, in Allen's analysis, doomed the rehabilitative ideal.

Whatever significance cultural radicalism may have had in initiating the breakup of the old penology in the mid-1970s, the emergence of the new penology in the 1980s reflects the influence of a more despairing view of poverty and the prospects for achieving equality (views that can hardly be blamed on the Left). Rehabilitating offenders, or any kind of reintegration strategy, can only make sense if the larger community from which offenders come is viewed as sharing a common normative universe with the communities of the middle classes—especially those values and expectations derived from the labor market. The concept of an underclass, with its connotation of a permanent marginality for whole portions of the population, has rendered the old penology incoherent and laid the groundwork for a strategic field that emphasizes low-cost management of a permanent offender population.

The connection between the new penality and the (re)emergent term *underclass* also is illustrated by recent studies of American jails. For instance, Irwin's 1985 book, *The Jail*, is subtitled *Managing the Underclass in American Society*. His thesis is that "prisoners in jails share two essential characteristics: detachment and disrepute" (p. 2). For Irwin, the function of jail is to manage the underclass, which he reports is also referred to as "rabble," "disorganized," "disorderly," and the "lowest class of people."

In one rough version of Irwin's analysis, the jail can be viewed as a means of controlling the most disruptive and unsightly members of the underclass. But in another version, it can be conceived of as an emergency service net for those who are in the most desperate straits. As other social services have shrunk, increasingly this task falls on the jail.

Whichever version one selects, few of those familiar with the jails in America's urban centers find it meaningful to characterize them only as facilities for "pretrial detention" or for serving "short-term sentences." Although not literally false, this characterization misses the broader function of the jail. The high rates of those released without charges filed, the turnstile-like frequency with which some people reappear, and the pathological characteristics of a high proportion of the inmates lead many to agree with Irwin that the jail is best understood as a social management instrument rather than an institution for effecting the purported aims of the criminal process.

Social management, not individualized justice, is also emphasized in other discussions of the criminal process. Long-time public defender, James M. Doyle (1992), offers the metaphors "colonial," "White Man's burden," and "Third World," in an essay drawing parallels between the careers of criminal justice officials and colonial administrators. Both, he argues,

> are convinced that they are menaced by both inscrutable, malign natives and ignorant, distant, policy-makers. They believe they are hamstrung by crazy legalities. Young Assistant District Attorneys, like young Assistant District Commissioners, hurriedly seize, then vehemently defend, a conventional wisdom as a protection against these threats. They pledge themselves to a professional code that sees the world in which people are divided into various collectives. Where they might have seen individuals, they see races, types, and colors instead. Like the colonialists before them, they embrace a "rigidly binomial opposition of 'ours' and 'theirs.' " In the criminal justice system as on the frontiers of empire "the impersonal communal idea of being a White Man" rules; it becomes "a very concrete way of being-in-the-world, a way of taking hold of reality, language and thought" (p. 74).

Sustaining his metaphor, Doyle parallels the corrupting influence of the White Man's effort to "manage" third-world natives with those of the criminal justice professionals' effort to handle cases. He concludes, "we have paid too much attention to the superficial exotic charms by which the reports of the colonial and criminal justice White Man entertain us, too little to the darker strains they also share" (p. 126).

Whether one prefers Irwin's notion of underclass or Doyle's "colonial" and "third world" metaphors, both resonate with our notion of the new penology. They vividly explain who is being managed and why. But in providing an explanation of these relationships, there is a danger that the terms will reify the problem, that they will suggest the problem is inevitable and permanent. Indeed, it is this belief, we maintain, that has contributed to the lowered expectations of the new penology—away from an aspiration to affect individual lives through rehabilitative and transformative efforts and toward the more "realistic" task of monitoring and managing intractable groups.

The hardening of poverty in contemporary America reinforces this view. When combined with a pessimistic analysis implied by the term *underclass*, the structural barriers that maintain the large islands of third world misery in America's major cities can lead to the conclusion that such conditions are inevitable and impervious to social policy intervention. This, in turn, can push corrections ever further toward a self-understanding based on the

470   FEELEY AND SIMON

imperative of herding a specific population that cannot be disaggregated and transformed but only maintained[35]—a kind of waste management function.[36] As the recent events in Los Angeles demonstrate, however, this kind of reversion is likely to be fatal to a democratic civil order.

CONCLUSION

Our discussion has proceeded as if the new penology—the new way of conceiving of the functions of the criminal sanction—has contributed to the recent rise in prison populations. Although we believe that it has, we also acknowledge that the new penology is both cause and effect of the increases. We recognize that those conditions we referred to at the outset as "external" have placed pressures on criminal justice institutions that, in turn, have caused them to adapt in a host of ways. The point of our paper, however, has been to show just how thorough this adaptation has been. It has led to a significant reconceptualization of penology, a shift that institutionalizes those adaptive behaviors. It embraces the new forms that have arisen as a result of this adaptation. As such, the new language, the new conceptualization, ensures that these new forms will persist independently of the pressures. They appear to be permanent features of the criminal justice system.

REFERENCES

Allen, Francis
    1981   The Decline of the Rehabilitative Idea. New Haven: Yale University Press.

Alschuler, Albert
    1991   The failure of sentencing guidelines: A plea for less aggregation. University of Chicago Law Review 58:901-951.

Anglin, Douglas, George Speckhart, Elizabeth Piper Deschenes
    1990   Examining the Effects of Narcotics Addiction. Los Angeles: UCLA Neuropsychiatric Institute, Drug Abuse Research Group.

Bennett, James
    1981   Oral History and Delinquency: The Rhetoric of Criminology. Chicago: University of Chicago Press.

Blumstein, Alfred, Jacqueline Cohen, Jeffrey A. Roth, and Christy A. Visher (eds.)
    1986   Criminal Careers and "Career Criminals." Washington, D.C.: National Academy Press.

---

35. However, those who work in corrections, whether they want to do social work or enforce laws, resist such deterministic ideas and resist conceiving of their jobs as recycling human beings from one level of custodial management to another with little reference to justice or social reintegration.

36. This term is more than metaphor. In 1989, then Governor Deukmejian of California proposed that prison inmates be used to process toxic wastes.

THE NEW PENOLOGY   471

Bottoms, Anthony
  1983   Neglected features of contemporary penal systems. In David Garland and
          Peter Young (eds.), The Power to Punish. London: Heinemann.

Bureau of Justice Statistics
  1989   Correctional Populations in the United States, 1988. Washington, D.C.:
          U.S. Department of Justice.

Burgess, Ernest W.
  1936   Protecting the public by parole and parole prediction. Journal of Criminal
          Law and Criminology 27:491-502.
  1974   The Basic Writings of Ernest W. Burgess, ed. Donald Bogue. Chicago:
          University of Chicago Press.

Cohen, Stanley
  1985   Visions of Social Control: Crime, Punishment and Classification. Oxford:
          Polity Press.

dan–Cohen, Meir
  1986   Persons, Rights and Organizations. Berkeley: University of California Press.

Doyle, James M.
  1992   "It's the Third World down there!": The colonialist vocation and American
          criminal justice. Harvard Civil Rights–Civil Liberties Law Review 27:71-
          126.

Duster, Troy
  1987   Crime, youth unemployment and the black urban underclass. Crime and
          Delinquency 33:300-316.

Foucault, Michel
  1977   Discipline and Punishment. New York: Pantheon.
  1978   The History of Sexuality. Vol. I, An Introduction. New York: Random
          House.
  1982   The subject and power. In Hubert L. Dreyfus and Paul Rabinow (eds.),
          Michel Foucault: Beyond Structuralism and Hermenuetics. Chicago: Uni-
          versity of Chicago Press.

Freeman, Alan
  1990   Antidiscrimination law: The view from 1989. In David Kaiyrs (ed.), The
          Politics of Law. New York: Pantheon.

Garland, David
  1985   Punishment and Welfare. Aldershot: Gower.

Garland, David and Peter Young (eds.)
  1983   The Power to Punish: Contemporary Penality and Social Analysis. London:
          Heinemann.

Gordon, Diana R.
  1991   The Justice Juggernaut: Fighting Street Crime, Controlling Citizens. New
          Brunswick: Rutgers University Press.

Greenspan, Rosanne
  1988   The transformation of criminal due process in the administrative state.
          Paper prepared for delivery at the annual meeting of the Law and Society
          Association, Vail, Colo., June 1988.

472   **FEELEY AND SIMON**

Greenwood, Peter
    1982   Selective Incapacitation. Santa Monica, Calif.: Rand.

Habermas, Jurgen
    1974   Communication and the Evolution of Society. Boston: Beacon Press.
    1985   Law as medium and law as institution. In Gunther Teubner (ed.),
            Dilemmas of Law in the Welfare State. Berlin: de Gruyter.

Hay, Douglas
    1975   Property, authority and the criminal law. In Douglas Hay, Peter Linebaugh,
            and Edward P. Thompson (eds.), Albion's Fatal Tree. New York:
            Pantheon.

Heydebrand, Wolf and Carroll Seron
    1990   Rationalizing Justice: The Political Economy and Federal District Courts.
            New York: State University of New York Press.

Ignatieff, Michael
    1978   A Just Measure of Pain: The Penitentiary in the Industrial Revolution,
            1750–1850. London: Macmillan.

Irwin, John
    1985   The Jail: Managing the Underclass in American Society. Berkeley:
            University of California Press.

Jacobs, James B.
    1977   Stateville: The Penitentiary in Mass Society. Chicago: University of
            Chicago Press.

Kelling, George L.
    1991   Crime and metaphor: Toward a new concept of policing. NY: The City
            Journal, Autumn:65-71.

Krygier, Martin
    1989   Law as tradition. Law and Philosophy 5:237–262.

Lipsky, Michael
    1980   Street Level Bureaucrats. New York: Russell Sage Foundation.

Maguire, Kathleen and Timothy J. Flanagan
    1990   Sourcebook of Criminal Justice Statistics 1989. U.S. Department of Justice,
            Bureau of Justice Statistics, Washington, D.C.: U.S. Government Printing
            Office.

Maltz, Michael
    1984   Recidivism. Orlando, Fla.: Academic Press.

Mathieson, Thomas
    1983   The future of control systems—The case of Norway. In David Garland and
            Peter Young (eds.), The Power to Punish. London: Heinemann.

Mauer, Marc
    1990   Young black men and the criminal justice system. Washington, D.C.: The
            Sentencing Project.

Messinger, Sheldon
    1969   Strategies of control. Ph.D. dissertation, Department of Sociology, Univer-
            sity of California at Los Angeles.

Messinger, Sheldon and John Berecochea
  1990   Don't stay too long but do come back soon. Proceedings, Conference on Growth and Its Influence on Correctional Policy, Center for the Study of Law and Society, University of California at Berkeley.

Moore, Mark H., Susan R. Estrich, Daniel McGillis, and William Spelman
  1984   Dangerous Offenders: The Elusive Target of Justice. Cambridge, Mass.: Harvard University Press.

National Institute of Justice
  1990   Research in Action—Drug Use Forecasting. Washington, D.C.: U.S. Department of Justice.

Nelken, David
  1982   Is there a crisis in law and legal ideology? Journal of Law and Society 9:177–189.

Pashukanis, Eugenii
  1978   Law and Marxism: A General Theory, trans. Barbara Einhurn, London: Ink Links.

Petersilia, Joan
  1987   Expanding Options for Criminal Sentencing. Santa Monica, Calif.: Rand.

President's Commission on Law Enforcement and the Administration of Justice
  1967   The Challenge of Crime in a Free Society. Washington, D.C.,: Government Printing Office.

Rainwater, Lee
  1966   Work and identity in the lower class. In Sam B. Warner (ed.), Planning for a Nation of Cities. Cambridge, Mass.: MIT Press.

Reichman, Nancy
  1986   Managing crime risks: Toward an insurance-based model of social control. Research in Law, Deviance and Social Control 8:151–172.

Rothman, David
  1971   The Discovery of the Asylum: Social Order and Disorder in the New Republic. Boston: Little, Brown.
  1980   Conscience and Convenience: The Asylum and its Alternative in Progressive America. Boston: Little, Brown.

Sharlet, Robert
  1978   Pashukanis and the withering away of law in the USSR. In Sheila Fitzpatrick (ed.), Cultural Revolution in Russia: 1928–1931. Bloomington: Indiana University Press.

Shaw, Clifford
  1931   The Natural History of a Delinquent Career. 1968. Westport, Conn.: Greenwood Press.

Simon, Jonathan
  1987   The emergence of a risk society: Insurance law and the state. Socialist Review 95:61-89.
  1988   The ideological effect of actuarial practices. Law and Society Review 22:771-800.
  1990   From discipline to management: Strategies of control in parole supervision, 1890–1990. Ph.D. dissertation, Jurisprudence and Social Policy Program, University of California at Berkeley.

474   FEELEY AND SIMON

Steiner, Henry J.
    1987   Moral Vision and Social Vision in the Court: A Study of Tort Accident
            Law. Madison: University of Wisconsin Press.

Stone, Christopher
    1975   Where the Law Ends. New York: Harper & Row.

Sutherland, Edwin H.
    1934   Principles of Criminology. Philadelphia: J.B. Lippincott.

Teubner, Gunther
    1989   How the law thinks: Toward a constructivist epistemology of law. Law and
            Society Review 23:727-757.

Wilkins, Leslie T.
    1973   Crime and criminal justice at the turn of the century. Annals of the
            American Academy of Political and Social Science 408:13-29.

Wilson, William Julius
    1987   The Truly Disadvantaged: The Inner City, the Underclass, and Public
            Policy. Chicago: University of Chicago Press.

Zimring, Franklin and Gordon Hawkins
    1991   The Scale of Imprisonment. Chicago: University of Chicago Press.

Malcolm M. Feeley is Professor of Law and Director of the Center for the Study of Law
and Society at the University of California at Berkeley. He received his Ph.D. in political
science in 1969, and he is the author of numerous books and articles. His book, *The Process Is the Punishment* (1979), received the American Bar Association's Silver Gavel
Award and was cited as one of the best books in the past five years by the American
Sociological Association's Criminal Justice Section.

    Jonathan Simon is Assistant Professor in the Department of Political Science at the University of Michigan and currently Visiting Associate Professor of Law at the University of
Miami. He received his Ph.D. and J.D. at the University of California at Berkeley, and he
writes on the criminal process. His articles have appeared in *Law & Society Review* and
Law and Social Enquiry, and he is the author of a forthcoming book, to be published by the
Univesity of Chicago Press, on the development of modern parole policies.

[12]

THE BRITISH JOURNAL

OF

CRIMINOLOGY

| Vol. 22 | July 1982 | No. 3 |

DANGEROUSNESS AND CRIMINAL JUSTICE

JEAN FLOUD (Cambridge)*

I AM glad to have this opportunity of introducing the Report of your working party.†

We were charged with the task of reviewing the law and practice relating to so-called " dangerous offenders " and were promptly dubbed " The Dangerous Offenders' Working-Party ". However, our terms of reference were not so wide. The Butler Committee had only recently reported on *The Mentally Abnormal Offender* and the " dangerous " offenders with whom we were to concern ourselves were mentally or, more precisely, legally sane. That is to say, whatever their mental state, they could not be said to be suffering from a definable mental disorder, treatable within the mental health system. They were, therefore, legally sane and the responsibility of the penal system, not the health system. In short, we were to look into the powers available to the courts and related authorities to protect the public from the exceptional, so-called " dangerous " offender, other than those provided under the Mental Health Act.

I say the exceptional, so-called " dangerous " offender and I hope that you can hear the inverted commas. Throughout the Report everything that inverted commas and qualifying adjectives can do is done, to remind readers that there is no such psychological or medical entity as a " dangerous " person and that " dangerousness " is not an objective concept. Dangers are unacceptable risks. We can measure risk—actuaries make a profession of it. Risk is, in principle, a matter of fact; but danger is a matter of judgment or opinion—a question of what we are prepared to put up with. People tolerate enormous risks without perceiving them as dangers, when their fears are not aroused or when it suits their convenience.

* C.B.E., M.A., Litt.D. Principal of Newnham College, Cambridge.

† *Dangerousness and Criminal Justice* Jean Floud and Warren Young, Cambridge Studies in Criminology XLVII Editor Sir Leon Radzinowicz, Heinemann 1981.

This talk was given at the Annual General Meeting of the Howard League for Penal Reform held on December 2, 1981.

JEAN FLOUD

What makes a risk of grave harm unacceptable? Why is it that when someone mentions " dangerous offenders " we do not immediately think of drunken drivers, keepers of unsafe factories, tippers of toxic waste, vendors of unsafe cars or harmful pharmaceutical products? Dangerousness is a thoroughly ambiguous concept and we may well ask whether it has any place in the administration of criminal justice; and, if it be conceded that it has, how we are to define and identify " dangerous " offenders for legal purposes. I will come to these questions, which dominated our work, but I must first say something about dangerousness and criminal justice in England.

The English sentencing system does not provide explicitly for " dangerous " offenders. The statutes contain no reference to them. There is mention of " dangerous " driving and " dangerous " drugs but the word " dangerous " is nowhere used to define *persons* for sentencing purposes. It is not that the courts do not recognise the difference between " ordinary " and " dangerous " offenders, for in practice they do. But in marked contrast to the position in most other countries, our arrangements for protecting the public from legally responsible serious offenders who present a continuing risk are almost wholly discretionary and *ad hoc* in character. The distinction between " ordinary " and " dangerous " offenders, recognised in practice by the courts, has not generated much discussion and rests on no established criteria.

The concept of the " dangerous " offender is to be found at three points in the English system of criminal justice. It comes closest to legal recognition through judicial practice in the use of the life-sentence for those few non-homicidal offences for which it is available as the maximum penalty; and to administrative definition in the arrangements for classifying prisoners for security purposes. But even in these circumscribed contexts, it is imprecise. Not surprisingly, it is still more so when ordinary, determinate sentences are used for protective purposes, whether they be sentences outside the normal range for a handful of abnormal crimes whose perpetrators are explicitly judged to be dangerous, or sentences within the normal range but more or less covertly longer than they would have been, had the court not perceived the need to provide the public with extra protection.

In short, the concept of dangerousness in English criminal justice is prevalent but elusive. It is not used consistently or with any precision and the nature of the risk to which it refers is never clearly defined. What is it that the English public is thought to need protection against? What must an offender do to place himself at risk of being judged " dangerous "? How much protection will the courts afford the public by means of exceptional sentences of one kind or another? It is possible, as we show in our Report, to piece together answers in broad terms to these questions, but nothing is explicit and there is little to go on.

It is impossible to determine precisely the size and composition of the class of dangerous offenders which emerges from the exercise of these discretionary powers. All that we can be sure of is that it is small and heterogeneous and it has not aroused controversy. It has not aroused controversy because sentences in the normal range are long and the permissible maxima are longer still.

DANGEROUSNESS AND CRIMINAL JUSTICE

There is no reason to suppose either that the public is not adequately protected or that large numbers of offenders are unnecessarily detained as dangerous for much longer than would be justifiable on other grounds alone. The problem is handled pragmatically and, one might say, discreetly. The public is as well protected as it can expect to be and there is no evidence of wholesale or systematic injustice to offenders. There seems little call to raise awkward and difficult questions about degrees of justifiable public alarm and the legitimate scope of protection against the risk of serious harm.

What, then, did the Howard League have in mind when they commissioned our inquiries? The Home Office was certainly mystified. They were nothing if not helpful to us in the course of our work; but, in reply to our Consultative Document, they remarked that they " were unaware of any pressing need for change arising from practical experience, either in the powers of the courts or in the arrangements made for the control and supervision of ' dangerous offenders ' apart from the special case of the mentally abnormal offender which [had] been remitted to the Butler Committee ". It is true that the Butler Committee had reported receiving a memorandum, prepared jointly by officials of the Home Office and the Department of Health and Social Security, which drew attention to the problem of the legal obligation to release at the end of a fixed sentence a small number of men " who are probably dangerous but who are not acceptable for treatment in hospital and for whom a life-sentence is not appropriate ". The Committee acknowledged " a defect in society's defences " and recommended that it be made good by means of a new form of indeterminate sentence—the so-called reviewable sentence. However, no attempt had been made to follow the post-release careers of the offenders in question; there was no evidence to show that they had caused serious harm which could have been prevented by delaying their release. No doubt, the case for the new sentence failed to impress itself on the Minister and his officials in the Home Office. It is certainly unlikely to have motivated the Howard League to set up a working-party. More persuasive, I think, must have been the desire not to duck the difficult issues raised by the existence of a few potentially recidivist serious offenders at a time when the campaign for shorter sentences was beginning to have effect.

Penal reformers object in principle not only to long prison sentences but also to the practice of keeping people in prison in the interests of public safety for longer than can be justified on other grounds alone. Yet, the shorter sentences become, the more difficult it seems to be to argue that there should not be a special protective sentence for the small number of exceptional offenders judged to present an unacceptable risk of further serious harm. Indeed, the provision of such a special sentence may well be a condition of securing shorter sentences overall.

This was recognised by the Advisory Council on the Penal System which proposed that legislation to effect a drastic reduction of maximum penalties should include provision for a special discretionary sentence, of unrestricted but determinate length, for a minority of exceptional, " dangerous " offenders. The proposed two-tier system was itself the target of objections of a

JEAN FLOUD

practical kind; but the suggestion that the distinction recognised in practice by the courts between the " ordinary " and the " dangerous " offender should be formalised and given statutory recognition aroused fierce opposition grounded in fundamental objections of principle. Our own proposals are attracting the same opposition.

It is worth noting that no-one dismisses the practical problem. That is, no-one denies the existence of a minority of serious offenders who present a continuing risk. The argument is all about degrees of risk, perceptions of danger and justifiable public alarm, the difficulty of deciding whether or not someone is " dangerous " and the legitimacy of confining people for what they *might* do as well as for what they have actually done.

The question of the legitimacy of protective sentencing goes to the root of the matter and we considered it carefully. We took seriously the fundamental objections raised by those who argue that it is never permissible to detain a legally responsible offender in anticipation of the harm he may cause, and that restraint must be justified in some other way (for example, as retributive punishment). We do not claim to have said the last word on a difficult ethical problem; but, for the reasons set out in our Report, we found these arguments unconvincing.

We found ourselves less resistant to the arguments of other critics who object that it is impossible to define and identify dangerous offenders satisfactorily for legal purposes and rest their case on the ambiguousness of the concept of dangerousness itself and the inherent unpredictability of human behaviour. They have a distinguished exponent in Professor Norval Morris; but we could not agree with his categorical verdict: " Since we cannot make reliable predictions of dangerous behaviour, considerations of justice forbid us to confine people against their wishes in the name of public safety for longer periods than we can justify on other grounds."

To reject protective sentencing, as morally unacceptable in principle and incapable of just administration in practice, completely avoids all the difficulties and dilemmas inherent in the practice—but it is the only way of doing so. Since we could not follow the critics to the end of the road, we were left with no alternative but to review the practical ethics of protective sentencing and to try to formulate the problems raised by the practice, in terms which would permit us to propose solutions that seemed to be both just and workable. Had we been persuaded by the critics, our Report would, of course, have looked very different. We would have been obliged to recommend that the practice as it exists, in any form, should be abandoned; and, as penal reformers, we should have found ourselves in a quandary.

Few serious offenders repeat their serious offences, so that there is no reason, in most cases, to keep them out of circulation on that account for very long periods of time. The question of penalties for serious offences—even for the worst cases of such offences—must not be confused with the question of protecting the public from the few serious offenders who *do* present a continuing risk and who *are* likely to cause further serious harm. So long as retribution is thought to require very long sentences for serious offenders, the problem of the risky minority is obscured and can be neglected; but if, as

DANGEROUSNESS AND CRIMINAL JUSTICE

is now widely accepted, the demands of retribution can be met with much shorter sentences, even for serious offenders, the problem of the exceptional minority is exposed and cannot be neglected. It seems irrational to tolerate longer sentences for serious offences than nowadays would meet the demands of retribution, in order to avoid the notorious difficulties and dilemmas of dealing justly with the exceptional few; but this seems to be the price of refusing to entertain the idea of bringing protective sentencing into the open and placing it under statutory control.

I need hardly remind this audience that our high maximum sentences are irrelevant and inappropriate for a modern penal policy. They are irrelevant because the normal range of sentences imposed is appreciably lower than the permitted maxima. Over the years, the sentences actually passed appear to have settled around an established average; but wide deviations in particular cases raise a risk of unequal treatment and are a source of unrest in prisons. They are inappropriate because a modern penal policy should clearly distinguish the main purposes of imprisonment and see that these are reflected in the sentencing structure: *viz.* protection, denunciation, and dealing with defaulters from the obligations imposed by other penalties. Long sentences of imprisonment are required only in the few cases which call for the separation of the offender for the protection of others; the requirements of denunciation or retribution can nowadays be met by short sentences even for serious offences (*e.g.* flagrant breaches of trust or offences of violence) so long as the offenders do not present a continuing risk to other persons; and more or less nominal sentences will serve to deal with defaulters from the obligations imposed by other penalties (*e.g.* fines). This is the pattern in most western countries. The Canadian Law Reform Commission in 1976 suggested a maximum sentence of six months for defaulters from the obligations of other penalties; and a maximum of three years for offences calling for denunciation. They proposed an upper limit of twenty years for protective purposes.

The practical difficulties and ethical dilemmas of protective sentencing are mutually reinforcing, as is clear from Professor Morris's statement quoted above. We paid a great deal of attention to the practical difficulty of identifying, with any degree of confidence, serious offenders against whom protection is needed because they present a continuing risk of serious harm. As will be evident from our Report, we sifted a considerable quantity of theoretical argument and empirical evidence bearing directly or indirectly on the state of the art of assessing " dangerousness ". We reached a conclusion which is not surprising, in so far as it amounts to saying that, since it is impossible to be sure how people will behave in the future, if only because of the working of chance, any attempt to apply precautions selectively against some persons for the sake of others is bound to be more or less wide of the mark. What *is* surprising—and very alarming—is to discover just how wide of the mark it turns out to be, whenever it is possible to put predictive judgments to the test by following the post-release careers of " dangerous " offenders. Statisticians have calculated the probabilities: so many judgments of *dangerous* falsified by the offender's subsequent behaviour (that is to say, by his failure to cause further grave harm) and so many judgments of *safe* falsified by the further

JEAN FLOUD

serious offences he commits. Not surprisingly, it tends to be the critics of protective sentencing who worry about the former and members of the general public who worry about the latter. But the former figure, the proportion of falsified judgments of *dangerous*, even at its lowest, is so uncomfortably high that no-one engaged in making predictive judgments in the administration of justice can fail to be impressed—or, more likely, depressed. As matters now stand, parole boards and similar bodies, to say nothing of courts, are, on average, at best as likely to be wrong as right in thinking that the offenders they decide to detain as dangerous will actually do further serious harm if left at large. Whatever be the prospects of improvement—and it must be admitted that, though they exist, they are not rosy and are forever constrained by a large factor of chance, it is likely that at least two persons are detained for every one person who is prevented from doing serious harm. This is to say that each offender in protective custody probably suffers, in addition to the usual hardships of imprisonment, at least a 50 per cent. risk of being unnecessarily detained. On what grounds are we justified in doing him this grave harm—for grave harm it undoubtedly is, on any reckoning?

The justification can only be that we are thereby relieving someone else of a substantial risk of grave harm—that we are justly redistributing a burden of risk that we cannot immediately reduce. This formulation of the answer, in terms of redistributing risk, seems to us to be more appropriate to the jurisprudence of protective sentencing than the one that is frequently given in terms of social utility. The objections to that approach, which involves the abstract and unacceptable concept of social defence, are by now familiar and I will not rehearse them, even briefly, here. Our own formulation has its difficulties and I prefer to say something about these—or at least about those of which we are aware. I will mention two fundamental problems.

We speak of redistributing risk between potential victims and potential aggressors. But we are all potential aggressors—differently placed and variously motivated to harm our fellows. Why shift the burden of risk, if any is to be shifted, only on to the shoulders of convicted offenders? Why confine tests of dangerousness to them? Why not, some critics ask, apply tests of dangerousness to us all and, in the interests of social defence, introduce what has been called " civil preventive confinement "? This is not a frivolous or even a purely academic question; the idea crops up to be taken seriously from time to time when some new piece of scientific or medical information seems to make it practicable: for example, the double X chromosome which apparently led the Nixon administration seriously to entertain the idea of screening the age-group of eight-year-old boys for potential delinquents. It is important to be able to answer the question: where is the barrier of principle to the extension of tests of dangerousness to citizens at large? This is not the place to expound our attempt at an answer. I want only to draw attention to the question and to point out that we attached importance to it and tried to answer it.

Another problem arises from the fact that we are talking about redistributing risk between two parties only one of whom—the convicted offender—is, generally speaking, actually and immediately identifiable and certain to bear

DANGEROUSNESS AND CRIMINAL JUSTICE

the cost of the redistribution in person. We have to make a moral choice between competing claims: the claim of a known individual offender, not to be unnecessarily deprived of his liberty; and the claim of an innocent (unconvicted), unknown person (or persons), not to be deprived of the right to go about their business without risk of grave harm at the hands of an aggressor. Where does justice lie? The debate has recently concentrated heavily on the rights of offenders. Civil libertarians have made the running, and not without reason; for the " protectionist " case has been both mis-stated and over-stated in the past.

Critics (for example, Professor Bottoms) argue that rights inhere in particu-lar individuals and are real only in so far as they may be asserted against the general welfare. This view of rights is acceptable in principle, but the " general welfare " is an unnecessary abstraction. We do not need to use this vague notion, when what we mean is a diffused right to protection against a diffused risk of grave harm from a particular source. Providing the risk is real and the anticipated harm is grave, the fact that it is diffused is no argument, prima facie, for refusing to take preventive measures. The claim to protection is a collective or communal one and the risk to particular indivi-duals need not be substantial. To cut a difficult argument short, we must not get ourselves into the position of denying the possibility of collective claims, or of arguing that, because any individual's claim to protection is stronger or weaker according to the risk he bears, the strength of the case for a protective sentence must vary inversely with the size of the population at risk from the offender concerned.

Of course, collective or communal claims are only logical constructions out of the claims of individuals generally; and there has been and continues to be much loose talk about the requirements of social defence and threats to " society " or the " fabric of society ". Nevertheless, it will not do simply to dismiss the idea of a collective claim of right to protection against a potential aggressor. To speak of protective sentences as being designed for the protec-tion of *society* need not be a misleading form of words which simply disguises the introduction into the balancing exercise of considerations of general welfare or popular preferences or unjustifiable public alarm—considerations which should not weigh against the right of an offender not to be detained unnecessarily.

This said, the fact remains that there is a standing temptation to over-state the collective claim to protection. It is easier to see ourselves as potential victims than as potential aggressors. But, as potential victims, we already have the protection of the criminal law, using ordinary forms of sentence. What is the case for extra protection? The courts have consistently rejected in practice well-meaning attempts by Parliament to provide extra protection against what is sometimes called the " social nuisance " of the habitual, petty offender. In this case we have had to learn to live with what we have got. Serious offenders who present a continuing risk represent, by the same token, a " social menace "; but we have not been denied extra protection against them. High maximum sentences have enabled the courts to deal at their discretion and without much debate with the small number of such

JEAN FLOUD

" dangerous " offenders. But a drastic reduction in maximum sentences would severely curtail, if not for practical purposes exclude, the discretionary power of the judiciary to deal with them, otherwise than by means of a life-sentence when it is available. We foresee the need, in such a situation, for a statutory framework for protective sentencing which would, in effect, rationalise and make explicit present practice.

I must make it clear that we are far from envisaging any expansion in the scope of present practice. Indeed, we would expect the introduction of a special sentence, under the conditions we propose, to result in some re-trenchment, notwithstanding the modest extent of present practice. We would wish to abolish the discretionary life-sentence; but we presume that few of those now given this sentence (53 in 1978) would escape the proposed new measure. The effect of the reduction of the gap between the permissible maximum and the normal range of ordinary determinate sentences is hard to estimate, since there is no means of discovering the number of such sentences which are at present fixed with protective considerations in mind. It seems likely that they are often imposed for offences against property, of a kind which would be excluded from the range of serious harm for which we think the protective sentence should be reserved. Since protective considerations in ordinary determinate sentencing are disavowed by the Court of Appeal, we may assume that a large proportion of the longer sentences—say, those of more than seven years (191 in 1978)—are likely to reflect only the gravity of the offence together with the offender's record. It is probably realistic to estimate that not more than half the annual total of long deter-minate sentences, plus most discretionary life-sentences, could be expected to be replaced by a special sentence. If so, the total in 1978 would have been about 140.

The general objective of our proposals is to bring protective sentencing under statutory control, while leaving ample scope for the necessary exercise of judicial discretion in the sentencing of a very heterogeneous group of exceptional offenders. To this end, we have formulated categories of grave harm, against which the public, in certain circumstances, may claim the protection of a special sentence outside the permitted maximum for a relevant serious offence; and we have defined a severely restricted class of offenders who might be eligible for such a sentence and mandatory evidential and procedural requirements within which judicial and executive discretion would be exercised in the administration of the proposed sentence.

I want to say something about three features of these proposals which are likely to attract criticism: our attempt to say what the public should be protected against (*i.e.* our definition of " grave harm "); our decision not to place a statutory upper limit on the proposed protective sentence; and not to give statutory expression to tests of " dangerousness ".

We took it as axiomatic that the public is entitled to the protection of a special sentence only against *grave* harm; and that no offender should be eligible for a protective sentence unless grave harm is manifested in his

DANGEROUSNESS AND CRIMINAL JUSTICE

criminal conduct. Our first thought was, naturally, that the interpretation of grave harm in this context should be as specific as possible.

The laws of many, if not most, western countries make provision for protective sentencing, but few codes specify the nature of the harm against which protective measures may be taken. Speaking generally and within the limits of our knowledge, we were very struck with the reluctance of legislatures to provide a substantive definition of dangerousness, by specifying the harm against which the public is entitled to special protection. In most cases, legislation relies heavily on the phrase " protection of the public ", or some equivalent, without indicating what the public needs protecting against. We, therefore, attempted a clarification of the notion of grave harm.

Grave harm is often simply equated with violence. Violence is almost universally regarded as the hall-mark of dangerousness. Dangerous offenders are presumed to be violent and violent offenders are presumed to be dangerous. But, of course, not all harm inflicted with violence is serious of its kind; nor does all harm against persons, which is by definition a serious kind of harm, involve violence. Some writers who take this obvious point try to resolve the difficulty by talking about white-collar or corporate violence, by which they mean decisions (usually but not necessarily corporate) which result in physical harm to employees, consumers or members of the general public. But this is no more than rhetoric. The question whether certain ills are tolerable and should be prevented, even by measures which carry the risk that some legally sane person will be unnecessarily deprived of his liberty, is essentially a moral one. Though, in practice, what people actually have to put up with is decided by government and the agencies of law enforcement and is in this sense a political matter, the question is one of principle. Are there any limits, in principle, to the kinds of harm, of sufficient degree, against which the public may claim protection, if necessary by very harmful measures such as protective sentences? I must refer you to our Report for an account of our attempt to arrive at a principled analysis. We spent some time, for example, considering Professor Walker's suggestion that we should agree that, since protective sentences involve serious and lasting hardship for the offenders concerned, they should be used only to prevent serious and lasting hardship to others of a kind which, once caused, *cannot be remedied*. But the idea of irremediable harm is troublesome, especially if you are unwilling to accept the conventional distinction between physical and mental harm and to set aside the latter as less important than the former.

In the end, we were forced to the conclusion that the problem of distinguishing between " serious " and other harm cannot be wholly objectified; that harms to the person are *sui generis* and enjoy special moral status, whatever their degree; but that a protective sentence, which carries the risk to the offender that he will be unnecessarily deprived of his liberty, should be used only where the victims of the anticipated harm are themselves exposed to the risk of unusual hardship (pain and suffering, shock and fear, injury to health or beggary). We therefore propose that grave harm for the purposes of protective sentencing should be interpreted as comprising the following categories: death, serious bodily injury, serious sexual assault, severe or

JEAN FLOUD

prolonged pain or mental stress, loss of or damage to property which causes severe personal hardship, damage to the environment which has a severely adverse effect on public health or safety, serious damage to the security of the state. This classification is similar in intended scope to that proposed by the Advisory Council on the Penal System, though it is formulated in somewhat more precise and concrete terms. Thus, we propose that the elements of grave physical and psychological harm should be specified and that serious sexual assaults, which we take to be harmful *sui generis*, should be given separate mention. We have added to the category of indirect, generalised harm, which is represented in their classification by serious damage to the security of the state, another, *viz.* damage to the environment resulting in serious damage to public health or safety. We rejected the category " damage to the general fabric of society " as being either redundant or too inclusive in its vagueness.

Though our categories are meant to be precise enough to become statutory law, we had intended, like the Butler Committee, to follow the example of the Danish legislature (among others) and confine protective custody to a restricted list of serious offences. As can be seen from our Consultative Document, we prepared ourselves to draw up a list of offences, using their legal definitions, which would serve to give precision to the categories of grave harm and to specify the offences which would make it permissible for a court to consider imposing a protective sentence. This seemed the obvious way of delimiting the scope of the protection to which the public was entitled and of restricting the class of eligible offenders, as well as safeguarding offenders against the imposition of long sentences when the offence for which they stand committed is not itself very harmful. Eventually, however, our view of the nature of the problem changed and, for the reasons given in our Report, we came to see the attractions of a list of justifying offences as spurious. We decided to abandon the idea of an " offence-condition " for the protective sentence. We propose that grave harm should be defined in terms of the categories we have specified and that it should be left to the courts to determine whether a particular offence comes within the definition and, if so, whether the circumstances in which it was committed give rise to reasonable anxiety about the future.

This is perhaps the point at which I should say something about our view of the role of discretionary powers in protective sentencing. The argument that these powers are indispensable but that they should be no greater than necessary and should be subject to reasonable guidelines applies, we think, with particular force to protective sentencing. Such sentences, I need not reiterate, represent a more serious infringement of the offender's rights than an ordinary retributive sentence and they should not be freely available to the courts. However, it may be argued, also, that they call for a greater degree of individualisation and indeterminacy than ordinary retributive sentences. We certainly think that, within the framework of a controlling statute, which would specify the harm against which the public may claim to be protected and define a restricted class of eligible offenders with reference to their age

DANGEROUSNESS AND CRIMINAL JUSTICE

and record, they call for a good deal of discretion if they are to be administered justly according to their purpose.

I have already mentioned our decision to give the judges a broad discretion to determine whether, in a particular case, grave harm within the meaning of the statute is at issue; whether the offence of which the offender stands convicted is an instance of such harm; and whether such harm is present in his criminal record. We also favoured giving them full discretion to determine the length of any sentence they judged it necessary to impose.

The Advisory Council on the Penal System have been much criticised for not stipulating an upper limit to the length of their proposed special sentence. However, we shared the Council's view that it is both unnecessary and unwise to circumscribe judicial discretion in the sentencing of a very hetero-geneous group of exceptional offenders. Moreover, we were unable to see on what grounds we could rationally prefer one maximum length of sentence to another. In the upshot, then, the protective sentence we propose may be of any determinate length and, like an ordinary sentence, will obey the pro-portionality rule. The court will have regard to the gravity of the anticipated harm and the risk of its occurring. The sentence will represent the length of time beyond which the offender could not justly be detained, even if he were still thought to present a risk; it will represent, so to say, the outside limit of the grant of additional protection to the public. The responsibility then rests with the executive to release the offender as soon as it becomes clear that control without custody is practicable.

I come now to the difficult question of determining an offender's dangerous-ness—*i.e.* making a predictive judgment about him. We had envisaged formulating restrictive criteria of dangerousness for the courts to apply; or, at any rate, guidelines for the making of predictive judgments. We had in mind, for example, indications of a pattern of behaviour or a mental condi-tion which would justify a conclusion of continuing risk; and a requirement that the court should be satisfied in fairly specific terms as to the level of the risk which would justify a protective sentence (for example, that the offender is all but certain to cause further serious harm; or, at least, is more likely than not to do so; or merely, perhaps, more likely to do so than others of similar age and circumstances). We spent a great deal of time on an extensive literature devoted to the problems of assessing " dangerousness ", including valuable papers written for us by the late Dr Peter Scott and our colleague Professor John Gunn. Our Report contains a careful analysis of the problem, together with a substantial appendix devoted to a discussion of the statistical and clinical problems of predicting behaviour, and a critical review of the findings of various attempts which have been made, by statisticians and sociologists, to put judgments of dangerousness to the test by following the careers of the substantial number of offenders who, at various times in the United States, have been released from detention by court order, against the advice of expert assessors.

The road to our conclusion was long and hard; but in the end we agreed that statutory tests of dangerousness were not feasible. The nature of predic-tive judgments, the limited scope for precision and confidence in such

JEAN FLOUD

judgments, the widely varying characteristics of the relatively few offenders likely to meet the qualifying conditions we propose for a protective sentence, call for the exercise of a broad discretion rather than the application of statutory tests.

I repeat that all the evidence indicates that, for the time being at any rate, those who make predictive judgments must realise that they have on average no more than an even chance, at best, of being right when they decide that a serious offender is likely to cause further grave harm and must be detained for the protection of the public. If this demonstrably low degree of confidence in predictive judgments leads you to the conclusion that the claims of potential victims to be relieved of the risk presented by certain offenders simply cannot be justly satisfied, except perhaps in the circumstances where the risk represented by an offender is so real and present as to amount to a threat of imminent harm, then there is no more to be said. If, however, you take the view that certain types of offence are so harmful that it is reasonable to regard even a low risk of their being repeated in the short or medium term as unacceptable, then you may be persuaded to conclude with us that the requirements of justice to the offender can be met by hedging the making of predictive judgments with procedural safeguards without regulating their scope and content. For example, we think it should be mandatory for the court to consider certain evidence, to provide for the defence to call their own expert witnesses, to make the assessment contestable, to require the court to give reasons for the sentence imposed, and to provide for every such sentence to be referred automatically to the Court of Appeal. We take the view that substantial justice in protective sentencing must depend on severely restricting the class of eligible offenders and on arrangements to ensure that each case is painstakingly adjudicated on its merits in accordance with mandatory evidential and procedural requirements.[1]

On the principle that a particular sentence should entail the minimum curtailment of the offender's liberty compatible with its purpose, we think he has the right, which should be given statutory expression, to be released from custody, assuming " tariff " conditions have been satisfied, as soon as it ceases to be necessary for the protection of the public to continue to detain him. Release on licence from a protective sentence is unlike parole from an ordinary sentence of imprisonment; it is not a privilege to be earned but a right to be claimed. The arrangements for reviewing the case for detaining a prisoner serving a protective sentence and for determining the conditions for his licence, if it is decided to release him, must reflect this conceptual difference. We therefore propose that the statute should provide for him to have access at frequent and regular intervals to an independent review tribunal of quasi-judicial composition and character.

We think, however, that the decision to release him should be retained by the Home Secretary for the duration of the determinate sentence imposed by

---

[1] " Since there is no truth of the matter and an offender's ' dangerousness ', insofar as it can be ascertained, is a matter of degree and there is a large element of chance in the outcome, it is more important to hedge the making of predictive judgments with safeguards than to stipulate precisely what level of probability that an offender will actually reoffend must be established before such a sentence can be imposed." *Dangerousness and Criminal Justice*, p. 111.

DANGEROUSNESS AND CRIMINAL JUSTICE

the court. This reflects our view that, whilst protective sentences should not be freely available to the courts, once imposed they must be administered so as to do justice to the public interest as well as to the rights of the offender; and that there is a risk, if the decision to release is removed from the executive, that less than justice may be done to the public interest.

This brings me to the end of the principal features of our Report and proposals to which I want, by way of introduction, to draw your attention. Before I conclude, however, I must refer to the charge which has been levelled against us, that we have failed to take account of the political implications of giving statutory recognition to the practice of protective sentencing.

I have put to you the arguments that weighed with us: the arguments that amount to a plea for a modern penal policy which would recognise the futility of long prison sentences for purely denunciatory or retributive purposes, and the desirability of a drastic reduction in the permissible maximum penalties for all offences, even serious ones, providing only for the possibility of putting a small number of offenders out of circulation for a substantial period in the interests of public safety. There are critics, however, who believe that the political price for a policy of this kind is too great: they are critics of what might be termed the " dangerousness of dangerousness " school. In this country, the most distinguished exponents of this point of view are Sir Leon Radzinowicz and Dr Roger Hood, who attacked the special sentence proposed by the Advisory Council to deal with the " dangerous " offender as " a dangerous direction for sentencing reform ". In their view, the concept of dangerousness carries inherent " potentialities for accelerating use and dangerous abuse " and ought never to be introduced into penal legislation. They find their fears realised in our own proposals, about which they write as follows [2]:

" [The] danger of the slippery extension of the criteria of ' dangerousness ' blatantly emerges from the inclusion of the category ' serious damage to the security of the state.'

" It is one thing to deal with offenders under the law of treason, or even sedition; it is quite another to open a hornets' nest at times of potential political and social unrest. It is one thing to allow the courts to sentence those who present a grave risk of ' loss or of damage to property which results in severe personal hardship ' to longer terms within a statutory maximum; it is another to give an open-ended power to the courts. It is one thing to make sure that those who cause havoc to the environment do not get off lightly, as they too often do now, and it is another to brand them as a special category of ' dangerous criminals ', subject to different penal provisions. Indeed in a different political climate the protective sentence could well become the engine of a system of preventive police. To introduce laws which can be abused in the belief that they will not be abused is not sound policy."

The precise thrust of this attack is not entirely clear though, of course, the

---

[2] *The Criminal Law Review*, November, 1981.

JEAN FLOUD

point that is being made is not in doubt. Despite the categorical statement
that the concept of dangerousness ought never to be introduced into penal
legislation, it seems that the target is *explicitness* in the use of predictive
judgments in criminal justice, rather than the use of these judgments as such.
The fear is that the explicitness required by any attempt to bring them under
statutory control will, as they put it, " release the beast into political and
judicial life "—presumably by encouraging the judges to make too much use
of the exceptional sentence. As they see it, the virtue of the present arrangements lies precisely in their diffuse and discretionary character. The concept
of " dangerousness " is indisputably present in our criminal justice system,
but it is, so to say, muffled; and, in their view, that is for the best. It would be
signally unwise to try to bring it under statutory control, except to the extent
of abolishing the discretionary life-sentence and replacing it with statutory
maxima for particular offences high enough to permit sentences outside the
normal range, in cases where the offender presents a continuing risk.

Abolishing the discretionary life-sentence would curtail the discretionary
powers of the executive to make and implement predictive judgments;
though, of course, the Parole Board and the Prison Department of the Home
Office would still retain a large measure of such powers in relation to the
administration of long determinate sentences and the classification of
prisoners for security purposes. The objection to the exercise of discretionary
powers by the executive is that it is difficult to ensure that decisions taken in
the exercise of those powers are not influenced by considerations, such as the
views of Ministers or public opinion, which the critics regard as being, in
principle, extraneous to the task of impartially balancing the rights of potential victims against those of potential aggressors.

There is room for argument here—for example, about the account to be
taken of public alarm and the need to preserve the discretion of the Home
Secretary to release on licence within the period of the sentence imposed by
the court. Nevertheless, we went quite a long way with the critics in their
desire to trim the discretionary powers of the executive; though possibly not
far enough for the European court and certainly not far enough for Sir Leon
Radzinowicz and Dr Hood.

Their attitude to the discretionary powers of the judiciary is less clear.
They believe that those judges are right who told us, in reply to our Consultative Document, that the largely unfettered discretion that they now enjoy to
make and act upon predictive judgments is a strength of the existing arrangements. This can only be because they feel that the judges may be trusted not
to extend and misuse the practice; and indeed, as we point out, there is good
reason to have this confidence in their good sense and restraint. But, this
being so, it seems odd to complain of proposals to bring the availability and
administration of protective sentencing under statutory control in the
context of a modernised penal policy, that they will encourage the judges to
extend and abuse the practice. It is surely a paradoxical stance that is
prepared to rely on the judiciary not to abuse its powers in a situation that is
de facto to all intents and purposes open-ended, but unwilling to trust them
in a situation in which the availability of a sentence is restricted but they are

DANGEROUSNESS AND CRIMINAL JUSTICE

given appropriately wide discretionary powers, subject to reasonable guidelines, in its administration.

For our part, we noted that the history of preventive detention, the extended sentence and the discretionary life-sentence in the hands of the judiciary does little to encourage the fear that, with more comprehensive provision, the courts would seek to extend the practice of protective sentencing. Nor do we know of evidence of abuse in other western countries whose penal codes provide for very low maximum sentences for ordinary offenders, with permission to go beyond them in special cases. It seems to us that an authoritarian regime determined to extend and abuse the practice of protective sentencing will find ways of doing so, whether or not it is under statutory control. Either way, a compliant judiciary will be needed; but our proposals for statutory control provide more opportunities for resistance to extension and abuse by a compliant judiciary than exist under present arrangements.

A more telling argument, it seems to us, would show that the drastic reform in our sentencing structure which is undoubtedly needed, could be achieved without disturbing the present arrangements for protective sentencing.

Sir Leon Radzinowicz and Dr Hood evidently believe that it could and so, I believe, does Professor Bottoms, who has expressed disapproval of a polarised sentencing structure such as we advocate. If these distinguished penologists are right then, as our Report makes clear, we are not disposed to press the case for statutory control. At the end of their review of our Report, in which they give voice to their apprehensions, Sir Leon and Dr Hood ask: " If there is no need to travel this thorny road, why begin ?". I had thought that our answer was clear: if there is no need, either in the sense that the problem itself is held not to exist, or in the sense that it can continue to be dealt with satisfactorily under the cloak of English-style high maximum sentences, then *don't*. As I have already remarked, no-one denies the existence of the problem. The disagreement, then, is over the question whether the sentencing structure can be reformed without polarising it—whether it is politically feasible or, more fundamentally, whether it is indeed just to deny members of the public special protection against serious offenders who present a continuing risk of grave harm.

I had also thought that it was abundantly clear from our Report that we perfectly understood that " the infrequency of really serious crimes of violence, their apparently random quality and the rarity of anything like a ' dangerous type ' offers little encouragement for a policy which aims to reduce serious assaults by selective incapacitation of those with violent records ". This is a quotation from the valuable Home Office Report published last year, *Taking Offenders out of Circulation*, to which Sir Leon and Dr Hood refer in their review as providing " striking empirical evidence of the futility of [our] enterprise ". Of course, it does nothing of the kind; for we were not seeking, as were the Butler Committee with the reviewable sentence, or the Scottish Council on Crime with the public protection order, to improve the protection of the public. We are in agreement with Messrs.

JEAN FLOUD

Brody and Tarling, the authors of the Home Office Report, that the public is as well protected as it can expect to be. Indeed, as I have said, we would expect that our proposals, if implemented, would bring about a reduction in the number of long sentences of seven years or more given to serious offenders.

I take issue on this point with Sir Leon and Dr Hood only to prevent the spread of misunderstanding of our work from an authoritative source and not, I need hardly say, in order to deflect or dismiss criticism of our approach or the particulars of our proposals.

[13]

Selective Incapacitation:
Sentencing According to Risk

John Blackmore
Jane Welsh

In October 1982, the Rand Corporation published Selective Incapacitation, *a sentencing proposal based on seven years of research by a team of Rand researchers under the direction of Peter Greenwood. In his report, Greenwood claims to have developed a classification scheme that would enable criminal justice practitioners to determine which offenders should receive long, "incapacitating" prison sentences and which can be sentenced to alternative programs or safely released to the community. If implemented in its purest form, he says, selective incapacitation could result both in a net reduction of crime in the community and in the number of offenders who would need to be incarcerated.*

Since the release of the Rand report, most criminologists agree that Greenwood's findings are incomplete, methodologically flawed, and do not justify his policy proposal. Some have also raised moral and legal objections to it.

In this article we outline the history, criticism and impact of selective incapacitation. We find that there are no clear and forceful answers to the dilemmas posed by the Greenwood saga. However, the pressure on the research community to come up with quick and easy answers to complex social problems, we suggest, is less than subtle, particularly when money, reputation and the ability to do research hang in the balance.

INTRODUCTION

In March 1982, a group of leading criminologists, corrections officials, and policy makers gathered in Sacramento, California to hear Peter Greenwood of the Rand Corporation present a remarkable new sentencing strategy, called selective incapacitation, to deal with career criminals. After seven years of study, Greenwood and his colleagues had developed a classification scheme that, he claimed, could reliably identify the most dangerous and persistent criminals among the offender class. Once identified, long, "incapacitating" prison sentences could be imposed on the "high-risk" offenders. Shorter jail terms and community-based sanctions could be applied, with some assurance of community safety, to those determined to pose less of a threat. If, he said, prison sentences for all high-risk offenders currently incarcerated in California were

JOHN BLACKMORE: Formerly contributing editor of *Corrections Magazine,* is Director of Court Operations, Victim Services Agency, New York City. **JANE WELSH:** Law student and executive editor of the *Brooklyn Law Review,* will join the law firm of Mudge Rose Guthrie Alexander & Ferdon following her graduation next year.

doubled in length, and the time behind bars for the "lightweights" (the low-risk offenders) were cut in half, "the state's crime rate would drop by 15 percent and the prison population by five percent."

Sweeping proposals to reduce crime and decrease prison populations are nothing new to the field. Many strategies have come upon the scene and reigned briefly as "the answer" to criminal justice problems. One after the other has proven ineffective in halting the spirals of crime and imprisonment. Each tends to enjoy but a short lifespan.

Those who came to Sacramento to hear Greenwood were veterans of the stormy debates of the past decade on the merits of deterrence, rehabilitation, the justice model, and alternatives to incarceration. They were skeptical of sweeping solutions. What Greenwood was proposing was something quite different, however. Selective incapacitation, he pointed out, is not an abstract theory or sentencing philosophy, but rather an administrative policy. It is pragmatic, cost effective, easily implemented, and likely to gain broad public support, he said. And, unlike earlier proposals, it faced squarely the dual dilemma of corrections policy makers: how to come to terms with prison crowding without sacrificing crime control.

After hearing Greenwood, some of the forum's participants, including a few skeptics, were clearly encouraged. "It's not the silver bullet that's going to get rid of crime, but it is a proposal that may help us do better at it," said Alfred Blumstein of Carnegie-Mellon University. Others could hardly contain their enthusiasm. "This proposal provides a unifying, driving theory for the whole criminal justice system," said Douglas Cunningham, director of California's Office of Criminal Justice Planning. "It will permit us to target resources for the entire system." Still others, after questioning Greenwood closely about the particulars of his theory and method, asked how such a scheme could be seriously considered. Sheldon Messinger, director of the University of California's Center for the Study of Law and Society, urged the other participants to consider the legal and moral ramifications of levying punishments according to indicators he called proxies for race and social class. "But gentlemen," he exclaimed, "we live in a society of laws!"

Since introduced, Greenwood's selective incapacitation scheme has been a major topic of discussion at every forum where crime control and prison crowding has been addressed. Dozens of scholarly papers on the topic are in print or in press. Friends and foes of the proposal routinely appear before crime commissions, state legislatures, and professional conferences to voice their opinions. Talk show hosts, news reporters, and editorialists have brought the public into the debate. For all the clamor, the issue is far from settled. And while the debate continues, the police, judges, and corrections officials already may be using Greenwood's findings to guide their decisions.

At issue is not so much the idea of selective incapacitation. There are few who oppose the premise that prisons must be used more selectively and efficiently. What is disputed is whether the Rand findings are sound, whether

Greenwood's method can actually accomplish its aims, and whether selective incapacitation can be fairly and lawfully implemented.

THE THEORY OF INCAPACITATION

> The ideas that shape public policy fit the temper of their times. Otherwise, they lack the currency necessary to legitimate and guide governmental action. The idea that crime could be more effectively attacked by incapacitating dangerous offenders has this quality.
>
> Mark Moore, Susan Estrich, Daniel McGillis and William Spelman in *Dealing With Dangerous Offenders*

Deterrence theory, rehabilitative sentencing, the just deserts model, and the other competing rationales for imprisonment are abstractions in the public eye, when the public is aware of them at all. As such, one or the other is unlikely to become the guiding rationale for corrections policy. By comparison, the notion that prisons incapacitate criminals, that is, prevent them from committing crime, is simplicity itself. When the criminal is in prison, he is not free to prey on law-abiding citizens, the conventional wisdom holds. The more criminals imprisoned, the less crime in the community. When politicians invoke the public's demand to get tough on crime, their most common solution boils down to removing criminals from the streets and incapacitating them (by imprisonment or death) from causing further harm to the community.

Criminologists and criminal justice policy makers, faced with a decade of discouraging findings on rehabilitation and deterrence, increasingly subscribe to the public's view. The ever-mounting fear of crime, whether rational or not, "gives impetus to collective action and, therefore, currency to proposals that plausibly address the problem," noted Moore and his colleagues. Some criminologists, notably Harvard's James Q. Wilson, have repeatedly called upon policy makers to launch massive prison building programs to create space to incapacitate more offenders for longer periods of time. Wilson's proposal amounts to unselective, or general incapacitation. Such a strategy might indeed prove effective in reducing crime; however, as a number of researchers have found, it would be prohibitively expensive to implement.

In 1975, Reuel and Shlomo Shinnar analyzed the costs and benefits of general incapacitation. Using a statistical model they had developed, they projected that the imposition of flat, five-year prison terms on all persons convicted of violent offenses would result in an 80 percent reduction in violent crime in the community. Other researchers who have looked into the strategy have predicted a somewhat lower, but nonetheless substantial, reduction in crime. However, in order to gain a reasonable reduction in crime through general incapacitation, prison populations would have to be increased to three to five times their current levels.

Selective Incapacitation   **507**

In 1978, Peter Greenwood and Joan Petersilia projected that the imposition of mandatory, five-year prison terms on all convicted felons in Denver would reduce violent crime in that city by nearly a third, but would result in a 450 percent increase in current prison populations. Stephan Van Dine, John Conrad, and Simon Dinitz, using Franklin County, Ohio as their test case, reported somewhat smaller crime-averting effects when they conducted a similar study. In *Restraining the Wicked,* they projected only a 17.8 percent reduction in violent crime. However, to obtain this relatively small reduction, the current prison population would have to be increased by 523 percent. As Michael Sherman and Gordon Hawkins noted in their 1981 Hudson Institute report, *Imprisonment in America,* general incapacitation strategies would result in "undramatic incapacitation benefits with unthinkable prison population costs."

Other authorities argue that we are already paying the cost of general incapacitation practices without any discernible effect on crime rates. Largely due to "get-tough-on-crime" attitudes among judges and legislators, the population of state and federal prisons has grown by 130 percent over the past ten years. However, there has been no concomitant reduction in national crime rates. In her study of incapacitation effects of current sentencing practices, Jacqueline Cohen of Carnegie-Mellon University concluded: "Crime reduction [due to these practices] is modest, at under 20 percent of crimes prevented."

The critical turn in incapacitation theory came when Greenwood and his colleagues at Rand began to refine this strategy by targeting incapacitative sentences to the few offenders who commit the greatest amount of crime. "In order to get the payoff of incapacitation [reduced crime] without breaking the bank, you have to impose long, incapacitative sentences on those who are likely to commit the greatest amount of serious crime," Greenwood argues. "We knew that the intensives [the high-rate offenders] were out there. We knew that [high-rate offending] was correlated with juvenile records and drug use, but we had no idea how strong these correlations were. . . . Once we saw how well the predictor variables distinguished among offenders, selective incapacitation was something that just leaped out at us."

The Discovery of Lambda

"In order to determine who will commit the greatest amount of crime, you need an accurate prediction model," noted Greenwood. It was to this task that Greenwood and his colleagues at Rand turned in 1978. Key to their efforts was the formula developed by the Shinnars in 1975. Their contribution was the invention of the variable "lambda," the number of crimes an individual commits in a year. Equipped with reasonable estimates of how much crime an individual commits and how long the individual's rate of offending persists, it becomes possible to estimate how much crime can be averted by incapacitating an individual for various lengths of time.

J. Blackmore, J. Welsh

Blumstein and Cohen of Carnegie-Mellon also contributed to Greenwood's cipher. In 1979, they developed a theoretical model of an individual's criminal career. The model they developed to describe the potential crime averting effects of various sentencing schemes provides a way to assess the effects of imprisonment.

Proponents of rehabilitation and specific deterrence, as well as those who say prison serves mainly to "criminalize" the inmate, believe that the prison experience affects an individual's criminal behavior following release from prison. If an individual's crime rate or criminal career length decreases after release from prison, this result could be attributed to either the rehabilitative or deterrent effects of imprisonment. If, on the other hand, an individual's crime rate or career length increases following release from prison, this result would lend support to those who believe that life in prison has a "criminalizing effect." In his *Research Perspectives on Selective Incapacitation as a Means of Crime Control*, Blumstein argues that "these two effects probably occur, but are roughly equal and so balance each other out."

If, as Blumstein suggests, incapacitation is the primary salutary effect of imprisonment, then the amount of crime averted would equal the product of the individual's crime rate (lambda) and the amount of time the individual is incarcerated. Incapacitation theorists generally hold that the prison experience has no lasting influence on an individual's criminal activities following release. Therefore, they assume that post-incarceration crime rates and career lengths are unaffected by imprisonment. Blumstein and other proponents of the "demographic effect" believe that once a criminal begins a life in crime, a major determinant of criminal career lengths and individual crime rates is the age of the individual. Most repeat offenders, they say, tend to reduce their criminal activities, and many "drop-out" of criminal careers, in their late twenties and thirties.

The Shinnars' model, and its elaboration by Blumstein and Cohen, is a theoretical one. Before it can be used with any assurance to estimate the incapacitative effects of imprisonment, one must be able to:

- accurately and reliably measure individual crime rates and criminal career lengths;
- show that individual crime rates are fairly constant over time;
- show that "replacement effects," the opportunities and incentives to commit crime encouraging other individuals to take the place of those incapacitated, are minimal; and
- discount or minimize the amount of crime that takes place in prison.

Ultimately, the selective incapacitation model rises or falls according to the validity of these assumptions. In recent years, criminologists are increasingly confident that individual crime rates and career lengths can be estimated with reasonable accuracy. However, no one has yet amassed the individual crime rates of a discrete group of offenders and shown their strict relationship to overall reported crime rates in any particular locality. The critical causal links implied by selective incapacitation theory have yet to be established. Furthermore, estimates of incapacitative effects vary widely according to which jurisdiction is studied and who is making the estimates.

Until recently, "researchers attempting to measure the incapacitative effects [of various sentencing strategies] were using estimates of average individual offense rates that ranged from one index crime per year to ten per year," Greenwood reported in *Selective Incapacitation*. With the firmer basis for estimating lambda provided by Blumstein and Cohen in 1979 and by Jan Chaiken of Rand in 1980, Greenwood believes that his own estimates are the most reliable to date.

In their study, Blumstein and Cohen calculated individual offense rates from official arrest records. Chaiken derived his by asking California inmates about their criminal activities prior to imprisonment. Despite different methods, they arrived at the same conclusion: the median number of offenses committed by individual offenders in a given year is quite low. The convicted robbers in Chaiken's sample committed an average of 1.5 per year. However, a few offenders had extraordinarily high lambdas. Some robbers reported committing more than 200 robberies per year. In statistical terms, they found the distribution of individual offense rates to be positively skewed.

In Rand's second inmate survey, the work on which Greenwood's proposal is based, Jan and Marcia Chaiken found that the shape of the distribution, this dramatic "skewness," was remarkably similar for all crime categories studied. "This means that the average offense rate for any group [of offenders] . . . is dominated by the activities of a very few," explains Greenwood. "Incarcerating one robber who is above the 90th percentile for one year [those who, according to the Rand survey, commit more than 57 robberies per year] would prevent more robberies than incarcerating 18 offenders who are below the median [those who commit less than five robberies per year] for the same period of time. The difficulty lies in identifying those with high rates."

The Chaikens' findings paved the way for Greenwood's proposal to target longer, incapacitating sentences for the most active offenders. Any change in current sentencing practices that increases the proportion of high-rate offenders in prison would bring about a significant reduction in crime. Furthermore, so long as the proportion of low-rate offenders behind bars was reduced to the same degree, crime reduction could be obtained without increasing prison populations. All that remained was to develop a method to reliably distinguish between high-lambda and low lambda offenders, and sentence them according to their risk to society.

The Predictive Instrument

In order to develop his classification scheme, Greenwood conducted his own analysis of Rand's second inmate survey. In that survey, 2190 male prison and jail inmates in Texas, California, and Michigan were asked about their personal and criminal activities. The Rand researchers recorded the age, race, employment history, education, drug use, prior arrests, convictions, and adult and juvenile commitments for each inmate. From these data, Greenwood selected 13 "candidate predictive factors," characteristics that had "possible legal relevance and appropriateness for the court's consideration [at sentencing and relevance on the basis of prior research or theory."

Greenwood then categorized the inmates according to their level of criminal activity during the two years prior to their current commitment. He limited his analysis to 781 inmates who were serving time for either robbery or burglary. Those who reported having committed robberies below the median rate during their last two years of freedom were classified as "low-rate" offenders; those who reported robbery rates between the 50th and 75th percentile were classified as "medium-rate" offenders; and those who ranked above the 75th percentile were classified as "high-rate" offenders. In the California sample, high-rate offenders reported committing an average of 30.8 robberies per year during their last two years at large; while those classified as low-rate offenders reported committing an average of less than two robberies per year in the same period. In Michigan and Texas, the mean robbery and burglary rates for the three categories were quite different from those reported in California. "Texas offenders were in every way less active—as juveniles, in drug use, in their possession of weapons, etc.," Greenwood noted in his report. "Whether this low rate of criminal activity is the result of generally harsher sentencing practices [in Texas] ... or the result of some other social forces, we cannot say at this time."

Greenwood then "cross-tabulated" the candidate predictor variables with the three offense-rate groups, and chose as his predictor variables those characteristics that were significantly correlated with high rates of offending. He assembled these characteristics into a seven-point, additive scale. If an offender was found to have four or more of these characteristics, he was classified as a high-rate offender deserving increased time behind bars. If the offender was found to have less than two of the characteristics, he was classified as a low-rate offender whose sentence length could be kept to a minimum.

The characteristics Greenwood found to be significantly correlated with high-rate offending were that the offender:

• had one or more prior convictions for the same crime as the current conviction;
• had been incarcerated more than 50 percent of the preceding two years;
• had been convicted one or more times prior to his 16th birthday;
• had served time at a state juvenile institution;
• had frequently used heroin or barbiturates during the preceding two years at large;
• had frequently used heroin or barbiturates as a juvenile; and
• was unemployed more than 50 percent of the preceding two years at large, excluding time spent in institutions.

Selective Incapacitation   **511**

COMMENTARY AND CRITIQUE

> [As] with any program touching on the rights of criminal defendants,
> the efforts must be consistent with ethical considerations and
> constitutional rights. . . . The proposal of selective incapacitation raises
> other concerns. Does the concept have undertones of racial and economic
> class distinctions; in punishment for possible future offenses; and
> punishment for status, such as drug addiction, unemployment, inadequate
> education, abuse as a child? Is there perhaps a greater potential for
> capricious sentencing by encouraging a disparity in sentencing? Will there
> be a perception of unfairness among prisoners themselves? Is there a class
> bias inherent in the criteria set forth for selecting those to be incapacitated?
> Is there a danger of excessive 'efficiency' in seeking the solution? . . . Is there
> a justification of the means by the end?
>
> > Lawrence Cooke, Chief Judge of the New York State Court of
> > Appeals, in Stephen Gillers's *Selective Incapacitation: Does It
> > Offer More or Less?*

Since the release of the Rand report, nearly every element of Greenwood's
method, findings, and proposal has been subjected to close scrutiny. Much of
the criticism has been negative. Criminologists and policy analysts agree that
Greenwood's findings, because they are incomplete and methodologically
flawed, do not justify his conclusions. It is therefore premature, they say, to
develop policy proposals on the basis of the findings. Others have raised moral
and legal objections to the entire idea of sentencing according to the socioeconomic characteristics associated with chronic criminal behavior.

Two of Greenwood's severest critics are Jan and Marcia Chaiken, his
colleagues at Rand who were responsible for much of the work on the second
inmate survey on which Greenwood's proposal is based. "Greenwood's work
adds nothing to the field," says Jan Chaiken. "It is a few hastily arranged facts
surrounded by intense verbiage. We think it is outrageous what he did with the
self-report data."

The Chaikens saw their work not as a basis for a policy proposal, but as a
contribution to the typology of offenders. Whether offenders specialize in
particular types of crime and whether criminal behavior is sufficiently stable to
permit reliable classification have been matters of long-standing dispute in
criminology. In their analysis of the self-report data, the Chaikens concluded
that there is indeed a hierarchy of criminal offenders and that offenders tended
to advance through the criminal "ranks" during their careers. Newly-initiated
juvenile offenders tended to start out committing low-level property offenses,
such as theft, credit card fraud, vandalism, and low-level drug dealing. Those
who continued to commit crimes tended to become more violent with age.
Furthermore, those who committed the most serious offenses had more
symptoms of social deviance than those who ended their criminal activities
early. According to the survey data, high-rate robbers tended to be unmarried,
chronically unemployed, heavy drug users, and to have a significantly higher

number of prior arrests and convictions for robbery than low-rate robbers. The Chaikens concluded that there is a degree of specialization among criminals, that the specialty tends to change with age, and that those who progress through the ranks to become robber-assaulters or "violent predators" (the most serious criminal types) tend to be the most deviant in other respects.

This information, said Marcia Chaiken, "may be a useful guide to practitioners and policy makers . . . in the discretionary areas—to confirm or negate assumptions they may hold and help them devise policy." However, what such policies should be "is not for us to decide. Our effort was to inform the research community and to encourage people to gather more useful information, *not* to have people implement a program now. . . . [Greenwood's proposal] is not realistic; it is not a justifiable use of the data."

In their summary report, the Chaikens addressed the policy implications of their research. Noting that 30 percent of those identified as high-rate robbers by their classification instrument "committed no robberies during the measurement period," they concluded:

> This margin of error allows for considerable false identification of some offenders as high-rate robbers—which is more than just a research problem if the criminal justice system acts on such identifications. Even if the models were foolproof, the legal and ethical ramifications of their use by the criminal justice system would be a matter of dispute. Sentencing offenders for past crimes that have never been adjudicated runs counter to the principle of just deserts, while sentencing them for predicted future crimes runs counter to the tenets of free will and justice. Therefore, we suggest that our findings should not be used simplistically as criteria for passing judgment on specific individuals.

In the year since the release of his report, Greenwood has become more measured in his policy proclamations. "The numbers hold up; the analysis is sound," he maintains. "But exactly what is to be made of our work is up to others, not me. All we meant to do is to pick up on a number of themes that had been floating around the field and put them together for discussion."

Nonetheless, researchers and policy makers have responded to the work as it was originally presented. The themes that they address are relevant not just to Greenwood's work, but to the shaping of policy through the use of statistical criminological data in a criminal justice system that operates to affect individual offenders.

The Offender Characteristics

Greenwood acknowledges that some of his predictor variables, particularly employment, drug use, and juvenile records, "are likely to be controversial" as a basis for sentencing. Sheldon Messinger has stronger words for the scale. "It treats people like animals," he says. "As if they can't change sometime in the future. I have a strong moral objection to this model of man. How much control does a person have over his employment status? And as for drug use as

Selective Incapacitation   **513**

a juvenile, that's nothing more than a proxy for race and social class. You might as well lock people up for being black."

David Lovell, the philosopher-in-residence at the Connecticut Department of Correction, also voices moral objections to the use of Greenwood's predictor variables. "The assumption here is that the only thing we can do with criminals [having these characteristics] is incapacitate them," he said at a recent forum on selective incapacitation at New York University Law School. "This falls to a *reductio ad absurdum.* That in order to be effective, you have to be selective; when in order to be selective, you have to be unjust."

In her monograph, *Incapacitation as a Strategy for Crime Control: Possibilities and Pitfalls,* Jacqueline Cohen notes that "status variables," such as age, sex, race, employment, and education, were "explicitly considered as potential criteria for sentencing by the Minnesota and Pennsylvania sentencing guidelines commissions." However, "the problems associated with these variables have led to their rejection as valid considerations in sentencing decisions. [The problem of individuals] having limited opportunities to affect their status outcomes ... contravenes the principle that punishment be based on the blameworthiness of the offender."

"As you go down the list [of Greenwood's predictor variables] you might get squeamish about using them for sentencing," says Alfred Blumstein. "And you might be tempted to cut out some of them because you consider them to be unfair or beyond a person's control. However, then you are in a Catch 22 bind. The nature of such a model is such that if you decide some of the predictor variables are unusable, you reduce the predictive power of the model. Many people would want to restrict the list to the current offense and prior adult convictions. But if you do that, you would be doing little more than what the system does now."

Sentencing For Future Crimes

A more fundamental criticism of Greenwood's scheme concerns the legitimacy of sentencing offenders according to a prediction of what they will do in the future. Even if Greenwood's scale possessed absolute predictive validity, that is, if his predictions were accurate in every case, its use would violate the venerable principles of law that punishment be commensurate to the crime and that all citizens, despite their station, should have equal standing before the law. "Some would argue that justice requires that punishment be based [only] on convicted crime," writes Cohen, "and that punishment for 'predicted' crimes would be unjust. [Greenwood's proposal] would result in the imposition of very different sentences on individuals convicted of the same current offense."

A number of observers have noted the resemblance between selective incapacitation and pre-trial preventive detention. Some support it for that very reason. "The public deserves to be protected," says Douglas Cunningham. "We have to account to them that they are getting the largest benefit. If selective incapacitation is a kind of post-conviction preventive detention, so be it. That's what the public wants." Those who subscribe to the just desert model strongly object to utilitarians who, like Cunningham, argue that the public must be protected even at the cost of some injustice.

Greenwood declines to take an absolutist position on the priority of public protection. "Desert is a constraint within which the system has to live," he says. "That's why, in my model, desert sets the acceptable boundaries for punishment for an individual offense. Within that range, those found to be high-rate offenders would be sentenced at the top of the range, and those determined to be low-rate offenders would get a break."

However, as Greenwood readily admits, his scale does not possess absolute predictive validity. "Any policy implementing the concept of selective incapacitation will inevitably result in some offenders being incorrectly classified," he wrote in a rebuttal to his critics. "In other words, some offenders who are incorrectly identified as high-rate will be incarcerated for longer periods of time than they deserve. It should be remembered that the model defined in this report should properly be tested not against completely accurate predictions, which we can never have, but against the current system [as it operates]."

In his report, Greenwood compared the predictive accuracy of his scale with how well the current sentence lengths being served by the inmates in his sample fit their self-reported crime rates. He found his scale to be superior to current practices. He reported that his scale correctly identified 51 percent of the high rate offenders, with a seven percent error factor, while the current sentence lengths correctly identified only 42 percent of them, with a 12 percent error factor.

Jacqueline Cohen reanalyzed Greenwood's data and found his figures in error. She determined that only 45 percent of high-rate offenders were correctly identified using Greenwood's scale, with a ten percent error factor. She concluded that the seven-point scale "does only marginally better overall" in identifying high-rate offenders than current practices and that misidentifications using the two methods were quite comparable (Figure 1).

The Applicability of Greenwood's Findings

Greenwood has proposed that his scale be applied not only at the sentencing decision, but as a guide to decisions about defendants and offenders throughout the criminal justice process, including decisions to arrest, set bail, prosecute, place on probation and parole. However, Greenwood's scale is based exclusively on a survey of currently incarcerated robbers and burglars at selected jails and prisons in three states, a small subcategory of the general criminal population. Andrew von Hirsch and Don Gottfredson of Rutgers University question whether the Rand sample was representative of the inmate population in the three states. "Caution is in order [when] generalizing to inmate populations other than those from the sites of data collection and

Figure 1. The Relative Predictive Accuracy of the Greenwood Scale: A Comparison with Current Sentencing Decisions on Sentence Lengths

Accuracy in Distinguishing Offenders by Their Crime Rates	Greenwood's Seven-Factor Scale		Current Sentence Lengths
	According to Cohen	According to Greenwood	
Predicted correctly	45%	51%	42%
Predicted to be High–Rate, actually Low–Rate (False–positives)	8%	4%	7%
Predicted to be Low–Rate, actually High–Rate (False–negatives)	2%	3%	5%

certainly to other jurisdictions," they wrote in *Selective Incapacitation: Some Queries on Research Design and Ethics.*

The question of the representativeness of Greenwood's findings extends further. At sentencing, judges see many more offenders than they will send to prison. If Greenwood's scale is to be applied to all offenders at sentencing, its applicability should be verified as well for those offenders who are not likely to receive prison sentences. If the scale is also to be a guide for arrest, bail, probation and parole decisions, then the relevant characteristics must be determined for all offenders, including those who have been arrested, but not convicted and those still at large. The currently incarcerated may have idiosyncrasies in their personal histories and criminal records that are not general to the common run of criminals. Until a larger, more general population of offenders is sampled, we will not know whether there are distinguishing characteristics among those who are and are not arrested, prosecuted, convicted, placed on probation or committed. In Greenwood's limited sample, which only included inmates, the variability of characteristics and rates of offending was sufficiently large to cast serious doubt on the applicability of his scale to the currently incarcerated, much less to the population at large.

Can the Self-Reports Be Believed?

Some observers have also questioned the veracity of the inmate self-reports. In the second inmate survey, the Chaikens compared the self-reports of arrests and convictions of the California inmates with their official records, and found close agreement between them. "But the respondents could be expected to be aware that the researchers had access to that information," note von Hirsch and Gottfredson. The problem, they say, is that the "self-reported crimes that had not led to official action exceeded by many times the crimes for which they were previously arrested and convicted, and there is not independent corroboration for those crimes."

> The research concentrates on the behavior of those who report themselves to be a troublesome minority; it is the high-risk offenders that the instrument is meant to identify. There seems to be a touching assumption here that these individuals (like the homicidal Irish maiden in Tom Lehrer's famous song) are happy to wreck the worst mayhem, but know that lying is a sin.

Greenwood acknowledges that the truthfulness of respondents is a valid issue, but believes that the official record check conducted by the Chaikens is sufficient to put it to rest. "Some of them overrepresent, some of them underrepresent [the amount of crime they committed]," he says. "But when we checked the records, we did not find any bias. The two tend to balance each other out."

Even if the inmates were absolutely truthful in their responses, they are less likely to be so if they know their responses will affect their interests. "Greenwood, particularly, is proposing to use those answers to develop a sentencing policy that involves much longer terms of imprisonment for supposed high-rate offenders," report von Hirsch and Gottfredson. "Once this fact is known . . . , the answers might change dramatically."

False Positives, False Negatives

The errors associated with prediction models are of two types: false negatives and false positives. In the context of recidivism, a false negative error is a failure to identify an offender who subsequently recidivates. A false positive error is an error of overprediction, that is, individuals are mistakenly predicted to recidivate, when indeed they do not.

For the past 50 years, high false positive rates have consistently bedevilled every effort to predict recidivism. False positive rates of 50 to 60 percent have been the rule. "It was these findings about the limitations of predictive instruments . . . [that] helped diminish the enthusiasm for predictive sentencing," note von Hirsch and Gottfredson.

Against these gloomy findings, Greenwood's report of a four percent false positive rate and a three percent false negative rate is very encouraging. For the utilitarians, the prospect of unfairly depriving the liberty of merely four percent of convicted offenders (who are, after all, guilty as charged) is an acceptable social cost in return for crime reduction benefits.

However, as a number of observers point out, Greenwood reported only offenders who were predicted to be high-rate when they were indeed low-rate, the most extreme category of false positives. He failed to report those predicted to be high-rate who were actually medium-rate. Since they, too, would receive longer, incapacitative sentences due to misclassification, they are false positives as well. According to Jacqueline Cohen's reanalysis of Greenwood's

Figure 2. Distribution of Offenders by Predicted and Actual Offense Categories

Predicted Offense Rate[‡]	*Self—Reported Offense Rate*			
	Low	Medium	High	Total
Low	20%	5%	2% [†]	27%
Medium	22%	12%	9%	43%
High	8% [*]	9%	13%	30%
Total	50%	26%	24%	100%

□Percent of offense rates accurately predicted by the scale. Total=45 percent. (Total percentage inaccurately predicted: 55 percent)

*Predicted high rate when actually a low-rate offender (false positive prediction). Total=8 percent.

†Predicted low rate when actually a high-rate offender (false negative prediction). Total=2 percent.

‡ Accuracy of Predictions When Examined by Lambda Groupings
  Total false positives among those predicted to be high—rate: 56.6%
  Total false positives among those predicted to be low—rate: 25.9%
  Total false negatives among those predicted to be high—rate: 26.6%
  Total false negatives among those predicted to be low—rate: 7.4%

Source: Derived from Jacqueline Cohen's *Incapcitation as a Strategy for Crime Control: Possibilities and Pitfalls*

data, this would raise the false positive rate to 17 percent (Figure 2). Both Cohen and von Hirsch and Gottfredson went one step further. They presented Greenwood's data in a format consistent with that used in earlier reports, examining just the group classified as high-rate offenders instead of all the predictions simultaneously, and found a false positive rate exceeding 55 percent (Figure 3). "Greenwood's technique ... shows little improvement over forecasting methods of the past," conclude von Hirsch and Gottfredson.

Predicting the Past

There is, indeed, a question whether Greenwood's method is a forecasting technique at all. Despite his frequent use of "predictor variables," "predictive index" and "predictive accuracy" in his report, Greenwood's scale is based entirely on retrospective data, that is, the past activities of offenders. Begging a lack of resources, he reported that a true predictive study, involving verified predictions of future criminal behavior, "was not feasible."

What he did instead was "postdict" the past criminal behavior of the inmates sampled by relating characteristics from the inmates' histories to their offense rates for their most recent two years at freedom. Six of Greenwood's seven predictor variables (juvenile and adult convictions, commitments, and drug use) are rather direct indicators of criminal involvement. They are not, as such, independent of the thing measured—recent criminal behavior. The only non-criminal indicator in Greenwood's scale is the individual's employment record. With that exception, his predictor variables are largely measures of persistence, rather than symptoms.

Not only are Greenwood's data retrospective, they are based on one set of measures (a single questionnaire) administered once to the subjects. At a minimum, confirmation of a prediction requires two independent assessments separated over time. Short of making a prediction at one point, and confirming it at another, the accuracy of a prediction cannot be ascertained. "The Greenwood study is not, in this sense, a prediction study at all," von Hirsch and Gottfredson report.

Furthermore, Greenwood made no attempt to confirm his findings using a new sample of offenders. Whatever other methodological flaws are apparent in his research, they pale in comparison to his failure to replicate the study and confirm his predictive index before using it as a basis for policy proposals. Greenwood again cites a lack of resources for his failure to conduct validation tests. Until the criminal behavior of an independent group of individuals is accurately forecast, there can be little value to his predictive instrument.

Once stripped of its predictive veneer, Greenwood's findings boil down to this: inmates who reported offending at high rates in the past (sufficiently high to have posted both juvenile and adult conviction and commitment records) also reported that they continued to offend at high rates in the two years of freedom prior to their current prison commitment. Those with long and strong criminal records also reported using hard drugs both as juveniles and as adults and experiencing difficulties holding down a job. The causal link between exhibiting these characteristics and recidivism has not been proven. It cannot be said that those who do possess them will indeed recidivate. Policy proposals based on such uncertain and incomplete findings are precipitous, if not irresponsible.

Selective Incapacitation Throughout the Criminal Justice System

Selective incapacitation was formulated specifically as a sentencing policy. Nearly all of the debate about the soundness of Greenwood's findings and the fairness and effectiveness of his policy proposal concerns its use in sentencing. Greenwood sees the relevance of the concept to be much broader. In this, he is not alone.

In his *Selective Incapacitation: A Means to Improve the Fairness of Existing Sentencing Practices*, Kenneth Feinberg, a Washington, D.C. attorney and former Special Counsel to the U.S. Senate Committee on the Judiciary and Administrative Assistant to Senator Edward M. Kennedy, notes the "financial advantages to a carefully crafted policy of selective incapacitation" throughout the criminal justice system. "The criminal justice system can no longer afford the luxury of scattering financial and technical resources in the direction of all suspected offenders," he writes. "There are not enough police to apprehend, not enough prosecutors to prosecute, not enough judges to try cases, and not enough prisons to house all those convicted. . . . In the long run, selective incapacitation can be a catalyst for the beneficial reallocation of resources." Since police and prosecutors are now concentrating their time and effort on those offenders they consider most dangerous, Feinberg argues, why not offer them Greenwood's "salient predictors," however imperfect, as the more reliable guide? Bail and parole decisions, now based on "flawed predictions," could likewise be informed. If selective incapacitation were implemented at every stage of the criminal justice process, the net effect would "reduc[e] current injustice in the criminal justice system."

Greenwood also proposes the use of predictor variables throughout the criminal justice process in his report. Using them, the police "could develop priorities concerning which cases they will investigate most thoroughly;" prosecutors "would have a more systematic means of identifying those who should be the target of [career criminal prosecution] programs;" and parole boards "could incorporate selective incapacitation concepts into their decisions."

Greenwood's and Feinberg's suggestion amounts to instituting a perverse version of triage in the criminal justice system. In the name of providing safety for the greatest number, Greenwood's scheme would allocate the scarce resources of the criminal justice system to the worst cases and curtail those for the merely slightly dangerous.

"Of course, such prioritizing may promote short-term political flak," noted Feinberg, "particularly among citizens who look to the police for the resolution of all disputes, however minor. But general maintenance of community order must be balanced against the need to investigate, apprehend, prosecute, and imprison the high-risk offender. In the long run, selective incapacitation can be a catalyst for the beneficial reallocation of resources." Therefore, the implementation of selective incapacitation should proceed, "but with caution. In the meantime, however, the perfect must not be allowed to become the enemy of the good."

By proposing that selective incapacitation policies should be extended beyond the realm of sentencing, Greenwood negates his earlier argument that the offender's score on the predictive index would operate as but one factor to be considered when establishing within the bounds of just desert the length of an offender's sentence. Yet, if investigation, arrest, bail, prosecution, probation, prison, and parole decisions are all based on selective incapacitation principles as well, classification as a high-rate offender would abolish the principle of desert. Treatment would be based on status, rather than related to the commission of a particular crime.

An individual classified as a high-risk offender would first be selected out of a pool of potential suspects for the full weight of the investigative resources of the police. Then, as the case proceeds, he would be the first selected out for arrest, for denial of bail and pre-trial release, for denial of plea bargaining, for prison commitment, for denial of early release and parole, for maximum security, and for denial of clemency. Once back in the free world as an ex-offender, he would be the first suspected of new crimes. The act of classifying an individual as a high-risk offender would not only stigmatize the individual at every level of the criminal justice process, but also that stigma would build with relentless momentum as he progresses through the system.

Nor does Greenwood's original scheme leave any room for the possible reformation of the individual. Once a person meets the criteria, he is tainted for life. He would have no escape. "The self report data [from the second inmate survey] has not been analyzed to the extent it should be to determine whether the criminal behavior patterns hold for any more than a short period of time," said Jan Chaiken. "We have, for instance, no explanation for those high-rate offenders who suddenly drop out of their criminal careers. We are aware that happens, but we have no idea under what circumstances." This explanation becomes critical if Greenwood's criteria are used to make long term decisions about individuals.

In response to his critics, Greenwood proposed modifying his predictive model to account for changes in criminal behavior. "It would be a simple matter to adjust the model so that a person's high-rate classification would be modified if that person posted a clean criminal record over a period of time," he said. "The high-rate classification only [would be again] invoked when the offender is again convicted for a serious crime."

Applications

In his report, Greenwood presents a step-by-step process for policy makers to implement selective incapacitation policies. It involves:

1. replicating the Rand study in the relevant jurisdiction in order to construct a distribution of individual offense rates and a set of predictor variables particular to the jurisdiction;
2. conducting an analysis of current sentencing practices in that jurisdiction in order to provide a basis for comparing current and alternative sentencing practices;
3. using the jurisdiction's current crime rates and prison and jail populations to project future crime rates and cell capacities;
4. establishing the minimum ranges of a determinate sentencing scheme, according to the tenets of just desert, deterrence, and prevailing notions of justice;
5. using the minimum sentences established and the crime rate projections to estimate the number of offenders who would be incarcerated during the next few years;
6. calculating the difference between the prison population generated by the minimum terms and the predicted prison and jail capacity; and
7. devising a selective incapacitation strategy for the use of the excess capacity created.

Selective Incapacitation   **521**

If indeed excess capacity were created by this method, the policy makers in the jurisdiction could use it in various ways. If the greatest priority were to reduce muggings, the excess capacity could be used to enhance the minimum sentences (and thereby reduce the "street time") of high-rate robbers. The predictive index could then be used to select those eligible for sentences above the minimum. If a stable or reduced prison population were the goal, the policy makers could adjust the minimum sentences downward to increase excess capacity. Using the formula devised by the Shinnars and Blumstein and Cohen, policy makers could determine in advance the impact of various sentencing decisions on the street time of various categories of offenders, on prison populations and on prevailing crime rates.

Since his report was released, Greenwood has become equivocal about his policy proposal. "I still see no problem of implementing selective incapacitation concepts in criminal justice decision making," he said earlier this year, "so long as it does not automatically invoke decisions. The [predictive] criteria should encourage closer scrutiny of an individual offender; they should not be used as part of a sentencing machine. We need much more research before we could think of doing that."

One of Greenwood's fears is that selective incapacitation will be seized upon by "the barbarians," those who would accept his work uncritically. In both his writings and his public presentations, Greenwood repeatedly warns that his predictive index should not be adopted without first independently verifying individual crime rate distributions and predictor variables specific to the jurisdiction in which they would be used. He also fears that some would use his index solely as a justification for meting out harsh and retributive sentences. As with general incapacitation, this approach would result in an enormous growth in prison populations.

To date, no state or local jurisdiction has formally adopted Greenwood's proposal. Language suggestive of selective incapacitation may be found in two sentencing guidelines bills, pending in California and recently enacted in New York State, and in an emergency overcrowding bill currently before the California legislature.

The California and New York sentencing guidelines bills, introduced in 1982 and 1983 respectively, are variants of Minnesota's Sentencing Guidelines Act of 1978. As in Minnesota, these bills would create state sentencing commissions to establish sentence ranges for offenses according to the type of offense and the seriousness of the offender's criminal record. The California bill, passed by the California Senate in Spring 1983, requires the commission to reserve whatever excess prison capacity is created by the guidelines for increased sentences for dangerous offenders. The New York bill, signed into law in July 1983, instructs the commission to take both the offender and the offense into consideration when determining guidelines and elevates to a "principle of sentencing" the proposition that confinement should be used "to restrain defendants and offenders" from committing new crime. Neither bill explicitly mentions the use of predictors for determining which offenders pose the greatest risk to the community. However, Greenwood did serve as a consultant to the California Youth and Adult Correction Agency, which helped draft the sentencing guidelines bill. He also testified before the California Senate that it is indeed possible to determine which offenders are most dangerous.

The use of Greenwood's predictive index and similar indicators of high-risk offenders does not, however, require the enactment of special legislation. Any police officer, prosecutor, judge, or parole officer who knows something of an individual's background could apply Greenwood's seven-point scale and guide his or her actions according to the result. Since all enjoy considerable discretion over decisions made about individuals in the system, they could simply inform that discretion by using Greenwood's index. Police and prosecutors now use various techniques for determining who will be the subject of full-scale investigations and who will be selected for career criminal prosecution programs. It would be a logical next step to apply "scientific" methods, such as Greenwood's, to guide these decisions.

At a recent meeting of New York City criminal justice officials, the idea of programming the city's criminal justice computer system to "flag" career criminals was proposed. It was suggested that certain selection criteria be entered into the computer, which would be programmed to inform its operators whenever "rap sheet" information on an offender, defendant or suspect who met the criteria was called up. Since the police, prosecutors, judges, and corrections officials will also have access to the computer, a career criminal "flag" could have a substantial effect on offenders so designated. During these discussions, prior arrests and the individual's pattern of serious offenses were discussed as candidate criteria. No mention was made of selective incapacitation or Greenwood's index. However, it would be an easy, additional step to program this or other criminal justice computer systems with Greenwood's criteria in order to select those offenders to be singled out for special treatment.

"This would be an entirely reasonable application of the basic concept," said Greenwood. "However, I would fear that the police and prosecutors might become too dependent on a computer flag and not look at the particulars of the criminal history. Also, the predictor variables would have to be verified specifically for the jurisdiction where they would be used."

Greenwood's model might also be used to identify incarcerated offenders who could safely be released from prison or to inform judges about who could safely be sentenced to alternative programs. The nature of the Rand findings, particularly the relatively low false positive error rate for those predicted to be low-rate offenders, makes this a more attractive possibility. Jan and Marcia Chaiken, who never subscribed to Greenwood's other policy proposals, consider the use of the index as a "deinstitutionalizer" to be the only possible application of the Rand findings.

"If the emphasis of the model were instead on identifying low-rate

Figure 3. Predictive Accuracy of the Greenwood Scale: Percent Correct Among Predictions

Predicted Scale Offense		Self-Reported Offense Rate			Distribution of Offenders Across Predicted Offense	
					Total	Percent of
Score	Rate	Low	Medium	High	n	Total
0–1	Low (100%)	76%	16%[†]	8%[†]	209	27%
2–3	Medium (100%)	52%	27%	22%	336	43%
>4	High (100%)	25%[*]	30%[*]	45%	236	30%

□Percentage of correct predictions.
[*]predicted high rate when actually a low or medium rate offender (Total: 55 percent).
[†]predicted low or medium rate when actually a high or medium rate offender (Total: 24 percent)

Source: Derived from Jacqueline Cohen's *Incapacitation as a Strategy for Crime Control: Possibilities and Pitfalls*

offenders, then it could serve as guide for selecting inmates who pose the least risk to the public for release from prison," said Marcia Chaiken. "The one thing we did find in the study was that a person who does not possess the characteristics Peter presented is extremely likely to be a low-rate offender."

"This would amount to a kind of back door selective incapacitation," said Greenwood. "Perhaps this is the best use for the work at this time. We did find much more precision at the low end [predicting low-rate offenders] and fewer false positives." (Figure 3).

As part of a multi-phased research project on the Illinois Department of Corrections "forced release" program, researchers from the National Council on Crime and Delinquency are planning to test the efficacy of Greenwood's index, along with other risk-assessment methods, in the selection of inmates for early release. Since forced release was instituted in June 1980, nearly 10,000 Illinois inmates have been released before the expiration of their minimum prison terms. NCCD's research will compare the recidivism rates of inmates released early with those of inmates who complete their full prison terms.

"The Illinois officials have released inmates convicted of property crimes under the state's 'good-time' statutes," explained Barry Krisberg, Senior Vice President of the National Council on Crime and Delinquency Research Center in San Francisco. "The amount of time cut from sentences depends primarily upon the level of crowding. We wondered what would happen if early release decisions were instead based on a risk-assessment model. So as part of our study, we're planning to use correctional records to code the inmates according to Greenwood's scale and apply it to a large sample of released offenders. From this, we will be able to see whether those identified as low-, medium- and high-lambda recidivated at different rates."

The study, Krisberg emphasized, will be entirely retrospective. Greenwood's criteria will be tested along with other risk-assessment models. "We're not proposing that Greenwood's index, or any other risk-assessment model be implemented," he said. "Rather, we're looking at such models to see if they can provide any improvement over across-the-board methods."

Legal Issues

The question of whether a statutory scheme employing Greenwood's seven point scale would pass constitutional muster is open to debate since any answer depends on the particularities of the statute under scrutiny. This much is clear: the answer depends on how Greenwood's scale would be used. Whether or not current case law would support the use of Greenwood's scale in a particular context, however, is not really the issue. The larger question is whether a court should permit the use of statistically-based judgments to determine the fate of an individual offender. This answer depends on the value that society and the judiciary place on the constitutional guarantee of due process of law under the fifth and fourteenth amendments.

As Mark Moore, Susan Estrich, Daniel McGillis, and William Spelman note in volume one of their recent report, *Dealing with Dangerous Offenders,* the Supreme Court has consistently held that a judge's power to impose a sentence is discretionary. The Court has rarely tampered with the length of a sentence properly imposed on a criminal offender. Furthermore, the federal courts have recognized that a judge may consider a wide range of factors when imposing a sentence. The United States Court of Appeals for the Eighth Circuit most recently reaffirmed this premise in *United States v. Moss* when it stated that "[t]here is no violation of due process . . . when the . . . court gives weight to . . . legitimate factors such as deterrence of future crimes [and] isolation of the offender from society. . . ." *United States v. Moss,* 631 F.2d 105, 107 (8th Cir. 1980). Moore suggests that proposals for selective incapacitation would advance the quest for justice and enhance due process guarantees by placing limits on unfettered judicial discretion. This would insure that "similar offenders who commit similar offenses receive[d] similar sentences—regardless of whose courtroom they find themselves in."

This is an appealing argument and one that has been used frequently in support of selective incapacitation. The argument goes: judges make these determinations already; selective incapacitation would only make their application more systematic and, therefore, more fair. Its proponents, however, ignore one basic precept of the Anglo-American common law tradition: *individuals* should be sentenced in proportion to the seriousness of the crimes they commit. Furthermore, there is something frightening about the notion of elevating the judicial practice of weighing individual factors in sentencing individual criminals to the level of official legislative policy. Echoing this concern, Professor Norval Morris has stated that there is a danger that "the selective incapacitation idea . . . will be taken by the barbarians and

Selective Incapacitation   **525**

misused." The basic theory behind selective incapacitation is that individuals can be classified into categories through the application of a set of statistically determined variables. As such, the individual is transformed into a statistical probability. Selective incapacitation places the emphasis not on the individual offender, but instead on a *class* of offenders.

The underlying constitutional difficulty with any scheme that uses a classification system based on statistical probabilities is that the reliability (in the common, not statistical, sense) of any such system is very poor. One of the strongest criticisms levelled at Greenwood's proposal is that its application results in an extremely high false positive rate. Some commentators, such as Moore, Feinberg, and Sherman and Hawkins, argue that this is a necessary trade-off if the crime rate is to be reduced. Others, such as Sheldon Messinger and Caleb Foote, believe that the price of such a trade-off is justice itself. "I start with the premise that we punish for crimes committed. ... Like offenses should be treated alike. [Greenwood] runs roughshod over this idea. [There is] no possible moral justification for [the imposition of] severe sentences for past convictions," states Caleb Foote, Professor of Criminal Law at Boalt Hall. The justification for imposing severe sentences for possible future convictions is even less supportable, he said.

The due process clause of the constitution is a guarantee of the individual's right to justice. The courts have indicated that reliability in the decision-making process is the cornerstone of this guarantee. Recently, in *United States v. Baylin,* 696 F.2d 1030,1046 (3d Cir. 1982), the court agreed : "Due process requires that there be something justifying dependence on a particular factor before a judge may make that factor a basis . . . [of a sentence. That factor must be] a reliable indicator of criminal involvement."

Thus, the legal issue before a court reviewing a statutory scheme using Greenwood's scale would be whether the variables in that scale are, in fact, reliable indicators of criminal involvement. No one disputes that a statistical correlation between high offense rates and the seven variables exists; however, it is very clear from Cohen's and von Hirsch and Gottfredson's reanalyses of Greenwood's false positive data, that the classification of one individual as a high rate offender on the basis of that person's having a number of the characteristics described in those variables is more likely than not an *incorrect* classification. In short, the use of Greenwood's variables to classify an individual as a high-rate offender is a less reliable method of prediction than flipping a coin. This would not appear to meet the standard of reliability imposed by the tenets of due process.

Classification of an individual as a high-rate offender would, furthermore, make that individual vulnerable to treatment specially reserved for those classified as such from the initial investigatory stage of the criminal justice process through sentencing. There is no escape for one so classified. Messinger has noted this danger: "To systematically assume that there are classes of people who can't be changed is to treat them as things." A court would be irresponsible, indeed, if it refused to recognize the difference between statistical correlation and legal reliability within the framework of due process and individual justice.

Some analogies can be drawn from current law. At present, agents of the Federal Bureau of Narcotics employ a Drug Courier Profile to target potential drug carriers for investigatory stops. Criminal defendants, arrested and tried on the basis of evidence seized as a result of reliance on this Profile, have challenged the use of such evidence at trial by claiming that the agents violated their right to be free from unreasonable searches and seizures under the fourth amendment of the constitution. In no case, has any court ever held that probable cause existed to stop and detain an individual on the basis of the characteristics contained in the Profile alone. In every case where the courts have held that evidence was legally seized and probable cause to stop and detain an individual existed, the courts have done so because the agent observed a particular circumstance on a particular occasion with respect to a particular individual *in addition to* the characteristics listed in the Profile.

The implication here is that the characteristics contained in the Drug Profile are not reliabile enough indicators that an individual is in fact carrying drugs to meet the probable cause standard imposed by the fourth amendment, even though, statistically, a *group* of people having the listed characteristics tends to be comprised largely of drug carriers.

One might also envision certain statutory schemes, such as recidivist statutes using Greenwood's scale. The Supreme Court has upheld the constitutionality of recidivism statutes in *Rummell v. Estelle*, 445 U.S. 263 (1980) so long as the statutory scheme merely enhances a sentence imposed as the result of a judgment of guilt for a specific crime. The authors of a recent Note in the Harvard Law Review (vol. 96) rightly point out that if the "scheme makes recidivism *itself* a crime or provides for a special term [of imprisonment] for purely incapacitive purposes, [that scheme would] be subject to the full range of due process guarantees, including proof beyond a reasonable doubt—a standard that no prediction scale [like Greenwood's] can possibly meet." In short, a statutory scheme using Greenwood's scale as the basis for making recidivism itself an offense would violate due process.

Another potential use for Greenwood's scale lies in the context of preventive detention statutes. The United States Court of Appeals for the Second Circuit recently declared New York's juvenile preventive detention statute unconstitutional in *Martin v. Strasburg*, 689 F.2d 365 (2d Cir. 1982). Judge Newman, in his concurring opinion, based his analysis on a belief that any classification system founded on statistical probabilities instead of individualized judgments, is suspect. The opinion speaks for itself:

> The governmental interest is the prevention of future crimes, obviously of great significance in general, but of high value in a particular case only to the extent that the pretrial detention of a person will prevent the commission of a crime that he would have committed if not detained, . . .significantly reduce the risk of his committing such a crime. . . . The proponents of preventive detention doubtless assess the risk of erroneous determinations somewhat lower than do the opponents, but *on the present state of knowledge concerning predictions of criminal behavior, only*

> *the foolhardy would deny that even with carefully circumscribed decision-making, a signi-*
> *ficant risk of erroneous prediction remains....* In my judgment, the Due Process Clause
> forbids the ... [infliction of] a deprivation as serious as loss of liberty in advance of
> trial on the basis of a highly uncertain prediction of future criminal behavior. 689
> F. 2d at 376-77 (emphasis added).

Thus, while it is impossible to predict what the Supreme Court would do if
presented with a challenge to selective incapacitation in a specific statutory
framework, it is clear that due process considerations must arise whenever
statistical information is used to make determinations about individual
suspects and offenders. The legal community must be sensitive to the dangers
of such an approach, even if politicians are not.

THE ETHICS OF RESEARCH

> There was corporate pressure [at Rand] to produce a policy statement,
> whatever its merits. It's a classic case of academic versus entrepreneurial
> research.
> *Marcia Chaiken, Jan. 17, 1983*

> The difference between Jan and Marcia [Chaiken] and me is not purely on
> policy grounds. We parted company over what to do with the remainder of
> the grant money.
> *Peter Greenwood, Jan. 18, 1983*

Greenwood's experience translates into a morality tale of relevance to all
academicians and researchers who, from time to time, venture out of their
ivory towers. The tale illustrates the competing and often irreconcilable
pressures felt by those whose research is at once a solid contribution toward a
solution to a large social problem and yet, in the context of that problem, a
proportionately small contribution. How does that person, without losing his
integrity, gain recognition for such a contribution without distorting its
context? The recognition is essential to the researcher's professional
advancement; indeed, the recognition is essential because any further research
in the area is often dependent on the financial support that he or she can muster
for the project. Must the researcher and/or his or her sponsoring institution
play politics? Or can they attempt quietly and carefully to formulate rational
social policy?

All too often, despite their similar linguistic roots, we forget that policy
and politics are two very different animals. The tragedy of the selective
incapacitation saga begins here and, as in similar situations where the policy and
politics of research have become hopelessly confused, it has led to some highly
irresponsible proclamations.

A year after the publication of his report, Greenwood is back at the Rand
Corporation headquarters in Santa Montica, California working on a totally
unrelated project on delinquents. Rand's selective incapacitation "dog and
pony show," which kept Greenwood and his colleagues on the road for many

months, has come to a halt. Greenwood is not a little weary of the episode that propelled him into the limelight, and he is glad that it is over. Although he continues to stand by his findings, he is considerably more cautious about his policy proposals.

"Without further verifying research, any explicit use of selective incapacitation principles is perhaps unwise," he said. "We still have much to learn about how well the predictors predict and what the long range effects of such policies would be."

But as the Rand Corporation research team winds down its seven-year stint with selective incapacitation, criminal justice officials, criminologists and policy makers are still grappling with the work and its policy implications. The clamor created by the proposal has hardly died down.

For Jan and Marcia Chaiken, the experience of working on the Rand studies has left them with some bitterness. After so much long and careful work, they feel that their contribution—their analysis of criminal behavior patterns and typology of offenders—was eclipsed by Greenwood's more dramatic policy proposal.

"There's a lot of political pressure to present quick and easy solutions," said Marcia Chaiken. "That's what grabs the funding. People do not want to hear nebulous conclusions. In this way, Peter was more politically astute than we were.... Peter wanted the entire body of our research to do his policy piece, but he didn't want our input. This resulted in an ideological split at Rand. One side thought the researchers ought to be responsible for the ways in which the research is used; others simply washed their hands of it."

"Jan and Marcia wanted to continue with their statistical analysis and give up on the policy piece," Greenwood responded. "It was my belief that if we didn't do the policy piece, which we had included in our original proposal, we might never do it. So we're left with the product of this bifurcation: a statistical analysis that doesn't go into as much detail as people would want to develop policy; and mine, which is a first cut, very simple prediction model that doesn't have all the fancy bells and whistles that it might."

Until the research community is given the resources to mount studies of scope and scale on selective incapacitation and is relieved of the burden of playing politics in order to receive those resources, the contributions made by Greenwood, and others like him, will continue to be obscured, and even distorted, by the political mind set that seeks quick and easy answers to complex and perhaps unresolvable social dilemmas.

[14]

Articles

Dangerousness, Risk and Technologies of Power *

John Pratt†

This paper provides a critical examination of the prevalence of dangerous offender legislation in modern criminal justice systems. The debate about this has been dominated by issues of ethics and effectiveness. Here, though, I want to examine the significance of this legislation and some of the theoretical issues that this raises. This involves discussion of the way in which 'dangerousness' as a social construct has changed historically and similarly the mode of its calibration. Ultimately, the dangerousness legislation today involves the use of a largely unnoticed strategy of control — actuarialism; and seems more likely to have an effect on the behaviour of potential victims of crime rather than dangerous offenders themselves.

'Dangerousness' appears to be one of the most prevalent themes in the criminal law jurisdictions of English speaking countries at the present time. That is to say, in the last few years, wherever we look in this part of the world, we find legislation that contains (inter alia) measures to allow the courts to sentence those judged to be 'dangerous offenders' to indefinite terms of imprisonment — usually known as preventive detention — while at the same time often imposing special restrictions in relation to their subsequent release on parole. For example: the Victorian State Sentencing (Amendment) Act 1993 and the Community Protection Act 1990; the Washington State Sexual Predator Law 1989; the Canadian federal legislation of 1993 — the Corrections and Conditional Release Act; and the New Zealand Criminal Justice Amendment Act 1993.

As such, the focus of interest on this subject noted by Bottoms (1977) seems to have continued apace since then. But dangerousness has not just kept legislators busy: it has also become a significant aspect of criminological research post-1970. Here, the preoccupation has been with how best to identify this group of offenders, usually thought to be small in number, and thus minimise the ethical problems that the sentencing of them to indefinite prison terms raises (see eg Floud & Young 1981) or, in opposition to this, the concern has been to argue that the ethical issues associated with the concept of dangerousness are insurmountable and, for this reason, legislation regarding it should be withdrawn (see eg von Hirsch 1972; Bottoms & Brownsword 1982).

In this paper, though, I want to move away from these issues of ethics and effectiveness that have dominated the dangerousness debate so far

---

* Received: 11 October 1993; accepted in revised form: 9 March 1994.

† Senior Lecturer, Institute of Criminology, Victoria University, PO Box 600, Wellington, New Zealand.

4   (1995) 28 The Australian and New Zealand Journal of Criminology

(Bottoms 1977 is a notable exception) and to consider instead the significance of the dangerousness legislation today, and some of the theoretical issues that this raises: about the concept of danger itself, about the management of crime risk, about patterns of social control in modern society. I should add that the paper is by way of an introduction to a more general study of the history of dangerousness laws in the English speaking world. It should thus be read as an attempt to raise questions and initiate divergent lines of inquiry rather than some definitive statement — and as a sketch of a theoretical framework that will receive more refinement at a later stage. As such, instead of taking the construct 'dangerousness' as a given, my starting point is to ask what has made possible its construction; how has it been possible for dangerous offenders to be constituted in criminological discourse? It is anticipated that the genealogical study that this approach entails will not be confined to analysis of an individual justice system but will present the development of this particular penal theme in English speaking societies as a whole (in the manner, say, of Cohen 1985).

Such an analysis does not dispute the fact that some offenders are dangerous. What I do want to suggest though is that, dangerousness, as a shifting criminological concept, has a significance that goes beyond the particular problems that the offenders targeted by this legislation may cause us from time to time. More generally, if we are to understand changes and shifts in penal policy at a given time, we must remember that:

> ... punishment is neither a simple consequence of crime, nor the reverse side of crime, nor a mere means which is determined by the end to be achieved. Punishment must be understood as a social phenomenon freed from both its juristic concept and its social ends. We do not deny that punishment has specific ends, but we do deny that it can be understood from its ends alone. (Rusche & Kirchheimer 1939:5)

In this respect, if we are to understand how dangerousness itself has been constituted today and the significance of this, then it would seem important that initially we turn to the origins of the concept and then examine and account for the subsequent shifts that have since taken place in it.

Dangerousness: the beginnings

When did a set of discourses urging special measures of confinement for those adjudicated to be a danger, or a menace, or some special risk over and above the ordinary, first enter the criminological universe? Perhaps the 1890 Congress of the International Union of Criminal Law at St Petersburg is the location, even if the apparent lateness of this date may come as something of a surprise to many[1]. Here, it was argued that special penalties should be introduced which would render habitual offenders 'incapable of inflicting harm for as long as possible' (Ancel 1965:47). In other words, the argument was for an indefinite prison sentence to nullify the particular harm or 'danger' that habitual offenders were thought to constitute. The immediate significance of the 1890 resolution was the way in which such a view ruptured the two then available modes of adult offender classification - there was no special residual category for the dangerous at this time. Instead, in the first, one was held to be legally sane and therefore fully responsible for one's actions: the penalty to be imposed was intended to be approximate to the harm done, while still acting as a deterrent − in line with the dominating principles of Victorian penology − classicism and less eligibility (Pratt 1992).

In the second, one was judged to be insane and therefore not responsible for one's actions. If this was the case, then the individual moved out of the clutches of the law and into those of psychiatry and the narrow space within criminal justice that it had been able to colonise for itself by this time. During the course of the 19th century, this had been achieved by siphoning off and proclaiming as its own, the most bizarre, horrendous cases that came to light.

> [Psychiatrists] justified their right to intervene, not by searching out the thousand little visible signs of madness which may accompany the most ordinary crimes, but by insisting − a preposterous stance − that there were kinds of insanity which manifested themselves only in outrageous crimes, and in no other way. (Foucault 1988:132–3)

Homicidal mania was one such example. Another would be the insanity laws in Britain at the end of the 19th century, where the defence of 'irresistible impulse' was made available − but only in murder cases (Wiener 1990).

The point about the perceived dangerousness of the habitual criminals was that it was the pettiness of their acts, rather than their demonstration of any signs of exceptional depravity that brought them to attention. What then seemed to separate them out from the rest of the criminal population was the fact that they continued to break the law: 'the real offence is the wilful persistence in the deliberately acquired habit of crime' (Report from the Departmental Committee on Prisons 1895:303). As such, they placed themselves outside of the then available modes of criminological classification. They were beyond the law − they continued to break it; and they were beyond psychiatry − they were not demonstrably mad, nor were they murderers. At this time, then, a special category had to be constituted to accommodate them. Prior to 1890, it seems to have been the case in English speaking jurisdictions that any attempt to do this, and by so doing begin to punish on the basis of who one was rather than what one had done, was resisted. The main sites of this resistance were the classically minded judiciary, liberal parliamentarians and the press (see Radzinowicz & Hood 1980, 1985). Hence the English 1869 Habitual Criminals Bill was forced to drop a proposal to sentence habitual criminals to seven years penal servitude (see Radzinowicz & Hood 1985:253–256).[2]

However, from around 1890 to 1910, growing attention was given to the issue of dangerousness and the threat to civil society that this created in the English speaking world; growing attention was given to the urgency of finding new methods of incapacitation for such offenders, as indeed it was for other forms of 'degeneracy' that such lawbreakers were

6   (1995) 28 The Australian and New Zealand Journal of Criminology

increasingly associated with: hence, in Scotland, the 1895 *Report from the Departmental Committee on Habitual Offenders, Vagrants, Beggars, Inebriates, and Juvenile Delinquents* (see also Garland 1985; Wearing & Berreen 1993). As we have seen, the category featured the habitual offenders. Thus in England, Sir Robert Anderson, former head of the CID claimed in 1901 that

> ... the community is being preyed upon by a gang of habitual criminals ...
> [N]o citizen's property is safe. Doors can no longer be left on the latch. Not
> even a window can be left unbarred. The whole community is thus kept in a
> state of siege. (Radzinowicz & Hood 1980:1358)

In New Zealand it was claimed that:

> ... these [habitual offenders] have from their young days preyed on society,
> and are not entitled to the rights of a citizen or their liberty. They boast that
> they have never done a day's work and never intend to ... They are no sooner
> released than they commence their nefarious mode of life again and return to
> gaol. In these cases reform appears to be out of the question, and although the
> problem of dealing with this class of person has exercised the minds of
> criminologists for a long period, they have not as yet arrived at any real
> solution. (Department of Justice 1906:2)

Furthermore, it was as if habituality itself was a sign of incorrigibility, thus placing the habituals beyond any redemption that the existing criminal justice system could offer. Again, as it was then constituted, they could not be accommodated within it. For example, in New Zealand:

> ... it is believed that these last mentioned [thrice or oftener convicted] include
> a class of person who were probably gaolbirds before they came to the colony,
> and who have spent the greater portion of their lives in prisons, and are so
> hardened and well versed in crime that no reformatory system, however good
> it may be, will ever alter their mode of life or induce them to forsake their
> criminal ways. (Department of Justice 1891:2)

But dangerousness also came to include another group: the professional criminals. Hence the subsequent 1908 Anglo-Welsh Prevention of Crime Act was also designed for:

> ... the professional criminal[s], men with an object, sound in mind − so far as
> a criminal could be sound in mind − and in body, competent, often highly
> skilled and who deliberately and with their eyes open, preferred a life of crime
> and know all the tricks and manoeuvres necessary for that life. (Parliamentary
> Debates, referred to by Radzinowicz & Hood 1980:1361)

Accordingly, crimes that constituted a danger 'must be of a serious character − such as burglary, housebreaking, coining, larceny from the person, robbery with violence and the like' (Report of Judges of King's Bench Division 1902, referred to by Radzinowicz & Hood 1980:1361). Then again, the judges wanted to ensure that this new classification included 'the happily rare ... habitual and dangerous crimes which are not crimes of "acquisitiveness" at all' as well as those 'weak and immoral beings who are not professional thieves or burglars, and generally have no sufficient cleverness or audacity for such a role, but whose abstinence from crime is so infrequent that society is justified in requiring special protection from their habits of depredation' (Radzinowicz & Hood 1980).

Certainly, dangerousness in its embryonic form was of a generic shifting nature, in itself demonstrating the changing social attitudes to the phenomenon. It does not exist, then, as some pre-given entity. Thus in the British 1908 parliamentary debates on the subject, the Home Secretary argued that legislation should be directed at 'a small and carefully selected category of the most formidable offenders' (quoted by Radzinowicz & Hood 1985:276). But perhaps what is most striking of all in the dangerousness debates of this period is the preoccupation with offences against property. The Report of the Gladstone Committee (1895) made no reference to violent offenders when discussing this concept. Instead, it had in mind;

> ... a large class of habitual criminals not of the desperate order who live by robbery and thieving and petty larceny, who run the risk of comparatively short sentences with comparative indifference. They make money rapidly by crime, they enjoy life after their fashions and then on detection and conviction they serve their time quietly with the full determination to revert to crime when they come out ...

In effect, 'what the committee was really concerned about was repetition of crimes against property, whatever their degree of seriousness (Radzinowicz & Hood 1985:266). As a result, the image of the dangerous offender, in the early years of this creature's existence, is made up of many little shades of light, the reflections of petty thieves, coiners, burglars and so on.

However, if until now, these dangerous offenders seemed to have broken free of the existing criminal justice system and its constraints and terrors, if they had placed themselves in some short lived terra nullius, beyond the reaches of both law and psychiatry, the impact of the new penology around the turn of the century (see eg Pasquino 1991; Pratt 1992) immediately colonised this space and brought its inhabitants under the regulatory powers it introduced to Western penal systems. The new penology both undermined the dominance of classicism and also made it possible to conceptualise modes of containment that went beyond the classical episteme. They could be indeterminate in nature without consigning those sanctioned in this way to asylums for the mad and deranged: to be judged dangerous was not necessarily to be judged insane. Thus, amongst the contributions to the new penology, free will and rational choice were denied by Ferri (1906). Garofalo (1914:xxxvii) wrote of the need to protect society against the depradations of dangerous criminals rather than allow the due process of law to offer them protection: 'the State does little for our protection [against the criminal]. Since, thanks to the legalists, criminal law is one thing and the measures necessary against malefactors another, action of the State has been rendered almost ineffective'. And the need for the individualisation of punishment, punishment on the basis of who one was rather than what one had done, was argued by Saleilles (1911).

8   (1995) 28 The Australian and New Zealand Journal of Criminology

Driven by such contributions, the possibility of indefinite confinement for dangerous criminals which had been, as we have seen, put on the penological agenda at the 1890 Conference, was finally endorsed, after much debate and opposition in succeeding meetings, at the 1910 Conference of the International Union of Criminal Law (Alper & Boren 1972). But by now, the convergence of anxieties about dangerous criminals and these changes in penological thought had made possible a range of legislation designed to identify and then entrap these creatures: the influence of 'the legalists' whom Garofalo had complained of, was now in decline. Thus the New South Wales Habitual Criminals Act 1905 allowed judges to impose an indeterminate sentence of detention following a finite prison term on habitual criminals and, similarly, the New Zealand Habitual Criminals Act of 1906. In England and Wales the Prevention of Crime Act 1908 introduced the sentence of preventive detention, prescribing imprisonment for those who qualified for it for a minimum period of 5 years and a maximum of 10. Similar legislation elsewhere can be found around this time, in the Victoria Indeterminate Sentences Act 1908, for example, and the Western Australian Criminal Code of 1913 and the Queensland Criminal Law Amendment Act.1914. The first such legislation in South Africa was the Transvaal Criminal Law Amendment Act 1909 empowering superior courts to declare certain persons habitual criminals.

All such laws were based on the assumption that those who qualified for these special measures had to demonstrate evidence of habituality – this was how dangerousness at this time was calibrated. Hence the criteria for eligibility under the 1908 Prevention of Crime Act were three previous convictions since the age of 16 and in addition it had to be proved that the offender had been 'leading persistently a dishonest or criminal life'. Similarly the Western Australian legislation defined as an habitual criminal anyone from '18 upwards who is convicted of any indictable offence, not punishable by death and has previously been so convicted on at least two occasions'. By this time then, the short-lived terra nullius that was the dangerousness concept had been colonised as the penological boundaries of classification and sanction were redrawn around its little bands of sad and wretched citizens.

Dangerousness: the renaissance?

In his paper of 1977, Bottoms argues that the current period, after these beginnings, has witnessed a resurgence of interest in the concept, a 'renaissance', in effect. By way of explanation, he argues in Durkheimian (and functionalist) fashion that, by focussing on supposedly dangerous individuals, governments hope to bolster a rather fraying conscience collective, the product of the economic and social crises and changes of these times: indeed, these are circumstances which are perhaps even more prevalent in the 1990s than they were in the late 1970s. Whatever, the result is that those labelled dangerous come to be useful scapegoats for society's ills and help to unify other citizens around the concerns that their conduct evokes. From this opening Bottoms (1983) and others (eg Matthews 1979; Chan & Ericson 1981) have gone on to argue that the contemporary interest in dangerousness is reflective of a bifurcation in penal policy: increasingly long periods of imprisonment for the dangerous/serious offender and (preferably) non-prison for 'the rest'. Here, the successive fiscal crises of the modern state are seen as crucial determinants. Prison becomes too expensive and control in the community will be a cheaper option for those who do not need to be in prison. Keep this latter sanction for those for whom it is essential to be locked up, the dangerous ones, so this argument goes.

Clearly, such contributions are helpful starting points in moving towards a sociology of the dangerousness laws. Having said this, though, I want to take the opportunity here to expand on these initial contributions both empirically and theoretically. First, let us consider the presumed 'renaissance' of interest in dangerousness. Undoubtedly, legislative attention has been keenly focussed on this concept in the last two decades and, if anything, this seems to be increasingly the case. However, to refer to this as a 'renaissance' perhaps cuts too sharp a division between the origins of the concept in the early part of this century and the dangerousness legislation of the modern period.[3] This is more than just a question of semantics since the impression could otherwise be gained that there was a completely vacant period in between the two areas. To do this, though, is to leave unproblematic the three themes that emerge in relation to the dangerousness laws between 1920 and 1970. These are:

1. The lack of use of the dangerousness laws

Despite the anxieties that helped to give birth to these laws, the laws themselves were hardly ever used. In New Zealand, for example, by 1945 only 605 habitual criminal declarations had been made in the 40 years of existence of the empowering legislation. Furthermore:

> ... notwithstanding that approximately 30% of total receptions in our prisons are of the petty recidivist type who are not deterred, or in respect of whom society is not protected, by repeated short sentences, there has been no recourse by the court to [habitual criminal declarations] at least during the past 20 years and possibly longer. (Department of Justice 1948:4)

In the USA, the concept of dangerousness, although linked initially to the problem of repeat offending mainly by professional criminals in the 1920s (Kramer 1982), shifted in focus between the 1930s and 1950s to encompass sexual psychopathy. Even so, Sutherland (1950:553) found that 'although these sexual psychopath laws are dangerous in principle, they are of little importance in practise. They are never used in some states and seldom used in the others ... ' In England and Wales, 'between 1922 and 1928 only 31 criminals, on average, were sentenced to preventive detention each year', (Radzinowicz & Hood 1980:1377); 'between 1928 and 1945 there were 325 such committals (only 7 for offences of violence)', (Morris 1951:65); and by 1962 the numbers had declined to only seven for that year' (Radzinowicz & Hood 1980:1383).

The position seems to have been the same in continental Europe (see Morris 1951), even though it might be thought that the more inquisitorial

10   (1995) 28 The Australian and New Zealand Journal of Criminology

systems of justice to be found would encourage the use of these measures, given the lesser opposition to be expected from the judiciary in these countries.[4] Indeed, in Western society as a whole it seems that the only three jurisdictions where any significant use was ever made of the power to award indefinite detention on the grounds that one constituted a danger to society were Soviet Russia, Fascist Italy and Nazi Germany (see Morris 1951).

2. The reluctance of legislatures in democratic societies to give up the powers of indefinite detention which they had introduced to the courts

If the laws were seldom used, governments nonetheless showed a marked reluctance to give up such powers. This was the case in spite of the growing weight of post war research which indicated that when these measures were used, it was usually nondangerous criminals who got caught up in their net. In England and Wales, the 1932 Report of the Departmental Committee on Persistent Offenders made the point that 'a large number of persistent offenders never commit a serious offence at all' (Advisory Council on the Treatment of Offenders 1963:10). Now, the 1963 review went on to claim, preventive detention was used mainly for offences of housebreaking. Furthermore, those given preventive detention were likely to be 'less of a danger to society than many given long term or other sentences of imprisonment'. West (1963:8) made the point that 'contrary to the popular stereotype of a persistent criminal, few of these prisoners were prone to violence and hardly any were efficiently organised professional criminals'. Nonetheless, the 1932 Report recommended the retention of the dangerousness legislation; the Criminal Justice Bill of 1938 and the Criminal Justice Act of 1948 extended the principle of indeterminacy by introducing the sentence of corrective training for appropriate offenders aged between 21 and 30. The Criminal Justice Act 1967, although abolishing the sentence of preventive detention, simply introduced the extended sentence to replace it.

Similarly, in New Zealand, the Criminal Justice Act 1954 replaced the habitual criminal declaration with the sentence of preventive detention: 'however, at no time did the courts impose the sentence freely' (Webb 1981:72), indeed, it was claimed that:

> . . . though designed mainly to remove persistent and dangerous offenders from the community for a long indeterminate period, the sentence has been applied to many who are merely irresponsible and inadequate, and its aptness in these cases is doubtful. (Department of Justice 1965:5)

Yet the sentence was retained in the Criminal Justice Act 1967, the Minister of Justice stating that 'the authorities should have the power to keep [appropriate] offenders out of circulation for a very long time' (NZPD vol 353, 1967:3629).

In the United States, the lack of use of the sexual psychopath laws of the 1950s did not prevent provision for 'dangerous offenders' being written into the Model Penal Code of 1962. Similarly, the National Council on Crime and Delinquency in 1967 maintained that 'confinement is necessary for offenders who, if not confined, would be a serious danger to the public'.

3. Shifts in the construction of dangerousness and its mode of calculation

As we have seen, dangerousness was originally a category that was designed to include, in the main, habitual and professional criminals, usually involving offences against property. The United States example above, though, again illustrates the shifting category of dangerousness itself, moving from the original target of professional criminals to that of sexual psychopath. In England and Wales, the 1932 Report (op cit) regarded as dangerous 'professional criminals who deliberately make a living by preying on the public' and that the danger lay not only in their offences but also in their contamination of other, particularly younger, men and now, specified for the first time, the category was also to include 'certain sexual offenders . . . particularly those who committed repeated offences against children or young persons and those who corrupt boys'. However, debates on the 1948 Criminal Justice Act reveal something of a reversion to the original concept of dangerousness. Preventive detention was specifically for 'the relatively trivial offender. This type of criminal presents one of the main problems of persistent offending' (Advisory Council on the Treatment of Offenders 1963:11). The subsequent researchers who claimed that only trivial offenders were being sentenced in this way missed the point. At various times, such offenders were intended to be the target but what had changed were the sensitivities of the particular researchers to what constituted a danger. Hall Williams (1967:07) again demonstrates the shifting category of dangerousness by arguing that indeterminate prison sentences should be restricted to offenders with an 'accumulation of convictions of a certain degree of seriousness', making particular reference to 'offences of violence, organised crime, drugs and child sex'.

In addition to these shifts in focus on the matter of who is considered to be dangerous, the calibration of dangerousness also begins to undergo change. It is no longer calculated solely on the basis of one's past offending but the extent to which the public need to be protected from such offenders. Earlier, it had only been in the English Prevention of Crime Act 1908 that these criminal law measures had been justified on the grounds of 'public protection'. After the war, this concept appears much more forcefully right across the various jurisdictions. In s 21(2) of the English Criminal Justice Act 1948, dangerousness is still linked to the amount of crime and regularity of offending that one has demonstrated. But what has now changed is that the grounds for the sentence are now tied more closely to social defence ('if the court is satisfied that it is expedient *for the protection of the public* that he should be detained in custody for a substantial period of time' (s 21(b); my italics). Similarly, in Canada, in the 1946 Criminal Code Amendment Act s 75(b), the criteria included three convictions for an indictable offence, leading a persistent

12   (1995) 28 The Australian and New Zealand Journal of Criminology

criminal life and that the offender is 'one whose criminal habits and mode of life require a special type of detention *for the protection of the public*' (my italics).

Thus Grunhut (1948:311) argued that 'the facts support the demand for a stronger protection of society against dangerous persistent criminals [ie 'habitual criminals proper and professional criminals']. In New Zealand, the Department of Justice (1954:6) declared that 'hardened criminals should be placed in custody for long period of time in order that the community may be protected from them, and in order that they themselves may realise the futility of their criminal activities'. In Britain, Hammond and Chayen (1963:187) spoke of the need 'to protect society from (i) professional housebreakers [and] (ii) violent/sexual offenders'. The 1967 Criminal Justice Act made provision for the imposition of the extended sentence 'having regard to his antecedents and the need to protect the public'. It was only to be used against those 'who were a real menace to society'.

By the 1970s then, I do not think it was necessarily the case that the dangerousness legislation had been allowed to fall into desuetude (Bottoms 1977). It had never become a significant sentencing option, even at times when fears of dangerous offenders were at their peak — the United States sexual psychopath laws being a case in point here (Sutherland 1950). One reason for this may simply be that such offenders could anyway be sentenced to long periods of imprisonment under existing penal measures. But, more symbolically, may it not be the case that these laws themselves were never intended to be a significant option? Any overuse of them, certainly in the post war period, would draw immediate resonances with totalitarianism. It had been in such societies where the rights and interests of the individual could be so dramatically eroded while those of the state were maximised. For example, the Italian penal code of 1930 had empowered the court to declare certain persons to have a *tendenza a delinquere* and to apply special segregative measures to them even though they had never before been convicted of a crime (Ancel 1965). Similarly, the Nazi gestapo were able to hold habitual criminals and 'asocial persons' in protective custody (Wolff 1993:5). Again, the way in which such legislation became explicitly tied to the interests of the state is seen in the work of the Nazi criminologist Mezger: 'the future administration of criminal law will consider its highest ambition to be to serve the racial improvement of the people. This task embraces two different things: the restoration of the responsibility of the individual towards the community and the elimination of elements which are detrimental to the people and the race' (referred to by Mannheim 1936:536).

And so, in the post war period, when the democracies began to legislate to ensure public protection there were limits as to how far these measures could go. Clearly the dangerousness legislation of this period (as with legislation regulating other areas of the social body) marked the greatly expanded role of the State in the welfare societies that began to emerge post 1945. Furthermore, the shift in the calibration of dangerousness from quantification of past criminality to public protection also signalled a further erosion of the principles of classical justice towards a framework which was ordered more by executive fiat.

Yet at the same time, the powers of indefinite confinement were residual. At one level, then, the judges and their liberal allies were still resisting the powers that legislatures were keen to give them. But even more so, perhaps, dangerousness itself, although colonised by the reforms in the early part of the twentieth century, and although now existing in an era when state powers were steadily increasing, represented some kind of hinterland between the democracies and totalitarian societies. To overpopulate it would be to blur the boundaries between the two that this legislation, with its quasi-abandonment of the rule of law, had helped to establish.

If we move now to the 1970s and beyond, what is perhaps most striking about the dangerousness debate from this point is the way in which its classification and assessment has changed again. Conduct which is regarded as dangerous is almost exclusively confined to (repeat) violent/sexual offending. For example, the Canadian draft legislation referred to earlier is targeted at:

> ... repeat, high-risk sex offenders ... there is clear consensus among Canadians that the government must have the power to keep these violent offenders in custody as long as their release poses a serious threat to society. (Solicitor General of Canada news release, 25 May 1993)

Proposed changes to the Canadian Criminal Code now define dangerousness as involving 'a serious personal injury offence' and that:

> ... the offender constitutes a threat to the life, safety or physical or mental well-being of other persons on the basis of evidence establishing (i) a pattern of repetitive behaviour by the offender [and] (ii) a pattern of persistent aggressive behaviour by the offender, of which the serious personal injury offence forms a part, showing a substantial degree of indifference on the part of the offender or (iii) any behaviour by the offender including behaviour associated with the serious personal injury offence, that is of such a brutal nature as to compel the conclusion that the offender's behaviour in the future is unlikely to be inhibited by normal standards of behavioural restraint ... (Proposals to amend the Corrections and Conditional Release Act and the Criminal Code 1993)

Similarly, the current New Zealand legislation makes the sentence of preventive detention specific to the commission of offences of sex and/or violence (s 34 Criminal Justice Amendment Act 1993)[5] and the Victorian Sentencing (Amendment) Bill of 1993 confines dangerousness to 'serious sexual offenders' and 'serious violent offenders'.

Indeed, even the term 'dangerous' now seems to have a much greater criminological specificity than before and is no longer interchangeable with such terms as 'habituality', 'seriousness' and so on. This contrast prior to and post 1970 is well demonstrated in the work of Nigel Walker. In *Sentencing in a Rational Society*, Walker (1969) makes virtually no reference at all to dangerousness, although there is a chapter entitled 'Protecting Society' where 'incorrigibility' (p 166) is seen as the underlying motif for measures such as preventive detention. However, in

14   (1995) 28 The Australian and New Zealand Journal of Criminology

Punishment, Danger and Stigma, Walker (1980) invests a whole chapter (titled 'Protecting') to consideration of the dangerousness issue, as well as making it part of the book's title.

If the post 1970 period has seen the dangerous offender thus reconstituted, what we also find is a further refinement in the mode of dangerousness assessment. Initially, the calibration of dangerousness had still obeyed the principles of classicism: the greater the number of crimes that were committed, the greater the penalty, until ultimately the boundaries of classicism itself were breached. We have already seen how, post war, 'protection of the public' was built into the criteria as the modern state continued to expand its duties and responsibilities. What we find around 1970 and beyond, though, is a growing interest in the kind of crime one might commit in the future, rather than the quantity of crimes one had committed in the past, as was originally the case. We first notice this shift in emphasis in the 1967 Anglo-Welsh Criminal Justice Act: 'the extended sentence could be imposed 'where [the court] is satisfied, by reason of the prisoner's previous conduct and of the likelihood of his committing further offences, that it is expedient to protect the public from him for a substantial time' (s 37). From this point on it can be said that the new element in the dangerousness equation is the probability of future crime. Thus the Scottish Council on Crime (1975, para 122) defined dangerousness as 'the probability that [the offender] will inflict serious and irremediable personal injury in the future'. In the United States case of *Jurek v Texas* (1976) it was decided that 'any sentencing authority must predict a convicted person's probable future conduct when it engages in the process of determining what punishment to impose' (quoted by Miller & Morris 1988:264).

In Australia, the Victoria Sentencing Committee (1988:47) recommended that 'the key consideration in dangerousness appears to be the threat of a repetition of serious behaviour involving physical or psychological injury to others and the means of preventing such behaviour occuring'. Similarly, the need to take into account the likelihood of future crime has been written into the Victoria Sentencing (Amendment) Bill (1993), s 18: 'the risk of serious danger to the rest of the community if an indefinite sentence were not imposed.' And the justification for the 1993 Canadian legislation is on the grounds that 'in order for the detention provisions to be invoked it is necessary that an offence be shown to have caused serious harm and that serious harm is likely in future offences' (Solicitor General of Canada 1993:2). And while, in New Zealand, the 1980's dangerousness legislation (Criminal Justice Act 1985; Criminal Justice Amendment Act 1988 no 2) merely reasserted that preventive detention would be available to the courts 'if it is expedient for the protection of the public', the 1993 Criminal Justice Amendment Act s 34(1)(b) includes the provision that the court must be satisfied 'that there is a substantial risk that the offender will commit a [qualifying] offence upon release' before imposing a sentence of preventive detention.

As such, to remark on the 'renaissance' of dangerousness post 1970 is to beg the question of why the category has actually changed in character in this time; why is it that the focus has shifted almost exclusively onto sexual and violent offenders? There are still, no doubt, habitual offenders, or the petty recidivists that the earlier commentators above regularly remarked upon, and professional criminals. Indeed, it seems to have been concern about professional crime in the 1960s that prompted a drive towards longer sentencing amidst the public anxieties that were so generated (Bottoms 1977). However, as we have seen, both the habituals and the professional criminals now seem to have dropped out of the dangerousness frame. Ultimately, then, to understand the significance of the dangerousness legislation today we have to address two issues:

(i) why the shift towards violent and sexual offending post 1970; and
(ii) what has made possible the assessment of dangerousness on the basis of a propensity to commit future offences?

Danger and modernity

Let us first consider, in very general terms, how such matters as danger and threat have been perceived and insured against in modern society. The way in which 'public protection' forced its way into the dangerousness legislative agenda in the 1940s was actually a rather late extension of the moves towards protection from risks and dangers of various kinds that Western governments, from around 1870, had been prepared to offer their citizens as a kind of social insurance: protection against sickness through the development of health services; protection against poverty in old age through pension provisions; protection against the consequences of unemployment through the provision of 'national assistance' benefits and so on; and, ultimately, in the penological context, protection against dangerous criminals.

One of the consequences of such initiatives, of course, was the growth of an elaborate administrative structure to regulate and distribute this 'continuous regime of assistance' (Castels 1991). It came to be the domain of the welfare expert, a new kind of judge, not so much interested in laws and their interpretation, as codes, standards, norms and the maximisation of human potential, whether this be to do with health, aging, scholarship or good conduct and so on. Departures from these standards were to be regulated through strategies of discipline and surveillance (Foucault 1977): discipline in the sense of transforming the souls of individual criminals – turning them into normal, useful, productive subjects through counselling, rehabilitative techniques etc; and surveillance – targeted at populations as a whole: the keeping of registers, surveys and various modes of classification and distribution. In this way, the power of judging individuals (hitherto, only matters of guilt or innocence in the courts) came to be connected to other powers such as classification, assessment, diagnosis and the power to judge came to be exercised in a multiplicity of sites, such as the case conference and the psychiatrist's office – no longer, then, just the courtroom. Hence in relation to the administration of criminal justice from the early twentieth century onwards, we find a shift from the legal formalism of the classical school to executive decision-making. For example, the release of

16   (1995) 28 The Australian and New Zealand Journal of Criminology

dangerous offenders from prison came to be decided not by judges (not sitting on their own at least) but by tribunals and parole boards. Between the different jurisdictions these would assume varying shapes and forms, but were likely to share one common feature: let them be staffed with experts in the pedagogy of human behaviour rather than the law. In New Zealand in 1910, when it was proposed that a judge be head of the newly constituted Prison Board, one MP claimed that 'I would not have a judge at all. What does a judge know about prison life? I admit he knows all about the law and inflicting a sentence for breach of the laws, but of gaol, well, he knows nothing' (NZPD vol 151, p 513).

This increased protection that governments were prepared to offer their citizens can be seen as having a twofold effect: (i) it maximised the potential of populations in general and (ii) it was a means of regulating their individual subjects by ensuring their conformity to the standards and norms that had thus been established (Foucault 1979). In this way, a relationship of dependency was created between citizens and governments. In return for conformity to a range of standards, governments would offer protection from dangers and risks. A set of assurances were given. A set of expectations were created, above all, perhaps, that the individual in modern Western society had a 'right to life' (Foucault 1979), a right which thus marks out modernity from both the pre-enlightenment era and other non-Western societies today.

This was not, though, a uniform and even tendency. As we have seen, protection against the perils of old age, against illness and so on, were well advanced before 'public protection' became a criterion in the dangerous offender legislation. Since this time, the threat to one's physical well-being has gradually displaced the threat to property that dangerous offenders constituted. Indeed, in the post-1970 period, alongside the economic and social changes designed to maximise life potential ('getting the State out of our lives' etc), sensitivity to personal violence and sexual attack has steadily increased. The growth of the women's movement, the development of women's refuges, and various forms of consciousness raising against the above types of crime, have all played a part in heightening sensitivities towards them, to the extent that the dangers and threat that they pose to human life have become intolerable (as opposed to being merely criminal).

However, if we accept the very stylised division that Foucault makes of the interplay between power and life in the pre and post-enlightenment eras, then, developing the argument further, it would seem to be the case that in the latter period, the investiture of the right to life has at the same time heightened sensitivities to forms of behaviour which might otherwise threaten it. As life itself became something to be cherished and protected, so did the dangers to it seem more abundant and threatening. If we are going to make more of life, then, inevitably, we are going to make more of the dangers to it. How has this come about? One of the immediate consequences of the fostering of life was the accompanying decline in security, as if life itself was never more precious nor more threatened. Increasing reliance on state protection in the modern period meant that this replaced the more intimate and personalised relationships of trust and dependence of the pre-industrial world:

> ... trust in abstract systems is the condition of time-space distanciation and of the large areas of security in day-to-day life which modern institutions offer as compared to the traditional world. The routines which are integrated with abstract systems are central to ontological security in conditions of modernity. Yet this situation also creates novel forms of psychological vulnerability, and trust in abstract systems is not psychologically rewarding in the way in which trust in persons is. (Giddens 1990:113)

In other words, this decline of the local community and its replacement with more abstracted systems of protection and order, inevitably led to a much greater privatisation of everyday life. In relation to our understanding of a particular phenomenon such as crime, this has meant a reliance on more remote sources of news and information — reliance on the mass media rather than neighbours, for example. In this way the presentation of the risks and threats from the phenomenon of crime become both more globalised and more localised (Giddens 1990). As is well known, the presentation of information about crime to us makes it appear to be 'everywhere' and at the same time localises its particular threat to us, however much the real threat of crime is unequally distributed across the population and however much the threat of particular crimes varies enormously. Nonetheless, the fact that our sources of information about crime highlight the existence of 'dangerous criminals' makes them a potential threat to all of us, however oblique and far removed the distance between 'them' and 'us'. In this way, it is as if a 'chronic and sporadically acute anxiety about crime ... ' (Sparks 1992:12) has become an institutionalised feature of modern society. And in this way, the right to life has been accompanied by the immanence of personal threat.

Risk Management and Insurance

The growth of and the particular emphases in the dangerousness legislation of the last two decades can be seen as a testament to this phenomenon. Yet, while these measures have been introduced, responsibility for the management of crime risks and others is in the process of undergoing dramatic change. Governments have begun to off-load many of their previous insurantial responsibilities of the last hundred years onto the private and voluntary sector. The economic rationales and fiscal imperatives associated with these moves are clear enough (see Gamble 1988) but they have also been justified by the collapse of faith in what had come to be the traditional strategies of life management of the same period (cf Giddens 1990): in relation to crime, a collapse of faith in the ability of policing and welfare institutions to safeguard their citizens and provide them with the security that had been their task. Rates of recorded crime continue to escalate in modern societies, sometimes dramatically so. Thus in New Zealand, for example, the general level of recorded crime has increased from 165,859 offences

18   (1995) 28 The Australian and New Zealand Journal of Criminology

in 1970 to 537,295 in 1992. More particularly, 15,253 offences of violence were recorded in 1979, as opposed to 29,120 in 1992 and over the same period reported sexual crimes increased from 2,552 in 1979 to 4,263 in 1992. This is in spite of the huge investment of public resources in experts of various kinds whose task it should have been to protect citizens from the risk of crime. The police cannot manage the problem on their own any more, it is now claimed — not least by the police themselves; parole boards are suspected of letting high risk criminals out of prison too early; probation officers are thought to write over-sympathetic reports, representing the criminal as a victim; judges are too lenient and so on. This collapse of faith has had considerable impact on the management of crime risk. Two distinct trends have emerged.

On the one hand, it is as if governments, through the dangerousness legislation, are offering their citizens a form of enhanced insurance against the risks they face from such criminals of today. Indeed, it seems that this is becoming a form of fully comprehensive insurance, in the light of legislation designed to reduce the 'blameworthiness' of the victims of such crimes, eg changing the rules of evidence and procedure in rape and child sexual abuse cases, both to try and shift any element of culpability away from the victim, as well as helping to make these offences easier to report and prosecute (see Sullivan 1985; Saphira 1992; New Zealand Crimes Amendment Act 1985).

Furthermore, the risk from such offenders is seen as intolerable, because of the affront and outrage that such crimes now evoke in the public sensitivity and because dangerousness has now come to be associated with life threatening behaviour. Thus in Canada the proposed new dangerousness legislation is justified on the grounds that:

> The federal government has come under increasing pressure to reform the correctional system to better protect society against dangerous offenders, such as repeat, high-risk sex offenders and those who have a history of violent offences ... The government has responded to this growing concern with a series of proposals that would tighten the system for these offenders and improve public protection. (Solicitor General of Canada 1993:1)

But it is also a risk that ordinary citizens cannot insure themselves against. This is because the threat from dangerous offenders is too unpredictable, too random, and its consequences too serious for citizens to insure themselves against in the usual way. And it is a risk with both generalised and localised effects: although (fortunately) it is a risk which happens to hardly anybody, it presents a danger that *could* happen to anybody, such is the nature of dangerousness. Historically, this legal construct 'dangerousness' was never considered to be a property of the demonstrably insane — people who could be identified and then avoided at all costs. This remains the case in the post 1970 period: 'what is a dangerous person? No such entity exists in the nosology of psychiatry' (Kozol et al 1972:379). As a consequence, this risk is all the more unpredictable since the danger is likely to come from otherwise ordinary people who continue to disregard the law until they are eventually discovered.

Dangerousness, Risk and Technologies of Power 19

Thus the crucial aspect of the insurance that the dangerous legislation offers is not financial compensation but the minimisation of risk from such offenders:

> What is insured is not the injury that is actually lived, suffered and resented by the person it happens to, but a capital against whose loss the insurer offers a guarantee. [This is because] the lived injury is irreparable: afterwards can never be the same as before. (Ewald 1991:204)

But this enhancement of insurance against dangerous offenders at one end of the penal spectrum should be seen in conjunction with the current focus on situational crime prevention at the other: how to insure against those crimes such as burglary, where the risk is significantly greater, those crimes *'to which we are all vulnerable'* (Victoria Police, referred to by O'Malley 1991:10, my italics). In this realm, responsibility for risk management is increasingly devolved from central administration to that at a local level, effectively limiting the form and amount of insurance that governments provide. This is not to say that they simply opt out of any responsibility for risk management, rather, the extent and nature of insurance cover is to be left to citizens and local organisations to decide amongst themselves. In effect, communities have been given 'ownership of the crime problem' (Prime Ministerial Safer Communities Council 1992:1). In relation to non-dangerous offending, they are increasingly expected to mobilise their own resources against the risks they face.

The nature of this mobilisation may take the form of citizens taking out their own cover through private insurance schemes or the hire of private security firms. They may buy into the defensible space architecture, join local community protection groups that offer surveillance of surrounding territory such as Neighbourhood Watch, or join citizens groups more actively involved in patrolling local areas, such as 'Crime Busters' and the 'Nighthawks'. Here, then, and in opposition to the 'stand alone' emphasis in police work on technology, specialisation and professionalism of the 1960s (Reiner 1985), a kind of partnership at a local level is forged with the police: citizens are exhorted to become 'the eyes and ears' of the police. Indeed, it is now claimed that 'crime prevention should be an essential part of the daily routine for the whole community, by making it second nature to consider crime prevention possibilities and weaknesses, the scope of the opportunistic, selfish and thoughtless petty offender can be drastically reduced' (Home Office 23 May 1988, referred to by King 1989:299). The redistribution of risk management involves the forging of new structures for the prevention of crime, or at least the prevention of non-dangerous crime, in the light of the perceived failure or inability to cope, of the more traditional methods of law enforcement and policing.

It might also be argued that this redistribution of risk informs the disposition of punishment and influences the bifurcatory trends referred to earlier. The current confinement of dangerousness legislation to violent and sexual offenders means that habitual and professional criminals are no longer thought to be sufficient a risk to justify the kind of insurance that such measures offer. Indeed, it would seem that in most jurisdictions it has become the intention to keep the habituals out of prison altogether rather than have them serve extended prison terms. It

20   (1995) 28 The Australian and New Zealand Journal of Criminology

was for this very purpose that day training centres, run by the probation service, were introduced in England and Wales in the mid 1970s (see eg Haxby 1978). The habituals, as characterised by West above, for example, came only to be an embarrassment within the prison - a sign of its inhumanity alongside the growing recognition that such expensive penal resources should not be wasted on them. Instead, let them wonder endlessly around our cities arm in arm with the other human relics that the modern state is no longer prepared to house or assume responsibility for. As for the professionals, it may now be that this group are likely to be the subject of longer finite prison sentences rather than be seen as appropriate for indeterminate prison terms, notwithstanding the lack of detailed empirical evidence in support of this contention (although see eg Radzinowicz 1968; Sparks 1971). It may thus be that here we find a relatively undisturbed space for the classical principles of responsibility, deterrence and proportionality. Long, but finite terms of imprisonment become a professional risk for this group (see Cohen & Taylor 1972).

The overall result would seem to be that governments *appear* to offer more insurantial protection, with the sharper focus and enhancement of the dangerousness legislation, while actually offering less overall, as a result of the devolution of the management of much more likely crime risk. Furthermore, sets of assurances by governments that they will offer enhanced protection against those regarded as dangerous may well serve the function of bolstering the *conscience collective* in the manner which I noted earlier; as indeed may the community crime prevention projects now coming into force: they may generate a form of social solidarity between respective social groups and individuals, rather than between citizens and government as has hitherto been the case. Indeed, in New Zealand, a recent crime prevention advert (sponsored by the police) states that 'your neighbours are your first line of defence against crime. Getting to know your neighbours is your first step in fighting back'. But more than this, these two themes — dangerousness and crime prevention — would seem to be representative of a more general reordering of the relationship between governments and citizens. It is not so much that they prop up a threatened *conscience collective* as being new forms of risk management in the post 1970 emerging social order.

New Technologies of Power

If the foregoing has attempted to explain the significance of and particular constitution of dangerousness today, let us now turn to the issue of its calculation: what makes possible the assessment of dangerousness today on the basis of a propensity to commit future offences? How is this to be gaged? The 1970s collapse of faith in criminal justice experts extended to the clinical psychologists and their powers of diagnosis and assessment. In reflection of this, Bottoms (1977:82) directs our attention to the now well-known diagnostic difficulties in determining the particular 'condition' of propensity to commit future crime:

> ... one must question the psychiatrist's assumption of the role of the scientific expert. Believing as he usually does that crime is a naturalistic category ... the

psychiatrist naturally believes in the natural science paradigm to the phenomenon in question, and that behavioural science experts can materially assist with the prediction and treatment of deviant behaviour.

In the USA the famous Baxstrom affair (see Steadman & Cocozza 1974) illustrated the way in which psychologists were likely to over-diagnose offenders as dangerous. In England, such a tendency posed a major ethical problem for the Butler Committee (referred to by Bottoms 1977:77): 'the tendency will generally be to err on the side of caution, with the result that some people will continue to be detained who, if released, would not commit further violent offences . . . '

However, what has become clear in recent years is that the predictive vacuum is now being filled by a new technology of power — actuarialism: that is, the application of base rate data and statistical methods to the task of categorising individuals by locating them within taxonomic subgroups. Such practises are expressed in discourses which see 'the replacement of a moral or clinical description of the individual with an actuarial language of probabilistic calculations and statistical distributions applied to populations' (Feeley & Simon 1992:452). Such techniques 'target offenders as an aggregate in place of traditional techniques for individualising or creating equity' (ibid p 450). In point of fact, these methods of classification, assessment and *prediction* have been present in many aspects of modern society for over a century now. If their use in such areas as insurance and taxation seems familiar and banal, they nonetheless represent an important tactic of control over the individuals and their categorisation and classification (eg credit worthiness and educational ability) and thus a tactic of control that exists *in addition to* those of discipline and surveillance referred to earlier. In the original sites of actuarial power, 'social insurance, worker's compensation, income tax and similar devices created forms of management that did not need to rely on the cumbersome techniques of individual discipline' (Simon 1988:774).

The application of actuarial methods to the administration of criminal justice has only recently begun to be addressed (see eg Reichman 1986; Feeley & Simon 1992; O'Malley 1992) as its techniques become increasingly sophisticated. The first significant criminological prediction study seems to have been by Burgess (1928) in relation to likely success or failure of parole cases; the higher an individual's score of independent variables thought to be important in determining parole success, the better the post release prognosis (Brown 1991:24). Glueck and Glueck (1930) then used actuarial methods to predict delinquency in young men released from a reformatory, this time weighting the independent variables rather than simply awarding them equal scores. Mannheim and Wilkins (1955) produced one of the first significant post war prediction studies, now using multivariate statistics, their subject being the likely success or failure of borstal trainees. But, in general terms, the deficiencies of the clinical approach in relation to the prediction of human behaviour has been well known for some considerable time. Meehl (1954) argued that actuarialism was both a more accurate and efficient method of prediction:

22   (1995) 28 The Australian and New Zealand Journal of Criminology

... arrived at by some straightforward application of an equation or table to the data. I do not mean the word in its usual pejorative sense. *This table, let me emphasise, does not have to be a table of individuals. The elements of such a table may be episodes or occasions in the life of one person. The defining property is that no judging or inferring or weighting is done by a skilled clinician. [Indeed] once the data have been gathered from whatever source and of whatever type, the prediction itself could be turned over to a clerical worker.* (Meehl 1954:15–16, my italics)

Yet, at this point, when dangerousness was being linked to public protection and, ultimately, future offending, the lack of adequate prediction methods to accomplish such tasks was quickly noted. Thus Morris (1951:29):

... prediction tables have not, as yet, been constructed in England. In the USA such tables have been prepared and tested in the light of experience, and it is certain that they are more efficient prognostic instruments than the 'magic eye' of 'sound common sense' on which we rely.

Similarly Hammond and Chayen (1963:177):

... what is required is information about the probability that a man who commits an offence of personal violence will commit another such offence; that a man who sexually molests children will do something of the same again. It is rather startling to find how little we have in the way of estimates of such probabilities.

And Simon (1971:13): 'in 1962 very few States in the USA were actually using prediction tables. This still appears to be the case'. One at least of the reasons for this was the lack of appropriate technology to carry out these tasks, as acknowledged by Mannheim and Wilkins (1955:144) in relation to their own research:

Since we had in all 60 zero order correlations we should have needed to calculate a total of over 1200 correlation coefficients if we were to examine the overlap of each of these with each other. Whilst this task in itself would have been formidable and well outside the budget which was available for the complete project, these calculations would have been only the first stage and the later calculations would have been almost impossible ...

As such, actuarialism as a *method* had yet to be linked to dangerousness; as a criminal justice *practise*, it was confined to respective and discrete sites of administrative decision-making — determining classification, early release and so on. In other words, it had yet to claim a space in the courtroom itself and operate arm in arm with juridical power. Up to this point, assessment of dangerousness was still the prerogative of clinical psychologists and the like. From the 1970s though, actuarialism begins to fill the predictive vacuum created by the subsequent collapse of faith in this form of expertise. Where clinical diagnosis was shown to be flawed, actuarialism would reduce the opportunity for human error by means of the statistical collation of profiles to fit the 'dangerous population' as a whole. More efficient, then as fewer wrong diagnoses would be made; but at the same time, it would be more liberal and humane. The clinicians, as we have seen, were thought too eager to classify offenders as dangerous. In the democracies, the whole point about such legislation and the powers it gave to groups of criminal justice professionals was that it was intended to be used sparingly as some kind of residual measure.

Able to do all that the clinical method could not do, able to remedy all that the clinical method was doing wrong, from this time on there is a growing shift towards actuarialism in the prediction of dangerousness. Thus, a prediction scale was devised for these purposes by Cocozza and Steadman (1974). The importance and implications of actuarial methods were recognised in Floud and Young (1981:276):

> ... the actuarial method has great practical advantages which we widely acknowledge. It is relatively cheap and it is exact and consistent. It is efficient in selecting relevant items of information and giving them weight according to their importance. It produces optimum classifications which yield the highest probabilities with the fewest mistakes.

Similarly, Morris and Miller (1985:3) make the point that 'present predictive capacities will prove to be the best we have for several decades ...' Most significantly for our purposes, Duckitt (1988:14), reviewing the shift from clinical to actuarial methods in this realm, was able to claim that:

> A decade ago the criterion being predicted was not violence risk but dangerous behaviour. The crucial concept was that of 'dangerousness', which was a real attribute of the individual — and more specifically, a clinical diagnostic category ... The shift which has occurred subsequently has been to discard the concept of dangerousness completely in favour of that of violence risk. *The latter is a frankly statistical and probabilistic concept, and does not indicate any real attribute of the individual at all.* (my italics)

In other words, actuarialism involves a shift away from the study of individual behaviour, the property of individuals and towards the calculation of risk, the presumed attribute of a population.

As the shift towards actuarialism has occurred, so too have its methods become increasingly sophisticated: 'disquiet with multiple regression led in the 1960s to the use of hierarchical clustering techniques, such as configural analysis ... and automatic interaction dector analysis. These techniques essentially aim to classify a heterogeneous population into homogenous subgroups' (Farrington & Tarling 1988:18–19). But, of course, what has helped to make this task more possible in the current era has been the introduction of computer technology to criminal justice administration. Indeed, the nexus it thus makes with actuarialism allows the drive towards the prediction of future crime in the dangerousness legislation of today. The efficacy of the computer over the expert was demonstrated by Hassin (1980) in relation to early prison release and crime prediction. Again, it was not just claimed to be more efficient; as human beings and their sentiments were left progressively out of both the calculation and the calculating, it was also claimed to be more humane. In this way the prediction of dangerousness becomes just one function of computerised justice systems. Armed with a computer, it becomes possible for a new type of expert — the criminal justice consultant — to predict crime patterns, sentencing trends and so on.

24   (1995) 28 The Australian and New Zealand Journal of Criminology

Clearly, though, this shift towards actuarialism has been an uneven development. In New Zealand, for example, the 1993 legislation stipulates that a sentence of preventive detention cannot be imposed before the court has obtained a psychiatric report on the offender which, by inference, is obtained by clinical methods. However, its use in the prediction of dangerousness may be gaining pace in the USA. In support of such trends, Gottfredson and Gottfredson (1988:262) claim that:

> [a] common feature of every major decision in criminal justice systems is the ubiquitous centrality of prediction. Often hidden, seldom verified and increasingly denied justifiable relevance, the forecast of future behavioural states ... is everywhere in evidence ... In elevating a model for the enhancement of rationality one must take cognisance of the central role of predictive judgements throughout the system and include mechanisms by which they can be improved.

Equally, Farrington and Tarling (1988:9) claim that:

> ... most of the advances in the use of prediction methods in criminology have occurred in the area of parole prediction, and prediction methods have had their greatest influence on parole procedures ... [but] there have been many other examples of the use of prediction techniques for individuals. Predictions can aid ... decisions to report a crime, to call the police, to arrest a suspect, to release on bail, to charge a suspect; and correctional decisions such as level of custody, treatment progress, after care progress and work assignment.

Actuarialism can bring 'rationality' to the world of criminal justice, the dream of all the reformers since the enlightenment. Actuarialism's logic, rather than human discretion, is the key to a more efficient, more just, justice system, its advocates seem to say. This power to classify and predict offers a new kind of expertise that has the potential to bring its adherents great status and prestige, outstripping that of their erstwhile, but now much discredited rivals, the clinicians. Indeed, the ability to predict — and thus it might seem prevent — future crime is never going to be reduced to the mere clerical performance envisaged by Meehl. But if this in itself will bring it out of the shadows of executive decision-making and allow it to take its place in the law courts, it seems likely to be a contested struggle: for example, between it and a judiciary which has never been keen to share power with newcomers.

Might it not be thought, in opposition, that such modes of prediction are a little too futuristic? Why, though, should this concern us, the actuarialists would argue. What is so different about using prediction methods to reduce the risk of crime, particularly the risk we face from dangerous offenders? Are not such practises already in use in other areas of the social body? For example, 'insurance companies set their premiums in accord with their experience of accidents or the frequency of the conditions against which they offer indemnity. If in the field of criminal justice there are decisions that are essentially similar to the insurance companies in fixing their premiums, then the experience or base expectancy tables prepared by similar means are similarly useful ...' (Wilkins 1988:39).

Discipline, surveillance and prediction

In conclusion, let us try and summarise the significance of the dangerousness legislation today. First, in terms of who is now considered to be a danger, the current laws reflect the way in which 'the right to life' in modern Western societies has been progressively both cherished and put at risk in recent times. The more value that is placed upon this expectation, the more it becomes besieged by the menace and threat that is thought to surround it. Second, in terms of the management of this threat, they form one aspect of the more general redistribution of risk management that has taken place in the post 1970 period and they represent an area where more protection seems to have been given. Yet the particular risk from the dangerous offender is not only slight, but the dangerousness legislation itself, it would appear, continues to be law that is hardly ever used. The Victorian Community Protection Act was directed at one offender (Craze 1992); in New Zealand, six sentences of preventive detention were imposed between 1982 and 1986; in 1987, coinciding with the fresh dangerousness legislation and concerns about violent and sexual crime, the number of such sentences rose to 10; in the succeeding years the average has been 5.5. As such, the legislation has more symbolic than real effects; it is not only a reflection of the abhorrence of what is felt to be the most reprehensible form of behaviour at any given time, but it is also a reflection of what the state is prepared to do to protect its citizens from such behaviour. By providing 'guarantees' against this risk, such as it is, the state is even prepared to move beyond the boundaries that mark the limits of law and punishment in democratic societies. Hence the laws themselves continue to be residual, symbolic powers, providing containment explicitly on the basis of such extra-legal criteria as public protection and propensity to commit future crime. To extend such criteria across the population at large would be to indicate that we had moved from democracy to totalitarianism; would be to threaten the value that is now placed on life. In relation to more general levels of protection from crime, though, governments have devolved responsibility for this onto local communities themselves.

In terms of the calculation of dangerousness, this brings to our attention the growth of actuarial power — the power to predict. As I have indicated, this power and the knowledge it produces has a history that goes back to the origins of modern society itself. Its emergence as a form of power in the criminal justice realm was, until recently, restricted to discrete administrative sites. In entering the domain of dangerousness, it begins to vie openly with juridical power itself. It does not displace strategies of discipline and surveillance: indeed, as I reflected earlier, it has had an integral role in the ordering and regulation of modern society — alongside these other tactics. But clearly, the particular importance and location of these three strategies of control is going to vary from time to time and the social and political changes of the post 1970 period make possible the growth of actuarial power in the control of crime. The collapse of faith in the ability of welfare expertise to manage the crime problem, the growth of computer technology, the reification of 'life', the

26   (1995) 28 The Australian and New Zealand Journal of Criminology

sensitivity to conduct endangering it, converge to make actuarial power appear to have the solution to the problems of crime prediction and management.

This would seem to mark an important shift in the regulation and control of crime and deviance. In contrast to tactics of discipline and surveillance, actuarialism involves a different mode of regulation. Its task is to be informative — to produce knowledge that others will then use, rather than attempt to control offenders' thoughts or keep a check on their whereabouts. In relation to dangerousness, it can provide us with a profile, so that we may then be able to gage the individual against this and make an appropriate judgement. Not though, so that we can change their behaviour (see Cohen 1985); but rather, so that we can identify and contain such individuals. As Reichman (1986:157) suggests, 'one way to manage the problem of crime is to prevent those who present high risks of offending from entry into certain types of social relationships'.

Contain, then, at one end of the spectrum and at the other: change the behaviour not of criminals any more, but of potential victims and change their behaviour not through the old techniques of counselling etc, but by allowing them to make choices through recourse to the information and identification of risks that actuarialism provides. Indeed, the role of actuarial power in the current social order seems to be predicated on an altogether different model of human behaviour from that to be found in the pre-1970 period. Then, there was a dependence on governments for protection, security and regulation. Now human beings are recast as atomised calculating machines. They must make 'rational choices' in relation to crime management and risk reduction. It is only where the risk is most minimal and most unknowable — the threat from dangerous offenders — that governments are currently prepared to increase their insurantial responsibilities.[6]

Acknowledgements

I would like to thank the following individuals who have variously provided me with helpful information, support, encouragement and new ideas during the preparation of this paper: Mark Brown, Kevin White, Arie Freiberg, Philip Stenning and John Meek.

Notes

1. In France, the sanction of relegation — committal to an institution for an indefinite time for vagrants, petty offenders etc — was introduced in 1885 and appears to be the forerunner of preventive detention.
2. However, the subsequent Act did introduce a register for those penal servitude prisoners released on license.
3. I must point out here that Bottoms (1977:76) clearly does cover some of the ground between the genesis of dangerousness and its formulation in the post 1970 period.
4. The inquisitorial systems of the European countries would seem to lend themselves more readily than those in the Anglo-Welsh

tradition to Tarde's (1912:450) injunction that 'even in the school of law perhaps it would be a good thing to compel young men who felt that they had a "criminological" calling to visit malefactors in prison and to make a psychological if not physical, and before everything, biographical and domestic study of some of these persons, a kind of moral vivisection'.

5. An exception to the rule here is found in the 1993 legislation. The crime of rape, even if a first offence, can be punished with preventive detention.

6. This paper was presented at the 9th Annual Australian and New Zealand Society of Criminology Conference, University of Sydney, September 1993.

References

Advisory Council on the Treatment of Offenders (1963) *Preventive Detention*, HMSO, London.

Alper, B & Boren, J (1972) *Crime: An International Agenda*, Lexington Books, Lexington.

Ancel, M (1965) *Social Defence*, Routledge & Kegan Paul, London.

Bottoms, A E (1977) 'Reflections on the renaissance of dangerousness', *Howard Journal of Penology and Crime Prevention* vol 16, pp 70–96.

Bottoms, A E (1983) 'Neglected features of contemporary penal systems', in *The Power to Punish*, eds D Garland & P Young, Heinemann, London.

Bottoms, A E & Brownsword, R (1982) 'The dangerousness debate after the Floud Report', *British Journal of Criminology* vol 22, pp 229–254.

Brown, M (1991) *An analysis of decision making in district prison boards*, PhD Thesis, Victoria University, Wellington.

Burgess, E (1928) 'Factors determining success or failure on parole', in *The Workings of the Indeterminate Sentence Law and Parole in Illinois* ed A Bruce, Springfield, Illinois.

Castels, R. (1991), 'From dangerousness to risk', in *The Foucault Effect*, eds G Burchell et al, Harvester Press, Brighton.

Chan, J & Ericson, R (1981) *Decarceration and the Economy of Penal Reform*, Centre of Criminology, University of Toronto, Toronto.

Cohen, S (1985) *Visions of Social Control*, Polity Press, Cambridge.

Cohen, S & Taylor, L (1972) *Psychological Survival*, Penguin, Harmondsworth.

Craze, L (1992) *The lure of relevance: The politics of crime research*, paper presented at 8th Australia and New Zealand Society of Criminology Annual Conference.

Department of Justice (1891) *Annual Report to Parliament*, Wellington.

Department of Justice (1906) *Annual Report to Parliament*, Wellington.

Department of Justice (1948) *Annual Report to Parliament*, Wellington.

28 (1995) 28 The Australian and New Zealand Journal of Criminology

Department of Justice (1954) *Annual Report to Parliament*, Wellington.

Department of Justice (1965) *Annual Report to Parliament*, Wellington.

Duckitt, J (1988) 'The prediction of violence', *South African Journal of Psychology* vol 18, pp 10–16.

Ewald, F (1991) 'Insurance and risk', in *The Foucault Effect*, eds F Burchell et al, Harvester Press, Brighton.

Farrington, D & Tarling, R (1988) 'Criminological prediction: An introduction', in *Prediction in Criminology*, eds D Farrington & R Tarling, State University of New York Press, Albany.

Feeley, M & Simon, J (1992) 'The new penology: Notes on the emerging strategy of corrections and its implications', *Criminology* vol 30, pp 449–474.

Ferri, E (1906) *The Positive School of Criminology*, Charles Kerr & Co, Chicago.

Floud, J & Young, W (1981) *Dangerousness and Criminal Justice*, Cambridge University Press, Cambridge.

Foucault, M (1977) *Discipline and Punish*, Allen Lane, London.

Foucault, M (1979) *The History of Sexuality, vol 1: An Introduction*, Allen Lane, London.

Foucault, M (1988) 'The dangerous individual', in *Politics, Philosophy and Culture*, pp 125–151, Routledge, London.

Gamble, A (1988) *The Free Economy and the Strong State*, Macmillan, London.

Garland, D (1985) *Punishment and Welfare*, Gower, London.

Garofalo, R (1914) *Criminology*, Little Brown, Boston.

Giddens, A (1990) *The Consequences of Modernity*, Polity Press, Cambridge.

Glueck, S & Glueck, E (1930) *500 Criminal Careers*, Harvard University Press, New York.

Gottfredson, S & Gottfredson, D (1988) 'Violence prediction methods: Statistical and clinical strategies', *Violence and Victims* vol 3, pp 303–324.

Grunhut, M (1948) *Penal Reform*, Clarendon Press, Oxford.

Hall Williams, J (1967) *The English Penal System in Transition*, Butterworth, London.

Hammond, W & Chayen, E (1963) *Persistent Criminals*, HMSO, London.

Hassin, Y (1980) 'Early release committees for prisoners versus the computer', *Criminology* vol 18, p 385–397.

Haxby, D (1978) *Probation: A Changing Service*, Constable, London.

King, M (1989) 'Social crime prevention à la Thatcher', *Howard Journal of Criminal Justice* vol 28, pp 385–397.

Kozol, H et al (1972) 'The diagnosis and treatment of dangerousness', *Crime and Delinquency* vol 18, pp 371–392.

Kramer, R (1982) 'From "habitual offenders" to "career criminals": The historical construction and development of criminal categories", *Law and Human Behaviour* vol 6, pp 273–293.

Mannheim, H (1936) 'The German Prevention of Crime Act 1933', *Journal of Criminal Law and Criminology* vol 26, pp 517–537.

Mannheim, H & Wilkins, L (1955) *Prediction Methods in Relation to Borstal Training*, HMSO, London.

Matthews, R (1979) 'Decarceration and the fiscal crisis', in *Capitalism and the Rule of Law*, eds B Fine et al, Hutchinson, London.

Meehl, P (1954) *Clinical versus Statistical Prediction: A Theoretical Analysis and Review of the Evidence*, University of Minnesota Press, Minneapolis.

Miller, M & Morris, N (1988) 'Predictions of dangerousness: an argument for limited use', *Violence and Victims* vol 3, p 263–283.

Morris, N (1951) *The Habitual Criminal*, Publications of the London School of Economics, London.

Morris, N & Miller, M (1985) 'Predictions of dangerousness', in *Crime and Justice: An International Review of Research 6*, eds M Tonry & N Morris, pp 1–50.

O'Malley, P (1991) 'Legal networks and domestic security', *Studies in Law and Politics 11*.

O'Malley, P (1992) 'Risk, power, and crime prevention', *Economy and Society* vol 21, pp 252–275.

Pasquino, P (1991) 'Criminology: the birth of a special knowledge', in *The Foucault Effect: Studies in Governmentality*, eds G Burchell et al, Harvester, Brighton.

Pratt, J (1992) *Punishment in a Perfect Society*, Victoria University Press, Wellington.

Prime Ministerial Safer Communities Council (1993), Wellington.

Proposals to amend the Corrections and Conditional Release Act and the Criminal Code (1993), Ottawa.

Radzinowicz, L (1968) 'The dangerous offender', *The Police Journal* vol 9, pp 411–467.

Radzinowicz, L & Hood, R (1980) 'Habitual criminals', *Michigan Law Review* vol 78, pp 1305–1380.

Radzinowicz, L & Hood, R (1985) *A History of English Criminal Law*, vol 5, Butterworth, London.

Reichman, N (1986) 'Managing crime risks: Towards an insurance based model of social control', *Law, Deviance and Social Control* vol 8, pp 151–172.

Reiner, R (1985) *The Politics of the Police*, Wheatsheaf Books, Brighton.

Report from the Departmental Committee on Prisons (1895), Cmnd No 7702, 56, Parliamentary Papers.

30 (1995) 28 The Australian and New Zealand Journal of Criminology

Rusche, G & Kirchheimer, O (1939) *Punishment and Social Structure*, Russell & Russell, New York.

Saleilles, R (1911) *The Individualisation of Punishment*, Little Brown & Co, Boston.

Saphira, M (1992) *Stopping Child Abuse: How Do We Bring Up New Zealand Children?*, Penguin, Auckland.

Scottish Council on Crime (1975), *Crime and the Prevention of Crime*, HMSO, London.

Simon, F (1971) *Prediction Methods in Criminology*, HMSO, London.

Simon, J (1988) 'The ideological effects of actuarial practises', *Law and Society Review* vol 22, pp 771–800.

Solicitor General of Canada (1993), *Proposed New Law to Protect Public from Dangerous Offenders*, Ottawa.

Sparks, R F (1971) *Local Prisons: The Crisis in the English Penal System*, Heinemann, London.

Sparks, R (1992) *Television and the Drama of Crime*, Open University Press, Milton Keynes.

Steadman, H & Cocozza, J (1974) *Careers of the Criminally Insane: Excessive Social Control of Deviance*, D C Heath, Lexington.

Sullivan, G (1986) *Rape Crisis Handbook*, Rape Crisis Centre, Wellington.

Sutherland, E (1950) 'The diffusion of the sexual psychopath laws', *American Journal of Sociology* vol 56, pp 142–148.

Tarde, G (1912) *Penal Philosophy*, Heinemann, London.

Victoria Sentencing Committee (1988), *Report*, Melbourne.

von Hirsch, A (1972) 'Prediction of criminal conduct and preventive confinement of convicted persons', *Buffalo Law Review* vol 21, pp 717–758.

Walker, N (1969) *Sentencing in a Rational Society*, Penguin, Harmondsworth.

Walker, N (1980) *Punishment, Danger and Stigma*, Basil Blackwell, Oxford.

Wearing, M & Berreen R (1993) *Disability, Crime and Classification in late 19th century and early 20th Century New South Wales*, paper presented at the 9th Annual Conference of the Australian and New Zealand Society of Criminology.

Webb, P (1981) *A History of Custodial and Related Penalties in New Zealand*, Government Printer, Wellington.

West, D (1963) *The Habitual Prisoner*, Macmillan, London.

Wiener, M (1990) *Reconstructing the Criminal*, Cambridge University Press, Cambridge.

Wilkins, L (1988) 'The politics of prediction', in *Prediction in Criminology*, eds D Farrington & R Tarling, State University of New York Press, Albany.

Wolff, J (1993) *Crime Policy against Juveniles and Crime Control during the Nazi-Period in Germany*, paper presented at the 11th International Congress on Criminology, Budapest.

[15]

When Have We Punished Enough?

Edwin W. Zedlewski, National Institute of Justice

Today's criminal justice system is in a state of crisis over prison crowding. Even though national prison capacity has expanded, it has not kept pace with demands. While capacity in state prisons grew from an estimated 243,500 bed spaces in 1978 to 365,817 bed spaces by 1983, state prison populations had grown from 270,025 to 399,072 inmates.[1] National attention has focused on prison crowding. But the common cry among corrections professionals is not a need for more prisons but a need for alternatives to incarceration.

The search for alternatives to prison is curious inasmuch as public sentiment calls for more punishment. Recent legislative changes to penal codes in the form of mandatory prison terms for drunk drivers and for gun crimes, plus calls for the abolition of parole boards, argue for more prison space. Yet many professionals resist, arguing that prison construction is too expensive and does little for the reduction of crime.[2]

Do we need more prisons or more alternatives to prison construction? Before such questions can be answered, we need more information on both the costs and benefits of punishment. Since so many elements of the sentencing decision, such as victim harm, justice, and public fear, defy quantification, any picture will be necessarily incomplete. Nonetheless, the data assembled here quantify many of the missing benefits of prison capacity and thereby contribute to debate over prison crowding and alternative sentencing.

Significantly, even discarding the emotional and psychological costs mentioned, the data strongly support the need for more prison capacity. Subsequent sections of this paper apply the social cost-benefit framework to alternate uses of scarce prison space and the choice of alternatives to incarceration. These sections are less prescriptive because research findings are less definitive. They are sufficient, however, to offer at least some recommendations for policy makers.

The Social Cost of Crime

Gary Becker first sketched an analytic framework for deciding upon optimal expenditure for crime control.[3] By advancing the notion that the criminal justice system ought to minimize the "net social harm" of crime, Becker recognized that while expenditures to reduce crime drained resources, crime imposed other costs upon a community. There is nothing mystical about

■ *Do we need more prisons or more alternatives to incarceration and prison construction? Based on available data, the analysis here suggests that greater social benefits are derived from prison incarceration than are usually assumed; it indicates overwhelming support for more prison capacity. The case for current use of probation and fines is less clear, since less data are available on the application of these sanctions. It, nonetheless, appears that social costs would be reduced if more probationers were given either prison terms or fines. This analysis also indicates that punitive fines for first offenders would have a deterrent effect and would reduce expenditures on prison supervision, while producing revenues and perhaps compensating victims.*

these so-called social costs. Home and business security systems, victim losses, and prematurely abandoned buildings are as much expenditures on crime as prisons and police salaries.

Three kinds of costs are involved: harm to victims, combating or preventing crime, and punishing offenders. Their sum represents the social cost of crime. These elements are interdependent in that an increase in punishment can simultaneously increase punishment costs and decrease victim and prevention expenditures. The trick is to find the balance among the elements that minimizes the total crime bill.

Available data cannot determine with precise accuracy what criminal justice expenditures ought to be to minimize net social costs. However, the logic of spending no more on a problem than one can realize in return is useful in examining sentencing decisions. There is now, moreover, sufficient data available to enable us to assess the direction—more or less prison—toward which sentencing should move.

Estimates of the social costs relevant to imprisonment decisions are generated using the notion of balancing the harm from crime against the costs of incarceration. Admittedly, this exercise is artificial in that defendants are imprisoned for a variety of reasons—retribution, rehabilitation, just deserts among them. Minimizing

Edwin W. Zedlewski is a staff economist for the National Institute of Justice, U.S. Department of Justice. Opinions expressed are solely those of the author and not of the Department of Justice.

PUBLIC ADMINISTRATION REVIEW

social harm may not even be among the reasons articulated by policy makers. Yet, judges and policy makers do in some sense weigh the safety of the community against the costs of punishment in their decisions and in that sense they are performing a social cost-benefit balancing.

Through their balancing, judges and corrections officials decide whether society will be better off if certain defendants are set free. They are concerned with the future: whether defendants will produce useful social products through jobs; whether the correctional system should expend several thousands of dollars to confine them; and whether society will be spared damage from future criminal acts. Two "costs," at least implicitly, are compared, the costs of imprisonment and the costs to society of setting a defendant free.

What Is a Year in Prison Worth?

What is the social cost of a year in prison? That figure can be obtained with reasonable accuracy. Custodial costs for a year in prison are about $15,000 according to the American Correctional Association. Construction and financing costs, if viewed improperly, can make building seem overwhelmingly expensive.[4] But construction financing costs are in fact like mortgage costs facing homebuyers who quickly find the relevant comparisons. To assess annual capital costs, one simply discounts future repayments into current dollars (to obtain the discounted present value of the investment) and then prorates total costs over the projected life of the facility. More simply, one can multiply the current interest rate times the value of the construction. Construction costs for new prisons average about $50,000 per bed space according to a recent General Accounting Office report.[5] Using a 10 percent interest rate on state bonds as the rental cost of capital, a prison space, with its share of the rest of the prison structure, costs about $5,000 per yer.

Lost social output from the defendant is somewhat more difficult to value. If a prisoner had been unique in his gainful employment, there would indeed be a loss. But, if imprisonment means that some unemployed person replaces him in the work force, then there might actually be a social gain. Added into these social dynamics are the net transfers of dependents, if there are any, into and out of other welfare support programs. A net social loss of $5,000 per year should generously account for lost social output.[6] Decisions to imprison, therefore, imply system costs of roughly $20,000 and total social costs of about $25,000. Subsequent development of this analysis shows that results are not sensitive to substantial errors in any one cost figure.

Letting Them Go Free, Is Not

The social cost of an imprisonment decision, about $25,000 per year, must be weighed against the social cost incurred by the release decision. That cost can be approximated, albeit crudely, by estimating the number

of crimes per year an offender is likely to commit if left free and multiplying that number by an estimate of the average social cost of a crime. We develop estimates of these two figures here, realizing in advance the substantial imprecision of the results. It is virtually meaningless to say that "the average criminal in the United States commits q crimes per year" or that "the average American crime costs X dollars." The numbers help focus attention on important issues, however. The number of crimes averted by imprisonment and the social costs attendant with crime are critical determinants of how much prison space we should have. The results here suggest the direction that sentencing policy should take, even if they do not suggest the magnitude of change.

Given that prison space is limited, judges try to reserve it for the most active criminals.[7] For expository purposes, we can envision omniscient judges trying to gauge a defendant's criminality in terms of past and future offenses per year. If he were to focus on crime control, the judge would send to prison those with the greatest annual offense rates, q. Since prison space is limited, he would eventually set free all those with offense rates greater than some q. The question is whether the q crimes saved is greater than the expenditure to save them.

FIGURE 1
Direct Benefit of Imprisonment

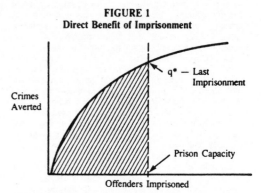

Judges are neither omniscient nor do they sentence offenders to prison solely on the basis of criminality. The average criminality of currently imprisoned offenders is, therefore, less than it would be under a pure and omniscient crime control sentencing policy. Still, knowing something about the criminality of current inmates at least helps us assess the benefits attained from current prison capacity.

In order to approximate the numbers of crimes likely to be committed by freed offenders, we used information about annual crime rates obtained from inmate interviews. Inmate characteristics should resemble those of marginal releasees—defendants that judges decided were almost but not quite deserving of a prison term. It

TABLE 1
Annual Inmate Offense Rates
(Rand Corporation, 1982)

Offense Committed	Average Per Committer
Burglary	76-118
Robbery	41-61
Other Theft	142-209
Fraud	174-238
Drug Deals	880-1300

is this group of borderline cases that would have been imprisoned if additional space were available and their crimes that would have been averted. Because of the severe limitations in predicting which defendants are most criminal, there is good reason to believe that inmate offense rates approximate those of borderline releasees.[1]

The estimates of annual offense rates here are taken from a survey by the Rand Corporation of 2,190 inmates who were housed in jails and prisons in California, Michigan, and Texas.[9] The average number of crimes per inmate serves well to assess the crime savings attained under current abilities to predict criminality (Table 1).

It would be inaccurate to say that a typical offender committed crimes at the rate and in the variety depicted. Rates varied from 1 to 1,000 offenses per year, and individual offenders specialized to varying degrees (a burglar, for instance, may have been involved in few other kinds of theft). Table 1 represents a composite of offenders rather than a typical offender in these state confinement systems. Two annual rates appear for each offense. These represent high and low estimates for each offender in the sample based on validity cross-checks of inmate answers. Inmates averaged somewhere between 187 and 278 property crimes of various kinds per year, excluding drug deals. Those who said they had committed no property offenses—some 18 percent of the sample—have been excluded in order to sidestep difficulties in valuing violent crimes.

The Victim's Bill

A final estimate is the value of a crime to society. It is the most troubling element in the exercise, partly because of the statistical errors, and partly because of the conceptual difficulties in defining social value. Rather than exhaust the reader with a long digression on the relationship between social value and market costs or between average expenditure on crime versus expected savings, we shall simply state our procedure. We counted every published expenditure on crime we could find and updated them to reach $99.8 billion (1983). We counted every victimization we could estimate for 1983 and obtained 43.4 million crimes. We divided

dollars by crimes to get expenditures of $2,300 per crime. Components are displayed in Table 2.

Admitting the inaccuracies involved in the estimation, does $2,300 per crime seem plausible, nonetheless? Expenditures have some merit as measures of value because people do not spend more for services than the value they derive from them. Because the figure is a gross average, it probably overvalues petty larcenies and undervalues rapes or vicious beatings. Some overestimation occurs because not all criminal justice expenditures are crime-related. On the other hand, many household and urban expenditures are uncounted. At any rate, even fairly large errors will not alter the conclusions reached.

The estimates indicate that if judges were to sentence 1,000 more offenders (similar to current inmates) to prison, they would obligate the correctional system to roughly $25 million per year. About 187,000 felonies would be averted through incapacitation of these offenders. These crimes would represent about $430 million in social costs. The conclusion is insensitive to rather large errors in estimates. If we were to double the annual cost of confinement, halve the average crimes per offender, and halve the average cost per crime, we would still conclude that $50 million in confinement investments would account for $107 million in social costs.

Since estimates of social costs were based on money spent, not costs avoided, what actual savings would be realized is open to speculation. One can, however, envision several kinds of savings from declining crime rates. If householders and businessmen are objective in their expenditures, they would divert some money from protection of goods to the purchase of more goods. Fewer buildings would be abandoned because of crime risks. Inner city businesses would enjoy lower operating expenses due to reduced incidences of thefts. Mass transportation would be safer and more popular. The potential savings seem large.[10]

The Fat Half of the Wishbone

Our cost comparisons were based on an implicit assumption that incapacitation of offenders was the only source of crime savings. An extensive literature[11] argues that in fact the majority of crime savings are attributable to deterrence. General deterrence is the crime savings accrued because potential offenders take into account the risks of punishment (as measured by the fraction of crimes that result in punishment) in their crime commission decisions. As the risk of punishment increases, the number of people willing to commit crimes decreases.

Estimates of the savings attributable to punishment risk vary with the data used and the crimes and sanctions studied. Ehrlich,[12] using state-aggregated data from 1960, estimated that a 1 percent increase in imprisonment risk (prisoners per crime) would produce a 1 percent decrease in crimes per capita. Wolpin,[13] using a national-aggregate time series of England and

PUBLIC ADMINISTRATION REVIEW

TABLE 2
Social Costs of Crime

Crimes—1983[a] (Millions)		Expenditures—1983[b] ($ Billions)	
Violence	5.0	Firearms	0.3
Robbery	1.4	Guard Dogs	4.2
Burglary	7.5	Victim Losses	35.4
Larceny	27.4	Criminal Justice	33.8
Theft	1.2	Commercial Security	26.1
	43.4		99.8
Missing: Homicides, white collar, underground economy		Missing: Residential security, opportunity costs, indirect costs	

[a]Personal and household victimizations are reported in *Criminal Victimizations 1983* (Bureau of Justice Statistics, 1984). Commercial victimizations were estimated by applying the 1976 (last-reported) National Crime Survey estimates to more current victimization and crime report statistics. Commercial robberies were 25 percent of personal robberies (0.25×1.1 million = 0.3 million); burglaries were 23 percent (6.1 million) of household burglaries = 1.4 million. Commercial larcenies were estimated at 13.7 percent of those reported to the FBI in 1983. Total larceny victimizations $X = 23,637,000 + 0.137X$, or $X = 27.4$ million.

[b]Source for firearms estimate, Cambridge Reports, Inc., in *An Analysis of Public Attitudes Toward Handgun Control* (Cambridge, Mass., 1978), found that 25 percent of all households owned at least one handgun. Some 20 percent of owners said guns were purchased for protection. Gun costs estimated at $75 per year for 5 percent of 83.1 million households.

Source for watchdog estimates, the 1976 National Election Study, G. Gerber et al., *Violence Profile No. 9, Trends in Network Drama and Viewer Conceptions of Social Reality 1967-1977* (Philadelphia: University of Pennsylvania, 1978), found 10 percent of households said they bought dogs for protection. Costs estimated at $500 per year for food, housing, and health care for 10 percent of 83.1 million households.

Victim losses estimated at $10.9 billion for property and medical in 1981 in *The Economic Cost of Crime to Victims*, Special Report (Bureau of Justice Statistics, 1984). Commercial losses taken from American Management Association (1975) study cited in W. Cunningham and T. H. Taylor, *Crime and Protection in America*, Final Report to National Institute of Justice, Grant No. 80-IJ-CX-0080. All costs inflated by consumer price index to 1983 dollars.

Source for criminal justice expenditures: Preliminary estimates for total system expenditure in 1981 from U.S. Department of Commerce, Bureau of the Census.

Commercial security expenditures estimated at $21.7 billion in 1980 dollars by Cunningham and Taylor, *op. cit.*

Wales, estimated that a 1 percent increase in imprisonment produced a four-fifths (0.839) percent decrease in crime rates. Wolpin also separated the deterrence savings from incapacitation or imprisonment savings and estimated that slightly more than half the savings were due to deterrence for both property and violent crimes.

Other studies suggest that the deterrent component is even larger. Cohen's[14] review of incapacitation research uncovered a range of 2 to 25 percent estimated for incapacitation's share. Nagin and Blumstein[15] estimated that if sentencing policies in effect in 1970 had been changed from a 25 percent chance of prison upon conviction of a serious crime to 100 percent and if prison terms had been reduced from 2.6 years on average to 1, crime rates would have been reduced by 25 percent while prison populations would have risen by 25,000 inmates. Focusing on the appealing concept of preventing crime through imprisonment misses most of the benefits of the punishment.

Deterrence estimates of crime savings help corroborate our findings. A 1 percent increase in 1983 state prison populations would amount to 4,390 more prisoners, or about $110 million in expenditures. Using Wolpin's estimate of a 0.839 percent reduction in crime rates means that 364,000 crimes would have been averted at an assumed value of about $837 million.

Not surprisingly, the cost-benefit ratio has fallen from about 17:1 to 7:1 as we moved from using inmate-based estimates of crimes averted to general population estimates; inmates are likely to contain a disproportionate number of high-rate offenders. So long as incoming prisoners resemble current inmates, the higher benefit ratio is pertinent. If incarcerations increased to the point that additional inmates more nearly represented the general population's propensities for crime, cost-benefit ratios would move toward the lower figure. Society is likely to receive a substantial rate of return on prison investments in either case.[16]

Selective Incapacitation

Some opponents of prison expansion have argued that improved identification of high-rate offenders coupled with a policy of "selective incapacitation" might obviate the need for additional capacity. Selective incapacitation emphasizes future criminality as a cornerstone of sentencing decisions. It argues that long terms for high-rate offenders and short terms or non-prison sanctions for lesser criminals can increase crime savings without construction. It is in contrast to what many perceive current policies to be; namely, a balance

FIGURE 2
Offender Crimes per Year
(All Crimes Except Drug Dealing)

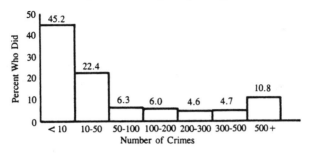

between the offense committed and the offender committing.

The potential for selective incapacitation can be seen in a histogram derived from the Rand survey data.[17] Nearly half the sample admitted to fewer than 10 crimes per year. At the other extreme, some 20 percent admitted to more than 200 crimes per year. Imprisoning more high-rate offenders for longer periods would increase the incapacitation benefits of prisons.

Enhanced prediction of criminality would be desirable even if current policies were maintained. Unfortunately, the near-term prospects for improvements are severely clouded.

Greenwood and Abrahamse[18] scored prison inmates on a scale of 0 to 7 on bases such as prior record, drug use, and employment history and then predicted which among a sample from the of 781 robbers and burglars from the Chaiken and Chaiken survey were likely to be high-, medium-, and low-rate offenders. They compared their predictions to inmate reports and concluded that they had predicted with fair accuracy. Unfortunately, this conclusion is sensitive to how their predictions are aggregated.

TABLE 3
Classifying Offenders
(Percent Classified, $N = 781$)

Predicted Activity	Actual Offender Rates		
	Low-Med	High	Total
Low-Med	58	13	71
High	14	15	29
Total	72	28	100

Table 3 recasts the data in the context of a selective incapacitation policy. The hypothetical policy under consideration gives long prison terms to high rate offenders and very short terms or probation to lesser offenders. This is consistent with a policy of targeting prison space for high-rate offenders. Using the study's classification scheme, judges would err by nearly 50 percent in both directions: every high-rate offender sentenced to a long term (15 percent) would be accompanied by a misclassified lesser offender (14 percent), and large numbers of high-rate offenders (13 out of 28 percent) would receive minor sentences.[19] One would expect classification errors to be even greater in any operational setting because a new set of offenders would differ from the study sample in terms of prediction characteristics.

Subsequent research in a decision-making environment reinforced pessimism over near-term prospects for identifying habitual offenders. Petersilia *et al.*[20] found that even comprehensive sentence investigations, which documented employment history, family structure, and criminal records, were poor predictors of the recidivists among a convicted population. Felons recommended for probation and felons recommended for prison but not incarcerated were back into the court system in nearly equal proportions. Only 3 percent of their sample of incoming prison inmates were predicted to be good probation risks.

Other problems requiring attention are the ethical questions raised for the nation's judiciary. Among them are the proportionality of punishment to the offense and the need to provide some sense of justice to victims. How should a judge decide between a first-time murderer and a career thief? Between imprisoning one habitual offender for 10 years and five lesser offenders for 2 years each? Such questions, largely resolved under current policies, must be reconsidered for selective incapacitation.

A final consideration is whether public sentiment would support long-term incarceration of juveniles. Youths under 18 accounted for over 30 percent of arrests for serious crimes in 1983; youths under 21 accounted for over 47 percent.[21] Thus, youths must figure into any crime savings calculated. Either current juvenile punishment policy, which minimizes the use of confinement, would have to be discarded or the hypo-

PUBLIC ADMINISTRATION REVIEW

thetical crime savings estimated from selective incapacitation would have to be revised.

The implications of this section are that selective incapacitation has many obstacles to overcome before it can be advanced as a viable policy. Besides the ethical issues of punishment structure and the social concerns over treatment of juvenile offenders, there is the distinct possibility that predicted crime savings are mythical. Increasing sentence lengths for some offenders means that bed spaces are taken away from other offenders. Reductions in punishment certainty are reductions in the deterrence power of sanctioning. Crimes saved through increased incapacitation may be fewer than those lost through reduced deterrence. Also, our current abilities to identify high-rate offenders from official statistics seem so limited that half the offenders sentenced to lengthy terms would likely be lesser criminals.

If Not Prison, What?

The same statistics that earlier argued for additional prison capacity support the notion that some offenders are not worth imprisoning. Indeed, most convicted offenders serve no prison time. Few who do serve prison time serve their full term. In 1983 American correctional systems were supervising 2.4 million persons. Some 73 percent of these persons were in the community, 252,000 as parolees from their prison terms and 1,502,000 probationers who had not been sent to prison. Jails, which house both convicted and some pretrial persons, held 224,000 and prisons held 439,000 inmates.[22] Persons who received only fines or suspended sentences are not counted in these figures because they receive no supervision. Incarceration is the extreme, not the standard, punishment for a crime.

The criminal justice system operates under a punitive philosophy nonetheless, and 20th century penologists have designed many alternatives to incarceration. Fines, restitution, forfeitures, community service, supervised and unsupervised probation, and suspended sentences are among the current alternatives. But despite the flexibility implied by the range of possibilities, alternatives to prison use either of two mechanisms: expropriation of assets (or work equivalent of assets) or monitoring of subsequent behavior in the community.

The World of Fines

Becker argued that fines were socially efficient because they punished offenders without draining significant amounts of resources for their administration. While correct in theory, the argument is eroded somewhat by two related considerations: a convict's ability to pay and the state's ability to enforce its fine policies. In *Tate* v. *Short*,[23] the Supreme Court ruled that fines could not be set beyond a defendant's ability to pay and then converted to imprisonment. This decision was buttressed by *Bearden* v. *Georgia*[24] in 1983 where the court ruled that unpaid fines could not be converted to imprisonment unless the state determined that the defendant had not made a *bona fide* effort to pay.

These decisions do not reflect disfavor of fines by the Supreme Court. In *Bearden,* the court explicitly recognized the enforcement of fines by imprisonment. What the court called attention to was the need for a rational and equitable fine structure. Amounts levied must be subjected to some sort of means test and enforcement must be tempered by subsequent considerations of ability to pay.

These restrictions do not appear to have severely restricted the use of fines. Hillsman *et al.*[25] found that fines were the predominant sanction for non-traffic violations in courts of limited jurisdiction (misdemeanors and lesser felonies) which handled 90 percent of all criminal cases brought and were also used in general jurisdiction felony courts. Only 2 of the 24 felony courts surveyed said they never imposed fines. The fraction of fine amounts actually collected, as much as 90 percent of the amounts levied, depended on the interest and persistence of the courts in collecting them.

Credible enforcement of fines requires the establishment and monitoring of payment schedules if the amounts set are anything but nominal. Setting fair but punitive fines requires information on the legitimate incomes of convicts. The equity problem has been solved in part in Sweden and West Germany by implementation of "day fines." Fines in these countries are levied in units of work days of the defendant. Defendant income is used to estimate the value of his work day and transform the days fined into a payable fine amount. Swedish and German courts enjoy easy access to a defendant's salary information, but it is not clear that easy access is an important ingredient of success. Simply asking the defendant his salary may be sufficient, particularly if the alternative to a fine is a jail term.

A popular American variation of the fine is restitution. Although the defendant is in essence fined, the fine amount is determined by the harm done to his victim and is paid to the victim, either in cash or labor. By combining punishment and compensation, restitution offers a strong sense of redress. But, only victims lucky enough to have a convicted assailant can receive compensation through restitution sentences. The large majority will have to look to other mechanisms. Victim compensation funds financed through fines and forfeitures, as established by the Victims of Crime Act of 1984, can offer more efficient and equitable restoration of damages.

Probation and Public Safety

While fines are popular in misdemeanor cases, the courts sentence the majority of felons and serious misdemeanants to probation. Table 4 shows that the relative use of probation and imprisonment has remained fairly stable despite perceptions of a large-scale shift toward imprisonment. What has changed is the absolute use of both sanctions and their use relative to the number of serious crimes.

As practiced in the early 1970s, probation was a cornerstone of rehabilitation. Probation officers

TABLE 4
Sentencing Trends, 1976-1983

Year	Probation[a] Population	Inmate[b] Population	P/I[c]	Crimes[d]	(P + I)/C[e] (Pct)
1976	923,064	278,000	3.32	11,315,600	10.6
1978	905,652	307,276	2.95	11,174,000	10.9
1980	1,118,097	329,821	3.39	13,366,100	10.8
1982	1,335,359	414,362	3.22	12,933,700	13.5
1983	1,502,247	438,830	3.42	12,070,200	16.1

[a]Sources: *State and Local Probation and Parole Systems,* Law Enforcement Assistance Administration, Report No. SD-P-1, February 1978; *Probation in the United States: 1979* (San Francisco: National Council on Crime and Delinquency, 1981); and *Probation and Parole—1981, 1982, 1983,* Bureau of Justice Statistics.

[b]"Prisoners in 1983," *Bureau of Justice Statistics Bulletin* (April 1984).

[c]Ratio of probationers to prison inmates.

[d]Serious crimes as defined by the Federal Bureau of Investigation, *Uniform Crime Reports, 1983* (Washington, D.C.: Government Printing Office, 1984).

[e]Percentage of probationers and inmates per number of serious crimes.

operated in part as social workers. They either gave referrals for job and family counseling, drug and alcohol treatment, and vocational training, or provided these services personally. As disappointment over the prospects for rehabilitation grew in the late 1970s, probation officers gradually took on more of a watchman's role even though many social services were still provided.

Whatever the underlying rationale, probation has been perceived to be a minor sanction. Polling college students, Sebba[26] found that they ranked one year's probation just below a 12-month suspended sentence and above a $250 fine in terms of severity. Surveying prosecutors, Jacoby and Ratledge[27] found that one year's unsupervised probation ranked between fines of $10 and $100; a year's supervised probation ranked on a par with a 30-day suspension of a driver's license.

Concern over the severity of punishment implied by probation and the threat to community safety has caused several states, among them Delaware, New Jersey, Georgia, and Washington, to implement special probation programs that have increased oversight and restricted freedom in varying degrees.[28] Perhaps typical, Georgia's Intensive Probation Supervision (IPS) is designed for prison-bound cases. IPS probationers must either hold a full-time job or be a full-time student, perform community service, and pay part of their supervisory costs. They average 16 contacts per month with their supervisors.

State officials regard the program as successful. Although IPS probationers have been more expensive to monitor than regular probationers ($1,595 versus $275 per year), they are still less expensive than confinement at $10,814 per year. Earnings and taxes paid by IPS probationers are offsets to program costs and their higher revocation rates—25.5 percent versus 16.7 percent for a matched group given regular probation—suggests that the increased supervision increases community safety.[29]

Many costs are not captured in this assessment, however. Among the missing are victim losses, repeated criminal justice costs for apprehensions and court procedures, and confinement costs for some of those revoked. Thus the efficacy of the program is unclear in a more complete cost environment.

Haynes and Larsen[30] made similar comparisons among correctional treatments under fuller accounting of costs. They estimated the social costs incurred from a cohort of Arizona burglars in three supervisory settings: confinement in prison or jail; community supervision under probation, parole, and halfway houses; and, unsupervised release, possibly after one of the aforementioned treatments. They captured a substantial number of the relevant cost components: corrections supervision, welfare and other social support, crime prevention, victim losses, and subsequent apprehensions. Costs were estimated for a variety of crimes and were applied to information on crimes committed obtained from interviews with the burglars. No attempt was made to estimate deterrence savings.

They found that incarceration was considerably less expensive than community supervision when identified crimes and costs were accounted for—$11,640 versus $26,868 per year. As previous studies found, small numbers of offenders (10 percent) committed most of the crimes (90 percent).[31] Haynes and Larsen also found that recurring system costs were substantial: $2,640 for arrest and prosecution of a burglary and $701 for a simple shoplifting, exclusive of general crime prevention and victim losses.

Twisting Punishment to Fit Crimes

Given that large numbers of convicted offenders are going to be released, how should one choose among alternatives to incarceration? Should a minor offense by a habitual offender receive the same sentence as a more

778   PUBLIC ADMINISTRATION REVIEW

FIGURE 3
Social Costs and Sentencing

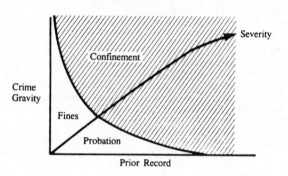

serious offense by a first offender? Should equal offenses be treated the same if the defendants differ in criminal record?

If the answer to the last question is no, then there must be combinations of offender characteristics and crime seriousness that deserve equal amounts of punishment. This does not mean that identical punishments should be handed down to dissimilar convicts. We suggest that differences in propensities to commit future crimes, perhaps as evidenced by prior record, argue for different forms of punishment. Extending the cost-benefit reasoning presented at the outset, it is suggested that defendants with low propensities to commit future crimes should be punished as inexpensively as possible. As perceived future danger increases, the punishment should provide an opportunity to curtail future social costs. This logic suggests fines for first offenders and appropriately supervised probation for repeat offenders. A sentencing policy based on cost-benefit principles is illustrated in Figure 3.

Absent evidence of habitual involvement in crime, the system should try to punish efficiently; that is, exact the penalty consuming the least resources. Properly set, fines can be made painful. If properly administered, nearly full payment can be extracted at low cost. Thus, fines produce economical deterrence. Evidence of future criminality, on the other hand, suggests that society may suffer additional crimes. The data presented here indicate that these costs are likely to exceed any reasonable costs of monitoring several times over. Supervised probation has a potential for detecting and limiting crimes.

Sanctions need not be administered separately. Judges can combine probation with a fine or with other forms of punishment. The important principle is that the punishment selected should minimize social costs while maintaining punishment equity.

Conclusion

The objective of this paper was to present research findings pertinent to the questions of how much offenders should be punished. Rather than rely on traditional but difficult to quantify *desiderata* of punishment such as retribution and justice, a cost-benefit perspective was used to investigate whether society spends more money punishing than it gains from punishment. Existing data are adequate only for a crude answer to that question. Yet, the results overwhelmingly support the case for more prison capacity. The case for current use of probation and fines is less clear because there is less data on the application of these sanctions. It appears, nonetheless, that social costs would be reduced if more probationers were given either prison terms or fines. Incapacitating borderline offenders now crowded out by today's space constraints would likely cost communities less in crime expenditure than they now pay in social damages and prevention. Punitive fines for first offenders would deter others and reduce system expenditures on supervision while producing revenues and perhaps compensating victims.

Notes

1. "Prisoners in 1983," *Bureau of Justice Statistics Bulletin*, April 1984.
2. See, for example, *Prison Crowding—A Crisis in Corrections*, a Report of the Task Force on Criminal Justice Issues of the Policy Committee of the Center for Metropolitan Planning and Research (Baltimore: Johns Hopkins University Press, December 1984), p. 6.
3. Gary S. Becker, "Crime and Punishment: An Economic Approach," *Journal of Political Economy*, vol. 76 (March 1968), pp. 169-217.
4. See, for example, Gail S. Funke, *Who's Buried in Grant's Tomb?* (Alexandria, Va.: Institute for Economic and Policy Studies, Inc., 1982).
5. *Federal, District of Columbia, and State Future Prison and Correctional Institution Populations and Capacities*, GAO/GOD-84-56 (Washington, D.C.: U.S. General Accounting Office, February 27, 1984), p. 30.
6. Clark R. Larsen estimated tax losses per prisoner at $408 per year and average welfare payments at $84 per year in *Costs of Incarceration and Alternatives* (Phoenix: Arizona State University Center for the Study of Justice, May 1983). The reason for such low average costs was that few of the inmates were employed in legitimate occupations or married at the time of imprisonment.
7. Some weight is undoubtedly given to a need for punishment of major criminal events rather than personalities. Justice demands that spouse killers be punished, for instance, even though repetition of the crime is unlikely.
8. Prior convictions alone have been found to be a weak predictor of underlying criminal activity. See Barbara Boland, *Age, Crime, and Punishment* (Washington, D.C.: The Urban Institute, 1978).
9. Jan Chaiken and Marcia Chaiken, *Varieties of Criminal Behavior*, R-2814-NIJ (Santa Monica, Calif.: Rand Corporation, 1982).
10. See William W. Greer, "What Is the Cost of Rising Crime?" *New York Affairs* (January 1984), pp. 6-16 for a comprehensive enumeration of social costs due to crime.
11. See A. Blumstein, J. Cohen, and D. Nagin (eds.), *Deterrence and Incapacitation: Estimating the Effects of Criminal Sanctions on Crime Rates* (Washington, D.C.: National Academy of Sciences, 1978) for an extensive review and assessment of the deterrence literature and evidence.
12. Isaac Ehrlich, "Participation in Illegitimate Activities: A Theoretical and Empirical Investigation," *Journal of Political Economy*, vol. 81 (May/June 1973), pp. 531-567.
13. Kenneth L. Wolpin, "An Economic Analysis of Crime and Punishment in England and Wales, 1894-1967," *Journal of Political Economy*, vol. 86 (October 1978), pp. 815-839.
14. Jacqueline Cohen, "The Incapacitative Effect of Imprisonment: A Critical Review of the Literature," in Blumstein, Cohen, and Nagin (eds.), *op. cit.*, pp. 187-243.
15. Daniel Nagin and Alfred Blumstein, "On the Optimum Use of Incarceration for Crime Control," *Operations Research*, vol. 26 (May 1978), pp. 381-405.
16. One cannot safely extrapolate too far from observed values of the data. A 50 percent increase in prison populations may generate more or fewer crime savings depending on how much deterrence is created by sizable increases in prison risks.
17. Table A.15 in Chaiken and Chaiken, *op. cit.*
18. Peter Greenwood and Allan Abrahamse, *Selective Incapacitation*, R-2815-NIJ (Santa Monica, Calif.: Rand Corporation, 1982).
19. From Table 4.8, *ibid.*, all robbers and burglars in the study. Definition of low, medium, and high rates of criminal activity differed with each state and crime in the sample.
20. J. Petersilia, S. Turner, J. Kahan, and J. Peterson, *Granting Felons Probation*, R-3186-NIJ (Santa Monica, Calif.: Rand Corporation, 1985).
21. Federal Bureau of Investigation, *Crime in the United States: Uniform Crime Reports* (Washington, D.C.: U.S. Government Printing Office, 1984).
22. Bureau of Justice Statistics, *Probation and Parole 1983*, September 1984; *The 1983 Jail Census*, November 1984; and *Prisoners in 1983*, April 1984.
23. *Tate v. Short*, 401 U.S. 395 (1971).
24. *Bearden v. Georgia*, 461 U.S. 660 (1983).
25. S. Hillsman, J. Sichel, and B. Mahoney, *Fines in Sentencing: A Study of the Use of the Fine as a Criminal Sanction* (Washington, D.C.: National Institute of Justice, 1984).
26. Leslie Sebba, "Some Explorations in the Scaling of Penalties," *Journal of Research in Crime and Delinquency*, vol. 15 (July 1978), pp. 247-265.
27. Joan Jacoby and Edward Ratledge, *Measuring the Severity of Criminal Penalties: Provisional Results* (Washington, D.C.: Jefferson Institute of Justice Studies, 1982).
28. The Delaware program is part of a comprehensive revision of its criminal sanctions. See former Governor Pierre S. duPont's *Expanding Sentencing Options: A Governor's Perspective, Research in Brief* (Washington, D.C.: National Institute of Justice, 1985).
29. Billie S. Erwin, *Evaluation of Intensive Probation Supervision in Georgia* (Atlanta: Georgia Department of Offender Rehabilitation, 1984).
30. P. Haynes and C. Larsen, "Financial Consequences of Incarceration and Alternatives," *Crime and Delinquency*, vol. 30 (October 1984), pp. 529-550.
31. See for comparison J. Petersilia, P. Greenwood, and M. Lavin, *Criminal Careers of Habitual Felons*, R-2144-DOJ (Santa Monica, Calif.: Rand Corporation, 1977).

[16]

Some Conceptual Issues in Incapacitating Offenders

Todd R. Clear
Donald M. Barry

Recently, growing attention has been paid to the concept of "incapacitation" as a crime-control device. Much of the increased interest in incapacitation has been the result of the existence of a developing consensus that other utilitarian punishment options, such as rehabilitation, are ineffective combined with an intuitive trust in the simple logic of incapacitation: incarcerated offenders can commit no crimes. An illustration of the importance of this growth in support for incapacitation is provided by the release in 1981 of the Report of the Attorney General's Commission on Violent Crime, which took a position staunchly supportive of incapacitation. The purpose of this paper is to point out some of the complexities underlying any attempt to implement a full-scale incapacitative model through the increased use of imprisonment. Our position is that, far from simple, the renewed use of incapacitative strategies is frought with difficulties. We expressly avoid a lengthy discussion of moral issues underlying the model, though we recognize their seriousness, as well. Instead, we point out technical concerns that make the effectiveness of an incapacitative approach problematic.

INCAPACITATION AS POLICY

As a penal policy, incapacitation attempts the prevention of offending behavior through the operation of some imposed physical or psychological restraint which renders the potential offender incapable of engaging in the offending behavior, so long as the restraint is continued (O'Leary, 1977). Thus, incapacitative methods are intentionally restricted to the duration of the restraint method and make no claims for effectiveness beyond this period of time.

For example, a broad incapacitative policy would incarcerate all youth from the date of the sixteenth birthday through the first day of the thirty-sixth year. Such a policy would have clear incapacitative effects, since it would result in the removal of potential criminals during the period of their highest crime-productive years, making the commission of crime (at least in open society) impossible so long as the youths were incarcerated.

Of course, no reasonable person would propose the incapacitation of all youth of a given age regardless of the impact on criminal behavior. Such a policy would violate several legal and intuitive principles. First, the law requires that due process standards requiring proof of past behavior be met, though the

TODD R. CLEAR: Rutgers University, Newark, New Jersey. DONALD M. BARRY: Rutgers University, Newark, New Jersey.

strictness of these legal standards varies from criminal to non-criminal statuses (Kittrie, 1971).

A second limitation is that not all crimes are seen as equally deserving of traditional incapacitative prevention: long term incapacitative methods used to prevent such offenses as auto theft, vandalism, and larceny would seem inappropriate to most people. As the seriousness of the offense increases in magnitude, so does the perceived appropriateness of incapacitative penal policies.

Moreover, we normally have a target-specific model in mind for incapacitative policies. That is, if an incarcerated thief continues to steal from fellow prisoners, we normally consider the thief to be incapacitated nonetheless. However, this target specification becomes more troublesome when the "incapacitated" offense is, for example, homicide.

The means used to incapacitate is also of concern. Too often it is assumed that imprisonment is the sole method for incapacitation, but clearly there are other methods: antabuse, prefrontal lobotomies, chemical behavior control and so on.

Related to the notion of incapacitation method is the degree to which error will be tolerated in the operation of an incapacitative system. One kind of error is the failure of a system to incapacitate after it has been set into motion: escapes from prison, ineffectiveness of drugs, etc. A second and perhaps more troublesome kind of error lies in the judgments made concerning the operation of an incapacitative system. The contingent probability of an event given application of a controlling device (and the comparative contingent probabilities of various devices) leads to the dilemma of Type I and II error. The permissible levels of error and changes in error rates permitted given changing seriousness of predicted events is a problem of major concern to those who implement incapacitative systems.

Thus, the simple concept of incapacitation is, not surprisingly, more complex in practice than is ordinarily thought: it is not merely a matter of locking up dangerous offenders. The National Academy of Sciences Panel on Research on Deterrent and Incapacitative Effects (Blumstein, Cohen, and Nagin (eds.), 1978) listed several priorities in this area, and numerous mathematical models of incapacitative effects have been proposed. Though slightly different approaches have been taken, the models are similar in many respects.

Most existing models characterize incapacitative effects in terms of a rate parameter lambda (λ), which reflects the number of crimes committed per year by the individual criminal. Knowing the value of λ makes it possible to estimate the number of crimes prevented by incapacitation for any specified time period and, more broadly, to evaluate the potential impact of proposed changes in sanctioning policy. To illustrate, if $\lambda = 20$ for, say, burglary offenses, then increasing the time actually served by convicted burglars by an amount of two years, in a jurisdiction where, say, 100 burglars are convicted annually, ought to decrease the number of burglaries by:

$$\frac{20 \text{ burglaries}}{\text{year}} \times 100 \text{ burglars} \times 2 \text{ years} = 4000 \text{ burglaries.}$$

While this logic may seem compelling, the approach does have some shortcomings. First, there is the problem of replacement, whereby incarcerated criminals are replaced by new recruits. Second, however, is the problem of obtaining an accurate estimate of λ, the numerical value for which has a drastic effect on estimates of the incapacitative effect. For obvious reasons, criminals are reluctant to divulge information about the true extent of their illegal activities, and so self-reports must be interpreted cautiously. In this regard, however, Manski (1978) has pointed out that self-reports need not be *true* in order to be useful; rather, they need only be *systematically related* to the truth. If it were known, for example, that offenders, on the average, divulged only one-third of the crimes they actually committed, and that the kinds of crimes divulged were representative of their criminal careers, then one would simply multiply the self-reported crimes per year by three to arrive at the "true value" of λ. Yet, we may not even assume that offenders understate their criminal behavior in self-report—a plausible argument can be made in favor of a model in which offenders overstate their criminal behavior.

The basic problem remains, therefore: how are we ever to produce the externally verifiable estimate of the true rate required to carry out the appropriate conversion? The behavior of sizeable numbers of unconfined persons, over an extended time period, simply does not seem to lend itself to direct observation.

Consequently, policy makers have tried to produce somewhat more general selection systems, in which the "most active" criminals are incapacitated regardless of their demonstrated level of activity.

The result is a series of difficult issues involving the selection of target behaviors and persons for incapacitation. One problem is the identification of offensive behaviors that are to be addressed through incapacitative policies.

Criterion behaviors—targets for incapacitative sanctions—do not exist in the abstract, but rather are exhibited in the context of social conditions, and these conditions may often be relatively highly correlated with the criterion behavior. The relationship between early delinquency and length of criminal careers (Wolfgang, 1972), violence, presence of handguns, and subcultural definitions (Wolfgang and Ferracuti, 1967), victim-offender situational interactions (Amir, 1971), and offense-specific role relationships and interaction patterns (Clinard and Quinney, 1968), have all been observed and described in criminological literature. The implication is that imaginative methods to prevent specific offenses through interventions into the lives of specific offenders and/or offense-prone situations may flow only from a detailed understanding of the nature of the event being prevented.

For example, researchers have speculated whether group delinquency has a pattern of member replacement which overcomes any real incapacitiative effect incarceration might have (Blumstein, 1978).

While grossly simplistic incapacitative methods such as imprisonment or brain alteration might have impact on a wide range of intended and unintended behaviors, a more clear idea of the target behavior helps to make this overzealously intrusive approach unnecessary. Schwitzgabel (1972) applied a situational understanding of child molesting behavior to develop a non-incarcerative incapacitative alternative method. Likewise, alcohol-based offensive behavior might be prevented by relatively unintrusive methods for restricting alcohol intake on the part of the control target. Simply because unimaginative, grossly over-intrusive and costly methods have dominated the fields of incapacitation technology does not mean this is necessarily the only approach. A more precisely effective set of methods may follow from a better understanding of the nature of the criterion behavior and its normal context. Of course, this also implies a need for knowledge about criminal careers as well as crimes.

PREDICTION AND INCAPACITATION

A more thorny set of problems arises from the task of selecting *individuals* once the criterion behavior is clearly identified. Unfortunately, there are a number of general misconceptions in the field of prediction. Commonly, it is believed that individual behavior "cannot be predicted," that "prediction is futile", or alternately, that people cannot clinically predict behavior though empirical "machines" can. Both of these beliefs oversimplify the current state of knowledge about prediction.

Before addressing these positions, however, some weaknesses in the current knowledge of research on incapacitation should be noted. First, "most so called prediction studies are in reality 'postdiction' studies, where the outcomes of the cases are already known prior to the 'predictions' of the raters." (Clear, 1978). What is tested is clinical or empirical differentiations of past cases using limited data, not "true prediction."

One of the closest tests of "true prediction" is provided by the famous Baxstrom studies (Steadman, 1973), in which a number of predicted "dangerous" patients were released from incarceration by court order. A follow-up of these patients showed a marked absence of harmful behavior. It should be noted that researchers have criticized this study because fully 42 percent of the Baxstrom patients had never committed a criminal act, and "to predict an act that has never occurred in an individual's history is an unwarranted test of clinical prediction" (Cohen, Groth, and Siegel, 1978).

This underscores again the significance of criterion behavior. Much of what is known about prediction comes from the field of educational psychology, where judges have been asked to predict "such multiple-choice criteria as grades and longevity in college" (McArthur, 1968). Obviously, the distribution of values of these variables in subject populations is likely to be much more even than the distribution of, say, rates of new convictions for serious assaults resulting in injury within a population of once-convicted felons.

A third problem has been that much of the research in prediction has focused on comparing clinical (human judgment) methods to actuarial (empirically-based, prior experience) methods. By viewing prediction as a contest between these methods, the real task of prediction has been obscured. First, it should be stressed that since the earliest comparative works on the topic (Meehl, 1956), clinical predictors have normally been at a handicap, forced to use only the discrete-category information available to the computer and sometimes even without the knowledge of the marginal values of the criterion behavior (McArthur, 1968). Obviously, under these conditions the clinician will likely fail. Experiments which have combined clinical and empirical methods, drawing on the strengths of each, have found that "the two methods together are likely to result in better classification than either one alone" (Mannheim and Wilkins, 1957).

A fourth problem is that as the frequency of the criterion behavior decreases, the rate of false positives increase. In a review of prediction studies Monahan (1976) found that:

> Violence is vastly overpredicted whether simple behavioral indicators are used or sophisticated multivariate analyses are employed, and whether psychological tests are administered or thorough psychiatric examinations are performed.

A simplistic approach to prediction counts false positives as errors equal to false negatives. From this point of view, the purpose of prediction is to improve accuracy in identification of outcomes over the marginal values. In the case of infrequent behaviors, improving upon the gross prediction suggested by the marginal values is difficult, as several studies have suggested (Meehl, 1959). However, all errors are not equal in negative value, as the seriousness (or cost) of the predicted value increases, the cost of Type I errors also increases. Since Type I and II errors are negatively related, one can employ a prediction error strategy (given a fixed ability to predict) which attempts to minimize total costs by increasing the amount of Type II erorr tolerated as the seriousness of Type I error increases (O'Leary and von Hirsch, 1975). Therefore, one area for study is the cost relationships of Type I and II error for serious, but infrequent behaviors. This point of view would generate prediction models which go beyond the generally held conclusion that "low base rates cannot be predicted to sufficiently warrant their use in clinical practice" (Schlesinger, 1978).

PREDICTION ERROR AND DECISION-MAKING VALUES: AN ILLUSTRATION

The problems of overprediction and balancing the relative costs associated with the two types of error might profitably be viewed in the context of the Theory of Signal Detectabilty (TSD), originally developed as a model of perceptual decision behavior (Peterson, Birdsell, and Fox, 1954; Green and Swets, 1966). In the original TSD paradigm, the decision maker observes an *event* (e.g., a brief visual stimulus or burst of white noise) and is required to indicate whether a *signal* (e.g. a dot in the visual field or a tone embedded in the white noise) is present. The signal is sufficiently inconspicuous to insure that the observer can rarely be certain of its presence or absence. The combinations of signal present or absent with the observer's possible responses to the event (claiming that the signal was present or absent) produce four possibilities: a signal is detected (hit), a signal is not detected (miss), a non-signal event is correctly perceived as not containing a signal (correct rejection), or a non-signal event is incorrectly perceived as containing a signal (false alarm). Each of the four outcomes is assigned a numerical utility which reflects the worth of hits and correct rejections, and the costs of misses and false alarms. The *prior probability* of a signal, reflecting the long-term base rate at which signals are present in a sequence of events, is asumed to be known.

Thus far, the TSD paradigm is equivalent to the familiar Neyman-Pearson "Type I-Type II Error" formulation of statistical decision theory. However, TSD goes on to quantify two concepts that occur naturally in the perceptual decision context, and which, as will be seen, are also directly applicable to the prediction of post-release behavior. The concepts are "sensitivity of the observer" and "optimal cutoff point" for deciding that a signal was present in a given event.

In the context of predicting violent behavior, the "event" is the individual offender about whom a prediction is to be made, and a "signal" is the future occurrence of violent behavior. The "observer" might be a clinician, a parole board, an objective rating scheme based on prior record, a battery of tests, or virtually any procedure that would yield, or could be modified to yield, a numerical index of the likelihood of future violence. Moreover, two or more such methods could be combined, perhaps via linear regression, to produce a broader-based, single index. Finally, the numerical utilities required would reflect the "costs" associated with predicting violent behavior for a non-violent individual, and with predicting non-violent behavior for a violent one, and the "benefits" associated with correct predictions of violence and non-violence.

We do not attempt a detailed description of the procedures and analytic techniques required for the TSD approach here, but rather illustrate some possible results of the approach via a hypothetical example.

Consider two competing techniques for predicting violent behavior: (a) a clinical interview with the offender, followed by the clinician's rating on, say a one to 100 scale, of the likelihood of future violence, and (b) a base expectancy technique employing the offender's prior record as the basis for prediction, and producing a numerical probability of future violent behavior.

TSD analysis would require that both techniques be applied to the same group of offenders, and that this group be followed up for some specified length of time to ascertain which individuals do in fact exhibit violence (however it might be operationalized) within the given time period.

One product of TSD analysis of such data would be a *sensitivity index d'* (d-prime), for each of the two procedures, reflecting the discriminatory power of each. When d' equals zero, the procedure has no discriminatory ability at all;

Incapacitating Offenders 535

the perceptual analogue would be an observer who, completely unable to perceive the signal, responds randomly to each event. The larger the value of d', the greater the ability to detect the signal, i.e., to correctly identify persons who will eventually exhibit violent behavior.

A similar analysis could be carried out without reference to TSD by using conventional statistics to characterize the relationship between predictions and outcomes, and the results would provide useful information about the validity of the procedures in question; i.e., one could say that Procedure A has greater predictive power than Procedure B. Conventional analysis stops short, however, of prescribing an explicit rule for converting assessment results to individual case dispositions, i.e., determining an appropriate *cutoff point*. Suppose, for example, that the clinician's ratings were found to be superior to the base expectancy approach. The question remains: *how high* a rating should be required to warrant a prediction of violence, with its associated constraints on the freedom of the individual for whom the prediction is made?

The TSD approach addresses this question explicitly by combining information about (a) the base rate of violent individuals, (b) the utilities associated with the four possible decision outcomes and (c) the sensitivity of the prediction method.

The result is an optimal cutoff point, termed β (beta) in TSD, which, if adopted as the criterion for predicting violence, guarantees that the overall "costs" associated with the procedure will be minimized. That is, TSD prescribes the appropriate trade-off between Type I and Type II errors ("false alarms" and "misses," respectively), consistent with the utilities provided to it.

The advantage of the TSD formulation, then, is in its explicit recognition and separation of two quantities (d' and β) which are confounded under traditional approaches. That is, an individual may be predicted to be violent because (a) a valid procedure indicates that he is likely to exhibit violence in the future (high value of d'), or (b) the values of decision makers are such that, even in the absence of a valid prediction device, a prediction of violence is preferable to one of non-violence because of the possible consequences of erroneous predictions (low value of β, i.e., better safe than sorry). Most likely, predictions of violence result from some combination of these two factors, but their relative importance does not seem to have been investigated because they have traditionally been confounded.

It should be noted that the "overprediction of violence" phenomenon referenced earlier might be an eminently reasonable consequence of decision makers' tendencies to view "misses" (predicting nonviolence for truly violent persons) as more serious than "false alarms" (predicting violence for truly non-violent ones).

Yet, we have no systematic way of confirming the relative values placed on these types of errors, and public pressure exists to seriously downplay the perceived costs of "false alarms." The problem is not so much arriving at a model, as it is deriving socially-defensible policy based on values that could support the model.

536   **T. Clear, D. Barry**

SCALING RISK AND DESIGNING POLICY OPTIONS: DECISION TECHNOLOGY

While prediction of individual outcomes is exceedingly difficult, methods exist to attach numerical values to offenders expressing, in probablistic terms, the chance that they will exhibit the behavior to be prevented. Rather than dichotomizing individuals into "yes" and "no" predictions, this approach allows subjects to be placed into rough "risk" groupings or classes to which different incapacitive policies can be applied (Wilkins, 1969). This probablistic approach draws on the earlier point that error costs are not uniform, but vary: one might accept a relatively high level of Type II error for an offender group characterized by a high risk of violent behavior, whereas this would be unacceptable for a low risk group.

A variety of multivariate methods exist for implementing these probablistic approaches, and there is some evidence that the predictive power, appropriateness, and general utility of these methods can be compared absolutely across all prediction situations and in terms of specific applied situations (McNaughten-Smith, 1965). Writers have compared simple points systems (Gottfredson, 1973) to regression strategies to approaches requiring less vigorous assumptions (Klecka, 1975).

In a report on prediction for probation, the General Accounting Office (1976) found that Association Analysis results for one population held up relatively well when applied to different populations of subjects. Though these results have recently been criticized (Ford and Johnson, 1977), the point is fairly clear that probability models which create groups of offenders based on risk can be used, and the reliable statistical methods already exist for this strategy. Further research will need to improve the power of these methods by increasing their sophistication, testing the degree to which their results can be generalized to more clearly identify methods appropriate for different kinds of data, and identifying additional variables as predictors.

One possible approach to resolving the second kind of error is to view the problem within the context of statistical decision theory (Raiffa and Schlaifer, 1961). In order to employ this scheme, several assumptions about the incapacitation process must be made. First, alternative courses of action must be delineated; this is not too difficult in the case of the imprisonment sanction, where the alternatives consist of possible sentences that can be imposed for a given crime in a given jurisdiction, e.g., zero, one, two, etc., through five years, say, for a first conviction on a robbery charge.

A second requirement is that all possible "states of nature" be identified; these consist of a set of mutually exclusive and exhaustive future conditions relevant to decision outcomes, over which the decision maker (sentencing judge) has no control, but which can be characterized in terms of their probabilities of occurrence. For the incarceration decision, the offender's post-release behavior constitutes the basis for defining relevant states of nature. The number of crimes per year that *would be* committed if the offender were released is viewed as a random variable; thus, probabilities associated

Incapacitating Offenders

with committing zero, one, two, three, etc., crimes within a specified time period need to be estimated. This is by no means a straightforward, objective procedure, but neither is it as arbitrary as it might first appear. We do have some knowledge, admittedly imperfect, about the likelihood of future criminal involvement for a given offender as characterized by a given criminal history. For example, a forger with numerous prior convictions is more likely to return to forgery than a second-degree murderer, with no prior convictions, is likely to return to murder.

The third requirement for applying statistical decision theory is that the costs and benefits, i.e., the *utilities* associated with any combination of a decision alternative and a state of nature be specifiable numerically. Again, the determination of such numerical values is far from an objective procedure, but the variability in subjective "costs" and "benefits" of any decision outcome can be attributed largely to real differences of opinion that exist among proponents of various approaches to the question of incarceration, and various value systems that co-exist within our society. The procedure advocated here, in other words, is objective in that it will dutifully incorporate any set of utilities which serve as inputs to it, and prescribe the "best" decision conditional upon those utilities. The procedure itself is indifferent to whatever subjective values are attached to available options.

A brief and admittedly simplified example may serve to illustrate the decision theoretic approach to incarceration decisions. Let us suppose that a judge has sentencing options of zero, one, two, and so forth, through five years imprisonment for a particular defendant convicted of robbery, where sentences reflect actual time served. These constitute the alternative course of action. Suppose also, to meet the second requirement, that the defendant, if not incarcerated, over the next five years will commit no new robberies with a 30 percent probability, one to nine robberies per year with a 30 percent probability, ten to 20 robberies per year with a 20 percent probability, and 21 to 30 robberies per year with a 20 percent probability. These constitute the various states of nature. Last, we assume that the utilities associated with each decision alternative/state of nature combination are specified by estimates of the dollar costs associated with (1) maintaining a person in an institution and (2) robbery victims' material losses.

Equating overall utilities with mere dollar costs is the most outrageous of the simplifying assumptions made for the sake of this example. Not considered, for instance, are the subjective but very real costs associated with the imprisonment of a possibly harmless, even productive person; and the psychological harm incurred by a robbery victim. The quantities required to summarize these "costs" are elusive and, as noted earlier, depend critically upon who is doing the estimating; nevertheless, techniques for extracting reliable utility estimates are in a state of steady development and refinement (Winterfeldt and Fischer, 1975).

So, (conservatively) assuming that the cost of incarcerating an offender is

Table 1. An Illustration of the Decision Theoretic Approach to Sentencing Decisions

	State of Nature (Robberies per year that would be committed)				Expected Cost (Dollars)
Decision Alternatives (Period of Incarceration)	None (p=.3)	1-9 (p=.3)	10-20 (p=.2)	21-30 (p=.2)	
No Incarceration	0	6,250	18,750	31,875	12,000
One Year	8,000	13,000	23,000	33,500	17,600
Two Years	16,000	19,750	27,250	35,125	23,200
Three Years	24,000	26,500	31,500	36,750	28,800
Four Years	32,000	33,250	35,750	38,375	31,075
Five Years	40,000	40,000	40,000	40,000	40,000

$8,000 per year, and that the dollar loss incurred in an average robbery is $250, Table 1 illustrates the decision-theoretic analysis under the present assumptions.

The entries in Table 1 represent the total cost of each possible sentence and state of nature combination. For example, the $13,000 entry in column two is obtained by adding the cost of one year's incarceration ($8,000) to four years' worth of robbery losses under the assumption of five (the midpoint of the one to nine interval) robberies per year ($4 \times 5 \times \$250 = \$5,000$). The last column in Table 1 contains the overall *expected* cost associated with each sentencing decision; these figures are weighted averages of the costs within each row, where the weights are the state of nature probabilities.

The best decision is the one that minimizes expected cost; thus "no incarceration" would be the prescribed sentence for the present utility and probability estimates. Different utilities and/or probabilities could, of course, produce different prescriptions. For example, higher probabilities for the "ten to 20" and "21 to 30" robberies per year categories (which correspondingly lower ones for "none" and "one to nine") would increase the overall appropriateness of incarceration, as would decreased costs of incarceration and increased average losses per robbery. In the present case, the relatively high costs of incarceration have overwhelmed costs asssociated with robbery occurrences. The picture would change markedly if the cost per robbery were estimated at, say, $500 or $1,000 to reflect the trauma of being victimized as well as the material losses incurred.

Thus far, the example has been kept simple for illustrative purposes, but the decision theoretic approach is entirely capable of taking as many complicating factors into account as may be warranted by knowledge of their effects. Special deterrence, for instance, could be incorporated by estimating two (or more) sets of probabilities: one set for the "no incarceration" decision, where the deterrent effect would have minimal chance to operate, and one or more additional sets for the various incarceration alternatives, where a deterrent effect would be reflected in higher probabilities for the crime-free and low-level crime activitiy states of nature. Conversely, if the "prisons-as-schools-for-crime" hypothesis were eventually borne out, probabilities of low level criminal activity would be *lower* for incarceration decisions than they would be for the decision not to incarcerate.

The problem becomes even more difficult when one factors the limits of existing resources into the model. That is, if we are merely attempting to redistribute existing bed space, our technical problem is simply that of identifying the *high probability* cases for incarceration. Thus, we are simply "spending" existing cell space differently, and our cost-benefit model is useful. When we must construct new cell space in order to reduce the crime costs of certain offense groups, however, the costs are substantially greater: to the order of ten to 15 times the operating cost figure we specified per inmate. Therefore, it is impossible to construct the maximum-benefit model without some idea of the limitations of current resources (fiscal and material) for implementing the policy eventually selected (Clear, Harris, and Record, 1982).

TECHNOLOGIES OF INCAPACITATION

The normally accepted technology for incapacitation is imprisonment. As an incapacitative strategy, imprisonment is based on "a reasonable presumption that offenders who are imprisoned would have continued to commit crimes if they had remained free" (Blumstein, 1978). However, as an incapacitative measure for convicted offenders, incarceration suffers from three primary limitations. First, there are real questions regarding the degree to which the "reasonable presumption" above is invalidated by "replacement of the criminal activitiy of an imprisoned offender by recruitment from an illegitimate labor market or because of the continued activity of a group of offenders (such as gangs) from which the imprisoned offender was removed" (Blumstein, 1978). Second, one can question the degree to which incapacitation has the qualitative effect of aggravating characteristics which led to criminal behavior thereby changing the post-incarcerative probability of the criminal event to exceed that which would have been true without the imposition of incarceration. Third, it stretches the meaning of incapacitation to say that offenses committed in prison do not count: when incarceration results in prison homicide, for example, it is a bit harsh to suggest that incapacitation has "occurred'" when in reality all that has occurred is that the population of potential victims has been limited to convicted felons and their guards.

This last point is important. Is it necessary to define incapacitative sanctions to include only those which actually resulted in prevention? To use such a *post hoc* definition of incapacitation would be of limited utility for research purposes; it is more useful to return to earlier definitions: incapacitation involves sanctions for which the primary intent is to use physical constraint to prevent certain kinds of behavior.

Under this definition, it is possible to construct overall measures of sanction effectiveness at incapacitation. For virtually all incapacitative sanctions then, there will also be a failure rate: escapes from prisons, variations in sensitivity to drug control, and so forth. From the standpoint of technologies, the research problem is to compare failure rates for various incapacitative methods in order to minimize costs, including social costs.

An example will help to illustrate the research problem: developing a policy of incapacitation for burglary offenses and choosing between weekend incarceration and, say, five year sentences for burglars as a general sanction. Simply by virtue of the more extreme isolation, the five-year incarcerative policy would seem to produce a higher degree of incarceration that has a lower failure rate than weekend incarceration.

However, this is not the sole criterion for a policy, since there are differential costs involved in these two strategies; there are hidden and straightforward financial costs, there are social costs which might be called externalities (for example, the "costs" of establishing a society with a larger proportion of citizens serving long sentences in total institutions is a "quality of life" cost issue). Assuming all of these costs can be quantified, the research question is: Which is greater, the prevented crimes in cost gains of incapacitation policy A minus the total costs of errors in A or the equivalent benefit-cost equation of policy B?

The point is that each prevented crime based on a technology represents cost associated with implementing the technology. Overall gain of a policy, then, is a function of the costs of various technologies and their incapacitative products (Hennessey et. al., 1977). This is a fairly simple issue so long as one considers only one technology, imprisonment: What level of imprisonment produces the maximum incapacitation for the amount of investment? The externalities here include the societal costs of more highly active social systems with the associated high rate of Type II error. In reality, however, there are numerous incapacitative devices, from solitary confinement to probation with heavy surveillance. From a policy standpoint, latter approaches comparing the difference in effectiveness/cost ratio may not be sufficient to justify use of solitary confinement. It is suggested that a *variety* of incapacitative measures be considered as researchable, including relatively high failure-rate approaches, in deciding optimal incapacitative strategies.

We have a need to develop new means for incapacitation. It must be stressed that this is not a developmental need which is valueless in scope. The problem with a policy of developing new technologies for incapacitating humans raises the spectre of increased state social control and a broader and deeper impact on freedom. In fact, it is the very crude nature of the current

Incapacitating Offenders   541

incapacitative method—imprisonment—which suggests the need for the development of less intrusive, less restrictive incapacitative approaches that are, perhaps, crime-specific in their impact. Moreover, by promoting new technology development, it will be more feasible to compare the relative utilities of various incapacitative approaches (including those operated while the offender continues to reside in the community) with calculations of direct and indirect costs of alternative approaches in order to arrive at more acceptable strategies. Imprisonment is sufficiently costly in indirect ways that more satisfactory approaches should be possible to develop.

IMPLEMENTATION SYSTEM

The broad potential of a penal policy of incapacitation is limited by the fact that existing bureaucratic agencies will be responsible for implementing such a policy in the context of the American criminal law. The problem is to articulate the manner in which legal agencies operate to limit the potential of incapacitation; this information will then prove useful in understanding the issues around selection systems and technologies.

One fundamental limitation on implementation was mentioned earlier: the due process requirements of the legal system. At the outset, this limitation requires that the state be put to a procedure of proofs before it can apply a negative sanction to an individual. In addition, it is ordinarily the case that an increased level of sanction, as may sometimes be the case for incapacitative strategies, requires an increased level of proof. This and other aspects of the due process requirement, taken together with a relatively natural selection process which produces a small number of convictions (and incarcerations) for a large number of crimes, places a parametric limitation on incapacitation which can only be overcome at great cost:

> When the current rate of imprisonment per crime and the individual crime rates are low, the percentage increase in prison population needed in order to achieve a given percentage reduction in crime is large (Blumstein, 1978).

Attempts to overcome the effects of legal tradition are frustrated by the "multiple-discretion" system of justice in this country (Zimring, 1977). Several proposals to strictly limit the impact of discretion on sanctions have been of limited success. Mandatory penalties for example, are frequently avoided by prosecutorial charging practices and judicial (and to a lesser extent jury) use of dismissals (Association of the Bar of New York, 1977). This same pattern of use of discretion to overcome the directive intentions of determinate sentencing has also been described by Clear, Hewitt, and Regoli (1978). The problem is that these limitations—due process, attrition of cases and discretion—tend to interact in intractable ways to limit the potentials of incapacitation. As an example, one study found that even such an extreme incapacitative policy as a mandatory five year flat sentence for *all convicted felons* might have produced only a negligible decrease in violent crimes of one community (Van Dine, Dinitz, and Conrad, 1977).

This is not to say that the agencies that implement sanctions make incapacitation impossible. To the contrary, a study of Michigan prisoners, classified by risk, showed that a limited policy of "penal quarantine" might have reduced the cost of an imprisonment system while keeping a greater number of high risk offenders incarcerated for a larger period of time (Johnson, 1978). The point is that it is essential to recognzie that the degree to which any policy of incapacitation is systematically effective, and that it will be so in part because its operation is consistent with the limitations of existing legal practices. This is particularly true since existing legal policies are themselves a social value which should not be overcome by incapacitative methods, but should be reflected by them. To find policies that can be operated in such a fashion requires, at the outset, an understanding of the nature and statistical impact of those agency limitations.

DISCUSSION

Our intention has been to point out some of the complexities inherent in the incapacitative approach to crime-control. Our point is not that incapacitation should (or should not) be given greater emphasis; rather our point is that the decision to adopt incapacitation carries with it a complicated array of technical problems to maximally benefit from the policy, at reasonable cost.

We know of very little systematic research being conducted to untangle these complex concerns. Instead, we see a kind of random, undirected trust in the efficacy of incarceration that is reminiscent of an earlier era's belief in reformation. As in the past, we will probably fail to be successful in the current crime-control movement, not so much because the idea is faulty, but once again because we have chosen not to give the *development* of the strategy sufficient thought and experiment. Unless we take a more careful view of the potential of incapacitation, we are likely to declare it a "failure," too, at a later date because of prediction errors and unmanageable costs. Ironically, cautious use of the policy would allow us to further develop the techniques necessary to implement it with due respect for the complexities it contains.

REFERENCES

AMIR, MENACHEM
   1971   *Patterns in Forcible Rape.* Chicago: University of Chicago Press.
BLUMSTEIN, ALFRED
   1978a   "Research on the Deterrent and Incapacitative Effects of the Criminal
           Law," *Journal of Criminal Justice*, 6(1):4.
   1978b   "Commentary," *The Criminologist*, 2(3):6.
BLUMSTEIN, ALFRED, J. COHEN, and D. NAGIN (eds.)
   1978   *Deterrence and Incapacitation: Estimating the Effects of Criminal Sanctions
           on Crime Rates.* Washington, D.C.: National Academy of Science.

CLEAR, TODD R.
1978 *A Model for the Supervision of the Offender in the Community.* Report to the National Institute of Correction.

CLEAR, TODD R, PATRICIA HARRIS and ALBERT L. RECORD
1982 "Managing the Costs of Correction," *The Prison Journal,* Spring-Summer, 62(1):1-64.

CLEAR, TODD R, JOHN D. HEWITT, and ROBERT M. REGOLI
1978 "Discretion and the Determinate Sentence: Its Distribution, Control and Effect on Time Served," *Crime and Delinquency,* 24 (4):428.

CLINARD, MARSHALL B, and R. QUINNEY
1967 *Criminal Behavior Systems: A Typology.* N.Y.: Holt, Rinehard, and Winston.

COHEN, MURRAY L, A. NICHOLAS GROTH, and RICHARD SIEGEL
1978 "The Clinical Prediction of Dangerousness," *Crime and Delinquency* 24(1):33.

FORD, ROBIN C. and S. R. JOHNSON
1977 *Probation Prediction and Recidivism,* Report to the Correctional Manpower Service, Illinois Department of Corrections.

GREEN, D. M. and J. A. SWETS
1966 *Signal Detection Theory and Psychophysics.* New York: Wiley.

GOTTFREDSON, DON M.
1973 *Paroling-Policy Guidelines,* Research reports no. 9, 10, U.S. Board of Parole.

HENNESSEY, TIMOTHY M., et. al.
1977 "Choosing Among Corrections Alternatives: A Political Economy Perspecitve," in Stuart S. Nagel, ed., *Modeling the Criminal Justice System.* Beverly Hills, California: Sage.

JOHNSON, PERRY M.
1978 "The Role of Penal Quarantine in Reducing Violent Crime," *Crime and Delinquency,* 24(4):465.

KITTRIE, NICHOLAS
1971 *The Right to Be Different: Deviance and Enforced Therapy.* Baltimore: The Johns Hopkins Press.

KLECKA, WILLIAM R.
"Discriminant Analysis," in Norman Nie et al., *Statistical Package for the Social Science.* N.Y.: McGraw-Hill.

MANNHEIM, HERMANN, and LESLIE T. WILKINS
1957 *Prediction Methods in Relation to Borstal Training.* Condon: HMSO, p. 47.

MANSKI, CHARLES F.
1978 "Prospects for Inference on Deterrence Through Empirical Analysis of Individual Criminal Behavior," in A. Blumstein, J. Cohen, and D.

Nagin (eds.), *Deterrence and Incapacitation: Estimating the Effects of Criminal Sanctions on Crime Rates.* Washington, D.C.: National Academy of Science.

MCCARTHUR, CHARLES C.
1968   "Comment on Studies of Clinical U.S. Statistical Prediction," *Journal of Counseling Psychology* 2:173.

MCNAUGHTEN-SMITH, P.
1965   *Some Statistical and other Numerical Methods for Classifying Individuals: A Home Office Research* Unit Report (Condon: HMSO).

MEEHL, PAUL E.
1956   *Clinical vs. Statistical Prediction* (Minneapolis: University of Minnesota).

1959   "A Comparsion of Clinicians with Five Statistical Methods of Identifying Psychotic MMPI Profiles," *Journal of Counseling Psychology,* 6(1):102.

MONAHAN, J.
1976   *Community Mental Health and the Criminal Justice System.* N.Y.: Pergamon.

NEW YORK ASSOCIATION OF THE BAR OF NEW YORK
The Nation's Toughest Drug Law: Evaluating the New York Experience. New York:ABA.

O'LEARY, VINCENT
1977   *Frames of Reference in Sentencing and Parole.* Hackensack, New Jersey: National Council on Crime and Delinquency.

O'LEARY, VINCENT and A. VON HIRSCH
1975   *Report of the Conference on Sentencing.* Mimeo, SUNY, Albany.

PETERSON, W.W., T. G. BIRDSALL, and W.C. FOX
1954   "The Theory of Signal Detectability," *Institute of Radio Engineers Transactions,* PGIT-4:171-212.

RAIFFA, HOWARD and R. SCHLAIFER
1961   *Applied Statistical Decision Theory,* Boston: Harvard University Press.

SCHLESINGER, STEPHEN E.
1978   "The Prediction of Dangerousness in Juveniles: A Replication," *Crime and Delinquency,* 24(1):47.

SCHWITZGEBEL, RALPH K.
1972   "Limitation on the Coercive Treatment of Offenders," *Criminal Law Bulletin,* 8(4):267.

STEADMAN, HENRY J.
1973   "Follow-up on Baxstrom Patients Return to Hospitals for the Criminally Insane," *American Journal of Psychiatry,* 130(3):317.

Incapacitating Offenders   **545**

U.S. GENERAL ACCOUNTING OFFICE
    State and County Probation: System in Crisis. Washington, D.C.: General
    Accounting Office.

VAN DINE, STEVEN, SIMON DINITZ, AND JOHN CONRAD
    1977   "The Incapacitation of the Dangerous Offender: A Statistical
            Experiment. *Journal of Research* in Crime and Delinquency, 14(1):22.

VON WINTERFELDT, D. and G. W. FISCHER
    "Multiattribute Utility Theory: Models and Assessment Procedures,"
    in D. Wendt and D.A.J. Vlek (eds), *Utility, Probability and Human
    Decision Making,* Odrdrecht, The Netherlands: Reidel.

WILKINS, LESLIE T.
    1969   *Evaluation of Penal Measures.* N.Y.: Random House.

WOLFGANG, MARVIN and FRANCO FERRACUTI
    1967   *The Subculture of Violence: Toward an Integrated Theory in Criminology.*
            N.Y.: Barnes and Noble.

WOLFGANG, MARVIN, et al.
    1972   *Delinquency in a Birth Cohort.* Chicago: University of Chicago Press.

ZIMRING, FRANKLIN
    1977   "Making the Punishment Fit the Crime: A Consumers Guide to
            Sentencing Reform," reprinted in *Senate Hearings on Reform of the
            Federal Criminal Law,* Part XIII, June 7-9, 22, 21.

[17]

The Howard Journal Vol 29 No 4. Nov 90
ISSN 0265-5527

Tagging Reviewed[1]

J. ROBERT LILLY

Professor, Department of Sociology, Northern Kentucky University,
Highland Heights, Ky. U.S.A.; Visiting Professor, School of Law,
Leicester Polytechnic, Leicester, England

*Abstract: Much of the confusion surrounding tagging has been created because the topic has yet
to be debated in the cultural context within which it has been developed. This paper identifies the
appropriate cultural context for an informed debate and asks that it begin. 'Our much vaunted
progress in technology, generally of civilization, is like the axe in the hand of a pathological
criminal' (Einstein 1917).*

While the Home Office has announced the end of its three small tagging
experiments and indicated that new plans are underway to begin one
large tagging scheme, it is still unclear whether tagging will have a future
of clouds or sunshine. Confusion about tagging abounds. Before proceeding
with additional tagging experiments and related legislative changes, it is
timely to examine how the first experiments were introduced and what
was neglected. This is important because they were the world's first
nationally sponsored tagging experiments and it will provide insight into
some of the problems with tagging. Attention is also given to the U.S.
experience with electronic monitoring. Together this approach will
illuminate some of the pitfalls to be avoided should the future bring
additional tagging. Hopefully this will add some perspective to a scene
that to date has been as befuddled as informed.

In this paper I contend that the recent experiments were gravely
misguided by a hubris expressing the age-old faith in technological
solutions to social problems (Ellul 1964; Grant 1986; Winner 1977; Hill
1988). This is exemplified by the Home Office and government
spokesperson's failure to recognise that tagging is part of the inclusive and
intrusive technology found in the *new age of surveillance*. At no point was
this recognised, at least not in print. This oversight was made easy by the
failure of tagging sponsors to have clear and consistent goals for the
experiments. The resulting confusion was further exacerbated by various
critics who themselves failed to recognise tagging's connection to the new
surveillance technology, and who in addition inaccurately represented the
U.S. experiences with tagging. Had the sponsors and the critics of the
experiments fully addressed these matters and dealt with tagging as one
element of a booming corrections industry, much confusion and expense
may have been avoided.

'House arrest' or 'home confinement' as it is better termed, and tagging

represent a relatively recent development in American and European
punitive policy. The growing popularity of electronic monitoring in the
United States and the English experimentation with it suggests the need
for critical analysis and caution lest it becomes another item on a long list
of unused and unusable penal reforms. This paper first reviews the major
features of the *new age of surveillance*. Second, the monitoring equipment
used in the United States is reviewed (briefly) against the backdrop of the
new age of surveillance technology. Third, the monitoring trends in the
U.S. are discussed, starting with locating tagging within the booming
corrections enterprise. These are offered as examples of some of the
problems that may be encountered should tagging enter England's
criminal justice system through privatisation. Last, the tagging trials are
examined and it is concluded they were ill-conceived from beginning to
end, including the Home Office's evaluation plans.

The New Age of Surveillance

The contemporary world is characterised by a new surveillance technology which has the potential to redefine the meaning of privacy and
human rights. A new regard for each is required because the new
technology includes the increasingly prevalent use of breath analysers,
motion detectors, polygraphs, electronic anklets, continuous monitoring
devices, bugs, wiretaps, light amplifiers, voice stress and brain analysis,
and the more recent identification process afforded by DNA research on
'genetic fingerprinting'. Each represents the spreading inclusiveness of
surveillance technology. This I argue is an extremely important element
of the cultural context within which tagging has developed, and it needs to
be discussed.

Although the causes, nature, and consequences of the various new
surveillance methods differ, the more important concern is how the new
forms of surveillance are distinguished from traditional ones. The new
surveillance transcends distance, darkness, and physical barriers. It can
look through closed doors, suitcases and far into the inner intellectual,
emotional, and physical regions of the individual. These technologies have
made intrusiveness and the new electronic incarceration easier. Sound
and video can be transmitted over vast distances and with the aid of infra-
red and light-amplifying technologies, night can be turned into day (Marx
1985a, 1985b).

The new surveillance also transcends time. Its records can easily be
stored, retrieved, combined, analysed and communicated. The information
it generates can be 'socially freeze-dried' and once stored it is available for
instant analysis many years after the fact and in totally different
interpretative contexts. This enhances data sharing on an immense scale.
Because it is capital rather than labour intensive, it has become much less
expensive to monitor people. It's economy is further enhanced because
persons have become voluntary and involuntary participants in their own
monitoring, which is often self-activated and automatic. Computerised
bank, credit, automobile, insurance and health records come to mind

here. One aspect of this is that persons are motivated to report themselves in turn for some benefit or to avoid a penalty.

The new surveillance triggers a shift from targetting specific suspects to categorical suspicion. Kafka's nightmare has been implemented; modern society suspects everyone. The camera, the tape-recorder, the identity card, the metal detector, the tax form that must be submitted even if one has no income and, pre-eminently, the computer make all who come within their province reasonable targets for surveillance. The new 'softer' forms of control are used to create a society in which people are permanently under suspicion, surveillance and incarceration. With the prevention of violation a major concern, control is extended to even more features of society and its surroundings. Rather than simply reacting to what is served up around us, anticipatory strategies seek to reduce risk and uncertainty. One result is that 'target hardening' (for instance, better locks) occurs, making violations more difficult (Marx 1985a, 1985b).

The new forms of surveillance are also decentralised and it triggers self-policing. In contrast to the trend of the last centuries, information can now in principle flow as freely from the centre of society's periphery as the reverse. Surveillance is decentralised too in the sense that national data resources are available to widely dispersed local officials. It also has either low visibility or it is invisible. Thus it becomes ever more difficult to ascertain when and whether or not we are being watched and who is doing the watching. Its instruments are often difficult to discover, either because they are something other than they appear to be or, as with snooping into microwave transmissions, there are few indications of surveillance.

It is also ever more intensive, continuously probing beneath surfaces and discovering previously inaccessible information. Much as we use drilling technology to bore ever deeper into the earth, today's surveillance prods ever deeper into physical, social, and personal areas. It hears whispers, penetrates clouds, walls and windows. It sees into the body – and attempts to see into the soul, claiming to go beneath ostensible meanings and appearances to real meanings.

At the same time, the new surveillance grows more extensive, covering not only deeper, but larger areas of human life. Previously unconnected surveillance threads now are woven into gigantic tapestries of information. The mesh of the fishing net has not only become finer and more pliable, the net itself now is wider (Cohen 1985). Broad new categories of persons and behaviour have become subjects for information collection and analysis, and as the pool of persons watched expands, so does the pool of watchers. Not only might anyone be watched, everyone is also a potential watcher. Mass surveillance and incarceration has become a reality. Tagging is part of and contributes to this development. Unfortunately, this has not been addressed.

Monitoring and the New Surveillance: United States

To what extent is monitoring part of the new age of surveillance? What is its 'degree of fit' with the new technology? What do we know about the tagging equipment?

The transmitting range of all tagging equipment is limited by distance and physical barriers and its signals often are foiled by weather conditions, radio frequencies, refrigerators and many other barriers, including different types of housing construction materials (Byrne and Kelly 1987). A recent national survey, in fact, reported that out of a total of 235 distinct problems identified by electronic monitoring programmes, 46.8% concerned equipment functions (Renzema forthcoming). Nor can it always transcend time, although a record can be made by the tagging equipment that otherwise would not have been made (Byrne and Kelly 1987). This is an important point because the newly created record permits officials to overcome 'ignorance' regarding the location and increasingly, the behaviour of the offender for a given period of time.

At first glance, it appears that the tagging equipment is more capital, than labour intensive. Records do indicate that electronic supervision can be approximately 75% cheaper than 'people' supervision. However, there is little if any evidence which demonstrates that labour has been replaced by the tagging equipment (Renzema forthcoming). What occurs instead is that additional employees are used to monitor the new categories of 'offenders' including AIDS victims, the elderly, juveniles and potential high-risk offenders, for example, soccer hooligans, and the massive amounts of information generated by the equipment.

Not everyone is suspect, only those connected to the tagging equipment (Byrne and Kelly 1987). Again, this is an important point but it eschews the fact that those monitored have homes, often with others living with them. The equipment is targetted not only on the offender, but their home as well, thus enhancing the family as a category for suspicion and incarceration. Tagging does seem to have an impact on violations while offenders are monitored. In the U.S. the rate of failures because of new offences while tagged ranges from 33% during the first month to a low of 2.1% through the 13th and 24th month of tagging (Renzema forthcoming). However, these rates may be an artifact of highly selective criteria for those considered suitable for tagging, and the lack of close supervision (especially from private companies driven by the profit motive and without statutory support for enforcing laws). Failures have increased as the selection criteria have been broadened to include greater risk offenders, including prisoners released on parole. The preventive value of tagging may also be enhanced by the fact that it does permit the flow of information to and from the periphery of society, allowing national data resources to be used at local levels and vice versa. This feature of the new surveillance and incarceration is strengthened by the activation of self-policing through the everyday processes of interaction with the tagging agencies.

There is no doubt that the new tagging equipment has low visibility for both the watched and the watcher. Critics have pointed out that this feature reduces stigmatisation, a dubious advantage for those who argue that stigmatisation has positive consequences especially in comparisons to the stigma associated with jail and prison terms. Because of its low visibility, however, the tagging equipment can be more intensive than 'people surveillance', a feature that will be further enhanced by coupling tagging to additional monitoring devices such as voice verification and blood alcohol analysis systems. Mitsubishi's Visual Telecom Division and other vendors in the U.S. are already doing this.

These distinctions and qualifications do not singularly or in combination exclude tagging equipment from the new surveillance. With the possible exception of intensive labour, each identified limitation can quickly be altered with relatively minor technological adjustments. Such adjustments have been made by vendors only too willing to repair and/or replace faulty or obsolete equipment (Renzema forthcoming). This has become a standard service from vendors with sales sufficient to sustain the cost. It is intended to keep clients satisfied and to maintain a competitive edge in the corrections marketplace. One consequence has been an enhancement of the power of the monitoring equipment while simultaneously increasing the capacity to increase the number of people incarcerated. Global Positioning Systems, Seattle, Washington, for instance, recently expressed confidence that with the help of cellular telephone technology, their satellite navigation system could within one year develop a cost-effective monitor that could track probationers and parolees throughout the U.S. within 30 feet of accuracy.

United States: Monitoring Trends

While tagging has developed primarily because of the unique confluence of new surveillance technology and prison/jail overcrowding, it is also but one element in a booming 'corrections enterprise' in an open market economy (Shover 1979; Shover and Einstadter 1988). Spending for corrections alone increased 115% between 1960 and 1980. In 1980 state and local government correctional employees numbered 260,722 at a monthly payroll of $338,325,000. By 1986 correctional employees number 372,899 with a monthly payroll of $392,027,000 (U.S. Dept. of Justice 1984, p. 32; 1988, p. 24). Total expenditures for state corrections in 1980 amounted to more than $4 billion. This increased to $9.8 billion in 1986. With some 3.4 million persons being supervised by correctional agencies as of 1 January 1988, there appears to be no end in sight to the 'boom time' in corrections. The following represents only the latest addition to this expanding economy.

Vendor Growth: Shareholder's reports profile an industry experiencing rapid turnarounds and expanding horizons. BI, Incorporated, a leading U.S. vendor, stated in May 1989 that 'Your Company achieved a meaningful turnaround in its business . . . [which] is testimony to the stability of our product . . .' (BI, Incorporated, 'BI Inc. sales up 143%', *Penny Stock Journal*, 1990). They envisioned accelerated expansion and by October 1989, BI, Incorporated announced record revenues of $2,237,000 and a net income of $251,000 (BI Incorporated 1989). This compares to revenues of $919,000 and a net loss of $700,000 for the same period in 1988. Corrections Services, Inc., the leading international tagging vendor based in the U.S., doubled its annual revenues between 1988 and 1989, and expected to do so again in 1990 (Corrections Services, Inc. 1989). Both vendors reported that business was strong and they expected annual revenues to increase dramatically for years to come. The expected growth is reflected in the expansion of monitoring programmes.[2]

Programme Expansion: The rate of growth of the number of offenders placed on house arrest with electronic monitoring between 1987 and 1988 was approximately 300% (Schmidt 1989). In February 1987 approximately 800 people on any given day were being monitored electronically. By February 1988 the number had increased to approximately 2,000. Altogether, 32 states in 1988 had at least one monitoring programme compared to 21 states in 1987. And according to Renzema (personal communication, 9 April 1989), the number of people being monitored per day in February 1989 had risen to 7,000; by October 1989 the number had increased to 12,000 and it has been conservatively estimated that the total number of offenders available for monitoring exceeds 70,000. By December 1989 the number of states with monitoring programmes had increased to 44 out of 50, with the total number of monitoring programmes throughout the U.S. exceeding 300.

Large programmes, for example, Michigan, Missouri and Florida, are still growing and nearly all programmes have expanded or plan to expand. Another 1989 development was the start of programmes with initial goals of large numbers, rather than the trend of 1987–88, which was to start small programmes with long-term plans to grow modestly. A question related to large and small programmes has been the extent to which purchased equipment has been utilised. One report stated that almost a quarter of the electronic devices purchased in Florida to keep tabs on offenders were on the shelf. In Miami, twice as many wrist monitors were on the shelf than being used, according to a February report by the state's Department of Corrections. In addition, 22% of the monitors statewide were not being used. Whether this represents programme failure is debatable, but it does suggest that full utilisation of acquired monitoring equipment is highly problematic. Regardless of the type (wristlets/anklets) or the extent to which equipment is used, the Florida Department of Corrections plans to double its usage of monitoring devices by 1990 at a cost of $1.3 million ('Many house-arrest devices not used' (Miami, Fl.), *El Miami Herald*, 3 March 1989).

For a variety of reasons approximately two dozen programmes have been abandoned, half of which were private ventures. These closed because they were unprofitable. A few have been closed because the equipment was not delivered expeditiously, or because it was unreliable. Some programmes were announced but never materialised. Other programmes failed because judges refused to consider monitoring a viable response to offenders.

Research: Research on offender's responses to electronic monitoring is unclear at this time. The programmes have not been in operation very long, thus hampering longitudinal evaluation (see Lilly, Ball and Wright 1987, pp. 189–203.) Only one descriptive research report has been written for the Federal government's evaluation projects; others are expected this year (see Beck and Klein-Saffran 1989).[3] Nor do most of the monitoring programmes have clearly stated goals and appropriate evaluation components. The reasons for this are two-fold. First, because most monitoring programmes have not been explicitly coupled with policies which guarantee that they are to be used as an alternative, they are only loosely connected to efforts to relieve jail/prison overcrowding. Second, only 13 states have statutory guidelines for monitoring. These are often deliberately vague or they reflect the successful lobbying of specific vendors. Also, they often lag behind technological developments. Consequently, there are few structured incentives for accountability and evaluation research, especially for private monitoring companies eager to increase caseloads with supervisory fees ('Reiner blasts house arrest as "utterly unreliable" ' (Los Angeles, Ca.), *Herald-Examiner*, 16 June 1988).

In a few instances monitoring programmes have been termed successful. In April 1989 the Cleveland, Ohio Detention Center reported that it had reduced its daily juvenile population by 23% through the use of monitors (Sanniti 1989). And a few states and cities have claimed that electronic monitoring has saved money because the pressure to construct new jails and prisons has been lessened because of the devices. One newspaper report stated that Arizona saved an estimated $10 million a year by keeping 700–800 offenders at home and out of jail ('Doing time electronically: good option for some offenders', *Reporters Dispatch*, 14 June 1988). And the Federal government's interim report concludes that monitoring is cost-effective relative to placing offenders in halfway houses. In addition to the reported economic advantages of monitoring, some public opinion polls indicated that only 15% of the public favour building new prisons. This too has been interpreted as evidence favourable to electronic monitoring ('House arrest, yes; more prisons, no', *Sun*, 22 May 1988). Yet, this does not offset the fact that the U.S. jail and prison population continues to increase by approximately 1,000 per week.

Fees: An interesting but not surprising development related to the economics of monitoring is that while open market competition among vendors in the United States has lowered the daily cost of the monitoring equipment, some programmes have increased the supervision fees paid by offenders. Santa Clara County, California, for example, increased its daily supervision fee more than 100%. The fee was increased from $4.80 to $10.00 because the administrative cost of the monitoring programme was $21 per day per inmate. The $10 daily fee is much closer to the fees charged by most of the monitoring programmes in the United States (' "Home" inmates now face higher costs', *Times Tribune*, 8 March 1989).

Unions: One of the more rare recent developments occurred in Rhode Island. This state's effort to hire a private agency to run home confinement programmes was attacked by two unions representing Rhode Island's prison guards and probation/parole staff. The unions reportedly supported the concept of home confinement, but objected to the private agency because the union could do the supervision of the offenders cheaper and better. They also claimed the private agency selected had a 'bad track record'. Plus, a former Rhode Island corrections director had also been the president of the private agency ('Unions attack at-home jail plan' (Providence, R.I.), *Journal*, 11 April 1989). The hint of conflicting interest is more than a passing concern.

Corruption: In Michigan, Illinois and Florida, criminal justice and corrections officials either have been embarrassed or resigned because of questionable behaviour connected with monitoring. In one case it was learned that correction officials held stock in a company they approved to provide monitoring equipment. Another official resigned because of unacceptable accounting practices and expenditures directly related to house arrest and monitoring. Other officials were investigated by the F.B.I. after allegedly taking bribes in exchange for placing particular offenders on a Work Release Program ('Sheriff fires ex-head of house arrest' (West Palm Beach, Fl.), *Post* (U.S.A.), 1 February 1989). One person in Illinois who had actually started a county-run monitoring programme ended up electronically tethered after pleading guilty to four felony counts involving unauthorised expenditures ('This prisoner's reputation rides on his not being able to escape', *Wall Street Journal*, 23 May 1989, B1).

Informed sources have reported that underneath these public scandals there are numerous others perking along, almost ready for public digestion. These include revelations of 'fixing' bids (tenders) for a particular vendor.[4] Another example includes the possible deliberate killing of a highly successful and lucrative county-sponsored home confinement programme by a high ranking elected official so that it could be replaced by a private company controlled by the same official and his brother. Another example involved a vendor hiring a probation officer to travel around the U.S. to attend probation and parole officers' conferences where he told others about the virtues of the equipment he was hawking, all along denying that his expenses were paid by the vendor.[5] And just four months after the Sheriff of Cook County (Chicago), Illinois, announced that its monitoring programme was going to be doubled from 400 to 800 at a cost of $2.2 million, Federal grand jury investigation focussed on the ties between private security guard business owned by the Sheriff, and the company selected to run the monitoring programme. The *Chicago Tribune* reported that the monitoring company shares office space and a telephone with the guard firm, which itself is owned by a former undersheriff. The Sheriff was reported to have said the revelation was 'biased reporting' ('More electronic bracelets approved', *Chicago Tribune*, 19 September 1989; 'O'Grady defends prisoner monitoring pact', *Chicago Tribune*, 4 January 1990).

A particularly egregious example of corruption involved the collusion of a county jailer, a judge, local criminal attorneys and the bank vice-president. Some of the local defence attorneys and the bank vice-president bank-rolled the leasing of the equipment, and the judge agreed that the jailer would select which inmates would be suitable for electronic monitoring. With the jailer agreeing that just about everyone in the jail would certainly be eligible for monitoring, he said: 'A man would be a fool if he couldn't make a barrel of money with this thing'. Except for the research, the efficacy of the profit motive for each trend is undeniable.

The New Prohibition: Threats to house arrest and monitoring, however, have not come from within the system alone. As the public has become increasingly intolerant of alcohol and nicotine abuse, they have become increasingly intolerant of public and private work places, habitats and official sanctions which tacitly permit if not actually approve of these abuses.[6] For example, as a result of a horrendous alcohol-related pickup truck and church/school bus accident in Kentucky which left a record 27 people dead in early Spring 1988 MADD (Mothers Against Drunk Drivers) announced opposition to the use of house arrest and electronic monitoring for Driving While Intoxicated (DWI) offenders ('MADD angered by house arrest for DWI's', *Kentucky Post*, 13 June 1988, 1k-2k). It made no difference that the truck driver never had been sentenced to house arrest and monitoring. The mere fact that alcohol was involved was enough to permit home confinement and monitoring to be guilty by association.[7]

One thing seems clear: house arrest and electronic monitoring has not yet reduced the nation-wide jail/prison overcrowding problem, and it may not. The United States has continued and accelerated its use of segregative confinement. Since 1973 the prison population has increased annually and a prison construction boom is underway (Shover 1990). There were 31 more state prisons and one more Federal prison in 1984 than in 1983, and in 1987 then-President Reagan proposed a budget for 1988 which would allocate $65.4 million 'to expand and repair the federal prison system, including $96.5 million to build two new medium-security prisons' ('Departmental priorities: highlights of the budget', *New York Times*, 6 January 1987, p. 9). President Bush's 1989 $1.2 billion 'plan to battle crime' continued the emphasis on prisons and added drug testing for Federal probation as well as 1,600 additional United States Attorneys ('President unveils $1.2 billion plan to battle crime', *New York Times*, 16 May 1989, p. 9). His 1990 budget contained $1.5 billion alone for 24,000 new Federal prison beds (U.S. General Accounting Office 1989). At the current rate of 13% annual expansion, the U.S. will have 1.13 million inmates and the states will need, $35 billion for prison construction by 1994 ('Czar vs. intellectuals', *New York Times*, 26 December 1989, p. 27).

None of these trends can be interpreted to mean that less people have been or ever will be incarcerated because of the availability and implementation of tagging. Nor do these trends indicate an awareness or concern that monitoring is part of broader developments in surveillance technology and the creation of new places of incarceration.

England

Until the 1988 announcement and the 1989 tagging trials, the English experience with tagging had been one of reluctance and caution. Now it appears that England is on the verge of imitating the U.S. experience, replete with a new 'hanging' Home Secretary, a new White Paper, 'tough

237

rhetoric' and claims of tagging successes with scant supporting evidence
('Patten toughens tagging trials', *Guardian*, 1 January 1990; 'Law reform
set to curb jailing' and 'Pick-a-penalty deal for courts', *Guardian*, 2
January 1990). Nevertheless, contradictions, confusion and a degree of
myopia has permeated the English tagging experience and there is little
reason to believe that this will change. The (Home Office 1988) Green
Paper on *Punishment, Custody and the Community*, and the government
officials' responses and explanations of it as reported in the media, and the
Home Office's 1989 tagging evaluation plans for the three trials are
offered as evidence. At no point was official recognition given to the fact
that tagging is part of the new age of surveillance. Nor was attention
directed to the implications of this for increasing the incarcerated
population.

What one finds in the Green Paper (Home Office 1988) is a relatively
broad and coherent statement of concerns. It opened debate on expanding
community corrections and providing punishment outside prison. It
suggested that electronic monitoring might be used to enhance punishment
in the community. It provided little reason to doubt that the government
was interested in different ways of organising punishment in the
community.

The Green Paper was less clear on whether too many people were being
sent to prison, except for thieves and burglars. The word 'remand' did not
appear in the report, while 'custody' did. A full paragraph was devoted to
the comparative cost of imprisonment and punishment in the community.
Private security and 'an organisation to organise punishment' in the
community received four paragraphs. No mention was made of the use
and efficacy of available alternatives to incarceration. Nor was any
mention made of the presence or absence of consensus on whether noncustodial responses to offenders should be punitive.[8]

Upon close examination of the Green Paper the government's position
on tagging revealed a 'profound ambivalence . . . about what tagging was
actually *for*' (Matthews 1988, p. 30; italics in original). It was not specific
as to whether tagging was to be used for early release *from* custody, or as a
sentence itself. The relevance, therefore, of tagging to other dimensions of
the criminal justice system was unclear. Its relevance to reducing
overcrowding and its meaning for the judiciary was equally unclear.
Officials' responses clarified little.

John Patten, then Minister of State at the Home Office, said tagging
was not to be seen as punishment (Patten 1988, p. 4). Then-Home
Secretary Hurd, however, referred to tagging as 'US-style punishment'
('Hurd decides to "tag" offenders', *Scotsman*, 10 October 1988), and 'a form
of punishment' ('Following the Hurd instinct', *Scotsman*, 10 October 1988).
He, however, was inconsistent on the theme of tagging as punishment as
witnessed by his reference to tagging as a means of tracking 'prisoners on
bail' ('Hurd declares war on crime', *Eastern Evening News*, 12 October
1988), and as a way of 'imposing curfew on offenders outside of prison'
('Hurd speech fails to placate the hanging lobby', *Scotsman*, 12 October
1988). He also referred to tagging as 'part of a new crackdown on crime'

('Tagging experiment in crime crackdown', *Sunderland Echo*, 12 October 1988), and part of his new tactics which 'call for a new spirit of active citizenship' 'to grub at the very roots of crime' ('Hurd to bring in electronic tagging', *Birmingham Daily News*, 13 October 1988). The lack of clarity regarding the purpose(s) of tagging lead more than one observer to refer to Hurd's announcement as 'vague' ('Tagging the trouble-makers', *Northern Echo*, 13 October 1988) and without 'any guiding philosophy' ('Hurd fends off critics with test for tagging', *Guardian*, 13 October 1988). No official mentioned the neo-Orwellian implications of tagging. Patten preferred to call it a 'human technological cure', a sentiment shared by David Davis, M.P., when he congratulated Patten 'on his humane innovation' ('Date fixed for remand tagging experiments', *Financial Times*, 9 May 1989; 'Bail (electronic monitoring)', *Hansard*, 15 December 1989).

Each of the Home Office's various evaluation plans were more explicit than the Green Paper and officials' explanations and interpretations of the tagging schemes. But these too were silent on the topic of how monitoring could increase the incarcerated population or its connection(s) to surveillance technology. Of the four research objectives outlined in early January, 1989, only one addressed a policy issue. It stated: 'Is monitoring being used as an alternative to a remand custody' (Mair 1989). The other objectives addressed operational issues and cost-effectiveness. No recognition was paid to the fact that even if tagging reduced the custodial population, the total number of persons incarcerated in *new places* would actually increase.

Draft two of the Home Office's Operational Requirements for electronic monitoring trials was equally myopic despite its grandiose objective to 'evaluate the social, administrative and technical aspects of the use of EM as an alternative to remanding in custody' (Home Office 1989, p. 3).[9] No definition or discussion of 'social' or 'administrative' appeared in this document. What attention was given was limited to specifying technical terms and describing services required from vendors.

In October 1989, some two months after the tagging trials began, Neil Clowes, Home Office project sponsor, summarised the evaluation objectives and plans. He stated: 'The question we are asking is "is there a place for electronic monitoring in our criminal justice system?" ' (Clowes 1989). More specifically, he said the formal objectives were:

1. To evaluate the extent to which the availability of electronic monitoring can enable defendants to be remanded on bail rather than in custody.
2. To evaluate current electronic monitoring technology.
3. To evaluate cost effectiveness and appropriateness of privatising electronic monitoring.
4. To inform consideration of the scope for widening the application of electronic monitoring to sentenced offenders who would otherwise have received a custodial sentence.

Objectives 3 and 4 are the most important for determining the government's intentions because objectives 1 and 2 are easily addressed with the plethora of U.S. monitoring experience. Objective 3 makes explicit the government's interest in using the logic of market forces to determine if monitoring is to be incorporated into the criminal justice system. The last objective indicates the government's increasing the number of persons monitored electronically. Again, no sensitivity was shown for how tagging can increase the total number of persons incarcerated, and how it is connected to surveillance technology.

The lack of clarity re tagging cannot, however, be blamed entirely on the government. The media, probation and parole officers, scholars and others each contributed to the confusion about what tagging might involve in England and what has happened with it in the U.S. The London *Sunday Times*, for example, reported the curfew radius for an offender wearing a monitor to be 100 yds. This distance is in fact much less, approximately 150 feet in the U.S. ('Electronic tagging trials to start in wake of Riseley', *Sunday Times*, 7 May 1988).

Matthews is quoted as saying: 'In America, only people charged with petty offences or soft crimes like drink-driving are given tags' ('Trial runs agreed for bail by electronic tagging', *Guardian*, 9 May 1989). In fact only 33.4% of the total offenders monitored in the United States have been convicted of major traffic offences, including drunk-driving. Other remaining offenders have been convicted of property offences (20.1%), drug offences (15.3%), offences against the person (9.7%), sex offences (4.0%), weapon offences (1.3%), frauds (3.8%), multiple offences (10.2%), other offences including murder (14.2%) (Schmidt 1989). In the same article that quoted Matthews, Labour's Home Affairs spokesman Sheerman, said he was concerned about the effects on defendants' families 'because enforced home confinement in the U.S. has resulted in domestic and child violence'. No evidence has been published which supports this claim.[10]

The National Association of Probation Officers (NAPO) said tagging was a 'costly irrelevance which would almost certainly be used disproportionately on black defendants' ('Date fixed for remand tagging experiments', *Financial Times*, 9 May 1989). And its general secretary is reported to have said that tagging had not reduced the prison population in America because 'most offenders were considered ineligible because they did not have a home, a telephone, or both' ('Private firms will tag prisoners to cut overcrowding', *Daily Telegraph* 9 May 1989). While disproportionate use of tags on blacks may occur in the future it did not occur during the tagging trials, and it has not happened in the U.S. The NAPO spokesperson is only partially correct about the reduction of prison populations. This population has not been reduced because only 12,000 are monitored per day at this time, which is 2% of the total state prison population (1988) of 627,402, and it is doubtful that monitoring has been initiated in order to reduce prison populations. He is in partial error also on the issue of ineligibility. Offenders without homes or phones either live with relatives, friends or they may be placed in halfway homes which have phones (Beck and Klein-Saffran 1989). The lack of phones represents a far greater hinderance to monitoring in England than in the U.S.

Another publication reported that 'American evidence showing that offenders confined to home frequently suffer from boredom or depression and often fall prey to alcohol and drug abuse' (*The Law Magazine*, 5 February 1988, pp. 23–4). The article failed to distinguish if such alleged problems preceded or followed tagging. Neither did the article explain that monitoring is almost always used in conjunction with drug and alcohol rehabilitation, if needed.[11] Again, as in the quote attributed to Sheerman ('Trial runs agreed for bail by electronic tagging', *Guardian*, 9 May 1989), no source was reported for the alleged information.

The various discussions of tagging were not limited to negative comments. One research article reported support for tagging, but it too presented erroneous information describing 'a typical scheme' (Frost and Stephenson 1989, p. 91). Frost and Stephenson imply that in America an offender may wear a monitor around the neck, which emits a signal to a cellular radio station, which in turn signals a computer thrice hourly. In fact, no such system exists in America, nor was such a system utilised in the three 1989/90 experiments in England. Rather, the description provided by Frost and Stephenson fits a 1984 proposal sponsored by the Offender's Tag Association.

Interest in this type of monitoring technology surfaced again in early 1990 just one day after release of the Taylor report on the Hillsborough tragedy which recommended among other things, the possibility of tagging soccer hooligans. At that time it was rumored that a Home Office employee in its Statistical Department had informally asked Marconi if they could develop a cellular monitoring system that might be used on soccer hooligans in the Newcastle area. Marconi was reported to have said 'Of course' (personal communication, 1 February 1990).

Conclusions

Despite the fact that tagging has been condemned by a wide range of individuals and organised voices, it has yet to be debated in terms of it's intrusiveness or in terms informed by the broader cultural context from which it has sprung. The condemnations, for instance, have instead been mostly in language reflecting *a priori* reasoning, professional self-interest, misinformation, fear and without the voice of the confined. These responses are not surprising because however widely the importance of technology has been acknowledged, it has seldom been a primary subject 'for political and social thought' (Winner 1977, p. 22). With rare exceptions this myopia has characterised the entire spectrum of contemporary criminology, especially the 'administrative criminology' of the last decade with its penchant for 'application'. A rare but brief exception is found in Taylor's (1988) work, but it otherwise has not often caught the criminological imagination.

To say that informed discussions of the intrusiveness of surveillance technology and tagging have been elided would be misleading, because they have not begun in earnest. This is not entirely the result of a lack of interest as it is probably the result of competition from other agendas and the lack of useful linguistic tools with which to enter into debate about technology in general, and tagging in particular. This reflects a form of cultural lag in which the 'linguistic resources of public discourse has changed little at all' (Winner 1977, p. 10). There can hardly be a better contemporary metaphor for this point than in recent England where those tagged sometimes had no phone. The language used to introduce and sell tagging, consequently, was more the product of technicians and sales representatives than members of the legislature, judiciary, academy, criminal justice practitioners and the public. It is not surprising therefore that the voices of opposition often resorted to value-laden words such as 'gimmickry' and pejorative comments that tagging was an idea that came out of a comic book ('Tagging trials are "just gimmick" ' *Liverpool Daily Post*, 14 August 1989; 'Scrap this tag trial gimmick', *Nottingham Evening Post*, 14 August 1989). One consequence has been calls for relegating tagging to the 'penological dustbin' (Rutherford 1989). As an emotional balm such responses may be satisfying to warring polarities, but it is hardly scholarly or realistic. The new age of surveillance technology is part of the post-modernism and it is not likely to go away. A middle ground is needed. The language of dichotomous thinking needs to give way to dialectical argumentation that provides something other than condemnation and cries of 'go away'. To avoid this confrontation is to allow tagging to be the new Trojan horse that gives additional access and power in criminal justice to corporate elites, which will in turn allow them to have additional access to our private life.

Notes

1   Special thanks are given to Dick Hobbs, Neal Shover, Nigel Fielding and anonymous reviewers for their helpful comments. For informants whose name I cannot print, I thank you too.

2   In an effort to follow the economic development of monitoring in the U.S. I purchased in the mid-1980s an extremely limited number of shares in four vendors. This gave me regular access to semi- and annual stock reports, some sales rhetoric and vendors' sales literature. More information on the 'selling of the image' of tagging is forthcoming.

3   One of the most interesting evaluation projects in the area of community corrections (called 'community control' in Florida) has been conducted in Florida by criminologists Ronald Akers and Linda Smith, Ph.D. student. They have completed a three-year follow-up study which compared the recidivism rates of offenders sent to prison with a matched group which had been sentenced to Florida's community control programme.

4   This may be done simply by specifying that the equipment have one particular feature, for example, 'water resistant' vs. 'water proof', 'tamper proof' vs. 'tamper resistant,' and 'battery life of 5 yrs.' vs. 'battery shelf-life of 10 yrs.'. These specifications have also appeared in some proposed state legislation.

5   Some of the claims and explanations have been remarkable. One shill claimed he liked the equipment so well that he used his holidays to travel and share the good news at his own expense. Variations on this theme have also appeared in the form of vendors paying for probation and parole officers, their supervisors and/or former corrections officials, to attend conferences where they speak

positively about their programme successes and therefore indirectly about the merits of the equipment used. One such speaker was a participant at the Second (1988) Annual Conference of Electronic Monitoring of Offenders, School of Law, Leicester Polytechnic, Leicester, England. As far as I have observed neither the vendors or the speakers publicly acknowledge such arrangements. Just as this paper was being finished a newspaper in Ohio reported that a judge said he saw no conflict of interest in a probation officer receiving $2.50 per day per each house arrest from the private firm that operates the computer and provides the monitoring equipment. The judge reasoned that the probation officer had no input into how many prisoners participate in the programme. The $2.50 is a commission from the $8.00 per day fee the defendant pays to the private company ('Judge sees no conflict' (Middletown, Ohio), *Journal*, 25 December 1989).

6   Several news accounts and government reports have acknowledged that the U.S. has entered a new phase of 'prohibitionism'. See 'Drinking going out of style in America', *Cincinnati Enquirer*, 9 March 1989, D-16; 'A new temperance is taking root in America', *New York Times*, 15 March 1989; 'Alcohol's last call', *Kentucky Enquirer*, 31 May 1989 and 'Koop does battle with liquor ads.', *USA Today*, 1 June 1989, p. 1.

7   As tagging continues to develop in England it will be interesting to learn if similar opposition comes from Parents Against Drunk Driving. With the recent extension of pub hours in England and Wales, coupled with the recent interest in drunk driving, this becomes more of a possibility. (See 'Brewers join drive against car drivers', *Daily Telegraph*, 25 October 1988, p. 7; 'Drink involved in 950 road deaths', *The Times*, 25 October 1988, p. 2; 'Kerb-crawling: an innocent victim pays a high price', *Independent*, 6 December 1988; 'For the pub crawler, more time to crawl', *New York Times*, 23 August 1988, p. 6. Ball and Lilly (1986, pp. 224–47) have examined the potential use of home incarceration for drunken drivers. A more elaborate discussion of 'tagging' can be found in Ball, Huff and Lilly 1988.

8   See Morris (1988) for brief but insightful discussion of the background against which the Green Paper should be interpreted.

9   According to private industry sources involved in the trials, there was never any doubt that the task at hand was to demonstrate that private industry could successfully introduce technology into the criminal justice system at the community level. Claims of interest in the 'social' aspects of tagging were referred to as 'PR. Nothing will come of it'.

10 To my knowledge this is the second time this claim has been made in England in the last year. This suggests two problems: (1) the lack of documentation for such assertions and (2) the near hysterical assertions made about offenders' responses to monitoring devices. While studying in England in 1988 I was asked if it was not true that one U.S. offender had become so frustrated with the monitoring anklet that he had amputated his own leg.

11 Again, no documentation was offered. However, the former Director of Corrections for Michigan, has stated that the electronically monitored felons serving their sentences at home are 'cleaner' than if they were in prison because they are frequently tested for drug and alcohol abuse (see Johnson 1989).

References

Ball, R. A. and Lilly, J. R. (1986) 'The potential use of home incarceration with drunken drivers', *Crime and Delinquency*, *32*, 224–47.

Ball, R. A., Huff, C. R. and Lilly, J. R. (1988) *House Arrest and Correctional Policy: Doing Time at Home*, Newbury, Ca.: Sage.

Beck, J. L. and Klein-Saffran, J. (1989) *Community Control Project* (Report Forty Four), U.S. Department of Justice, U.S. Parole Commission.

BI, Incorporated (1989) *First Quarter Report FY 89*, Boulder, Co.

Byrne, J. M. and Kelly, L. M. L. (1987) 'The use of electronic surveillance in the criminal justice system: the marketing of punishment' (Presented at the annual meeting of the Society for the Study of Social Problems, Chicago, Il., U.S.A., 14 August).

Clowes, N. (1989) 'Electronic monitoring: the Home Office trials' (Presented at the III International Conference on Electronic Monitoring, School of Law, Leicester Polytechnic, Leicester, 13 October).

Cohen, S. (1985) *Visions of Social Control*, Cambridge: Polity Press.

Corrections Services, Inc. (1989) *Shareholders Report*, Ft. Lauderdale, Fl.

Ellul, J. (1964) *The Technological Society*, New York: Knopf.

Frost, S. M. and Stephenson, G. M. (1989) 'A simulation study of electronic tagging as a sentencing option'. *Howard Journal*, *28*, 91–104.

Grant, G. P. (1986) *Technology and Justice*, Notre Dame, In.: University of Notre Dame Press.

Hill, S. (1988) *The Tragedy of Technology*, London: Pluto Press.

Home Office (1988) *Punishment, Custody and the Community*, Cm. 424.

Home Office (1989) 'Home Office trials of electronic monitoring' (Draft Two, Version 2.2, 26 January), Scientific Research and Development Branch, Science and Technology Group.

Johnson, P. (1989) 'A home as a prison: can it work?', in: K. Russell and J. R. Lilly (Eds.), *The Electronic Monitoring of Offenders* (School of Law Monograph), Leicester: Leicester Polytechnic.

Lilly, J. R., Ball, R. A. and Wright, J. (1987) 'Home incarceration with electronic monitoring in Kenton County, Kentucky: an evaluation', in: B. R. McCarthy (Ed.), *Intermediate Punishments: Intensive Supervision, Home Confinement and Electronic Surveillance*, Monsey, New York: Criminal Justice Press.

Mair, G. (1989) 'Electronic monitoring: a research proposal' (Home Office, unpublished).

Marx, G. T. (1985a) 'I'll be watching you', *Dissent*, Winter, 26–34.

Marx, G. T. (1985b) 'The new surveillance', *Technology Review*, May–June, 43–8.

Matthews, R. (1988) 'Privatisation of punishment', *New Statesman/Society*. July.

Morris, T. (1988) 'Punishment, custody and the community', *Criminal Justice*, *6* (4), 5–6.

Patten, J. (1988) 'Punishment, custody and community', *Criminal Justice*, *6* (4), 4.

Renzema, M. (forthcoming) 'Electronic monitoring survey'.

Rutherford, A. (1989) 'Why the electronic tag leads back to the ball and chain' (Editorial), *The Independent*, 9 August.

Sanniti, C. (1989) 'House arrest and electronic monitoring: human and technological responses to prison and jail overcrowding' (Presented at the 50th annual meeting of the American Society for Public Administration, 8–12 April, Miami, Fl.).

Schmidt, A. (1989) 'Electronic monitoring of offenders increases' (NIJ Reports No. 212) (Jan/Feb), Washington, D.C.: Department of Justice, U.S. Government Printing Office.

Shover, N. (1979) *Sociology of American Corrections*, Homewood, Ill.: Dorsey Press.

Shover, N. (1990) 'Institutional correction: jails and prisons', in: J. Sheley (Ed.), *A Handbook of Contemporary Criminology*, Belmont, Ca: Wadsworth.

Shover, N. and Einstadter, W. J. (1988) *Analyzing American Corrections*, Belmont, Ca.: Wadsworth.

Taylor, I. (1988) 'Left realism, the free market economy and the problem of social order' (Presented at the annual meeting of the American Society of Criminology. Chicago, Ill., November).

U.S. Department of Justice (1984) *Sourcebook of Criminal Justice Statistics*, Washington, D.C.: Bureau of Justice Statistics.

U.S. Department of Justice (1988) *Sourcebook of Criminal Justice Statistics*, Washington, D. C.: Bureau of Justice Statistics.

U.S. General Accounting Office (1989) *Prison Overcrowding (November)*, Washington, D.C.: General Accounting Office.

Winner, L. (1977) *Autonomous Technology*, Cambridge, Mass.: MIT Press.

18

8

Actuarial Justice: the Emerging New Criminal Law

Malcolm Feeley and Jonathan Simon

Introduction

In a recent article we argued that there is a paradigm shift taking place in the criminal process. Focusing on selected issues of penology, we examined what we termed the Old Penology and the New Penology (Feeley and Simon, 1992: 449). In this chapter we broaden this argument, and outline the features of this new development, which we term *actuarial justice*. In the earlier paper we argued that the Old Penology is rooted in a concern for individuals, and preoccupied with such concepts as guilt, responsibility and obligation, as well as diagnosis, intervention and treatment of the individual offender. It views committing a crime a deviant or antisocial act which is deserving of a response, and one of its central aims is to ascertain the nature of the responsibility of the accused and hold the guilty accountable.

In contrast the New Penology has a radically different orientation.[1] It is actuarial. It is concerned with techniques for identifying, classifying and managing groups assorted by levels of dangerousness. It takes crime for granted. It accepts deviance as normal. It is sceptical that liberal interventionist crime control strategies do or can make a difference. Thus its aim is not to intervene in individuals' lives for the purpose of ascertaining responsibility, making the guilty 'pay for their crime' or changing them. Rather it seeks to regulate groups as part of a strategy of managing danger.

In our article (Feeley and Simon, 1992) we addressed the general logic of the New Penology in terms of discourses, techniques and objectives. Here in our more general enquiry we explore how 'actuarial justice', is being institutionalised and survey the broader intellectual, political and social contexts which have facilitated its emergence. This shift, we believe, is shaping and will continue to shape the agenda of criminology. Indeed, as we show here, and in our earlier article, a new actuarial criminology has already emerged and made itself felt.

In the first part of this chapter, the basic characteristics of actuarial justice are analysed. We begin with an examination of three practices that most clearly exemplify the qualities of actuarial justice: incapacitation, preventive detention and drug courier profiles. These are far from the only locations where actuarial justice is present, but an examination of these forms reveals important features they have in common. Next, we look at some examples of how traditional practices in the criminal justice system are being reshaped by the imperatives of actuarial justice. Finally, we explore how the logic of actuarial justice is influencing the application of constitutional norms which might have acted as a constraint on its expansion.

The second part of this chapter is an exploration of the intellectual, political, and social contexts of actuarial justice. This falls far short of a causal explanation, but by linking actuarial justice to emerging practices elsewhere we can identify some of the forces that are facilitating the growth of actuarial justice.

THE ELEMENTS OF ACTUARIAL JUSTICE

Actuarial justice is nebulous, but it is significant. Actuarial justice involves how we conceive of and talk about crime policy, but it is not an ideology in the narrow sense of a set of beliefs and ideas which constrain action. It involves practices, but is not reducible to a specific technology or set of behaviours. Indeed it is powerful and significant precisely because it lacks a well-articulated ideology and identification with a specific technology. Its very amorphousness contributes to its power. Below we outline an account of actual practices and discourses which are giving shape to this emerging formation in the criminal process.[2] Following that we abstract some of the critical features of these developments. However, it is important to keep in mind that what we describe is not a mentality or a blueprint that can be cleanly separated from the material it analyses.

New practices

It is somewhat misleading to speak of new practices, since the practices we discuss are, in fact, partial practices which have had long and varied histories. Their newness lies in their particular combinations and the particular micropractices they are embedded in and the functions which they perform.

Incapacitation

Possibly the clearest indication of actuarial justice is found in the new theory of incapacitation, which has perhaps become the predominant model of punishment (see Greenwood, 1982; Moore et al., 1984). Incapacitation promises to reduce the effects of crime in society not by altering either offender or social context, but by rearranging the distribution of offenders in society. If the prison can do nothing else, incapacitation theory holds, it can detain offenders for a time and thus delay their resumption of criminal activity in society.

According to the theory, if such delays are sustained for enough time and for enough people, significant aggregate effects in crime can take place although individual destinies are only marginally altered. In this sense, incapacitation is to penology what arbitration is to investments, a method of capitalising on minute displacements in time; and like arbitration it has a diminished relationship to the normative goal of enhancing the value of its objects.

These aggregate effects can be further intensified by a strategy of *selective* incapacitation. This approach proposes a sentencing scheme in which lengths of sentence depend not upon the nature of the criminal offence or upon an assessment of the character of the offender, but upon risk profiles. Its objects are to identify high-risk offenders and to maintain long-term control over them while investing in shorter terms and less intrusive control and surveillance over lower risk offenders.

First articulated as a coherent scheme for punishing in a report by the RAND Corporation (Greenwood, 1982), an operations research-oriented R&D organisation, it was quickly embraced and self-consciously promoted as a new justification for punishment by a team of scholars at Harvard University (Moore et al., 1984), who were keenly aware that it constituted a paradigm shift in the underlying rationale for imposing criminal sanctions.[3]

The focus on the group rather than the individual is not, of course, completely new. The 'group' has been an organising unit in many societies from time immemorial, and in Western liberal society since the eighteenth century thinkers have been concerned with the general preventive effects of criminal punishment, sometimes called general deterrence (Andenaes, 1974). But general deterrence is essentially a theory of communication. Through punishment the political sovereign is able to communicate to the public as such and signal the degree of prohibition to be associated with various forms of proscribed conduct. The broadcast is general, but the receivers are individuals who will presumably integrate the information in their rational management of their own lives. In contrast, incapacitation (selective or otherwise) attempts to manipulate the public as a demographic mass or aggregate, bypassing the *res cogitans* of individuals altogether. The aim is not to induce altered behaviour as a result of rational calculations by individuals, but the management-through-custody of that segment of the population that is dangerous. Length of custody is determined by calculated risk factors not seriousness of offence.

Preventive detention

Pre-trial decision making in the United States has always made evident a concern for preventive detention as well as for the task of assuring the presence of the accused at trial. Both concerns were pursued on an individual basis, albeit one which embodied plenty of collective stereotypes. The new logic of pre-trial detention operates in a manner similar to selective incapacitation. Preselected categories of information about an arrestee are collected and run through a collective algorithm.

The origins of this development are found in the bail reform efforts of the early 1960s, when liberal reformers and the courts rejected a constitutional 'rights strategy' for bail reform in preference to an 'administrative strategy'. The rights strategy called for clarification of the Eighth Amendment's prohibition against 'excessive bail'. Arguing that the purpose of bail was to assure appearance at trial, it called for clarification and expansion of the standard of 'least restrictive conditions' and assurances that bail would not be used as a form of preventive detention or summary punishment. It saw the right to bail as an undeveloped constitutional issue in need of development, and called upon the courts to clarify it. In the United States, this strategy was set forth in a series of path-breaking articles by Caleb Foote in the 1950s who foresaw a 'coming constitutional crisis in bail' and set forth its agenda. However, liberal reformers and judges rejected the constitutional revolution and the rights strategy that Foote advocated, and instead developed an alternative administrative strategy. Agreeing with Foote that the purpose of pre-trial release was to assure presence at trial (as opposed to detaining 'dangerous individuals' or imposing summary punishment), they conceived of pre-trial release as an administrative matter to be handled by scientific not legal expertise. The alternative administrative strategy sought to base conditions of pre-trial release on models of 'predictors' of appearance and non-appearance. The US Department of Justice vigorously promoted the establishment of specialised pre-trial release agencies which developed multivariate models to predict appearance and non-appearance at trial and report their findings to the courts. These developments stunted constitutional clarification of the *right* to bail.[4] As one of the authors noted a decade ago:

> Professor Caleb Foote's hope that a crisis in bail would be resolved through constitutional law reform has not been fulfilled. . . . [L]egal challenges to current bail practices have met with . . . numbing defeats. Perhaps these defeats have been conditioned by the conservative tenor of the Burger Court, but they may also be due to a sense of complacency about the administrative approach to bail reform as reflected in pretrial release programs. (Feeley, 1983: 77)

Once established 'pre-trial release agencies' developed a life of their own. What began as a reform calling attention to the problems of unnecessary pre-trial detention, quickly became 'part of that problem'. Seemingly without effort the pre-trial release agencies moved from developing actuarial-like models to predict appearance at trial to developing models to predict dangerousness and on to models to predict the consequences of testing dirty to various types of drugs (Feeley, 1983: 79). Once a rights strategy had given way to an administrative strategy, each of these moves was but a small step along the path of actuarial justice.

The conventional explanation for shifts in pre-trial release policy in the United States and Western Europe from the 1960s to the 1990s is that due process-oriented liberals were displaced by law-and-order conservatives. But this explanation is incomplete if not altogether wrong. Pre-trial release policies do not divide neatly along these lines. Indeed it was well-known liberal reformers who were responsible for first promoting actuarial justice in the form of administrative strategy of pre-trial release agencies. They set aside issues of rights, and once having claimed the ability to predict appearance at trial, it was a small step to applying their risk assessment models to the issue of dangerousness, the consequences of testing dirty, and the like. In hindsight one can trace the development of actuarial justice in this area and see how it cuts across traditional liberal-conservative lines.

Drug courier profiles

Over the last two decades law enforcement has utilised a variety of objective and quasi-objective 'profiles' to identify suspected criminals in specific settings. The first such profile to be widely used was for hijackers at airports. Developed in 1969 by a federal task force, the profile includes 24 to 30 characteristics which the task force concluded could be used in selected combinations to differentiate potential hijackers from other air travellers (Cloud, 1985: 874).[5] In 1974, the federal Drug Enforcement Agency developed a 'drug courier profile' which contained a list of behavioural factors which in combination were believed to differentiate individuals transporting illegal narcotics by air from other air travellers. The profile and variants have been widely used to identify suspects for further surveillance or brief detentions and interrogations (Cloud, 1985: 844–5). Similar profiles have also been used to identify drivers transporting drugs on the nation's highways and illegal aliens across the border (Cloud, 1985: 854).

The drug courier profiles that have been revealed in court proceedings provide evidence of the form of actuarial prediction, but lack the substantive data and methods which generally support their use. Factors such as the city the suspect is travelling from, his or her type of luggage, order of departure from the plane, and nervousness and many other factors have been included in such profiles. While government agents have often defended the relevancy of these factors on the witness stand, they have never presented systematic statistical analyses of their individual association or aggregate efficiency as predictors.

Despite these shortcomings, their popularity suggests that actuarial justice fits well with prevailing ideologies of what makes the exercise of power rational although its actual use may be riddled with subjectivity and prejudice. In the future we may expect pressure both to validate the profiles statistically, refine them and to expand their use.

Analysis of actuarial justice

What these forms have in common is not the repetition of a singular structure but a set of overlapping features.

The population itself, in its biological and demographic sense, is taken as the target of power The emergence of criminological positivism in the late nineteenth century divided between those who focused on crime as a set of prohibited acts (whether understood economically or morally) and those who focused on criminals as a set of dangerous individuals (embodied in both classicism and moral philosophies of punishment). As late as the 1970s it seemed as if the central tensions in criminal justice policy could be understood as a dialectic between these positions.[6] We argue that the new practices radically reframe the issues, and target something very different, that is, the crime rate, understood as the *distribution* of behaviours in the population as a whole. In this sense actuarial justice should be seen as a part of the general movement noted by a number of scholars towards the exercise of state power as 'governmentality'.[7]

This does not mean that individuals disappear in criminal justice. They remain, but increasingly they are grasped not as coherent subjects, whether understood as moral, psychological or economic agents, but as members of particular subpopulations and the intersection of various categorical indicators.

Power is aimed at prevention and risk minimisation   Rather than seeking to respond to past offences, these techniques are mainly aimed at preventing future offences. Prevention has always been a concern of the criminal process and a justification of punishment. Some of the new techniques – selective incapacitation and pre-trial detention – present a possibly purer form of prevention. More important, however, prevention is aimed less at halting proscribed activities than reducing the likelihood and seriousness of offending.

Justice is increasingly understood not as a rational system but through the rationality of the system   Criminal justice has always been concerned with how to distribute its own considerable powers. The classic theorists, such as Beccaria and Bentham, worried about the distribution between legislators, prosecutors and juries. Positivists defined the scientifically trained expert as the obvious repository of power. Until recently our debates on sentencing and other topics have operated as if this was still the fundamental set of choices. The new techniques discussed here suggest the rise of formal systems of internal rules, analogous in many respects to computer programs.

The new techniques we discussed above are a small subset of all criminal justice practices. They are attached to institutions that seem largely to operate in 'the old fashioned way', that is, responding reactively and often brutally to crime. Yet, while these measures are all in varying degrees defined as new and controversial, an examination of how the logic of actuarial justice has penetrated more venerable practices in criminal justice suggests that the future is already here.

New functions for old forms

New formations rarely grow on ground totally cleared of the past. They develop alongside practices created at various times which have accrued social and political weight against the demands of coherence and reform. The significance of actuarial justice is not only to be found in the development of the new practices described in the preceding section, but as well in the reorientation and redefinition of older practices. Below we explore several of the new functions for old forms.

Recidivism

Although the term 'recidivism' is used in penology and continues to be used in actuarial justice, its function has undergone an important metamorphosis. Once used extensively as an indicator of programme effectiveness (such as, 'Did the programme reduce recidivism, and if so, by how much?'), now it is much more likely to be used as an 'indicator' of another sort, as data to be considered along with still other indicators to make judgements about risk classification, incarceration and surveillance.

Drug testing

The traditional aim of drug tests was to identify deviance, self-destructive behaviour – in itself an individual failure that should trigger a concern for intervention. In actuarial justice, such tests are data in a flow of information for assessing risk. To the extent that drug use (and type, frequency and amount – all of which can be roughly calibrated by the tests) is an indicator of social dangerousness, information revealed by drug tests can be folded into the decision-making algorithms of the system. Drug use – like other indicators which once were more easily obtainable, such as residency, marital status, employment status, criminal record, education and the like – can also be systematically included in developing profiles of dangerousness.

Prison, probation and parole

Actuarial justice invites new justifications for, and hence new forms of, custody and surveillance. Increasingly imprisonment and 'supervision' assume new functions and forms. Actuarial rationales for imprisonment and supervision are not anchored in aspirations to obtain restitution, rehabilitate, reintegrate, train and the like. Rather they are justified in more blunt terms: variable detention and surveillance depending upon level of risk assessment. They invite low-cost, no-frills prisons – custody centres – without education and vocational training services. And they invite expanded and variable use of detention, and especially greater reliance on short-term detention with little or no accompanying educational or training opportunities.[8]

The small boom in private prisons in the United States has largely been aimed at providing such no-frills, short-term 'custody centres', institutions whose value is in the aggregate, as institutions for marginally reducing danger in society by detaining high-risk offenders.

Similarly, probation and parole have assumed new functions. Once conceived of as 'half-way' stages whose aim was to reintegrate offenders back into their communities, parole and probation are now simply alternatives to custody for lower-risk offenders. 'Supervision' consists of monitoring levels of risk as determined by several indicators, most prominently drug testing. Moreover, with large portions of the non-incarcerated population in some of the poorest and most crime victimised communities in the country, probation, parole or some form of community supervision are becoming a lower cost alternative to traditional justice (Simon, 1993).

For instance procedures for revoking parole and probation in most American states and the UK are far lower than those for criminal conviction. Given that in many American states a substantial proportion of all new inmates entering prison are people whose probation or parole has been revoked, a new, managerial process of incarceration already has been established and is functioning. And even here revocation hearings are often waived as part of a rapidly expanding new form of plea bargaining where even truncated revocation hearings are waived (and the probationer returns to custody voluntarily) in exchange for dropping new charges (Greenspan, 1991).

Adoption of new models of rationality in judicial review

The courts are one force that could do much to slow the development of actuarial justice. The criminal jurisprudence embodied in the Constitution and the Bill of Rights is loaded with values of individual autonomy and social equality which clash with the logic of actuarial justice. And indeed many of the landmarks of American constitutional criminal procedure throughout the 1960s elaborate this social vision. However, an analysis of more recent Supreme Court decisions suggests that this development has been reversed. The Court is engaged in rethinking the values of constitutional criminal jurisprudence from an orientation deeply informed by actuarial justice. This has, we believe, even more profound implications than the appointment of more conservative, 'law and order' federal judges that has been the object of so much concern among the liberal community. An actuarial social vision, clothed in familiar language, is powerful precisely because it subtly restructures concepts and language. In the long run, we suspect that it will be more powerful than the 'law and order' political movement precisely because it will be more deeply ingrained in the law.

Preventive detention

In *United States* v. *Salerno* (1987) the Supreme Court upheld preventive detention provisions of the Bail Reform Act of 1984 which permitted pre-trial detention to protect the 'safety of the community' based on a set of prescribed factors including the seriousness of the charge, the extent of the evidence and the nature of the threat posed. Then Associate Justice William Rehnquist, the author of the Court's opinion, argued that preventive detention does not trigger the same level of protection as other penal detention decisions because pre-trial release is intended to manage risks rather than punish.[9] So long as Congress intended to regulate (and hence subject its provisions to review by the traditional rationality test), rather than punish dangerous people, due process standards were not offended (*Salerno*, 1987: 748).

While the Court's distinction may appear disingenuous to some, it does have the virtue of openly acknowledging that the Court is constructing a new way of thinking about criminal justice. The risk factors considered by the trial court in *Salerno* were different from the purely actuarial associations employed in selective incapacitation, or even in the quasi-actuarial methods of the drug courier profile. In *Salerno* the government claimed that Mr Salerno was the boss of the Genovese family of the New York ' Cosa Nostra' (*Salerno*, 1987: 743). The Court's analysis does not dwell on methodology in its rush to affirm confinement based on dangerousness. Actuarial factors may even be fairer bases. The important point is that the Court openly and explicitly recognised a regulatory exercise of power operating in and through the criminal justice process that aims at *managing* a population of dangerous people at an appropriate level of control. This decision stands in stark contrast with the social vision informing its earlier pre-trial release rulings (see, for example, *Stack* v. *Boyle*, 1951).

Mass surveillance and probable cause

The line between regulatory power and punishment has been further blurred in the Court's Fourth Amendment jurisprudence. Where the Court once treated probable cause to believe that a suspect has committed or is committing a crime as a prerequisite to police intervention, more recently it has described a broader area of police intervention as falling outside the protections of the Fourth Amendment or requiring only general rationales. Indeed it has come close to turning the Fourth Amendment on its head and treating it as an affirmative grant of power to the police (Wasserstrom, 1984).

Normalising a surveillance society One way of accomplishing this is by treating less formal encounters between police and citizens as consensual rather than detentions. The Court has described as 'consensual' and increasingly coercive set of encounters – airport stops where individuals are asked for their ticket and identification, sweeps of factories, random inspections of intercity buses, and the like. Thus in *Florida* v. *Bostick* (1991) the Court held that a person was *not* detained by the police even though it was reasonable for him to believe that he was not free to terminate the encounter.

The border is everywhere Similarly the Court has enlarged the border 'exception' to expand the power of the police to stop and search people. In

Michigan State Police v. *Sitz* (1991) the Supreme Court approved a sobriety checkpoint set up by police. The case was the first to approve a police stop without any individualised suspicion in a non-specialised setting. Prior cases had limited such stops to airports, and at or very near international borders. These special settings, most especially the border, represent those liminal spaces of the political community where its democratic internal life comes into contact with its quite different ethos as a sovereign subject seeking to minimise its risk in international affairs. The recognition that anyone who enters these spaces is operating within a domain of generalised suspicion is justifiable because of this liminality. In contrast, *Sitz* represents the expansion of the mentality of the border to virtually *all* the interior spaces of the United States.[10]

Profiles in suspicion   And as mentioned earlier, the Court has embraced the use of 'profiles' as the basis for detaining persons. In a series of 1980s cases,[11] often employing the language of a 'war against drugs', the Supreme Court endorsed the use by the Federal Drug Enforcement Agency (DEA) of drug courier profiles, and in so doing greatly enhanced the capacity to detain and search people. In *Reid* v. *Georgia*, the US Supreme Court reversed a state high court ruling upholding a stop made on the basis of a drug courier profile. In so doing the US Supreme Court rejected detention based upon factors such as 'drug source city departure, early-morning arrival, no luggage other than shoulder bag', and the like (*Reid*, 1980: 441) as an acceptable basis for detaining persons because these factors 'describe[ed] a very large category of presumably innocent travellers'.

However, in *Sokolow* (1989) a majority on the Supreme Court changed course, and upheld a stop based on the same sort of information. While *Reid* suggested that the Court was at least sensitive to the special nature of actuarial knowledge, *Sokolow* took the path of avoiding any explicit analysis of the significance of this knowledge, treating it instead as an ordinary instance of inevitably probabilistic evaluation. In declining to even engage a lower court's strongly argued concern about the implications of using actuarial-like profiles, it signalled a new willingness to allow the expansion of search and seizure powers of the police without any corresponding adjustment of constitutional protections to the individual. In short it represents a significant expansion of what we call actuarial justice.

The particulars of the case are revealing, especially when contrasted with the lower appellate court's ruling to the contrary, and the Court's earlier case attempting to define carefully the conditions under which police can stop and frisk someone in the absence of probable cause. Because *Sokolow* represents a significant endorsement of a powerful actuarial technique, it is worth reviewing them at some length.

In *Sokolow* a traveller had been detained in the Honolulu airport by DEA agents who had been alerted to him by the following factors which matched their current drug courier profile:

(1) he paid $2,100 for two airplane tickets from a roll of $20 bills; (2) he traveled under a name that did not match the name under which his telephone number was listed; (3) his original destination was Miami, a source city for illicit drugs; (4) he stayed in Miami for only 48 hours, even though a round-trip flight from Honolulu to Miami takes 20 hours; (5) he appeared nervous during his trip; and (6) he checked none of his luggage. (*Sokolow*, 1989: 3)

A lower appellate court rejected this use of actuarial justice, arguing that the relationship between the knowledge and police action in *Sokolow* were distinct from a narrow test of suspiciousness that would justify detention enunciated by the Supreme Court in *Terry* v. *Ohio* (1968) itself. Rejecting the theory that the profile elements were fragments of a larger picture assembled by the government of crime in action, the lower appellate court characterised the information as forming: 'a vaguer shape resulting from the improper attempt to define not ongoing criminal activity but a class of people that is predominantly criminal' (*Sokolow*, 1987: 1419). This lower court went on to acknowledge that some information used in the profile might bear independently on the likelihood of a criminal activity being afoot, but went on to argue that other elements only identified a population which might be deemed more likely to be involved in crime. The Supreme Court swept such reasoning aside, and allowed the type of categoric information used in *Sokolow*, failing to note that in its earlier decision in *Terry*, it had treated as crucial the fact that the officer had observed the behaviour of a particular individual which led him, because of his training and experience, to believe that a robbery might be unfolding. It had not allowed the stop and frisk merely because Terry and his cohorts 'looked like' robbers, but because they acted like robbers. In contrast they upheld the detention of Sokolow simply because he possessed some of the characteristics contained in the profile of risky persons (*Sokolow*, 1987: 1419).

Reversing the lower appellate court, Chief Justice Rehnquist declined to acknowledge any significant difference between actuarial information which identifies a class of people more likely to be involved in drug trafficking, and evidence of trafficking itself. Indeed, from his perspective all information in the criminal process is 'probabilistic'. In the light of this, he regarded the lower court's effort to separate different kinds of information as an exercise in 'unnecessary difficulty in dealing with one of the relatively simple concepts embodied in the Fourth Amendment' (*Sokolow*, 1989: 8–9). The fact that information here was part of a drug courier profile was irrelevant to his (and the majority's) analysis (*Sokolow*, 1989: 10).

Justice Brennan's dissent in *Sokolow* characterised the distinction between actuarial information and more individualised forms of suspicion in strong terms.

In my view, a law enforcement officer's mechanistic application of a formula or personal and behavioral traits in deciding whom to detain can only dull the officer's ability and determination to make sensitive and fact-specific inferences 'in light of his experience.' . . . Reflexive reliance on a profile of drug courier characteristics runs a far greater risk than does ordinary, case-by-case police work of subjecting innocent individuals to unwarranted police harassment and detention. (*Sokolow*, 1989: 13)

Unfortunately none of the opinions succeeded in specifying the concrete effects of the use of actuarial knowledge in defining targets for police investigation. Both the lower appellate court and Justice Brennan saw the use of the profile as creating an unreasonable risk of innocent persons being subject to police intrusion. If this is true it is surely no more than a matter of degree since many indicia of suspicion will end up touching on innocent individuals. Moreover, neither makes an effort to wrestle with the claim that a profile at least places some restraints on what is as likely to be subjective prejudice as 'sensitive and fact-specific inferences'.

A comparison of *Terry* with *Sokolow* reveals one important difference. In the former, the arresting officer observed Terry and his compatriots repeatedly walking in front of a store and then conferring with each other. As the Supreme Court recognised, the suspicious behaviour in *Terry* fits the 'hypothesis' of a burglary in progress. But because a pattern of behaviour was at issue, there are imaginable actions that could have disproved the hypothesis. For example, had a young woman come running out of the shop and said to Terry, 'I'm sorry dad, I was trying on a dress', Officer MacFadden would have shifted his attention elsewhere. In contrast, there was nothing Sokolow or anyone else could do that would throw off the suspicion (other than the police search itself).

Rehnquist's opinion in *Sokolow* also illustrates the features of the pervasive private security networks that increasingly provide the background for public justice. The Chief Justice noted the fact that Sokolow paid for his ticket in cash from a roll of bills as especially probative: 'Most business travelers, we feel confident, purchase airline tickets by credit card or check so as to have a record for tax or business purposes' (*Sokolow*, 1989: 8–9). Thus, to fail to already be part of the practices of private security and scrutiny is itself a mark of dangerousness.

Sokolow stands for the Court's unwillingness to recognise the special features of actuarial knowledge. The majority's unwillingness to directly confront the issue is disappointing for two reasons. First, it is far from clear that the sinister view of actuarial knowledge and the glowing view of individualised expert judgment drawn by Justice Brennan is accurate. Brennan noted with approval the *Terry* Court's concern about 'police conduct carried out solely on the basis of imprecise stereotypes of what criminals look like' (*Sokolow*, 1989: 12). But what if actuarial profiles turn out to be more precise stereotypes than those of the ordinary officer's working assumptions. The opinion might have provided a real analysis of the relative merits of both kinds of knowledge in the criminal process.

Second, the lower appellate court's opinion, far from offering a 'luddite' rejection of actuarial technology just because it is new and different, actually sought to define new forms of evaluation, including having the government provide empirical proof of the associations drawn in the profiles. While these devices take the form of actuarial prediction, their actual statistical validity has rarely been confirmed. The Supreme Court, by avoiding any recognition of the special features of actuarial knowledge, permits the exercise of power on the basis of such knowledge to go forward with no adjustment in constitutional protection.

As this extended examination of the *Sokolow* case reveals, criminal procedure, influenced by the absorption of administrative law rationales, is becoming a jurisprudence of actuarial justice. Government action against criminal activity, even when mixed with traditional punitive functions, is increasingly subject to a different constitutional standard because instead of emphasising the goals of public justice, it emphasises the goals of risk management. It is preventive rather than responsive. It seeks not to punish but to exclude those with criminal proclivities. It is directed not at a general public norm but at security within a specialized and functionally defined arena.

THE CONTEXT OF ACTUARIAL JUSTICE

Our claims about the emerging constellation of discourses and practices, knowledge and power, in the criminal process can be further illuminated by looking briefly at the intellectual, political and social contexts in which that constellation has emerged. Such an examination helps clarify the importance of this emerging constellation and distinguish it from less important developments. This enquiry, if developed, may offer the basis of a causal account of the emergence of actuarial justice, but at present this is premature. Here we simply attempt to locate the emergence of actuarial justice in a broader intellectual and social context. It remains to be seen, how far these connections can be developed.

The intellectual origins

Foucault's (1977) study of the emergence of the prison, *Discipline and Punish*, was really about the rise of a technology of power, the disciplines.[12] The historical transformation in the practices of punishment represented not only an opportune site to explore the disciplines in general, but also a significant social locus wherein the practices of discipline were forged. There is nothing in Foucault's account, however, to lead us to the conclusion that punishment must always be the site where new technologies of power develop.

In fact it appears to us that the factors accounting for the rise of actuarial justice in the criminal process have their origins in technologies developed elsewhere. We see three factors as especially important: the emergence of a concern for managing risks in other fields of law, particularly torts; the practical application of systems engineering to manufacturing and warfare; and the rise of the law and economics movement.

186   *The futures of criminology*

Legal theory

Although social utility analysis or actuarial thinking is commonplace enough
in modern life – it frames policy considerations of all sorts – in recent years
this mode of thinking has gained ascendancy in legal discourse, a system of
reasoning that traditionally has employed the language of morality and
focused on individuals (Simon, 1987, 1988). The new mode of reasoning is
now commonplace in the law.

Thus, for instance, it is by now the conventional mode of reasoning in tort
law. Traditional concerns with fault and negligence standards – which
require a focus on the individual and concern with closely contextual
causality – have given way to strict liability and no-fault. One sees this in
both doctrines, and even more clearly in the social vision that constitutes the
discourse about modern torts. The new doctrines ask, how do we 'manage'
accidents and public safety. They employ the language of social utility and
management, not individual responsibility.

This development was noted in the early years of the century by visionary
legal academics such as Young B. Smith and William O. Douglas (Simon,
1987). More recently, in an enterprise which seeks to trace the shifts in
modern tort law, and the 'social vision' that underlies them, Professor Henry
Steiner has observed:

> [Judges employing modern tort doctrines] visualize the parties before them less as
> individual persons or discrete organizations and more as representatives of groups
> with identifiable common characteristics. They understand accidents and the
> social losses that accidents entail less as unique events and more as statistically
> predictable events. Modern social vision tends then toward the systemic-group-
> statistical in contrast with the vision more characteristic of the fault system, the
> dyadic-individual-unique. (Steiner, 1987: 8)

In developing this theme, Steiner traces shifts in the doctrine, justification
and the social vision and in so doing provides a conceptual framework for
understanding the 'dynamics of change that informs other bodies of law [as
well as torts]' (Steiner, 1987: 1).

Although Steiner's analysis of developments in torts focuses almost
exclusively on shifts in discourse, and the social vision underlying it, he as
well as other commentators on recent developments in torts are not
unmindful of social processes that have affected this transformation. In
particular, they all emphasise the importance of insurance, and high
transaction costs in determination of fault in accidents. If injured parties are
covered by insurance and as well if the cost of assessing blame under
traditional fault doctrines is high (relative to the injuries caused), modern
tort lawyers hold, it makes little sense to employ these doctrines. Thus they
advocate an accident-management policy, and in some places, for example
New Zealand, have replaced tort coverage with mandatory accident
insurance schemes (Sugarman, 1989).

The practice of tort law, in fact, remains much more messy. Efforts to
intensify the risk management rationality of tort law through reforms have

met with mixed success in the face of fearsome resistance by trial laywers and the recent successes of individual responsibility discourse in political life. Yet, as Steiner has shown, actuarial discourse has become *the* language of tort law and is likely to endure and push practice further along when less enduring political contingencies shift.[13]

Systems analysis and operations research

By systems analysis we mean the application of operations research techniques and approaches which conceive of the criminal process as a 'system' which can be analysed as such for purposes of policy analysis and management, and to which overarching and integrated goals can be assigned. Systems analysis posits a synoptic (even if hypothetical) vantage point for assessing goals and efficiency. When the history of twentieth century American criminal justice is written, the rise of 'criminal justice system-thinking' may be regarded as the single most important contribution of criminology and criminal justice policy discourse.[14]

Although there is nothing inherently antithetical to traditional conceptions of individual justice in the techniques employed by systems analysis, the latter is fundamentally concerned with rational management and the regulation of aggregates, and the former with individual-focused justice. Indeed the distinct claim of operations research is that it offers generic insights and techniques for managing seemingly different phenomena – systemic processes – airports, communications, manufacturing, criminal justice.

Systems theory evolved out of the fields of mathematics, physics and electrical engineering during the 1950s and early 1960s (Ruberti, 1984: xi). It was first introduced into the practice of government in the early 1960s by US Secretary of Defense, Robert McNamera, to rationalise Pentagon procurement practices. It was quickly applied to a host of other areas, including the criminal process. This step was bold and deliberate; a group of 'whiz kid' consultants to the Department of Defense were appointed to staff a Task Force for the President's Commission on Law Enforcement and Administration of Justice, and subsequently published the *Task Force Report: Science and Technology* (1967b), which became one of the Commission's most widely read reports. In the midst of an escalating war on crime, modern systems analysis, the latest Defense Department technique, gained instant credibility and appeal.

The most stunning symbol of this rapid and dramatic addition to modern American criminology is the near instant and widespread acceptance of the 'funnel of justice' flow chart published in the Report of the President's Commission on Law Enforcement and Administration of Justice (1967b: 8–9). This chart, no doubt the most frequently reprinted and distributed 'chart' in modern American criminology, captures the essence of the new criminology, a shift away from concern with individual-focused justice to a concern with the efficient management of danger.[15] It constitutes the new symbol of justice in the newly announced criminal justice *system*.[16]

The chart does much more than provide a pictorial overview of the criminal process. The 'funnel of justice' fosters a perspective that invites us to think about the elimination of bottlenecks, pre-trial diversion, 'early case assessment' bureaux to weed out 'junk cases', 'fast track' prosecution bureaux to go after 'career criminals', use of probation and parole revocations to avoid the 'trial loop', 'selective incapacitation' to deploy limited prison space more efficiently, and the like. It suggests new forms of plea bargaining; drop new charges if the arrestee agrees to return a revocation of parole or probation and a return to custody (Greenspan, 1991). It invites the creation of categories and the specification and rationalisation of goals, ideally reduced into a single metric scale, which we suggest is the 'management of danger'. Thus it is possible to weigh the relative benefits of, say, increased investment pre-trial diversion for low risk offenders and expanded use of selective incapacitation for high risk offenders.

Contrast the implications of the chart depicting the 'funnel of justice', the new symbol of (actuarial) justice with another traditional symbol, which represents Justice as a blindfolded woman holding scales. This earlier symbol captures the aspirations if not the reality of individual-focused justice. Justice is a woman to represent mercy; the blindfold symbolises disinterest and impartiality, and the scales suggest carefully weighed individualised assessment. As Curtis and Resnik (1987) have noted, such iconography is no longer in fashion. In criminal justice it appears to have been replaced by the flow chart of systems analysis.

Law and economics

An important movement in contemporary jurisprudence with possible links to actuarial justice is law and economics. Economic thinking has a powerful influence on contemporary scholarship in a variety of substantive law fields, especially torts, contracts, environmental law and anti-trust, and in turn this has influenced the courts.[17] Some scholars have also applied it to the analysis of criminal law and procedure (Becker, 1968; Posner, 1985; Shavell, 1985). Economic analysis and actuarial justice share several important features. They both emphasise utilitarian purposes of punishment over moral considerations. They both prefer quantitative analysis over qualitative analysis. They both focus on the performance of the criminal process as a *system* in which the effects of various stages have implications for each other and for the overall operation of the criminal law.

However, these similarities hide important differences. To say that they are both hyperutilitarian highlights certain similarities, but to contrast utilitarianism against morality-based analysis obscures a great deal. Indeed in our view the superficial similarities of economic analysis and actuarial justice obscures crucial differences.

However useful the contrast between utilitarian and moral reasoning may have been in the eighteenth century when utilitarianism was first introduced as a system of reasoning, today it embraces such a range of considerations, that it can no longer be easily contrasted to 'moral' reasoning. Indeed the systemic logic of economic analysis and actuarial justice is a good example of the inability to make such simple comparisons. The differences can be illustrated by contrasting the deterrent (economic) and incapacitative (actuarial) approaches to punishment. Although both are utilitarian, they are also quite different. Deterrence is economic analysis par excellence since it focuses on the behaviour of individuals as rational actors responding to socially broadcast pricing signals.[18] It treats the offender as a rational economic actor to be influenced by the pricing system of punishments. Incapacitation, in contrast, treats the offender as *inert* from the point of view of influencing decision making. Thus deterrence theory views criminal punishment as only one end of a broad spectrum of incentive signals produced by government and various markets to influence individual decision making (as well as the aggregation of these individual decisions). In contrast, incapacitation theory marks punishment off as a special form of power appropriate to specific categories of people. Its aim is not to influence the decisions of individual would-be criminals, but simply to identify and incapacitate a designated high-risk population.

As Posner recognises, the criminal law's deterrence capacity is a power intended to be deployed largely on a special portion of the population – the poor. The affluent in contrast, he argues, are kept in line adequately by tort sanctions (1985: 1205). Since the poor have too little available wealth to be adequately deterred through the traditional monetary sanctions of the tort law system, imprisonment and the stigma of punishment have a special role to play in their social control. Posner does not pursue this analysis too far because it would seem to undermine his insistence that the criminal process is best understood as a system aimed at attaining efficiency. Since efficiency only has meaning in relation to value in economic theory, and since value is only measurable by willingness to pay, it follows that those outside the cash economy are outside of the efficiency maximisation process.

This suggests that the rise of incapacitation and the other instruments of actuarial justice as a reflection of social forces are pushing a larger portion of the population out of the range of normal economic signals. Deterrence in the end relies on the existence of alternatives for the population being deterred. Posner's major hypothesis is that the criminal law is aimed at preventing forced transactions outside the marketplace (1985: 1195). Ultimately deterrence can only do so to the extent that the people being deterred have basic access to market allocation through participation in the labour market and the cash economy.

Despite these crucial differences, however, economic analysis still may facilitate actuarial justice in two ways: its emphasis on collective goods (rather than individual rights) is deeply compatible with the normative assumption of actuarial justice. And, by undermining the claims of

190   *The futures of criminology*

traditional moral (individual-focused) analysis of crime and punishment as forming the basis of the criminal process, it weakens a source of resistance to actuarial justice.

The pendulum swings of crime politics

At first impression there appears to be a strong and obvious connection between the rise of conservative political stances and towards crime actuarial justice, and liberal stances and a traditional due-process focus. Although there may be some connection, it is neither obvious nor strong, and it is our contention that actuarial thinking represents deeper 'pre-political' thought that cannot easily be associated with conventional political labels. As a new technology, no doubt it can be employed somewhat differently by those with any number of different political perspectives. For instance, it was the due-process-oriented liberals of the Great Society era who provided much of the impetus to bring operations research into criminal justice, and it was the reports of the liberal-oriented members of the President's Commission which did much to promote this view. In contrast the 'lock-'em up' conservatives who held sway in the 1980s often employed traditional, individual-focused discourse (although their propensity to increase imprisonment placed such strains on prisons that it no doubt contributed pressures to expand actuarial rationalisation of the criminal process) (Feeley and Simon, 1992). In the long run, however, the implications of actuarial justice are much more far-reaching than are the periodic pendulum-like shifts in emphasis between liberal and conservative policies.

Liberal due-process values and the emergence of actuarial justice

The 1967a report of the President's Commission reveals the connection between liberal values and actuarial justice. The tone of the report, especially its sections on corrections, drugs and crime, was overwhelmingly liberal. Indeed, from a 25-year perspective, the Commission's report must be seen as one of the high water marks of postwar liberalism, and a reminder of what federal policy might have looked like in the 1970s and 1980s had contingent political events played out differently. But at the same time the President's Crime Commission provided the launching pad for the operations research discourse discussed above. The central statement of this innovative approach was found in the volume authored by the Commission's Task Force on Science and Technology (1967b), but it was more pervasive. In turn the Science and Technology Task Force had significant influences on each of the several other volumes produced by the Commission. The new discourse modelled on the operations research paradigm it introduced permeated the entire work of the Commission and its staff.

Another important sector of liberal criminal policy formation was through the constitutional jurisprudence of the federal courts. During the 1960s and

1970s the courts specified reforms in law enforcement, courts and corrections. In a way which was hard to see contemporaneously, judicial mandates to regularise procedures contributed to the effort to systematise the criminal process and rationalise the system. The exclusionary rule required major investments in monitoring and training police conduct, the right to counsel spurred the formation of bureaucratically organised public defender services in some (but by no means all) localities, and prison suits compelled the state to monitor population and coordinate the flow of arrestees and prisoners in jails. While each of these developments spawned effects that cannot be catalogued here, it is important to recognise how much they stimulated the formation of a professional class of criminal justice managers and the adoption of technologies that would permit greater coordination.

Conservative crime control policies seal the deal

As we suggested earlier, despite a 'lock-'em up' stance, conservative crime policies appear to repudiate much of the logic of actuarial justice. Yet there are features of the conservative policies that have also facilitated the expansion of actuarial justice. Two of the most conspicuous are support for the death penalty and enthusiasm for imprisonment. Both have increased reliance on actuarial techniques.

The consequences of these policies on the system are only now being taken stock of (Blumstein, 1993). In the short run the propounders of the get-tough approach are being blamed with distending the system for uncertain gains. In the long run, however, the conservative build-up in the 1980s has facilitated the dependence upon actuarial justice. Distention when it does not truly result in the collapse of a system forces important adaptations, which in the case of the criminal process has meant greater systemic thinking and planning. The swollen size of the process has facilitated institutionalisation of actuarial solutions. By creating an enormous population of persons under criminal custody,[19] the conservative policies of the 1980s in the United States and some European countries has made 'system' perspective all but inevitable as governments struggle to deal with consequences. One sees these developments in any number of new penal policies, which increasingly are designed to manage risks rather than punish or rehabilitate (Feeley and Simon, 1992).

Another indication of the consequences of expanded reliance on systemic thinking is the developing link between civil and criminal processes. For instance Section 5101 of the Anti-Drug Abuse Act of 1988 requires that leases in federally funded public housing contain a provision providing that 'criminal activity, including drug-related criminal activity, on or near public housing premises' by 'a public housing tenant, any member of the tenant's household, or another person under tenant's control . . . shall be cause for termination of tenancy.'[20]

When taken together, these and other actions provide an impressive arsenal not for identifying the guilty and holding them accountable, but for 'managing' populations, the 'dangerous class'.

Social factors: the discovery of the 'underclass'

An old term, 'underclass', has been revived to characterise a segment of society that is increasingly viewed as permanently excluded from social mobility and economic integration.[21] It refers to a largely black and Hispanic population living in concentrated zones of poverty in the centre of US cities, separated physically and institutionally from mainstream American social and economic life. In contrast to others who may be poor and unemployed, the underclass is a permanently dysfunctional population, without literacy, without skills and without hope; a self-perpetuating and pathological segment of society that is not integratable into the larger whole, and whose culture fosters violence.[22] Actuarial justice invites it to be treated as a high-risk group that must be managed for the protection of the larger society.[23]

The underclass and crime

Building on Wilson's (1987) book, *The Truly Disadvantaged*, and the earlier ecological studies of juvenile delinquency by Chicago sociologists Clifford Shaw and Henry McKay (1969), Sampson and Wilson (1993: 24) have developed a theory of race, crime and urban inequality, which links persistent high crime among black youth to both structural and cultural concepts. They conclude that community-level social disorganisation may go a long way towards explaining how current patterns of crime have been shaped by rapid social change in the macrostructural context of inner-city ghetto poverty. 'In our view', they comment, 'the unique value of this community-level perspective is that it leads away from a simple "kinds of people" analysis to a focus on how changing social characteristics of collectivities foster violence' (Sampson and Wilson, 1993: 11).

They portray the 'concentration effects' of an urban underclass which sustains and reinforces a 'culture of violence' through 'structural social disorganization and cultural social isolation that stem from the concentration of poverty, family disruption, and residential instability', and which associates an increasingly entrenched urban underclass with violence (Sampson and Wilson, 1993: 14). To the extent that the underclass is understood as a permanent feature of modern urban society, and that it sustains a culture of violence and social disorganisation, it resonates with the discourse of actuarial justice, which is couched in terms of collectives.[24]

The underclass and criminal justice

But if the emergence of the term underclass reinforces the salience of actuarial justice, the links to practice are even more significant. Sampson and Laub (1992) argue that intervention by criminal justice officials is differentially applied to various segments of the youth population as determined by their position in the social structure. Members of the black underclass are, Sampson and Laub show, 'managed' more stringently than others accused of the same offences. Although they react to this as a demonstration of the 'inequalities' in the juvenile courts, their own conceptual framework leads to an even more chilling conclusion: when framed in terms of their own theory of the culture of violence of the black underclass, *and* seen in the light of actuarial concerns of danger-management, the pattern reveals a new and different social logic – danger management, not individualised criminal justice.

It is not that officials are 'merely' violating traditional ideals of equality when dealing with or intervening in underclass communities, it is that they are animated by a powerful new social logic, risk management. When married with the emerging conception of actuarial justice, the concept 'underclass' sets concerns with individualised justice, and its correlates of equality and inequality, to one side. In this new and emerging formulation, the emphasis is on groups and aggregates and danger management, not individualised justice.[25]

The concept of an underclass, with its connotation of a permanent marginality for entire portions of the population, has rendered the traditional goal of reintegration of offenders incoherent, and laid the groundwork for a strategy that emphasises efficient management of dangerous populations.[26] Imagine for instance how ludicruous it is to think of a parole officer attempting to 'integrate' an offender back into his or her community. One can work through any of several other institutions in the criminal process and come to much the same pessimistic conclusion: likelihood to appear at 'trial' versus risk of dangerousness, adjudication of guilt versus risk management, punishment versus population control, and the like (Irwin, 1986; Doyle, 1992).

Conclusion: some notes on crime and civil war from the *intifada* to South Central Los Angeles

It may seem odd to conclude an examination of developments of largely American (and European)[27] criminal processes with a digression on an international problem, the *intifada*, the Palestinian uprising in the Israeli occupied territories (Judea and Samaria and Gaza). Yet, as we will attempt to show, the metaphoric discussion of 'two societies' that often goes on in the United States is illuminated by looking at a situation where there is nothing metaphoric about it.

In responding to violence and illegality, in both the United States and in the territories held by Israel since the 1967 war, the language of rights is employed. But in both settings, this discourse is commingled with another language, that of actuarial justice. In the United States it is muted; the rhetoric of liberal legal discourse still predominates; actuarial discourse is

194   *The futures of criminology*

found only at the margins. In contrast in Israel in reference to the territories, the language of the danger-management is as prominent, if not more so, than the rhetoric of rights.

Although when confronted with criticism of preventive detention, collective punishment, aggressive interrogation, extensive surveillance, street sweeps for weapons and law-breakers, truncated procedure, extensive road blocks, a system of passes, use of colour-coded licence plates, and pressed for clarification of long-term objectives, Israeli officials struggle to characterise policies in the familiar language of rights and judicial officials oblige. But such efforts are seen as the charades they are. Everyone – Palestinians and Israelis, hawks and doves – acknowledges that what is taking place is a war, 'a war that is not a war' in the words of one prominent official, and that the overwhelming task at hand is the management of danger and not the identification and sanctioning of guilty individuals.

Thus despite a facade of the language of rights, there exists another more powerful discourse in which the conflict is described: it is group conflict. It employs actuarial language: preventive detention, aggressive surveillance, mass arrests, collective punishments, curfews, censorship, mass deportation, identification papers and passes, decisions based upon profiles and symbols are all justified in terms of the management of 'danger'. The techniques to pursue these aims include decision making based upon profiles, constructs pieced together from partial bits of information and designed to provide assessment as to a person's – and a group's – risk; extensive surveillance; preventive detention; mass detention; aggressive interrogation. For instance age is, at times, an important variable. And so too is employment. Young unemployed males are high risks and their mobility – as opposed to older employed males and women – may be more severely restricted. A variety of identity cards indicating one's status as defined by these and other characteristics facilitates regulation of movement.

All of this is, of course, commonplace to war. After all, war is conducted between groups and not individuals. And 'offence' is about belonging, belonging to the 'enemy' group, and not individualised conduct. Furthermore, it is young men who constitute the main combatants in war. And although there are emerging 'rules of war', no one argues that it is to be conducted according to due process.

The Israeli dilemma is, of course, that although the *intifada* is a sort of war, it is also 'not a war'. Control in the territories has become a sort of permanent struggle woven into the fabric of civil existence (but not quite a civil war which could signal a prospect of a resolution). This precarious situation no doubt accounts for the effort to normalise policies by employing the rhetoric of rights. But such an effort is widely acknowledged for what it is, a veneer on the effort to manage a permanently dangerous population.

This comparison obviously invites more careful consideration of the metaphors being used in America today, such as 'war on crime' and 'war on drugs', than is usually given. But it also does more. The readily apparent actuarial considerations in Israel unwittingly provide a basis for appreciating how actuarial American criminal processes have become. Apart from the frequency with which the metaphor war is used in both societies, a comparison also reveals that many of the policies employed by the Israelis in managing danger in the territories have their counterparts in the American criminal process as well. And it reveals a similarity in rhetoric as the new aims and techniques of actuarial justice are described and justified.

In recent years both the Israeli and the American governments have endorsed 'preventive detention', and (in at least selected areas of organised crime and drug sales in the United States) collective sanctioning. Both have come to rely extensively on 'profiles' and 'associations' as predictors of dangerousness, and employed 'sweeps', 'checkpoints' and other technologies to target entire populations. And both employ 'balancing' tests and 'reasonable-under-the-circumstances' standards to justify aggressive patrolling, and frequent questioning searches in the absence of probable cause (the new 'reasonableness' standard), and expanding reliance on preventive detention.

Of course, one can press this comparison too far. After all, Israel must control an alien population which no one wishes to be integrated into the larger society and which aspires to national self-determination. Under the circumstances, it is hardly surprising that a risk management strategy crowds out liberal legal principles in shaping policy. However, before we discard the comparison because of the vast difference in political situations, it is interesting to reflect on just how similar – in certain respects relevant to this chapter – the American situation is to the Israeli situation. Both the Palestinian population in the territories and the American urban underclass (although for profoundly different reasons) are alienated and cut off from the larger dominant society and social institutions, and both present seemingly intractable problems of violence for this order. In fact violence by (both within the group and against others) the black underclass population in the United States is much greater than violence in (again, both within and against others) Palestinian communities in the territories. Per capita there are more deaths of young black males in American cities than there are of young Palestinians. And at any given time a higher proportion of young black American males are in custody than are Palestinian males of the same age group from the territories. After the April 1992 civil disorders in Los Angeles, few can doubt the potential for much more overt forms of urban warfare. Indeed, Los Angeles already strikes some observers as embodying much of the urban form and social structure of Third World cities (Davis, 1990; Cooper, 1993).

Many defend the Israeli policy of aggressive danger management as necessary 'under the circumstances'. We need not enter into this debate about the propriety of Israeli policy here, but we do wish to note that the 'circumstances' in the United States are in some important respects much worse. Indeed by itself the Israeli policy on violence in the territories might be understood as an ad hoc response to a distinctive and complicated international dilemma, an ill-defined military matter. But juxtaposed against even greater American violence, these policies may also be seen as a harbinger of things to come in the criminal process of Western societies more generally. Danger management may be the wave of the future, and the Israeli experience, admittedly wrenched out of context here, may provide a glimpse of that future. In other countries the 'recalcitrant population' may be an underclass. Although indigenous and formally part of an inclusive national community, it nevertheless still may be perceived as unintegratable and dangerous to the dominant communities.

Indeed the internal status of the underclass may mean that solution to the American dilemma is even less tractable than the Israeli issue which at least everyone agrees requires a 'political solution' to foster normality and reduce danger. In contrast the 'dangerous class' in America is indigenous; and neither expulsion nor divestiture nor any form of separation and autonomy nor any other political solutions appear viable. The very term 'underclass' comes close to suggesting that it is a permanent condition to be managed rather than solved or eliminated.

To the extent that this pessimistic assessment is accurate, actuarial justice may be regarded by a growing number of people as an obvious and practical – the only – response to an intractable problem involving at least certain types of dangerous people. Actuarial justice may be seen not as an emergency policy to deal with an anomalous situation, but an effort to normalise the situation. It may become an integral part of – rather than an embarrassing adjunct to – the process of justice. If this is true, ironically we may now see the future in a setting where in the future it may not be present.

Notes

An earlier version of sections of this chapter was presented by Professor Feeley at the Drapkin Lecture, Hebrew University, 5 December 1992, and a subsequent faculty workshop at the School of Law, Hebrew University in March 1993. The authors wish to acknowledge the helpful comments of a number of people, including Stanley Cohen, Alon Harel, Menachem Horowitz, Mordechi Kremnitzer, Michael Maltz, David Nelken, Robert J. Sampson, Yoram Shachar. They also wish to express their gratitude for support from the Daniel and Florence Guggenheim Foundation and the UC Berkeley Committee on Research.

1 Both European and North American scholars have noted the recent rising trend within criminal justice agencies to target categories and subpopulations rather than individuals, and for scholars to formulate analyses which follow suit (Bottoms, 1983; Matthiesen, 1983; Cohen, 1985; Ewald, 1986; Reichman, 1986).

2 We acknowledge that the term actuarial justice is nebulous, and that our analysis lacks sufficient analytic clarity. But the phenomenon is relatively new, not well developed and is emerging. Writing a 'history of the present' is always dangerous. However it is real, growing and, we maintain, significant. The general form of our thesis is readily apparent to anyone familiar with Marxist theories of law. Like us, they too assert that the criminal process does not provide liberal, individual-oriented justice, but is best understood as one element in a scheme of class repression. There are, of course, many variations to this theme. Although our analysis has some affinity with this perspective, we reject the notion of any 'grand theory' of society or any master plan for the criminal process. This, of course, makes actuarial justice more nebulous,

The emerging new criminal law   197

but in our view also more convincing. In addition, we argue that we are witnessing a decline of liberal legalism, that is a shift away from individual-oriented jurisprudence to one that is oriented towards aggregate considerations. This is not the place to put forward the theoretical bases which inspire our perspective. However, our debt to Michel Foucault will be obvious to the reader, and he or she should note that one of Foucault's enduring contributions will be his insistence that we treat knowledge and power as inextricably bound up in complex relations of reciprocal expansion (so that one might simply speak of 'knowledge/power' or a specific complex of 'knowledge/power' like medicine) (Foucault, 1977, 1980). And, like him, we note that discourse and knowledge emerge in decentralised, not directed ways, but nevertheless can congeal in ways that exert powerful 'strategies', though these strategies are not master plans (Simon, 1992).

3 Selective incapacitation is still largely an 'idea', and is not widely incorporated in sentencing laws. Some may regard it as a bad memory from the 1980s but we suspect it will continue to reappear in more subtle forms within sentencing systems that do not highlight the centrality of selectivity. The United States Sentencing Commission, *Supplementary Report on the Initial Sentencing Guidelines and Policy Statements* (Washington DC: United States Sentencing Commission, 1987, 197–8), emphasised the predictive powers of the criminal history score in the guidelines and suggested that further research would improve its selectivity.

4 For an account of this see Chapter 2, 'Bail reform', in Feeley (1983: 40–80).

5 The task force drew upon social science methodologies, but the specific analysis and the specific factors are classified secrets (Cloud, 1985: 879).

6 Herbert Packer's (1968) two models of the criminal process – the due process model and the crime control model, and the tension between them – continue to dominate discussion of the underlying social vision that shapes crime policy.

7 In this respect criminal justice is not leading but following trends laid down in health care, employment policy and social welfare. See generally the essays in Burchell et al. (1991).

8 In the American states, state prisons are designed for housing the more serious offenders who are serving sentences of one year or longer. Less serious offenders serve their time in local jails. Yet in recent years, an increasing proportion of inmates in state prisons are there for short periods, of six months or less. These inmates have been returned to custody after revocation of parole or probation.

9 Then Associate Justice Rehnquist made this distinction in *Salerno*. Although critics scoffed at this distinction and the reasoning in this case, it does reveal an acknowledgement of the shift in objectives we have emphasised and openly redefines rights more narrowly accordingly.

10 The immigration context has long been one of policing 'masses' rather than individuals (Auchincloss-Lorr, 1993: 111). The Court has recognised that limiting enforcement by individualised suspicion would make much of the immigration function impossible. Increasingly the Court seems to be recognising and endorsing the shift of regular law enforcement towards mass surveillance. Sweeps, checkpoints and airport stops are the police forms of actuarial justice. The Court has not only upheld these measures but diluted the strength of Fourth Amendment protections in order to do so.

11 *United States* v. *Mendenhall* (1980), *Reid* v. *Georgia* (1980), *Florida* v. *Royer*, (1983), *Florida* v. *Rodriguez*, (1984) and *United States* v. *Sokolow* (1989).

12 A similar perspective has also been put forward by David Garland in his book *Punishment and Modern Society* (1990).

13 Parallel developments are taking place in other legal fields including business associations, employment rights relations and environmental law.

14 Indeed, that history is already being written. Samuel Walker has painstakingly charted the first steps of this 'innovation' in thinking (1992, 1993).

15 Both authors can attest to seeing copies of the chart in the offices of an astounding variety of criminal justice operatives from judges to parole officers, a perception shared by many other researchers we have spoken to about this.

16 We are not the first to note shifts in iconography about the criminal process (see, for example, Curtis and Resnik, 1987).

198   *The futures of criminology*

17 The seminal statement of the contemporary variety of law and economics remains Posner (4th edn, 1992).

18 Posner (1985) recognises that deterrence is insufficient to account for the system of criminal punishments in use. He suggests that the place of incapacitative sanctions, which seek to suppress certain individuals altogether rather than alter their calculations is understandable when it is recognised that unlike the treatment of accidents by tort law, the criminal law seeks to attain complete suppression (1985: 1215). According to Posner this has an overall economic logic since unlike behaviour that leads to accidents crime has no overall social benefit (1985: 1215).

19 An accumulation that will endure and even widen as the effects of over arrest, prosecution and imprisonment have their effects on future sentencing, detection of crime through surveillance of known offenders, and the reproduction of criminal life styles through the loss of fathering for another generation of male children.

20 Anti-Drug Abuse Act of 1988, Pub. L. No. 100–690, Section 510:, 102 Stat. 4181, 4300 (codified as amended at 42 U.S.C. Section 2437d(1)(5) (1988)).

21 William Julius Wilson first began talking about 'the underclass' in the late 1970s. The term was popularised first by journalist Ken Auletta (1982), and later presented in its most influential form by Wilson himself (1987). Wilson is Professor of Sociology at the University of Chicago and a recent President of the American Sociological Association. His book provoked immense and intense comment, precisely because it was read to suggest that there was a segment of American society that has all but been written out of the social contract, a permanent 'underclass'. Although in subsequent writings Professor Wilson has expressed some regret about using the term because of the permanence and hopelessness that it conveys, it is nevertheless powerful precisely because it does convey such profound problems.

The term, of course, has a much longer history, and some variation of it has long been used by Marxists. In German, the term *untermenchen* has long been used to characterise a segment of the population that is in but not really of the community because of deprivations and depravity. The term 'dangerous classes' was widely used in the late eighteenth and early twentieth centuries to convey that portion of the population that is 'rabble' and inherently dangerous (Irwin, 1986). Indeed discussion of crime in late-eighteenth-century England may closely parallel recent developments in actuarial justice, a period when criminal justice administration was largely privatised.

22 There is by now considerable criticism of the political assumptions behind the 'underclass' talk, much of which we agree with. Here we use this term mainly because it is the talk as such that we want to highlight.

23 A recent study estimated that on any given day in 1988 roughly one in every four young (between ages 20 and 29) black males was under some form of correctional custody in the United States (Mauer, 1990). More recently, a similar study calculated that on a randomly selected day in 1990, some 42 per cent of all young black males in Washington, DC, were in custody (reported in Terry, 1992). The growing visibility of the link between criminal management and race is likely to reinforce the sense that crime is the product of a pathological subpopulation that cannot be integrated into the society at large, as well as the perception that the penal system can do no better than maintain custody over a large segment of this population. See also, Austin (1992: 1782).

24 This formulation of issues is hardly new to us. Wilson himself has expressed reservations about his use of the term 'underclass' precisely because it tends to imply hopelessness and permanence, something that as a committed social reformer he rejects (1991: 475).

25 Our characterisation of law enforcement tactics in the black community is hardly distinctive. We draw on the standard field work studies on urban neighbourhoods, the drug culture and gangs, which routinely describe mass arrests, frequent street sweeps for drugs, weapons and violators. See, for example, Austin (1992) and Davis (1990) – matter of fact descriptions of massive gang crackdowns by Los Angeles Police Department; Jankowski (1991) – describing routine anti-gang sweeps in South-Central Los Angeles.

26 The underclass is not the only feature of the contemporary social scene that seems linked to actuarial justice. One powerful influence is the growth of illegal immigration into the United

The emerging new criminal law   199

States and the techniques that have been deployed against it by the Immigration and Naturalisation Service (INS). Katharine Auchincloss-Lorr (1993) worries that the Supreme Court has been influenced by the use of techniques of mass control ('sweeps' and 'surveys') by the INS in accepting their increasing use in the criminal process. Another important source of new technologies and ideologies for the criminal process is the problem of regulating organisational behaviour. The spectre of elite criminality in the form of white-collar crime invites assimilation of regulatory methods to detecting and prosecuting criminal acts. The emergence of civil forfeiture and the panoply of prosecutorial devices under the federal Racketeering and Corrupt Organizations Act are examples. We do not have space here to discuss these sources further but plan on addressing them in a future article.

27 Our discussion here has been overwhelmingly American but see the citations in note 1.

References

Andenaes, Johannes (1974) *Punishment and Deterrence*. Ann Arbor: University of Michigan Press.

Auchincloss-Lorr, Katharine (1993) 'Police encounters of the third kind: the role of immigration law and policy in pre-seizure interrogation strategies', *Search and Seizure Law Reporter*, 20: 105–12.

Auletta, Ken (1982) *The Underclass*. New York: Random House.

Austin, Regina (1992) '"The Black Community", its lawbreakers, and a politics of identification', *Southern California Law Review*, 65: 1769–1817.

Becker, Gary (1968) 'Crime and punishment: an economic approach', *Journal of Political Economy*, 76: 169–87.

Blumstein, Alfred (1993) 'Making rationality relevant – the American Society of Criminology 1992 Presidential Address', *Criminology*, 31: 1–16.

Bottoms, Anthony (1983) 'Neglected trends in contemporary punishment', in David Garland and Peter Young (eds), *The Power to Punish*. London: Heinemann.

Burchell, Graham, Gordon, Colin and Miller, Peter (eds) (1991) *The Foucault Effect: Studies in Governmentality*. Chicago, IL: University of Chicago Press.

Cloud, Morgan (1985) 'Search and seizure by the numbers: the drug courier profile and judicial review of investigative formulas', *Boston University Law Review*. 65: 843–921.

Cohen, Stanley (1985) *Visions of Social Control*. New York: Oxford University Press.

Cooper, Marc (1993) 'Falling Down', *Village Voice*, 23 March: 24–9.

Curtis, Dennis E. and Resnik, Judith (1987) 'Images of Justice', *Yale Law Journal*, 96: 1727.

Davis, Mike (1990) *City of Quartz: Excavating the Future of L.A.* New York: Vintage.

Doyle, James M. (1992) '"It's the Third World down there!": the colonialist vocation and American criminal justice', *Harvard Civil Rights – Civil Liberties Law Review*, 27: 71–126.

Ewald, François (1986) *L'etat Providence*. Paris: Grasset.

Feeley, Malcolm M. (1983) *Court Reform on Trial: Why Simple Solutions Fail*. New York: Basic Books.

Feeley, Malcolm M. and Simon, Jonathan (1992) 'The new penology: notes on the emerging strategy of corrections and its implications', *Criminology*, 30: 449–74.

Foote, Caleb (1965) 'The Coming Constitutional Crisis in Bail', *University of Pennsylvania Law Review*. 113: 959–1185.

Foucault, Michel (1977) *Discipline and Punish: The Birth of the Prison*. New York: Pantheon.

Foucault, Michel (1980) 'Truth and Power', in Colin Gordon (ed.), *Power/Knowledge: Selected Interviews and Other Writings 1972–1977*. New York: Pantheon.

Garland, David (1990) *Punishment and Modern Society*. Oxford: Oxford University Press.

Greenspan, Rosann (1991) *The Transformation of Criminal Due Process in the Administrative State*. PhD thesis, University of California at Berkeley.

Greenwood, Peter (1982) *Selective Incapacitation* (with Alan Abrahmse). Santa Monica, CA: Rand.

Irwin, John (1986) *The Jail: Managing the Underclass in American Society*. Chicago, IL: University of Chicago Press.

Jankowski, Martin Sanchez (1991) *Islands in the Street: Gangs in American Urban Society*. Berkeley: University of California Press.

Matthiesen, Thomas (1983) 'The future of control systems – the case of Norway', in David Garland and Peter Young (eds), *The Power to Punish*. London: Heinemann.

Mauer, Marc (1990) *Young Black Men and the Criminal Justice System*. Washington, DC: The Sentencing Project.

Moore, Mark H., Estrich, Susan R., McGillis, Daniel and Spelman, William (1984) *Dangerous Offenders: The Elusive Target of Justice*. Cambridge, MA: Harvard University Press.

Packer, Herbert (1968) *The Limits of the Criminal Sanction*. Palo Alto, CA: Stanford University Press.

Posner, Richard A. (1985) 'An economic theory of the criminal law', *Columbia Law Review*, 85: 1193–1231.

Posner, Richard (1992) *Economic Analysis of Law* (4th edn). Boston, MA: Little Brown.

President's Commission on Law Enforcement and Administration of Justice (1967a) *The Challenge of Crime in a Free Society*. Washington, DC: US Government Printing Office.

President's Commission on Law Enforcement and Administration of Justice (1967b) *Task Force Report: Science and Technology*. Washington, DC: US Government Printing Office.

Reichman, Nancy (1986) 'Managing crime risks: toward an insurance based model of social control', *Research in Law and Social Control*, 8: 151–72.

Ruberti, A. (1984) 'Introduction', in A. Ruberti (ed.), *Systems Sciences and Modelling*. Boston, MA: Reidel Publishing.

Sampson, Robert J. and Laub, John H. (1992) 'Crime and deviance in the life course', *Annual Review of Sociology*, 18: 63–89.

Sampson, Robert J. and Wilson, William Julius (1993) 'Toward a theory of race, crime, and urban inequality', in John Hagan and Ruth Peterson (eds), *Crime and Inequality*. Stanford, CA: Stanford University Press.

Shavell, Steven (1985) 'Criminal law and the optimal use of nonmonetary sanctions as a deterrent,' *Columbia Law Review*, 85: 1232–61.

Shaw, Clifford and Henry McKay (1942; rev. edn 1969), *Juvenile Delinquency and Urban Areas*. Chicago, IL: University of Chicago Press.

Simon, Jonathan (1987) 'The emergence of a risk society: insurance, law, and the state', *Socialist Review*, 95: 93–108.

Simon, Jonathan (1988) 'The ideological effects of actuarial practices', *Law & Society Review*, 22: 772.

Simon, Jonathan (1992) ' "In another kind of wood": Michel Foucault and socio-legal studies', *Law & Social Inquiry*, 17: 49–55.

Simon, Jonathan (1993) *Poor Discipline: Parole and the Social Control of the Underclass, 1890–1990*. Chicago, IL: University of Chicago Press.

Steiner, Henry (1987) *Moral Argument and Social Vision in the Courts: A Study of Tort Accident Law*. Madison: University of Wisconsin Press.

Sugarman, Stephen D. (1989) *Doing Away with Personal Injury Law: New Compensation Mechanisms for Victims, Consumers, & Business*. Westport, CA: Greenwood.

Terry, Don (1992) 'More familiar, life in a cell seems less terrible', *The New York Times*, 13 September.

Walker, Samuel (1992) 'Origins of the contemporary criminal justice paradigm: the American Bar Foundation Survey, 1953–1969', *Justice Quarterly*, 9: 47–76.

Walker, Samuel (1993) *Taming the System: The Control of Discretion in Criminal Justice, 1950–1990*. New York: Oxford University Press.

Wasserstrom, Silas (1984) 'The incredible shrinking Fourth Amendment', *American Criminal Law Review*, 21: 257–401.

Wilson, William J. (1987) *The Truly Disadvantaged: The Inner City, the Underclass, and Public Policy*. Chicago, IL: University of Chicago Press.

Wilson, William J. (1991) 'Public policy research and the truly disadvantaged', in Christopher Jencks and Paul E. Peterson (eds), *The Urban Underclass*. Washington, DC: Brookings.

Table of cases

Part IV
The Politics of Crime Risk Management

[19]

Warnings to Women

Police Advice and Women's Safety in Britain

ELIZABETH A. STANKO

Brunel University

This article examines police and other governmental crime prevention literature advising women about personal safety. Through a radical feminist perspective, my personal narrative includes a historical context for developments in Britain that give rise to a social and political climate within which individual responsibility for avoiding violence is paramount. The purpose of this article is to raise theoretical questions about the effect of this context on us as women. As a feminist, I also argue for the usefulness of a radical feminist perspective to inform our thinking about avoiding men's violence and ensuring women's safety.

Common sense tells you that not every man approaching you in a lonely place will do you harm. But it still pays to be wary. (*Positive Action*, 1995)

Through the traditions of an approach to women's safety as developed in Britain from radical feminist critiques of violence against women (Kelly, 1988; Stanko, 1985, 1990b), I raise concerns with the assumptions about women, violence, and crime avoidance embedded in police and other governmental crime prevention literature that ultimately find their way into the popular press. This article offers a textual analysis of police advice literature to women on crime and its avoidance. During the years, I have watched as this advice has been reproduced by the media in its coverage of violence against women. Do the public police and popular media converge in their views of men's violence to women? Do such views give advice to women that may assist them in avoiding or minimizing (or both) men's violence?

I ask: Have women's experiences of sexual and physical violence and its avoidance been used to inform women's safety pamphlets issued by the police, who are credited for finally taking

VIOLENCE AGAINST WOMEN, Vol. 2 No. 1, March 1996 5-24

violence against women seriously? What are the lessons about
safety we can glean from media accounts of violence against
women? Is such advice likely to assist in assuaging women's fear
of crime (Stanko, 1990b; Young, 1992) or women's avoidance of
men's violence?

SOME CONTEXTUAL BACKGROUNDS

WOMEN'S FEAR OF CRIME

During the 1980s, women's fear of crime, as measured by the
influential British Crime Survey (Hough & Mayhew, 1983),
opened up another dimension of the debate about women and
violence in the United Kingdom. Stanko (1987) suggested that
women's fear of crime is an expression of women's fear of men
and of men's violence. Radical feminists interpreted women's fear
of crime as a barometer of our actual and perceived vulnerability
to men's physical and sexual violence (Hanmer & Maynard, 1987;
Hanmer & Saunders, 1984; Kelly, 1988; Stanko, 1987, 1990a, 1992;
in the United States, see Young, 1992). As such, we began to
document our anticipation of men's violence, which results in
"policing ourselves" (Radford, 1987). Accumulated research suggests that (a) women are more likely to restrict their activities in
public because of anxiety about encountering the potential of
men's violence (Burgess, 1995; Crawford, Jones, Woodhouse, &
Young, 1990) and (b) women use more safety precautions than
men do (Stanko, 1990b; for the United States, see Gardener, 1980,
1990; Gordon & Riger, 1988).

The British Home Office, the government ministry responsible
for all domestic affairs including law and order in Britain, also
became concerned about fear of crime, and women's greater fear
was acknowledged. It convened a working group in 1989 to
consider the problem and recommend solutions to people's fear
of crime.[1] One of the findings of the Working Group on the Fear
of Crime was that the media exaggerated the fear of crime and, as
part of a concern for public responsibility, the media were asked
to be "more responsible" in their coverage of crime and violence.
Although some media (such as the BBC) adopted guidelines for
their handling of crime, there is little evidence that the media have
muted their spotlight on violence, in particular sexual violence.

POLICING AND THE CRISIS OF PROTECTION

In the early 1980s, the police came under public scrutiny for their treatment of women as victims of violence (Radford & Stanko, 1991). The police were criticized for their handling of women who complained of rape. Public pressure initiated internal police reforms (Blair, 1985). Police suddenly seemed to be taken by a zealous concern about violence against women: They established domestic violence teams; initiated training about sexual assault; and became active spokespeople, advising women about criminal assault. Today, many of these reforms are still in place, and police crime prevention literature remains an important component in an overall publicity strategy to involve individuals, and especially women, in crime avoidance.

WOMEN'S SAFETY AND THE AGENDAS
FOR STATE RESPONSIBILITY

In Britain, the Conservative government was elected in 1979. One central component of their campaign was a "law and order" agenda (Downes & Morgan, 1994). Concern for victims, and the development of a national agenda to meet their needs, was given special emphasis with the establishment of a National Association of Victim Support Schemes (see Rock, 1990). The Women's Movement was also active; refuges for battered women arose in the early 1970s and most major conurbations had rape crisis centers (see Dobash & Dobash, 1992).

By the late 1980s, local government authorities hosted a variety of women's units, equality units, or community safety units, many of which put women's fear of crime, domestic violence, and sexual violence on the agendas for innovative social policy. Although not exclusively in Labour authorities,[2] many of the mostly women working on issues of women's violence and safety were informed by radical feminist campaigns and were theorizing about violence against women. Underpinning the work on women's safety, therefore, was a commitment to confront the climate of victim blame so prevalent within the criminal justice approaches to violence against women (Dobash & Dobash, 1979; Stanko, 1985; see, in particular, Dobash & Dobash, 1992, for a history of the rise of domestic violence as a social problem in Britain).

A decade later, by the 1990s, many local authorities, police forces, and central government departments had taken on the issues of women and violence, in its broadest sense.[3] The Association of Women's Units in Local Government released *Responding With Authority* (National Association of Local Government Women's Committees, 1991) as a call to action for local governments to become actively involved in discovering support systems to alleviate all kinds of violence against women, including women's fear of crime. Edinburgh City Council sponsored a highly visible public education campaign, *Zero Tolerance*, which confronted myths about rape, child sexual abuse, domestic violence, and women's safety from a feminist perspective (see Stanko, 1995). All of these initiatives served to reinforce the importance of catering to the needs of women in the communities—and violence was shown to be high on the agenda of the needs of women.

However, the mid-1990s find Britain, after 16 years of Conservative party rule, amid a cash crisis in public expenditure, with a decline in the welfare state (with severe cutbacks in basic provision of services such as health, education, social services, transportation, and public policing). It is essential to view police advice within the context of the wider changes in British public services—and as a metaphor for the abdication of the state for collective responsibility toward its subjects. Crime prevention advice is a centerpiece of the Conservative government's campaign against crime; advice to women flourished in the context of the developments in prevention of crime (Pease, 1994), not the prevention of violence against women (Stanko, 1990a).

My ongoing research suggests that police advice dominates community safety work. As part of a nationwide crime prevention initiative, crime avoidance and safety have become popularized, with the so-called "active citizen" taking center stage (O'Malley, 1992; Pease, 1994).[4] Individual prudence (O'Malley, 1992) prevails;[5] as individuals, we are responsible for our own safety.

A METHODOLOGICAL AND THEORETICAL APPROACH FOR ANALYZING SAFETY ADVICE

As a feminist academic, I am consciously trying to influence change through a radical feminist perspective (see, e.g., Stanko,

1985) on how we think about violence against women: through involvement in devising strategies for local government officers to introduce programs addressing violence against women, and in training police on issues of rape and domestic violence.[6] I am interested in discovering ways of changing police practice, thinking, and attitudes toward violence against women. My critique of this literature is in the spirit of such activism.

Since 1991, I have collected safety advice generated by government bodies, statutory and voluntary agencies, and the police. The initial study began in 1991 when I contacted more than 80 local governments in England, Scotland, and Wales to discover whether these bodies distributed information about women and safety to their local residents.[7] I asked for pamphlets, posters, and other relevant material to advise women about issues of their safety. I received information from 66 separate agencies.[8] A significant proportion of these local authorities forwarded the literature produced by their local police or by the Home Office's crime prevention campaign, *Practical Ways to Crack Crime*,[9] or had local models adapting these official approaches.

The analysis in this article first examines the literature distributed by police, then illustrates how this advice appears within the press coverage of men's violence against women. I am using content analysis, choosing particular passages of the texts to illustrate the approach to crime prevention advice that permeates this literature. The advice contained within these documents cannot be read with indifference to gender. To analyze them, police must be treated as socially situated within legal and ideological structures that take the provision of safety and its distribution as gender-neutral. In many ways, women—the supposed audience of these booklets—are largely silent, presumed unified in their needs, and are treated as simultaneously needlessly frightened, yet rationally wary, the voiceless objects in the negotiation of our own safety. It is an ambivalence that, I suggest, can only arise because the theoretical basis of such crime advice removes women from their position as intentional targets for men's violence (Stanko, 1990b). As such, my interpretation of these booklets is necessarily my own, informed by my 20 years as a radical feminist criminologist and an analyst of the everyday practices of personal safety of women and men.

ADVISING CAUTION:
A LOOK AT THE SAFETY ADVICE

My 4-year collection of available advice literature can be assigned to five categories:

1. Advice concerning sexual assault, rape, or both.
2. Advice concerning personal safety for women, notably a pamphlet that first appeared in 1982 titled *Positive Steps*, produced by the London Metropolitan Police and reproduced by numerous local police forces. In 1995, such pamphlets were still being used and were often available at front desks of police stations, distributed at neighborhood meetings, or posted as general advice from community police officers.
3. General advice about crime prevention in the community, including personal and household safety. Although some communities authored their own guidelines, by and large the central government crime prevention document *Practical Ways to Crack Crime* (known in Scotland as *Don't Give Crime an Open Invitation*) was the literature provided.
4. Advice concerning domestic violence. Some of this information was directed at women themselves; other information received included information to workers in local government, such as housing officers, social workers, or teachers.
5. Guidelines and advice concerning sexual harassment, aggression at work, or both.

As such, women's safety from men's violence has become divided into discrete problems, which are fragmented, with advice about domestic violence separated from that of crime, and particularly, rape avoidance. Kelly (1988) warned us against separating forms of women's abuse at the hands of men, preferring instead to remind us of the "continuum of sexual violence." Without such an understanding, I believe, thinking about violence against women becomes a distortion of individual men's behaviors, when, according to a radical feminist analysis, such behavior is indicative of women's subordinate status to men.

A word about the booklets: Their structures are similar; the types and kinds of illustrations show remarkable likenesses. Men are shadowy characters, police are kind and reassuring figures, and women deserve to be reassured. These booklets (and there were many different booklets issued in Scotland, England, and Wales) tend to be organized around three sections:

1. Suggestions about how to conduct oneself when home alone, fending off exterior intrusion.
2. Advice about how to walk on the street, carry one's handbag, and how to travel by car or public transport.
3. Reassurance if an assault happens, with a description of the partnership the victim has with the police to solve the crime.

I will explore each of these in turn.

HOME ALONE: WOMEN BEWARE

Section 1 of *Positive Steps* (PS), an example of the first (and current) booklet specially devised for women and safety by the London Metropolitan Police in the early 1980s, and *Practical Ways to Crack Crime* (PWCC), the Home Office's crime prevention guide, emphasize the special risks of being at home, at risk to strangers. States *PS*: "You probably think that you are only at risk when you're out—in side streets or up dark alleys. . . . Many incidents occur just where you might expect to feel safest—at home."

The safety suggestions revolve around the fitting of security hardware: chains on doors, windows, and so forth. The booklet gives tips on safe courses of action: Ask for identification of callers who wish access to the house; dial 999 if you are at all suspicious of the caller; and seek special advice if you are trying to sell a house ("Try not to show people around on your own"). The booklet continues:

> You can never be too careful. Every woman living alone should be especially safety conscious, and take these simple precautions to improve her security. Get into the habit of "doing the rounds" before you leave home. Lock every outside door and window—*one lapse could put you at risk.* (emphasis mine)

Similarly, "Although attacks on people do occur in their own homes, many citizens fail to take precautions to reduce such risks" (*Taking Care*).

Directed at women living alone, the suggestions include keeping the fact that one lives alone as obscure as possible. The pamphlets add that one might "wish to keep a dog," "draw curtains at night and remove clothes from outside line to deter peeping toms," keep a whistle by the telephone for pestering callers, and demand identity cards of strangers at the door. At every stage, reminders about the availability of the police to provide advice and protection appear. Throughout, there are constant references to join a Neighborhood Watch group, advice that ignores the research that suggests that Neighborhood Watch participants report higher levels of fear of crime (Mayhew, Dowds, & Elliot, 1989) and are confused about how to participate (McConville & Shepherd, 1991), and that overall such schemes have a doubtful effect on crime reduction (Bennett, 1990).

The view of "woman" is a reflection of assumptions about which women are likely to be frightened unnecessarily: single, home owning, incompetent, perhaps elderly, and naive about strangers, and especially women living outside of the supposed individual protection from individual men. Two points to emphasize here: First, the research about women and safety (Gardner, 1980, 1988, 1990; Gordon & Riger, 1988; Stanko, 1990b) suggests that most women already have fairly elaborate strategies to minimize risk of danger from strangers and are already wary of male strangers (Burgess, 1995). Of course, women could always learn different, creative strategies but many of the ones suggested—for example, do not walk in dimly lit alley ways—are ones women already adopt (Burgess, 1995; Stanko, 1990b), and if we do not, we do so for our own reasons (e.g., we may live down dimly lit alleys!).

Second, as all the research suggests, it is known that men, partners or former partners of women, pose the greatest threat to women. Advice about this type of violence is limited in these booklets: Women, it is proposed, might ask for police or court interventions, but there is no recognition that women are already actively negotiating men's violence day in and day out. The fourth and current edition of *PWCC* suggests:

> If the violence is within your family, the courts have powers to help you, regardless of whether you press criminal charges. They can, for example, require a husband not to enter your home, and in some cases, even your neighborhood.

The actual protection provided by civil injunctions has been questioned by research (Barron, 1992). The focus on strangers found in the safety literature continues to capture the imagination of the advisers as they turn to tips for women walking and driving in public. Moreover, it is also interesting to note that we ourselves have strongly held beliefs that we are most at risk in public places

(Pain, 1993). Such beliefs, suggested from an overall evaluation of my collection of safety advice, influence the literature produced by local government women's units as well as by the police. As more women live outside male control/protection by choice, is it possible to advise women about men's violence without somehow belittling different women's perceptions and experiences of dangerous men?

OUT AND ABOUT: WOMEN KEEP VIGILANT

> Obviously, no one deliberately puts themselves at risk, but the thought of becoming a victim can still be a constant worry. (*Positive Steps*)

Consolation for women's anxieties begins the next major section on women-in-public. Women are told to walk confidently, to avoid lingering at darkly lit bus stops, to keep to well-lit roads, to walk facing the oncoming traffic—all practical steps the advisers assume women do not already do. Women are encouraged to plan ahead if they are going out for the evening: Have taxi numbers on hand or trusted friends and acquaintances for company on the way home and, if walking, keep hands free for self-defense. Booklets state that handbags, carried carelessly, expose women to the opportunist thief, as does the wearing of expensive-looking jewelry. Precautions about how to travel on public transport, how to travel in a car, and how to park safely in well-lit public areas are also included.

This advice is especially ironic, given the ruthless abandonment of public expenditure to services such as transport and the staff employed by transport. The wholesale privatization of bus companies has resulted in limited and unpredictable provision of bus services and in the elimination of staff on underground trains in London and on British Rail (which is itself scheduled for privatization, hence the reduction of more staff).

The pamphlets attempt to reassure women by alerting them to their potential as targets of theft, personal assault, or worse in public places. Returning to the sanctuary of one's home is presumed. Are homeless women or women fleeing violence in the home merely overlooked? Having options, choices, daily plans, and detailed strategies are obligations: These are the armaments of the responsible woman. But many of us are excluded from being responsible before we start. What if we feel we are targets for men's violence? What happens if a man really wants to hurt us because we are women?

IF THE WORST HAPPENS: SYMPATHETIC PARTNERSHIP

> It is sensible to think about what you would be prepared to do if you were physically attacked. Could you fight back or would you play along and wait for a chance to escape? Preparing yourself for all possibilities could provide a split-second advantage. (_Taking Care_)

> If the worst happens and you are raped or sexually assaulted, turn immediately to the police. It's vital to report quickly what has happened, and you can do so in complete confidence. You will need all the special care and attention the police are anxious to give. (_Positive Steps_)

The booklets encourage the woman to report the assault to the police and assure her that she will be treated sympathetically. Police practice, however, does not ensure such sympathetic treatment. More than 10 years after this booklet was first issued, the police practice of "unfounding" rape complaints—in effect, nullifying the crime report—still exists (Lees & Gregory, 1993). No matter how sympathetic the police, if the woman gives evidence in court, she is still likely to be aggressively cross-examined by a defense attorney in a way that relies on stereotypical images of "the responsible woman" (Matoesian, 1993) and that contributes to the likelihood that her assailant will be acquitted.

Inspector Shirley Tulloch, "personal safety adviser" of the London Metropolitan Police, recently commented in a 1994 article in the widely read popular London weekly guide _Time Out_ that women's fear of crime is unrealistic ("Cosh or Cheque," 1993). She noted that most women imagine potential attackers as strangers who jump out at them from bushes but this type of crime is actually rare.

She suggested that police advise women to be on their guard and avoid potentially dangerous situations: Do not take shortcuts and stay in well-lit areas. She also recommended that women carry rape alarms. Her comments are meant to comfort, but they illustrate both the confusion in the way women's safety is promoted by the police and their actual concern about it. On one hand, there is an effort to debunk the stereotype of women's danger (see Stanko, 1988; Young, 1992)—the stranger—whereas on the other hand, offering advice about how the prudent woman should behave to avoid the potential danger of the (presumably) male stranger.

This contradiction, I suggest, can be understood through an analysis of the creation of the responsible woman. Police advice exists within a context that takes for granted the responsible woman—the woman who commonsensically takes all necessary precautions to avoid the violence of men and treats the violence of men to women as encounters that can, given responsible precautions, be avoided.

In addition, the conscious use of pictures and sketches of women and children in the care of women officers invites women's trust in the police as sensitive interviewers of women reporting rape or sexual assault, as crusaders in child protection, or as dedicated domestic violence workers. Clearly, these images illustrate how the police are using women police as a public relations tool, the acceptable face of police protection, and aim specifically at reassuring women they will be treated sympathetically should they need to contact police. What is important here is the use of imagery about victims. Only the deserving and unfortunate victim is the legitimate recipient of care. Presumably, she is responsible.

Over the past few years, police have extended this approach to advising women in highly publicized crimes against women. For instance, when a young mother was brutally killed in a London park, police suggested women avoid parks until the killer was arrested.[10] In one recent study of the use of urban fringe woodland (Burgess, 1995), all of the women interviewed mentioned this horrific murder, some adopting precaution without police advice.

Long-standing allies of the police in their fight against crime, the media cover much crime within a legacy of its own distortions (see, e.g., Ericson, Baranek, & Chan, 1991; Saward, 1991; Soothill & Walby, 1990). Police advice to women appears as part of the story, as a public service cautionary tale. How this assuages women's fear is unclear, for the fact that women are attacked, and are attacked because they are women, is a subtext, within both the safety pamphlets and, as I argue next, in the news.

POPULARIZING DANGER:
MEDIA AND POLICE ADVICE

Clearly, women's fear of crime has captured, and continues to capture, the imagination of the popular press. Images of women walking down dark alleys clutching their handbags abound; news stories of women attacked in parks, cabs, and dimly lit streets mirror these images of danger. Within this arena of crime, prevention initiatives embrace individual obligation and specify the burdens of individuals to protect themselves and their property from the opportunist thief and assailant. Within this opportunity-reduction initiative, gender has particular salience. Women—the generic audience of the advice about personal safety—represent a stereotypical, gendered vulnerability. There is, for instance, no special advice for young men, the population, according to official data, that is most at risk from assault in public.

The production of news has metaphorical import: It presents the police as sympathetic, caring professionals who are knowledgeable about what frightens women. It is only recently that police public relations officers have spotlighted the symbolic import of women police as protectors of women and as specially qualified to service the needs of women's emotional turmoil (Soothill, 1993).

The use of the police by the media as experts in women's safety stems in part from the ideological import of the police in societal protection, which is based in their crime fighting abatement, their role as gatherers of evidence and apprehenders of suspects, and their moral obligation to protect the public from the vagaries of those dangerous few, who the police, given their ownership of expertise, can identify. This is paradoxical because the media have also spearheaded the discussion of the role of policing and public confidence in that role in contemporary Britain. Concerns about confidence in the police to protect the public against crime—fostered by the civil disturbances of the 1980s, feminist campaigns about police responses to rape and domestic violence, Black people's campaigns about racial harassment, escalating crime statistics, and a host of miscarriages of justice—have been raised by the popular press in Britain.

However varied the explanations of the decline in confidence in the police though, such coverage uses the police forces throughout the country to assuage women's anxiety. In doing so, the news media actively give credence to police as servicers of the needs of vulnerable or victimized women. Although the police may privately assail the media for focusing on the most salacious of crimes against women—murder or sexual assault of young, often White, women—and for raising women's anxiety about safety, police also use the publicizing of such crime as occasions for issuing encouraging advice about how to avoid similar misfortunes and for confirming their position in the public's eye as the experts on women's safety and protection. But what they suggest as responsible precautions are usually safety measures that women already take (Stanko, 1990a) or that may increase women's fear of crime. Pain's (1993) study of women in Edinburgh found that 1 in 6 said they worried more about their safety because of police advice.

Ironically, radical feminists are still being accused of unnecessarily frightening women by publicizing the prevalence of violence against them (Roiphe, 1993). To me, though, the awareness of men's violence through a radical feminist perspective intends to spotlight the problem of men, not the problem of individual, imprudent women. The police advice fails to condemn male violence as indicative of women's subordinate position in society. As such, it individualizes responsibility, without collective comment on *the problem of men*.

So, too, the media individualizes the problem of violence against women. Violent crime committed by male strangers against women is a popular folktale of danger. The police use publicity to appeal to the public for clues to the identity of an unknown attacker. Take, for instance, a story that appeared in the *Daily Telegraph* ("Don't Go Out Alone," 1992). An Oxford undergraduate who was raped on her way home from a party was interviewed about the incident in an attempt to catch the attacker. The attack, it was noted, had created an atmosphere of tension among the thousands of women students in the city. With a victim-support counselor and a "specially trained police woman at her side," the young woman warned others not to walk alone at night. She praised the police for treating her well, and a detective working on the case advised students to avoid walking alone at night, because the crime appeared to be opportunistic and "spur of the moment."

What then are women to do? Do such news stories reassure women that the police are on the suspect's trail? This story contains a standard recipe: a random attack, an innocent victim grateful for her sympathetic treatment at the hands of police and for victim support, a police search for the perpetrator, and offers of public service follow-up to women, such as advice and police seminars on self-defense.

Another tale in *The Independent* ("Taxi Driver," 1992) reported on a taxi driver jailed for rape in a cab. The news story reported the conviction of a man for rape of a passenger. The final paragraph of the story contained a statement by the detective who headed the investigation, reassuring women that they should not be afraid to take a black cab, because this was an isolated incident.

An August 1992 story in *The Guardian* contained an appeal by police for a witness to an attack on a woman by a "bogus" minicab driver (Johnson, 1992). The detective heading the investigation stated that he was sure that the rapist had found the woman by listening to calls to the firm she had phoned, and he warned other women to be on their guard against rogue cabbies who may eavesdrop, telling women readers to always use a reputable firm and to check that the driver who arrives is from the company they called. *The Independent* also carried a story about this incident in which the final paragraph also contained a warning to women to be vigilant, to always use reputable taxi companies, and to be certain that when a cab arrives, it is from the firm called (Braid, 1992). This article also stated that there had been no publicity about this case until this point because police feared that reports might hamper their investigation. Here, it is interesting that the requirements of the police—catching the suspect—may collide with the need to warn women about similar incidents. What is the message about safety here?

Finally, consider a story that appeared in *The Independent* in July 1992 with the headline, "Fantasy World of a Murderer." In a journalistic biography of Scott Singleton, recently convicted killer of a 17-year-old woman, cautionary advice for young job applicants was included in the story. The last two paragraphs were devoted to lessons about men's tactics for luring women for abuse. The detective leading the murder investigation was quoted as saying that he was disturbed by the number of phone calls the police had received from women who had had experiences similar to the victim, but had managed to escape. He noted that this made the police realize how widespread the practice of recruitment is, especially during a period of economic recession. His advice to women applying for jobs through agencies was to check the credentials of all prospective employers by using such techniques as looking for agency letterhead, taking the agency's phone number and calling back to see if it really exists, and being suspicious of any job that sounds "too good to be true."

When I asked senior police officers at a recent seminar on service to women given at Bramshill Police College about the appearance of the above advice in the newspapers, they suggested that the reporters ask police "what advice they have for the public" subsequent to an act of random violence. The scripts for the social construction of the responsible woman are readily available: Prudent women avoid men's violence.

The messages contained within the advice booklets and the news stories suggest that we should, and can, be individually accountable for our own safety. To be a responsible woman is to display a healthy suspicion of men who appear to be ordinary men: cab drivers, potential employers, passers-by, doctors, co-workers and so forth.[11] Such wariness is never-ending and resonates in the questions we ask ourselves when we have been attacked: if only I did not walk home, open the door, shop at this store, and so forth. Even more curious, all of this advice is supposed to ease our anxiety about our safety-in-public.

CONCLUDING REMARKS

In this article, I have argued that police advice to women about personal safety fails to question why we are at risk. The feminist efforts to put violence against women on the state's agenda has also led to police turning the problem back on us. Although the police may be taking violence against women seriously, the form of their practice and thinking often reinforces the assumption that we can, given correct and responsible behavior, avoid the violence of men. As the research continues to verify, violent men want to attack a woman, whether at random or with foresight. Even assailants rationalize their behavior by blaming us for bringing on the assault ourselves (Scully, 1990; Smythman, 1978), or minimize the actual harm they cause us (Hearn, 1993).

Police advice to women implicitly reflects an understanding of our risk to men's violence: Presumably, we are vulnerable because we are women. What continues to be ignored, however, is the feminist-inspired interpretation of our vulnerability, embedded in an appropriation of our sexuality: "that which is one's own, yet most taken away" (MacKinnon, 1982, p. 515). We take many precautions because we acknowledge such potential violence as a condition of being a woman. Publicized advice, generated by in-house police publicity or through media attention to salacious crime, reinforces the message of our sexual vulnerability. It does so without the wider context that radical feminism sought to expose. Our anxiety may be raised: By placing the responsibility for avoiding men's violence once again on our shoulders—for it is our behavior that can minimize the chances of becoming a target of men's violence—we are responsible for sorting safe from unsafe men.

Given that much abuse arises within women's friendship, intimate, kinship, and daily relationships with men (Stanko, 1990a; Young, 1992), women routinely risk misjudging men's trustworthiness. Given that we may wish to live our lives without constantly thinking about our protection, we are questioned about being prudent and sensible when we stray from the rigid guidelines that will never entirely assure safety. The failure to recognize the contradictions within the subtext of police advice and the daily media accounts of violence to women, I suggest, diminishes the potential to assuage women's "fear of crime." Police are not guaranteeing—and can never guarantee—us safety within a world that takes for granted our perceptions and our experiences of sexual vulnerability. But the police are trying to do just that, resulting in a failure to truly confront the devastating personal consequences of our subordination (nor do I think they can). Thus Inspector Tulloch's advice mentioned in this article is not meant to aid us in eluding violence, but is meant to reassure. So if personal alarms make some of us feel better, regardless of whether they actually work in attracting assistance ("Calls for Alarm," 1994) or fending off attackers, then alarms work as long as they reduce our anxiety.

In sum, the advice booklets and the media accounts of police advice following horrific incidents subscribe to a standard narrative: Women are unduly afraid; if we were to adopt a set of basic safety precautions, we would reduce an already small risk of crime; police are our protectors and will treat us seriously and sympathetically; men, when they encounter us "duly protecting ourselves," will not act on impulse and foresight and attack, rob, beat, or rape us.

What would radical feminist-inspired safety advice look like? If we suggest women-only parking lots, women-only buses, or women-only bars, would we be ridiculed? Is this even realistic, given the many differences among us? How would we offer advice about minimizing the violence within intimate relationships? If we drew up a list of the "dos" and "don'ts" of safety, would it minimize the violence of men we experience? Certainly, women-designed environments, which increase the likelihood that other people "look out for them" (Burgess, 1995), are contributing to more woman-friendly environments in public. But we are still left with the problem of men. I welcome any and all suggestions to find some method of discovering collective ways to minimize our encounters with men's violence. After all, the research suggests that ultimately it is men who decide to attack us—and we need to find ways of stopping them collectively, not individually.

NOTES

1. The working group was convened in 1989, chaired by Michael Grade, chief executive of Channel 4 Television. I was a member of the working group, which was dominated by members of the media.

2. Three parties dominate the political scene in mainland Britain: Labour, Tory, and Liberal Democrat. From 1979 onward, the Tory party has controlled Central Government, but local authorities were controlled largely by either the Tory or Labour parties. Much of the so-called progressive work took place within Labour authorities, who incorporated special units within the local government, such as women's equality units or police units (which monitored the activities of police delivery of community protection).

3. See, for instance, Smith (1989a, 1989b). The Home Office issues two circulars to police concerning their treatment of women complainants of rape and domestic violence. Home Office Circulars 69/1986 and 60/1990 were issued to the police forces of England and Wales, serving as guidance in their responsibilities to provide more adequate care and attention to violence against women. A handful of local authorities, for instance, hosted conferences bringing together local agencies, interested women, and the police to discuss available remedies to domestic violence, women's fear of crime, or sexual safety.

4. Not only is such advice available throughout Britain, but I have seen versions of this crime prevention document in Australia, Canada, and the United States (see DeKeresedy, Burshtyn, & Gordon, 1992, for an analysis of the Canadian pamphlet).

5. As both Stanko (1988, 1990b) and Young (1992) argued, traditional approaches to women's fear of crime neglect the domestic nature of a vast majority of men's violence to women, which may contribute to women's fear and anxiety about their own safety.

6. These training sessions took place at the Hendon Police Training College, home of the Metropolitan Police training operations. Later, I participated in the training of senior officers at Bramshill Police College, a national training ground for officers facing promotion.

7. I did so as a prelude to a national conference on women's safety, bringing together then junior Home Office Minister John Patten (Tory) and the late Shadow Minister for Women Jo Richardson (Labour)—a demonstration that both parties treat the issue of violence against women high on their agendas.

8. I did not receive replies from 10 queries; 4 responded, informing me that they did not distribute any information to women.

9. First published in 1988, this pamphlet is the premier crime prevention literature produced by central government and distributed through local police stations throughout England, Scotland, and Wales.

10. A man was arrested and acquitted of this murder. The police were accused of entrapment.

11. Even more curious, when radical feminists suggested that all men could be rapists, they were castigated for tarring all men with the same brush.

REFERENCES

Barron, J. (1992). *Not worth the paper*. Bristol: Women's Aid.

Bennett, T. (1990). *Evaluating neighbourhood watch*. Aldershot: Gower.

Blair, I. (1985). *Investigating rape*. Aldershot: Gower.

Braid, M. (1992, August 18). Woman raped by bogus cab driver. *The Independent*, p. 1.

Burgess, J. (1995). *Growing in confidence*. Walgrave, Northampton: Countryside Commission.

Calls for alarm. (1994, December). *Which? The Independent Consumer Guide*, pp. 12-13.

Cosh or cheque. (1993, September 8-15). *Time Out*, pp. 29-30.

Crawford, A., Jones, T., Woodhouse, T., & Young, J. (1990). *The second Islington crime survey*. Middlesex, UK: Middlesex University.

DeKeseredy, W., Burshtyn, H., & Gordon, C. (1992). Taking woman abuse seriously: A critical response to the Solicitor General of Canada's crime prevention advice. *International Review of Victimology*, *2*, 157-168.

Dobash, R. E., & Dobash, R. P. (1979). *Violence against wives*. Milton Keynes: Open University Press.

Dobash, R. E., & Dobash, R. P. (1992). *Women, violence and social change*. London: Routledge.

Don't go out alone, warns rape victim. (1992, June 9). *The Daily Telegraph*, p. 3.

Downes, D., & Morgan, R. (1994). "Hostages to fortune?" The politics of law and order in post-war Britain. In M. Maguire, R. Morgan, & R. Reiner (Eds.), *The Oxford handbook of criminology* (pp. 183-232). Oxford: Oxford University Press.

Ericson, R., Baranek, P. M., & Chan, J.B.L. (1991). *Representing order: Crime, law and justice in the news media*. Milton Keynes: Open University Press.

Fantasy world of a murderer. (1992, July 23). *The Independent*, p. 3.

Gardner, C. B. (1980). Passing-by: Street remarks, address rights and the urban female. *Sociological Inquiry*, *50*, 328-356.

Gardner, C. B. (1988). Access information: Public lies and private peril. *Social Problems, 35,* 384-397.

Gardner, C. B. (1990). Safe conduct: Women, crime and self in public places. *Social Problems, 37,* 311-328.

Gordon, M., & Riger, S. (1988). *The female fear.* New York: Free Press.

Hanmer, J., & Maynard, M. (Eds.). (1987). *Women, violence and social control.* London: Macmillan.

Hanmer, J., & Saunders, S. (1984). *Well-founded fear.* London: Hutchinson.

Hearn, J. (1993). *How men talk about men's violence to known women.* Conference Report, Masculinities and Crime, Centre for Criminal Justice Research, Brunel University. Uxbridge, Middlesex, UK.

Hough, M., & Mayhew, P. (1983). *The British crime survey.* London: HMSO.

Johnson, A. (1992, August 18). Rapist driver intercepted radio cab call. *The Guardian,* p. 5.

Kelly, L. (1988). *Surviving sexual violence.* Oxford: Polity.

Lees, S., & Gregory, J. (1993). *Rape and sexual assault: A study of attrition.* London: Islington Council.

MacKinnon, C. (1982). Feminism, Marxism, method and the state: Toward a feminist jurisprudence. *Signs, 8,* 635-658.

Matoesian, G. M. (1993). *Reproducing rape.* Oxford: Polity.

Mayhew, P., Dowds, L., & Elliot, D. (1989). *The 1988 British crime survey.* London: HMSO.

McConville, M., & Shepherd, D. (1991). *Watching police, watching communities.* London: Routledge.

National Association of Local Government Women's Committees. (1991). *Responding with authority: Local authority initiatives to counter violence against women.* Manchester: Author.

O'Malley, P. (1992). Risk, power and crime prevention. *Economy and Society, 21,* 252-275.

Pain, R. (1993). *Crime, social control and spatial constraint: A study of women's fear of sexual violence.* Unpublished doctoral dissertation, University of Edinburgh.

Pease, K. (1994). Crime prevention. In M. Maguire, R. Morgan, & R. Reiner (Eds.), *The Oxford handbook of criminology* (pp. 659-704). Oxford: Oxford University Press.

Radford, J. (1987). Policing male violence—policing women. In J. Hanmer & M. Maynard (Eds.), *Women, violence and social control* (pp. 30-45). London: Macmillan.

Radford, J., & Stanko, E. (1991). Violence against women and children: The contradictions of crime control under patriarchy. In K. Stenson & D. Cowell (Eds.), *The politics of crime control* (pp. 186-202). London: Sage.

Rock, P. (1990). *Helping victims of crime.* Oxford: Clarendon.

Roiphe, K. (1993). *The morning after.* London: Chatto & Windus.

Saward, J. (1991). *Rape: My story.* London: Pan Books.

Scully, D. (1990). *Understanding sexual violence.* London: Unwin Hyman.

Smith, L. (1989a). *Concerns about rape.* London: HMSO.

Smith, L. (1989b). *Domestic violence.* London: HMSO.

Smythman, S. D. (1978). *The undetected rapist.* Unpublished doctoral dissertation, University of California.

Soothill, K. (1993, January). Policewomen in the news. *The Police Journal,* pp. 25-36.

Soothill, K., & Walby, S. (1990). *Sex crime in the news.* London: Routledge.

Stanko, E. (1985). *Intimate intrusions: Women's experience of male violence.* London: Routledge.

Stanko, E. (1987). Typical violence, normal precaution: Men, women and interpersonal violence in England, Wales, Scotland and the USA. In J. Hanmer & M. Maynard (Eds.), *Women, violence and social control* (pp. 122-134). London: Macmillan.

Stanko, E. (1988). Fear of crime and the myth of the safe home: A feminist critique of criminology. In K. Yllo & M. Bograd (Eds.), *Feminist perspectives on wife abuse* (pp. 75-88). Beverly Hills, CA: Sage.

Stanko, E. (1990a). *Everyday violence*. London: Pandora.

Stanko, E. (1990b). When precaution is normal: A feminist critique of crime prevention. In L. Gelsthorpe & A. Morris (Eds.), *Feminist perspectives in criminology* (pp. 171-83). Milton Keynes: Open University Press.

Stanko, E. (1992). The case of fearful women: Gender, personal safety and fear of crime. *Women and Criminal Justice, 4*, 117-135.

Stanko, E. (1995). Women, crime and fear. *Annals of American Political and Social Science, 539*, 46-58.

Taxi driver jailed for rape in cab. (1992, July 23). *The Independent*, p. 4.

Young, V. (1992). Fear of victimization and victimization rates among women: A paradox? *Justice Quarterly, 9*, 421-441.

Elizabeth A. Stanko, Reader in Criminology, Lecturer in Criminology, Department of Law, Brunel University, United Kingdom, received her Ph.D. in sociology from the City University of New York Graduate School in 1977. She worked for 13 years, teaching sociology and women's studies at Clark University (U.S.), moving to London in 1990 to take the position of Director, Centre for Criminal Justice Research, and Convenor, M.A., in Criminal Justice. She is the author of Everyday Violence *(Pandora, 1990) and* Intimate Intrusions *(Routledge, 1985), editor of texts on gender and crime (most recently,* Just Boys Doing Business: Men, Masculinities, and Crime, *coedited with Tim Newburn (Routledge, 1994), and has published widely on issues of prosecutorial discretion, violence, violence against women, and crime prevention. She is currently writing a book, tentatively titled* The Good, the Bad and the Vulnerable: Victims, Victimization and Gender *(Sage).*

BRIT. J. CRIMINOL VOL. 37 NO. 1 WINTER 1997

RISK AND CRIMINAL VICTIMIZATION

A Modernist Dilemma?

SANDRA WALKLATE*

Over the last 15 years or so the study of criminal victimization has proceeeded apace. That study has frequently drawn together an understanding of the nature and extent of criminal victimization with the question of risk from such victimization. Yet while what is actually meant by criminal victimization has been subject to considerable scrutiny, what is meant by risk in this context has been less closely examined. The purpose of this paper is to suggest that thinking about risk through a gendered lens might better inform those wider concerns of criminal victimization in general.

Research has shown that repeatedly victimized people and places account for a significant proportion of all crime. One study found that of the 1992 British Crime Survey respondents, half of those who were victimized were repeat victims and suffered 81 per cent of all reported crimes. Of these 4 per cent were chronically victimized. That is, they suffered four or more crimes in a year, and accounted for 44 per cent of all the reported crime. Effectively preventing crime against these people and places should ultimately have an impact on overall crime levels. (National Board for Crime Prevention 1994: 2)

The quote above epitomizes what is considered to be current 'state of the art' policy thinking on crime prevention. The targeting of 'repeat victimization' as a suitable case for treatment has proceeded apace in the UK and elsewhere as the struggle to combat rising crime rates has become more acute. Of course other factors have also played a part in this process; targeting repeat victims can constitute an argument in support of more efficient resource allocation in policing, for example. However, such a focus of policy concern arguably constitutes a logical outcome of what Karmen (1990) has identified as the movement from crime prevention to victimization prevention which has occurred over the last decade or more in criminal justice policy as those policy processes have searched for solutions to the 'crime' problem. There are a number of issues, however, which have been (and still are) deeply embedded in these policy processes; namely, what kind of criminal victimization is being targeted, what kind of understanding of risk is presumed in that targeting, and what kind of assumptions underpin the criminological and victimological discourses which have permitted such a focus of concern to emerge in such an unproblematic fashion. In order to examine some of these issues particular attention will be paid to the way in which the gender blindness associated with each of the disciplines of criminology and victimology has led to an implicit acceptance of particular ways of thinking about the concept of risk and the way in which that concept has been related to criminal victimization. The main purpose of this paper, then, is to problematize the criminological use of the concept of

* Reader in Criminology, Department of Criminology, University of Keele.
    The author is grateful to Wendy Hollway and Tony Jefferson for comments on an earlier draft of this paper. The faults which remain are entirely her own. An earlier version of this paper was presented at the American Society for Criminology Conference, Miami, November 1994.

SANDRA WALKLATE

risk. It will be argued that a continued acceptance of a gender-blind way of thinking about risk not only impoverishes criminological and victimological understandings of criminal victimization but further perpetuates the gender blindness already inherent in both those disciplines.

Criminological Conceptions of Risk

Some time ago, Short (1984: 713) made the following observations about the links between criminology and modern risk analysis:

The technical aspects of crime management and the management of risks to human health and life have much in common. In the latter, levels of risk are determined, often without firm knowledge of results which might follow from policies based on them, or of causal processes ... Distinctions between causation and control, and between determination of risks and judgements of safety, are neither straightforward nor simple. The results of neglect of such distinctions are similar for risk analysis and for criminology. Separation of causal theory and research from social policy in both areas condemns the latter to the treatment of symptoms.

These observations capture some, though not all, of the essentially problematic assumptions embedded in the criminological (and victimological) use of the concept of risk and its application. As the quote with which this paper began illustrates, risk assessments in criminology have certainly become preoccupied with the symptoms of crime (the nature and extent of criminal victimization and the kind of crime prevention strategies which can be built upon that knowledge) rather than the causes of criminal victimization per se. Moreover such risk assessments have been focused on particular kinds of crime, for example, household burglary and street crime. Much less attention has been paid, within criminology, to risk assessments of fraud or corporate crime. More importantly, arguably, one of the dangers which emanates from downgrading the search for causes in preference for upgrading the targeting of the criminally victimized is that they also become the locus through which criminal behaviour, in and of itself, is explained. Such generalized 'victim blaming' may enhance the policy agenda in new and ever more imaginative ways, but leaves criminology (and victimology) treating the symptoms but never finding the cure, as Short so aptly states.

Arguably, the drive to address crime prevention in this way emanates from criminology's (and victimology's) well-documented and central commitment to a modernist project. Such a project embeds criminological theory with criminological practice and policy (see for example on criminology, Garland 1985; Smart 1990; and on victimology, Mawby and Walklate 1994). This project sees the role of the (social) scientist as finding answers to social problems in order better to control the social world, and is connected with broader social processes which displace knowledge based on belief with knowledge emanating from scientific practice. It is through these wider interconnections that criminology, and later victimology, became entwined in a particular version of what counts as scientific knowledge. This statement requires further explication.

The key characteristics of criminology and victimology have been itemized in different ways by different writers. Taylor *et al.* (1973) for example, identify the quantification of behaviour, an understanding of the determinant nature of human behaviour and a belief in the unity of the scientific method as constituting criminology's essential characteristics. Roshier (1989) suggests the following determining characteristics for criminology: determinism, differentiation, and pathology. Similar characterizations of victimology have been proffered by Miers (1989) and Walklate (1994). A common thread in these characterizations is the implicit and/or explicit highlighting of the influence of a particular conception of what counts as scientific knowledge: a conception of science which can not only be identified as positivist but also as masculinist.

The influence of positivism within criminology and victimology can be traced in a number of different ways. It can be identified as positivist in the Comtean sense, that is as constituting a search for ways of gathering universally applicable knowledge in order to assert a positive influence (and thereby control) on the processes of modernization. It can also be identified as positivist in a philosophical sense as espousing a particular set of methodological concerns which centre the pursuit of '... regularities, successions of phenomena which can be systematically represented in the universal laws of scientific theory' (Keat and Urry 1975: 3), objectively gathered. This conception of science has also been identified as masculinist (Harding 1991). That is to say, not only has it been an activity which has been dominated by men and in which men have set the agenda so identifying what is and is not worthy of investigation, but also it is an activity which is deeply rooted in ways of thinking about the relationship between reason and nature which privileges a masculine world-view. Seidler (1994: 6) expresses these links in this way:

Science was to be an objective activity that worked with impartial laws. As men in their rationality were to remain unmoved by emotions and feelings, so were the sciences that were created in their image.

Thus the processes emanating from the Enlightenment were not only about challenging the existing social order through a commitment to reason, they were also about privileging the maleness of that reason. In this way male knowledge became deeply embedded in the knowledge gathering process called science; a process also deeply embedded in the development of modern societies. As a consequence these ideas also became linked to the central concerns of criminology and later victimology. These deep rooted assumptions are evidenced and articulated in a number of different ways, one of which is found in criminology's conceptualization of risk and the manner in which that conceptualization has been related to criminal victimization—the central focus of this paper. So what constitutes a criminological conceptualization of risk?

Criminological Assumptions on Risk and Risk Analysis

There has been an implicit acceptance of the idea of risk as a forensic concept within criminology. In other words, there has been an acceptance that in the possibility of understanding risk and risk analysis lies risk management: that is, the management and control of outcomes. The control of outcomes: the calculation of probabilities which determine the likely consequences of particular courses of action is what Douglas (1992) argues is expected, culturally, from the scientific enterprise. This scientific enterprise is also implicitly connected with the desire to control the environment and simultaneously valorize masculine knowledge (Harding 1991, and see above). It is assumptions such as these from which criminology has drawn the parameters of its debate on the relationship between risk and criminal victimization. What this comprises needs to be spelt out a little more clearly.

SANDRA WALKLATE

In a different context Dake (1992) has argued that 'perceived probabilities of harm are not merely subjective but may best be viewed as inter-subjective—a matter of shared cognition'. If this is the case, as Dake (1992: 33) argues:

Such world views provide powerful cultural lenses, magnifying one danger, obscuring another threat, selecting others for minimal attention or even disregard. (p. 33)

If Dake's view is correct, by analogy it is possible to argue that it is cultural processes which underpin the risks and dangers we see as opposed to the ones we do not see (a tension cogently argued by Adams 1995). Here it is held that these cultural processes control those risks that we see and that lie at the root of science, technology and policy in general, including criminology. Of course, as both Beck (1992) and Wildavsky (1988) have intimated, the threats posed by what we see as risks and what we fail to see as risks are in themselves culturally constructed, though Beck's (1992) position might be somewhat more diffuse than this. In one sense the particularities of this debate concerning the role of science and technology in general are not directly relevant here. However recognition of this cultural imperative provides one insight into how the understanding of risk has become equated with identifying technical rather than human strategies of risk avoidance within criminology.

It was argued earlier that the social construction of science, of challenging authority on the basis of reason rather than emotion, privileged a masculine world-view. The desire to control nature through science and consequently through the increasingly technical management of risk, articulates one link between science, risk analysis and masculinity. Understanding this link requires an acceptance of the view that the disciplines of criminology and victimology share a particular form: a malestream view of what counts as science. The search is on for a situation of zero risk, of risk avoidance: the ultimate control by man of his environment.

Acceptance of this view reveals in a telling way the extent to which both criminology and victimology have absorbed a conceptualization of risk which foregrounds risk avoidance and backgrounds risk seeking. As Douglas (1992) has stated:

In spite of evidence to the contrary, avoiding loss is written into the psychology textbooks as the normal, rational, human motive. But all this means is that the commercial, risk-averse culture has locally vanquished the risk-seeking culture, and writes off the latter as pathological or abnormal. To ignore such a large segment of the human psychology tells us more about assumptions upholding the modern industrial way of life than about human nature's risk-taking propensities.

In one sense, it could be argued that this emphasis on risk avoidance through the knowledge of risk management reflects a version of (masculine) knowledge which prefers to assert control via reasonable and rational argument rather than by brute force. In other words, this version of knowledge values reason, and as risk avoidance is presumed to be reasonable, risk-seeking behaviour is downgraded, obscured, hidden from the debate although not from social reality or experience. These values concur with those which support a conventional view of science and what counts as scientific knowledge.

To summarize: criminology's implicit acceptance of a conventional scientific agenda and its associated masculinist stance has resulted in that discipline's failure to work more critically with the concept of risk. This failure, it will be argued, has impover-

38

ished criminology's understanding of the experience of criminal victimization by tying that issue, and by implication any associated explanation of criminal behaviour, to a presumption of risk avoidance. This has resulted in a masculinist interpretation of what counts as risky behaviour, thus endorsing some behaviours for men as acceptably risky and some behaviours for women as unacceptably risky.

This view, then, suggests that men and women will experience quite different messages about their relationship to and experience of criminal victimization. Understanding these differences requires exploring possible alternative gendered conceptualizations of risk; but first how might an alternative view of risk be constructed?

Risk: Exploring Some Alternatives

Sparks (1992) rails against criminology's simplified use of the terms fear, risk and danger. He points out that these terms, in their everyday usage, connote far more complex and subtle an understanding of day to day experiences, than any survey technique is capable of detecting. Moreover, Sparks goes on to suggest that it is important not to presume the significance that feelings of risk and danger have for people and in what context. He states that:

Crime presents people with certain dangers of which they must take account as best they may. In taking account of these dangers each of us engages in some version of risk analysis. But the resources available to us in making the necessary judgements are both enormously extensive, varied, complex and inherently incomplete. (1992: 132)

Sparks's analysis, then, fundamentally challenges criminology's presumption that there is a straightforward connection between fear and risk, mediated by rationality and/or irrationality, as articulated in the 'fear of crime' debate, for example. Such a challenge follows logically from the position espoused by Douglas (1992) quoted above; but it needs to be taken further. As Douglas observes, and as some of the work cited earlier illustrates, it is misleading to address the concept of risk as though it only refers to risk *avoidance*. Douglas's (and others') work raises the question: what do we do about risk *seeking* behaviour and its relationship with fear and danger?

Understanding the phenomenon of 'risk seeking' behaviour equips us with a view of human beings which, as Douglas has pointed out, appears to be less tenable in the modern world. Risk avoidance as a key social and psychological strategy appears to have become an increasingly predominant cultural view as the technological world has advanced. Yet despite the control of the environment and the consequent reduction of risk which is presumed to accompany improved technology, it is clear that we accept routinely and implicitly that being human is about *taking* risks. Moreover we accept that it is a culturally embedded requirement for (young) men to seek out pleasure and excitement, i.e. positively to take risks.

It is, of course, not a prerequisite that such (young) men should also be criminal. The phenomenon of (young) policemen engaged in a high-speed car chase of other (young) men is coupled to a shared desire for excitement, pleasure, fear and risk. The behaviour may be the same and the individual motivations may be different, but the legitimacy attached to the behaviour is obviously different. However the deeply held cultural expectations that it is acceptable for young men to engage in this kind of

SANDRA WALKLATE

behaviour (and not young women) are rarely explored. And for criminal victimization, risk appears to have been equated only with with risk avoidance.

Here as elsewhere, criminology (and victimology) ignores gender.While the general
reluctance of the discipline to engage critically with gender is lessening, there remains
an inability to address the pervasive effects of masculinity: not only in terms of understanding and explaining crime but also reflexively; that is in understanding the nature
and structure of these disciplinary areas in and of themselves. In the context of the 'fear
of crime' debate, for example, this reluctance has not only impacted upon the way in
which much criminological work hides men's fears (and their thrills) but the way in
which this also simultaneously consigns women to possessing 'legitimate fears'.

These deeply embedded assumptions within criminology and victimology have,
therefore, resulted in a failure to explore risk as a gendered concept as well as a gendered experience. The question remains: how might that be rectified? The answer to
this question can be formulated in a number of different ways. In the general context of
offering an understanding of the processes of criminal victimization, one way is to
rethink the relationship between men, 'fear' and risk; and women, 'fear' and risk. It is
to such a formulation that we shall now turn.

Men, 'fear' and risk

Conventional criminal victimization survey work, emanating from the Home Office
and elsewhere, clearly identifies young men as being at a greater risk from street crime
than any other category of people. Moreover, Crawford *et al.* (1990) and Stanko
(1990) have both pointed to men's greater unwillingness to admit to or talk about their
fears relating to criminal victimization in general. As Stanko and Hobdell state:

Criminology's failure to explore men's experience of violence is often attributed to men's
reluctance to report 'weakness'. This silence is, we are led to believe, a product of men's hes-
itation to disclose vulnerability. (Stanko and Hobdell 1993: 400)

Indeed, on the face of the evidence frequently discussed in the fear of crime debate, it
could be argued that it is (young) men who behave irrationally given their greater
exposure to risk from crime and their reported lower levels of fear of crime. But this
view accepts unquestioningly the notion that men, by virtue of being male, do not
experience fear.

How men experience, understand and then articulate their relationship with risk,
'fear' and danger is relatively under-explored in the context of criminology and victimology. However, in a more general context Lyng (1990: 872–3) suggests that:

Males are more likely to have an illusory sense of control over fateful endeavours because of
the socialization pressures on males to develop a skill orientation towards their environment.
Insofar as males are encouraged to use their skills to affect the outcome of all situations, even
those that are almost entirely chance determined, they are likely to develop a distorted sense
of their ability to control fateful circumstances.

This process leads Lyng to conclude that this is the reason why more males are
involved in 'edgework', which he defines as behaviour on the edge: between order and
chaos; living and dying; consciousness and unconsciousness.

40

RISK AND CRIMINAL VICTIMIZATION

Lyng's observations stem from ethnographic work carried out with a group of sky-divers. However, what Lyng has identified there, perhaps, is something much more deeply rooted. His insight also taps readily available ideological and cultural images which deem males and females capable of different things. These images emphasize a positive relationship between men and such risk taking behaviours, and a negative one for women.

On the other hand, the interviews with men who were victims of different kinds of violence, reported in Stanko and Hobdell's (1993) work, provide a somewhat different emphasis. The men in this study clearly proffered a range of responses to violence, not a single preoccupation with danger in the form of personal violence.

It is important to note that the responses of these men—Lyng's skydivers and Stanko and Hobdell's victims of violence—need to be understood as being not only a part of, but also fundamentally connected with, a more general understanding of masculinity. This is a masculinity which values excitement, adventure, power and control as what men do. This is a masculinity to which all men relate to a greater or lesser degree: an aspect of what Connell (1987) has called 'hegemonic masculinity'. So while it is possible that Lyng's skydivers might have been *asserting* control over the uncontrollable in a very positive and ego-enhancing way, Stanko and Hobdell's work might be viewed as being much more about how men *lost* control in an ego-damaging way. The question of the motivation for, and experience of, each of these different types of behaviour and responses to it is, of course, a highly individual one. The central concern here, however, is to draw attention to the way in which each of these responses captures what is culturally expected of a man, and how the variable responses to those cultural expectations may be rendered silent in the discourses which claim to be speaking about them.

One implication of this argument is, then, that it is necessary to locate men's relationship to fear and anxiety within a broader cultural context of the values associated with masculinity. Campbell (1993) offers one way of analysing these interconnections in her concern to understand the mechanisms underpinning the civil disturbances which occurred in several areas in England in 1991. One of the features of this was the predominant involvement of young men. She states:

In the 1990s young men were schooled in unprecedented displays of personal and public force ... Going to war was what nations did to each other—they recruited their young men to kill and they rounded up women to be raped ... The lads' problem was not that they were starved of male role models, it was that they were saturated with them. That was the problem with no name that set the estates on fire in 1991. (Campbell 1993: 323)

A cultural context which promotes certain expressions of masculinity in preference to others can provide a framework in which to understand both the inhibition and the expression of fear and of risk-taking behaviour in (young) men. That cultural context might not, however, provide the complete picture. It is important to recognize that thrill and excitement frequently go alongside risk, fear and danger; and that all of these are frequently talked about in male terms. This 'talking' frequently not only silences women's experiences but also silences the experiences of some men.

The recognition of the interconnections between these threads of masculinity—risk, fear, danger, excitement—raises further questions about some of the processes which underpin current conceptualizations of criminal victimization. First, given that it has

SANDRA WALKLATE

been argued that these interconnections are mediated by what has been identified as masculinity; the question has already been raised whether or not this is a set of genderized cultural norms and values which can only be experienced by men. Putting this question another way, what are the implications of this discussion for understanding the relationship between women, 'fear' and risk? Moreover, how does this discussion better our understanding of the way in which the concepts of fear, risk and danger have been articulated within criminology in particular and modern western societies in general? But first, what about women, 'fear' and risk?

Women, 'fear' and risk

Let us take as our starting point that women's 'fear' of crime needs to be connected to their experience and knowledge of what might happen to them. We can take this to mean it is important to recognize the radical feminist position which asserts the centrality of not only understanding women's expressed 'fear' of crime as measured by victimization surveys, but also the nature and extent of 'domestic' violence including 'wife' rape, 'date' rape, and murder which is not measured by such surveys. This view emphasizes the idea that women are exposed to much greater levels of risk of criminal victimization from some kinds of crime than are men. If to this we add women's experiences of what Crawford *et al.* (1990) call 'public' abuse, i.e. sexual harassment on the street and in the workplace, the main offenders under all circumstances are men. The radical feminist position seems more than justified.

In the light of the kind of evidence mentioned above, it would be difficult to mount a convincing argument that women's 'fear' of crime is not connected to their public and private experience of men (Warr 1985; Stanko 1985). This does not mean that all women are always afraid, or that women are always or only afraid of men that they know. The point is that for women threats of sexual danger permeate their public as well as their private lives.

One way to theorize this is to locate women's experiences of criminal victimization in the context of what Brittain (1989) has called 'masculinism'; that is, in the ideological beliefs which naturalize the differences between men and women. Understanding these ideological beliefs means that it is necessary to understand the experiences of both men and women by reference to deeply held social expectations. These expectations legitimate the differences between men and women as if they were inevitably natural differences. One of the areas in which such differences are naturalized pertains to both male and female responses to risk and danger. This view asserts that such differences are ideological rather biological. In other words, it would postulate that there are no innate biological reasons for men's reluctance to articulate their fears, and women's greater willingness to do so.

Locating women's 'fear' of crime within such ideological imperatives raises at least two related questions. Both require us to consider the tensions between the unifying effects of a notion of masculinism, and the potential difference and diversity of subjectively constructed experience. More specifically these questions pose a challenge to the radical feminist presumption that women fear all men because 'all men are potential rapists'. The first question to be asked is: do women fear all men? Secondly, if they do not fear all men, do women work with knowledge which renders some situations, some men, some places as being more uncertain than others, and how do they do this?

42

RISK AND CRIMINAL VICTIMIZATION

This latter question not only problematizes 'fear', it also renders problematic any all embracing usage of the term 'woman'. What does this imply for our view of the relationship between 'fear', risk and danger for women?

First: do women 'fear' all men? Intuitively the answer to this question must be 'no'. Women have access to their own experiences and knowledge, some of which will be shared (probably with other women) and some of which will be unique to them. This knowledge will be partial and incomplete, and is likely to reflect a range of different experiences with different men they have known. While women may not 'fear' all men, their sense of security will be informed by the sex of the person(s) they are with at any one point in time, the place they are in, their structural location, and so on. Thus while all women may not fear all men, some have considerable knowledge about men that they know, places they deem dangerous, and the potential for sexual danger from men that they know, and men they do not know. Some might also be afraid of some women as evidenced by work on bullying in schools. However, this does not necessarily mean that there is a symmetrical relationship between 'women's' fears of 'men', and their fears of other women (Dobash and Dobash 1992).

In pursuing this it might be useful to use a framework which puts to the fore an understanding of masculinity/ies. For example, women have a good deal of knowledge about men and men's expression of their masculinity/ies. Asking women as well as men about their understanding and experience of masculinity/ies might facilitate the development of a framework which de-centres a masculine-defined, risk-avoiding agenda, in favour of identifying the greater subtlety and diversity of experiences which are possessed by (both men and) women in their relationship with each other and in their relationship with risk and 'fear' in a risk-seeking agenda. Arguably, this is the point at which a gendered understanding really replaces one focused on sex differentials.

This view, however, begs a further question: whether or not women only experience their day-to-day lives in relation to the perceived threat of sexual danger, or whether they too, rather like the young men exemplified earlier engage in 'risk-seeking' behaviour? In other words, how and under what circumstances do women seek pleasure, excitement, thrills; take risks, make choices?

A major area of excitement and danger seeking for women is around sex (usually with men) (Hollway 1984). The way in which those excitements might be expressed are highly circumscribed (Holland *et al.* 1994) given the powerful influence of 'passive femininity', the norms of heterosexual behaviour, and the ways in which (young) women's sexuality is policed. This is nevertheless the arena in which the 'Russian roulette' of sexuality and pregnancy is certainly played. It is not the only arena in which women might seek thrills and excitement, of course, it is used here merely to illustrate that women unquestionably seek pleasure, excitement, thrills and risks. How and under what circumstances this occurs, however, has been explored relatively infrequently, and when it has it has often been pathologized. Women are after all the 'Other'; typically defined as being outside the discourse of risk and risk seeking, but not as I have shown here outside the risk and risk-seeking experience.

One danger introduced by asking such a question is the interpretation that if women seek risky situations, then they 'ask for' what happens to them. This is a very powerful rhetorical device which certainly takes its toll on women in all kinds of situations and especially in their relationships with men. In raising this issue, I do not intend to imply

43

SANDRA WALKLATE

that women 'ask for it'. But unless the male conceptualization of risk is challenged, women will be forever deemed as 'asking for it'!

Conclusion

This paper has tried to argue that not only is 'fear' a gendered phenomenon (not a new observation), but that the concepts of 'risk' and 'danger' are also gendered (a relatively new observation). This does not downgrade the importance of women's likely chances of being murdered, of being raped in marriage, or of finding themselves in a violent relationship. Indeed, the intention has been the opposite. By drawing attention to these new issues we can see that the common feature is not only women's 'fear' and the threat to women's personal security, but the sense in which all of these processes are permeated by versions of masculinity expressed by the men in their lives. Blindness to this not only takes its toll on individual men, but also on the way in which the criminological use of the concept of risk is defined.

While here has been an increase in the concern with criminal victimization as evidenced by the kinds of issues politicians and policy makers now attend to, however inappropriately (Stanko 1990), the debate in the policy field frequently marginalizes the 'reality' of women's relationship to 'fear' and risk and also renders invisible aspects of the relationship between 'fear', risk and danger experienced by men. Challenging the hitherto simplistic conceptualization also has implications for repeat or multiple victimization. These implications raise both specific and general questions. For example, how can policy initiatives be put in place which do not presume that risk avoidance equates with risk management? How can we develop a theoretical framework for criminology which captures a structurally and reflexively informed conceptualization of risk, which might erase the victim-blaming connotations currently embedded in the context of multiple victimization? But perhaps most fundamentally, given the argument presented here, can we or should we be concerned with risk managment at all?

As this paper has argued, part of the answer to these questions may lie in a reconceptualization of the concept of risk. This is a task which has hardly begun within criminology or victimology but from which both might gain. There has been no real explication of risk as a gendered concept subjectively experienced, and subjectively and reflexively understood in either of these disciplinary areas. It is time to consider the value of pursuing such an analysis further in the interests of both 'victims' and 'offenders'.

REFERENCES

ADAMS, J. (1995), *Risk*. London: UCL Press.
BECK, U. (1992), *The Risk Society*. London: Sage.
BRITTAIN, A. (1989), *Masculinity and Power*. Oxford: Blackwell.
CAIN, M. (1989), 'Feminists Transgress Criminology' in M. Cain, ed., *Growing Up Good*. London: Sage.
CAMPBELL, B. (1993), *Goliath: Britain's Dangerous Places*. London: Virago.
CONNELL, R. W. (1987), *Gender and Power*. Oxford: Polity.

RISK AND CRIMINAL VICTIMIZATION

CRAWFORD, A., JONES, T., WOODHOUSE, T., and YOUNG, J. (1990), *The Second Islington Crime Survey*. Middlesex University: Centre for Criminology.

DAKE, K. (1992), 'Myths of Nature: Culture and the Social Construction of Risk', *Journal of Social Issues*, 48/4.

DOBASH, R.P., and DOBASH, R.E. (1992), *Women, Violence, and Social Change*. London: Routledge.

DOUGLAS, M. (1992), *Risk and Blame: Essays in Cultural Theory*. London: Routledge.

GARLAND, D. (1985), *Punishment and Welfare*. Aldershot: Gower.

HARDING, S. (1991), *Whose Science? Whose Knowledge?* Buckingham: Open University Press.

HOLLAND, J., RAMAZANOGLU, C., SHARPE, S., and THOMSON, R. (1994), Power and Desire: The Embodiment of Female Sexuality. *Feminist Review*, 46, Spring.

HOLLWAY, W. (1984), 'Gender Difference and the Production of Subjectivity', in J. Henriques, W. Hollway, C. Urwin, C. Venn and V. Walkerdine, *Changing the Subject: Psychology, Social Regulation and Subjectivity*. London: Methuen.

KARMEN, A. (1990), *Crime Victims: An Introduction to Victimology*. Pacific Grove, CA: Brooks Cole.

KEAT, R., and URRY, J. (1975), *Social Theory as Science*. London: Routledge.

LYNG, S. (1990), 'Edgework: A Social Psychology of Voluntary Risk Taking', *American Journal of Sociology*, 95/4.

MAWBY, R., and WALKLATE, S. (1994), *Critical Victimology: The Victim in International Perspective*. London: Sage.

MIERS, D. (1989), 'Positivist Victimology: A Critique', in *Victimology: An International Review*, 1/1.

NATIONAL BOARD FOR CRIME PREVENTION (1994), *Wise After the Event: Tackling Repeat Victimization*, 2, May.

ROSHIER, B. (1989), *Controlling Crime*. Milton Keynes. Open University Press.

SEIDLER, V. (1994), *Unreasonable Men: Masculinity and Social Theory*. London: Routledge.

SHORT, J. (1984), 'The Social Fabric at Risk: Toward the Social Transformation of Risk Analysis', *American Sociological Review*, 49, December.

SMART, C. (1990), 'Feminist Approaches to Criminology; or Postmodern Woman Meets Atavistic Man', in L. Gelsthorpe and A. Morris, eds., *Feminist Perspectives in Criminology*, 70–84. Milton Keynes: Open University Press.

SPARKS, R. (1992), 'Reason and Unreason in 'Left Realism': Some Problems in the Constitution of the Fear of Crime', in R. Matthews and J. Young, eds., *Issues in Realist Criminology*. London: Sage.

STANKO, E. (1985), *Intimate Intrusions; Women's Experience of Male Violence*. London: Routledge.

—— (1990), *Everyday Violence*. London: Virago.

STANKO, E., and HOBDELL, K. (1993), 'Assault on Men: Masculinity and Male Victimization', *British Journal of Criminology*, 33/3: 400–15.

TAYLOR, I., WALTON, P., and YOUNG, J. (1973), *The New Criminology*. London: Routledge.

WALKLATE, S. (1994), Can There Be a Progressive Victimology? *Victimology: An International Review*, 3/1 and 2.

WARR, M. (1985), 'Fear of Rape Among Urban Women', *Social Problems*, 32/3.

WILDAVSKY, A. (1988), *Searching for Safety*. Oxford: Transition.

45

[21]

Who Gets Probation
and Parole: Case Study
Versus Actuarial Decision Making

Daniel Glaser

Probation and parole decisions have traditionally been based upon case studies, governed by informal norms prescribing base rates, and made with overconfidence in their wisdom. Actuarial tables that statistically identify the best predictors of past violations, then convert information from them into a prediction score, have repeatedly been shown to classify offenders into future risk categories more accurately than do case study prognoses. Although such tables have been available since the 1920s, they were only widely adopted by parole boards during the 1970s with the development of decision guidelines that also take offense severity into account and that prescribe for any current case not a specific penalty but a choice within the range of punishments previously imposed for cases similar in actuarial risk and in offense severity. Application of actuarial prediction to sentencing decisions by use of guidelines analogous to those for parole has been attempted, but in practice thus far has had little impact due to the custom of determining sentences by pretrial plea bargaining.

Traditionally, the granting or denial of probation or parole to an offender has been based upon the decision maker's subjective impressions from studying case records and reports, and perhaps from direct observations and interviews with the person whose fate must be decided. Unfortunately, the officials who grant or deny liberty seldom receive systematic feedback on the wisdom of their judgments, so they tend to drift in their practices and to be governed by informal norms of which they are unaware, rather than guide policies according to evidence on the effectiveness and consistency of their actions. Why this drift in routine decision policies occurs in many respected professions as well as in everyday life will be indicated, as well as how its correction by actuarial tables was shown to be feasible decades ago, but only began to be achieved in probation and parole recently.

DANIEL GLASER: Professor of Sociology at the University of Southern California and Past-President of the American Society of Criminology.

CRIME & DELINQUENCY, Vol. 31 No. 3, July 1985 367-378
© 1985 Sage Publications, Inc.

368   **CRIME & DELINQUENCY / JULY 1985**

PRESCRIPTIVE BASE RATES

A valuable lesson might be gained by judges and parole board members from the outcome of an experiment conducted by the New York City Board of Health in the 1930s, when it was more customary than it is now to remove a child's tonsils if they were inflamed. The Board had 1000 sixth-grade students examined by physicians, who found that 611 of the children already had their tonsils removed, and recommended tonsillectomies for 174 (45%) of the remainder. The 215 with tonsils for whom no action had been recommended were then sent for assessment to a second group of physicians, who did not know that these students had already been examined, and they recommended tonsillectomies for 99 (46%). This left 116 children now twice-diagnosed as not needing this operation who were sent to a third set of physicians without disclosing the previous medical judgments, and these doctors recommended tonsillectomies for 51 (44%; American Child Health Care Association, 1934).

These physicians thought that the conservative decision was to recommend a tonsillectomy because it was presumed to prevent more serious ailments, but because it involved some risk and cost, they recommended it only for the worst cases that they saw, apparently unaware that these tended to be about 45% of any group of children sent to them. The logical policy for physicians who know of no benefits from retaining tonsils but only of risks in not removing those that are infected, and who also know that infection is probable for everyone, would be to operate readily. They probably were unaware that a norm had developed for them to operate on the worst approximately 45% of the cases that they saw in any brief period. This base rate probably changed only slowly until evidence persuasively questioning the effectiveness of tonsillectomies was promulgated; before then, if New York physicians were to change their diagnostic practices suddenly it would have had a conspicuous effect on the economy of local hospitals.

An inertia or only slow drift in decision practices also occurs because, as Nobel laureate Herbert Simon (1965: 108) pointed out in economics, we tend to make decisions that satisfy—that relieve us of immediate concern—rather than making an extensive attempt to determine what decisions would optimize our benefits. As he pointed out, "The limits of rationality . . . derive from the inability of the human mind to bring upon a single decision all the aspects of value, knowledge and behavior that would be relevant. The pattern of human choice is often more nearly a stimulus-response pattern than a choice among alternatives."

Like the physicians, judges and parole board members generally get feedback about the consequences of their decisions only from bad news; in the criminal justice situation it is when someone commits a serious crime while still on probation or parole. Therefore, these officials also tend to prefer a conservative reaction, which is to deny liberty. The logical policy for them if they only learn of the bad results from releasing serious offenders—rarely of the successes—would be to impose maximum penalties in most cases. However, norms exist in each courthouse and for each parole board on the traditional proportions usually granted a supervised release there; if the proportion released abruptly deviates much from these norms, there are soon either unusually crowded or exceptionally empty institutions. Also, parole board members are usually informed, at least annually, whether the number of persons whose parole is revoked has changed as a percentage of the number who were granted parole. This is their usual method of assessing their violation rate because it is more quickly procurable than rates based on follow up of the cohort of prisoners paroled in a past year. From this imperfect feedback, without officials usually being aware of it in their separate decisions, traditional base rates evolve locally as to the proportions of eligible cases for whom probation or parole is granted.

Another major factor in the persistence of unofficial base rates for case decisions in many fields is the tendency of humans to become overconfident about the wisdom of their past judgments. Psychologist Leon Festinger (1964: 4-5) explains: "The greater the conflict before the decision, the greater the dissonance afterward. Hence . . . the tendency to justify that decision (reduce the dissonance) afterward. The dissonance can be justified by increasing the attractiveness of the chosen alternative and decreasing the attractiveness of the rejected alternative, and one would expect a post-decision cognitive process of occur that accomplishes this spreading apart of the attractiveness of the alternatives." He cites experiments in which subjects asked to make choices in hypothetical problem situations rated the alternatives as more similar in merit before they made their decisions than when they were asked to recall the problem some months later and again rate the alternatives. Further evidence of this tendency to reduce cognitive dissonance over past decisions is the report that persons planning to buy an automobile tend to read advertisements for all makes that they are considering before they make their purchase, but afterward read advertisements only for the car that they bought.

A further impediment in efforts to increase the rationality of probation and parole decisions is the fact that officials have multiple considerations in reaching release decisions. The risk of the offender committing new crimes if released is only one of their chief concerns, and is often secondary to the question of whether the severity of the punishment imposed is proportional to the seriousness of the crimes for which the offender has been convicted. Social scientists studied the risk assessment problem repeatedly, beginning decades ago, but only when they developed statistical tables that addressed the risk and punishment considerations simultaneously did they have a clear influence on many release decisions.

METHODS OF
RISK ASSESSMENT

Over 60 years ago Sam B. Warner (1923), comparing the prerelease files of 300 Massachusetts Reformatory parole violators with those of 300 who had been successful on parole, concluded that of 67 categories of information available on each inmate before release, the only one that markedly differentiated the two outcome groups was their classification by the board's "alienist." This official was a psychiatrist, or sometimes another type of physician, whose designation of a prisoner as an "accidental offender" predicted success, but whose labels "recidivist" or "feeble-minded" forecast failure. Hornell Hart (1923), however, calculated that 15 of Warner's categories differentiated successes from failures to an extent that had less than one chance in a hundred of occurring by chance. He estimated that if a prediction score derived from several such factors was assigned to each prisoner, and parole decisions were based on this score, the Massachusetts Reformatory's parole violation rate could be cut in half.

Ernest W. Burgess in 1928 compared Illinois parole successes and failures on every type of prerelease information he could find routinely in their files, and constructed a table that scored each prisoner one point

for each of 21 attributes—for example, no prior offenses, or married—
that were statistically associated with below average violation rates. Of
those who scored 16 to 21 by this system, only 1.5% violated parole, but
of those with scores lower than 5, 76% violated.

The Burgess research soon resulted in the establishment of the
Sociologist-Actuary position in each major Illinois prison to conduct
research that would update and improve on what were called his
"prediction tables" or, perhaps more accurately, "experience tables."
These appointees, however, were mainly occupied with interviewing
prisoners eligible for parole consideration each month and studying
their case files in order to give the state's parole board a prediction based
on these tables for every prisoner being considered for parole (described
in Ohlin, 1951).

Similar research to develop prediction tables for probationers and
parolees soon followed in several other states, and in other nations
(Schuessler, 1954; Simon, 1971). Sheldon and Eleanor Glueck (1946:
68-69), in their numerous longitudinal studies of released offenders
whom they and their staffs interviewed in the community, developed
tables that predicted not just recidivism but rates of total adjustment to
conventional behavior standards, and they urged that such tables be
used by judges in sentencing decisions as well as by parole boards.

The Illinois tables were shown to predict parole outcome more
accurately than the prognoses of psychiatrists, sociologists, and others
who made case study summaries and recommendations for the state's
parole board (Glaser, 1962). Mannheim and Wilkins (1955) showed that
their experience tables on parole outcome for inmates of British Borstal
institutions more accurately predicted recidivism than did the case study
prognoses of either the heads of these institutions or the staff in charge
of the unit to which the inmate was assigned. As far as I have been able to
determine, all other published comparisons of case study versus
statistical prediction of probation or parole outcomes also found the
case study method to be the least accurate. Most recent are a study done
with Pennsylvania parolees (Carroll et al., 1982), and a Canadian study
that not only found that an actuarial table based on objective data from
the record files predicted parole outcome better than did the subjective
parole prognoses of clinical staff, but that tables devised to integrate the
clinical case judgments with the actuarial table components did not
significantly improve on the predictive accuracy of the actuarial table
taken alone (Wormith and Goldstone, 1984). All of these findings were

also consistent with long-established findings in almost all tests of clinical (case study) versus statistical prediction in psychology and education (Meehl, 1954; Sawyer, 1966), and with the findings of insurance companies that it is more profitable to rely on estimates from actuarial analyses of past experience than on case judgments alone in assessing risks of all types.

Despite this overwhelming evidence from almost all rigorous tests, and despite decades of exhortations by many prominent researchers that sentencing and parole judgments should be guided by actuarial tables, the Illinois parole board was until the 1970s the only criminal justice agency that routinely procured a statistical risk estimate on almost every case for which it made a release decision. Even in that state, however, the actuary's report only supplemented case study prognoses that the board procured from prison classification staff and others, and it was never evident that the statistical risk figure was the dominant influence in most parole decisions.

In justifying their not procuring actuarial risk predictions to guide their decisions, judges and parole board members offered many arguments. I suspect that the most influential one was simply that they are not just interested in the risk of parole or probation violation, but in determining that the punishment imposed is appropriate for the offense. Parole boards routinely "retry" each case at the beginning of their deliberations, considering not just the crime for which the prisoner was convicted, but the file's entire description of the alleged offenses, including those that were reduced to lesser charges in the course of plea bargaining. Perhaps their most successfully achieved function has been to offset disparities in judicial sentencing. A California study found the following: its parole board members focused primarily on the seriousness of the most recent offense in making their decisions; the prison case workers gave greater attention to recidivism-related variables than did the board in making their reports and recommendations on parole; only the case worker assessments were statistically related to the subsequent violation rates of parolees; and much more accurate predictions could be made by an actuarial "base expectancy" table (Holland et al., 1978; the "base expectancy," as the term was used in California correctional research, is a statistical estimation of parole outcome derived from analysis of past experience, but using information only available at an inmate's admission to prison, hence not considering behavior in prison or other postadmission events).

Parole board members and judges have often criticized the actuarial tables for disregarding what these officials regard as unique evidence of good or bad character, or of postrelease intentions, in many offenders. The evidence that they cite usually consists of particular remarks or gestures by the subject or by others who testify or submit reports on the case, communications that officials believe indicate the character or the postrelease plans of the subject that have great prognostic significance, but for which no statistics can be procured because these are not objectively classifiable attributes of individuals. Officials also contend that in those cases for which they have no special information, their prognoses would not differ greatly from the actuarial risk estimations, but such officials cannot rigorously demonstrate the validity of such claims because they do not record their prognoses and check their accuracy later by the behavior of releasees. Until the past decade—and in some states still today—these officials have seemed unaware of the research evidence that statistical experience tables predict parole outcome more accurately than case study assessments by any type of presumed expert who prognosticates on offenders before their release. Perhaps their resistance has mainly reflected the fact that researchers are outsiders who seem to ignore the concerns of judges and parole board members with pleasing those on whom their job security and advancement depends—the public and its politicians. Most of this resistance vanished, however, when researchers finally began to collaborate with judges and parole board members to develop new types of statistical tables.

PAROLE AND SENTENCING GUIDELINES

Early in the 1970s, researchers Don Gottfredson and Leslie T. Wilkins worked with the United States Board of Parole to develop tables that would not only reflect the best possible actuarial predictions of parole outcome for different offenders, but would also indicate the Board's past practices in deciding on appropriate penalties for different offenses. This interest was inspired both by growing public criticisms of the apparent arbitrariness of parole decisions and by the burgeoning movement to make just deserts the primary basis for determining criminal penalties. It was especially accelerated, however, by a court ruling that the Board should articulate its policies, *Childs v. United States Board of Parole,* 371 F. Supp. 1246 (D.D.C. 1973), *modified,* 511 F.2d 1270 (D.C., Cir. 1974).

The United States Parole Guidelines are statistical tables that have four columns headed "Parole Prognosis," with the separate columns designated "Very Good (9-11)," "Good (6-8)," "Fair (4-5)," and "Poor (0-3)." These numbers in parentheses indicate the range in "Salient Factor Score" that determines into which of these four categories a prisoner's parole prognosis falls. The scores come from actuarial research originally directed by Gottsfredson and Wilkins, but since that time updated by the Board's research staff, and shown to make highly dependable predictions (Hoffman and Stone-Meierhoefer, 1979). In these scores, up to 3 points are assigned for absence of prior criminal convictions or delinquency adjudications, up to 2 points for absence of prior institutional confinements, up to 2 points for being of mature age at the behavior that led to the first institutional confinement, and 1 point each for absence of prior violations of probation or parole, no record of opiate dependence, verified full-time school or work record for six months in the last two years of freedom, and the offense in the current commitment not being auto or check theft or check forgery.

Multivariate statistical research that began with a much larger number of different kinds of information for classifying offenders demonstrated that the items used for the Salient Factor Score and the points assigned to them yielded the most reliable and useful risk classifications. In a 2-year follow up, 92% of those in the "Very Good" (9-11 point) category had favorable outcomes on parole, as did 78% of those with "Good," 66% of those with "Fair," and 56% of those with "Poor" prognoses by the scores for these categories indicated above (Hoffman and Adelberg, 1980). A long-term follow up of an earlier actuarial prediction table for federal prisoners showed that the risk categories into which it ranked inmates forecast their relative reconfinement rates well two, five, ten, and fifteen years after their release (Kitchener et al., 1977).

The Federal Parole Guidelines table supplements its four columns for actuarial prognosis categories by seven rows that classify the cases in each column into seven categories of severity of offense. Each federal crime is placed in one of these severity categories on the basis of the harshness of the average penalty imposed for it in past years; the categories range from "Low," which include tax evasions and property offenses of less than $2,000, to "Greatest II," which includes aircraft hijacking, kidnapping for ransom, and treason. Thus any federal prisoner can be classified into one square of the Guideline table by the column into which his Salient Factor Score prognosis places him, and by the row for the severity classification of the most serious crime for which he has been convicted (these tables were only developed for males, who make up about 95% of federal prisoners). Each square of the table gives the range of confinement that the Board imposed in the past for most prisoners with that particular combination of prognosis and severity. Thus for prisoners with an offense of Low Severity but with a score indicating a Poor Prognosis, the range is 12 to 16 months, but for prisoners with offenses of High Severity (for example, passing or possessing $20,000 to $100,000 in counterfeit currency) and with a Fair Prognosis the range is 26 to 34 months.

With four columns for actuarial prognosis and seven rows for offense severity, the Guidelines provided the federal parole board with 28 different recommended ranges of confinement, but for each separate prisoner considered for parole it only prescribed that range that was used by the Board in most of its past actions in cases with the same combination of prognosis and offense severity. The Board could still impose any legal term of confinement on a prisoner, but if the term were shorter or longer than the range in the Guidelines, the Board members were expected to record their reasons for making an exception in that particular case. In meetings every six months, the Board reviewed compilations by its research staff of the average term that it had imposed for cases in each of the 28 categories of the Guidelines, the number of deviations from the Guidelines' ranges, and the reasons recorded for these deviations. This information permitted the Board to decide when it wished to alter the recommended range of penalties in the Guidelines for a particular category, and thus to change from its past policies.

Decision guidelines, generally based on the federal model, were adopted during the 1970s by a majority of state parole boards (Bohnstedt and Geiser, 1979), and have remained in use by almost every board that adopted them. They bring actuarial predictions to bear on case decisions, but in almost all states they do this only while also

376   **CRIME & DELINQUENCY / JULY 1985**

considering just deserts for the severity of the offense. They make parole decisions more consistent with prior practice, and more rational with respect to the goals of risk reduction and achieving just deserts. Currently, however, the federal parole board is being abolished, and several states have also eliminated their boards or reduced the range of parole discretion.

Soon after they created the parole guidelines, Gottfredson and Wilkins, with Jack Kress and others, undertook with the aid of a federal grant the development of sentencing guidelines for the courts of Denver and Philadelphia, with some pilot studies also for courts in other jurisdictions. These guidelines were modeled on those established for parole decisions in having recidivism prognosis and offense severity as their two dimensions, and in indicating not a specific sentence but the range of sentences most often imposed by the court in the preceding years for each combination of prognosis and severity categories. In each court, however, they developed several guidelines, one for misdemeanors and one for each of several broad classes of felonies under state laws. For categories with favorable offender prognosis scores and the less severe offenses, the designation in the table was "Out," which meant that a penalty other than confinement had usually been imposed, such as probation, fines, restitution, or some combination of these.

Although each set of sentencing guidelines was developed with close consultation between the researchers and the local judges (described in Kress, 1980), a follow-up of experience with them in Denver and Philadelphia revealed that they were largely ignored by the judges (Rich et al., 1982). The main reason seems to have been that sentencing in these courts is usually determined in pretrial bargaining between the prosecution and defense counsel, with the judge approving almost all agreed penalties for which a plea of guilty is offered. Judges often failed to record their reasons for imposing sentences outside the recommended range in the guidelines, or gave only very brief and glib explanations for their deviations from customary penalties.

It appears that guidelines are unlikely to produce major reductions in the disparity of sentencing in American courts as long as plea bargaining is the principal method of guilt determination. However, it is conceivable that guidelines could be promulgated as official limits to the sentences for which plea bargains will be accepted by the judges unless exceptionally persuasive reasons are given for penalties outside the guideline ranges. Meanwhile, guidelines appear likely to bring actuarial predictions into parole decisions in most states where parole still exists.

REFERENCES

American Child Health Association
   1934   Physical Defects: The Pathway to Correction. New York: The Association.
Bakwin, H.
   1945   "Pseudosocial pediatrica." New England J. of Medicine 232: 691-697.
Bohnstedt, M. and S. Geiser
   1979   Classification Instruments for Criminal Justice Decisions. Washington, DC: Department of Justice, National Institute of Corrections.
Burgess, E. W.
   1928   "Factors determining success or failure on parole," Part IV of A. A. Bruce et al., The Workings of the Indeterminate Sentence Law and the Parole System in Illinois. Springfield, IL: The Board of Parole.
Carroll, J. S., R. L. Wiener, D. Coates, J. Galegher, and J. L. Alibrio.
   1982   "Evaluation, diagnosis, and prediction in parole decision making." Law & Society Rev. 17, 1: 199-228.
Festinger, L.
   1964   Conflict, Decision and Dissonance. Stanford, CA: Stanford Univ. Press.
Glaser, D.
   1962   "Prediction tables as accounting devices for judges and parole boards." Crime and Delinquency 8 (July): 239-258.
Glueck, S., and E. T. Glueck
   1946   After-Conduct of Discharged Offenders. New York: Macmillan.
Hart, H.
   1923   "Predicting parole success." J. of Criminal Law and Criminology 14 (November): 403-412.
Hoffman, P. B. and S. Adelberg
   1980   "The salient factor score: nontechnical overview." Federal Probation 44 (March): 44-52.
Hoffman, P. B. and B. Stone-Meierhoefer
   1979   "Post-release arrest experiences of federal prisoners: a six-year follow-up." J. of Criminal Justice 7 (Fall): 193-216.
Holland, T. R., N. Holt, and D. L. Brewer
   1978   "Social roles and information utilization in parole decision making." J. of Social Psychology 106 (October): 111-120.
Kitchener, H., A. K. Schmidt, and D. Glaser
   1977   "How persistent is post-prison success?" Federal Probation 41 (March): 9-15.
Kress, J. M.
   1980   Prescription for Justice. Cambridge, MA: Ballinger.
Mannheim, H. and L. T. Wilkins
   1955   Prediction Methods in Relation to Borstal Training. London: Her Majesty's Stationery Store.

Meehl, P. E.
    1954   Clinical versus Statistical Prediction. Minneapolis: University of Minnesota
            Press.
Ohlin, L. E.
    1951   Selection for Parole. New York: Russell Sage Foundation.
Rich, W. D., L. P. Sutton, T. R. Clear, and M. J. Saks
    1982   Sentencing by Mathematics. Williamsburg, VA: National Center for State
            Courts, Publication No. R-071.
Sawyer, J.
    1966   "Measurement and prediction: clinical and statistical." Psychological
            Bulletin 66 (September): 178-200.
Scheff, T. J.
    1966   Being Mentally Ill. Chicago: Aldine.
Schuessler, K. F.
    1954   "Parole prediction: its history and status." J. of Criminal Law and Criminology
            45 (November): 425-431.
Simon, F. H.
    1971   Prediction Methods in Criminology. London: Her Majesty's Stationery Store.
Simon, H. A.
    1965   The Shape of Automation for Men and Management. New York: Harper &
            Row.
Warner, S. B.
    1923   "Factors determining parole from the Massachusetts reformatory." J. of
            Criminal Law and Criminology 14 (August): 172-207.
Wormith, J. S. and C. S. Goldstone
    1984   "The clinical and statistical prediction of recidivism." Criminal Justice and
            Behavior 11 (March): 3-34.

[22]

The Journal of Drug Issues 21(4), 713-737, 1991

SOCIAL CONSTRUCTIONS OF BLEACH IN COMBATING AIDS AMONG INJECTION DRUG USERS

Robert S. Broadhead

Following decades of corporate strategy promoting common household bleach as essential for peoples' health and happiness, a use for bleach was finally discovered in 1986 that actually achieved life-saving proportions for a certain population: injection drug users in preventing the spread of AIDS. Since then, substantial promotional efforts have surfaced — corporate, governmental, and community-based — to downplay or obstruct the public definition of bleach as a major AIDS prevention weapon. An analysis is offered of four competing social constructions of bleach that have emerged since 1986: bleach as a public health breakthrough; bleach as a liability; bleach as an endorsement for drug abuse; and bleach as a social policy copout.

There have been substantial efforts over several decades in the United States to construct a public belief that a 5.25% solution of sodium hypochlorite — common household bleach — plays an essential part in peoples' private and family lives; indeed, that it is crucial for their health and happiness. Such promotional efforts have been primarily corporate in nature, especially by Clorox, a name that has become synonymous with bleach itself in consumers' minds.

For example, since the 1950s, Clorox has promoted bleach in family and women's magazines by ascribing virtues to the product that go far beyond its

Robert S. Broadhead, Ph.D., is an associate professor in the Department of Sociology, University of Connecticut, Storrs, CT 06269. His professional interests include the Sociology of Deviance, Health Sociology and Qualitative Research Methods. He is presently writing a book entitled "The Significance of the Gesture: AIDS Outreach Among Injection Drug Users." For reprints of this article, please write to the above address. This research was funded by a grant from the National Institute on Drug Abuse (R01 DA05517).[1]

BROADHEAD

use as a disinfectant in kitchens and bathrooms. Examination of claims and photographic images in advertisements reveals that Clorox not only cleans and whitens: It makes little girls dance with their bright skirts billowing; prompts husbands to kiss their wives in appreciation for a sparkling appearance and wonderful marriage; "brightens the home and the whole family too!" and gives babies "99% less to cry about."

However, in 1986, following decades of corporate strategy promoting bleach as essential not only for clean clothes and floors, but for peoples' health and happiness, a group of researchers in San Francisco discovered a use for bleach that actually achieved life-saving proportions for a certain population. Bleach became "the product of choice" to recommend to thousands of injection drug users (IDUs) for disinfecting their needles to stop the spread of HIV. Ironically, since then, substantial promotional efforts have surfaced — corporate, governmental, and community-based — to downplay or obstruct the public definition of bleach as a major AIDS prevention weapon. These efforts have met with relative success. For example, in dozens of American cities, outreach workers have been distributing hundreds of one ounce bottles of bleach per week on the street directly into the hands of IDUs. Yet, in many other cities, very little or no bleach distribution has been permitted. Various groups have been working to stop distribution and educational efforts to teach users how to protect their health while shooting up.

Opposition to common household bleach in combating AIDS issues from several competing ways in which the product and its distribution have come to be defined. Bleach is no longer the innocuous household disinfectant that can whiten laundry and "get out dirt that suds leave in." Since 1986, in many quarters, the possession of bleach in small amounts indicates drug addiction, and its distribution is seen as promoting drug abuse.

The analysis below examines four competing social constructions of common household bleach that have emerged since 1986: bleach as a public health breakthrough; bleach as a liability; bleach as an endorsement for drug abuse; and bleach as a social policy copout.

This analysis is part of a three-year, ethnographic study that began in June 1988 of a model outreach project in the San Francisco Bay area. The findings are based on a year and a half of participant observation with outreach workers. During this time the author and two full-time research assistants were trained as outreach workers and actively served as members of different teams. The author joined a three-member outreach team deployed in a large Latino community that worked primarily with street IDUs and prostitutes. Kathryn J. Fox worked in two communities: with a three-member team involved with homeless and runaway youth who engage in various drug and sex trade activities; and with a six-member team deployed in the city's largest adult sex trade, homeless, and drug-using zone. Gayle N. Williams accompanied a four-member outreach team that worked city-wide with the female sexual partners of IDUs.

SOCIAL CONSTRUCTION OF BLEACH

In addition to our experience as outreach workers, combined with months of observing others conducting outreach, this analysis is based on formal interviews with twenty-four of the thirty-three outreach workers employed by the project between 1988 and January 1990. All of the principal researchers (about ten) who conceptualized, implemented and directed the outreach project at various times since 1986 were also interviewed, along with other important AIDS prevention professionals, (e.g., the director of Public Health in San Francisco, and officials of the National Institute on Drug Abuse [NIDA] in Washington D.C.). *As an ethnography, the analysis is based upon and uses the points of view of the outreach project staff as an analytic baseline for examining the different constructions of bleach that have emerged nationwide since 1986.*

Bleach as a Public Health Breakthrough

In the early 1980s, drug researchers in San Francisco became increasingly concerned by reports from New York City and northern New Jersey about the spread of AIDS among IDUs. In 1985, a combined epidemiological/ethnographic study by Watters and associates (1986) of approximately 300 addicts in treatment, and 100 out of treatment, found an HIV seroprevalence rate of 9% and 16% respectively. While this was substantially less than the 50% + rate found in the New York area, the findings were nevertheless sobering. The ethnographic observations found that needle sharing among IDUs was ubiquitous, alleged to be due to state laws prohibiting the sale of hypodermic syringes over the counter, which in turn creates a large underground market for "points" at inflated prices (Newmeyer et al. 1989). The researchers were convinced that, unless some kind of innovative actions were taken quickly, an explosion would occur in the spread of HIV among the estimated 15,000 IDUs in San Francisco. Many of these users, mostly heterosexual men, would then pass the virus on to their sexual partners, who in turn would perinatally infect their newborns. The scenario was grim. As Newmeyer (1988: 152) wrote,

> The opportunity in early 1986 to avert a disaster could be lost
> in as little as 6 months or a year. The experiences of other cities
> — Edinburgh and New York in particular — suggest that an
> HIV contagion, once well established in an IVDU population,
> can explode to a 50 per cent level in a year or two.

Funded largely by demonstration grants from the National Institute on Drug Abuse (NIDA) in 1985, the researchers, in cooperation with the San Francisco Department of Public Health, plunged into what everyone involved described as a collaborative, brainstorming period designing an innovative intervention. The consensus early on was that drug treatment programs could not serve as a vehicle for implementing a fast strike intervention because the majority of IDUs

BROADHEAD

were not in treatment. In addition, users were not likely to enter treatment even
if slots became available (which they were not):

> Out-of-treatment IVDUs[2] expressed no great desire to enter
> treatment. Enrollment in a treatment program was generally
> viewed as a temporary respite from a career on the street
> (Newmeyer et al. 1989: 169).

In addition, between one-third to one-half of IDUs claimed stimulants as
their drug of choice, while "the treatment portfolio in San Francisco is heavily
dominated by programs that are specifically geared to the opiate addict"
(Watters et al. 1986: I-37).

The researchers discussed implementing a community-based,
needle-exchange program, but dropped the idea because, as Biernacki (1988a)·
noted, "We would have all gone to jail," given the aforementioned state law.
The idea of trying to change the law was also dropped. The researchers felt
strongly that they were in a race against time, and courting legislators would be
a consuming and protracted process, with uncertain hope of success.

The researchers concluded that the intervention would have to rely primarily
on educational materials like flyers, brochures, billboards, cartoon strips and
so on. Early on, the group planned to invest a considerable portion of their
limited demonstration funds in mass media messages, thinking that doing so
offered the best way to reach their targeted audience. But ethnographic
observations began to suggest otherwise, as Watters (1988) explained:

> The findings from the research were that these guys don't
> watch tv, they don't read newspapers, they don't get their
> information from posters. They get their information from
> one-to-one contact.[3]

Funds were therefore reallocated for deploying outreach workers to walk
the streets and teach methods of risk reduction directly to IDUs on their own
terms and turf. One important advantage in this approach was that outreach
workers could shape the intervention message on the spot, and, by taking into
account different clients' education levels, gender and sexual orientation, and
cultural backgrounds, their effort would be enhanced. This is something that
mass media messages cannot do, which is one reason they frequently miss their
intended audiences.

Still, even the direct approach was problematic. The outreach staff
discovered quickly that many IDUs would listen to their message, but then walk
away and discard the literature. Also, in early 1986, the prevention information
that outreach workers had to give to users was not particularly appealing or
helpful. It was not appealing because IDUs had heard enough of dire warnings

SOCIAL CONSTRUCTION OF BLEACH

such as "don't use drugs," "don't shoot up" and "don't share needles." Messages encouraging users to disinfect their needles by boiling them in water for fifteen minutes between use were not helpful. IDUs frequently pool their resources, cop together, and share syringes in places such as cars and back alleys that do not allow boiling water (Battjes and Pickens 1988).

The researchers began to wonder whether there was something that IDUs could easily incorporate into their injection routine no matter where they injected. The ethnographic data indicated that IDUs commonly rinsed their "works" with water if it is around to prevent blood from clogging the syringe. Perhaps there was a portable disinfectant they could recommend that users could carry with them. If so, they reasoned, it would have to meet specific criteria if users were going to use it. The disinfectant would have to be very inexpensive, easily obtainable, effective at killing the virus, fast acting, and generally safe to the user in the event of accidents or misuse (Newmeyer et al. 1989). Further research led to three options: isopropyl (rubbing) alcohol, hydrogen peroxide, and sodium hypochlorite (in a 5.25% dilution — common household bleach).

Hydrogen peroxide seemed to fit all of the criteria. But under inspection it forced an additional criterion that made it ineligible: the disinfectant had to be durable. Hydrogen peroxide has a short shelf-life. Rubbing alcohol seemed to meet all the criteria, but it too forced an additional criterion: the disinfectant should not be easily confused with other products. As Newmeyer and associates (1989: 172) explained:

> After much discussion, we eliminated alcohol and hydrogen peroxide. Although isopropyl alcohol is an effective disinfectant, we were concerned that issuing too many qualifiers would confuse the message: many IVDUs would take recommending alcohol to mean, "any alcohol is OK," which might result in the use of gin, whisky, or other alcoholic beverage...which would not be effective.

Thus, through a process of elimination, the researchers hit on what they came to consider as a breakthrough in AIDS prevention: common household bleach. It was cheap, convenient, effective, safe, fast-acting, long-lasting, and unmistakable. Coincidentally, an article by Resnick and colleagues (1986), reported that common household bleach, even diluted ten times, effectively destroyed HIV on contact.[4] To be safe, the outreach workers instructed users on the street to use full strength bleach to disinfect their needles, and to "flush twice with bleach, twice with water." The procedure took no more than fifteen seconds. But, problems still remained, as Biernacki (1988) described:

> They started distributing [the information] and it didn't take us a week to see that there was a real disjuncture between

BROADHEAD

> [IDUs] getting this information and having the wherewithal to
> go to the store and buy some bleach. This may seem simple to
> us, but if you're a drag queen, meth freak, prostitute, living in
> a single room in a hotel with two other people in the Tender-
> loin, it isn't the simplest thing to do...Our observations said,
> this isn't going to do it.

Again, as Biernacki (1988) described: "Our method [ethnography] kept us close to what is happening. As soon as we saw the problem, we changed our theory."[5] The researchers decided, if they wanted IDUs not only to accept their recommendation, but act on it immediately, the outreach workers would have to give out small bottles of bleach on the street, and instruct users how to use it.[6] Still, beginning a systematic program of giving users materials to make shooting illicit drugs "safer" in the community was bound to be controversial, and the researchers worried about the potential unknown liabilities that could threaten their efforts and professional careers.

For example, what if people shot up the bleach and injured themselves? The researchers found two cases in the medical literature: one was a woman who was accidently injected with a quantity of bleach while on dialysis; the other was a boy who tried to commit suicide by injecting bleach. Both patients recovered, apparently without complications (Froner et al. 1987). The researchers felt confident that bleach was safe, even if used improperly. Still, they worried IDUs might think that if bleach kills AIDS in the needle, it will kill AIDS in their body if injected. Thus, before starting a mass distribution, the researchers printed up a label for the bottles that included explicit instructions. Then they field tested the idea and found no problems of improper use.

But the potential legal and political repercussions were still difficult to envision. The researchers discussed whether they should seek some form of authorization or approval, perhaps from the mayor's office, or the Department of Public Health. Interestingly, interviews in 1988 — two years after the bleach distribution began — revealed that some of the researchers' recollections had become romanticized about the decision to distribute bleach. For example, one of the researchers asserted:

> We didn't ask anyone's permission. If we had asked permis-
> sion from any authorities, we might not be doing it to this day!
> When people elsewhere ask us about bleach, we say: "Do it!"
> If you ask permission, it'll be delayed. If you ask for it, they
> can deny it.[7]

Another researcher claimed that they decided to follow the immortal advice of movie idol Mae West: "It's better to beg for forgiveness than to ask for permission."

SOCIAL CONSTRUCTION OF BLEACH

However, officials with the city's Department of Public Health (DPH) tell a substantially less heroic story. The director of DPH, in particular, emphasized that the researchers had discussed the bleach distribution proposal with him and members of his department on several occasions, and that his department encouraged them to proceed. As Werdegar (1989) recounted his testimony before the city's Health Commission in 1986, concerning a grant that the researchers had applied for:

> I was quite grateful to [the group] because they had a way of approaching the I.V./AIDS problem in a way that we could do quickly, that we could do legally, and that made good sense...At some point along the way I was called upon to lend my support for their efforts before a health commission that had its skeptics, and a mayor who got very — you know the previous Mayor would get very skittish on anything that had to do with needles and drug users.

The director also noted that he contacted the chief of police, and ran interference for the researchers, who were anxious about whether the police would confiscate the small bleach bottles as drug paraphernalia, using them as evidence to search or arrest IDUs. The researchers also had a meeting with the chief of police and his commanders in the summer of 1986, and they received a memorandum of understanding from the police that bleach would not be confiscated. Essentially, the chief of police agreed to have his force treat bleach like they do condoms, as Werdegar (1989) explained:

> I remember calling the police chief and explaining to him that prostitutes got condoms from us at our city clinic, and why they shouldn't [confiscate them]. That actually we were protecting both the prostitutes and their customers just by encouraging them to have condoms. And he was most sympathetic, and eventually got it written into the standing orders to policemen not to confiscate condoms.

This was obviously important for the researchers because, as Newmeyer and Des Jarlais (1986: 4) put it:

> We regard the Bleach Bottle as the moral equivalent of the condom — that is, it provides Americans who still engage in unsafe needle use with a cheap, quick, handy means of avoiding infection, just as the condom provides similar protection for Americans who still engage in unsafe sex.

BROADHEAD

The moral significance of the "discovery" of bleach, and the decision to distribute it on the streets, took on even greater importance thereafter. By 1988-89, the researchers as a group generally felt that the "reach, bleach and teach" model was nothing less than a major public health breakthrough for several reasons.

First, data based on systematic blood sampling and in depth interviews of IDUs in San Francisco every year since 1986 found that the seroprevalence rate of HIV infection had held relatively constant — around 13% to 15% (Watters, Newmeyer and Cheng 1986a; Watters 1987; Watters et al. 1988; Watters 1989; Evans et al. 1990). Since the beginning of the bleach outreach program, drug injectors reported an increase in using a disinfectant to clean their needles from 13% use rate in 1986, to 80% in 1989. A substantial percentage of users also indicated that they had stopped sharing needles altogether. At the Sixth International Conference on AIDS in 1990, Watters and colleagues (1990:4) made a point of emphasizing: "Major behavior change [among IDUs] occurred immediately following the implementation of outreach and bleach distribution."

Second, the researchers believed they had achieved a major breakthrough because, to their knowledge, no other program in history like the outreach project had as suddenly and dramatically changed the behavior of IDUs — a population widely believed to be *the* most unreachable and uncooperative in society.

Finally, the researchers' sense of having achieved something heroic was reinforced by other researchers nationwide, and officials from NIDA, who praised them for having demonstrated a model project that cities elsewhere should emulate. One NIDA officer, Hartsock (1989), characterized the San Francisco research group as the "flagship" for the following reasons:

> They were the flagship early on — the way [they] worked together. They became a de facto research institute, the way they shared data and expertise with one another, and col-laborated. Damn right! They began the bleach thing, they combined the epidemiology with ethnographic methods, and began the [serological] testing. And they tied ethnography with outreach. Because they worked together like they did, they set the standard.

Most of the researchers involved gave similar testimony when interviewed. The "discovery" of bleach, and the decision to distribute it on the streets, was described as the product of a very creative, brainstorming *collaboration* that lasted about nine months. All of the researchers, except for one, were hesitant to claim any individual credit for themselves, to say who did what, or which idea belonged to whom.

SOCIAL CONSTRUCTION OF BLEACH

However, the researchers' very success, and the question of whether any one member actually deserved special credit for it, became a threat to the group itself. A rupture in the flagship occurred with the news that the Names Quilt Project, founded years earlier by Cleve Jones in San Francisco, was nominated for a Nobel prize.[8] In a small but telling gesture that utterly confirmed the group's belief in having achieved a breakthrough, one of the researchers began commenting that, if not the actual prize, it would be fitting if he at least received a similar Nobel nomination on behalf of the group. Shortly thereafter, the researcher began insisting that it was he who had assumed the responsibility for the "risky" decision to begin bleach distribution, rising above the apprehension and cowardice of the others, and that he also deserved the credit for conceptually linking the methodology of ethnography to the conduct of street-based outreach.[9] The researcher even confronted professionals with other agencies in the city and accused them of trying to steal the flagship model. Such arrogance, paranoia, and clamoring for credit, among other factors, importantly led to the breakup of the flagship in the summer of 1990. By then, however, bleach was being distributed throughout the city by "over 40 outreach workers from various agencies within San Francisco" (Watters et al. 1990: 1).

Bleach as a Liability
The social construction of bleach as a major AIDS prevention weapon for use by IDUs led others to see it as a liability. On one hand, companies that manufactured and promoted bleach, especially Clorox, had worked for years to establish a wholesome image of bleach in the public's mind about its usefulness and importance in peoples' lives. Now, with public health campaigns and mass media stories associating bleach with drug abuse and addicts, companies sought to minimize the potential liability such associations ostensibly posed — for soiling their good name and their product's wholesome reputation.

For example, in 1988, the San Francisco AIDS Foundation, picking up on the researchers' bleach innovation, created "Bleachman," a superhero who began appearing "live" on the streets periodically in targeted neighborhoods, handing out bleach bottles and encouraging IDUs to disinfect their needles. Early on, elements of Bleachman's image was borrowed from Clorox bottles and bleach ads, including his head — a large plastic bottle — and Clorox logo and insignia on his uniform (which indicates how much Clorox had become generic for bleach). Shortly after Bleachman's creation, the San Francisco AIDS Foundation was contacted by the Clorox corporation, as Bleachman (Pappas 1989) explained:

> [Clorox] felt that the way we represented the bleach bottle was
> an infringement on their copyrights, trade marks, and trade
> dress...They just told us that if we didn't stop, they would sue
> us. We did copy their stuff.

BROADHEAD

The researchers who "discovered" bleach also confronted Clorox's reluctance to promote bleach to reduce the spread of AIDS among IDUs. For example, Biernacki (1988) described contacting the corporation early on to inform them of the outreach project's plans to distribute bleach on the street, and to obtain further information about the product: "We just wanted a letter saying, generally, that bleach is an effective disinfectant. I contacted the Clorox Foundation. They about flipped out!" Clorox has attempted to distance itself ever since from the "reach, bleach and teach" program. Other organizations have defined bleach as a liability following the discovery of bleach as an AIDS prevention weapon. Outreach workers report that they have been asked by managers of some businesses, cafes, bars and so on, not to distribute bleach on their premises because they do not want the public to think that IDUs patronize them or congregate on their premises. Outreach workers find their commitment to being nonjudgmental is put to the test when they work with community members who *are* judgmental toward drugs and users, and who *are* against *any* efforts that appear to make it safer for people to shoot-up in their community. Sometimes outreach workers must make adjustments in deference to the wishes of the larger community and curb their distribution of bleach and other AIDS prevention materials.

Other AIDS prevention projects, and/or their funding sources, have also determined that bleach is a liability, perhaps of unknown proportions. For example, some prevention organizations have prohibited their outreach workers from distributing bleach to users because of fears that a client will later sue them for contracting HIV, claiming that bleach was ineffective. Many feel that this fear is preposterous because a person with a history of shooting drugs will be hard-pressed to make a credible case that bleach was to blame for their infection. Nevertheless, the fear has stopped some prevention agencies from distributing bleach.

Some funding agencies have also attempted to minimize their liability by requiring applicants to avoid any mention of bleach, or bleach distribution, in their grant applications. For example, the California State Office of AIDS sent prospective grant applicants a list of answers to typical questions that organizations might ask in preparing their applications (Ford 1988: 3):

Q. When preparing a proposal do we need to avoid language about cleaning needles if the target group is IV
Drug Users?

A. We cannot advocate the use or distribution of bleach.
There are other products that you can use as a disinfectant...

SOCIAL CONSTRUCTION OF BLEACH

> Q. Why won't the Department approve of the distribution of
> bleach?
> A. California AIDS Leadership Committee endorses the
> concept of using a disinfectant to clean the works if
> they share needles, [but] not one specific product, [or]
> even a reference to a common name such as bleach.

Apparently the idea of requiring grant applicants to use the term
"disinfectant" rather than bleach was necessary to protect the state, and
agencies it funded, against lawsuits in the event that bleach, by some strange
turn of events, proved not to be a true disinfectant. For the state to require the
word "disinfectant" apparently meant that, ipso facto, it could not be held liable
by people who used a product that did not effectively disinfect.

Outreach workers have also found bleach to be somewhat of a liability to
them under certain, unusual circumstances. Workers attempt to teach users
how to engage in safer sex and needle use, instead of admonishing them to "just
say no" to sex or drugs. To demonstrate this, they distribute bleach for cleaning
needles, and condoms for protection while having sex. They hand out these
materials in order to communicate that they are nonjudgmental about others'
sexual practices and drug use, and that they are not trying to "reform" people.
They want clients to see them as on their side and looking out for their health
interests (Broadhead, Fox and Espada 1990). Outreach workers, in fact, think
of bleach as a "gift" which they give in order to develop a relationship with IDUs,
by virtue of which they can provide AIDS prevention counseling and education.

However, if not done sensitively, the mere act of handing out bleach to IDUs
can become a liability. For example, outreach workers must learn to identify
appropriate candidates on the street for prevention materials, which is difficult
given that IDUs do not conform to simple stereotypes. But offering a bottle of
bleach to a non-drug user can be taken as an insult, as Fox reported in her field
notes while working as an outreach worker:

> This guy got right in my face and said, "Why are you asking
> me that?...You think I'm a hype just because I'm black!" He
> suggested that I ought to be able to tell, and that my inability
> was due to racism. On the other hand, I can't just go on some
> stereotypical image of a dope fiend.

Outreach workers have found that bleach can be a liability if, in offering it,
the recipient feels that s/he is being identified as a drug addict. Thus, one
outreach worker, standing in a small community park full of users, noted:

BROADHEAD

> There was a policeman standing right in the middle, so I didn't
> think it would be right if I started handing out bleach. I just
> stood there and didn't know what to do.

In accompanying outreach workers on the streets, the authors observed that
people sometimes appear defensive and nervous in accepting the bleach.
"That's why," a veteran outreach worker explained, "I just hold it in my hand
and pass it to them - just like it was a drug deal." If outreach workers do not
observe such street etiquette, handing out bleach can become a liability for
them. Because most outreach workers are streetwise, it is extremely seldom that
any problems arise (see, however, Broadhead and Fox, in press). More often
than not, clients are extremely appreciative of outreach workers' efforts and
gifts.

Finally, there are small liabilities associated with bleach for IDUs
themselves. First, users have noted that bleach is corrosive, and flushing their
syringes with it hastens the deterioration of the rubber plunger and the "outfit"
itself. Obviously, given the scarcity of needles due to their illegality in many
states, bleach's side effect of shortening the life of syringes is a concern to users.
One reason why bleach was chosen as the ideal disinfectant was because of its
long shelf-life; one liability of using bleach for users' is that it shortens the life
of their equipment.

Secondly, while the police have agreed not to define bleach as drug
paraphernalia, or use it as evidence to obtain drug convictions, many users
report that officers sometime search them if they are found carrying bleach.
Possession of bleach can make IDUs more vulnerable to police suspicion, and
accepting bleach from outreach workers can be read by others as indicative of
persons' connection to drug scenes.

Finally, users commonly express gratitude in being given bleach, but
occasionally they also say they will be using it in their laundry. Bleach is both a
powerful disinfectant and a whitener, which makes it highly desirable for
cleaning clothes. However, as a weapon in AIDS prevention, the whitening
powers of bleach become a liability when the small bottles, which IDUs
conscientiously carry around with them, leak in their pockets. The bottle caps
occasionally break or come loose. IDUs generally are not known to have large
wardrobes or to be sharp dressers. When the bleach leaks in the pockets, and
down the crotch and legs, their clothes look even more unsightly. And the stains
are permanent. Because they are also highly visible, the stains become flags to
trained observers, like narcs or ethnographers, that someone is an IDU. This
makes bleach a liability of sorts to IDUs, albeit a small one, in light of their much
larger appreciation of outreach workers, and their knowledge of bleach as a
AIDS prevention weapon.

SOCIAL CONSTRUCTION OF BLEACH

Bleach as an Endorsement for Drug Abuse

In the beginning of their collaboration, the researchers were aware that their proposed efforts in teaching users how to disinfect their needles using bleach — and thereby shoot up more safely in the community — might be read as encouraging drug abuse. As acknowledged in an early grant proposal to the National Institute on Drug Abuse:

> The major problem we anticipate in implementing this project is the ethical concern we and others have about presenting materials to I.V. drug users which carry a tacit approval of continued drug use through injection... We realize that in recommending these measures that a contradiction exists since our national policy is one that discourages rather than encourages drug consumption (Biernacki and Feldman 1986: 51).

The researchers argued, however, that stopping the transmission of AIDS was more urgent than stopping drug use. In order to make the "reach, bleach and teach" program appear to be more consistent with the national anti-drug policy of "zero tolerance," the researchers devised a "bleach protocol" which they included in later grant applicants (Evans and Feldman 1987; Biernacki 1988b):

- Don't use drugs.

- If you use drugs, don't shoot them.

- If you shoot drugs, don't share needles.

- If you share needles, clean them with bleach between use.

In the grant proposals, outreach workers were described as trained to follow closely this step-wise format in interacting with IDUs, beginning always with a strong statement against drug use. Thus, on paper, the researchers' construction of the bleach program made it appear to be consistent with the dominant, anti-drug policy of "zero tolerance."

However, in working the streets, the outreach staff reverse the order of the bleach protocol in virtually all interactions. They do so in order to convey an impression of being nonjudgmental, and to cultivate trusting relationships with drug users. By far the most common and strongest encouragement outreach workers convey in their many exchanges with IDUs is to disinfect their "works" with bleach when they shoot up. Foremost in outreach workers' minds is the goal of stopping the spread of HIV. After that, they are interested in trying to help their clients in any way they realistically can. As Margolis (1990: 389) explained:

BROADHEAD

> They do what they can to intercede on behalf of their clients
> in their relations with the social service agencies that control
> and circumscribe their lives — housing, food stamps, detox
> programs, medical and legal systems, and so on. Outreach
> workers' clients have innumerable problems, drug abuse
> being only one of many and, perhaps, one that is not par-
> ticularly pressing.

Outreach workers emphasize that, in working with specific individuals, their objective is to help IDUs identify and work on specific problems that they have some chance of resolving.

As news spread about the success of the bleach program, and IDUs' impressive acceptance of bleach in their needle-sharing practices, the researchers began to hear a criticism directed at them — one they anticipated but most dreaded.

First, beginning in 1988 in various communities, AIDS prevention projects began experiencing implementation problems because public officials refused to authorize bleach programs, alleging that distributing bleach caters to drug abuse. For example, county officials in Los Angeles spurned the advice of their own health experts and refused to authorize county distribution of bleach and condoms to slow the spread of AIDS. In voting against the distribution of prevention materials, one board supervisor said, "We're creating an illusion of safe drug use to those individuals who have a drug habit. It's a myth, and it's only camouflaging the problem that we have."[10]

More ominous rumblings then surfaced in early 1989. The researchers received phone calls from NIDA indicating that officials at the U.S. Department of Justice were asking questions about federal monies being used to distribute bleach to IDUs. The researchers were asked to tabulate quickly what percentage of their overall budget was devoted to bleach. The amount proved to be insignificant, but that did not quell the controversy.

In April, legislation was introduced in the United States House of Representatives, and an identical bill in the Senate two months later, prohibiting the use of federal money for the "provision of sterile hypodermic needles or bleach to intravenous drug abusers."[11] The ensuing debate throughout the winter focused more on needle exchange programs than bleach, but both were alleged to encourage drug abuse. Senator Jesse Helms declared, "Let's get tough on drugs, not condone drug use."[12] Bleach itself was construed as encouraging drug abuse, as Senator Dan Coats explained in a backhanded reference: "The language in the amendment only prohibits distribution of bleach, not dissemination of information relative to bleach."[13] In general, both bleach and needle exchange programs were alleged to promote drug abuse and death, as Rep. Charles Rangel was quoted as saying: "Needle distribution puts public authorities in the business of death on the installment plan."[14]

SOCIAL CONSTRUCTION OF BLEACH

The social construction of bleach as an endorsement of drug abuse, and the threat of defunding AIDS prevention projects throughout the country, generated a significant public reaction. A *New York Times* editorial[15] came to the defense of bleach and asserted that Helms' amendment erroneously lumped the disinfectant in with needle exchange: "There is no basis for asserting, with Mr. Helms, that giving out bleach condones drug abuse in the same way giving out needles might." The *Times* called the proposed ban on bleach "murderous mischief."

Several senators also resurrected the definition of bleach as an effective weapon in AIDS prevention, rather than an endorsement of drug abuse. Senator Alan Cranston[16] read the *Times* editorial directly into the *Congressional Record*, quoting the published findings of one of the researchers in San Francisco who was a member of the flagship:

> Dr. John Watters, assistant professor at the School of Medicine, UCSF, reports that, among individuals who participated in the [bleach] program, demand for drug treatment increased from 40 to 60% over from 1986 to 1989... Dr. Watters reports that HIV infection among heterosexual IV drug users in San Francisco has remained stable since 1986 when the program was introduced. That's a remarkable finding.

Finally, Rep. Henry Waxman[17] defended bleach by reading testimony into the *Congressional Record* from Dr. Louis B. Sullivan, Secretary for the Department of Health and Human Services:

> Mr. Waxman: We have had critics introduce legislation which would prohibit not only needle exchange but bleach programs...Do you see a distinction between those efforts?

> Secretary Sullivan: Yes, Mr. Chairman. The distinction is that a bleach program does not put into the hand of an addict an instrument which would tend to support his drug habit, whereas a bleach program is one that really works...to really try and prevent the spread of AIDS.

Following this testimony, the language banning bleach was removed from the joint congressional appropriations bill and, for the time being, the construction of bleach as a weapon in AIDS prevention, rather than an endorsement of drug abuse, was sustained.[18] Indeed, as debates began in communities over the implementation of needle exchange programs, representatives of various community groups started asking the question, as one

BROADHEAD

did in a September 1989 health commission meeting in San Francisco: "Why do we need a needle exchange when we have a successful bleach distribution program?" In this way, different constructions of bleach are used as devices to fend off support of needle exchange programs. At the most, bleach is seen as a major AIDS prevention weapon; at the least, it is construed as the lesser of two evils.

Bleach as a Social Policy Copout

The San Francisco project celebrated bleach outreach because, as the researchers said, it was cheap, effective, and so on. In August 1990, about three years after NIDA began funding demonstration outreach programs in targeted cities throughout the United States, the Centers for Disease Control (CDC) held a press conference to announce the impressive success of the overall effort. The CDC spoke of "strong evidence of the considerable impact this approach can have," and, as *The New York Times* reported:[19]

> The Centers said a recent study in San Francisco... found that
> the start of community outreach program for IV drug abusers
> in 1986 corresponded with a community-wide increase in
> users' use of bleach to clean their drug equipment.

However, two months before the CDC announced the success of bleach outreach, the Black Leadership Commission on AIDS in New York announced that bleach distribution was hardly a success: It was an outrageous, social policy copout. As reported by the *New York Times*,[20] the Commission "criticized public health officials in the city for the bleach distribution, saying they were giving the poor a sop rather than real help"; and,

> Bleach distribution amounts to endorsing inexpensive ways to
> stop AIDS from spreading among users but failing to come up
> with the millions of dollars needed to help users get off drugs.

Bleach was also denounced as "just a quick fix" by a Harlem Hospital physician. (See Quimby and Friedman [1989] for an extended analysis of the African-American community's response to AIDS and IDUs.)

Having worked the streets for over four years, the outreach workers in San Francisco were used to hearing opinions and allegations about the dangers or foolishness of handing out bleach to IDUs. In their own local area, outreach workers had long heard what they regarded as outlandish and silly objections not only to bleach, but also to condoms and even educational brochures and flyers. For example, in 1986, the California State Office of AIDS would not allow agencies receiving state funds to distribute a pamphlet to IDUs and prostitutes that gave instructions on how to use condoms because its illustrations showed

SOCIAL CONSTRUCTION OF BLEACH

pubic hair and testicles. Similarly, the outreach workers were amazed to learn in 1989 that, because the L.A. Board of Supervisors had prohibited the distribution of bleach, outreach workers were distributing small, *empty* bleach bottles which IDUs could fill on their own. The outreach workers shook there heads in disbelief when they discovered that the city of San Francisco would not permit the distribution of condoms to inmates in jails because it was illegal for them to have sex while incarcerated. They literally howled when the city later reversed its policy and decided to distribute condoms to jail inmates, but, as reported by the *San Francisco Chronicle*[21]

> In a strange twist to stay within the law, any prisoner who says he is having sex will not receive a condom... Inmates will get one prophylactic at a time with counseling on the spread of AIDS and a stern reminder that sex in jail is illegal.

About that time, the outreach workers also learned that the Board of Supervisors in a neighboring county had banned the distribution of mint-flavored condoms by health workers "for fear they might promote oral sex."[22] Outreach workers emphasize that people generally dislike condoms, finding them unpleasant and morally incriminating when introduced into an intimate relationship. The outreach workers feel that anything that can be done to make condoms more appealing and fun to use — glow in the dark or taste great — should be eagerly supported by any intervention effort hoping to stop a deadly, sexually transmitted virus.

The outreach workers' perspective toward all prevention materials, but particularly bleach, was exactly the opposite of groups like the Black Leadership Commission on AIDS. In working with IDUs, outreach workers see giving out small bottles of bleach not as a cheap maneuver to deny users real help while appearing to save them. They emphasize strongly that they do not develop relationships with users in order to just give them bleach; they give them bleach in order to develop trusting, nonjudgmental relationships. The distinction is not merely a play on words. If the goal of outreach is the former, then outreach workers' interactions with clients, and their responsibilities toward them, will be minimal and tightly circumscribed. However, if the goal in distributing prevention materials is to cultivate relationships with users, then the work leads to a progressive expansion of responsibilities and efforts to help people.

In addition, outreach workers emphasize that there is a substantial amount of assistance they can provide clients, without necessarily requiring the expenditure of vast sums of money. First, they help clients to establish priorities and identify problems they can do something about. Second, outreach workers help others take advantage of existing resources, programs and opportunities that they may not know how to access, or even know are available (Margolis 1990). As one outreach worker said, "You begin with small steps, not giant ones.

BROADHEAD

And you make sure that the client meets you half way. That's important."
Another worker explained, "You realize that even a small change can be a big
success, so you work hard for it. Some people are so beaten down they don't
think they can do anything."

In helping clients, outreach workers become walking encyclopedias of
invaluable local knowledge. They collect insider information on programs and
services, special telephone numbers, who to speak to, what to say, how to jump
a queue or get restrictions waived — basically how to get things done. Outreach
workers would argue that such work is hardly a sop, and it does not require
throwing massive sums of money at complex problems.

The outreach workers' perspective is nearly identical to the recent findings
of the Special White House Study Group on Infant Mortality, another serious
national health problem. Two of the main findings in the report are reported in
the *New York Times*.[23]

> Government programs can reduce infant mortality, experts
> say...through home visits [i.e., outreach] by nurses, social
> workers and other counselors...Home visits could reduce in-
> fant mortality by insuring that pregnant women received
> prenatal care.

Such efforts do not require the expenditure of enormous sums of money.

> The fate of the project is puzzling because its recommenda-
> tions are relatively modest and seem well suited to an Ad-
> ministration that says it is eager to attack social problems but
> unable to finance big new programs. A central theme of the
> report is that the U.S. could substantially reduce infant deaths
> without redistributing income, eradicating poverty or spend-
> ing billions of dollars.

Conclusion

Clorox bleach now contains a label warning: "It is a violation of Federal law
to use this product in a manner inconsistent with its labeling." Clorox has taken
steps to ensure that its image and brand product do not become associated with
efforts to help IDUs shoot up more safely in the community. On the other hand,
although it appears that NIDA will no longer be funding outreach projects,
some city councils, like in Los Angeles, have been reversing themselves and
approving the distribution of bleach and condoms by outreach workers.[24]
However, where the funds will come from for the outreach effort is unknown.

In fact, the irony for outreach workers, not only in San Francisco but in other
major cities, is that, right on the heels of the White House Special Study Group
on infant mortality, and the CDC's announcement of the impressive success of

SOCIAL CONSTRUCTION OF BLEACH

outreach in combating the spread of HIV, outreach projects supported nationwide by NIDA are being defunded, scaled back or closed. Most programs were originally funded as demonstration research projects to run for three years, like the San Francisco project which began in 1987. As such, in early August 1990, the outreach workers in San Francisco were informed that half of their group of approximately twenty-two would be laid off in thirty days, and the remainder at year's end. As Rep. Ted Weiss (1990:1) said as chairperson of a recent congressional subcommittee:

> There is convincing evidence that strategies such as outreach programs to IV drug users and their sexual partners can prevent HIV transmission. One excellent program, conducted by NIDA...is ending, however, after serving the purpose of demonstrating effectiveness. There is an irony to that; it is effective and it must end...But because this program was designed as research, not service delivery, its time is up.

Rep. Weiss continued by emphasizing:

> No other agency has stepped forward to request funds for a replacement or to offer other forms of aid to those who will no longer be helped by NIDA's outreach program. So where does this leave us? Where should those persons at greatest risk turn for help? The futility of the Federal Government's efforts is maddening. No one wants to claim responsibility.

As outreach workers now find themselves laid off and looking for work, and innovative prevention projects closing their doors, outreach workers cannot help but wonder about what they see as the *real* social policy copout towards the AIDS epidemic — the defunding of an inexpensive, nationwide program that was successfully combating the spread of a deadly disease.

NOTES

1. I wish to thank the entire project staff who participated in the study: the outreach workers, researchers and the administrators. *All* of the interview subjects cited by name in the analysis read drafts of the paper, and I thank them for their reactions. I thank Kathryn J. Fox and Gayle N. Williams for their assistance in collecting the field and interview data, and Christine Zak-Lewis for transcribing the taped materials. Kathryn Fox also helped conceptualize much of the analysis. I also wish to thank the following for their thoughtful reactions to the paper: Michael Aldrich, Joyce Rivera-Beckman, Patricia Evans, Samuel Friedman, Jerry Mandel, Eric Margolis, Lawrence Ouellett,

BROADHEAD

Marsha Rosenbaum, Leonard Schatzman, Anselm Strauss, Dan Waldorf, Eddie Washington, John Wiley, and the anonymous reviewers.

2. Over the last few years, the term IVDU (intravenous drug user) has been largely replaced with IDU because of the common practice among needle users of "skin popping" or intramuscular injection. Such injection tends to occur after most of a user's veins have collapsed or become inaccessible.

3. Much of this may be true about IDUs while they are on the street, busy hustling, "takin' care of business" and "ripping and running" (Preble and Casey 1969; Agar 1978). However, substantial research indicates that most IDUs spend considerable time incarcerated. For example, Watters and colleagues (1990:2) reported that 64% of the 3,431 heterosexual drug injectors his team interviewed, in seven cross-sectional sampling waves beginning in 1986, had been incarcerated during the last five years. During their time locked up, inmates' main past-times are watching tv and reading. These periods, therefore, provided excellent opportunities for AIDS prevention counseling to occur using videos, comic books, and group presentations.

4. A mini-controversy continues over whether bleach actually kills HIV, or HIV-infected blood cells, and whether it can thoroughly disinfect all of the equipment that IDUs use (see AIDS Strategy for Addicts is faulted, *New York Times* 24 December 1989; Black group attacks using bleach to slow spread of AIDS *New York Times* 17 June 1990).

5. As Berg (1988), Margolis (1989) and Kotarba (1990) discussed, ethnographers have played a major role in the United States in designing and implementing outreach programs to work with IDUs in combating AIDS.

6. It was not until two years later that the researchers began considering that they also needed to distribute water along with bleach, since water too is scarce in many of the places in which people shoot up. In addition, other recommendations surfaced over time that needed to be conveyed: IDUs should be encouraged to use the bleach to cleanse their skin at the point of injection each time to prevent dermatological staph infections which frequently develop into large, open ulcers; IDUs should ensure that they flush the back of the syringes and the plunger with bleach, since traces of blood can collect there; they need to clean their "cookers" with bleach between use, and not share them or the cotton ball/cigarette filter used to strain a fix in drawing it into the syringe (see *New York Times* 24 December 1989).

7. There is some truth to this point. Two years after bleach distribution began in San Francisco, public health officials in Los Angeles were denied permission by the Board of Supervisors to distribute either bleach or condoms.

SOCIAL CONSTRUCTION OF BLEACH

8. AIDS Quilt in the running for peace prize. *San Francisco Chronicle*, 2 February 1989.

9. Other discoveries in AIDS research and prevention have been similarly marred by conflicts over scientific authorship, credit and allegations of profiteering at the expense of AIDS victims (see Culliton 1990; Rubinstein 1990; Shilts 1987).

10. L.A. condom giveaway rejected, *San Francisco Chronicle*, 31 August 1988.

11. Congressional Record April 25, 1989: HB28.

12. Helms, J., Senate Testimony. Congressional Record, 21 September: S11597.

13. Coats, D., Senate Testimony. Congressional Record, 16 November: S15791.

14. Helms, J., Senate Testimony. Congressional Record, 21 September: S11597.

15. Murderous mischief on AIDS, *New York Times*, 23 October 1989.

16. Cranston, A., Senate Testimony. Congressional Record, 16 November: S15792.

17. Waxman, H., House Testimony. Congressional Record, 17 November: H8887.

18. Substantial evidence has, and continues to, accumulate substantiating that *neither* bleach distribution or needle-exchange programs encourage drug use or increase rates. Indeed, the data from many different national sources indicates that such programs impact in reducing both rates of use, and the incidence of needle sharing and injection frequency, by users (see Francis 1991; Watters et al. 1990).

19. AIDS programs are successfully enlisted in drug addiction fight, *New York Times*, 10 August 1990.

20. Black group attacks using bleach to slow spread of AIDS, *New York Times*, 17 June 1990.

21. Condoms ok'd for prisoners in S.F. jail, *San Francisco Chronicle*, 19 July 1989.

22. Contra Costa rejects mint-flavored condom, *San Francisco Chronicle*, 5 August 1989.

BROADHEAD

23. The hard thing about cutting infant mortality is educating mothers, *New York Times*, 12 August 1990.

24. L.A. give addicts AIDS kits of condoms, bleach, *Los Angeles Times*, 4 April 1990.

REFERENCES

Agar, M.
1973   *Ripping and Running: A Formal Ethnography of Urban Heroin Addicts.*
          New York: Seminar Press.
Battjes, R.J. and R. Pickens
1988   Needle-Sharing Among Intravenous Drug Abusers: National and
          International Perspectives. National Institute on Drug Abuse,
          NIDA Research Monograph 80, Washington, D.C.: U.S.
          Government Printing Office.
Berg, E.
1988   Reach out and touch someone: A report on AIDS. *ASA Footnotes*
          16 (April): 4.
Biernacki, P.
1988a   Interview. Biernacki Research and Associates, San Francisco, July 22.
Biernacki, P.
1988b   AIDS community outreach demonstration research. Grant proposal
          to the National Institute on Drug Abuse, March 29.
Biernacki, P. and H.W. Feldman
1986   Methods to stop the spread of AIDS among IV drug users. Grant
          proposal to the National Institute on Drug Abuse, Washington,
          D.C., January 24.
Broadhead, R.S. and K.J. Fox
1990   Takin' it to the streets: AIDS outreach as ethnography. *Journal of
          Contemporary Ethnography* 19:322-348.
Broadhead, R.S.N. and K.J. Fox
in press Occupational health risks of harm reduction work: combating AIDS
          among injection drug users. In *Advances in Medical Sociology Vol.
          III: The Social and Behavioral Aspects of AIDS*, G.L. Albrecht and
          R. Zimmerman (eds.). Greenwich, Connecticut: UAI Press.
Broadhead, R.S., K.J. Fox and F. Espada
1990   AIDS outreach workers. *Society* 27:66-70.
Congressional Record
1989   "HR2097." April 25: HB28.
Culliton, B.J.
1990   Inside the Gallo probe. *Science* 248:1494-98.

SOCIAL CONSTRUCTION OF BLEACH

Evans, P.E. and H.W. Feldman
1987   AIDS community outreach project - San Francisco/Oakland. Grant proposal to the National Institute on Drug Abuse, April 1.
Evans, P.E., K.F. Hembry, B.P. Bowser, S.A. Gross and T. Dasher
1990   Epidemiology of HIV seropositive African-American injection drug users in San Francisco. Paper presentation, Sixth International Conference on AIDS, San Francisco, June.
Francis, D.P.
1991   The virus of the people: Whose side are we on? An evaluation of our prevention strategies. Fourth National AIDS Update Conference, San Francisco, May.
Ford, D.L.
1988   Letter to prospective grant applicants. California Department of Health Services. November 22.
Froner, G., G.W. Rutherford and M. Rokeach
1987   Injection of sodium hypochlorite by intravenous drug users. *Journal of the American Medical Association* 258:325.
Hartsock, P.
1989   Interview. National Institute on Drug Abuse, September 22.
Kotarba, J.A.
1990   Ethnography and AIDS *Journal of Contemporary Ethnography* 19:259-270.
Margolis, E.
1989   Using ethnography to combat AIDS: The theoretical underpinnings of San Francisco's NIDA demonstration project. Paper presented at the Western Social Science Association meeting, Albuquerque, New Mexico, April.
Margolis, E.
1990   Visual ethnography: tools for mapping the AIDS epidemic. *Journal of Contemporary Ethnography* 19:370-391.
Newmeyer, J.A.
1988   Why bleach? Development of a strategy to combat HIV contagion among San Francisco intravenous drug users. In *Needle Sharing Among Intravenous Drug Users: National and International Perspectives*, R.J. Battjes and R.W. Pickens (eds.) 151-159. NIDA Research Monograph 80. Washington, D.C.: U.S. Government Printing Office.
Newmeyer, J.A. and D. Des Jarlais
1986   Providing IV drug users in four cities with legal means to sterilize their "works." Concept paper, Haight Ashbury Free Medical Clinic, San Francisco.

BROADHEAD

Newmeyer, J.A., J.K. Watters, P. Biernacki and H.W. Feldman
1989   Preventing AIDS contagion among intravenous drug users. *Medical Anthropology* 10:167-175.
Pappas, L. (Bleachman)
1990   Interview. San Francisco AIDS Foundation, January 9.
Preble, E. and J.J. Casey
1969   Taking care of business - the heroin user's life on the street. *International Journal of Addictions* 4:1-24.
Quimby, E. and S. Friedman
1989   Dynamics of black mobilization against AIDS in New York City, *Social Problems* 4:403-15.
Resnick, L.K., K. Veren, S.Z. Salahuddin, P.D. Tondreau and P.D. Markham
1986   Stability and inactivation of HTLV-III/LAV under clinical and laboratory environments. *Journal of the American Medical Association* 255:1887-1891.
Rubinstein, E.
1990   The Untold story of HUT78. *Science* 248:1499-1507.
Shilts, R.
1987   *And The Band Played On: Politics, People and the AIDS Epidemic*. New York: St. Martin's.
Watters, J.K.
1987   Preventing human immunodeficiency virus contagion among intravenous drug users: the impact of street-based education on risk behavior. Paper presentation, Third International Conference on AIDS, Washington, D.C., June.
Watters, J.K.
1988   Interview. Urban Health Study, San Francisco, 4 August.
Watters, J.K.
1989   Instituting change by direct action: seroprevalence among IV drug users in San Francisco. Paper presentation, Fifth International AIDS Conference, Montreal, Canada, June.
Watters, J.K., J.A. Newmeyer, P. Biernacki and H.W. Feldman
1986   Street-based AIDS prevention for intravenous drug users in San Francisco: Prospects, options and obstacles. *Community Epidemiology Work Group Proceedings*. vol. II: 37-43. Rockville, Maryland: U.S. Department of Health and Human Services.
Watters, J.K., J.A. Newmeyer and Y. Cheng
1986   Human immunodeficiency virus infection and risk factors among intravenous drug users in San Francisco. Paper presentation, American Public Health Association, Las Vegas, October.
Watters, J.K., P. Case, K.H.C. Huang, Y. Cheng, J. Lorvick and J. Carlson
1988   HIV seroepidemiology and behavior change in intravenous drug users: Progress report on the effectiveness of street-based intervention.

SOCIAL CONSTRUCTION OF BLEACH

Fourth International Conference on AIDS, Stockholm, Sweden, June.

Watters, J.K., Y. Cheng, M. Segal, J. Lorvick, P. Case, F. Taylor and J.R. Carlson
1990   Epidemiology and prevention of HIV in heterosexual IV drug users in San Francisco, 1986–1989. Paper presentation, Sixth International Conference on AIDS, San Francisco. June.

Weiss, T.
1990   Strategies to Prevent Transmission of HIV Among Intravenous Drug Users. Opening statement before the Human Resources and Intergovernmental Relations Subcommittee of the Committee on Government Operations, 18 September.

Werdegar, D.
1989   Interview. San Francisco Department of Public Health, 25 September.

Drug and Alcohol Review (1993) 12, 369–375

Social change and the control of psychotropic drugs—risk management, harm reduction and 'postmodernity'

STEPHEN MUGFORD

Department of Sociology, Faculty of Arts, Australian National University, Canberra, Australia

Abstract

This paper argues that in order to understand the broad tide of change in drug control in recent times, we need to link these changes to a general understanding of social change. The paper sketches out how modern society arose and how it is giving way to the postmodern. Two themes are then developed. The first concerns the way that the state shrinks in postmodernity and links this to drug control, mentioning the example of random drug testing in the workplace as a good example of the change. It then moves to looking at the related shift in social control regimes from the 'corporal' regime of the premodern through the 'carceral' regime of the modern to population and risk management in the postmodern. It argues that in society in general there is a tension between carceral discipline and the amoral management of risk and that this is exhibited in drug control as a struggle between individual treatment and law enforcement on the one hand and 'harm reduction' on the other. This is illustrated by reference to a persistent tension within the NCADA enterprise. [Mugford S. Social change and the control of psychotropic drugs—risk management, harm reduction and 'postmodernity'. *Drug Alcohol Rev* 1993; 12: 369–375.]

Keywords: drug control; drug policy; harm minimization; law enforcement; postmodern.

How should we understand drug control?

Drug policy is not an autonomous sphere of debate and activity in which changes are initiated in ways unconnected to the broader historical context. Moreover, drug control is historically a recent phenomenon, a child of the modern world. Thus, it is vital to have some sense of what modernity consists of and how it is changing. Unless we can do that, our analyses of drug control will miss the 'big picture'. This paper sketches an understanding of drug control—the way in which governments seek to monitor and affect the pattern of drug use—in terms of large scale social, political and legal changes. The thesis is developed in a general way, and illustrated briefly by reference to specific examples—random drug testing and the National Campaign Against Drug Abuse (NCADA).

In exploring the issue, I do not purport to answer more than a few of the questions that might arise about drug control and drug policy. But this is a very brief paper and I have explored many related issues which are connected with the present theme in an array of other recent publications on drug policy,

Stephen Mugford, BSc. (Hons), PhD, Senior Lecturer, Department of Sociology, Faculty of Arts, Australian National University, Canberra, ACT 0200, Australia. Correspondence to Dr Mugford.

drug law, harm reduction and so forth [1–16] which would need to be considered in a full account of drug control.

Drug policy and modern society

In recent centuries, the world has been massively transformed. Driven by internal upheaval and external colonialism—intertwined in complex ways—'Western' ideas and culture have spread around the globe in 'the growth of modernity'. But that process is not finished. No sooner has modernity arrived than it too is being transformed. The key features of modernity—a global system of nation states, a worldwide system of capitalist production, trade and consumption, a culture of rationality, mass communications, mass transportation, centralized bureaucratic management and increasing metropolitanization—are beginning to give way to a new pattern of 'postmodernity'[17].

In the change from modern to postmodern, the centralizing tendencies of the previous three or four centuries—the results of which were mentioned in the previous paragraph—now show marked signs of reversal. As Crook _et al._ show, the three central processes producing modernity—differentiation of social roles and functions, rationalization of activities and the commodification of more and more aspects of life—have not altered. But further development leads to hyper-differentiation, hyper-rationalization and hyper-commodification and as this occurs a series of 'reversals' emerge. Of these, the reversals that concern the domain of organized political activity that we conventionally label 'the state' is of greatest relevance to drug control.

According to these authors, the typical form of the state is undergoing major change. For some centuries, Western nation states grew in size, scope and complexity to become the main arena within which social problems were identified, described, studied, responded to and controlled. The size of bureaucracies grew concomitantly and with it the taxation base needed to maintain the vast range of projects—in health, education, welfare, defence, economic infrastructural development, economic management and so on—that the government and the bureaucrats undertook. At the same time, the scope of representation—conceived in terms of enfranchisement—expanded. In short, the modern state can be understood as broadly corporatist and liberal democratic.

This corporatist, liberal democratic state, however, is now shrinking. Faced with criticisms that it has failed in many areas, and beset with a persistent fiscal crisis, state functions are moving in four analytically separable directions—upwards, downwards, sideways, out. Upwards, we see a tendency to move functions to supra-state organizations, such as the EC, the UN, GATT, the World Court and various other international bodies established by treaty agreement. Even within composite, federalized nations like Australia we see the development of bodies which move functions 'upwards'—either by attempting to transfer the functions of the separate State governments to the Federal government (hence the repeated cry to abolish the former in the interests of efficiency) or by creating new bodies to carry out tasks that sit astride boundaries, such as the Murray Darling Basin Commission, a body which seeks to co-ordinate the ecologically relevant actions of the Commonwealth and four state governments.

Downwards, we see a tendency to devolve many activities to local governments and communities. Indeed, 'involve the community' has become a catch-cry of the 1980s and 1990s and many social control activities—ranging from Neighbourhood Watch to school based drug education programs—are designed to shift initiative and responsibility 'back' to the 'community' (even though both the notion that communities once exerted such functions and the notion that communities exist in the unitary sense implied are both problematic).

Sideways, there is a tendency to shift functions to a variety of bodies which exist parallel to the state. Unions, business associations, conservation bodies, professional associations and voluntary associations are receiving more functions as the once omnipresent state begins to shrink.

And perhaps the most striking case of state shrinkage has concerned the movement _out_ to the market place. Through privatization and the sale of state owned assets, governments of a variety of persuasions—conservative in the USA, the UK and Canada, labour oriented in Australia and NZ—have undertaken a dual movement. First, by selling these assets they have raised money to help in the short run with immediate fiscal crises. Second, in the longer run, by divesting themselves of such things as power generation, telecommunications or air transport they have obviated the need to find more taxes, or more government raised loans, with which to support and recapitalize these enterprises. In the area of social control, for example, policing has been supplanted as a principally state based activity by the growth of private security and private policing organizations, systems in which private financing of security activity replaces taxation based action by government agencies.

In the postmodern situation, then, we expect to find that social control of any area—and drugs would merely be one example—will be gradually moving away from the control of central state bodies, such as publicly funded police forces, government bureaucracies and the criminal court. Instead we should expect to find that drug control is increasingly being exerted by other bodies. We should expect to find nation states looking to supra-state bodies (such as the United Nations agencies) to control trafficking. At the same time, we should expect to find that there will be devolution downwards to local control through links to interest groups, a sideways shift to control by enlisting the energies of other agencies and some movement out to the market place.

I suggest that there are clear examples of all of these things going on in Australia and other countries. A striking example which illustrates several aspects of the change is the growth of, and advocacy for, random drug testing (RDT) of employees. While it is easy to make a moral justification for performance related drug testing in occupations where safety is an issue (pilots, drivers, etc) it is much harder to see how one makes the same justification for occupations such as shop floor workers or clerical staff. Yet, in the USA in particular, the introduction of RDT is clearly linked to a wider concern to prosecute the so-called 'war on drugs' [16]. There is every reason to suppose that this represents a moral crusade, masquerading as the enlightened pursuit of safety. But even more interesting is the fact that this is an activity driven by the state but not carried out by the state. In the USA where the system is most developed, it has been moved outwards, sideways and down by a simple legal mechanism. This is that companies are barred from obtaining government contracts unless they guarantee drug free workplaces, and RDT is the 'proof' needed to establish that the company has met this requirement. In this way, we see political activities that have recently been pursued by state agencies—compare the role of policing in the US during Prohibition—being transferred to non-state agencies.

The idea of postmodernity and the shrinkage of the state is not the only way that we can offer relevant theories that help link social change and drug control. A second profitable way to do this is to examine the general process of social control itself in greater detail.

Central to this endeavour are some ideas originally proposed by the French writer Michel Foucault [18,19] and more recently developed by Jonathan Simon and others [20–24].

Foucault has argued that the way in which social control has operated has undergone a process of change that has taken modernizing societies through three major phases—the corporal, the carceral and risk management. In the corporal phase, characteristic of premodern society, punishment centres upon painful revenge carried out on the body of the perpetrator, in full view of the public gaze. In the Roman amphitheatre, in the town square or wherever, miscreants are exposed to punishments that are humiliating, excruciatingly painful, mutilating and, in extreme cases, fatal. By whipping, burning, breaking on wheels, dismembering and many other actions too horrible to recount, wrong-doers are made to pay in pain for their wrongdoings. At the same time, Foucault argues, the on-lookers are reminded, albeit in ways they find entertaining and we today find repellent, that the power of the emperor (king, lord, whatever) is both great and fearsome. Power is not merely exercised, it is seen to be exercised.

For complex reasons which we cannot trace out here, this process is gradually transcended during the growth of modernity and is replaced by a phase of intense 'discipline'. In this 'carceral' phase—the Victorian workhouse and 'panopticon' style prisons, such as the one at Port Arthur being quintessential examples—the deviant is subject to the most intense scrutiny during the period of punishment. Every movement, gesture and word is watched for signs of disobedience or recalcitrance, for the idea is that the soul of the deviant will be reconstructed by reconstructing the minutiae of behaviour. While the system sounds appalling when described this way, it is important to remember that it is underpinned by a particular view derived from Protestant Christian understandings of sin: sinners could only be saved by renunciation of their sinning ways and a return to a righteous path. However we may now interpret the ideology, it is clear that 'discipline' was a deeply

moral, as well as moralizing and moralistic, enterprise.

In the third phase, Foucault argues, the moralizing enterprise of discipline fades, to be replaced by
the management of populations and the 'risks' that
populations create. This movement, which has been
labelled the move to a risk society or the rise of an
'insurential' logic, has been elaborated by other writers [22–24]. Now the ideology is seen to centre
neither upon a vengeful punishment for crime nor
upon punishing in order to reform. These concerns
wither away and we are left with the amorally
pragmatic tasks of preventing crime, reducing its
impact, disabling criminals so that they cannot reoffend and so forth. As always, the introduction of
such changes is accompanied by a variety of
justificatory rhetorics, such as the view that crime
will not go away, that older ways of controlling the
problem did more harm than good and that instead
of concerning ourselves with fine polemical
flourishes we should simply deal with the real costs
of crime with a minimum of fuss. Furthermore,
following this logic, when such crimes are 'victim-
less' there is every reason to decriminalize them for
by removing the crime from the statutes and 'letting
the police catch the real criminals' we reduce the
problem for everybody.

It should not be hard to see how the shift from
discipline to risk management might be thought to
be connected to the more general shift within the
state sphere. Driven partly by fiscal crisis and partly
by a conviction that with crime 'nothing works', the
move away from reformism and moral concern towards simply coping with the problem by
containment and damage reduction makes good
sense.

It is also easy to see how we can apply this to drug
control. Someone who understood the issues of the
shrinking state and the move towards risk control
should be able to predict that 'harm reduction'
would be a major plank of modern policy, and of
course it is. Harm reduction might indeed be
thought to be a classic instance of the type of
punishment/control mode that is coming into vogue
today.

One of the central axes of debate would therefore
be expected to be between advocates of older modes
of control (for example, those working in therapeutic
communities or law enforcement) and advocates of
harm reduction. Located within a more 'disciplinary'
and morally concerned enterprise and drawing on a

'modern' view of the state, we could predict that
critics of harm reduction would argue against its
amorality, would claim that harm reductionists are
prepared to 'abandon' problem users and would
characterize harm reduction as giving up a moral
struggle that we have no right to quit—precisely the
kind of claim that critics of harm reduction do make.
At the same time, we would expect to find harm
reductionists criticizing the older position for its
morally self righteous stance and its refusal to come
to terms with the fact that the disciplinary strategy
has not worked well where drugs are concerned and
pointing out that it will never work well now because resources for the enterprise are shrinking not
increasing. And that is again what we find.

Thus the tension between these positions, which
is all too easily understood in terms of personalities
or of the political agenda or 'interests' of particular
groups, is much better understood as linked to a
much broader pattern of social change, within which
it is embedded.

NCADA—an example

A good example of the tension between different
views in drug control can be seen in the development in Australia of the National Campaign Against
Drug Abuse (NCADA). From its inception, there
has been a persistent conflict between those who
would pursue a more disciplinary policy, emphasizing individual treatment of users and law
enforcement against drug selling and those who
emphasize a more 'medical' model, the latter stressing the fact that harm reduction is now the official
central tenet of policy.

It would be simplistic to assume either that all
who favour a disciplinary approach to drugs are in
the law enforcement area or that all who favour
harm reduction are in the medical area. Furthermore, there are ways that law enforcement can be
harm reductionist and certainly many medically
based drug programmes have a strongly disciplinary
character (such as many methadone programmes
and therapeutic communities). Nonetheless, the
rough grouping of law enforcement advocates with a
disciplinary stance and of health and medical personnel with harm reduction is not far from the truth.

And it is along these lines that tensions have
continued to surface within NCADA. Even in the
official evaluations, where as we all know one commonly needs to read carefully between the lines of

the bland, passionless language to find what might really be meant, these tensions are clearly visible.

For example, in the more recent evaluation [25], which appeared in 1992, the Task Force—operating from within a model strongly influenced by health and medical interests—states bluntly at p. 55 that:

> The Task Force is concerned that the Commonwealth Attorney-General's Department, which at SCO [the Standing Committee of Officials] formally represents all Commonwealth law and enforcement agencies including the Australian Federal Police, does not see NCADA as relevant to their area of interest. The Department has distanced itself from community policing and alcohol and tobacco issues thus creating an impression that it is substantially out-of-step with general policing strategies. It is of further concern that the Attorney-General's Department provides the sole law and enforcement representative on a number of SCO working parties and other national and advisory working groups relating to alcohol and other issues.

In this passage we are invited to understand the attitude of Attorney-General's as out-of-date (a quintessential insult in postmodern culture) but not beyond rescue, if only they will come to the harm reduction party. Given this view, it is perhaps not surprising to find that elsewhere (p. 56) the authors lament the fact that:

> ... it soon became evident to the Task Force that while there was a need for integrated strategies between health, education, law and enforcement agencies at local through to national levels, this had not worked as well as most had hoped. Too often it was perceived that health was the dominant decision maker, while the law and enforcement sector was sidelined and forced to set separate agendas ...

We are left wondering who were the 'most' who 'hoped' and how the perception that health was dominant occurred 'too often', given that the whole thrust of this report is about defending the dominance of a harm reduction model over the disciplinary model which lies at the core of policing in a modern (as opposed to postmodern) nation state. Nonetheless, the authors continue in an optimistic vein, when they argue that "... it has not been recognized that supply control can be seen as a as

harm minimization strategy, in relation to both licit and illicit drugs, and that supply control is and will remain the primary role of policing".

Here we see a subtle shift, for police activity that is desirable under a harm reduction model is recast as if it were traditionally the major thrust of police work, as opposed merely to one theme among many other disciplinary themes.

In short, the tensions between discipline and risk management remain strong inside the NCADA enterprise. As often occurs in such debates, the proponents of the newer view (here, harm reduction) like to imagine that they have found the truth about an issue, casting aside old misunderstandings and offering an improved and liberating view of the problem. While I prefer and advocate this view over the older view that emphasizes moralizing discipline I want to emphasize the limits of such a view.

First, harm reduction logic is essentially a logic of utilitarian cost-benefit analysis, except that the familiar view that we should aim for the 'greatest happiness of the greatest number' is transformed into the 'least harm for the least number'. Unfortunately, this appealing simple logic does not overcome problems endemic to utilitarianism, especially its failure to prioritize types of happiness (here, harm). How do we choose between the deaths of some drug users under one regime of drug control or the illness of others under another? As I have argued [15], failure to resolve the complex problems of utilitarianism, including the difficulty of valuing 'benefits' in the cost-benefit analysis, means that harm reduction positions remain more committed to rhetoric than detailed policy.

Second, the alleged move to risk management of which harm reduction is a part is often more a mirage than a reality. While NCADA seems to be a program in which rhetoric and reality are well integrated, many efforts, such as the implementation of RDT in American industry purportedly to control risks cannot seriously be seen as other than a traditional moralizing enterprise.

Finally, it is important to link the decline of disciplinary enterprises not only to the rise of risk management, but also to another factor—a shift away from punitive models emphasizing surveillance towards a system of self monitoring underpinned by the organization of pleasure—from *1984* to *Brave New World*, as it were. In many locations in modern society we see this shift, perhaps best epitomized by the slick social control exercized in Disney World and similar locations [25]. Indeed, in postmodern culture it seems more and more that surveillance, discipline and overt punishment occur more and more with people on the margins of society while those in the mainstream are controlled more and more through the organization of pleasure. In such a context, drug control policies that are disciplinary are seen as relevant only to marginal people—such as unemployed addicts—while more 'humane' policies are needed for the mainstream person.

Conclusion

This paper has sketched only a few themes, and those quite superficially in the space available. What I hope, however, to have demonstrated is not so much a complete analysis of drug control so much as an illustration of the opening thesis. That is, that while when we are close up to drug control and concentrating on the detail, then we can easily lose perspective; we cannot 'see the wood for the trees'. My argument is that the broad tide of changes in drug control have little to do with drugs and their properties *per se*, and not an awful lot to do with the personalities, politics and interest of the policy players. Rather, such a broad tide is much better understood in terms of large scale changes in society and in systems of social control. If we grasp the general pattern of changing social control in a postmodern society we will be much better able to get the 'big picture' of drug control and then, in turn, understand how the specific details might fit into that picture.

References

[1] Mugford SK. Alternative methods, alternative realities. In: Wardlaw G. ed. Proceedings of the Second National Drug Indicators Conference. Canberra, Australian Institute of Criminology 1991:333–55.

[2] Mugford SK. Controlled drug use among recreational users: Sociological perspectives. In: Heather N. Miller WR, Greeley J. eds. Self control and the addictive behaviours. Sydney, Maxwell MacMillan, 1992:243–61.

[3] Mugford SK. Policing euphoria: the politics and pragmatics of drug control. In: Moir P, Eijckman H, eds. Policing Australia: Old issues new perspectives. Sydney, MacMillan, 1992:183–210.

[4] Dance P, Mugford SK. The St. Oswald's Day celebrations: 'Carnival' versus 'sobriety' in an Australian drug enthusiast group. J Drug Issues 1992;22:591–606.

[5] O'Malley PT, Mugford SK. The demand for intoxicating commodities: Implications for the War on Drugs. Soc Justice 1991;18:49–75.

[6] O'Malley PT, Mugford SK. Crime, excitement and modernity. In Barak G, ed. Varieties of criminology. New York, Praeger; in press.

[7] Mugford SK. Drug policy and harm reduction: Towards a unified policy for legal and illegal drugs. Carne T, Drew L, Matthews J, Mugford SK, Wodak A, eds. An unwinnable war: The politics of drug decriminalization. Sydney, Pluto Press, 1991:22–35.

[8] Mugford SK. Drug legalization and the Goldilocks problem: Thinking about the costs and control of drugs. In: Krause MB, Lazear EP, eds. Searching for alternatives: Drug control policy in the United States. Stanford, Hoover Institution Press, 1991:33–50.

[9] Mugford SK. Least bad solutions to the drug problem. Drug Alcohol Rev, 1991;10:401–415.

[10] Mugford SK. Crime and the partial legalization of heroin: Comments and caveats. A NZ J Criminology 1992;25:27–40.

[11] Mugford SK, O'Malley PT. Heroin policy and the limits of Left Realism. Crime, Law & Soc Change 1991;15:19–36.

[12] Mugford SK. Licit and Illicit drug use, health costs and the 'crime connection' in Australia: Public views and policy implications. Cont Drug Probs 1992;19:351–85.

[13] Mugford SK. Towards a harm reduction strategy: the conceptual foundations of policy change in Australia. Newsletter Council on Illicit Drug Policy, 1991;1:4–6.

[14] Mugford SK. Harm reduction—What is it and how could one achieve it? In Touch, 1991;8:5–8.

[15] Mugford SK. Harm reduction: Does it lead where its proponents imagine? In: Heather N, Wodak A, Nadelmann EA, O'Hare P, eds. Psychoactive drugs and harm reduction: From faith to science. London, Whurr Publishers 1993:21–33.

[16] O'Malley PT, Mugford SK. Moral technology: the political agenda of random drug testing. Soc Justice 1991;18:122–46.

[17] Crook S, Pakulski J, Waters M. Postmodernization: Change in advanced society. London, Sage, 1992.

[18] Foucault M. Discipline and punish: The birth of the prison. New York, Vintage Books, 1984.

[19] Foucault M. The history of sexuality: Volume 1. London, Peregrine Books, 1984.

[20] Donzelot J. The poverty of political culture. Ideology and Consciousness, 1979,5:71–86.

[21] Ewald F. L'etat providence. Paris, Grasset, 1986.

[22] Reichman N. Managing crime risks: Toward an in

surance based model of social control. Res Law Soc Control 1986;8:51–172.

[23] Simon J. The emergence of a risk society: Insurance, law, and the state. Socialist Rev 1987;95:61–89.

[24] Simon J. The ideological effects of actuarial practices. Law Soc Review 1988,22:772–800.

[25] Second Task Force on Evaluation. No quick fix: An evaluation of the National Campaign Against Drug Abuse. Canberra, Ministerial Council on Drug Strategy, 1992.

[26] Fjellman SM. Vinyl leaves: Walt Disney World and America. Boulder, Co., Westview Press, 1992.

Name Index